Praise for *Einstein, Micha(...)*

"I love it! A work of lyrical ecstasy and prim(...)
penetrating insights, very, very absorbing, lea(...)
reader's mind this energy/thing called rock an(...)

—MARK LAMONICA, winner of the Southern California Booksellers Association
Nonfiction Award, photographer for *Rio L.A.: Tales from the Los Angeles River*

"Fantastic, every chapter is an eye-opener. Amazing. Exciting, secret, and unbelievable revelations. I sit here spinning. Every chapter keeps you wanting more. I
eat, breath, and live your every word; I see through your eyes; I feel through your
energy. You are able to grab my by the balls and the brain at once. To pierce my
soul and my rationality in one single move."

—SUZIE DOVE MILES

"This is amazing! What a life Bloom has led! The names in Bloom's book have
really given me what I can only describe as whiplash down memory lane! What a
long strange trip it's been."

—SUE STEINBERG, former PR manager for Foreigner,
one of the founders of MTV

"*Einstein, Michael Jackson & Me: A Search for Soul in the Power Pits of Rock and Roll*
is a masterpiece. . . . It is fun, intelligent, deeply insightful, and humorous. From an
author who has written about God, the Global Brain, the history of Capitalism,
Islam, and of course how he invented the '60s, Howard Bloom adds another volume to a long shelf of great books. I lift the lighter and demand an encore!"

—DAVID HOULE FUTURIST, author of
Moving to a Finite Earth Economy—Crew Manual: The Three Economies

"Great lessons, insights, and inspirations."

—STEVE MILLER, artist, exhibited at the National Academy of Sciences,
the Hong Kong Arts Centre, Rose Art Museum,
the Centre International d'Art Visuels CARGO in Marseilles,
and the CAPC musée d'art contemporain de Bordeaux

"Fabulous! Read in one sitting."

—Mike Sigman, former editor, *Record World* magazine,
former CEO, *LA Weekly*

"A fun masterpiece, full of insights and ideas. A great work."

—Jose Cordeiro, international fellow of the World Academy of
Art and Science (WAAS), author of *La Muerte de la Muerte: La posibilidad
científica de la inmortalidad física y su defensa moral* (The Death of Death)

"*Einstein, Michael Jackson & Me: A Search for Soul in the Power Pits of Rock and Roll*
is an astonishing, compelling, and super accessible read."

—Jamilee Baroud, In a Click podcast

EINSTEIN,
MICHAEL JACKSON
& ME

EINSTEIN, MICHAEL JACKSON & ME

A SEARCH FOR SOUL IN THE POWER PITS OF ROCK AND ROLL

HOWARD BLOOM

Backbeat
Books

Guilford, Connecticut

Published by Backbeat Books
An imprint of The Rowman & Littlefield Publishing Group, Inc.
4501 Forbes Blvd., Ste. 200
Lanham, MD 20706
www.rowman.com

Distributed by NATIONAL BOOK NETWORK

Library of Congress Cataloging-in-Publication Data available

ISBN 978-1-4930-5167-0 (paperback)
ISBN 978-1-4930-5168-7 (e-book)

♾™ The paper used in this publication meets the minimum requirements of American National Standard for Information Sciences—Permanence of Paper for Printed Library Materials, ANSI/NISO Z39.48-1992

CONTENTS

FOREWORD

This book is amazing. There are many who believe Howard Bloom is a yoda. He can certainly seem to summon an inexplicable Force. His disciples call it THE FORCE. I remain agnostic. But there is undeniable evidence. I saw it myself. I was lucky that one of the people he summoned that love for was me.

Howard was the first media giant to create a boutique public relations empire dedicated to the rock 'n' roll pop culture and its icons—the baby boomers' generation of power. He didn't come cheap. And he took Kenny, the Blackhearts, and me on without charging us for over a year, while we struggled to survive.

In *Einstein, Michael Jackson & Me*, Howard explains how he got that power. In his twelve years as a legend in the music business, Howard Bloom was on a hero's journey. A spiritual and a scientific hunt. A hunt riddled with adventures that go from funny to profound. He was on what he calls "a quest for soul in the power pits of rock and roll."

If Howard Bloom believed in you, you had it made. He went to the mat for you. He put everything he had into your career. And there was a magic to his instincts. If you watched the charts of hits, one Bloom client after another made it to the top. Michael Jackson, Prince, Bob Marley, Billy Joel, Simon & Garfunkel, Peter Gabriel, John Mellencamp, Styx, and REO Speedwagon—they all worked with Howard Bloom. And they all went to number one. So did I.

I first met Howard in 1979. I was struggling. I'd left the band I'd founded, the Runaways, and started a solo career. A Swedish record company had given me $25,000 to record an album. It was produced by Kenny Laguna. Here's how Howard describes Kenny's track record: "He had written songs for Tony Orlando, the Ohio Express, and the Lemon Pipers. He had played on Tommy James and the Shondells' 'Mony Mony,' Crazy Elephant's 'Gimme Gimme Good Lovin',' the Lemon Pipers 'Green Tambourine,' and Jay and the Americans 'This Magic Moment' and 'Walking in the Rain.'"

But my Swedish album had been turned down by 26 record companies in the United States. And I was playing in the sort of German clubs where the Beatles got their start. But I wasn't booked into hotels. I slept on the floor of the club after everyone had left for the night.

Kenny Laguna jumped in to rescue me. And he became a believer. He became a kamikaze for my cause. He put everything he had and everything he was into helping me.

Kenny had met Howard Bloom when Howard was East Coast head of public and artist relations for ABC Records. I never knew it until I read this book, but when Kenny first met Howard, Howard had done something strange with the manager of a band with a number-three hit.

Bloom explains how the manager was due to fly in to New York from LA at 5:00 p.m., rush hour. Bloom picked up the manager up at LaGuardia Airport in a limousine. Bloom knew that he'd have the manager trapped for at least an hour while the limo was baked into traffic. Why did Howard need to make sure that he had the manager's undivided attention? The band prided itself on its democracy; every member was equal to every other member. But Howard told the manager that if he'd allow Howard to pull the lead singer to the forefront and to focus the spotlight exclusively on her, and if the manager would cover his ass with the other group members, Bloom would give that manager a star. Bloom confesses in this book that this was the first time he'd ever made the promise to deliver a star.

Bloom came through. The lead singer's name was Chaka Khan.

The second and only other time Howard made that promise was with me. Kenny went to Howard hoping that Howard would do him a favor and get a line about me in *Cashbox*, the number three trade paper in the music industry in those days. Kenny figured that a sentence in *Cashbox* would finally help me get me a record contract.

But Howard said no.

Instead, Howard sat Kenny down on the low-slung couch in his office, pulled up a chair that loomed over Kenny, and said, "If you work the way I do, 17-hour days, seven days a week, and if you do everything I tell you to, within two years, I will help deliver you a star."

Remember, I'd been tossed on the reject heap. No record company would touch me. But 18 months later, I had a number one hit single and an album that went double platinum—an album that sold seven million copies.

In this book, Howard tells the story of how he helped make this miracle happen, not just for me and for Chaka Khan. He tells the story of how he did it over and over again.

Ten years later, Kenny and I went to visit Howard in his bedroom. By then he was sick with ME/CFS, the illness that yanked him out of his position as a legend in the music business and kept him bed-bound for 15 years. 15 years in which he'd write three books and found two international scientific groups. That's when I discovered that Howard had been in disguise in the record business from the very beginning. His real roots were in science. But he was on a hunt for something far deeper than science alone could uncover.

I had just read Neil Donald Walsh's *Conversations with God*. And, sitting on Howard's king-sized mattress in his Park Slope, Brooklyn brownstone with him, *Conversations with God* is what we discussed. That's when I discovered that Howard was far more than just a music industry wizard. And far more than just a scientist. He had the wisdom of an elder. He was on the prowl for the experience we call divinity, using the tools of his science. And using the resonance of his own soul with the souls of those he cared about.

In *Einstein, Michael Jackson & Me*, Bloom shows that when you are dedicated to truth, you have an eerie power. You have The Force.

I was lucky that one of those he loved was me. He and his many believers will tell you he used The Force. I can't tell you there is any other explanation.

Joan Jett
January 2020

1

MICHAEL JACKSON IS DEAD

It was just past midnight on June 25, 2009, my birthday. I had left the café in Park Slope, Brooklyn, where I wrote my books, and was on the two-mile walk that loops me up to Prospect Park, through the dark and starry meadow, then takes me back down the hill the three long blocks to my brownstone. Two hours earlier, I had been hit with a gut-punching birthday present—the death of Michael Jackson. My body was still processing the loss. It was too much for my verbal mind to handle. For me, the permanence of the separation was savage. I had unfinished business with Michael. I had conversations I wanted to complete. More important, I had signed on with his brothers for a mission that I had not been able to accomplish. Deep in me, I still wanted to deliver on that commitment.

What's more, because of the negative press about Michael's supposed sexual interest in children, I wondered if others were still as deeply attached to Michael Jackson as I was. Had others become disgusted and abandoned him? Had he been despised and forgotten? Was he a cultural has-been?

The streets and sidewalks of Park Slope at 12:30 a.m. are normally empty. Devoid of human beings. But that was not the case on this black night. Sitting on the very top stair of a brownstone stoop were two eighteen-year-olds. The guy had long, dark black curly hair, and the girl had a short, blonde haircut and was wearing shorts. The male said something to me as I passed. I was listening to a book on my Kindle and couldn't make it out. I ignored it and walked a hundred feet further down the sidewalk. Then I turned around, walked back, took off my headphones, and asked him to repeat it. He said, "Michael Jackson is dead."

I asked him why he said that to me. I wondered if he knew me from the Tea Lounge, the café where I wrote in those days, or from the streets of Park Slope, and if he knew my Michael Jackson connection. No, he didn't. He was announcing that Michael Jackson was dead loudly and with a strange urgency, a strange sense of command, to everyone he saw. He wanted no one to ignore it.

He was particularly emphatic about making sure that no one over the age of twenty-five pass it by or dismiss it. Michael Jackson's death, he felt, was a loss to all of us, whether we realized it or not. And he was afraid that those over twenty-five would fail

to recognize that one of the beating hearts of our culture had just stopped. A greatness
had just died. He was determined that no one forget Michael Jackson. That no one fail
to realize that a piece of flesh had just been ripped from the body of mankind. So no,
Michael was not a has-been. Far from it.

* * *

How did I get involved with Michael Jackson and his brothers? It was the fall of 1983,
and the Jacksons were planning to go on the road for their Victory Tour. They were
getting the whole family together for this fifty-five-city extravaganza, including their
dad, who had originally engineered the rise of the Jackson Five to the top of the charts
in 1969 and in the 1970s.[1] This would be their first tour as a family since 1981. The first
since Michael's career had exploded in a way that no one had seen since Elvis Presley
and the Beatles.

I was a science nerd in a field I'd initially known nothing about—popular music.
But six years into my scientific expedition into pop, five years into my hunt for soul in
the power pits of rock and roll, I'd founded and headed what had become the biggest
publicity firm in the music industry. The manager that Tito, Marlon, Jackie, and Randy
Jackson had hired for the Victory Tour called me over and over again for four months,
asking me to work with the Jacksons. I said no. Over and over again. By this point,
I'd helped Amnesty International establish itself in North America. I'd worked with
Simon and Garfunkel when they'd reunited for an audience of four hundred thousand
in a free concert in Central Park. Then my staff had handled Simon and Garfunkel's
national reunion tour. I had done Queen's massive tour of 120,000-seat soccer stadiums in South America. And I'd been working since 1981 with a brilliant manager, Bob
Cavallo, to build the career of an unknown Minneapolis twenty-two-year-old named
Prince.

I liked to do crusades—to fight for truths that others didn't see. I didn't like to
work on sure things. And, in 1983, the Jacksons were a sure thing. Michael had just
sold roughly thirty-two million copies of just one album—*Thriller*. That was almost
three times as many as the previous record holder, Peter Frampton. I didn't feel the
Jacksons needed me. Or, as I kept explaining to their manager, if you hired a talking
dog to say Michael Jackson's name on the phone, you'd get coverage from any magazine
editor or TV producer you wanted. So I kept turning the Jacksons down. Then, in a
phone conversation, their manager cornered me. The Jacksons were coming into New
York and wanted to meet with me, despite my no's.

I hadn't grown up among other human beings. I'd grown up in a bedroom stocked
with guinea pigs, guppies, and laboratory rats. So I didn't know the rules of politeness.

But I'd learned a few human norms from observation. One was the idea that if you're going to say no to someone, at least you owe them the decency of saying it to their face. So, when the Jacksons' manager asked me to meet with Michael's brothers at the Helmsley Palace hotel in Manhattan, just a subway ride away from my Brooklyn brownstone, I was forced to say yes. Even though the meeting was at midnight on a Saturday night, and Saturday and Sunday were my most precious working days of the week—the only days when the phone didn't ring, and when I could go over every detail of every campaign, assemble an overview, and determine what my staff, the biggest PR staff in the music industry at the time, needed to do during the coming week. On weekends, I worked from 9:00 a.m. until I dropped. A midnight interruption was going to hurt.

But on that Saturday, two minutes before midnight, I stepped out of a Helmsley Palace Hotel elevator on a top floor, walked down the richly carpeted corridor, knocked on the correct, white, elegantly gilded door, and everything changed. It changed when the door opened a mere inch. Why? I saw four men sitting up against a wall in a suite they'd rented for meetings only. Something was wrong. Deeply wrong. There was an ad for a cassette-tape company way back then that showed a man with long hair sitting in a big, stuffed easy chair. His hair was blown straight back, and he was plastered up against the back of the seat as if he were in a hurricane and the wind was blasting him with the force of a flying brick. This brutal wind supposedly represented the power of the music recorded on the sponsor's tape. That was exactly how Marlon, Tito, Randy, and Jackie Jackson looked. Plastered up against the wall by an unknown force. A dark force.

But there was more. Something in the Jacksons' body language said that these were four of the most decent people you'd ever met in your life. And that they were in trouble. They didn't know what that trouble was. I didn't know what it was. But I did know this: here was a challenge. There was a wrong to be righted. A wrong all of us could feel but none of us could name. I said yes.

By 2:00 a.m., the brothers crowded around me, each handing me his private phone number on a scrap of paper. "You start," said Randy, "at 10:30 tomorrow morning, Sunday."

* * *

Actually, I should have had an inkling of the Jacksons' trouble. My meeting with the brothers at the Helmsley Palace Hotel took place in roughly December 1983. Two months earlier, in October, *Rolling Stone* magazine had run a story announcing that the Jackson Victory Tour's promoter would be Don King, the wild-haired, ultra-theatrical black promoter who had pulled off a miracle. King had almost singlehandedly re-vived a dying sport—boxing. He'd turned something old and dull into theater. But the *Rolling Stone* story didn't focus on King's creative achievements. Instead, it zeroed in on King's background as a thug. In particular, it told the tale of King's conviction for second-degree murder. In 1966, a man named Sam Garrett owed King six hundred dollars in a gambling debt. How did the future boxing genius handle the problem? He pistol-whipped, stomped, and kicked the man in the head until Garrett was dead.[2] In other words, the very first word about the upcoming Jackson tour in the top taste-mak-ing music publication in America blasted a single message—the message of an ethical cancer. Then, in November, Don King threw a press conference to unveil the Victory Tour at the Tavern on the Green in Manhattan's Central Park. The Tavern on the Green in those days was a place that, like King, flared with theatricality. The Central Park thicket of trees surrounding the place was turned into a fairy wonderland by the tiny stars of white Christmas tree lights.

How did *Rolling Stone* cover this press conference? It said that Don King, the murderer, had dominated the event, hogging the podium as if he were really the singer of Michael Jacksons' hits and the star of Michael's amazing videos. In other words, the clues had been there before I ever took the elevator to the top of the Helmsley Palace Hotel. Something was wrong with the Jackson tour. Something was wrong with its press. Something was not only inaccurate but malevolent. But what?

* * *

My first meeting with Michael didn't come until four months later. I was with Michael's brothers at Marlon Jackson's pool house in Encino—a tiny, two-story building with one room per floor in the backyard to the left of Marlon's pool. By then, I'd done my homework. I'd read thousands of articles on Michael. I'd compiled a dossier on the Jacksons' lives. One thing all the articles agreed on was this: Michael was not a normal human being. The articles called him a bubble baby, a person who would shrink from your touch.

But the fact is that neither Michael nor I had experienced a normal childhood. Neither of us had been raised among other kids. As I said, I didn't know the common rituals of normal life. I had to teach myself by watching other people, as if they were laboratory specimens and I was a scientist from Mars. One of the rituals an acquain-tance had taught me when I was nineteen was the handshake between strangers. You know, you see someone you've never met before but who others want you to meet. You walk up to him or her, you stick out your hand, and you say, "Hello, my name is [*fill in your name here*].” And he or she says her name back. This was a ritual I'd never used. But when Michael opened the pool house's screen door, I walked up to him, stuck out my hand, and said, “Hi, I'm Howard.”

I knew what would happen. The articles had explained it. Michael would recoil from my touch. But that's not what occurred. Michael put out his hand, shook mine, and replied, “Hi, I'm Michael.” Michael's voice was normal. And so was his handshake. The media stories were false. But thousands of press people had parroted them as truths. Something strange was happening in the sphere of press perception we are handed as fact—at least as it pertained to Michael Jackson.

A few minutes later, Michael and I climbed the cramped stairs to the tiny second-floor room where Marlon Jackson kept his recording equipment. I'd written a press release, and I wanted Michael's approval. We found places to sit on the stacks of amplifiers and keyboards. I read the press release out loud to Michael. As I did, Michael's body softened and slid a bit more horizontal with each paragraph. And his face opened with, well, with awe. “That's beautiful,” he said, in a soft, emotional voice, when I was finished. “Did you write that?” The fact was that I had. And the fact was that writing press releases was not just a hack job for me, it was an art. I'd edited a literary magazine that had won two Academy of American Poets prizes. And, in the decades since my involvement with the Jacksons, the *Washington Post* has called the writing in my books “beautiful.” But no one else had ever seen the art hidden in the craft. Michael had.

* * *

Once Michael had approved of the press release, we went back downstairs to the one-room first floor. Lining the walls were boardwalk video-game machines—machines only amusement arcades could afford in those days. And in the center of the room, hogging most of the space, was a billiard table. The Jacksons were scheduled to have a meeting with an art director from their record company, CBS, so the group could decide on the cover for the Victory Tour album. They wanted me to be in on it.

When the art director arrived, she bore the portfolios of five artists—portfolios she stacked at one end of the pool table's green felt playing surface. These were not the black vinyl portfolios most commercial artists use to display their work. Every one of them was a custom-made presentation case of hand-tooled leather or rich cherry wood. And every one was from a legendary artist, an artist at the very top of his field. I knew. I had snuck out of my four graduate fellowships in neuroscience and into a field I knew nothing about, pop culture, by co-founding a commercial art studio and making it onto the cover of *Art Direction* magazine. I used to carry a portfolio like these from one art director's office to another. Not the hand-tooled variety. The vinyl. And the artist portfolios on the table were from former competitors who were legends.

We were all bunched together on the opposite side of the pool table from the art director. Michael was in the center. I stood next to him on his left. And the brothers were crowded around us on either side. Which meant my right arm was up against Michael's, and my knee was next to his knee. The CBS art director slid the first of the portfolios toward Michael. He opened the first page, slowly . . . just enough to see perhaps an inch of the image. As he took in that postage-stamp-sized corner, his knees began to buckle, his elbows bent, and all he could say was, "Oooohhhhh." A soft, orgasmic "ooooh." In that one syllable and in his body language, you could feel what he was seeing. You could feel it from his arm to yours.

You know the poem by William Blake:

To see a World in a grain of sand,
And a Heaven in a wild flower,
Hold Infinity in the palm of your hand,
And Eternity in an hour . . .

The intense ambition of that poem, the overwhelming desire to see the infinite in the tiniest of things, was alive in Michael Jackson. More alive than anything of the sort I'd ever witnessed. Michael saw the infinite in an inch. As Michael opened the page farther, inch by inch, his knees and elbows bent even more, and his "oooh's," his sounds of aesthetic orgasm, grew even more intense. Standing elbow-to-elbow with him, you could feel him discovering things in the brush-and-ink strokes that even the artist never saw. By the time Michael had opened the full page, his body and voice expressed an ecstasy. An epiphany. Michael felt the beauty of the work with every cell of his being. I'd never encountered anything like it in my life.

Look, I've worked with Prince, Bob Marley, Peter Gabriel, Billy Joel, and Bette Midler—some of the most talented people of my generation. Not to mention the astronauts Buzz Aldrin and Edgar Mitchell, and the eleventh president of India, Dr. APJ Kalam. And not one of them had the quality of wonder that came alive in Michael Jackson. In the coming months, I would slowly learn that Michael saw the wonder in everything. His quality of astonishment was beyond anything most of us humans can conceive.

* * *

Put yourself in my position. Above all other things, you are a scientist. Science is your religion. It's been your religion since you were ten years old. And the first two rules of science are:

1. The truth at any price, including the price of your life.
2. Look at the things right under your nose as if you've never seen them before, then proceed from there.

Rule number one is the rule of courage. And rule number two is the rule of awe. The rule of amazement and wonder. These are not just rules of science. They are rules of art. And they are rules of life. Very few people know it. Even fewer people live it. But Michael WAS it.

You would learn step-by-step that Michael Jackson incarnated those two rules in every follicle of his being. Michael was the closest you'd ever seen to an angel or a saint.

* * *

It seems strange to say this, but Michael Jackson will always be a part of me. No other superstar I worked with wound himself into the threads at my core the way he did. As you've glimpsed, Michael opened a window to a quality of wonder unlike anything I'd ever been exposed to in my life. For that gift, I felt I owed him. I felt we all owed him. And we still do. We owe him an honest view of who he was. We will owe him that until we finally sweep away the garbage of sensationalist headlines and clearly see why those who never met him but love him know more about him than any expert or journalist who claims to have probed Michael Jackson's life. Those journalists and experts do not know Michael Jackson. But, if you love him, there's a good chance that you do.

* * *

But why was Michael Jackson in trouble? Why was he on his way from the twenty-five years that made him great to the twenty-five years that would nail him to the cross and would crucify him? The twenty-five years in which every thorn in his crown and nail through his flesh would be a headline? Why had I said yes to the Jacksons when my intention was to say a solid no?

And how would I discover a very different Michael than any you've ever read about before?

2

CONFESSIONS OF A MUSICAL KLUTZ

I was the least likely person on planet earth to get involved with music—much less to work with stars like Michael Jackson, Prince, Bob Marley, Bette Midler, Billy Joel, Paul Simon, AC/DC, Aerosmith, Queen, and KISS. I hated the popular music of my childhood. Once I did become interested, I tried to play music . . . and failed. Three times.

When I was eleven, my mom persuaded the second violinist at my hometown symphony orchestra—the Buffalo Philharmonic—to teach me violin. He tried. Lord knows, he tried. But one day, when I was in my living room for my weekly music lesson, I scratched away at something that had been music before it came into my hands. Suddenly, I saw a huge fist moving from my far right to the center of my vision, where it smashed into my violin and sent the fragile instrument soaring to the left across my living room to the front windows, hitting the thick, wine-red velvet curtains, then falling to the crumple of velvet at the curtains' base. It was the fist of my high-prestige, second-violinist teacher. That was the last time I ever saw him.

In eighth grade, I tried again. I'd gotten into jazz. I wanted to be J. J. Johnson and Kai Winding, a duo who both played the trombone. So I signed up at school for a trombone class. That sounds simple enough, right? I lasted two weeks. Then the teacher threw me out. Have you ever heard of a child being thrown out of a grammar-school musical-instrument class? I haven't.

Then, in the summer between eighth grade and my freshman year of high school, I was foolish enough to try again. New improvisations in the style of Fats Waller and Erroll Garner were constantly playing in my brain. I wanted to perform them on an instrument, where other people could hear them. So I got my mom to find me a piano teacher. The teacher and I had a wonderful time. Once a week we'd get together in his studio, and for half an hour he'd teach me piano. Then, for an hour, we'd discuss philosophy. That began in June. When we reached the end of August, my piano teacher finally admitted why he had not followed the example of my violin teacher and my trombone teacher. "When I first saw you," he said, "I knew you'd never be able to play the piano. But I was desperate." The students he depended on for an income, he explained, had all been sent to summer camp. He needed to pay the rent. I was his only source of cash. So he took me on. Despite the clear fact that I was hopeless. "But you've worked so hard at this," he concluded, "that I now believe if you continue to work this hard, you will be able to play the piano."

Alas, I couldn't afford to continue to work that hard on a musical instrument. My parents had offered me a choice: to go either to the local public high school—a place that felt to me like a penitentiary—or to a private school that felt like liberation. But if I went to the private school, they said, I'd have to make a promise. I'd have to promise that I would do my schoolwork. Since I was ten, I'd read two books a day—one in class and the other at home. Which means I'd read books under the desk and had never paid attention in class. So this was going to take all of my time and energy.

You'd think that when it comes to playing musical instruments, I should have simply given up. But twenty years later, I would discover a musical instrument that very few people in the music business even know exists. And I would learn to play it like a virtuoso. That instrument is the star-making machine. An instrument as complex as a cathedral organ. What's more, I would learn to play that instrument with something every great musician from Beethoven to the Beatles would have approved of—soul.

* * *

This book is the story of how that musical accident came to be. It's the story of my work launching or sustaining the careers of people like Michael Jackson, Prince, Bob Marley, Bette Midler, Billy Joel, Paul Simon, AC/DC, Aerosmith, Queen, KISS, Billy Idol, and Joan Jett. It's the tale of how I helped put the *soar* into people who can do the musical things I never could. People for whom I was able to do things they never would have been able to do for themselves.

It's the story of my adventures in the dark underbelly where new myths and movements are made. It's the story of how I developed a peculiar skill I called secular shamanism. It's the story of my search for soul in the power pits of rock and roll.

3

HUNTING THE GODS INSIDE

I grew up as an alien, a perpetual outsider, in Buffalo, New York. Other kids wanted to have nothing to do with me. And my parents didn't have time for me. So, as you've seen, I read two books a day. One under my desk at school. The other when I got home. Science was my life. Science and music. Yes, I was too klutzy to play an instrument. But I couldn't live without music. I marinated myself in it. Zeroing in on classical and jazz. Everything but popular music and rock and roll, the music of the kids who despised me. When I got home from Public School 64, where I was too busy reading to pay attention to my teachers, I put six LPs on an automatic turntable in my beige bedroom and listened while I read until the time for lights out. Then I stacked another six LPs on the turntable so the music would keep going while I slept. I ate, breathed, and slept two things: my science and my music. Way, way down the line, I would discover that eating, living, and breathing music was one of the keys to stardom.

As for science, when I was twelve, I built my first Boolean algebra machine, co-conceived a computer that won some science-fair awards, and was tutored in outside-the-box scientific thinking by the head of research and development for the Moog Valve Corporation, the company that made cutting-edge valves for the rocket engines that took planes like the Bell X-1 and the Bell X-2 on mankind's first trips to the edge of space. And, when I was still twelve, I was granted an hour-long session with the head of the graduate physics department at my local university, the University of Buffalo, to discuss *big bang* versus *steady state* theory of the universe and the interpretation of the Doppler shift. When I was sixteen, I became a lab assistant for a summer at the world's largest cancer-research facility, the Roswell Park Memorial Cancer Research Institute. I tended to photo spectrometers and particle counters for advanced work on the immune system.

But there was something far more important—and far more subversive—going on. It took place in the institute's cafeteria. I was the leader of a brainstorming session at lunch in which, over the course of two and a half months, I came up with a theory of the beginning, middle, and end of the universe that predicted something that would not be discovered for another thirty-eight years: dark energy.

Doesn't sound like it has anything to do with music, does it? Guess again.

* * *

Way back when I was thirteen years old, something light years outside the box happened that would prove crucial to my future career. And crucial to my understanding of people like Michael Jackson, Bob Marley, and Prince. It came just after my realization that I was an atheist. It was the discovery of the gods inside. Here's how I told the tale in my book *The God Problem: How a Godless Cosmos Creates*.

When you are twelve, you become an atheist. But you refuse to confess that to yourself. Confession will kill your Bar Mitzvah, and a Bar Mitzvah means presents and one of the first parties you've ever been invited to. When the Bar Mitzvah is over, when the checks are deposited, when the presents are unwrapped, and when you've sent two hundred thank-you cards, you are finally free to confess that you don't believe in God. A mere ten weeks after your Bar Mitzvah and your confession of atheism, the Jewish High Holidays arrive. Your parents believe in God so deeply that they literally try to wrestle you into a car to take you to Temple Beth El on Buffalo's Richmond Avenue. Why? Because High Holiday services are the most important services in the Jewish year. But, when it's time to leave the car, you refuse. So your mom and dad literally grab you by the ankles and try to drag you from their blue, four-door Frazier while you hold on to the rear right doorframe for all you're worth. Or at least that's the way you remember it.

What's more, by then you've been in science for a whopping 23 percent of your life. Since the age of ten. So you've read a considerable amount of anthropology. And every tribe you've ever read about agrees with your parents. Every tribe believes that there is some sort of supernatural power. Yes, the gods of each of these strange clans scattered across the face of the earth and sprinkled through history have been different—gods who create, gods who keep things running, gods who destroy, gods with faces on the front and back of their heads, gods who handle heaven's paperwork, and gods who file reports on your behavior. Or merely ancestors hovering in the ceilings of the family hut. Nearly every tribe and nearly every human being has ancestors, spirits, or gods. Belief in one form of spirit or another is all over the place. It's universal. It squeaks and squoozes from every pore of humanity.

Your parents are trying to yank you out of the car with an urgency you've never seen before. You are an atheist. Which means that you believe there are no gods in the sky, on the mountaintops, or in rivers, rocks, and underworlds. Yet there are gods in this scene. Where are they? In your parents. And, in all probability, in you. The gods are in our imaginations. The gods are in our passions. The gods are in our hearts and minds.

But what are they? Why are they? And what do they do? You would find the answers in the least likely place of all. In a form of music you didn't listen to. Rock and roll.

And science would be your perceptual lens.

What's more, in finding the source of deity, you were certain you'd find the forces of history. But why is a subject we'll save for later. What else would you discover by peeping tomming the gods within? You'd discover the secrets of stardom.

* * *

Finding the gods inside had a forefather.

When I was fourteen, I heard about a book called *The Varieties of the Religious Experience*, a 1902 work by one of the founders of American psychology, William James. This title galvanized me. There was no Amazon.com in those pitiful, primitive days, so it took me four months to hunt down a copy of the tome. But, when I got it, it was one of those volumes that reaches a hand out from the pages and grabs you by the collar. In the book, James lays out the extreme experiences of folks like Saint Teresa of Avila and George Fox, the man who founded the Quaker movement in 1652. James saw a deep validity in whacko visitations that, under ordinary circumstances, would be deemed what he called "psychopathic."

For example, Saint Teresa was a nun, a bride of Christ, in Spain in the 1530s. Laying in her monastic cell late at night, she would feel Christ coming through the stone walls, penetrating her body, and filling her with rapture. Or she would be caught up to heaven in an out-of-body experience, an ecstatic experience. As she described one of these experiences, an angel came toward her in the dark of the night and thrust a spear through her gut, leaving me "all on fire with a wondrous love for God. The pain was so great that it caused me to utter several moans; and yet so exceeding sweet is this greatest of pains that it is impossible to desire to be rid of it, or for the soul to be content with less than God. What empire is comparable to that of a soul who, from this sublime summit to which God has raised her, sees all the things of earth beneath her feet."[3]

But these moments of mystic madness, explains James, can be harvested. They can turn those they visit into some "of the most powerfully practical human engines that ever lived." Or at least that's how William James saw it. And he was right. Men and women like Saint Teresa can turn mystic raptures into new realities. Into the formation of new social groups, into forces of history. Saint Theresa reformed the Carmelite order of nuns and helped create the order of the Barefoot Carmelites. The structure she catalyzed in the 1560s, over four hundred years ago, became so strong that today it has four archbishops and seventeen bishops.

So where are the gods? In the margins just outside of sanity, in the dark outskirts of the psyche where lunacy lies. In your psyche and mine.

The ecstatic experience would be a clue to the real nature of stardom.

* * *

I'd soon have one of the ecstasies I was seeking when dancing on a stage at my private high school, the Park School of Buffalo.

I was elected the chairman of the program committee, despite the fact that the students hated me. My responsibilities included going before an audience of three hundred and fifty people five times a week as the MC of our 8:00 a.m. morning assemblies and programming two of these assemblies a week. Here's the utter shock that hit me one morning when I least expected it, a tale I told in *How I Accidentally Started the Sixties*.

The juniors came to me with a request. They were going to have a dance. Could I please find some way of advertising it to the assembled multitudes in the morning assembly? Little did they see the irony. Kids all over Buffalo made it abundantly clear that if there was something resembling a terpsichorean gathering anywhere in the city, I was kindly invited to park my feet as far away as possible—say, Cleveland. What's more, I had learned from a year in dance class that I was so clumsy at the basic ballroom steps of the late 1950s—the box step, the fox-trot, and the waltz—that if you put three hundred girls on any dance floor anywhere in the world, I could step on all three thousand dainty, nail-polished, female toes with just a few swift, tripping movements of my dress shoes. Do I have the math on the number of podiatric digits right?

And the juniors wanted me to advertise their dance? I mean, really! But I said yes.

So I picked a piece of music, put it on a record player at the back of the stage, then went center stage with absolutely nothing planned. And let loose. Moved. Wriggled. Jiggled. Writhed. Whumped. Bumped. Jumped. Stumped. Whipped my shoulders up and down. Let my arms fly. Squoonched my facial muscles. Interpreted the music in a way that apparently no one had ever seen before. I looked like a Loony Toon drawn under the influence of something that would not appear on the scene for another two years—LSD. Yes, I looked like a cartoon drawn by Chuck Jones of Wiley Coyote, Pepe Le Pew, Daffy Duck, and Tom and Jerry fame himself. On a night when his brain was chemically whipped, beaten, mashed, boiled, and fried.

This maniacal spasm of movement had consequences. It did something strange to the audience. Three hundred and fifty people who hated me—seven hundred spite-filled eyeballs worth—had a look I'd never seen before. The ocular orbs of the girl who hated me the most were zeroed in with disbelief. Six hundred and ninety-eight other irises were glued with an intensity I'd never seen. Pupils dilated—they grew wide. Yes, seven hundred of them. Faces went limp. Three hundred and fifty physiognomies flaccidified. Everything that those spellbound students had, were, and felt was concentrated in their gaze. And that gaze was lasered onto the least likely object in the room—me.

The power of those seven hundred emotionally focused fovea sent a strange force coursing through me. It was as if the energy of the individuals in the auditorium had merged into one big collective thundercloud; as if that cloud had aimed its bolts straight through the core of me; as if those ribbons of lightning had slammed up my backbone from my tail to my throat on their way to a transformer just above my head, a transformer in which the voltage was converted into something bigger, stranger, and more powerful, then was channeled back down through me as if I were a coaxial copper cable, zapped out to those three hundred and fifty transfixed faces, then sizzled from them back to me again for further amplification.

Meanwhile, I had an out-of-body experience. No kidding. I was on the ceiling watching this whole thing from above. And what I saw was a reverberatory circuit. A feedback loop of human spirit. A feedback loop of naked soul. When the music was over and my fit of dancing ceased, the crowd did something it had never done before in my three years at the Park School, and that it never did again. Not for football players, homecoming queens, or exchange students just back from Italy. All three hundred and fifty Park Schoolers surged down to the foot of the stage, picked me up off the proscenium, put me on their shoulders, carried me out of the auditorium door, and transported me up the sidewalk to the building where our classes were held.

Not only had my frantic rapture seized me in a whole new way, it had pulled together three hundred and fifty students into an unplanned but unitary mass. I was amazed.

This dance-trance was one of those Varieties of the Religious Experience that William James had attempted to capture. An experience of the sort that he couldn't explain. In fact, accidentally fire-balling on the stage at Park School would prove to be a massive clue to the gods inside. A massive clue to everything from the rise of disco and *Saturday Night Fever* to Prince.

4

HOW I ACCIDENTALLY STARTED THE SIXTIES

Then came the 1960s and yet more adventures that would lead to a hunt for soul in the power pits of rock and roll. I dropped out of Reed College in Portland, Oregon, in 1962, at the age of nineteen, and accidentally helped lay the base for the hippie movement. The whole sordid tale is in my book *How I Accidentally Started the Sixties*, whose first draft was called "a monumental, epic, glorious literary achievement" by 1960s icon Timothy Leary. But Leary's opinion is not trustworthy. He may have been on acid.

I hitchhiked and rode the rails from Seattle to San Diego, seeking Zen Buddhist satori. Satori was allegedly one of those transcendent, ecstatic inner states. One of those connectors to the gods inside. As I and my two companions, Dick Hoff and Carol Edson, inadvertently gathered followers, music was not an important part of the group forming around us. Or, to put it differently, classical music was my thing. It had been since I was ten. Plus a bit of jazz.

Then came the Beatles.

* * *

Hairstyles give a subculture an identity. From the middle of World War II until 1964, men wore something called "crew cuts"—short, military haircuts with only one and a half inches of hair.[4] Fairly close to bald. Wearing your hair long was something only women did. If you were a male in 1962 and you had long hair, you sparked outrage. Your fellow men got very upset when they saw you from behind. They thought you were a girl, and they lusted after your buns. Then they felt like horse puckey when you turned around and they discovered their mistake. How did they deal with this appalling sensation? They got mad.

So mad that out in California in 1962, in my hitchhiking and riding-the-rails days, five guys picked me up in their car, threatened to gang rape me, and swore they were going to tie me to the rear fender of their Pontiac and drag me to a barber shop. My offense? I hadn't cut my hair in a year, and it had grown out in a wildly corkscrewing Jewfro, something no one alive at the time had ever seen. Hairstyles were tools with which groups like mine expressed their identity, their right to be. Hairstyles were a way of saying "screw you" to the generations that had come before. I'd soon discover that music, too, was one of those identity tools. A tool for the identity of a group. But what in the world is the identity of a group?

* * *

There is a concept that would prove crucial to my work with people like Prince, John Mellencamp, Joan Jett, and Billy Idol. It's loosely derived from a lyric in Arlo Guthrie's 1967 song "Alice's Restaurant." If one person shows up with an odd passion, folks ignore her. If two people show up with an odd passion, folks suspect they are gay. But if fifty show up with an odd passion, folks "may think it's a movement."[5]

Sometimes you have a vague emotional undertow that makes you feel weird and alone. You don't have words for it. And you have a hard time expressing it to your friends. In fact, you think it is a personal insanity and that something is wrong with you. You think it's something that you should hide. Even from yourself. Then a social signal like music helps you discover that you are not alone. It helps you realize that other people feel the way that you do. And it helps you realize that other people want to behave the way that you do.

There's a metaphor that's helpful in understanding this. I can go out to the kitchen, pour twelve ounces of water into a Pyrex beaker, and, where you can't see it, I can heat the water to a boil and dissolve nearly five ounces of table salt in it. A whopping big amount. Then I can let it cool and bring that nice, clear beaker of water into the living room and give it to you. If you don't taste it, it will look like an ordinary beaker of water. Clear as clear can be. But if you drop a single tiny crystal of salt into it, something remarkable will happen. Suddenly, all that salt dissolved in the water will find its common identity. An identity it didn't know it had. The separated salt molecules will rush over to your single tiny crystal and will cohere into a giant mass—a huge, complicated, single crystal of salt. A community of individual molecules. A molecular social group. The water with the salt invisibly dissolved in it is called a supersaturated solution. And, from time to time, we are all lost molecules invisibly separated in a supersaturated solution. Molecules waiting for something that will bring us together. Something that will give us a voice.

My subculture's voice didn't arrive until 1964, with the Beatles.

* * *

The early music of the Beatles was pop. It had nothing to say. "I Want to Hold Your Hand" was not a deeply meaningful message. But in 1964, with their wildly unacceptable long hair, the Beatles helped us discover that we were not alone. They helped us find something we hadn't known existed: our collective soul. As I was about to discover . . . over and over again.

* * *

Where was I in 1964, the year the Beatles outraged our parents? I'd stopped riding freight cars and hitchhiking and had gone back to school. I was a student at NYU. I majored in English literature. That doesn't sound like something that would lead to a career in music, does it? But it would.

Why English literature?

5

THE EINSTEIN IMPERATIVE

When I was twelve, one of the girls in my eighth-grade class swung her gaze in my direction and said, "I told my mother you understand the theory of relativity." It was the first time that any girl in class had ever made eye contact with me. It was startling. And the statement presented a challenge I could not ignore. In those days, it was said that only seven men in the world could understand the theory of relativity. And I certainly didn't understand it. But I wasn't going to confess that to the only woman who had ever looked in my direction in my entire eight years of schooling. So, when classes let out, I jumped on my bicycle, pedaled to the local library, where the librarians knew me better than my mother did, and asked them for everything they had on the theory of relativity. They gave me two books: a great big fat book written by Albert Einstein and two collaborators, and a little skinny book written by Einstein on his own. I started with the fat one.

I had learned that if you plow through something you don't think you understand and you make it to the end, by the time you've reached the last page you actually understand something. Even if you've only understood it in your gut. But when 8:00 p.m. rolled around, I was still only fifty pages into book one—a book with thirty-five equations on each page and very few words of English. I realized that I only had two hours before my mom was going to put me to bed in which to understand the theory of relativity.

So I reluctantly picked up the little skinny book, the one that Einstein had written on his own. In his introduction to the book, it felt as if Albert Einstein had reached out through the page and grabbed me by the collar, then put his nose to mine and said, "Schmuck, listen up. If you want to be a genius it is not enough to come up with a theory only seven men in the world can understand. To be a genius you have to be able to come up with that theory, then express it so clearly that anyone with a high-school education and a reasonable degree of intelligence can understand it." In other words, through the pages of a book, Albert Einstein had told me that to be an original scientific thinker, you have to be a writer. And a good one.

When I entered NYU in 1964, science had been my life for more than half the time I'd been alive. So I felt I could take my science for granted. But I couldn't take for granted what Albert Einstein had demanded of me: the ability to write. If I majored in English literature, I thought my professors would stand over me with a whip, making sure that I learned how to express myself in glowingly delicious syllables. Again, what does this have to do with the music business? Everything, as you are about to see.

One more thing. I loved poetry. I had been obsessed with it since the age of fourteen. I had spent an entire year writing just one four-page poem. So I took a series of poetry courses from the poet-in-residence at NYU, Robert Hazel, known for starting the careers of authors like Wendell Berry, Bobbie Ann Mason, James Baker Hall, Ed McClanahan, Gurney Norman, Charles Simic, and Rita Mae Brown.[6] Authors I had never heard of. One day in poetry class with Hazel, at the end of my junior year, this august poet-in-residence said, "Bloom, wait until everyone leaves this classroom, then close the door and sit," and he pointed to the chair opposite his desk, the balling-out chair.

So I waited until the room emptied, closed the door, and sat in the designated torture seat. Hazel said, "Look, last year I asked you to be on the staff of the literary magazine. You never even showed up. This year I'm telling you, the minute you walk out that door, you *are* the literary magazine. You are the editor. You don't even have a faculty advisor. Now walk out that door." When I stepped into the corridor, I looked as if my guppies had just been strangled. I hated literary magazines. The mere color of their cover, a pale and sickening blue, was enough to stop an orgy and empty a room. The choices of typeface were horrendous. Literary magazines were soul-deadeners.

As I stood in the hallway, looking as if I had just been impaled on a stake, a student I didn't know walked up to me and said, "You look disturbed about something. Could I help you?" "Yes," I said, "I've just been made the editor of the literary magazine." But I said that as if I had just been condemned to be dissolved in a vat of acid in Washington Square Park, opposite the NYU library, at midnight. "Why don't you come down and have a cup of coffee with me?" said my Good Samaritan.

What happened next, bizarre as it sounds, was destined to shove me onto a tangled path that would lead to the superstars.

* * *

Remember, I had not grown up around human beings. The kids in Buffalo, New York, had wanted nothing to do with me. And my parents didn't have the time. My companions were the lab rats, lizards, and guinea pigs I kept in my bedroom. So I didn't know basic human rituals. Among those rituals I did not know was having a cup of coffee.

But I dutifully followed this rescuer down two flights of stairs to Waverly Place and one or two buildings east to—guess what?—a coffee shop. We sat down. He ordered a cup of coffee. I requested a glass of water. And he asked me one of the most important questions I have ever been asked in my life: "If you could do anything you want with this magazine, what would it be?" I scratched my head and said, "A picture book."

Problem solved. I went on a hunt for talented students who wanted to make their way through vast quantities of incoherent student poetry hoping to find something moderately readable—in other words, I started to track down a literary staff. But that wasn't all. I also went on a hunt for visual artists. A friend and fellow NYU student was a member of the Andy Warhol scene and a student in art. I told her my dilemma—I needed artists. "You've got to meet my friend Michael Sullivan," she said. "He's a genius." So we set up a meeting in one of the NYU art school's classrooms. It was in a building I'd never entered, and to a liberal-arts student like me, even the classroom was weird. Instead of desks you could write on, or just plain chairs, it had long, high tables with high stools. Work surfaces for sculptors who wanted their work to be truly elevated? Who could tell. But the room was distinctly alien. What's worse, I arrived at precisely the appointed time—4:00 p.m. But when I entered the room, it was empty. Not a soul in sight. Or so it seemed. Suddenly, from behind one of the worktables, a figure emerged. A very Tolkienish figure. Four feet five inches tall. Round. A hobbit. Shorter than the worktables that had hidden him. It was Michael Sullivan. And, as advertised, his work was (and still is) brilliant.

I walked with Michael over to the apartment he shared with his parents, his brother, and his sister on Tenth Street, between Fifth and Sixth Avenue, a very ritzy West Village block, and learned more about Michael's work. He was a filmmaker, photographer, and model maker who had invented nineteenth century spaceships—steampunk spaceships—long before the days of steampunk, and who today is known in cult circles for his RoboPorn. And for his work as a model maker on the fifth *Star Trek* movie.

Then, through a student who doubled as a drug dealer, I heard of a weaselly little guy with a long, thin, Snidely Whiplash mustache living over on Tenth Street and Second Avenue in the East Village—a neighborhood that was a dangerous slum with a few old Jewish theaters but had rents that an artist could afford. His name was Peter Bramley, and he was brilliant. Sullivan and Bramley became the nuclei around whom I organized a visual team.

The literary magazine—now an experimental graphics and literary magazine—became a smash hit. The poetry won two Academy of American Poets prizes. Or so the poet who won the prizes told me. The NYU art department bought forty copies for their archive—something they had never done before. And the Student Activities Committee was so bowled over that it doubled our budget for the second issue.

When it became obvious that our second issue would be dedicated to sex and death, half of my literary staff quit. And when the sex-and-death issue emerged in the spring, no one on campus would talk to me, including the poet-in-residence who had suckered me into this to begin with. But I got phone calls from:

- the art director of *Look*, one of America's two big, glossy, gorgeous weekly photo-news magazines;
- the art director of the *Evergreen Review*, the leading avant-garde magazine in North America; and
- the art director of *Boy's Life*, the big, full-color, glossy magazine of the Boy Scouts of America.

So our sex-and-death issue was hated at NYU, but it was a hit in the world of high-placed art directors. How would this lead to people like Michael Jackson, Bette Midler, and Prince? How would it lead to the ultimate adventure in the dark underbelly where new myths and movements are made? Hang in with me.

* * *

A few months later, I graduated NYU *magna cum laude* and Phi Beta Kappa with four fellowships in psychology and what is now called neuroscience at four universities. But I had a problem. I had married a woman with a five-year-old daughter just after my freshman year of college. Her previous husband, the father of her child, had been a student at Dartmouth, and she made it very clear that she was tired of having student husbands. If I went to grad school, I was likely to lose my wife.

What's more, as you know, since I was twelve years old, I'd been fascinated by the mass passions that power the forces of history. I'd been fascinated by the mass ecstasies and the strange states of mind that churn out a Renaissance, a Reformation, the idea of democracy, the rise of Marxism, and more. I was on a hunt for the gods inside. There was no way in hell that I was going to see those ecstatic emotions, those wild exaltations of the crowd, if I became a graduate student and gave paper-and-pencil tests to twenty-two college students in exchange for a psychology credit. Academia had begun to look to me like an Auschwitz for the mind.

A solution to this conundrum would soon appear. At the beginning of the summer before I was supposed to start grad school at Columbia University, I walked into the apartment of Peter Bramley, my brilliant artist, and I was shocked. There was no furniture in the apartment. Peter and his wife were sitting on the wall-to-wall carpet with their three-year-old son. All three of them were crying.

What was the matter? They had no money. Their furniture had been repossessed. Their electricity and phone were about to be cut off. And they were about to be thrown out of their apartment. *This is crazy*, I thought, *this guy's a bloody genius*. If I took Peter's work around for as little as two weeks, I was sure that I could get people to buy it—enough people to pay Peter's rent. Then I could find a legitimate summer job to carry me over until grad school in neuroscience at Columbia University in September.

Peter made a demand. If I was going to carry his portfolio, I would also have to carry the portfolio of his best friend, with whom he had moved from Boston to New York after art school in the hope of founding an art studio. Peter's friend's work was horrible. In my opinion, it wasn't art. But I said yes. So Peter, his best friend, and his best friend's wife—whose work was good—all put their art into a single portfolio, and I consulted the *Yellow Pages* and began to take that big, black vinyl portfolio with the crystalline pages to everybody that I thought might be able to buy art. Again, I thought this would be finished in two weeks. It wasn't. In fact, it wasn't finished in two months. But fifteen years later it would be relevant when I worked with Michael Jackson.

The end of the summer came. I had gotten *New York* magazine interested in doing a feature about our studio, but I hadn't sold a single piece of art. And two Swords of Damocles were hanging over my head. If I showed up in September at Columbia University, I stood a good chance of losing my wife. And women sufficiently desperate to marry you are not that easy to find. Or, at least, it is not that easy to find women desperate enough to marry me.

My dad had talked about the importance of what he called the real world. My mom had been a fan of academia. But I had never been prepared for life in the real world. Everyone in my hometown, Buffalo, New York, had known I would be a college professor from the time I was ten. And one of the world's most absent-minded college professors at that. But the real world seemed to be the place where I could find the extraordinary borderline passions that shape and reshape human destiny. And our art studio, Cloud Studio, seemed to be a doorway into the real world. Even more, the studio seemed likely to give me a periscope position from which I could scope out the dark underbelly where new myths and movements are made. So I called Columbia University and said I would be delayed for a year.

* * *

One more thing was crucial to my splashdown in, of all places, rock and roll.

Remember I had majored in English literature in order to learn how to write. When I was twenty, before I returned for my second attempt at a freshman year of college, I had had my first real writing job, proofreading and editing for Sol Gordon, the head of the Middlesex County Mental Health Clinic in New Brunswick, New Jersey.

Sol had been so pleased with my work that he'd proposed that I write a book with him. But instead I went into my freshman year at NYU. (Sol wasn't kidding about writing a book. He would go on to write twenty-six of them.)

When my freshman year at NYU ended, I wanted a summer job that would bring me close to writing. So I looked up every employment agency in the *New York Times* that offered jobs in "editorial." Precisely ninety-eight agencies advertised editorial jobs. I listed every single one of them on a yellow legal pad. Then I called the first ninety-seven agencies. Every one of them turned me down. Finally, I got to the last agency on the list, agency number ninety-eight. I explained myself to the person on the other end of the phone, and she said, "I think we've got something for you." That's how I got a genuine summer writing job—writing for the Boy Scouts of America in their headquarters in New Brunswick, New Jersey. What in the world would this have to do with entering the power pits of rock and roll? Far more than you might think.

* * *

My first assignment was to rewrite the *Boy Scout Handbook*'s chapter on masturbation. Why my editor felt I might be an expert in this subject is beyond me. Then he put me to work rewriting the Boy Scout handbooks on camouflage and stalking and tracking. And he went even farther. He assigned me the task of editing and rewriting *Ten Steps to Organize a Boy Scout Troop*, a handbook adults would use to establish Boy Scout beachheads in neighborhoods that had never hosted a real, live brigade of Scouts before.

The odd thing is this. I had been thrown out of the Boy Scouts for incompetence at Morse code at the age of eleven. Yes, I've been ejected from quite a few endeavors that you'd think would be foolproof. If the Boy Scouts hadn't thrown me out for my inability to grasp Morse code, they could easily have tossed me out for my inability to tie knots. As a Boy Scout I was a complete failure. But writing for Boy Scouts was another matter. I was absolutely determined that if I taught you how to stalk and track, my instructions would serve you so well that you could creep up on a bunny rabbit and it wouldn't see you until you were rubbing noses. So I loved my audience, and I researched my ass off to serve them. This, believe it or not, would prove crucial to my career in rock and roll.

* * *

Now back to attempting to feed a few starving artists. Peter Bramley and his friend, the artistic incompetent, had named us Cloud Studio. For the first year, us Cloud Studio members made a total of seventy-five dollars a week each. That's $533 in today's dollars. But, one way or the other, it seemed pitiful.

Nonetheless, eventually we built our visibility and credibility in the community of New York's art directors. *Art Direction* magazine put me on the cover. I invented a new animation technique for NBC TV. We did book covers for every major publisher, and illustrations for odd magazines like Adam Smith's *Institutional Investor*. Then we hit the big time. We hit music! And not just any music: we bumped into a musical revolution.

We were asked to do an advertising campaign for ABC's seven FM stations. Yes, all seven of them. The corporate HQ that owned these stations wanted us to help them with something risky: the launch of an entirely new radio format, progressive radio, otherwise known as "album radio" and "rock radio." Instead of sticking to a rigid playlist like the Top 40 stations that poured a tiny number of pop songs over and over again into America's five hundred million overworked ears, progressive rock allowed DJs to pick any cut they wanted from any record, and, if it moved them, to play entire albums from beginning to end.

This was a radical innovation. And there was no guarantee that it would succeed. We had a tall, blond, lanky eighteen-year-old artist, Bradley Johannsen, who had literally wandered in off the street one day, hoping that we at Cloud Studio might give him a job, then had lived with my wife, my step-daughter, and me for the next year. He was a brilliant psychedelic surrealist whose work was unlike the art of any other human I have ever seen. Brad created new worlds—wonder worlds—with paper and fluorescent ink. So he drew and colored a separate wonder world for each of ABC's seven FM stations. Seven delicious, nonexistent planets with mermaids and twelve-year-olds with wings.

There was a craze for the psychedelic posters being used to promote rock concerts at places like the Fillmore West and the Fillmore East. In fact, the Fillmore East was a mere two blocks from our art studio's headquarters in New York's East Village, on Fourth Street and Second Avenue. Brad's work not only fit the psychedelic poster craze, it radically outpaced it in imagination. Because Brad's work was so intense and three dimensional, it made the flat graphics of traditional psychedelic artists look, well, flat. And it gave an irresistible look to ABC's spanking new progressive stations from New York, LA, and Houston to San Francisco. In fact, when the guys from the Houston station rolled up to one college campus with the back of their station wagon filled to the ceiling with posters, the college students gathered 'round and grabbed the

posters until they were all gone. The radio-station folks were left without a single poster for their original purpose—to hang in public spots on campus.

The result? ABC asked me to found an advertising agency to handle their account.
I did not want to learn time-buying, a craft with no soul, and we continued to work
on just ABC's art.

Meanwhile, whenever I walked into ABC-FM Radio's headquarters on Sixth
Avenue and Fifty-Fourth Street in Manhattan, there was music playing. Rock music.
In those days—1970—the two leading rockers were Carole King and James Taylor. I
could tell them apart by the fact that James was a male and Carole was a female. That's
how little I knew of rock music. Remember, my main fare was Beethoven, Bartok, and
Stravinsky. But the head of promotion for ABC Radio, Penny Ross, was extremely
kind to me. She gave me records. She told me about the rockers. And, one day, she
invited me to a concert.

* * *

ABC was going to host a piano player in its Studio B, a studio with enough seats for
roughly two hundred people.[7] I had only been to two rock concerts before in my life:
the Jefferson Airplane, and Country Joe and the Fish. But I thought Peter Bramley,
my star artist, might enjoy the experience, so I took him to the concert. Peter sat on
my right. And he embarrassed the fecal material out of me. He stood, he whooped, he
hollered, and he whistled. I was hoping that no one would notice that he was with me,
but that was impossible because he was seated directly next to me, and it was obvious
that I had brought him. Talk about humiliating.

Eventually, the performance came out as a record album. The name of the piano
player? Elton John. And that live album became a classic, Elton's *17-11-70*. When
I heard it on the radio, over and over again, in the years afterward, I realized that
Peter Bramley had made the concert. He had given Elton John the energy that every
performer needs in order to reach the level of a transcendent performance—an ecstatic performance of the kind that I had been searching for in my quest for the mass
passions that power the forces of history. The sort of performance I'd had at the Park
School of Buffalo when I'd been carried out on the shoulders of the audience.

Then came another really big job. Matty Simmons was a man who had participat-
ed in the invention of a brand new thing in the 1960s. He had helped create this innovation for an old company that specialized in getting money to travelers—American
Express. Matty's new invention was called the credit card. Then Matty had left the
credit-card business. Now that he had a small fortune, there was something else he
wanted to do. He wanted to be a publisher. He bought a monthly magazine for young

women, *Ingénue*. Good, he was now in the magazine business. But he had his eye on something a little more off-kilter. There was a gaggle of kids at Harvard University who churned out a once-a-year magazine. That annual magazine sold out every single copy on newsstands all across America. In hours! And it was an institution. Every year, another group of kids from Harvard would churn out another edition of the magazine. And it, too, would sell out every copy. Everywhere that fine magazines were sold.

Matty flew up to Boston, searched out some of these Harvard kids, and made two of them an offer. He would set them up in an office in Manhattan and would bankroll them to churn out a new copy of the magazine every month. And he would pay them nice, fat salaries. The two Harvard kids, Doug Kenney and Henry Beard, took him up on the offer.

But what was the new magazine going to do for art direction? Matty Simmons treated me like a father. So he hired us, Cloud Studio, to handle the task. That meant there would be a big, fat check—$17,200 a month in today's dollars—rolling in every month.

Now, remember, we had one artist whose work was sickeningly bad. I had accepted him because he was an undetachable tumor on one of our most charismatic artists, Peter Bramley. However, this artist, who will go unnamed to protect me against his attorneys, was better with words and persuasion than he was with visual art. Far better. He lobbied the other artists with two messages. First of all, that I should be voted out of the studio. After all, with that big fat check coming in, I was unnecessary. And if they didn't have to pay me my percentage, there would be more money to go around. That was message number one. Then there was message number two: that he should art direct the magazine.

The name of the Harvard student magazine that had started all of this? The *Harvard Lampoon*. And the name of the new monthly magazine based in New York City? The one our incompetent artist had just hijacked? The *National Lampoon*.

So I was voted out of the studio. And the first seven issues of the *National Lampoon* were appallingly art directed. Then the *National Lampoon* fired Cloud Studio. A wise decision, since art direction establishes the identity of a magazine, and Cloud Studio was botching the job terribly. But, very strangely, this move would come out in my favor. It would wedge me into rock and roll.

* * *

During my three years laboring to establish Cloud Studio, Einstein's demand that I become a writer had sledgehammered the back of my brain. For some reason, Einstein's voice was telling me that writing for the head of the Middlesex County Mental Health clinic about issues in psychology was a nice first step, but now, to write in a style that anyone with a high-school education and a reasonable degree of intelligence could understand, I needed to reach a mass audience—I needed to become a magazine writer. Which, frankly, looked impossible.

Yes, I was encouraged by someone with *Esquire*-magazine contacts to go out to a suburban town in Connecticut every weekend for two summer months with spiral notebooks and a tape recorder to interview teenagers about sex and drugs in their lives. It was amazing. The sex-and-drug revolution I'd helped pioneer on the West Coast in 1962 had gone from nineteen- and twenty-year-olds down to eleven-year-olds. And the kids of suburban Connecticut broke down into four separate subcultures—preppies, jocks, heads, and greasers. But this deep dive into the wilds of the normal didn't result in an *Esquire* story. So how in the world was I going to break into magazine writing? While running an art studio? The answer? My clothes.

* * *

There's something I haven't told you. I do not like to wear suits. To me, a suit jacket is a straitjacket. Jackets and dress pants wrap around you like boa constrictors. They won't let you move. Try catching a falling squirrel in a suit. You can't. You can't lift your arms above your head. And as for ties, well, how in the world has modern Western fashion convinced men to tie their own nooses? So I'd found a designer in the East Village near our studio, Susan Harris, who made unusual looking outfits out of Indonesian cotton batiks—outfits in which you could easily dive for second base or reach up and catch a fly ball. Well, *you* could. I couldn't. I can't throw or catch a ball. But if I'd wanted to, I could have made a good try. What's more, the batiks were so light that if you were carrying, let's say, a black vinyl art portfolio on your way to, let's say, a midtown Madison Avenue advertising agency and it poured, your clothes would get soaked, but when you were out of the rain, waiting for the elevator, they would dry before the elevator came.

I designed a broad belt and a leather pouch to go on the outside of any outfit I wore, so I could carry cash, subway tokens, and a small, leather-bound, custom-made, three-ring notebook. And I bought a five-dollar used fur coat on St. Marks Place in the East Village, a red fox coat in which I had Susan Harris install a red paisley lining. Problem was that the pelt was so old it was dried and crackling, which meant I left red tufts of fox fur in every major advertising-agency waiting room in Manhattan. Then there was the gorgeous black Persian-lamb coat that my wife's mother gave her on one condition and one condition only, that she not let Howard get his hands on it. With help from Susan Harris, I had it turned into a Henry VIII–style jacket with huge Persian-lamb epaulets on the shoulders, striped aquamarine and gold crushed-velvet sleeves, Persian-lamb gauntlets at the cuffs, a striped crushed-velvet bodice, and a short Persian-lamb skirt angling down from the hips like armor, emphasizing the slender waist. Sounds feminine. With its assertive shoulders, it was the opposite. At least I hoped it was the opposite.

Then, one day, I walked into the garment-district office of an underground fashion magazine bankrolled by Baron Wolman, one of the founders of *Rolling Stone*. I was wearing one of Susan Harris's batik outfits when I stepped out of the freight elevator and walked into the industrial loft that served as an office, prepared to lay the Cloud Studio portfolio on a desk and get the show underway. But the show never began. Instead, the three female editors of *Rags* stared at my clothes. "Do you have more of those?" asked Mary Peacock, the editor in chief. "Yes," I said, "I have a whole closet full of them." "Do you think you could write an article about them?" asked Mary. *Hmmmmmm*, exactly what the spirit of Albert Einstein had been urging me to do.

So, when I went home from the art studio that night, I made dinner, fed my wife and daughter, sat down at our big 1940s manual Remington typewriter, and hammered out my first magazine article. It was a cry of freedom for those of us who want to throw off the shackles of suits and ties. Then *Rags* made me a contributing editor, and I slammed out 174 more pieces for them, some of them very tiny, some of them reasonably big. Next, another of *Rags'* contributing editors decided to start her own magazine, *Natural Lifestyles*, and asked if I'd be a contributing editor to that, too.

The result? I'd get up at six in the morning, naked, go directly to the typewriter, write until eight, put on one of my Susan Harris jumpsuits, head for the studio, spend the morning calling art directors, spend the afternoon visiting art directors with our portfolio, go home to Cobble Hill in Brooklyn, make dinner for my wife and daughter, and type on the kitchen table, with a coffee pot a quick arm-stretch away. It was becoming exhausting. Then my artists tossed me out and started savaging the poor, helpless *National Lampoon*.

Half my artists left with me, and we started another studio, Muggles, the Sybaritic Studio. But that meant building another business from scratch. And I really wanted to write. Remember, Einstein had said you can't be an original scientific thinker without sparkling prose.

Meanwhile, a crazy hippie friend leading a commune in Saratoga, New York, called and told me about a guy named Cleve Baxter.[8] Cleve was a CIA lie-detector expert. He'd hooked his lie detector's input up to a leaf of one of his plants. And he'd hooked the lie detector's output up to his stereo. Then he'd discovered that whenever the plant sensed death, it screamed. Or that's how he interpreted things. For example, the plants screamed when Baxter washed some baby shrimp from his aquarium down the drain. And the plants screamed when he stirred his cup of yoghurt, killing its bacterial inhabitants with the preservatives in the jam at the bottom of the cup. So I did what may have been the first ever interview with Cleve and wrote it up for *Rags*. Later, Cleve would become famous, appearing on national radio and providing the focus for a book called *The Secret Life of Plants*—a book that was made into a documentary film.[9] This wasn't science. Far from it. But it was a great story.

Then, one day, *Natural Lifestyles* assigned me the job of covering a parapsychology convention here in New York. You know parapsychology—telepathy, mind reading, telekinesis, bending spoons with your thoughts, and other such seriously not-scientific stuff. But there are sometimes hints to unspoken realities in the most unexpected things. There I was, milling around with a crowd of mind-readers, my notepad in my hand—a notepad that often seemed like a fifth limb that had emerged from the womb with me—and a kid a few years younger than I was walked over and popped a question: "Would you like to edit a magazine?"

Hmmmmmm, if I edited a magazine I could do my writing during the day. No more 6:00 a.m. and 11:00 p.m. manual typewriting. What's more, it didn't matter what the magazine was about. If I, a person who can't find his way into a forest much less out of one, could edit Boy Scout manuals on stalking, tracking, and camouflage, surely, with enough love for my audience and a sufficient quantity of research, I could write about anything in the cosmos. So I said yes. And this person from out of the blue set up a meeting with a publisher.

Now, in those dim and distant days of 1971, we didn't have Google, so you couldn't look up the publisher's name and see his accomplishments. In fact, you couldn't even look up the name of his magazine and check out its subject matter. Which means I went totally unprepared to an interview in a high-rise Manhattan office and residential building at One UN Plaza on the East River with a view up the river, down the river, across the river, and south to the United Nations, which was on the same plot of land. When I walked in, there was a windowless converted storage closet to my right. In it were two editors who had just quit, packing up their things. To my left was the door to an executive office. I was ushered through the door to my left to meet my interviewer, publisher Gerald Rothberg, the man with six windows and a view of roughly five miles of the East River. It was from Gerry that I got the lowdown on what the magazine was. Its name was *Circus*. But it wasn't a magazine about elephants and clowns. It was a magazine about rock and roll.

Did I know anything about rock music? Not a stitch. Yes, I knew the difference between Carole King and James Taylor. By sex. And I had seen Elton John perform live. But that, along with a little Jefferson Airplane, Janis Joplin, and Buffy St. Marie, was about it. Did Gerald Rothberg care? Not really. His editors were leaving. He was due to have a complete magazine at the printer in two weeks or he would lose his distributors and his income. Not a word of that coming issue of the magazine had been put together. Gerry did not ask me about the fine points of the Rolling Stones, the Beatles, and the fleas on Eric Burden and the Animals. He had only one question: can you give me a finished magazine in two weeks?

Well, I'd learned quite a bit putting together the NYU literary magazine, the *Washington Square Review*. But that certainly wasn't the kind of deadline-pressure publication Gerry was talking about. Nonetheless, something deep inside of me told me unequivocally that the answer was yes. And when I uttered that answer, Gerry hired me on the spot.

Lord knows how I put together that first issue of *Circus*. There were articles I could use laying around the converted utility closet. Gerry pointed me to two British rock weeklies, *Melody Maker* and *New Musical Express*, and suggested that I steal news from them. I took huge heaps of paper down to the library where my wife was working on Manhattan's West Twenty-Third Street, laid them out on a big, wooden library table, and started editing. And writing.

Two weeks later, I had a completed magazine. Gerry accepted it with relief and went down to the printer in Pennsylvania to get it inked in mass quantities on genuine paper and shipped to the distributor. Then Gerry's wife called to say her husband was very uncomfortable with me working at my big library table with thirteen-foot-high windows on Twenty-Third Street. Could I please soothe Gerry's anxiety and work out of the windowless utility closet across from his many-windowed, luxury office? I didn't want to give another human panic attacks, especially one who was paying me a salary that looked substantial at the time—the equivalent of $61,000 a year in today's dollars. And who was paying me to write and edit by day. So I moved to the closet, which had a Remington manual typewriter from the 1940s almost identical to the one I had at home.

From day one, I studied rock and roll like a Talmudic scholar. I brought lunch to the office in the traditional brown bag, laid out *Melody Maker* and *New Musical Express* on a table, and, while I ate lunch, read them from cover to cover. I talked on the phone to the team of writers I pulled together. They helped educate me. Then Sony came out with a new gadget—a pair of huge, silver earphones with antennae that extended two feet into the air like the antennae of a creature from Venus. The gizmo had a package of electronics that fit in a narrow, black box on the top of your head. Sound weird? It was. But it was a portable AM/FM radio. And its stereo separation and high fidelity were stunning.

I listened obsessively to the Sony radio when I was peddling into *Circus* from Brooklyn and back home again on my bicycle. That's two hours of listening time a day. I discovered a show called *Casey Kasem's American Top 40*, a rundown of the forty hottest songs on the charts. And I taped *Casey Kasem's American Top 40* and listened until I could identify every hit by its first two notes. In other words, I ate, breathed, and slept music. For the second time in my life. Again, remember that phrase, eating, breathing, and sleeping music. It will prove crucial.

* * *

Meanwhile, Gerry Rothberg had another challenge even bigger than going from utter ignoramus to sizzling expert in a matter of months. When I finished work at six o'clock, he would summon me to his office with six windows. And we'd have a ball. He showed me two magazines from Europe—Germany's *Bravo* and France's *Salut les copains*. Gerry had come from *Esquire*, and he had high ambitions. *Bravo* and *Salut les copains* each had a circulation of a million. And each was in a market a fifth the size of the population of the United States. So it was as if each magazine sold five million copies per month. America's biggest-selling music magazine was *Rolling Stone*, and it sold a measly 250,000 copies a month. A piffle by comparison. How, Gerry wanted to know, could you goose a magazine so it would sell its theoretical equivalent to *Bravo* and *Salut les copains*?

Sometimes, says my book *The God Problem: How a Godless Cosmos Creates*, a good question is more valuable than a brilliant answer. And Gerry had asked a very good question.

But that wasn't all. Gerry wanted his magazine, *Circus*, to read like *Time* magazine. It just so happened that I had grown up reading *Time* magazine from cover to cover. Every year, *Time* had a national promotion designed to get high-school students to beg their parents for a subscription to *Time*. The marketing and promotion folks would have a *Time* Magazine Current Events quiz in your high school. Yes, yours. The winner of this competition in each school would win a genuine, big, glossy, full-color book from the amazing series on history, archaeology, and god-knows-what all else that Time-Life publications churned out. I was lucky. I had a friend when I was in high school. Yes, just one. And, every year, he and I would tie as winners of the *Time* magazine quiz. Since our school did not want to saw a Time-Life book in half and give a slice to each one of us, our teachers had to work out an egalitarian way to handle this tie. They did it by not handing out any prize. Despite this deprivation, when it came to *Time* magazine, I was an addict.

So, in addition to studying the rock world and its denizens over lunch, I took home copies of *Bravo* and *Salut les copains* (I already had *Time*), and, at night and on weekends, dissected them like frogs. The workload—the study plus the story-assigning and editing process—was so intense that on Saturdays and Sundays I would sit at the Remington typewriter on the kitchen table in my Brooklyn apartment from the time I got up to the time I went to bed. My wife would make me a sandwich for lunch and quietly place it next to the typewriter so I could hold my train of thought and not lose my concentration. Editing an article so the story reads like a drama is like putting together a jigsaw puzzle while you're juggling the pieces in midair. You have to hold all the sentences in your head at once so you can string them together in a way that makes a compelling narrative. A narrative that comes across in the style of *Time* magazine.

Normal kids grew up with rock and roll. And normal kids hated me. So, as I mentioned briefly, I'd grown up with Beethoven, Bartok, Rachmaninoff, Stravinsky, and jazz. Which meant I was going to have to understand normal kids. Ahhhh, a perfect opportunity for urban anthropology. A perfect opportunity for participant/observer science. A perfect opportunity to search for the gods inside. So I began to invent no-cost ways to get to my audience's heart and soul. Ways that often derived a lot from Martin Gardner's "Mathematical Games" section in the *Scientific American*, a magazine I'd read from cover to cover when I was a child.

What's more, *Salut les copains*, the French magazine Gerry Rothberg wanted to emulate, had a way to feel out its readers' interests. *Salut les copains* ran a Top 20 chart with a ballot beneath it asking you to vote for your five favorite acts. Then it compiled the Top 20 based on reader ballots. And readers did everything in their power to make sure their favorite groups made it to the top. So I convinced Gerry Rothberg to let me run a similar ballot and a reader-based Top 20 in *Circus* magazine. In fact, Gerry went a step farther. He hired someone to tally the ballots every day. Ironically, this new assistant worked in a room with a window. I continued pounding away at my Remington manual typewriter keys in my windowless closet. Our ballot-counting assistant's wife would someday manage Donna Summer. But I digress.

We were swimming in record albums. Every day, a stack of a dozen or more albums would arrive in the mail. They were a nuisance. No one had time to listen to that much music. So I offered a free album to the first five readers who would tell me their favorite paragraph in the magazine. Turned out that my kids, my readers, favored paragraphs that told stories in vivid detail, and, most important, that had hints of sex or violence. I shaped our style to suit their hungers. Happily. Remember, I'd made an entire issue of NYU's literary magazine the sex-and-death issue. So my audience and I were in sync.

On our Top 20 ballots, you had to fill in your city, your sex, and your age. Turned out our audience was 80 percent male and averaged 16.5 years old. Yes, we had readers who went from twelve to twenty. But the bulk of the audience was precisely 16.5.

I talked Gerry into giving me sales figures per issue, something he'd never previously divulged and that he didn't part with very easily. Then I ran rough correlational studies to see what factors corresponded with increased or decreased sales. It pays to come from the world of science. It turned out that we sold best when we had easily visible headlines on the cover—headlines about acts that were hot on the *Billboard* sales charts when we hit the newsstands. Well, not just hot on the charts. The acts that sold magazine copies for us had to have one other factor. They had to be touring bands, bands giving live concerts all across America. If a singer had a hit at No. 1 but hadn't toured America from coast to coast at least three times, it was the kiss of death. Our readers weren't interested.

Why? It turned out that there was a huge difference between "singles acts" and "album acts." A singles act could be an absolutely terrific vocalist, like Leo Sayer, who had two No. 1 smash hits, one hit at No. 2, and could sing like a castrated angel. But he was a girls' act. A girls' act like David Cassidy, Bobby Sherman, or Donny Osmond. Our audience of young males wanted nothing to do with groups that girls swooned over. Confessing that you liked one of these pop stars would have destroyed your newly hatching image of machismo.

Album acts were bands you heard about from your friends. And how did your macho male friends and their friends' friends discover testosterone-pumping bands? Not from their parents. Not from their sisters. From their male friends. Male friends who knew someone who knew someone who knew someone who had seen the band in one of the world's greatest bonding rituals, a concert.

All this would be crucial, eight years later, in saving the careers of Billy Idol and John Mellencamp. And in establishing the career of Joan Jett.

* * *

I was in search of the gods inside. And I found them.

One day in 1971, just after I'd been named editor of *Circus*, I was required to attend my first rock concert. The band was one of a flush of British blues groups that had been big in the late sixties but were now on their last legs. The two most important of these bands had been Chicken Shack and Fleetwood Mac. This concert was Fleetwood Mac at Carnegie Hall.

The performance began normally enough. There were three thousand of us in the audience. While the lights were up and there was no band onstage, we were all insanely self-conscious, aware of how the people behind us and on either side of us viewed us. We were trying to look intelligent and under control. In other words, we were trying to look cool. Then the lights went down, the band took to the stage, the music began, and I got my first glimpse of that mystical thing that happens at concerts. We lose our sense of performing for the folks near us and are sucked into the performance onstage. We lose the self-consciousness of our interior makeup department. We are lifted out of our selves. We become a part of something bigger.

Then, half an hour into the show, something strange happened. The power went out onstage, and the house lights, the lights over our heads in the audience, went on. The magic that had sucked us out of our selves was in danger of disappearing.

The stage had no lighting at all. And no sound. But Mick Fleetwood, a tall, gangly string bean of a man, came to the very lip of the proscenium, getting as close to us as he could without jumping down and breaking a leg. He raised his fist in the air, and said, "Fuck this. We're going to rock and roll." The audience was galvanized. Yes, including me. We were all in this together, riding over the forces of calamity and telling them to go intercourse themselves. We were a part of something higher than ourselves. We were exhilarated and exalted.

We were what Hitler's torchlight parade audience in Berlin in 1933 had been. Six-hour nighttime marches of twenty-five thousand SA and SS men, nine abreast, carrying torches and goose-stepping down the Unter den Linden boulevard through Berlin's massive triumphal arch, the Brandenburg Gate, to the Presidential Palace and the Reich Chancellery. During those marches, the sidewalk was packed, and each individual on the boulevard felt lifted above his or her self and turned into a salt molecule in the collective crystal of *ein Volk, ein Reich, ein Führer*—one people, one state, and one leader.

We, too, were a group with a collective soul, a soul uplifted by challenge and fired by ecstasies. But we were elevated and galvanized without a hint of scapegoats, violence, and war. By total accident, I had found my way into the land of the gods.

* * *

"But where there are gods, there are demons," says writer Liza Lentini. That became clear in another one of the first concerts I was invited to as editor of *Circus*. Pakistan was bogged down in a nasty civil war. One part of Pakistan wanted to secede and make itself an independent state. The main Pakistanis were not going to take that lying down. The result was war. And, thanks to that war, children were starving to death, dying by the thousands, in the brand new rebel country of Bangladesh.

George Harrison, the Beatle, wanted to do something to help these kids. He wanted to raise money to feed them. So he took over Madison Square Garden for a night and staged a concert starring himself, Eric Clapton, Bob Dylan, and the most famous player of the Indian sitar in the world, Ravi Shankar. Not to mention Ringo Starr, Leon Russell, Badfinger, and Billy Preston. My seat was in a center VIP section, about twenty rows from the stage. Before the concert began, there were two huge screens flanking the stage. And those screens showed horrific scenes of starving kids. I was moved to the gut by these massive photos. But the couple behind me was not.

It was two guys. One of them was bragging to the other, "I was up at Danny Ellsberg's place last week." Daniel Ellsberg was a superstar in politics for giving the *New York Times* a trove of secret documents on the Vietnam War called the "Pentagon Papers." "Danny had this dynamite organic cocaine," continued the person behind me. "Then someone told me about this concert," he said, "The tickets were sold out. So I called Mick [yes, Mick Jagger, the leader of the Rolling Stones] to see if he could get me tickets. Mick said the only way to get them was from scalpers. And the scalpers were charging $200 a ticket [$1,200 in current dollars]. So I bought tickets and flew down from Boston. You should have seen the face on the stewardess when I offered her organic coke from Danny Ellsberg."

Pictures that would have tortured the heart of Jack the Ripper were flashing on the screen, and all this goofball behind me could do was brag about his super-rich celebrity lifestyle. Who was the guy behind me? Abbie Hoffman, leader of the Yippies, a man who publicized himself as one of the most feeling, compassionate leaders on planet earth. And who was the person next to him? Jerry Rubin, Hoffman's partner in leading left-wing events like the protest that turned the 1968 Democratic presidential convention in Chicago into an embarrassment. The protest that helped the Democrats lose to Richard Nixon. The gods inside can be mobilized for good or they can be mobilized for evil. From this conversation, I'd guess that Abbie Hoffman was just a tiny bit on the side of evil. But there would be far harsher evils to come. Much harsher.

6

A TALE OF TWO HORMONES— A BRIEF HISTORY OF POP

What's the difference between stars who become icons and stars who disappear overnight? What's the difference between singles acts and album acts? To understand that, you have to understand three things:

1. soul,
2. screaming girls versus rebellious boys, and
3. the Great Sex Shift.

Let's start with soul. We owe the meaning of the word "soul" to American black culture. We also owe black music for feeding the human spirit, even in white music, whether that food for the spirit is served up as a vital spice in country and western, punk, rap, or just plain rock and roll. Or, to put it differently, pop music thrills not because of its black or white components. It rocks because it makes something new from black and white combined. Why has black music had a soul that white music often lacked? Because of the gods inside. As you would see when the most astonishing percussionist of the twentieth century, Ralph MacDonald, would bring you face to face with the Yoruban god of thunder. But that's for later.

Black rhythms have been breaking through the boredom of white music since the birth of the cakewalk among slaves in the 1850s, ragtime in 1895, and the blues in Mississippi in 1903. All three of these became musical crazes. And they became crazes not just among blacks but among whites, too.

Then, in 1904, a new music crept out of New Orleans. In those days, New Orleans had a thriving red-light district, Storyville, a neighborhood where prostitution was king. In the houses of ill repute where the wealthy went to buy upscale sexual services, ambitious madams attracted the powerful by providing extra luxuries, extra touches of forbidden deliciousness. One of those deliciousnesses was forbidden entertainment. In 1902, a seventeen-year-old black piano player named Jelly Roll Morton added to the glamour of New Orleans's sex-for-sale mansions by introducing a black breakthrough: jazz.

Just how forbidden was this new, syncopated musical form? There was a clue in Morton's first name. "Jelly roll" meant the sweetness that your tongue discovers when it slips between the labia of a young woman. And Jelly Roll Morton's new music was so subversive that it got its name from the unmentionable scum of the houses of ill repute where Morton played. I'm talking about the crusty scuz the laundry women had to use extra effort to wash off of the brothel sheets. The new music was named after sperm—in the street language of the day, "jizz." Misspelled and mispronounced, that came out as "jazz."

In 1917, the Original Dixieland Jass Band was the first to headline this scandalous new music to an audience in New York City. Ironically, the Original Dixieland Jass Band was not original. It was an imitation. It was white and came from Chicago. And it was not from Dixie. It merely imitated the unmentionable black New Orleans sex-work music.

But put yourself back into 1917 as a teenager. Your parents are so shocked by this music playing at Reisenweber's Café near New York City's Columbus Circle that they will wash your mouth out with soap and water if you even pronounce its name. Does that make you want to avoid the new music like leprosy, or to adopt it as your own? A year later, jazz would become the official music of youthful rebellion. In fact, in America, the period from the end of World War I in 1918 to the Stock Market Crash of 1929 would be called the Jazz Age.

What accounted for this smashing success? Jazz wasn't just a music, it was a lifestyle. If you were seduced by jazz and you were a woman, you shocked your parents by cutting the hair that you'd previously worn down to your waist. You bobbed it, as in the 1920 F. Scott Fitzgerald story "Bernice Bobs Her Hair." Your mom knew exactly what that new hairstyle meant. You were a whore. Even worse, you wore a dress that your mother told you made you look naked. It was silk-thin. It clung to your butt, your hips, and your breasts, and it hinted at your slender waist. If you were lucky enough to have one. For Chrissake, whatever happened to corsets and bustles? Not to mention modesty?

Then you gave your mom a further heart attack by going out in a new form of transport, a car, to dance with a young man . . . without a chaperone. Yes, you stepped into a mobile bedroom, a rolling pair of couches, with a sex-starved male. And to wave it all in your parents' face, you called yourself a flapper. It was a miracle that your parents survived. Jazz was an identity tool. A crystal of salt. A voice for the soul of a group.

But as jazz seeped into the hands of white musicians like the superstar conductor of Caucasian jazz orchestras, Paul Whiteman, the music slowed down and lost its edge. By the 1930s, young people needed a new music with which to give their parents coronary fibrillation. And they got it in a sped-up version of big-band jazz called swing. A music that, as usual, came courtesy of black culture.

Swing, like jazz, was far more than just a sound. Like the music of the Jazz Age, it was a lifestyle. Young men horrified their parents by wearing pegged pants, whatever those are, and heading for swing-dance halls. Young girls sent their parents into paroxysms by joining the young men. And the Episcopalian bishop of New York wrote in the pages of *Billboard* magazine that swing was leading the youth of America down the primrose path to hell, and strongly urged that all swing records be destroyed. What's more, the Archbishop of Dubuque, Francis J. L. Beckman, called swing music "a degenerated musical system . . . turned loose to gnaw away at the moral fiber of young people."[10]

One generation after another, parents panic about a fact that threatens them profoundly. Their kids have grown hormones and are about to make what Shakespeare called the "two-backed beast." And music helps those kids find a collective identity—a togetherness that validates their rebellion. Which means that, at its base, music is about sex. And sex and soul go hand in hand. So do sex and rebellion. And so do sex and ecstasies. In sex we sometimes reach a jet stream of passion best described by the word divinity. Sex and the gods inside are sometimes one.

More about the moral panics of parents later. Meanwhile . . .

* * *

After swing and jazz, popular music rode a sexual seesaw. First it was big with females. Then it was big with males. First it worked to rouse estrogen. Then it appealed to testosterone.

That sexual seesaw started rocking back and forth in the 1940s. The singers of the 1920s, like Rudy Vallee, had shouted their songs to reach the folks in the seats in the back of a concert hall. Vallee even used a megaphone. In the 1930s, Bing Crosby had invented a new way of using three new gadgets: a microphone, an amplifier, and speakers. Thanks to amplifiers, shouting was no longer necessary. Crosby nearly whispered to the microphone. He was intimate with it. He seduced it. But the real social earthquake didn't happen until December 30, 1942.

In 1942, the nation's young men were away at war, leaving young women without boyfriends they could neck with. No sexual partners to squirm with in the backseats of cars or on their parents' living-room furniture when Dad or Mom had gone out for the night or were asleep. Which means that World War II left the young women of America horny. Sex-starved and making money. Those who weren't still students labored as telephone operators, typists, secretaries, and Rosie the Riveter industrial hands. For example, in just one industry, aviation, "women made up 65 percent of the workforce."[11]

On December 30, 1942, 3,664 young women gathered at a concert in the Paramount Theater near New York's Times Square.[12] It is said that many of the girls in the audience were famished because they had not eaten lunch. More important, they had hit their years of prime fertility. Their bodies and brains were dying for sexual action, and most of the males eligible to satisfy those needs were off in Europe or the Pacific. Fighting World War II. The 3,664 girls at the Paramount came to see a twenty-seven-year-old male onstage who was whippet thin and, like Crosby, could seduce using a microphone. In fact, he sang as if he were seducing each young lady in the audience personally. Whispering his romance lyrics in her ear. The result? Girls did in public things they were only supposed to do in the privacy of the bedchamber during their honeymoon. And a few things they weren't supposed to do even there. They quivered, they quavered, they creamed, they screamed, and they fainted.

Said the singer at the heart of this, "The sound that greeted me was absolutely deafening. It was a tremendous roar. Five thousand kids, stamping, yelling, screaming, applauding. I was scared stiff." Jack Doyle, author of the *Pop History Dig*, calls this explosion of feminine energy a "riot."[13] So the singer was booked first for one more night, then another, until he finally played the Paramount for almost four weeks of these "riots."

When the girls at the Paramount screamed and fainted, a new form of pop stardom was born. In evolutionary biology, it's called a "supernormal stimulus." What's a supernormal stimulus?

* * *

In the 1940s and 1950s, Niko Tinbergen studied herring gulls on the cliffs of Walney Island,[14] off the west coast of England. Herring gulls are seabirds. They fly out over the ocean to scoop up fish. To minimize their commute, their nests are on the flats just a few feet inland from the tops of cliffs overlooking the sea. Those nests are wide and shallow. So when a seagull comes home, squats, and wriggles to position herself on her eggs, she often shoves an egg outside the low, curved hump that passes for the wall of the nest. Tinbergen noticed that mother gulls stick out their beaks to recover an escaped egg, then tuck those beaks in toward their necks, over and over again, to move the wayward egg back into the nest. Tinbergen figured that the tucking might be a simple reflex. He guessed that reflexes are triggered by simple stimuli, and he wondered what those stimuli might be. So the mean researcher started to put egg-like objects near the escaped eggs, to see if any would do a better job of stimulating the mother than the real egg. Turned out that Tinbergen could make colorful and spotted eggs that were more egg-like than the real thing.

How could Tinbergen tell? When he put one of these artificial eggs next to the mother's very own live, biological egg with her very own private, personal offspring gestating inside, the herring-gull mom chose to scoop up the phony egg and to tuck, tuck, tuck until it was safely in her nest. Tinbergen had made a super egg. He had fashioned the first supernormal stimulus. A trigger that sets off a reflex better than the real thing.

Herring gulls were not the only species suckered by supernormal stimuli. Tinbergen tricked songbirds into ignoring their own eggs and rolling in "black pol-ka-dot Day-Glo blue dummies so large that the birds constantly slid off and had to climb back on." And he lured graylag geese into ignoring their own eggs and trying to roll in a volleyball.[15]

The singer onstage at the Paramount was a supernormal stimulus. No, he was not an egg. But he stimulated sexual centers without penetration. Not to mention without impregnation. And he did it better than the real thing, a boyfriend. Thus began the era of the pop star as a birth-control device. The singer causing the hormonal commotion at the Paramount? The walking sex toy pulling young females together like a grain of salt in a supersaturated solution? The man demonstrating the powers of a supernormal stimulus? Frank Sinatra.

* * *

Thus did popular music go from providing anthems for rebellious young men and women dancing with each other to providing sexual outlets for girls and girls only, young ladies tidal-waved by hormones. Music mobs changed from crowds of young men and women doing the Charleston with each other in an upright imitation of cop-ulation to masses of young women wetting their panties and going orgasmic. But, one way or the other, music was about two things: rebellion and sex.

Music was still in the screaming and fainting phase thirteen years later, in 1955, when a white man singing music with black roots came along—Elvis Presley.

Why? The 1940s and 1950s saw the popularization of a concept first invented in the 1920s—the idea of the teenager.[16] A girl becomes ripe for childbearing at roughly twelve years old. But the new notion of teenagehood said that much as she lusted after male penetration, a pubescent girl had to sit on a shelf until she finished something else relatively new—high school. And maybe even college. Which meant that, in the 1950s, the level of sexual frustration among girls was almost as high as it had been during Frank Sinatra's start in World War II. But Sinatra had a problem. By now, he was forty, and performing for an "older" audience. What was the new crop of young American women going to do? They would have to find their own supernormal sexual substitute. They would have to come up with their own talking, walking, crooning birth-control device. And they did.

In 1955, a new twenty-year-old singer took over Sinatra's position as a sexual releaser. He made his role as a sex toy obvious by the way he gyrated his hips. Not to mention the way that authority figures tried to ban those hips from mainstream outlets like TV's biggest variety show, *The Ed Sullivan Show*, and the way that the new singer's promoters capitalized on that censorship. After all, we really, really want to see what we've been told we can't. Don't we?

Why were mere hips offensive? Because this new singer gyrated as if he were in the throes of intercourse. Even worse, his music accumulated a name that in black slang meant, well, it meant fucking. That name was rock and roll. The new sensation's name was Elvis Presley. And, when he sang, girls did precisely what they had done for Sinatra. They screamed and fainted.

During the period from 1945 to 1964, girls dominated the pop music audience. Show-business experts did everything in their power to manufacture imitation Sinatras and Presleys. They did everything they could think of to excite the legions of young girls who would scream and faint. That's why they came up with artificial pop stars like Fabian, Frankie Avalon, and Rickie Nelson. Pop was a girls' world. And pop makers worked their fingers to the bone trying to craft the ultimate super egg.

The result: Fabian and Frankie Avalon were artificial concoctions designed to stoke the estrogen of screaming, fainting girls. Designed to make money. Idol-maker Bob Marcucci told Fabian how to cut his hair (in a pompadour), what shoes to wear (white bucks), and even where to sit in a movie theater (the middle of the row . . . and they had a fistfight about this one). Fabian and Avalon did not write their own songs. Marcucci picked the tunes and tweaked the sound of Fabian's voice in the studio. Said Fabian, who finally bought himself out of his contract with Marcucci for $65,000, "I felt controlled. I felt like a puppet."[17] More important, Fabian wasn't a touring sensation. He appeared on *American Bandstand* twenty times, and popped up on *The Ed Sullivan Show*. He even played a few record hops. But he lip-synched his songs. He was shoved down throats from above, not built from below. More about that later.

In other words, like Nikko Tinbergen making Day-Glo super eggs—eggs so huge that birds slid off of them and had to climb back on top to "hatch" them—Bob Marcucci and his ilk were fashioning supernormal stimuli. Or trying to.

Then came the next big flip. As you know, Elvis Presley had been heavily influenced by America's black music. But the Beatles and the Rolling Stones were obsessed with it.[18] The Beatles and the Stones haunted British record stores looking for obscure "race records"—records from little-known American black guitar players and singers. In particular, singers of the blues. That's what these pale white English kids imitated. Pallid limeys with names like Lennon, McCartney, and Jagger. What secret made black music so essential to these kids? What would continue to make it so essential for white rock and pop? Soul and the gods within. But that's a tale for later.

Meanwhile, these British kids were also influenced by Elvis Presley and the rock-and-roll music that had come along in Presley's wake. Presley was an icon. And icons have powers that we'll dig into farther down the line. So when John Lennon first spotted Paul McCartney "at a fair in the field behind St. Peter's Church in Woolton, a suburb of Liverpool," wearing tight black pants and a white jacket with silver threads, Lennon was impressed because McCartney looked so much like Elvis.[19]

But in the audience, girls were it. So when the black-music-loving Beatles came to America for the first time on February 7, 1964, on Pan Am Flight 101, their promoters did everything in their power to imitate the Sinatra and Presley signs of stardom—mobs of fainting, screaming girls. The Beatles' promoters made sure there was a mob of fainters and screamers at JFK airport when the Beatles flew into New York City.[20] Three thousand of them.[21] And publicist Connie de Nave will gladly tell you her fond memories of rounding up crowds of girls to be at New York's John F. Kennedy airport when the Rolling Stones came to the United States for the first time four months later, on June 1, 1964.[22]

But the publicists and promoters were missing something. The audience for popular music stars was about to flip. Dramatically. Popular music celebrities were about to shift from providing a sexual substitute for girls to providing something equally vital for boys. Something for which the twelve-to-twenty-year-olds of the 1960s had an unseen hunger: rebellion. Individuation. Demonstrating independence from your parents. Independence, in fact, from your parents' entire generation. The emphasis was about to flip from solo males crooning into the microphone to small gangs of young men deliberately defying convention.

To really understand the Great Sex Switch, the switch of popular music from an audience of girls to an audience of boys, you have to understand something else: langur monkeys. When us primates—monkeys and apes—hit adolescence, we begin to smell bad to our parents, and they begin to smell bad to us. Why? Because we are about to become sexually active. If we are male, nature does not want us to copulate with our mothers. And if we are female, nature does not want us to have affairs with our dads. No one is entirely sure why this is true. We think it's evolution's way of keeping us from incest. Incest, it is said, produces monsters. Without genetic variety, we are said to develop all kinds of problems, like the unstoppable bleeding—the hemophilia—that ran in the last Russian czar's family. Why the hemophilia? Because the royals of Europe, it is said, were all related, and tended to marry their cousins. The Czar and his wife, for example, were both first cousins of Britain's King George V. The royal hemophilia was a product of inbreeding. Or so the current scientific story goes.

One way or the other, when we hit puberty, our biology begins to eject us from our family and to distance us from our parents. How do young langur monkeys handle this? The juvenile males get together in gangs. Then those gangs, like gangs of human juvenile delinquents, roam the territory checking out the males of the previous generation. Specifically, they look for older males with harems and kids. Why? Because if they find a dominant male who is slipping, who is getting weaker, who is losing the enthusiasm of his wives, that male is ripe for attack. The gang of youngsters will challenge him. Most of the time, the older male will be able to stand up to that challenge. But occasionally, the gang of youngsters will luck out. They will find a male who is too weak, too insecure, or too poorly supported by his family. In that case, they will stride into the harem and attempt to knock the dominant elder off his throne.

If they succeed, the gang members will kill the former ruler's babies. Why? Because as long as the females are suckling young, they will not be sexually receptive. And what the gang of young males wants is sex. In fact, though they don't see it at the moment, what the gang of males really wants is what comes as a consequence of sex—the ability to reproduce. The ability to have kids and a family of their own. Once the young males have done away with the infants, they fight among themselves until one of the rebels comes out on top. That one takes over the harem. Which leaves the rest of the young male gang to go back to roaming. And to looking for another vulnerable alpha male. Another male they can knock off the top of the heap. Evolutionary biologists refer to these groups of young males as "bands."

What does this have to do with the switch in popular music from singers mobbed by screaming, fainting women to rock bands? A rock band is a roaming group of post-adolescent males, just like the roaming groups of langurs looking for an elder to knock off his perch. Sinatra and Presley surfed the wave of hormones in females. But the rock bands that appeared with the Beatles and the Rolling Stones rode the back of another deep hormonal need, the need of young men to challenge the previous generation . . . and to get sex.

So the Beatles and Rolling Stones arrived in the United States in 1964, packaged to attract mobs of hysterical girls. But, in a very short time, something surprising happened. They attracted mobs of passionate boys, passionate young men. In fact, the sixties was the age when langur monkey principles ruled. A movement that I had accidentally helped found, the hippie movement, did exactly what bands of young langur monkeys do. We challenged our elders. We tried to knock them off the top of the heap. We called them the Establishment. And we declared war on that Establishment. We said that the Establishment had to be driven out of power. And if our attack upon dominant elders wasn't clear enough, we had a slogan: "Don't trust anyone over thirty." Meanwhile, we used a violent, profoundly threatening term over and over again: revolution. Do you notice the langur monkey just beneath the skin?

Again, the biggest statement the Beatles made when they hit the United States for the first time was not in standard pop lyrics like "I Want to Hold Your Hand." It was not in the mobs of fainters and screamers at the airport. Or in the fainting, screaming females drowning out the music on their first *Ed Sullivan* appearance. As you've read a few minutes ago, it was in the Fab Four's haircuts. John, Paul, George, and Ringo's long hair was a deliberate provocation of parents and authority figures. Yes, it was good for publicity. It got the "Four Mop Tops" headlines. But it also said "fuck you" to the powers that be.

What's more, the Beatles did something unheard of for a band of touring musicians. They wrote their own music. They did what adolescent males need the most—they took control of their own lives.

* * *

By roughly 1967, the Beatles had declared that they were angry young men out to topple the norms. John Lennon compared himself to Jesus Christ. The song "Norwegian Wood" made it clear that the Beatles occasionally smoked a forbidden substance called marijuana. Which is what the bohemian kids of my generation smoked. I didn't. I had horribly bad trips on the stuff and avoided it like the plague. But my friends loved to whiplash their minds with a good joint. The Rolling Stones went even further than the Beatles to declare themselves rebels. In one song, Mick Jagger made it clear that he had "Sympathy for the Devil."

The Beatles and the Stones were rewarded for their bravado with every pubescent male's fantasy: unlimited sex.

7

INVENTING THE HEAVY-METAL MAGAZINE

I started at *Circus* magazine in 1971. By then, as you know, it was extremely clear that rock music was no longer the stuff of crooners, it was the territory of young, brash, rebellious males. Yet there was a kink. A big one. I found this strange twist out when the assistant Gerry Rothberg had hired began to total up the votes on the ballots we printed in the magazine. One musical act was twice as popular with our readers as the closest runner-up. That band whomping the stuffing out of its rivals with our *Circus* audience was not the Beatles. And it was not the Rolling Stones. It was a band that rebelled by using androgyny. In other words, it was a band whose lead singer was, in fact, a male, but he would go onstage wearing mascara and a dress. Then, to show that he was just as rebellious as anyone else, he would chop up baby dolls with an axe. His name was Alice Cooper. And the runner-up, the act in second place on our poll, was almost as androgynous as Alice. He, too, had started his career in London wearing a dress. That was before I reached *Circus*. Now he wore clothes that had a little bit of the masculine and a little bit of the feminine. His name was David Bowie. To our audience, it was all Alice and Bowie. No one else really mattered.

Why the appeal of androgyny? It was a great way to shock your parents.

Now remember, Gerry Rothberg had wanted me to turn *Circus* into the *Time* magazine of rock and roll. As a person marinated in *Time* from the age of twelve, I was up for it. But in my coming year dissecting *Time* magazine, I would discover something. *Time* magazine had an A-track, a B-track, and a C-track. Only one person was on the A-track: the president of the United States. *Time* magazine had at least one story on the president every single week. *Time* covered the unfolding events in the president's life as if they were episodes in a soap opera. Every episode left you hanging. Every episode left you wondering how in the world the president would get out of this one. On the B-track were people like Henry Kissinger, President Richard Nixon's high-profile National Security Advisor and Secretary of State. Folks on Kissinger's level would be covered every other week. Then there was a lazy Susan tray full of extra characters who would get coverage every three months, every four months, or once a year.

So I made a proposal to Gerry. We, too, would have an A-track, a B-track, and a C-track. Since Alice Cooper was our most popular artist by two to one, we would cover Alice Cooper every issue. And, like *Time* magazine, we would turn Alice's unfolding life into a soap opera. We would leave you hanging at the end of each article, wondering what in the world would happen to Alice next. Our B-track would be David Bowie. Then I wanted to do a two-page feature in each issue on six artists, testing them to see if any of them got votes, and if any of them deserved to be moved up to the B-track. The new format broke all of Gerry's rules. Up until then, he had refused to cover any artist more than once a year. He'd been convinced that variety was the key to sales. But he very kindly allowed me to make this rather massive change.

And there was something else. Those cover lines that correlated with magazine sales. I showed Gerry how *Cosmopolitan* magazine's covers were art-directed so that the magazine could have cover lines going down the left side of the cover and down the right side of the cover without blocking your view of the sulky cover girl and her cleavage.

More important, we had a four-month lead time. If our cover lines were going to zero in on artists who were in the Top 10 on the charts when we hit the newsstands, I was going to have to figure out how to predict who would be where on the charts four months in advance. So I called all of the record-company publicists and asked them for something that had been top secret—the schedule of their upcoming discs. The record-company publicists were extremely reluctant. They said no. They had never given out anything of this sort before. But I explained that this information would be vital to getting their artists covered in *Circus*. All of them were good souls, and they eventually relented. Well, almost all of them. There was Bob Merlis. But the menace of Merlis would come up much, much later.

Simple correlational studies helped me work out the formula that would allow me to predict chart-toppers long before their time. It turned out that I could do that by using two bits of information: how high a band's previous album had gone on the charts, and how much touring the group had been doing. Surprisingly, most people in the record industry thought that hit songs in the Top 40 were the key to success. As you know, what I discovered was that touring was the key to success. You could sell humongous numbers of albums even if you never had a hit single. You could do it by going out on the road and bonding with your audience in that ecstatic ritual called the rock concert. The rock concert did for bands and their audiences what dancing onstage had done for me and for the high-school kids who hated me. Yes, the kids who had carried me out of the auditorium on their shoulders. It had welded us together in an experience that went way outside the emotional bonds of normal life.

In those days, there was no Google to help you figure out where a band's previous album had peaked on the charts. I was left with only one memory device to rely on: my memory. Which was a problem. I have no powers of retention. But, within months, I could tell you the highest charting position of any band currently showing a reasonable degree of success in North America. Lord knows how.

Gerry Rothberg let me apply the formula I'd worked out. Our audience—my kids—liked it. We increased in sales 211 percent in twelve months. Gerry had been a man of modest means living in a small apartment in the 60s on Second Avenue when I went to work for him. But that changed. Gerry and his wife moved to a huge, modern, aircraft hangar–sized apartment overlooking the East River. Why? As the distributors saw our sales figures skyrocket, they offered Gerry more and more money.

But something strange was about to take place in the office suite Gerry Rothberg occupied . . .

8

THE KENNEDY ASSASSINATION, THE WATERGATE BREAK-IN, AND, WELL, UMMM, ME . . . SORT OF

How do the Kennedy assassination, Richard Nixon, Howard Hughes, and the Mafia get into all of this? Through a man named Art Ford.

Originally, *Circus* had started as a magazine offshoot of a teen music TV show called *Hullabaloo*. *Hullabaloo*'s founder had created *Hullabaloo* the TV show, *Hullabaloo* the magazine, and one other entity—a chain of Hullabaloo teen music clubs all over America. But it was the 1960s, and parents were afraid that clubs meant alcohol, drugs, and unsavory doings of all kinds. In other words, sex. The *Hullabaloo* founder wanted some way to give his clubs a *Good Housekeeping* Seal of Approval, validation as friendly, PG locations where you could trust that your kids would be in the hands of virtue, not vice.

To figure out how to make his operation appear whiter than the driven snow, the *Hullabaloo* founder turned to a guy named Art Ford. Art, who had a room in the *Circus* office complex along with his wife Renee when I got there, gave the following account of why he had been picked for such a task.

He had grown up in Newport, Rhode Island, a town in which every major residential building is a mansion. He showed me a picture of the mansion he'd grown up in to prove it. But with Art you could never be sure. When he was sixteen, Art said, he had become a speechwriter for a presidential candidate who dared run against Franklin Delano Roosevelt—the Republican Wendell Willkie. Then Art had become a New York City radio DJ at a time when DJs were the new superstars. Art had presided for twelve years over a show, *The Milkman's Matinee*,[23] that brought him into contact with everyone from Marilyn Monroe and Billie Holiday to Nikita Khrushchev. How did I know? Because when I was about to leave *Circus*, Art threw a going-away party for me. Art had always been extremely secretive about where he lived. I don't believe he even told Gerry Rothberg. But he claimed to have four apartments in Manhattan. He invited my wife Linda and me to one of them, an apartment done all in white. White rugs, white walls, and white furniture. Art claimed he had purchased the apartment complete with the decor from the legendary French novelist and film director Jean Cocteau. But again with Art you never knew.

Then Art had shown a slide show of what he said were all the celebrities that had turned out to wish me goodbye when I left *Circus*. And there were the pictures slide-showed on the wall: Art Ford with Elizabeth Taylor, Art Ford with Marilyn Monroe, Art Ford with Nikita Khrushchev, Art Ford with half a dozen other stars, and, finally, Art with the MGM lion. It was very impressive. And it was not Photoshopped. In those days, Photoshop did not exist. So how did this ability to hob nob with the most famous people on earth make Art the consultant of choice in turning *Hullabaloo* into a family-friendly enterprise?

Art was a fixer. He used his connections to get a photo of the *Hullabaloo* founder with the president of the United States—Lyndon Johnson—handing over some certificate of presidential approval. Very impressive. From that point on, Art and his wife Renee were permanent consultants to *Circus*, with an office of their own, an office with windows. Remember, my converted closet had none.

When Gerry Rothberg acquired the *Hullabaloo* magazine, he changed its name to *Circus*.

* * *

Why was Gerry Rothberg's office so opulent—with its views up the river, across the river, and down the river, and its ritzy address at one UN Plaza? Because in the early twentieth century, there was a family that had made its money utterly revolutionizing the grocery business. It had created something new, the supermarket. And it had made a fortune.

The founder of the company—George Gilman—had inherited his father's prosperous leather tanning business at 98 Gold Street in Lower Manhattan in the 1850s. Then, in 1858, to present a more genteel face to society, Gilman had started a wholesale tea business. Also in roughly 1858, Gilman had hired a new clerk, George Huntington Hartford. It would prove to be an astonishing manpower acquisition.

Hartford and his sons radically expanded the company, taking advantage of new technologies like the transcontinental railroad, which allowed the firm to go from just the Great American Tea Company to the Great Atlantic and Pacific Tea Company. In 1912, when George Gilman died without a will, his heirs realized that, without the Hartfords, there would be no business. So they kept a passive ownership of just a tad more than 50 percent of the company, but gave control of the operation to the

Hartfords. And, thanks to the Hartfords, by 1912, the Great Atlantic and Pacific Tea Company had four hundred stores, a host of private brands, its own warehouses, a mail-order business, and its own distinctly branded red and black horse-drawn wagons selling Atlantic and Pacific Tea Company products on five thousand routes in the countryside.

Then, in roughly 1912, the Hartfords looked over the American retail landscape and saw that groceries were sold in small local shops with poor variety, poor lighting, and a hard time keeping things like meat and vegetables fresh. So the family invented a grocery market so big and with such a low overhead that it could offer fresh meat and vegetables every day. At a tremendous discount. A grocery market with something relatively new—huge plate-glass windows. Not to mention refrigerated display cases to keep food fresh. By 1925, the company operated 13,961 of these big, low-cost, well-lit stores. And, as time went on, the stores added another convenience—a parking lot out front or in back—to take advantage of another high-tech culture-shift: Americans in the mid-twentieth century had these new luxuries called cars.

The Hartford family named the grocery chain after its original tea business—the Atlantic and Pacific Tea Company. For short, the supermarket chain was called the A&P. And in the 1940s and 1950s, A&P was the dominant supermarket chain in North America. Says Wikipedia, the most comprehensive repository of our current common wisdom, "No retail company had ever achieved these results. A&P was twice as large as the next largest retailer, Sears, and four times that of grocer Kroger."[24]

The family that took the A&P to such lofty heights, as you know, was the Hartfords. And, by 1940, the Hartfords had one of the biggest fortunes in America.[25] Then the family produced an heir who had none of the family's talents and all of the family's deficiencies. He was a spendthrift who came up with project after project that lost money. And who embarked on romantic relationship after romantic relationship that would make great reading in a comedic novel, but all of which were simply awful. This poor heir literally had to pay women to marry him, then to sleep with him, then to bring him to climax (they got a $200 bonus for this), then to divorce him. He was the victim of one predatory relationship after another.

How do I know? This heir would read the *New York Times Magazine* every Sunday, use the lingerie ads as a shopping catalogue, call his secretary on Monday mornings, order the girl on page eleven, then the secretary would track down the model's agency, call the model, and ask if she wanted to have lunch with the heir, who at the time happened to be one of the most famous men in North America. His name was Huntington Hartford.

Again, how do I know all of this? Because roughly six feet to the right of the door to my converted closet was the door to Huntington Hartford's secretary, the secretary who would get Hartford the woman on page eleven. And because one of Huntington Harford's wives—a wife who insisted that she would marry Hartford only if her boyfriend could move into his mansion and continue to sleep with her—ditched him. She was Swedish. And behind her she left a diary. Our *Circus* accountant was Swedish. So Hartford sent the diary over to be translated. And our blonde, female accountant, whose office was six steps to the left of mine, let us in on a few of the details.

Why was Huntington Hartford's assistant located in our office? Because it was Huntington Hartford's office. Gerry Rothberg's svelte office overlooking the East River was Huntington Hartford's personal workspace. But Hartford did not really work. He ran his few entrepreneurial projects from his mansion. Those included a ping-pong table for six players and a place called Hog Island that he wanted to turn into a resort. And they all lost money. At least they lost money as long as Huntington Hartford was running them.

Even changing Hog Island's name to Paradise Island, reconstructing a French monastery previously owned by William Randolph Hearst brick by brick on the spot, flying in fireworks for the opening of the resort from France, and landing the place articles in *Time* and *Newsweek*, couldn't save the venture. The folks who tried to make a go of Paradise Island next—a paint company that diversified its business and re-named itself Resorts International—cleaned up. Keep that name in mind—Resorts International.

What was Hartford's problem? He had great ideas, but he apparently had the attention span of a gnat. He'd make you fly from China to meet with him and hear his next terrific brainstorm, then he'd forget his brilliant new idea and would be too busy to see you when you arrived.

How had Gerry Rothberg—my boss at *Circus*—obtained the Huntington Hartford office? Apparently through Art Ford. In exchange for Gerry's overseeing a magazine Hartford had begun in 1961, *Show* magazine. But there was more to Art Ford than this.

* * *

On June 17, 1972, when I'd been at *Circus* for a year, Richard Nixon's Watergate scandal seized every headline in America. Five Nixon operatives had broken into the Democratic National Committee's headquarters in Washington's luxurious Watergate Complex in the middle of the night to bug its phones. But they'd been caught. And

Art, who often let me eat my brown-bagged lunch in his office, went into high alert. Like most Americans, he wanted to know every juicy detail of the Watergate debacle. But, unlike most Americans, he seemed to have a personal stake in the action.

Art predicted that certain people would be discovered to be members of the Plumbers, the gang that had pulled off the botched break-in. And, indeed, as the names of the Nixon team members who had broken into the Democratic Party's headquarters oozed out, Art's predictions proved to be on target. In fact, Art seemed to know each of the players. What's more, for reasons I simply couldn't see at the time, Art was hyper-alert to the story of a book by author Clifford Irving—a book that later was exposed as phony in a big scandal of its own. It was a biography that its author claimed had been authorized by Howard Hughes. And the whole affair had Art obsessed with the hermit-billionaire Hughes, a man who most of us poor American chumps would have thought was totally irrelevant to the Watergate scandal.

Nearly every day, Art told me about the fact that Howard Hughes had let him stay in one of the secretive billionaire's posh hideouts in LA: a bungalow at the Beverly Hills Hotel. Every night at 3:00 a.m., just to show his mastery of everything in the universe, Hughes, said Art, had a piping-hot hamburger delivered to the crotch of a tree just outside this luxury nest's door. A slightly lukewarm hamburger would not do. It had to be kitchen fresh and piping hot. Most of the year, this bit of splendor in the LA grass—Hughes's bungalow—went empty. Except when Hughes showed up. Or when Art took advantage of Hughes's generosity and stayed in the Hughes hideout. A bungalow at the Beverly Hills Hotel will come up again when we get to one of my most important conversations with Joan Jett.

Art was on to something. His connections appeared in an astonishing exposé of the alleged conspiracy behind the Kennedy assassination that, as I remember it, appeared in *Rolling Stone* in roughly 1973, just as I was finishing my two years at *Circus*. Today, neither I, my assistant, or the two people who volunteered to help me can find the story. But as best I can recall the tangle of details, it goes something like this. The CIA had an unquenchable appetite for laundered money. From the 1940s until 1959, it cleansed its funds in the gambling casinos of Havana, a rip-roaring gaming capital of the Western world—a capital established in part by the member of the Mob with the greatest gift for earning money and counting it, Meyer Lansky. The CIA had ties with Lansky and the Mob that went back to World War II, when the national intelligence-agency crew had used the boys with crooked noses to keep dockworkers from striking, and to make sure that America's ports were free of saboteurs. In other words, the CIA had longstanding ties with the Mafia. When Fidel Castro threw his revolution in 1959, he created a problem for the CIA and for organized crime. Fidel closed down the gigantic gambling operations in Havana, leaving the CIA with no way to rinse and soak its funds.

Meyer Lansky had made a fortune from Cuba, but now the loss of Havana was draining him dry. The Mafia counted on an operation planned under President Dwight D. Eisenhower to put it back in business in Havana. That operation was the Bay of Pigs. But at the last minute, a new president, John F. Kennedy, canceled the air cover for this invasion of Cuba by CIA-trained and -supported Cuban patriots. And, without the air cover, the Bay of Pigs operation failed. Utterly. Because J.F.K. wasn't sufficiently interested in regaining control of Cuba, the Mob had the young and dashing president assassinated. With a little help from the CIA. Or something of the sort.

Meanwhile, back in real life, the CIA turned to Howard Hughes, and asked him to upgrade a gambling mecca in an impossible desert—Las Vegas. A new place to launder cash. Hughes complied. And who provided Howard Hughes with his security, his muscle, and his men with guns? Resorts International, the former paint company that had diversified into security and, more important, into casinos. A former paint company that had bought guess what piece of real estate? Paradise Island.[26] The former Hog Island. What's more, in 1970, Howard Hughes moved from Las Vegas to, of all places, Paradise Island.[27] And who did Resorts International buy Paradise Island from? Huntington Hartford. Art Ford's friend and occasional client. The man in whose broom closet I had the privilege of editing *Circus* magazine.

Oh, and that Clifford Irving book that turned out to be a hoax? A hoax that landed Irving in jail for seventeen months? A hoax that fascinated Art? Who was the phony book about? Howard Hughes. The man who had a hamburger delivered nightly to the crotch of a tree outside a Beverly Hills Hotel bungalow. Irving claimed that the book had been dictated to him by Hughes. That was apparently a lie. But, if I recall this correctly, who did Art Ford think Clifford Irving really got the information from? Robert Maheu. And who was Robert Maheu? A CIA operative who worked as Howard Hughes's right-hand man. In other words, the book for which Clifford Irving was jailed was not a phony. Why was Irving jailed—something that in a land of freedom of speech should never happen, and almost never does? Irving's book was based on legitimate information that Hughes did not want leaked. And Hughes had buddies in the CIA who owed him favors. At least according to Art Ford. If my totally swoggled memory has it right.

One more little after-note. Resorts International would go on to build a casino in Atlantic City called the Taj Mahal. And guess who would buy the Taj Mahal when

Resorts International had burned through three quarters of a billion dollars and run out of funds, and when the place was still unfinished? Donald Trump.

* * *

On my last day at *Circus*, Art Ford would take me into his office, close the door, and say, "You are going into a very big company, Gulf and Western. If that company ever gets into trouble with the government and needs some help, tell Judelson and Bluhdorn [the two men at the top of Gulf and Western] that I have a team of cleaners—former generals and CIA people who can scrub the situation up for them." This was exactly the sort of team that the magazine article illuminating the Kennedy assassination said had helped pave the way for Howard Hughes as he built Las Vegas. Did Art really know such a team? Well, he apparently knew the Plumbers who had broken into the Democratic suite at the Watergate. And he had known Marilyn Monroe, Elizabeth Taylor, Nikita Khrushchev, and the MGM lion. So my guess is, yes. And my guess is that Resorts International's security division—the guys who had kept Howard Hughes safe, had bailed out Huntington Hartford, and would someday sell the Taj Mahal to Donald Trump—was the team Art had in mind.

* * *

Other highlights of my time at *Circus*? A man through whom I would get a preview of the way that Michael Jackson may have been imprisoned by evil. That man was a manager named Dee Anthony. A manager who had nothing to do with Michael, but who, much later in this book, would provide a disturbing clue to Michael's difficulties.

In my first months at *Circus*, before my input from our readers forced me to focus on Alice and Bowie, Emerson, Lake, and Palmer had been one of my personal favorites. Keith Emerson was a wonderful piano player who combined rock, classical music, and showmanship. He was famous for throwing daggers into the keys of his piano onstage. And he even played one of my classical favorites—Modest Mussorgsky's "Pictures at an Exhibition." Emerson, Lake, and Palmer's manager was Dee Anthony. At first, I picked up news on Dee's bands through phone calls to one of Dee's road managers, John Doumanian, who would go on to have a career as an actor in Woody Allen movies. John was wonderful to me. But I'd decided to do a story on Steve Marriott, the leader of England's Small Faces and leader of another band called Humble Pie. Steve was one of Dee's clients. What none of us quite realized at the time was that Marriott was developing an utterly unique vocal style. A few years down the road, that vocal style would be adopted and advanced by a band from Australia who would make this high-strained, R&B-based heavy-metal vocal approach its signature sound. That band would be AC/DC. And AC/DC would be one of my clients. But I'm getting ahead of myself.

Marriott had a new album coming up. John Doumanian and I decided that I should interview Marriott. But Marriott was in England, and I was in New York. In those days, transoceanic conversations were expensive. Gerry Rothberg would not have been able to afford the phone bill for an hour-long call to the UK. So Doumanian offered to set up the call at his office. That's how I met Doumanian's boss, Dee Anthony. Dee was a little round man of high energy. He was all excited to host me when I arrived at his office in the West Fifties in Manhattan. And he had, how shall we say this, a slight Mafia flavor. "Know who makes the best pizza in Manhattan?" asked Dee in his deep, raspy growl. I didn't have a clue. "Gino's down on Thirty-Fourth Street," said Dee, with a twinkle in his eye. "Why don't I send my Rolls-Royce down to Thirty-Fourth Street and get you a slice?"

Then Dee "leaked" me the real story of Marriott's next LP. Marriott and the Small Faces toured ferociously. Which meant that they were away from home most of the year. While he was gone, Marriott's wife had started a relationship with another man. One who was more physically available. This tore Steve up inside. And you could see it in the lyrics of every song on the upcoming album. By this time, I'd figured out something about journalism. As a reporter and writer, you have to be able to create a scene so vivid that your reader feels as if he is in the room with your subject. So I made a point of getting physical details. Where was Steve when we talked? In his house. Where was the house? What sort of neighborhood? What did the room where Steve was sitting with the phone in his hand look like? Et cetera. When I wrote the piece, Marriott was angry. How did I know about his wife? And how in the world did I dare make the interview feel as if I'd been in the room with him as we talked, even though I'd never made that claim?

Ten years later, I would run into Dee Anthony's influence again. In a sinister way. Via Peter Frampton. And, as you know, Michael Jackson. But that's a story for later.

9

HOW VINCE FURNIER BECAME ALICE COOPER

Remember the new formula I'd worked out for *Circus*? We'd have an A-track, a B-track, and a C-track. Every day, I'd go to the office next to mine where the assistant Gerry Rothberg had hired tabulated our ballots. And every day, Alice Cooper was ahead of David Bowie, his nearest competitor, by two-to-one. Which meant that Alice Cooper had to be in every issue of my magazine.

So, now that I was determined to cover Alice Cooper as if he were the president, I wanted to know more about just who and what Alice was. To find out, I made an appointment to meet Alice's manager, Shep Gordon, at his headquarters on Thirteenth Street in the West Village. Shep's office was a small converted two-bedroom apartment on the basement floor of a brownstone, the floor that gets access to the garden out back. I was ushered into Shep's office. It was in the front of the building. You could see the legs of attractive women walking by the window. Walking past on the sidewalk. Unfortunately, because it was the basement, you couldn't see above the knee.

But Shep was amazing. He gave me my introduction to a concept I didn't know . . . rock-and-roll management. And he taught me that managing is the discovery of human souls. I'm not sure if that is the message he intended to get across. But Shep is both sweet and bright. So that may, in fact, be a way of putting it that he would approve of.

* * *

Shep explained that he'd gone to the University of Buffalo, my hometown college, the university where I'd been allowed to bat around Doppler shifts with the head of the graduate physics department when I was twelve, and where I'd been allowed to take a course in philosophy—in Aristotle and Nietzsche—when I was sixteen. But Shep's approach to the University of Buffalo campus was a little less cerebral than mine. He spent his time playing poker. And he was devilishly good at it. Shep claimed he had made a lot of money with his straights and flushes. I didn't believe him. I figured he'd probably been dealing drugs and didn't want to admit it. After all, drug dealing was an accepted entrepreneurial practice for middle-class white kids on college campuses at the end of the sixties and the beginning of the 1970s.

Then I talked to the leader of the gang that had chased me around the block and humiliated me in Buffalo when I was four. My former tormentor had gone to the University of Buffalo during Shep's poker days. And he'd played poker with Shep. What's more, he'd lost. Consistently. To the tune of a lot of money. So Shep, he assured me, was telling the truth. He had made a bushel basket of money playing poker.

With his gambling winnings, Shep said, he had bought a car. Then he and a bunch of friends had done the hip thing to do in those days: they'd headed for the California sunshine. As in the Mamas and the Papas' song "California Dreaming." In LA, Shep and his friends had dropped into a music club. The first band to play had an audience of less than reasonable size. The second band onstage drove every single member of that tiny audience out. The listeners simply couldn't stand what they saw. Or what they heard.

Then a sudden insight thwacked Shep over the head. Just a few years earlier, a Jewish kid from Minnesota had shown up in New York City singing the most Waspy music on earth, folk music. But this intruder from the Midwest had a nasal approach that seemed designed to scoop the earwax out of creatures on some distant planet. What's more, in a field based on traditional melodies and words, this guy had the au-dacity to write his own songs. So when he made his first appearances in the folk clubs of Greenwich Village, every potential listener walked out. And the tables didn't follow the listeners for one reason and one reason only. Their wooden legs were too stiff to bend at the knee. The singer everyone hated was Bob Dylan.

Absolute disgust, thought Shep, could be a sign of impending stardom. So Shep waited until the show was over, then convinced the lead singer to let him manage the band. What experience did Shep have in management? None. Except managing to out-bluff college kids when holding onto a hand with no knaves or royals. But that didn't matter. The lead singer had almost no experience singing. And his band was a bunch of high-school football players. But how a band of football players made it to LA is, believe it or not, a story of soul.

* * *

Here's how Shep and Alice told the tale. Or how I remember it. Back in the 1960s, there was a kid in Phoenix, Arizona, named Vincent Furnier. Vince was a scrawny little thing with a big nose whose mother used to dress him in a suit and tie before she sent him off to school. Vince behaved so perfectly that he became the teacher's pet. And you know what happens to teachers' pets.

The other kids hated the way Vince looked, hated the way he dressed, hated his perfect behavior, and hated the fact that the teachers loved him. So, during recess, they called him "the schnoz" and kicked him around the playground mercilessly.

When he was sixteen, Vince was sitting at his kitchen table. In front of him was a Ouija board piloted by a nice, suburban neighbor who said she had the knack of contacting spirits from a higher plane. Vince was skeptical but willing to go along and play the game. Sure enough, a spirit showed up and began to get personal. It said it was a seventeenth-century witch who had been burned at the stake, and that Vincent Furnier was her current incarnation. The witch's name was Alice Cooper. That hit a nerve. It touched something buried deep inside of Vince waiting to come alive. It touched a buried self that had more passion than anything Vince had ever known.

So Vince put a rock routine together and went onstage during a high-school talent show. But he didn't appear as the well-behaved, scrawny little kid his high-school classmates loved to hate. He wore mascara and a dress and chopped up baby dolls. He did it with passion. He did it with fury. He did it with a conviction and a power that his classmates had never seen. Why? Because the real Vincent Furnier was Alice Cooper!

The mascara-wearing, gender-bending axe murderer inside of Vince had an emotional reality more powerful than the nice kid dressed in a suit. The newly unmasked killer-witch tapped something buried deep in the members of Vince's audience, too. The high-school kids who had hated Vince cheered and applauded his act. They went crazy over it. And the jocks—the same athletes who'd kicked him around the schoolyard—came to him, begging. They wanted to be members of his band. Ten years later, the lucky former football players who'd made it as Alice's bass players and drummers would be millionaires. All because Vincent Furnier had connected with a source of passion buried deep inside of him.

Or at least that's how Shep and Alice told me the story. Or, as I said, how I remembered it. Not to mention how I carried the key meaning of that tale into my future work in rock and roll. I hugged tight to the lesson of the hidden personalities inside of us. Personalities with more power than the self of everyday life. One of my first lessons in soul, and in the gods inside.

* * *

Since then, some avid Alice Cooper fans have corrected me on Facebook. In fact, they've said, Vince Furnier's father was a preacher. Vince was an athlete, particularly good at track. He was popular. He and his fellow track stars put together a band. The high-school talent show did take place. And the band were well received. But it wasn't until they left Arizona and went to LA that the Ouija board incident took place and Vince started to go onstage in mascara and a dress.

One way or the other, Alice Cooper gave something valuable to society. He helped his audience live out its violence and its anger without hurting a single soul. And he did it by finding a self more real and more passionate than the self of "Hello, how are you?" and "Fine, thank you very much."

* * *

That led to a conclusion: what you're selling in the music business isn't an inanimate "product," like a cornflake. In the music business, you are not selling pieces of plastic, streaming, or downloads. You are not branding, marketing, or selling "image." You are selling soul. You are selling raw human emotion. You are selling a sense of self-validation. You are selling a chance to make contact with normally hidden parts of your self. And you are selling the right to feel that even in your weirdness you are not alone. You are selling a salt crystal for the human spirit. You are selling honesty of a very strange kind—honesty that comes from centers that don't have normal voices in the human mind. You are selling the gods inside.

* * *

There were other lessons I learned at *Circus*. None of them quite this deep. David Bowie's managers kept me at a distance. I covered Bowie every other month, but his management team never let me meet him. Instead, once a month, they'd send a gorgeously dressed, beautifully made-up young woman with a stack of slide sheets, sheets with thousands of pictures. And each month, those pictures told a different story. One month there was the flurry of amazing new costumes created by a hot new Japanese designer, Kansai Yamamoto.[28] Including an outfit that could be ripped off onstage, revealing another costume underneath it.[29] Another month, there was Bowie's trip on the Trans-Siberian Railroad from Vladivostok on the Sea of Japan, 3,986 miles across Central Asia to Moscow.[30] I was allowed to pick one or two dozen pictures and have their exclusive use.

But two things were obvious. David had a spectacular ability to find hot new talents who were about to explode in the art scene, to bring them into his entourage, to get them to help him reinvent himself, then to throw those talented people away and find new ones. He was a brilliant creative vampire. And he knew the sort of unusual adventures that made for perfect photojournalism. David Bowie was a P. T. Barnum of the avant-garde.

* * *

My actual interactions with Alice were minimal. Shep ensconced the band in a mansion in Greenwich, Connecticut. He claimed it was the Warner Mansion, the former property of one of the Warner brothers. A quick Google indicates that this claim may have been a bit of fabrication. But Shep knew how to make headlines. He knew how to play what one of my books, *The Genius of the Beast: A Radical Re-Vision of Capitalism*, calls "the name game." Mention as many famous names as you can in a sentence, and you get attention. So Shep volunteered to ship me out to the mansion to interview Alice and the band. The interview with Alice was uneventful. My fault. A good interviewer should be able to get a gripping tale out of a pebble. But the most amazing thing about the mansion was this. It was 1972. American families were struggling to buy a single color TV. Then they were parking it in the living room, so everyone could see it. But Alice and the band were rolling in such luxury that they were able to have toaster-sized portable color TVs in every bedroom. And there were enough bedrooms for all the band members. By the early 2000s, that was normal. Back in 1971, it was unheard of.

But I learned far more from Shep than I learned from the band. And what I learned would make a huge difference for people like John Mellencamp and Prince.

* * *

One morning, when I had taken the subway from Brooklyn to Manhattan instead of biking, I was walking from Grand Central Station to *Circus* magazine's office, pondering a problem. Alice Cooper chopped up baby dolls onstage. He was violent. Was his violence going to encourage violence in his fans? Or was it going to prove an outlet for the instinctual violence in all of us? An outlet that would satisfy our internal demands for bloodshed, but do it in fantasy? And would that fantasy violence decrease the violence in the real world? Was Alice's violence going to be exercise for the animals in the brain?

What did I mean by "exercise for the animals in the brain"? In roughly the 1970s, the Seattle Zoo acquired an ocelot, one of the most gorgeous cats on the planet. But the big feline insisted on yanking out clumps of its fur and leaving bloody sores. This was not the gorgeousness the zoo executives had counted on. The keepers tried everything they could think of to get the ocelot to stop. They changed its food. They changed the temperature in its cage. When they ran out of solutions, someone had an idea. In the wild, ocelots hunt birds. But birds come wrapped in a packing material that does terrible things to your mouth—feathers. Maybe the ocelot had a feather-plucking instinct—an instinct like the yanking-your-egg-into-the-nest instinct of seabirds. So the zookeepers gave their prize cat an unplucked chicken. It worked. The ocelot methodically yanked the feathers off of the dead bird, stopped plucking itself, and resumed its beauty.

Evolutionary psychology says we come prewired with instincts that have helped us survive. Among them are instincts we rein in, ban, restrict, hide, and sometimes loathe. In some cases, the loathing is absurd. And in some cases, it's on target. The two most important of these prewired instincts are sex and violence. As in your sex-and-violence issue of the *Washington Square Review*. And in the sex-and-violence paragraphs *Circus* readers loved.

Is violent entertainment a harmless substitute for real-world violence?

Here are the facts. Violence has plummeted since Alice Cooper's axe-and-baby-doll days. By one measure, violent crimes have gone down to half of what they were in 1993. By another, violent crimes have plunged 75 percent. In other words, violent crime in America has fallen to between a half and a quarter of what it was in 1993.[31] That's astonishing.

Could Alice Cooper's violence have been exercise for the animals inside of you and me? Exercise that made violence unnecessary? We shall have to see.

* * *

Now, remember, I had never worked for anyone else in my life for longer than a summer vacation. I knew as little of the rituals of normal work as I did about having a cup of coffee. I'd been working at *Circus* for a year and a half when my boss, Gerry Rothberg, approached me with a strange question. "Don't you think," he said, "that it's about time for a raise?" A raise. Hmmm, I admit I had heard about such a thing somewhere in my life. But I had no idea of an appropriate answer to Gerry's question.

So I called my friends for advice. Specifically, my friends the editors from *Rags*, the underground fashion magazine for which I'd cranked out 175 stories. Mary Peacock, the founding editor, had shuttered *Rags* when the publication ran out of money, and was now helping Gloria Steinem found a new magazine called *Ms*. Other members of our team had gone to *Vogue*. I called and asked each of them what I should ask for in the way of a raise. And each asked the same question, "Tell me what you do." So I told them. Remember, I had replaced two editors.

My editor friends did a little calculating and all came back with the same answer. I should be paid 60 percent more than my current salary. In other words, I was making $10,000 per year—$61,000 in today's dollars. I should be getting $16,000—roughly $96,000 in today's dollars. That didn't sound unreasonable to me. So I went to Gerry, agreed that he might be right, and that a raise might, indeed be a good idea, and hit him with the $16,000 figure.

I don't know whether he was shocked by the notion. I don't know if he went home to his wife and begged that she once again save him from paralyzing stress. But the next day he came back and said that was unacceptable. In those days, I did not know how to negotiate. And Gerry may have been lacking in that skill as well. We did not discuss a lower figure . . . a compromise. Which backed me into a corner. I could continue at $10,000 a year, or rescue what little dignity I had and quit. Much as I loved brainstorming with Gerry, then turning our brainstorms into realities, I gave six months' notice.

I had discovered a few really terrific writers. One of them was Steven Gaines, who would go on to write for the *New York Times*, *New York* magazine, and *Vanity Fair*. Not to mention writing books about the Beatles, about the ultra-rich in the Hamptons, and about the Manhattan real-estate adventures of Tommy Hilfiger, Donna Karan, Jerry Seinfeld, Steven Spielberg, and Madonna. I suggested that Gerry hire Steve as the new editor. Then I helped put the magazine together and hid away for hours a day in my converted broom closet across the reception area from Gerry's cruise liner–like office. What was I doing? Writing a fifty-seven-page booklet on the magazine format I'd invented to give Gerry the rock magazine of his dreams. A fifty-seven-page booklet on how to turn out *Circus* magazine.

And I trained Steve Gaines.

* * *

Let's do a quick reprise. It was 1973. I'd increased the circulation of *Circus* by 211 percent, had handed Gerry Rothberg six months' notice, had trained Steven Gaines to replace me, and had written a fifty-seven-page handbook on how to turn out *Circus*. At the end of six months, I was in a pickle. I needed to make a living to support my working wife and her twelve-year-old daughter. But how?

I applied for magazine editing jobs, but no luck. Then Steven Gaines, the writer I was training as my replacement at *Circus*, said, "I want to introduce you to someone." That someone turned out to be Seymour Stein. I'd been to Seymour's office in my art-studio days. Seymour had founded Sire Records, whose big acts in those days were the classical rock band Renaissance, and the Climax Blues Band. Eventually, Seymour would sign and build careers for Madonna, the Ramones, Talking Heads, the Smiths, Tom-Tom Club, Depeche Mode, Echo and the Bunnymen, Ice-T, the Pet Shop Boys, and Brian Eno's collaborations with David Byrne. Now, it appeared that, if I was in luck, Seymour might sign, of all people, me.

10

THE CASE OF THE
HEADLESS RECORD COMPANY

Seymour Stein and his wife, Linda, adopted me and my wife, also named Linda. Seymour and Linda had grown up in Brooklyn, where I, my wife, and my wife's daughter were now living. But Seymour was shocked to discover that I was utterly ignorant of the real Brooklyn, its beaches and its cultural landmarks. So Seymour and his wife volunteered to take my wife and me on tours of the cultural highlights of Brooklyn, like Lundy's, a restaurant where the Brooklynites in the neighborhood of Seymour's childhood had made ritual pilgrimages on the weekends.

Unlike most New Yorkers, Seymour owned a car.

For our sightseeing trips, Seymour wanted my Linda and me to meet him at his apartment. And his apartment was an eye-opener. Seymour lived near Seventy-Fourth Street on Central Park West. His fourth-floor windows had a terrific view just over the tops of the Central Park trees. Paul Simon, I believe, lived in the same building. And John Lennon lived a very short walk away. Not only was this one of New York's most expensive neighborhoods, but Seymour had an apartment the size of a football field. The living room alone was the size of two studio apartments. But that living room felt peculiarly unlived-in and empty. There was one couch—a couch that looked as small as a pill because it was engulfed by so much empty space. That's where Linda and I would sit. Leaning against the wall were stacks of, well, I couldn't quite tell what. Something flat and a little less than waist-high. Since Seymour left us waiting in that room quite a bit, I ventured off the couch, went over to one of these leaning stacks, and tilted back one of the flat objects. It was a picture. But not just any picture.

Art nouveau, the art that reigned in Paris from roughly 1880 to 1910, was wildly fashionable in 1973. Everybody you met in New York had posters on their walls by the most famous of art nouveau's poster artists: Mucha, Alphonse Maria Mucha. The Parisians had just invented the full-color poster in Mucha's day.[32] And every Paris surface in sight was soon covered with these blazing, full-color beauties. Some Parisians saw this as enlivening the city. Some saw it as desecrating the place. But now, in 1973,

Mucha was the unofficial artist of everyone who lived in Greenwich Village and every-one who had ever wanted to live there.

So there I was in Seymour Stein's living room, tilting back a flat object whose nature I did not know. When I took its upper edge in my hand, it became obvious that it was the back of a wooden frame with a heavy cloth stretched over it—canvas. And when I moved it farther from the wall and was able to see what was on the other side, I was astonished. It was THE Mucha poster that every college student and would-be creative had on her wall. Yes, the original painting. And there were roughly forty of these originals staggered in one stack after another against Seymour Stein's living room wall. A fortune in paintings.

There was also a telephone on a tiny table on the opposite side of the room from the couch where Linda and I waited. It was twenty feet away, next to the windows. While Linda and I were parked on the couch, Seymour would get on that phone and have long conversations. They would go something like this. "Sotheby's is auctioning a piece tomorrow. It's an art-nouveau sculpture of a girl. Look it up in their catalogue. It's going for $18,000. But if you buy it and hold on to it for a year, it'll be worth $36,000." Who was Seymour talking to? A pudgy kid who had been a tea boy at Dick James Music in England when Seymour had first met him. A tea boy is a gofer. That kid had made it with his own songs. In fact, he had driven my Cloud Studio artist, Peter Bramley, into a frenzy. The former tea boy was Reginald Dwight, the piano player who had changed his name to Elton John.

Finally, Seymour and Linda would bundle Linda and me into their car and take us across the Brooklyn Bridge to the highway that loops around the Brooklyn shore. And the shore came as a surprise. I had no idea that Brooklyn is a giant beach community with water on three sides. One more thing became obvious during our conversations in that car. Seymour had been a geek like me. But instead of diving into science, Seymour had become obsessed with music. So obsessed that he could give you the record com-pany, publisher, songwriter, and catalogue number of any song you cared to mention. And he'd been able to do this since he was fifteen. Eating, sleeping, and breathing music indeed.

Steve Gaines must have talked me up heavily, because Seymour had decided to get me a job. Sire Records had a distribution deal with the music arm of the biggest conglomerate in the world, Gulf and Western. Gulf and Western's music operation, in fact, distributed fourteen record labels. Remember the two editors who had been packing their bags and quitting the day I went to meet Gerry Rothberg? One of them was Danny Goldberg. Danny had gotten a job heading the PR department for Gulf and Western's fourteen record companies. But Danny had long since abandoned that job, leaving a big, empty office. Seymour had an idea. He wanted me to take over that empty space. And he wanted me to build a new public and artist-relations department for Gulf and Western's fourteen record companies from scratch. Which meant I'd be doing the publicity for his artists.

Why did Seymour think I'd be able to do something I'd never done before—publicity? "I've always believed in you," he explained to me recently. I had come into *Circus* knowing nothing about rock and roll. The only publication I'd ever edited was NYU's literary magazine. And I'd made Gerry Rothberg temporarily rich. (We'll get into "temporarily" later). Seymour Stein apparently thought I could do the same for him. And he turned out to be right.

* * *

Seymour Stein talked Gulf and Western into going with his plan—hiring me to start a public and artist-relations department for G&W's fourteen record companies. And Connie de Nave, the wrangler of screaming girls for the Rolling Stones' first landing at New York's JFK Airport, called to give me a crucial piece of advice. "You're going into a big corporation," she said, "and you're a talker. But when you sit down at corporate meetings, control yourself. Keep your mouth shut and listen." That advice would prove to be more powerful than it sounds.

* * *

On my first day in the Gulf and Western Building, someone ushered me into an empty office with very little furniture and a couple of empty file cabinets up against the wall. It was clear that Danny Goldberg had departed leaving nothing behind. But the office was gorgeous. For a reason. It was on Columbus Circle, at the southwest corner of Central Park. In a high-rise office building, the Gulf and Western Building, a building that now belongs to Donald Trump. It was on the twenty-third floor, overlooking the park. I would later learn that the publicists for another giant in the record industry, CBS, had one window each in their high-rise, super-modern office building, Black Rock, a fifteen-minute walk away. But the office into which I was ushered had three windows. Three. And the sight of greenery way down below was amazing. Not to mention the sight of birds flying not above you but below you. Because you were so high. And not on drugs.

* * *

Meanwhile, back at *Circus*, Gerry Rothberg decided to abandon the formula I had created for him. I felt jilted. So when I got calls from Barry Kramer, the founder of the gonzo-rock magazine *Creem*, and from Shelton Ivany, the editor of *Hit Parader*, asking if we could have lunch, I said yes. At a restaurant table I explained to each of them exactly how the abandoned *Circus* formula had worked. And they used my *Circus* secrets to alter the format—and the sales—of their magazines. Meanwhile, moving away from the magic formula was not good for Gerry. He went into Chapter 11 bankruptcy. When he came out of it and continued to publish *Circus*, I don't know whether he used my formula or not. But the lunches with Kramer and Ivany spread the approach, and it became the sort of magazine format that can occupy its own shelf at 7/11, Walmart, or on a newsstand. Keep those shelves in mind. We'll need them when we get to the story of the Witches of Washington. But I digress.

One day, a messenger arrived at my office in the Gulf and Western Building with a big manila envelope. It was from Chet Flippo, one of the founding editors at *Rolling Stone*, the man who had set up *Rolling Stone*'s first New York office. Being a rock editor wasn't enough to satisfy Chet. In his spare time, he was going through a PhD program in journalism at the University of Texas in Austin, doing his homework from his office in New York. Chet's PhD thesis topic? A history of rock-and-roll journalism.

Normally, publicists send things by messenger to writers, not the other way around. Messengers cost a lot of money. Why was Chet indulging in this expensive extravagance? I opened the manila envelope. In it were six pieces of paper with neatly double-spaced type. It was the story of a mysterious munchkin who had labored in a converted windowless closet near the UN, weaving straw into gold for a magazine publisher. This figure straight out of *Rumpelstiltskin*, said Chet, had invented a whole new magazine genre—the heavy-metal magazine. And who was that genre creator? Well, ummm, yes, you wrung the confession out of me. It was me.

* * *

Meanwhile, I made a rapid discovery at Gulf and Western. Though we had fourteen record companies on paper, eleven of them were phantoms. They had no staff. We didn't have phone numbers for the company presidents. Without a team, their records were doomed. There was no point wasting effort on them. One of those phantom companies, alas, was Paramount Records. But two of our companies had teams that simply would not quit. They were Seymour Stein's Sire Records, and a country-music record company in Nashville called Dot Records. Seymour's bands did that magic thing that I'd discovered at *Circus* sells records. They toured. They built an audience. And Dot was extraordinary. They were number three in country music. But they wanted to be number one. I'd soon discover that they had the team, the organization, the motivation, the work ethic, and the smarts to pull it off. What's more, they also had access to a TV show. But we'll get to that ace up their sleeve in a bit.

Thanks to an accident of fate, I was free to ignore the ghost-companies and to focus on the two that really mattered: Sire and Dot. With an occasional exception. How did I get that freedom?

Here's how I told the story in my book *The Genius of the Beast: A Radical Re-Vision of Capitalism.*

Gulf and Western was one of the mightiest conglomerates of the mid-twentieth century. Corporations were in a feeding frenzy. They swallowed smaller firms alive, discarded the parts they felt were unimportant—like the people who'd built the firms from nothing—and either kept the remains or sold the dismembered pieces for a profit.

Time magazine called it the era of "Voracious, Inc." The worldwide business community summed it up with an even more threatening nickname, "Engulf and Devour."[33] The term "Engulf and Devour" was coined specifically to describe one of the worst of these mega-predators—the company in whose offices I was ensconced: Gulf and Western Industries.

Gulf and Western had chewed up a venerable giant of the film business, Paramount Pictures. Along with the meat had come the feathers and the beak. One of those feathers was a music lightweight called Paramount Records.

Music was a hot property in 1973. It was the boom time of psychedelia and rock. CBS was making a fortune off of tie-dyed stars like Janis Joplin. RCA was hauling in profits from the Jefferson Airplane, and RCA was still riding high on the greatest solo rock-and-roll revenue producer of all time, Elvis Presley. Atlantic Records was getting rich with new albums from a beachhead act of the British Invasion, the Rolling Stones, and with Led Zeppelin, the central band in an even newer movement, heavy metal. And Capitol Records was raking in profits from the foursome that had landed the British Invasion on American shores—the Beatles.

Teenagers were the fastest-growing market on the planet. Since 1968, platinum-priced executive newsletters had sprung into being, promising to explain this puzzling cash-explosion, the emerging "youth phenomenon." And in my days at Cloud Studio, I had spent time with the founder of the first of these newsletters, probing the newly detonating demographic.

The forces underlying the youth explosion were simple. America had just been through the longest peacetime period of prosperity in its history. The trickle-down effect had carried the wealth from the pockets of parents to the allowances of their kids.

Kids have no necessities to spend on, so every cent a teen received was squandered as "disposable income."

What were the first things teens with money in their pockets plunked down their coins and dollars to buy in the early 1970s? Usually those antique twelve-inch vinyl music Frisbees called LPs (short for long-playing records) with roughly ten songs apiece. And much smaller records with two songs each called singles or 45s.

So a foothold in the music business was a necessity for a conglomerate, especially one dedicated to engulfing and devouring. Paramount Records, Gulf and Western's entry to the music industry, was scarcely even a single toe-rest, much less a solid footing. Paramount Records had once been a firm that sold the soundtracks from Paramount's movies. But soundtracks had stopped selling way back in the mid-1960s. Now, in 1973, Paramount Records had just one lonely star—a singer/songwriter who'd sold tons of records in the late 1960s but was on her way to oblivion. Her full name was Melanie Safka Schekeryk, but she went under just her first name, Melanie.

As Melanie sank from her former heights, the only Paramount Records replacement in sight was a band from Austin, Texas, the press loved but the public did not, Commander Cody and His Lost Planet Airmen.

So Gulf and Western acquired the distribution of another thirteen record companies. And it plucked a president to run this operation from the golden nest of CBS—one of the most successful firms in the twentieth century music business.

That CBS executive, Tony Martell, had made his name by aiding in the launch of a most unlikely success story—a strange "concept-record" with an even stranger subject matter. The "concept" was a holy grail several had striven for but none had yet been able to achieve—a "rock opera." The music's writer was the twenty-three-year-old son of a church organist from London's All Saints Church. He had staged a minor musical called *Joseph and the Amazing Technicolor Dreamcoat* in a London School at the age of nineteen.[34] Now he'd moved into something seemingly even more alien to the music of the day: a rock-and-roll version of the story of Christ, told from the point of view of Judas Iscariot. The upstart composer without a band and without an electric guitar in his hand was Andrew Lloyd Webber. His preposterous project was called *Jesus Christ Superstar*.

And *Jesus Christ Superstar* sold like crazy.

That may have been an accident.

* * *

Thanks to my art studio, I had been at ABC's flagship New York FM station, WPLJ, one afternoon in 1970 when one of PLJ's most popular DJs—Dave Herman—stood chatting with his arm resting on a tall stack of promotional albums that had come in that week's mail. When a pause arose in the conversation, Dave looked down to see what his left elbow was propped on. The album cover caught his eye. "What's this?" he said, his right eyebrow lifting with curiosity. He picked the album up, read the title on the front jacket, slid the record halfway out of its sleeve, skimmed the list of songs on the label, and said, "Hmmmmm, it looks interesting. I think I'll play it as soon as I get on air." Then he slid the LP back into its sleeve again. Fifteen minutes later, *Jesus Christ Superstar* made its radio debut on Dave Herman's turntable. The rest is history.

Jesus Christ Superstar went to No. 1 on *Billboard*'s charts. And its composer, Andrew Lloyd Webber, went on to write musicals like *Evita*, *Phantom of the Opera*, and *Cats*—productions that would earn him a knighthood and land him a fortune of over a billion dollars.[35]

The idea of music about Jesus Christ as a rock singer of sorts, a superstar, had fired an influential DJ's imagination. Was this the sly work of CBS executives like Tony Martell? Or was it just a fluke? In business, many make the mistake of crediting you with a success you didn't create. They fail to ask whether you were one of those who had built and driven the locomotive or whether you had merely been along for the ride.

Gulf and Western had snatched Tony Martell away from CBS and had made him the president of its struggling flock of fourteen record companies in the hope that he could replace the tin in its music with platinum. And Tony Martell had been kind enough or crazy enough to hire me.

But Tony Martell's greatest gift to me would be . . . his absence.

11

YOU FUCKING NUN . . . STEPHANIE MILLS, NAPOLEON, AND *THE WIZ*

Shortly after he was hired by Gulf and Western to repeat the success of *Jesus Christ Superstar*, Tony Martell encountered a problem. A big one. His sixteen-year-old son was diagnosed with leukemia. In those days, the early 1970s, leukemia was a death sentence. There was no cure. But Tony would not take the death of his son lying down. He was determined to save T.J.'s life.

So, every day, Tony came into the office at 9:00 a.m., an infernally early hour for record company types, most of whom had to be out at night seeing bands and meandered into the office closer to 10:00 a.m. Tony would close the huge wooden doors that led to his corner office and lock them. We were not quite sure what he did in there all day. He may have been drinking. But, in fact, with or without alcohol, Tony was researching his ass off to save his son. He was tracking down the world's most advanced leukemia specialists, trying to turn up clues and cures that would save T.J.'s life.

Which meant that Gulf and Western's record company was operating headless—a tremendous advantage for a person like me, who insists on doing things in his own strange ways. And who can sometimes give you whopping successes based on that strangeness. But all this means that, as my book *The Genius of the Beast* explains:

When I first arrived at Gulf and Western's music operation, this HQ of tunes was a most peculiar place. There were no staff meetings—ever. There were no lists of the records we were putting out. No one gave us any sense of what to do from day to day. Heck, no one even gave us the names and addresses of our fourteen record labels.

Our company was by no sense a team. And one thing intuition revealed quickly: it takes teams to make stars. It takes teams to make companies. Twelve of our fourteen labels had no teams—none at all. Even the presidents of the labels seemed elusive, as if they'd been invented by some lowly staffer on LSD.

But, as you know, there were two gems in our stack of chaff and dandruff—two companies with teams that had a work ethic and a passionate determination to succeed:

Sire Records and Dot. So I tried to give the singers and musicians from Sire and Dot that extra boost they needed to make it.

When the Paramount Records talent scout, its A&R (artist and repertoire) guy, came into my office frothing with enthusiasm over whatever surefire star he'd found that day, I loved his hyperbolic energy. But when he left, I went back to work strategizing, directing my growing staff, landing roughly six hundred stories a month for Sire acts like Renaissance and the Climax Blues Band, and getting feature stories in a new magazine called *People* for folks like Donna Fargo and Roy Clark—now-forgotten entertainers who paved the way for country-music's charge from its ghetto in the Bible Belt into the mainstream of American culture. More about that great escape in a few minutes.

Then I encountered an unexpected twist.

* * *

One day, the Paramount Records A&R guy trapped me. His gonzo-megastar tale of the day, told with the usual wild excitement, concerned a thirteen-year-old girl from Crown Heights in Brooklyn—a very marginal black and ultra-orthodox Jewish neighborhood. This kid, his new discovery, was going to be a monster, a superstar, a gorilla, a smash. Sure, just like Augie Meyers and the rest who'd slipped into utter invisibility. "And guess what," the A&R maestro said, "I've set her up to do a showcase at the Plaza Hotel tomorrow at noon."

Yikes. This was a smart bomb I couldn't dodge. The Plaza Hotel was just a short and pleasant walk away. I was the head of the public and artist-relations department. That meant that on the rare occasion when a singer or musician actually made it to a nearby stage, I had to be there to make the artist feel that we were paying attention to him or her. If the company was not doing a thing for a singer, I told him so. But, still, I owed him or her the courtesy of my presence.

So, the next day, at fifteen minutes to noon, I left my office and my growing staff and walked at top speed along the lusciously green lower margin of Central Park, not stopping to take in the springtime scenery, straight into the white-with-gold-trim elegance of the Plaza Hotel, into one of the Plaza's nightclubs, and sat down at a small, round table, expecting to hear some unfortunate kid who couldn't carry a tune if you put it in a bucket and Krazy Glued the handle to her palm.

The room darkened. The lights came up on the small, semicircular stage. Out walked a squashed-looking African American thirteen-year-old a mere four feet eight inches tall with a microphone in her hand. Her eyes swept the room, seeming to peer with intensity directly into your face and into the face of everyone else in the

mini-amphitheater-like curve of tiered nightclub tables. There was something ferocious and commanding about those eyes, as if she'd reached through your skin, grabbed
you by the esophagus, pulled your nose up to hers, then given you a silent command to
sit, to stay, to pant, and to obey.

Then she opened her mouth and sang. For half an hour she gripped you and everyone else your peripheral vision could see. Her hold on your ears, eyes, and throat
extended to your body, and to those gods of bone-deep passion I'd been hunting for.
She dragged you at high speed through hell and heaven, through the exaltation of
being dipped, thrown, lifted, and flown.

The team it would take to turn this exquisitely controlled raw power into a career
did not exist. Paramount Records, her label, was a name on paper, not a thriving company. But two minutes after she began to sing, I opened a space for her on my priority
list—a very big space.

* * *

Meanwhile, Dot Records and Sire Records were steadily upping their revenues, their
profits, and their prestige. But our other twelve labels remained anonymous sinkholes
into which maintenance dollars flowed, never to be seen again. And we continued to
operate without leadership as our president tried obsessively to save his son. But another company that Gulf and Western Industries had swallowed, Paramount Pictures,
was a giant in the film industry—a studio run with deftness, precision, and artistry.

So Paramount Pictures' president, Frank Yablans, did a bit of maneuvering, and
one day, roughly two weeks after I first saw Stephanie Mills, I came to work and
discovered that our president now answered to a new boss. From this day forward,
Tony Martell would be slid under the thumb of Paramount Pictures' president, Frank
Yablans.

I'd never seen Frank Yablans. None of us on the twenty-third floor of the Gulf and
Western Building had. All we knew was that he had a reputation akin to Adolf Hitler's
and Attila the Hun's. Gossip implied that intimidation was his game, and that he could
turn you into ash and powder simply by looking your way.

The news of this earthquake on the corporate-organization chart brought about
something unprecedented—a meeting of our department heads.

* * *

There was a room in our twenty-third-floor complex that all of us thought was for
storage. Or at least I did. The lights were never on. It was heaped inside with boxes of
extra xerox paper. It was where you went when you needed to replenish your copying

machine. Or, more properly, where your secretary went when she needed to feed the paper tray. But one morning, we came in and discovered the lights were on. What's more, the boxes of xerox paper had been cleared out. To our surprise, what had been below them was a long table. The mystery chamber turned out to be a conference room. One we'd never used while I'd been there. And on this particular morning, there was a yellow pad, a pencil, and an eight and a half by eleven sheet of paper with type on it in front of each of the seats around the table—seats we had never noticed before.

We, the chief honchos, were summoned to plonk ourselves down at eleven o'clock that morning in this windowless, previously unoccupied deliberation chamber. And we discovered that the neatly typed and copied sheet before us was a list, a list of records our company was allegedly planning to release during the next few weeks—all discs none of us had ever heard of. Five minutes after eleven, our president seated himself at the far end of the table, cleared his throat, and prepared to take charge. Then the door opened, you had the feeling that laser lights and the sound of trumpets had streamed into the room, and, as if walking on a path of lightning bolts, in strode a small man with a $4,000 suit and an expression masterfully contrived to strike terror into even a titanium armored heart.

As this multi-megaton Napoleon walked the length of the room, Tony Martell, our illustrious president, slumped back in his chair, little by little, until his chin seemed to dip almost below the line of the conference table's top. When the mini-Napoleon reached the conference table's head, Martell slid out of his seat like a flattened jellyfish. Then the newcomer took over the power chair from which our noble leader had just oozed.

This was the human Godzilla we'd all heard of, Frank Yablans. Yablans glanced at the list of upcoming releases on the table in front of him, picked the first one, turned to the first executive on his left, and said, "You. What are you doing to promote this record?"

In reality, nobody was doing much to promote *any* record, much less a record not a soul had heard. But I don't think the executive upon whom the withering stare was fixed wanted to admit that. So he mustered all the brain cells he had used in college to answer essay questions about matters he'd never studied, and made up an elaborate story on the spot, a fictional saga of his heroic efforts.

Then Yablans turned to the next executive in line, opened his Howitzer mouth, and fired the same question. Executive number two followed executive number one's creative example. About two executives later, Yablans finally got to me.

Now remember, I was new to the corporate world. Science was my religion, and the first commandment of science, as I'd learned it, is "The truth at any price, including the price of your life." Galileo had spent his last nine years under house arrest and the Italian astronomer Giordano Bruno had died at the stake so that I might have the privilege of infiltrating the corporate world.

"I'm not doing anything about this record," I said. "In fact, I'm not doing anything about any of the records on this list. Ninety-nine percent of the music we sign doesn't stand a chance of success. Working on it would be a waste of effort and of time. But there's a girl one of our labels has just signed who is getting 40 percent of my attention." And I proceeded to describe the thirteen-year-old wonder from Brooklyn, Stephanie Mills.

When I finished, Yablans abruptly walked out of the room, his face frozen, leaving five executives unquizzed but still quaking like the Oakland overpass during an earthquake. As we squeezed through the doorway to exit the conference chamber, the vice president I allegedly answered to grabbed me by the arm with a grip designed to take my humerus bone to the breaking point and hissed, "You fucking nun. If you ever do that again, you're fired." I had the red marks of his fingers on my right bicep for the rest of the week.

When I arrived back at my office, my secretary told me that I'd received a phone call. It was not my exit notice. It was Frank Yablans's secretary. Mr. Yablans had set up a meeting for the next day at noon with all of his East Coast vice presidents and department heads. He wanted me there. And he wanted me to bring Stephanie Mills.

* * *

Thus began an expedition into the power of sheer honesty. An expedition into the power of the first rule of science: the truth at any price including the price of your life. An expedition that would eventually reveal the powers of something strange: using tuned empathy, using your own feelings as a mirror of those you serve—your customers, your audience, your clients, your flock. A lesson in using the gods inside.

* * *

From that point on, the Paramount Pictures people treated me as a member of their staff. They called me in whenever they were planning a campaign to break a major film. They were laying the ground for a blockbuster, a 1974 version of *The Great Gatsby* based on a script by Francis Ford Coppola, starring Robert Redford and including Mia Farrow, Sam Waterston, Bruce Dern, and Karen Black. All massive names in the film business at the time. Paramount had made deals with an expensive hair-cutting chain to give Gatsby haircuts, a prestige clothing company to sell Gatsby outfits, and an upscale dinnerware company to sell Gatsby plates and saucers. They let me put together a press assault for the orchestrator of the soundtrack—Nelson Riddle, the legendary producer and orchestrator who was given something unheard of, equal credit, on the labels of records by Frank Sinatra. And the Paramount staff gave me full control of the press effort for *The Life and Times of Sonny Carson*, a film directed by Frank Yablans's little brother, Irving.

No one at Paramount dared get near *The Life and Times of Sonny Carson*. Why? They thought Frank had simply tossed his brother a few million dollars of production money to keep him out of trouble. What's more, the film was about a controversial black activist. But they were wrong about the little brother, Irving Yablans. He would eventually make a fortune creating *Friday the 13th*. What's more, Carson would resurface in the early 1990s as a leader of an anti-Korean, anti-Semitic movement in the New York black community.[36] And I'd become the leading "black" publicist in the music industry. But that's a story for later.

Apparently, Frank Yablans saw me as a secret weapon. Bless him. After directing *The Last Picture Show* and *Paper Moon*, Peter Bogdanovich was the hottest property in the film industry. He was regarded as a genius. Every studio wanted him. But Frank Yablans had an ace up his sleeve. Why? Peter had a high-profile girlfriend—supermodel Cybill Shepherd. There was a strange backstory circulating about the Bogdanovich-Shepherd relationship. Peter, the genius, was the puppet master, said the street gossip. Cybill Shepherd was a mindless beauty, an empty vessel, a Pygmalion. Peter was her puppeteer. It was thanks to Peter that Cybill appeared to have a brain. Nonetheless, Cybill wanted something . . . to become a singer.

Yablans set up a meeting in his office—an office with roughly seven windows on the thirty-second floor—to convince Peter that of all the film studios pursuing him, the one he should settle on was Paramount. I was summoned to be present. Why? Because Paramount Pictures had a record label. A label Cybill could record on. A label that could get her success and show just how brilliant Peter was as a puppeteer. Exhibit A was the only person from the record company in the room, Yablans's secret weapon: me.

Which meant that I would get to spend quite a bit of time in Peter and Cybill's suite at the Plaza Hotel. Well, not exactly one suite. Two suites with the folding doors between them wide open. I watched as Peter directed exactly where the furniture should be moved. And I watched as Peter had a meeting with a high-powered figure in the Madison Avenue art-gallery world about his father. Peter's dad was a painter in Woodstock, New York. A painter who had never gotten any recognition. A painter Peter wanted to make famous. The art gallery potentate was brutally honest. The most important thing an artist can do to increase his visibility is . . . to die. Not what Peter wanted to hear.

But my time with Cybill and Peter revealed one thing. Cybill actually had a brain. She was no empty puppet. And Peter was not as bright as he thought he was.

Oh, and one more thing. You can't build a star without soul.

* * *

Things did not turn out as you might suspect.

The corporate VP who'd threatened to fire me for being "a fucking nun" was tossed out of the company two weeks after the appearance of Frank Yablans in our conference room. Which sickened me, since beneath this VP's gruffness was a deep commitment to his people and to his work. Whatever work that was. I could never quite tell.

As for Stephanie Mills, potential stars are people who eat, breathe, and sleep music. You cannot stop them from making music, no matter how hard you try. Stephanie was one of this rare breed. When she was a little girl, she would stand on the top of her Brooklyn stoop and sing, trying to imitate all three of the Supremes at once. Role models are crucial in the life of a would-be star. So is outdoing them. As we'll see in a minute.

Meanwhile, our department got Stephanie Mills into everything from the *New York Times* to *Seventeen* magazine, with a whole bunch of television shows in between. Then Stephanie landed the lead in the Broadway production of *The Wiz*, the first black-written, black directed, black-produced Broadway musical. A musical based on *The Wizard of Oz*. A brilliant idea. There was a professional Broadway PR firm on the case. But to my highly prejudiced eyes, it looked as if they were doing nothing. So my staff and I did most of the publicity for *The Wiz*, using the musical to pull in a landslide of additional press for Stephanie.

Stephanie never became the household name I would have liked. But the base for her career was well laid. Mills would have three No. 1 R&B records in the late 1980s—"I Feel Good All Over" (1987), "If I Were Your Woman" (1987), and "Something in the Way (You Make Me Feel)" (1989)—and three gold albums, and would sell several million LPs and CDs.

And I came away with a lesson. Rule of science number one—the truth at any price, including the price of your life—was a powerful tool in business. I'd soon learn more about why.

* * *

A few more Gulf and Western lessons before we plow into yet another great adventure: ABC Records. Let me start with the peculiar case of Bill Chinnock, from which I learned massively. Bill was a guitarist signed by Paramount Records, one of our twelve radically unsuccessful record companies. He was a sweet guy. A wonderful person, in fact. But his songs were unremarkable, and his voice was nothing special. So why had our talent scout, our A&R guy, signed him? Because of his guitar work.

When Bill Chinnock played New York, it was my job as head of artist relations to go see him. Backstage after the show, I had to confess that there was not much we were doing for him. And not much we were likely to do. But I needed to know Bill's story, just in case there was something spectacular in it. And there was.

Bill had grown up listening to Les Paul's records. He'd been amazed by the blazing speed of Paul's guitar work. He'd wanted to emulate it. So he'd gotten a guitar and sat himself next to the record player in his bedroom, diligently attempting to play Les Paul's machine-gun fusillade of notes. Day after day. Year after year. It wasn't easy. But after roughly six years, Bill finally got it down. Like Les Paul, he could play at a speed that was mind-boggling. Then, years later, Bill made records and played in clubs. One night, Bill was playing a club in New Jersey. A little old man was sitting in the back during the whole performance. When the show was over, the little old man came to the foot of the stage. "How in hell did you do that, son?" the generously wrinkled gentleman asked Bill. "Do what?" said Bill. "Play that blizzard of notes all at once," said the amazed listener. So Bill told him the story of learning to play like Les Paul.

"Son," said the little old man, "I am Les Paul. Don't you realize that I invented multitracking?" In other words, it had taken eight Les Paul's laying down track after track to make the sound that Bill Chinnock had imitated. Bill Chinnock had learned to play like eight Les Paul's. So Les Paul invited Bill over to his house to play once again . . . in his den. And he was once again amazed.

* * *

Les Paul had set a standard—even though it was an impossible one to achieve. Bill Chinnock had absorbed that standard, wrapped his brain around it, and made it his role model. Then Bill Chinnock had achieved it. He'd achieved the impossible. Like Stephanie Mills out-singing all three Supremes. Bill Chinnock, Stephanie Mills, and Les Paul had given a lesson in how society climbs. One generation fixes on the highest achievement of the previous generation then tries to live up to that extreme accomplishment. In the process, the new generation brings the nearly impossible into the realm of the real. And it sets a few new records of its own. The next generation of strivers grabs that next rung of the impossible, hoists itself up, makes the unbelievable ordinary, and sets yet another bar for the generation yet to come. The ceiling of one generation becomes the floor for the next.

In 1950, running a four-minute mile looked impossible. It was a fantasy. Then a medical student named Roger Bannister organized a small team, applied "scientific training methods and thorough research into the mechanics of running,"[37] and, in 1954, ran a mile in three minutes and fifty-nine-point-four seconds. From that point on, breaking the four-minute mile became easy. Says Wikipedia, today it is "the standard of all male professional middle-distance runners."[38] In other words, breaking the four-minute mile is now ordinary. That's the value of a record-breaking role model. First you fantasize. Then you work persistently to achieve the impossible. Once you've achieved the impossible, others follow. And the fantasies of those who come after aim even higher. That's the lesson of Bill Chinnock. It's a lesson about the role of stars in our lives. A lesson that will become clearer when we get to the peculiar ways of ducks. Yes, ducks.

But before we get to animals that quack, another quick story about achieving the impossible: solving a problem with country music.

12

DOT RECORDS AND COUNTRY CROSSOVER— BREAKING OUT OF THE BIBLE BELT

When I was three years old in my parents' tiny apartment on Hartwell Road in Buffalo, New York, I went out to the living room to enjoy the sunshine at six in the morning when everyone else was asleep. I turned on the radio, and the local station, WBEN, was deep into something very different than what it programmed from 8:00 a.m. on. It played a form of music that unnerved me—country music. Sandwiched in between alien-sounding farm reports. Why did that disturb me? It smacked of a culture very different from my Jewish urban roots. It smacked of a culture that would not accept me. Not that my Jewish urban culture would accept me. It wouldn't. But at least it felt like the right culture to be rejected by. This was a strange experience to have at the age of three. But it was my first lesson in the fact that music expresses the identity of a tribe, the identity of a subculture.

And I was wrong about country music. Its culture would accept me.

* * *

Dot was doing something few of our other labels achieved. They were getting records on the charts. Over and over again. Week after week. Yes, most of their big scores were not on the main pop charts, where the big sales were. They were on the country charts. But most of our other record companies were not getting on any charts at all. So I flew down to Nashville to spend a week getting to know Dot.

Dot Records was located in a small, totally residential-looking house on a totally residential-looking street of three-story houses, Sixteenth Avenue South in Nashville. The building at 111 did not look like it could possibly hold offices. A middle-class family of four with two kids, yes. Offices, no. I walked from the sidewalk up the concrete path that cut the lawn in half to the front door, rang the doorbell, and was ushered into a living room converted to an office—a living room with some of the most ferociously driven people I'd ever seen. Jim Foglesong, the president of the company, was a regal fifty-three-year-old of the Kentucky Colonel variety. He wore a suit, cowboy boots, and a bolo tie—one of those western thongs of braided leather with silver tips. He was tall and slender, and his bearing was so erect that he had to look down his nose to see you. Yet he managed to seem friendly. Sort of. Jim introduced me to his promotion man.

What's a promotion man? A promotion man is the diesel engine of a record company. The promotion man deals with the radio stations from one coast to another. He works to get radio stations to play your records. If he succeeds, the rest of the company succeeds. If he fails, you are in trouble.

Back home in New York City, in the Gulf and Western building, we, the Gulf and Western music operation, had a promotion man, too. He was charming. But he was a married man having an affair with his secretary. And he got us almost no airplay. We had a total of one hit in an entire year.

That wasn't true of Dot Records' promotion man. He had gone to Yale, then come back to the Bible Belt, because that's where his heart and roots were. He was a quiet man. No hype. But he was deeply analytic. And deeply driven. The result? He got airplay. Week after week. As you've heard before, Dot Records was already the number three label in the country-music business when I flew down to Nashville—despite the overwhelming success of giants like CBS and RCA. And both Jim Foglesong and his promotion man were absolutely determined to change that. They wanted to be number one. Period.

I'd set aside a full week for this Nashville trip. Why? Because while I was down in Tennessee, I wanted to interview every Dot artist and get his or her story. Stories sell. And I was determined to get Dot's stars publicity. So I sat down for a day each with people like Donna Fargo, Roy Clark, and Eddy Raven. Eddy taught me the most. In fact, the lesson he taught me was about collective passion—group soul. Eddy Raven was from Louisiana, and he explained to me what a Cajun actually is. It's not just a spice. It's an ethnic group. It's a people.

Have you ever read the classic nineteenth-century poem "Evangeline" by Henry Wadsworth Longfellow? Surely some grammar-school or high-school teacher must have threatened you with it. "Evangeline" is the tale of a man and woman in a French colony located off the coast of Canada on an island in the Atlantic. It's set in a time of transition, 1755 to 1764. The French seemed on the verge of dominating a hefty slice of North America. They had what we call French Canada. They had New Orleans, Louisiana, and all of what later became the Louisiana Purchase. Which means they had a massive third of North America. But there was a war afoot between the French and its allies on one side and the English and their allies on the other—the Seven Years' War. It was a war that spanned the globe, a world war. A war to dominate the territories taken by European imperialism—from India to the West Indies. In America, the French and Indian War of 1754–1763 was a small part of that global war. In the French and Indian War, the British turned the tables on the French. And France's losses had big consequences for the island inhabitants Longfellow was writing about in his fictional poem. The entire population of the French island that Longfellow focused his heroic couplets on was expelled by the British in 1755, driven from their homes in an ethnic cleansing.[39] They fled to the French city of New Orleans and fanned out around French Louisiana, bringing their cooking, their music, and their culture with them. The name of the frosty Atlantic island from which these people had been expelled? Acadia. From which we get the word "Cajun." Acadian.

Eddy was a Cajun. He told me this story as he was making me coffee in his kitchen. And something hit me. Ethnic groups often derive their sense of identity from a deep scar in their collective past. The Irish were driven into the hinterlands and made to serve British masters in 1650, but they carried the concept of what they had been in their hearts and used it to reassert their independence in 1916. My people, the Jews, had carried the scar of five ethnic expulsions—the escape from Egypt, and four expulsions from Israel by the empires of the Babylonians,[40] the Assyrians, the Romans, and the Muslims. That memory kept us together even as we were scattered across the face of the world. And the folks in Serbia are held together by their memory of a defeat at the battle of Kosovo in 1389 and the loss of their independence to conquerors—to the Turks, to the empire of Islam. What does the identity of ethnic groups have to do with music? Everything.

The Cajuns clung together using the social glue of two markers of their cultural heritage—their cooking and their music. The Irish held together with their unique music. And the Jews had many musics, from Yiddish songs and klezmer to Mendelsohn. Music was often the voice of a group asserting its right to be. That's a lesson whose meaning would reveal itself tiny step by tiny step the farther I got into music.

* * *

Meanwhile, a day with country star Barbara Mandrell in her suburban Nashville home taught me one more thing. The night before, burglars had broken into Barbara's home. She had called the police. The police had caught the thieves. Then they'd come to Barbara and asked her a question: did she want these first responders to take the crooks down to her basement and beat the crap out of them before they deposited them in a jail cell? Barbara said no. The lesson? Police brutality is for real. Or was.

* * *

What else made Dot Records different from the rest? Its artists toured. Incessantly. And Dot had another ace up its sleeve, a nationally syndicated country-music TV show—*Hee Haw*. *Hee Haw* did extremely well all across America. It gave a sense of identity to those in the Bible Belt, a sense of a right to exist in a culture that was very different from theirs. And it did unexpectedly well in the ratings in northern cities like New York, Boston, and Chicago, not to mention way out west in Los Angeles. Roy Clark was a co-host on *Hee Haw*. Donna Fargo appeared at least half a dozen times on the show. And Roy and Donna were two of Dot's biggest stars.

I flew back to New York with the stories of these artists, complete with a list of all their accomplishments. As you've seen, Time-Life publications had just hit the news-stands with a new magazine—*People*. So I got Roy and Donna into *People*. It was the first time that Dot Records artists had gotten major national press.

Then Jim Foglesong and one of his artist managers, an amazing man named Jim Halsey, laid out a bold plan. Country music got no airplay on pop radio stations. Remember, G&W was confined to the ghetto of the Bible Belt. The two Jims wanted to take country music national. No, not just national. International. They wanted to make country music global. In the background was something no one said. If country music went national and international, it would elevate the pride of an entire group of Americans who were often despised. That, I was discovering, was one of the key roles of music. And of stars.

Slowly an idea dawned on me. I still did not like listening to country music. But I was damned certain that the people this music represented had a right to their dignity. And that their stars deserved recognition. What's more, something strange was happening to my department, the public and artist-relations department of G&W's music operation. Because the Gulf and Western music organization was losing money, other people were told to save pennies on things like notepads and pencils. But I was given bigger and bigger budgets. And I was able to grow my staff to five. I made those five people spend a significant amount of time on Dot.

Then it hit me. Why not have a publicity office in Nashville, to be in direct contact on a daily basis with Dot's stars, the news those stars were generating, and the country-and-western press? I proposed the idea, and guess what? Despite the fact that we were supposed to be saving on paper clips and yellow pads, I was given the money. So I scouted Nashville's country journalists, looking for a talented workaholic, and hired Jerry Bailey, who I believe I found at the trade magazine *Cashbox*. It was the first record-company PR department in the history of Nashville. And it was my first experience using music to give a downtrodden minority a right to be. But there would be more.

13

BLOOD IN THE CORRIDORS

Seymour Stein's bands, Renaissance and the Climax Blues Band, were touring their tiny tails off. And my staff was getting them newspaper and TV coverage in every city they hit. Behind both bands was a man I would come to love, Miles Copeland. Miles was the founder and head of British Talent Management, the firm that managed both bands. And, like me, Miles was a total workaholic. I loved the way he handled phone calls. Like a person with Asperger's syndrome, Miles had no idea of how to say niceties like "Hello, how are you?" and "Nice talking to you, goodbye." He got you on the phone and went directly into what he wanted you to do, listened to what you had to say, replied, then jumped off without a single salutation. You could look at this approach as unspeakably rude or unbelievably efficient. I chose efficient. I loved it. Miles, his brothers, and his dad would play a mind-boggling role in my life a little further down the line. I'll give you a hint. The key word is "CIA."

Because of all the touring and the press, Seymour Stein's bands did something that defied the laws of gravity, the laws that weighed down Gulf and Western's other record labels: Seymour Stein's groups sold albums. They made money. And they made good music. Annie Haslam, Renaissance's lead vocalist, had a five-octave range. An astonishment. And Renaissance's music was so good that I got the Joffrey Dance Company interested in doing an annual Christmas event choreographed around a piece of Renaissance's music.

Then we had an interruption. The story, as I told it in *The Genius of the Beast*, goes something like this.

Gulf and Western finally tired of the music business. It sold its record holdings to ABC Records. ABC flew a vice president to New York from LA. He gathered all fifty-seven employees in the New York office, told us to go on working in our normal manner, and promised us that our jobs were safe. "No blood," he said, "will flow in the corridors of this company."

I did not find his words persuasive. New brooms sweep clean. I put my staff into emergency mode. For the next five days, our sole job was to account for every bit of press coverage we'd ever gotten. Our job was to find out how much the equivalent magazine or newspaper space or radio or TV time would have cost if it was purchased with advertising dollars. Our job was to demonstrate what G&W had gotten in exchange for its investment in our department. At the end of five days of research, the figure was startling. For every dollar Gulf and Western had spent on our department, it had gotten eleven dollars in exposure.

Then, late one snowy evening, I shared a cab from work out to Brooklyn with an executive from one of the major ad agencies. I told him what we'd discovered—for every dollar spent, our company had gotten eleven dollars' worth of space or airtime. "No," said the ad executive, "you've calculated that wrong." Uh oh. This sounded bad. The executive explained that, "In advertising, we figure that every inch of editorial is worth five times as much as an inch of advertising. Every inch of copy filed by a journalist is worth five times as much as a paid ad. People believe journalists. They don't believe ads. So, for every dollar your company has spent on your PR department, you've delivered fifty-five dollars' worth of exposure." Heady stuff.

It didn't matter. Two Fridays after the "no blood in the corridors" speech, everyone in the company, every one of our fifty-seven staff people, received a pink slip in the mail. Everyone with a single exception—me. And I resigned. Why? The company had fired my staff. I had learned my lesson at *Circus*, where eventually they had replaced me with five people, including future star rock writers Kurt Loder and David Fricke. Meaning that I'd been doing the job of five talented humans. Without the team I'd built at Gulf and Western, there was no way I'd be able to accomplish a thing.

The VP who had made the "no blood in the corridors" speech took the redeye in from the LA and appeared unannounced in my office the morning after I tendered my resignation. He laid a blank piece of paper on my desk, told me to write my name at the top, to write the names of the employees I wanted to keep, then to fill in the salary I wanted for myself and the salaries I wanted for the members of my team. I gave us all a 20 percent raise, and we went to work for ABC.

A year later, I got a call from the attorney who had negotiated the sale from Gulf and Western to our new owners. "You know why ABC was willing to pay so much for Gulf and Western's record holdings, don't you?" he said. I confessed that I didn't have a clue. "The reason," he said, "is you."

This was preposterous. I was a novice to the corporate world. I was a scientific thinker learning the hard way that the politics around me only made sense if you saw it in terms of wolf packs—with alpha males, beta males, and with small, competing, carnivorous gangs whose members were bound to each other by instinctual loyalty. I was on a scientific expedition into the land of the gods, into the dark underbelly where new myths and movements are made, an expedition into the shadowy menagerie of group soul. I told the attorney he was wrong. There was no way I could have triggered a profitable sale of a company.

His answer: "No, listen to me carefully. What did you do for Dot Records? And what did you do for Sire? You increased their cash flow, their profits, and their market share. I'd say you doubled or tripled their worth." The rest of his explanation suddenly made the puzzle pieces fall into place.

Why had ABC not fired me? Because, the lawyer explained, "The president of Sire Records, Seymour Stein, and the president of Dot Records, Jim Foglesong, both flew out to California to meet with Jay Lasker, the president of ABC Records. Do you know what they told him?" As usual, I didn't have a clue. "That without you they would bolt . . . they'd find a way to leave ABC."

Astonishing!

At ABC, I was back from a twenty-third-floor office with three windows overlooking Central Park to a cubicle with clear glass walls but no windows. In the ABC building at Sixth Avenue and Fifty-Fourth Street. On the tenth floor. If you walked out of the door of my glassed-in cage, turned right, and marched fifty feet, you reached a window from which you could see the view. And what did you see? Not acres of green. The glass and steel walls of other skyscrapers. Talk about sterile.

More important, I had adopted a phrase from economics—good money drives out bad. In my case, it would be good information drives out bad. Truth drives out lies. It would take thirty years for me to discover that I'd gotten the phrase wrong. In economics, it is said that bad money drives out good. It's called Gresham's law. And it's the 180-degree opposite of what I preached. Yet the Gulf and Western experience would hint that truth can, indeed, drive out lies. If you work hard enough. In fact, truth can drive out evil motives and misrepresentation almost every time. Almost. But I'm getting ahead of myself.

* * *

Once I had my full staff in place again, I looked over ABC's artists and made two amazing discoveries. Number one, we had a record at No. 3 on the pop singles charts, "Tell Me Something Good." That was a privilege I'd never experienced at Gulf and Western. Ever. Second discovery: no one on ABC's main PR staff in Hollywood wanted to work on this record. No one was touching it. Why?

Because the lead singer was black. Outrageous!

The publicists on the West Coast felt they were part of the same elite from which the rock press was carved. And, if you feel part of an elite, you define yourself by what you despise. It was obligatory in this self-proclaimed aristocracy to despise black music. Yes, I know it sounds insane. Black music is the heart and soul of American and British pop. Without black music, we wouldn't have had Elvis Presley. Without black music, we wouldn't have had the Beatles and the Rolling Stones. And the publicists at ABC's LA office literally turned their noses up at a No. 3 hit because its singer was black? Appalling!

There was another reason for this outrageous behavior. Record companies, like all human societies, are based on a pecking order. The tradition in the music biz was to have a black music department with an all-black staff. These people were often hired for one talent only: the ability to be bagmen, the ability to hand out bribes. Bribes to the black press to cover your artists. Bribes to black DJs to play your artists. Bribes to influential preachers to praise your artists to their congregations. A black artist, based on skin color alone, was thrown to this small black department. And that department was despised in its own record company. It was at the bottom of the pecking order.

What's worse, ABC didn't even have a black department. It had a black A&R man, a single black talent scout, and that was it.

I had no such prejudice. I'd helped build Stephanie Mills not because of her skin color but because of her talent. I was ready to pick up the voice behind this ABC hit single and run with it. The band responsible for the chart-ripper was called Rufus. They were a group of three white and two black musicians with a black lead singer. And their official bio made something very clear: the band was a democracy. Every member was equal to every other member.

I had a friend who had been one of my best writers at *Circus* and was now writing for publications like the *New York Times*. He gave me a passionate lecture about the power of taking a female lead vocalist and putting all of the attention on her. It made total sense. So I tracked down the band's manager, Robert Ellis Silberstein, a nice Jewish boy who just happened to be married to Diana Ross. And who just happened to be the father of a three-year-old named Tracee Ellis Ross. And I found that he was about to fly from LA into New York. So I volunteered to pick him up at the airport. In a limousine. After all, I was the head of East Coast public and artist relations. It was my job to make our artists and their managers feel we were paying attention to them. The manager said yes. But I had an ulterior motive.

The manager's plane was due to arrive at 5:00 p.m. That's rush hour. I'd have him as a captive audience for at least an hour and a half while we were baked into motionless traffic on the Van Wyck Expressway. In that landlocked limo, I told Rufus's manager something simple. Something I'd never said before. If you cover my ass, if you let me forget about the band's democracy, and if you let me put all of the attention on the lead vocalist, I will deliver you a star. I had never said such a thing in my life. And I would only say it once more in the future. The manager said yes. He promised he would cover my tiny heinie with the band. So, over the coming year, I built the biggest press campaign I was capable of around the lead singer. Her name was Chaka Khan.

* * *

Three more tiny things of significance at ABC. First, a lesson from the King of the Blues. One of our artists was B.B. King, perhaps the most influential bluesman in the history of music. I was not supposed to do his publicity. That was being handled by an outside PR firm. But I was head of artist relations. I was ABC Records' ambassador to our musicians. And B.B. King had a date out on Long Island, a forty-five-minute drive from Manhattan. I rented a car and drove out to see him perform, then go backstage and show him that we, ABC Records, his label, cared about him.

B.B. had a manager, Sid Seidenberg. And B.B. had a complaint. Another of Sid's acts was breaking big time: Gladys Knight and the Pips. Knight and her Pips had just gone to No. 1 on the pop charts with "Midnight Train to Georgia." Said B.B. King, "When you have a new baby, never neglect your first child." Sid must have gotten the message. He was still working with King twenty years later. Here are a few of the things that *Variety* says Seidenberg pulled off for King: he got King a concert at one of the meccas of 1960s white rock music, the Fillmore East. He landed King the biggest TV shows of the day, from the Ed Sullivan and Johnny Carson shows to the newer, hipper David Letterman and Jay Leno shows. He pulled in a State Department–sponsored tour of Africa and a 1979 tour of the Soviet Union. Most important, Seidenberg landed King a Rolling Stones tour in 1970, and a 1990s tour with U2.[41]

So Sid must have understood B.B.'s advice. Pay more attention to B.B. King or you will lose him. And Sid understood two other things—the magic of touring, and the sorcery of the name game. Pair King with the Rolling Stones and U2 and you lift King's name to a new level. What's more, you reach a whole new audience.

The result? While classic blues-makers like Howlin' Wolf, Lead Belly, and Muddy Waters were known only by the blues cognoscenti, B.B. King became a household name. He became "the King of the Blues."

* * *

Tiny detail number two: a clue to the mystery of the gods inside. And to what gives black music its gut-level power. Among the key triggers that had shaped my vision of the gods inside were James Baldwin's description of being possessed by Jesus at a

Holy Roller church ceremony, which I'd read at fourteen, and Marcel Camus's picture of the same thing in his film *Black Orpheus*, a film that came out when I was fifteen. *Black Orpheus* showed a black Macumba ritual in Brazil. A ritual in which a drumbeat grabbed a man in a fist of rapture and dropped him to the ground writhing in mystic transport. The Holy Roller and Macumba frenzies were ecstatic experiences in which a god took you over and your normal self stepped aside or disappeared. James Baldwin had called this rib-shivering ecstasy of possession "shouting." And the first time I would see it in the flesh, I would be too dense to know it.

One of my acts at ABC Records was the Mighty Clouds of Joy, an absolutely fabulous gospel group. When the Clouds came into Manhattan, they played a date at Columbia University. I cabbed uptown from 54th Street to roughly 112th Street to see them. The audience consisted of blacks and whites. I was enjoying the music when suddenly one of the black female members of the audience about twenty people off to my right stood up. Not a big deal. People are inspired to stand up at concerts all the time, right? But that was just the beginning. Her body trembled and shook. It looked like she was in serious trouble. It looked, in fact, like she was having an epileptic fit. Or a personal earthquake.

I've been raised to believe that if you see someone in trouble, you go over and help them out. And before the Boy Scouts tossed me out, they had taught me that you roll up a handkerchief and put it in the victim's mouth so she won't bite her tongue off. But no one looked the least bit alarmed. And no one was grabbing for a handkerchief. Except for me. Then another person off on my left stood. And trembled uncontrollably. Then a person four rows in front of me. What was happening here? An epidemic of Parkinson's disease? A breakout of an uptown palsy? A neurodegenerative manifestation caused by too much studying in Columbia University's library?

When I got backstage, I told the Clouds what had happened. They could see how concerned I looked. But they broke out laughing. "Haven't you seen shoutin' before?" they said. And they laughed some more. I'd just come face to face with James Baldwin's Holy Roller possession and Marcel Camus's Macumba ritual. I'd just been given one more lesson on the gods inside.

I'd soon get another lesson on those gods with a percussionist who had the precision of an atomic clock. But that's for later.

*   *   *

Tiny detail number three is a clue to an evil that would inflict itself on Styx and, just possibly, on Michael Jackson.

Joe Walsh, a superb guitarist and an extraordinary songwriter, was one of ABC Records' biggest-selling artists. He'd been in the James Gang, Ringo Starr's All Starr Band, and the Eagles. He'd just written an amazing Eagles hit, "Life in the Fast Lane." Two years later, he would play guitar solos on one of the Eagles' most astonishing songs ever, "Hotel California." And he would eventually be named by *Rolling Stone* one of the hundred greatest guitarists of all time.

Joe was coming into New York City to play out on Long Island, at Nassau Coliseum. He was staying at the Warwick Hotel across the street from the ABC Building. The Warwick had been my dad's favorite hotel in Manhattan. But, of slightly greater significance, it was the hotel the Beatles had stayed in on their first trip to the USA.

I got the usual call from Jay Lasker—I didn't have to worry about Joe's publicity. That was being taken care of by the leading PR firm in rock publicity, Gibson and Stromberg. More on Gibson and Stromberg's disturbing use of sex and drugs in a minute. But could I please go across the street and show Joe that we, his record company, cared about him? So I had my secretary make an appointment, I put on my coat, and I headed across the street to the Warwick. Joe was staying on the fourth floor. I took the elevator up so I wouldn't be out of breath when I arrived.

I walked down the corridor to the room at the end of the hall and knocked. A minute later, the door opened three inches. Behind it was a man about five foot four. I could only see one of his eyes through the opening. And behind him was a man on his hands and knees, muttering incoherently. Joe Walsh. It was the first time I'd ever seen this particular manifestation of cocaine and alcohol. I'd see it again a few years later, with two of the members of KISS.

The tiny man behind the crack in the door told me to get lost. It was not a good time to pay a courtesy call on Joe Walsh.

This would be my first introduction to the man who I would later suspect of setting off the avalanche of negative press that would help kill Michael Jackson. It would be my first introduction to the Darth Vader of the music industry.

* * *

I had no idea of how in the world Joe Walsh would sing his songs the next night at Nassau Coliseum. He seemed incapable of uttering a single syllable of the English language. The next night, when I went backstage to see him at the Coliseum, Joe was at least vertical. He was standing on two legs. That was a hopeful sign. Even if he was swaying back and forth ominously. And even if he still could not speak an entire sentence. When Walsh took to the stage, that all changed. He was able to enunciate his lyrics.

That may be a testament to one of the most impressive powers of music—the power to integrate even the most scrambled mind. The phenomenon that pulls together even people with senile dementia, people who cannot speak, and allows them to seem normal for three minutes—the three minutes in which they're playing an instrument and singing a song. Joe pulled off the seeming normal—or at least the seemingly rock-star-ish—for a whole seventy minutes. Not bad. Thank god for the invisible self, the soul that comes alive in front of an audience. And thank god for the gods inside.

* * *

Which brings us to the thirty-fourth floor of ABC. On that floor was an executive who was pondering one of the same questions I was. What magic allowed CBS to dominate the record business? What secret allowed it to pull in a full 33 percent of the record industry's revenues? So, Martin Pompadur would summon me up to the thirty-fourth floor from time to time to pick my brain. I'd explain the importance of album artists. The importance of touring. The importance of artist development—having a strategy for building the artist and growing his or her audience during a minimum of three years. The importance of the star-making machine. It looked like I had the ear of one of the folks in power—one of the top executives above all of ABC's operations. But looks can be deceiving. In the end, Pompadur drew his own conclusion. And that conclusion was ridiculous. CBS's miracle president, Clive Davis, had been a lawyer. So what ABC really needed was to hire a lawyer to head its music operation. Simple, right? Yes, simple. And wrong.

Jay Lasker was fired. A lawyer with a new style of hair—artificially silver-gray and meticulously coifed—was hired, Jerry Rubinstein.[42] Rubinstein spent a year wrecking the company. Among other things, he brought in a new head of the publicity department in LA, Michael Ochs, whose major claims to fame were that he was the brother of legendary folk singer Phil Ochs and that he had a tight friendship with Dave Marsh, one of the cardinals in the church of rock criticism. Michael fired me, being careful to do it the day before my pension rights would kick in, thus saving the company money. And he hired Dave Marsh's girlfriend to replace me. Very smart.

After a year of sack and pillage by the new president, the one with the law degree and the fancy silver haircut, ABC realized it was losing everything Lasker had built, and doing something more: losing a fortune. ABC corporate fired the lawyer-president. But because he was a lawyer, rumor said he had written himself a contract that gave him one of the first golden parachutes in the history of the corporate world. If he were fired, his contract reportedly said, ABC would have to pay him $20 million. Yes, he'd get $20 million if he completely floogled up the company. That's $95 million in today's dollars. At that point, ABC appears to have thrown its hands up in the air, sold what little was left of its music operation to MCA, and accepted the fact that it no longer owned a record company.

All because ABC had killed the soul of a company.

So there I was, fired. For the second time in my life. The first time was when I'd been tossed out of my own art studio. What was I going to do?

* * *

Well, one day, while I was still firmly ensconced in my glass cubicle at ABC Records available for all in the world to see, Seymour Stein had passed my door on his way to a meeting. Seymour poked his head into my cubicle and said one simple sentence. "Schmuck, if you're so smart, why don't you have your own company?" That bit me to the quick. I mean, I can't catch or throw a baseball. I don't know how to date. I fumble tragically with a knife and fork and hope that no one else at the table notices. The one thing I have going for me is a reasonable degree of intelligence. So tell me I'm brainless and you steal my only legitimate reason for being.

But I avoided taking Seymour up on his challenge for a year. Yes, ABC fired me. But thanks to the kindness of someone I had known at G&W, I got a call from the president of the eleventh-largest PR firm in the world—ICPR. He asked if I'd meet with him in LA. So I flew out. I met with this ICPR president, John Strauss, in a tiny, four-story Hollywood building on La Cienega Boulevard, near Santa Monica Boulevard, that looked like it had been built last week and would be torn down next week. A common feature of LA architecture. One fact was on instant display. Strauss, the ICPR head, was a generous man.[43] His receptionist was handicapped and answered the phones at the front desk in a wheelchair. When I sat down in his office, John Strauss asked if I could develop any aspect of PR I wanted, what would it be? I said I'd do PR in science. John hired me anyway and tasked me with building an East Coast music department. I brought in Renaissance, the Climax Blues Band, and Stephanie Mills as clients. Then I snagged another client—ZZ Top. But ZZ Top is a story for later.

One of ICPR's hotshots on the West Coast, a flamboyant gay guy who showed no ability to do PR that I could see, landed a band called Queen. And I got Queen into *Newsweek*, the only story ICPR landed in one of the high-prestige, high-readership weekly news magazines in the entire time I was there. It would not be my last encounter with Queen.

I was a problem for a PR firm. When the president of Paramount Pictures had summoned me to appear along with Stephanie Mills at a meeting with his department heads, he had done something else. He'd told his staff to call me up from the twenty-third floor whenever Paramount Pictures was planning a new blockbuster. So, a mere six months after I'd started in music publicity, I'd been kidnapped into film publicity. And in film publicity I'd learned something. A film PR campaign gets a budget four times the size of the PR budget allocated to a rock star. And, as a consequence, a movie gets four times as much attention from the staff. Four times as much attention and four times as much publicity.

I wanted to see that same super-intense concentration applied in the rock-and-roll business. But that's the opposite of what was happening in rock. First off, record-company presidents had a phrase, "Throw the shit up against the wall and see what sticks." In other words, sign ten times as many artists as you intend to take all the way to stardom. Then see which ones develop a momentum of their own and hop on their bandwagons. There was something deeply wrong with this approach. A musician makes an extremely risky decision sometime in his or her teen years. She makes a million-to-one bet. She dedicates her entire life to her music. So if you sign that musician, then ignore her, you are flushing away someone's life. That is not acceptable.

But there's more. The leading PR firm in the rock-and-roll business when I arrived at *Circus* in 1971 was a company you've glimpsed a few minutes ago, Gibson and Stromberg. Gibson and Stromberg had all the hottest acts. One act of particular importance to me at *Circus* was Jethro Tull. And Jethro Tull's publicist at Gibson and Stromberg in LA was Bobbi Cowan, who was prompt, reliable, and attentive. But that was not the norm. There was a reason.

Gibson and Stromberg's Bob Gibson and Gary Stromberg had a disturbing sales technique. To woo a record-company president, they would take him (and, yes, it was all hims) out to dinner, buy him the drugs of his choice, buy him girls or boys (whichever he preferred), and make him an outrageously happy man. For a night. In exchange, the record-company president would promise to sign a Lollapalooza-sized contract naming Gibson and Stromberg the PR firm for the company's seven or eight biggest acts. Then what would happen? Gibson and Stromberg's PR staff would have so many musicians on their roster that they would have no time for 80 percent of them.

How did I know this? One day at ABC, I'd gotten a call from our president, Jay Lasker. John Klemmer, a saxophone player, was coming into New York City. I didn't need to do anything, said Jay. John Klemmer was being handled by Gibson and Stromberg. Just call Gibson and Stromberg and see how they're doing. So I called

Gibson and Stromberg. I knew all their staff. I'd worked with them for two years at *Circus*. "What are you doing for John Klemmer?" I asked. Said the account executive I was talking to, "John who?"

Gibson and Stromberg had approximately sixteen artists on their roster for every publicist in the company. In the film business, that ratio was more like three clients for each account executive. That three-to-one ratio was what I wanted to provide. What's more, the "booze, cocaine, and broads" approach to sales disgusted me. I wanted nothing to do with it.

But my approach to PR was more expensive than anything ICPR—the publicity firm that had just made the mistake of hiring me—was used to, even though they were in the film business. So, after eight months, ICPR asked me to leave. I was snapped up immediately by another firm, Bob Levinson's Levinson Associates.[44] But when Bob saw the intensity with which I worked—actually going out on the road two days a week with ZZ Top—he realized he could not afford me, either.

That's when Seymour Stein's "shmuck, if you're so smart, why don't you have your own company" smacked me upside the head. For some reason I cannot remember, I called Danny Goldberg, the editor I'd replaced at *Circus*, then at Gulf and Western. Danny, too, urged me start my own company. In fact, he made me an offer. I could work out of his living room on Manhattan's West Seventy-Ninth Street. I could use half of his coffee table. He was trying to start a hybrid PR-and-management firm of his own. So if I paid half the salary of his assistant, he said, I could use half of her time. I took him up on the offer.

And I took my faithful clients with me: Seymour Stein's Renaissance and Climax Blues Band, Stephanie Mills, and my new client, ZZ Top. Again, more on ZZ Top in a minute.

Meanwhile, I was still working on another mystery. What is artist development? What is the star-making machine? And how do you operate it? How do you help deserving artists become huge?

The person I would finally learn the key secrets of artist development from—the secrets of the star-making machine—had just appeared in my life: a man few have heard of, but many more should: the genius behind ZZ Top, their manager, Bill Ham. How would I get involved with ZZ Top? How would I discover a group soul even more powerful than that of the Cajuns? And how would ZZ Top's Bill Ham make me the Ambassador of Texas Culture to the World?

For that, alas, you will have to read on.

* * *

When I arrived at *Circus* magazine in 1971, I seldom had lunch with anyone outside of Gerry Rothberg's office. Lunchtime was my most intense study period. You remember, I took my brown-paper-bagged tuna sandwiches to a table where I could spread out the latest issues of *Melody Maker* and *New Musical Express*, the British music weeklies, and study them like a religious scholar studying the Talmud. Or I'd schlepp my sandwiches into Art Ford's room and listen to his stories. Oh, and one more thing: no one invited me to lunch.

There was one exception. Decca Records was the company that launched rock and roll in 1954 with Bill Haley and the Comets' twenty-five-million-selling "Rock Around the Clock." Eight years later, Decca auditioned the Beatles, rejected them, and signed Brian Poole and the Tremeloes instead.[45] So, by the early 1970s, Decca Records' American operation was a spent force. It was one of the bare survivors left in the backwater when CBS and Warner Bros rose to dominance, with a full 66 percent of the industry's revenues between them.

But two guys at Decca wanted to take me to lunch—Bob Small and Ray Caviano. Normally, when you are invited to your first lunch with someone, it is a one-on-one. After all, that's the best way to get to know someone. Aside from laboring to survive in a lifeboat with someone for three months after your ship has gone down. So why two people were taking me to lunch I didn't quite understand. And I didn't quite catch their titles. Ray was apparently head of publicity for Decca. But what was Bob? And how did their work mesh? Bob and Ray (not the 1950s comedy duo of the same name) were all excited about something. They had this new artist named Al Green, and they spoke of him as if he were a messiah. By that time, I'd done enough work with my *Circus* audience to discover something. My kids did not like black artists. They were suburban white teens who regarded the subculture of the inner city as alien and threatening. Something that would change eight years later.

Look, every inch of my magazine, from the cover to the pages inside, had to sell. It had to make the hearts of my kids beat fast. I had run features on Stevie Wonder and Roberta Flack, then learned my lesson. For my kids, those were wasted pages. They did not sell magazines. They didn't quicken my kids' spirits.

So trying to sell me on Al Green for *Circus* was not going to work. And Bob and Ray had nothing else to offer. Plus they were a little bit odd. I couldn't quite figure out why. One reason, I'd discover, was that they and I shared something in common. We were kamikazes. We were utterly devoted to our work. If given a choice of leisure or labor on behalf of our goals, we'd choose labor. And Bob and Ray must have had their eyes on me.

A few years later, when I was ejected from ABC and went over to ICPR, Bob Small called me. He had a band he was working with. He wanted me to work on it with him. It was ZZ Top. And ZZ Top would reveal some of the strangest clues you would ever see. Clues to the mysteries of group soul and to the puzzles of the gods inside. Massive clues.

* * *

In 1975, ZZ Top was one of the most hated bands in America. At least it was hated by the people who were convinced that they counted most, the rock critics. Robert Christgau, chief music critic and senior editor of the *Village Voice*, had named himself the pope of what he would eventually call "a rock-critic establishment," a rock-crit elite.[46] All wannabe critics, he let it be known, would have to come to him for approval. Or at least would have to sit at his feet, lick his toenails, and learn. Learn to write in the style he demanded. And no one objected to his self-anointment.

My introduction to Christgau came one night shortly after I'd been asked to found a public and artist-relations department for Gulf and Western. Back in my *Rags* magazine days, one of my areas of expertise had been finding the least expensive way to handle the basics of living, from grocery shopping to buying designer clothes. I'd needed that skill badly. My wife, my daughter, and I had been forced to live on the barest whiff of a budget. Remember, for my first year at Cloud Studio, I'd earned a measly seventy-five dollars a week. A staffer at the *New York Post*, Susan Rogers, had found this fascinating. She'd asked if she could do a story on me. Sure, I said. The story was "How to Feed a Family on Fifteen Dollars a Week." From that point on, I invited Susan every year to my annual Passover Seder—a Seder I'd rearranged so it would tell the story of the Exodus from Egypt as written in the Bible, but as a drama, a narrative, a clear and vivid tale. A tale of the formation of a group's identity.

In exchange for the Seder, Susan invited me and my wife Linda over to her Twenty-Third Street place on Manhattan's East Side for dinner. To us, a Manhattan apartment that wasn't in a slum was a luxury we'd seldom experienced. Susan had just married Gary Giddins, a kid who had started as a copy boy at the *New York Post* and was on the very lowest rung of his future career as one of the most prominent jazz critics in America.[47] I believe Gary was younger than Susan was. Susan went all out to display her gifts as a hostess. We had a lovely meal: a white tablecloth, ambitious food, the whole nine yards of dinner mastery. Then the doorbell rang. It was an unscheduled appearance by Gary's editor and mentor, Bob Christgau.

Because Christgau was a pope and Gary was a mere petitioner in the church of rock criticism, Gary immediately assumed a stooped submission posture. Bob was not much to look at, much less to bow at. In fact, if given a choice, you'd gladly have looked away. His facial features were anything but pretty. His attitude made those features downright ugly. His shirt was untucked. The upper rim of his underwear was on display. So, if you weren't averting your eyes, was back hair, stomach hair, and more skin than you really wanted to see.

Bob treated me as if I were a leper. After all, I was now a part of a subhuman species, one born to be shat upon—publicists. Rudeness is something I can take without difficulty. Snubbed is my usual position in life. But Susan was so mortified that she ended up in the bedroom, sobbing. Bob Christgau had ruined her dinner.

Yes, that was the king of the critics, the pope of the music press from the Atlantic to the Pacific. When Robert Christgau set forth one of his edicts, it was dutifully repeated by rock critics from coast to coast. And when it came to ZZ Top, Christgau had pronounced his verdict. In fact, he'd done it in a thirty-two-point, bold-type headline: "ZZ Top Has the Sound of Hammered Shit."

How in the world was I going to get ZZ Top out of this pickle?

14

ZZ TOP—TAKING TEXAS TO THE WORLD

I didn't really like to work with popular acts. I felt they didn't need me. But give me an act that no one else wants, and my heart catches fire. Especially if that act has something worth telling the world about. And ZZ Top had a lot to tell the world.

First off, out in the lost cities like Atlanta, Memphis, and Houston, out in the flyover towns, ZZ Top had broken concert attendance records set by the Beatles and the Rolling Stones. Second, ZZ Top represented a culture as foreign as the Trobriand Islanders. They came from a state that is less a part of the USA than it seems—Texas. And they were proud of it. Or at least they were about to be proud of it. They weren't quite proud yet, when Bob Small recruited me to work on them.

In other words, there was more to ZZ Top than I imagined. But it would take six months to find that out. My first step with a band was to find a story so compelling that the press would be forced to tell it. So I studied every article I could get my hands on about ZZ Top, and every interview that had ever reached the light of print. Then I flew down to Houston to meet the band. I drove to a one-story ranch house somewhere in the Houston suburbs, though my impression was that Houston was one giant suburb trying to pretend it was a city. In this nice, low-slung, middle-class ranch house was the office of Lone Wolf Management, a company owned by a man named Bill Ham. Ham, as his name might indicate, was a big man. Roughly six feet tall, which in those days was lofty. And he looked broad and strong. He didn't talk much. He tried to be gracious. But he was actually somewhere between shy and mysterious. And it was from Bill Ham that I would learn two of the most important and best-hidden secrets of artist development, two of the most vital elements in the star-making machine. First, a little-known form of wizardry called touring strategy. And second, another crucial factor—another lesson on the soul of a subculture.

Remember, I wanted to know what unique story was in ZZ Top. Bob Small had reeled off the concert records ZZ Top had broken. Bill Ham had reeled off a few more. Smashing attendance records set by the Beatles and the Rolling Stones. But what about these three guys—Billy Gibbons, Dusty Hill, and Frank Beard—made them a story?

Billy Gibbons seemed to have a tale to tell. His dad had been THE society orchestra leader in Texas. If you were going to throw a debutante ball, Billy's dad was the man you wanted to have. Because Billy's pop had spent most of his time making music for the upper crust, Billy's mom possessed exquisitely lofty society contacts, too. When John F. Kennedy was shot in Dallas in 1963, another man was sworn in as president of the United States on Air Force One while it flew back to Washington. That man, Lyndon Johnson, was from Texas. So Billy's mother became one of Lyndon's assistants and worked for the president in Washington, D.C. In the White House.

There was a problem with this story. It made Billy an overdog. And the rock audience preferred underdogs. People like themselves who have to struggle to mount the ladder of success.

But there was more. Texas had a hidden cultural edge of a very strange kind. Billy explained that, back in 1919, a doctor with questionable medical credentials, John Brinkley, had begun working with the gonads of goats and felt they had all kinds of restorative properties. Mostly the ability to pep up your sex life and the male organ responsible for it. So, rather than take the active ingredient from these testicles—testosterone—and put it in pills, the iffy medical doctor tried to pep you up or stand your organ upright by sewing the testicular glands of goats into your body. The medical board of the state where Brinkley was headquartered, Kansas, revoked his medical license and concluded that he "performed an organized charlatanism . . . quite beyond the invention of the humble mountebank."[48] Not exactly a compliment. So the banished goat-gland doctor, Brinkley, moved his practice to Del Rio, Texas, on the border with Mexico.

Though his clinic generated a ton of traffic, it was his advertising medium that changed Texas's culture. In Kansas, Brinkley had owned a radio station that interspersed regular programming with all-goat-glands-all-the-time. When he had been stripped of his medical license, he'd also been stripped of his license to broadcast. So he'd gotten a broadcasting license from the country of Mexico and set up a station across the bridge from Del Rio, in Mexico's Villa Acuña. It was a radio station with ten times more power than the maximum allowed in the USA—a 500,000-watt station with 300-foot high antennas that could reach all the way to Canada and across the North Pole to Russia on a good night.[49]

Brinkley died in 1942. But his station lived on. To attract a listenership, it hired DJs. In the 1950s, one of those DJs, a Brooklyn lad named Bob Smith, renamed himself Wolfman Jack. And Wolfman Jack played "race records"—the kind of nitty-gritty black music that no major pop station dared play. The sort of music that the Beatles and the Rolling Stones had been obsessed with in their teens.

Meanwhile, the Japanese had taken a strange invention developed in the USA at Bell Labs and had built a small, simple entertainment device around it—the transistor radio. Transistor radios were so cheap that kids could afford them and so small that you could hide one under your pillow. Which is exactly what Billy Gibbons did. Night after night, when lights-out came, he listened to strange black music under his pillow. From that came his blues-based guitar and his strained, strangled vocals.

Okay, this was a bit of a ZZ Top story. But I was missing something. And I couldn't figure out what. Then, six months later, Bob Small called with a hint. ZZ Top had talked to a writer from Atlanta named Jim Pettigrew, and Jim might have something for me. When I called him, Jim did, indeed, have a story. Here's how it goes. When Billy Gibbons was a teenager, a friend of his owned a ranch. On that ranch was an old black man with a strange form of sorcery. He was a welder. A welder of what? Windmills connect the gears high in the air behind their blades to the pump way down below in the depths of a well. To make that connection, windmill builders use roughly thirty feet of something called "sucker gauge" steel. Long, thin, incredibly tough steel rods. The elderly black welder could bend those sucker-gauge steel rods, weld them together, and make just about anything you could conceive. So Billy and his friend gave this maker of the exotic and the strange an assignment. Make a six-foot-wide spherical cage of sucker-gauge steel. Weld a bucket seat and a safety harness into it. Then pack it onto the back of a pickup truck. Wait until late at night, when the highways are empty. Drive it to the emptiest piece of tarmac around, Jack Rabbit Road. Let Billy or his friend open the cage door, squoonch himself inside, and safety-harness himself into the bucket seat. Then take the truck up to its top speed, pull a cord outside the driver's window, open the truck's flap, let the spherical cage roll out onto the highway, and enjoy the ride. When the cage hit the asphalt at fifty miles an hour, said Gibbons, it sent up a rooster tail of sparks higher than the trees by the side of the road. And the bucket-seated kid inside turned end over end as the cage bounced down the highway, sometimes going off road, encountering a barbed-wire fence, and wrapping itself in a quarter-mile of spiked wire. This sounded a bit more authentically Texan. It was a start. But it still lacked a heart, a core. It still lacked soul.

After I'd worked with ZZ Top for eight months, I was sitting with them in a hotel suite somewhere out on the road. When you tour, all you see is the hotel you're in and the arena where you're performing. Cities blend into each other. It is hard to remember which town you are in so you can shout, "Howdy Cincinnati," when you hit the stage. We could have been in Dallas–Fort Worth, Memphis, or Atlanta. But there we were in a big and luxurious suite somewhere above the eighth floor, with a view of the city and beyond. And Billy Gibbons, Frank Beard, and Dusty Hill finally revealed both the heart of their story and the reason it had taken me so long to detect it.

* * *

Texans back in 1976 had an inferiority complex—a big one. If you admitted you were a Texan in polite company, people looked down on you as a form of life somewhere below toilet algae. So when Texans tried to make it on the national scene, Billy explained to me, they pretended they were from someplace else. Janis Joplin was from Port Arthur, Texas. But she pretended to be from San Francisco. Johnny and Edgar Winter, two fabulous blues guitarists, were from Beaumont, Texas. But they pretended to be from Connecticut. Explained Billy Gibbons, the world saw Texans as ignorant ranchers who had struck it rich with oil then had ordered custom-made Cadillac convertibles with squirrel-fur covers on their steering wheels and longhorn steer horns mounted above the front bumper. Texans were assumed to have a brainpower just slightly above that of an oil pump.

In reality, Billy confessed, Texas was not an ordinary state. It was its own nation with its own history. In the remaining forty-nine states, schoolchildren learned of our founding fathers, George Washington, Thomas Jefferson, James Madison, and Alexander Hamilton. But that wasn't the history Texan kids learned. Texans had another founding father entirely: Sam Houston. What's more, if you took a chain saw, sawed straight across the border connecting Texas to the rest of the USA, and set the entire state afloat in the Gulf of Mexico, Texas would have the sixth largest economy in the world. Oh, and one more thing. The Texas constitution, Frank Beard added, says that the state can declare independence and secede from the Union any time it wants. What had we here?

Meanwhile, Texans hid all of this and suffered a secret shame.

It was the era of pride movements. Black pride was giving the African American community permission to claim freedom from old prejudices and to reach for a higher status, not to mention respect, rights, and dignity. The gay community was about to come out of the closet, a story we'll get to in just a minute. And Texans were aching for something they did not yet possess—a Texas pride movement. That movement would soon come to be. And who would it come from? ZZ Top. And it would come from the man whose humiliation as a Texan was hidden beneath his silence and his size—ZZ Top's manager, Bill Ham.

A few months later, I got a call to come back down to Houston. Bill Ham and the band were planning something big. They were plotting to fling a finger in the face of America. They were going to undo their humiliation, stop the pretense of coming from somewhere other than the Lone Star State, and make a statement. They called it their Worldwide Texas Tour. Otherwise known as Taking Texas to the World. A tour that was going to travel with four trailer trucks painted with murals of Texas, all of them dovetailing into a giant panoramic view of the Texas landscape. One hundred and forty feet of Texas topography, blazing its image on the retinas of motorists from Winston-Salem to Seattle. What's more, Ham and the band were building a seventy-five-foot-wide stage shaped like the state of Texas and tilted forward so you could see that shape from any seat in a stadium or arena. They were having scrims painted and lighting designed to show a Texas landscape onstage at sunrise, noon, and sunset. They were going to carry a buffalo, a longhorn steer, two turkey vultures, and a small passel of rattlesnakes—Texas animals—to every city they visited.

And, just to show that they were finally going to make Texas loud and proud, Bill Ham had me carted to the Houston City Hall to be named the official Ambassador of Texas Culture to the World. The city hall turned out to be a pair of white, aluminum, one-story buildings that looked like temporary shacks on a construction site. I was ushered into the office of a woman who I was told was the mayor. And she handed me an official certificate, formally naming me the Ambassador of Texas Culture to the World. Thus, like Moses's brother, Aaron, I was made the voice of a people, the tongue of Texas pride.

What's the role of music in human life? It binds us to others. It helps us realize that we are not alone. It helps us feel that we are part of a group. A movement. And music gives our subculture a voice and an identity. Along with clothes and hairstyles, music expresses group soul.

* * *

It was my approach to publicity with ZZ Top that convinced Bob Levinson and John Strauss, the head of ICPR, that I didn't belong in their companies. When I took you on as a client, I became a warrior for your cause. ZZ Top wanted me out on the road with them. Which meant that for two days of the week I was in whatever city ZZ Top was playing that weekend. And for five days of the week I was back in New York. Working. Frankly, I was never happy with five-day workweeks. I hate leisure. It depresses me. Work is my salvation. So seven-day weeks of work were perfect for me.

Bill Ham and his booking agent had done an incredible job of tour packaging. A ZZ Top concert was an event. And for more than just the shape of the stage and the sight of the buffalo and the longhorn steer. The opening acts were the J. Geils Band, a terrific blues-rock outfit from Worcester, Massachusetts, fifty-three minutes outside of Boston; and Aerosmith, another Boston band that would become one of the most popular in the heavy-metal firmament (and a band I would later work with). This meant that we were no longer performing in mere arenas—indoor halls with a capacity of 18,000. We were performing in stadiums—outdoor football fields with seats for roughly 60–70,000. ZZ Top was using the newborn audiences of two other hot, new bands to build its base. And those two bands were doing something equally synergistic—they, too, were taking advantage of ZZ Top's draw to expand their audiences. They were playing the name game.

Meanwhile, other stories of ZZ Top's youth in Texas started inching out. There was a used-car hawker in Houston who had made himself a celebrity with his TV ads. One of his gimmicks was selling a used car every week for a mere fifty dollars. The privilege of purchasing that used vehicle for pocket change went to the winner of a weekly drawing. One week, ZZ Top managed to win that contest. The car wasn't a clunker. Yes, it was aged. And some frills—like the windows—barely worked. But the car could eat its way down the highway at an acceptable speed.

Now, in Texas, there is a tradition. A rite of passage. An entry into manliness. You allow a fourteen-year-old's friends to drive him south of the border into Mexico. For what? For one of his first madly alcoholic binges. And to go to a whorehouse and get laid.

Since the three ZZ Toppers now had a fifty-dollar car, they decided to head for Mexico. I suspect that this wasn't their first time. On the way, the trio spotted some cattle in a pasture. They stopped the car. Frank Beard—the drummer, and the only member of the trio who never wore a beard—jumped over the barbed wire fence, strode out into the pasture, and demonstrated his cowboy manliness by wrestling a calf to the ground, putting it over his shoulders, carrying it back to the car, and tossing the poor baby into the back seat. The calf, which was not enthusiastic about a trip to Mexico in a vehicle propelled by horsepower, not cow-power, bucked and kicked. With every kick, it destroyed another piece of the fifty-dollar car's carefully appointed interior—the rear seat, the ceiling, the covering of the back of the front seats. The guys in the band decided to continue on to Mexico without the calf. And without most of the functional parts of the car's interior. They let the innocent bovid out. God knows how—or if—it ever found its way back to its mother.

Then there was the time the boys were driving the Texas roads and spotted every adolescent male's dream: two girls hitchhiking by the side of the highway. The ZZ Toppers gallantly stopped the car, swung the rear door open to indicate a welcome, and got excited as the girls stepped into the car. But it very quickly became apparent that these were two ladies you did not want to mess with. One of them had acne scars so bad that, as Billy Gibbons explained, it looked as if her face had been set on fire with lighter fluid, then someone had tried to stomp out the flames with a spiked football shoe. The lovelies were hitchhiking because they had just gotten out of prison and were headed home. At the girls' request, the ZZ Topniks drove the mademoiselles down the highway to a cutoff and turned onto an unpaved dirt road, then to a shack in the woods, where they met one of the dads. He stood there with a shotgun, making it clear without a word that if you messed with his daughter, you were either going to marry her and stick with her 'til death do you part, or you were about to become richer by two dozen shotgun pellets conveniently implanted in your flesh. The beauties were named Precious and Grace. And "Precious and Grace" became a song.

A picture was emerging of a hidden culture. And that suppressed culture was crying for its right to be, through the music of ZZ Top. In other words, ZZ Top had authenticity. And authenticity is something that the snooty rock-crit elite respects. If you manage to tell them the tale. And that's not easy.

* * *

Why are the top rock writers so hard to reach? Before we go farther into the hidden culture of ZZ Top, let's take a look at something even better hidden—the mysterious culture of the rock-crit elite. As nose-in-the-air as that rock-crit elite is, its behavior is based on something primitive. The story of that primitive impulse leads through the brains of sheep. Sheep? Sheep don't listen to music. Surely, Mr. Bloom, you must be joking. Bear with me. Or ewe with me.

Where do sheep come into the tale of the rock-critic brat pack? Back in roughly 1832, the social commentator Thomas Carlyle was trying to explain how the pop-culture elite of his day worked.[50] He was trying to explain the behavior of critics. The pop culture back then was dominated by theater and books. And theater and books had their passel of reviewers who made a living by trashing novels, shredding plays, and tearing writers, actors, and actresses to pieces. In print. In magazines like the *Spectator* and the *Athenaeum*.[51] Was there a hidden dynamic powering this group of highbrows? A dynamic you might be able to see naked in animals? Thomas Carlyle believed the answer was a big yes.

Carlyle told a tale that my memory embellished, then held on to. Imagine that you are a naturalist, fifty years before Darwin's *On the Origin of Species*. More specifically, you are the German writer Jean Paul Friedrich Richter, a man Carlyle praises for his "quick eye." It's a Sunday. You have been on a long walk and are standing in a pasture, admiring the view. Meanwhile, a hundred feet or less away from you is a narrow, blackened, deeply trodden path running next to the road. The sort of path you do not want to take a date on. Why? Because you would have to walk it single file, which makes holding hands tricky. What wears these paths down to thin black gullies? Sheep. Herds of sheep walking in single file under the supervision of a shepherd. And, sure enough, a convenient herd of sheep comes down the path. In single file.

You decide to try an experiment. You lift your walking stick and hold it out in front of the lead sheep, the bellwether. The lead sheep jumps over your cane. Then you withdraw your cane. What happens? There is no longer an obstacle blocking the path. But the remaining thousand sheep jump at precisely the spot where their leader jumped. A thousand sheep jump, even though there is nothing to jump over. The sheep follow the leader. To quote Carlyle, the vast mass of us are a "dull flock." We "roll hither and thither, whithersoever," we "are led; and seem all sightless and slavish."[52] We are sheep.

How does that work with rock critics? Remember, Bob Christgau spun a name, "the rock-critic establishment," the rock-crit elite.[53] And Christgau anointed himself as that elite's pope. The rock-crit establishment included a tiny handful of initiates. Remember, Christgau wrote and assigned record reviews for the *Village Voice*, an instrument of influence back in the 1970s. Who had equal influence? Those who wrote for the biggest lead-sheep-publication in the nation's flock of daily newspapers—the *New York Times*. And the writers for the most prestigious publication in rock and roll—*Rolling Stone*. But did these high priests really have the impact they hoped for, the position of lead sheep? Did others imitate their every move?

On July 22, 1976, I flew out to Minneapolis to see ZZ Top in the sold-out Sports Coliseum. Not only did I rep ZZ Top, I also handled the PR for a musical group called Dr. Buzzard's Original Savannah Band. The rock-crit elite back in New York loathed ZZ Top and loved Dr. Buzzard's Original Savannah Band. The Minneapolis arena was, as I mentioned, packed. It was filled with eighteen thousand ZZ Top enthusiasts. My seat was in between the seats of the two leading music critics in Minneapolis—critics for the city's two competing daily newspapers. While we waited for the show to begin, each critic killed time by reading. And what did they read? The critic on my left was reading the *New York Times*. The critic on my right was reading the *Village Voice*. Each was reading a wildly appreciative review of Dr. Buzzard's Original Savannah Band. A review of one of my clients.

When the lights went up on the stage, the critics stopped reading. For the next seventy minutes, the audience went wild for ZZ Top. But the critics seemed blind to the frenzied appreciation the band received. Each went back to his electric typewriter late that night and spat out a review of ZZ Top. And a review of Dr. Buzzard's Original Savannah Band. The reviews of Dr. Buzzard's Original Savannah Band were ecstatic. Why? Because the *New York Times* had been ecstatic. The reviews of ZZ Top were terrible. Why? Because the *Village Voice* had made the papal pronouncement that ZZ

Top's music was on a par with hammered shit. These two Minneapolis rock writers were sheep.

My job was to keep the opinion of Dr. Buzzard's Original Savannah band high. And to turn the rock-crit verdict on ZZ Top 180 degrees. How would I do it? Telling stories. The story of the Master of Sparks—the sucker-gauge steel cage that shot sparks high into the air when it hit the highway. The story of Precious and Grace. And the tale of the trip to Mexico in the fifty-dollar used car. But the real meat was what those stories indicated—that Texas had a hidden culture, a culture that had been suppressed and humiliated, and a culture that was crying out for its right to be, for its right to exist. The real meat was group soul.

Remember, the *New York Times* and the *Village Voice* were not the only lead sheep. There was another big ram in the rock-crit flock: *Rolling Stone*. What *Rolling Stone* wrote, lesser journalists imitated. So I pounded *Rolling Stone*'s editors with ZZ Top tales. For roughly a year. And, finally, *Rolling Stone* caved in to the stories of ZZ Top's authenticity and suppressed lone-star identity.

In roughly 1977, ZZ Top was going back to its home, Houston, for the first time in years. It was playing a football stadium. Bill Ham, the group's manager, gave me a travel budget to fly journalists down to see this triumphal homecoming. By then I'd been in music publicity roughly four years. And I'd realized that there are three things rock journalists can't resist: fine food, alcohol, and . . . travel. With help from the travel budget, I got *Rolling Stone* to assign a writer to do a major feature. Not just any writer but Timothy Ferris.

Why was Timothy Ferris special? He was about to help Carl Sagan put together a pair of golden records that would be launched into deep space on two Voyager spacecraft to tell alien species about us. And he was about to become one of the most lauded writers of science books in America. A writer who would be rewarded with a position teaching science writing at Berkeley. And with his own special on PBS. So I flew down to Houston with Timothy Ferris sitting on my right. He had no suspicion of my scientific background. And I had no suspicion of his. We had just one major focus—taking Texas culture to the world. And because he wrote for *Rolling Stone*, Timothy was a lead sheep. Once he wrote positives about the ZZ Top phenomenon, we were home free. From that instant on, ZZ Top had respect. And more. The rock-crit elite defended ZZ Top. Because we had successfully made the case that ZZ Top represented a legitimate subculture. A subculture that had been suppressed. Because we had shown that ZZ Top was an underdog. And because we had shown that ZZ Top were spokespeople for a group's soul. And for that soul's right to be.

* * *

Bill Ham, ZZ Top's manager, had a handle on the herd nature of music fans. Without the benefit of Carlyle's tale of sheep.

Let's return to the fact that, in 1964, when the Beatles and the Rolling Stones first hit the United States, huge crowds of girls showed up at the airport in New York to greet them with screams. And that another horde of girls had screamed for the arrival of the Rolling Stones. Bill Ham watched this process and wanted to duplicate it. One of ZZ Top's first dates outside of Texas had been in New Orleans. Ham wanted to make sure that the New Orleans audience screamed. How did he do it? He packed buses with girls from Texas—girls who loved ZZ Top. He planted those girls in the audience in New Orleans. And, like the girls who had greeted the Beatles and the Stones, they screamed.

ZZ Top's girls were lead sheep. They were oversized eggs. They were supernormal stimuli.

* * *

Rock and roll horrified parents and nearly every other sort of elder. That was one of its appeals to the young. But this meant that the press was primed for stories of violence at rock concerts. In general, rock dissipated violence. It didn't generate it. When I researched the topic, it turned out that the rate of violent incidents inside a rock concert was less than the rate of violence on the sidewalks and in the homes of the folks outside the concerts. It was less than the rate of violence per person of the city outside the arena or stadium.

But there were exceptions. On its Worldwide Texas Tour, ZZ Top played an outdoor concert near one of the Marine Corp's biggest training facilities, Camp Lejeune in North Carolina. Many of the security people who toured with ZZ Top were policemen from Texas—big guys who loved to brag about what pussies non-Texans were, and about their own bravery and willingness to face violence . . . and to use it. So the backstage area had a considerable number of swaggering Texas tough guys whose job it was to prevent murder and mayhem.

But it turned out that this particular ZZ Top concert had attracted more than just thousands of marines. It had also brought in a gathering of Hells Angels, pack after pack of them. At some point, a marine and a biker had a disagreement. The biker pulled out a massive knife and literally eviscerated the marine. When the serviceman was rushed backstage for medical treatment, his guts were hanging out, and we didn't know if he was dead or alive. I scrambled with the press contingent to get accurate information and to not let this incident overshadow the enthusiasm of the fifty thousand concertgoers having a great time. But it looked like a war might break out at any second between the bikers and the military guys.

What did the brave Texas policemen doubling as security superheroes do? They hid.

Then there were M-80s. M-80s are three grams of explosive used as a firecracker. They are so dangerous that you can only buy one if you have a special license. At least legally. Why? They are deadly. On June 12, 1976, we played a date at Three Rivers Stadium in Pittsburgh.[54] That's three weeks before the Fourth of July. But, alas, some of the kids brought M-80s. And some tossed these mini-dynamite-sticks into the air, not thinking of where they might land. One tore off a concertgoer's face.

Thank goodness our big concerts had medics.

* * *

Three years later, in 1979, ZZ Top had become huge. But it was still stranded on a dead record label, Decca Records. ZZ Top had sold records in spite of Decca.

Now a label that knew how to build superstardom had come to ZZ Top offering oodles of money—$5 million, which in those days was a jackpot. Worth over $18 million in today's dollars. Bill Ham, Bob Small, and ZZ Top were jubilant. They flew me out to LA first class to meet with the Warners team.

The trip was extraordinary. Sitting next to me in first class was a slender, tall young woman wearing black pants and a black blouse. Turns out that she was the assistant to a new CEO at a film company that had been failing for decades and was looking to a new pair of heads for a turnaround. Her name was Jane Rosenthal. And her boss's name was Jeffrey Katzenberg. What antique company were they about to attempt to drag out of the ditch? Disney. But that is a story for much, much later, when we get to Bette Midler.

When we arrived in LA, I checked in to my hotel near Sunset Boulevard, then drove northeast through the Hollywood Hills toward Burbank[55] and the Warners headquarters, one of my favorite pieces of interior design in the record biz—with the chocolate browns and bare woods that I would adopt for my own office back in New York City. We sat at a big round table in one of Warners' sunny conference rooms. And I watched a bonding ritual of a kind I'd never seen before.

Bill Ham was Texas. He spoke slowly and infrequently. The Warners chief honchos were LA. They spoke a heck of a lot faster and a heck of a lot more. The two groups, Bill's team and the Warners team, did not share a common rhythm, a common body language, or a common vocabulary. They did not sync. They came from very different subcultures. How in hell were they going to communicate? The answer: football. They turned to the weekend's football games and analyzed the strategies of the winning and losing teams. Suddenly they were on the same planet . . . and the same page. Aha, I thought, so that's what sports is all about. A continent-wide common vocabulary. One of the tiny secrets of group soul.

A few months later, I was told I was no longer working for ZZ Top. Why? After years of reflection, I arrived at a hypothesis—Bob Merlis.

Merlis was VP of publicity for Warner Bros Records. When I'd been hired by *Circus*, he'd just started at Warners.[56] I was a very strange bird in those days. I still am. But you recall that I was locked in a windowless closet with a manual typewriter, turning out a monthly magazine that it had taken two people to crank out before I arrived and that it would take five people to generate after I left. Being locked in a closet all day long does strange things to your mind. Especially if your mind is strange to begin with.

I avoided calls most of the time. I had to stick to the typewriter if I was going to get *Circus* to the printer on time. But when I did answer a phone call, I sounded as if I were a Martian on amphetamines. My tongue rushed at three times the normal human speed. And I wasn't on drugs. I seldom even drank coffee.

Merlis was forced to call me a few times each month. And he must have hated it. I mean, he lived not far from me—in Cadman Plaza in Brooklyn Heights. I was fully prepared to like him. But apparently that liking was all one way.

In blood-hounding the evidence over the decades, I was forced to a strange conclusion. Merlis did more than merely dislike me. He wanted me out of every career over which he could gain influence. We will see more evidence of that when we get to a major showdown over John Cougar Mellencamp.

But in the three years I worked with ZZ Top, my staff and I had made the band headline material. And, more important, we had given the band legitimacy. Merlis wanted to step on our fingers and climb the remaining rungs of the ladder we had built. Even though he didn't have a clue to ZZ Top's secret. Speaking for a collective identity. Expressing a group soul.

Meanwhile, I was about to get another off-the-wall lesson in just how powerful group soul could be.

15

THE BIRTH OF DISCO—
FIREMEN COME OUT OF THE CLOSET

Back to 1976, when ZZ top had the mayor of Houston anoint me the Ambassador of Texas Culture to the World. Bob Small was my daily connection to the Texas band. He was, like me, a passionate workaholic. Cast your mind back to when Bob had taken me out to lunch while I was at *Circus* and he had brought along another executive from his record company. That fellow Decca-Record man was Ray Caviano.

Ray, too, was a workaholic. The kind of person who doesn't use the normal rituals of small talk—"Hi, how are you?" at the beginning of a phone call, and "Thanks, talk soon" at the phone call's end. Bob and Ray both launched directly into what they wanted done, then hung up. As you know, I liked that approach. I liked it so much that one Thanksgiving, I invited Bob and Ray to the holiday dinner I prepared for my wife and my stepdaughter. They were the only record-industry people I ever invited to one of my family's celebrations. Why? Because of their passionate intensity.

So here I was, working my butt off with ZZ Top and building a staff and a client roster for the Howard Bloom Organization Ltd., and one Sunday afternoon in the middle of the summer of 1976, I got a call from Ray Caviano. "I know how important your Mondays are to you," he said. "I know you go over every campaign with each of your account executives and focus on what needs to be done in the coming week. And I know that ritual is sacred. But you have to be at my apartment tomorrow, Monday morning, at 10 a.m., when I get off the seaplane from Fire Island. I have something we need to discuss." No other person had ever been allowed to jostle my Monday schedule.

But this Monday, I walked from my office on East Fifty-Fifth Street to Ray's apartment on East Fifty-Sixth Street in Manhattan. When Ray came in, he was all excited. First, he shifted the ground on me. He and his roommate, Bob Small, had taken me to lunch together and showed up at my Thanksgiving together for a reason. They were about as macho as you can be without wearing a plaid flannel shirt and carrying a dead deer over one shoulder and an assault rifle over the other. Turns out they were roommates because they shared more than an apartment. They shared a bed.

They were gay. They were lovers and committed partners. Also turns out that there was something I didn't know about Fire Island. Yes, it was an upscale summer island retreat for Manhattan art directors, editors, advertising execs, and other creatives who were climbing the corporate ladder. But it had a gay community. A community that hid itself discretely, and pretended not to be. A community that in its shame and secrecy was like the humiliated Texans I was helping to ease out of the closet.

But all that hiding was about to change. Why? Ray was no longer at Decca Records. He was independent. He worked out of the office of Allen Grubman, soon to be the most powerful attorney in the music industry. And he was a New York operative for two of Allen's clients. One was Miles Copeland, the London-based manager you met with the Climax Blues Band and Renaissance, and who you will meet again. The other was TK Records, a Florida-based company with one big act—KC and the Sunshine Band. In his spare time, Ray had been collecting a new kind of music—high-tempo electronic dance music from Europe. Music made to invoke ecstasies—the out-of-body experiences you have when you're in the middle of a crowd, you have a few drinks in you, the rhythm is pumping away, your dancing becomes frantic, and you become a wildly lapping flame of energy. The sort of experience you have when something inside of you that you don't know takes you over and dances you like a puppet on a string. The sort of experience in which you are seized by the gods inside.

When the summer came and a substantial slice of New York's creative community took up summer residence on Fire Island, Ray packed a suitcase full of his European electronic dance music discoveries and, after he arrived and settled in, played the music at gatherings of his gay tribe—gatherings where drugs and alcohol were probably abundant.

A strange thing happened. Gay men who had always avoided revealing their sexual preference in public shed their attempts to seem straight. Men—even gay men—had traditionally danced only with women. But the gay men of Fire Island began to dance with each other. In public. A shocking thing to do in 1976. And, sure enough, they went ecstatic. They were taken over by something deep inside of them. A second self. The gods inside.

But the real surprise was not the taboo-shattering fact that men danced with other men in public. It was the form of the secret selves, the form of the inner gods, that took these men over. Up until then, if you adopted an openly gay identity, you went *swish*. Your wrists went limp in a classic submission gesture. You swayed your hips when you walked. You walked like a woman. And, when you could get away with it, you wore makeup and a dress.

But what came out of the gay men of Fire Island in their dance music–driven ecstasies was a gut-grabbing surprise. It was not an inner woman. It was an inner man. The dancers were driven by the need to be cowboys, Indians, and fire chiefs—the ultimate male icons of masculinizing little boys. Like Bob Small and Ray Caviano, who were masculine straight through, the hidden gods of the gay men of Fire Island were the role models of maleness those little boys had imprinted on at the age of five. More about imprinting in a few minutes. And more about these hyper-masculine inner souls of men who were gay.

Remember dropping a crystal of salt into a supersaturated solution? Ray had dropped that crystal on Fire Island. He described the scene he had catalyzed. And he explained what it meant. Gay men were ready to emerge from hiding. As you know by now, it was an age of subcultural pride—black pride and, thanks to ZZ Top, Texas pride. It was an age of liberation of group soul. Now it was time for something radically new—gay pride. Who did Ray make the spokesperson for this new movement? A straight, married guy from Buffalo, New York. Me.

Ray rattled off the names of roughly twenty publications I'd never heard of. And he ordered that when I exit the elevator in his building, I take a right and walk straight over from Fifty-Sixth Street to two of the biggest newsstands in North America, newsstands on New York's West Fifty-Seventh Street. And that I buy every one of these sleazy little rags. How could there be twenty publications that I, a public-relations pro, had never heard of? Easy. They were as hidden as the gay community had been on Fire Island. They were by gay men and for gay men.

So I went over to Fifty-Seventh Street and, with massive embarrassment, asked for the publications Ray had insisted on. Sure enough, the newsstands had them. Hidden behind the counter. I asked for a shopping bag in which to carry them. A brown paper bag. Then I headed back to my office, blushing all the way, and wondering how my staff would respond to these publications printed cheaply on even cheaper paper. By now, my staff was entirely made up of women. Because a TV show called *Charlie's Angels* was popular, they called themselves Howard's Angels. Every one of the shoddy magazines I was carrying in my shopping bag had a black-and-white centerfold of a male's naked sexual equipment—balls and prick, testicles and penis. Garnished with a bit of pubic hair. Would my employees be shocked? Would they be paralyzed by embarrassment? Would they refuse to look at something so obviously indecent? Worse, would they refuse to work on it?

When I arrived at my office, I put the shopping bag with the magazines in a corner next to the couch in my room, seated myself at my massive desk with seven

Rolodexes, and went on the intercom to tell the girls that I'd just brought in some publications I felt they should see. How did they respond to the two-page penis spreads that I thought would shock them? They loved them. They couldn't get enough of them. They clustered around the shopping bag of publications like bees on honey. Excitedly pointing out the differences between one penis and another.

So I'd been named the Ambassador of Texas Culture to the World and the spokesman for the gay community in the same month. I wondered what the mayor of Houston would have thought if she had known.

* * *

Would there be a name for the sort of music Ray Caviano had introduced to the gay community, the music that had become the anthem for gay liberation? Yes. A name stolen from a two-year-old breed of Hispanic dance club: disco.

Music, once again, had shown the power to bring together a group—to unite a subculture—and to speak for that subculture's right to be. It had shown its capacity to sing the hidden soul of a group, and to make that group-soul soar.

* * *

It was still early days for the Howard Bloom Organization Ltd., and I had extra space in my office. To help pay the monthly check to the landlord, I rented an extra room out to Ray Caviano's twin brother, Bob, a music-industry booking agent. Bob, like Ray, was gay. Every two weeks or so, two gay guys from the French music industry would pop across the Atlantic to visit and would make Bob's room their headquarters. They would do the rounds of the new gay clubs popping up in the abandoned buildings of the Meatpacking District near Tenth Street and the Hudson River docks. Clubs marinating gay men in disco music. In fact, the rapidly growing New York disco club scene must have seemed to these two Frenchmen like a gay paradise. A pornographic paradise. Finally, the duo put together a studio project of their own in the new musical style. It was themed around a song about the cowboys, firemen, and Indian chiefs flickering like flames from the ecstacized bodies of men in the raptures of dance. The group the two would send out on the road to sing the song live would be dressed, in fact, as a cowboy, a fireman, and an Indian chief. The club scene was in the West Village. So the Frenchmen called their group the Village People. And the group's key song, the one that put the Village People on the map, was "Macho Man." As in "macho, macho, macho man." A celebration of the hidden selves of the gay community. A celebration of the butch hunks within. A celebration of the gods inside.

* * *

One other peculiar experience emerged from the gay club scene exploding in the empty industrial buildings of the Meatpacking District around Tenth Street and West Street overlooking the Hudson River. I worked with a tiny record company called Roadshow. Roadshow's president was Fred Frank, and, according to his official bio, Fred has been involved with records that have sold a total of twenty million copies. Fred coined a peculiar new description for me: "Howard Bloom reeks of integrity."

Apparently, Fred felt that integrity had power. At about the same time that the new gay disco dance clubs were going nuclear, Fred called. Tina Turner was looking for a new record label. Fred wanted to sign her. Remember how Frank Yablans had wooed Peter Bogdanovich using me as bait? Fred Frank wanted to do the same to win Tina Turner. Fred was about to have dinner with Tina. Could I please come? And could I dress as an hors d'oeuvre? No, I made that up. Dressing as an appetizer. Ignore it.

So Fred and I had dinner with Tina. And we heard one of the most astonishing stories I've ever been privy to. Tina was gorgeous. And she had eyes that shined like laser beams. More about that laser-beam effect when we meet Natalie Cole and super-star photographer Francesco Scavullo. But Tina's story outdid even the gleam in her pupils. When she was sixteen, in St. Louis, the charismatic leader of a hot local band, Ike Turner, spotted her, then turned her into a sex-and-singing slave. He imprisoned her in a building with a studio on the first floor and a great big bedroom on the second. The bedroom had a circular bed with a mirror on the ceiling.

Ike was very big on recruiting new talent. Specifically female talent. He packed those talents into the backup singing group he put together for Tina's recording sessions and for her onstage appearances—the Ikettes. And Ike also packed those talents one by one into his bedroom—the one where Tina was trapped. At least I think it was one by one. But whatever his preference, Ike made his way through the inner chambers of every single Ikette. While Tina apparently watched. Ike Turner lived out a classic male fantasy.

Ike was more than possessive and controlling, he was physically violent. Finally, Tina got into a fashionable new spiritual discipline, chanting the Buddhist mantra *Namu Myōhō Renge Kyō*. The mantra gave her courage. The courage to escape from Ike. And an escape it was. Tina holed up in a house in god knows what suburb of god knows what city. She kept her whereabouts top secret. But Ike found her. And to deliver a message, he had small bombs—M-80s—planted in her front lawn, then had them set off all at once. A sort of "You belong to me and you cannot get away" communiqué.

So Tina had experienced the strange.

I was due to go to one of the new disco dance clubs later that night on the instructions of Ray Caviano, the man who started disco. Ray wanted me to get the feel of the place. So I asked if Tina would like to come with me. She said yes. Tina and I grabbed a cab around Fifty-Seventh Street and Madison Avenue and barreled down to the grim and lowering, factory-like buildings and empty concrete streets and sidewalks of the Meatpacking District. We found the address. It wasn't easy. The street was dark and the massive industrial building looked abandoned. But we went inside and found ourselves in a long, narrow corridor leading to a speck of light in the distance. Since we were in unknown territory, I walked ahead. And as I advanced farther down the hallway, the speck of light at the end expanded. What did it turn out to be?

A two-story-high room, a room with thirty-foot-high ceilings. Flaming, swirling Magic Marker murals on the walls, murals blazing with color, murals two stories high. And men. To paraphrase the singing group the Tons of Fun—the backup group for another of my future clients, the transvestite star Sylvester—it was "Raining Men."

There were big men with skimpy leather vests and no undershirts. Men with perfect tans, oiled muscles, and lots of naked skin. At least above the navel. Men flexing their biceps and showing off their pecs. And tiny men. Mousy, skinny little men. Hanging from the biceps of the big men as if those upper arms were chinning bars. And the farther we got, the more of this Gomorrah on the Hudson Tina could see. Now remember, Tina had been forced to watch while Ike fornicated the Ikettes. She should have been inured to this kind of thing. But she wasn't. She was shocked. So shocked that she spun around on her seven-inch stiletto heels and fled like a gazelle escaping a jaguar.

Fred Frank and Roadshow Records did not land Tina Turner. And Kurt Loder of *Rolling Stone* got Tina to tell her story to him, used it to write a *Rolling Stone* article, then turned it into a book, Tina's autobiography, *I, Tina*. A book that became a film and a Broadway musical. Tina's story helped Kurt become a rock-writing superstar.

And my dive downtown to the clubs where gay disco was roaring would lead me, a white publicist, to help reopen a black monument on a par with the pyramids . . . the Apollo Theater.

16

RALPH MACDONALD—
THE MAN WITH ATOMIC CLOCK FINGERS

Ray Caviano, as you recall, was working for TK Records, a label in Florida best known for hitting the charts with KC and the Sunshine Band. A label Ray convinced to sign on to disco. Then Ray brought me one of the very first American disco acts, TK singer George McCrae.[57] And Ray put me to work on one of the most important artists he would ever give me: TK's Ralph MacDonald. Ralph MacDonald would change my life.

Ralph would show me why black music connected to the gods inside.

* * *

Ralph MacDonald was a percussionist. Not the sort of person who normally gets any press. But on any given week, if you looked up the top twenty albums on the jazz charts, Ralph was on ten of them. If you turned your attention to the top five singles on the pop charts, Ralph was on two. That is staggering.

Ralph's rhythm was more precise than an atomic clock. How do I know? One day, I was sitting across from Ralph at his desk in a shabby building on Manhattan's Broadway near Fiftieth Street. Ralph decided to reset a clock. He called the time service. Ralph's finger hovered over a button on the clock. And when I say hovered, I mean that it held its place without the slightest waver. When Ralph finally punched that button, you saw a commanding gesture that made the accuracy overwhelmingly exact. Ralph seemed to have more precision than the time service's cesium-beam frequency standard clock.

But Ralph had more than precision going for him. He had melody. He'd co-written three hits:

- "Where Is the Love," a song that was turned into a Top 5 chart smash by Roberta Flack and Donny Hathaway. "Where Is the Love" won a Grammy and was No. 1 on the R&B and Easy Listening charts.
- "Just the Two of Us," recorded by Grover Washington Jr. and Bill Withers. "Just the Two of Us" went to No. 2 on the pop charts and would be covered by over

twenty other recording artists, including the rapper Will Smith. It, too, would
win a Grammy.

- "Mister Magic," the title track of an album from saxophonist Grover Washington
  Jr.—an album that would go to No. 1 on the R&B and jazz charts and would hit
  the Top 10 on the pop chart—highly unusual for an album by an instrumentalist.

Why does writing a hit song that is covered over and over again for decades change
your life? Much less writing three of them? Let's flash back to my days at Gulf and
Western, my first days, when I was still getting my bearings. A man named George Pincus
called me and invited me to lunch.[58] He was the owner of one of the fourteen record labels
we distributed. So I sat at a posh restaurant near Manhattan's Columbus Circle in a booth
across from George. He was in his eighties, with white hair and a wrinkled face, but with
ruddy cheeks, cheer, and energy. "Do you know why I look so good at the age of eighty?"
he asked. I didn't have a clue. Said George, "Publishing." He explained that a music publisher collects the royalties on songs. Royalties from record sales, from radio airplay, from
play in supermarkets and dentist offices, and even from play by bands at weddings and bar
mitzvahs.[59] And, if you are the publisher of a standard like "Happy Birthday" or "Rudolph
the Red Nosed Reindeer," you will collect money for the rest of your life. While scarcely
lifting a finger. The magic of publishing. A magic that may have eventually motivated
someone to torpedo the life of Michael Jackson. But we'll get to that later.

A quick Google hints that the songs George Pincus owned were worth a fortune.
They include six Beatles songs: "She Loves You," "I Saw Her Standing There," "From
Me to You," "Misery," "I Wanna Be Your Man," and "There's a Place." Not bad.[60]

But back to Ralph MacDonald. How could you see the magic of publishing
in Ralph's life? Just go up the elevator to the fourth floor of the office building on
Broadway where Ralph was headquartered, turn right, walk forty feet down the dark
and grubby corridor, and look at the name in gold on the frosted glass door: Antisia
Music, the publishing company Ralph founded with his songwriting partner, Bill
Salter. The publishing company with a sign hung in the xerox room:

They must think I'm a mushroom. They keep me in the dark and feed me shit.

How many musicians can afford a four-room office in Manhattan? And how
many can sum up the tricks and traps of the record industry with such a simple phrase?
Another hint of Ralph's approach to life came from a line he liked to repeat to me:
"Don't stop to pick up the pennies when the dollars are flying over your head." I loved
the line, but alas it didn't apply to me. I was looking for something very different than
dollars. I was looking for soul. And, with Ralph, I found it.

* * *

How did Ralph MacDonald change my life? It wasn't the education he tried to give me about money. It was the education he gave me about black culture. No, he wasn't the man who explained CPT to me. That was someone backstage at a Stephanie Mills showcase in LA roughly two years earlier. Whoever it was was black and taking very good care of me. He was leading me across the stage before showtime on our way to the dressing rooms on the other side. "You know what CPT is, don't you?" he asked. No, I didn't have a clue. "Colored people's time," he explained. Then he laid it out. If you made an appointment with a white person for 2:00 p.m. on Tuesday, he might show up at 2:05. And he'd apologize. But if you made an appointment for 2:00 p.m. on Tuesday with an African American, that pleasantly colored individual might show up on Wednesday. Or sometime in the following week. Colored people's time.

We are not supposed to mention such things today. But this was a black man talking about a common perception in black society. A common perception that I suspect most black professionals were working hard to correct. By the way, none of my black clients ever showed up more than five minutes late. Well, none of them except Al Greene. But we'll get to Al and his strange ways later.

* * *

Ralph MacDonald's parents had come from Trinidad, an island at the furthest southern extreme of the Caribbean, so far south that it's off the coast of a South American nation, Venezuela. And Trinidad had developed its own music. How? As Ralph told it, during World War II, Trinidad had been a base for the US Navy. To feed the hungry engines of naval war vessels, Trinidad was stocked up with oil imported from the USA. Literally tons of it. In barrels. When the barrels were empty, they were tossed away. But the Trinidadians found a use for this refuse. They hammered the flat barrel tops into hemispheres pointed inward, creating a concave shape like a colander, a spaghetti strainer. A half-bubble of steel with its center curved toward the bottom of the barrel. Then, with a mallet, they struck the hollowed out steel shell they'd just made. Each part of the curved barrel top yielded a different note. But the notes had a strange, metallic ping—a sweetness no other instrument had ever produced. This was the birth of the steel drum. A product of one of the most important gifts humanity possesses: the ability to turn garbage into gold. A gift that shows up over and over again in black culture. And that will show up once more when we get to rap.

* * *

Trinidad had another tradition, a tradition its former slaves had been able to carry from Africa. In North America, said Ralph, slaves had been stripped of their African culture. But that wasn't true in Trinidad. One result: the tradition of the griot had stayed alive. The griot was a storyteller and news-conveyor who went from one village to another spreading the latest headlines, gossip, and myths. Another way of conveying the news, said Ralph, was through drumbeats. Drums in Africa told stories and conveyed those tales from one village to another within hearing distance. The result in Trinidad was calypso, a new form of music whose lyrics were ripe with the news.

Ralph's dad was the leader of a calypso band when Ralph was growing up on 127th Street in Harlem in the late 1940s. Ralph's earliest memories were of crawling around under the kitchen table while his dad and his dad's key bandmates sat at the table and plotted how to sell tickets to their annual Christmas dance. Their plan was diabolically clever. First the band members would recruit as many family members and friends as they could. Then the full squadron would go out on the street and sell raffle tickets. To buy a ticket, you had to write down your address. The list of addresses was a mailing list. A mailing list to which Ralph's dad and his companions snail-mailed advertisements for their dance. Way back then, there was no email.

At the dance, Ralph's father would bring little Ralph onstage, put him on a stool, give him a drum, and let Ralph whale away. For most kid musicians, this would have been a sloppy performance. But in Ralph's case, I suspect he already had a wicked precision. How old was he? Five.

Meanwhile, one man would ride calypso to the top of the pop charts and all the way into film. His name was Harry Belafonte. In the 1950s, when Ralph was still growing up, Harry Belafonte would top the charts with calypso songs like "Matilda" and "The Banana Boat Song." When Ralph was twelve, Belafonte would have the first LP ever to sell a million copies—an album that would stay at No. 1 on the *Billboard* album chart for an astonishing thirty-three weeks. Belafonte would also have his own TV special, would star in three films, would win three Grammys, and would receive a Grammy Lifetime Achievement Award, an Emmy, and a Tony. Frank Sinatra would recruit Belafonte to perform at the inauguration of president John F. Kennedy. Belafonte would be named a UNICEF Goodwill Ambassador. And Belafonte would work behind the scenes to help shape the career of a civil rights activist and articulator of group soul named Martin Luther King Jr.

In other words, Harry Belafonte would use calypso to become huge in two areas: music and social activism. We'll encounter Belafonte's activism when we hit "We Are the World."

In 1963, Ralph was nineteen years old and working in the kitchen of an insane asylum on Randall's Island in the Harlem River.[61] Then a flyer was posted on the Harlem streets. It announced that Harry Belafonte was looking for a percussionist. When Ralph showed up at the Belafonte audition, there were hundreds of other talented Harlem kids lined up, waiting to show their chops. The odds of landing the job were impossible. But when Ralph went onstage and began to drum, Belafonte must have seen what I would later see—that atomic-clock precision. Ralph got the job.

Thus did Ralph MacDonald enter what he called the University of Harry Belafonte. The first lesson in that school: stop using cuss words like *fuck* and *shit*. Speak in a manner that the other people of the world can respect. The second lesson: the world has many forms of music. Learn as many of them as you can. For example, Belafonte toured in India. And Ralph learned the secret of Indian rhythms, which are very different from the rhythms of the West. More about these rhythms in a minute. Third lesson: when you are touring the United States, you will run into segregation. You will often not be allowed to stay in the hotels where you are playing. For example, in Las Vegas. Why ban your overnight presence? Because you are black.

But, through his own action, Harry would show what you could do about it. Belafonte was one of the most effective crusaders in the history of the civil rights movement. He worked behind the scenes with a white Jewish activist named Stanley Levison[62] to build the content and influence of a talented preacher with a thunderous superstar potential. And through that orator's career, Belafonte and Levison helped end segregation. You already know the pastor's name: Martin Luther King Jr. One of the greatest tongues of group soul in modern history.

One of my favorite treats was bringing the author John Storm Roberts over to Ralph's Broadway office to interview the percussion master. Roberts, a Brit, had written a book called *Black Music of Two Worlds: African, Caribbean, Latin, and African-American Traditions*. That book laid out the relationship between the music of Africa and the music of the Western Hemisphere. Ralph loved the book. When he and Roberts got into intense discussion, they would leave the realm of words. They would communicate by tapping out rhythms on their thighs. Ralph, for example, would discuss the difference he'd learned in India between Indian rhythms and Western rhythms. To illustrate his points, he would tap out the Indian rhythms on his leg. Then the Western rhythms. Soon, most of the verbal discussion would stop, and Ralph and John would speak to each other almost entirely in thigh taps. I didn't understand a bit of it. But it was fascinating.

* * *

In January 1977, a TV series would wrench Ralph's attention in a new direction. It was Alex Haley's *Roots*, a series that showed the African roots of American black culture. Ralph was riveted. He decided to trace the African roots of his own family . . . and of his own music. God knows how he did his research—I suspect that New York's Schomburg Library, a library of black culture, played a role. I learned about the existence of that library from Ralph. But by roughly June, Ralph had a seventeen-minute composition called "The Path." Ralph explained to me that it started with the culture of the Yoruba tribe in Africa, Ralph's ancestors. The Yorubas, said Ralph, were among those who used drums to communicate messages from one village to the next. But there was something more. The Yorubas had a god of thunder, Shango. And they used their drums to bring Shango into the bodies of men and women. They performed trance rituals in which the drumming became furious and in which a few tribesmen would go into what looked like an epileptic fit, their arms shaking, their heads thrown back, their faces in a grimace, sometimes with foam coming from their lips. Then they would fall to the ground and writhe for hours. This visitation would be, of all things, prized and welcomed. Why? It was possession by the god Shango, the god "with a voice like thunder and a mouth that spewed fire when he spoke."[63] Shades of the ecstasies of gay men dancing at clubs and being taken over by their inner cowboys, Indians, and fire chiefs. Yes, with Ralph and Shango, you'd walked straight into the Varieties of the Religious Experience. You'd walked straight into the gods inside.

* * *

As Ralph explained it, Shango and his rhythm made the transition from Africa to the Americas along with Yoruban slaves—Yoruban slaves who were Ralph's ancestors, Ralph's roots. Shango's trance rituals appeared in Brazil as Macumba; in Uruguay as Candombe; in Cuba, Puerto Rica, and the Dominican Republic as Santeria; in Haiti as Voodoo; and in North America as Holy Roller Christianity. Yes, when a Holy Roller rises from her seat, shakes convulsively, then falls on the floor writhing, he or she believes that she has been taken over by Jesus. But the wings transporting her to the heights of spiritual ecstasy were fashioned by an African god.

Ralph's composition, "The Path," showed how the Shango rhythm evolved, appearing in the music of Cuba, Haiti, and the Caribbean as Chango. It appeared in South America as the Tango and the Samba. And it later influenced the blues, jazz, funk, and pop.

Ralph told me the tale of "The Path," and it grabbed me deeply. He needed someone to tell the story in the album notes. So I volunteered and wrote those notes, telling the tale of the hunt that had produced "The Path" and the saga of musical history that Ralph had assembled. It was an honor.

Ralph had revealed the origins of a trail to the ecstasies that free souls. A trail I'd been seeking ever since I realized that the gods were inside of my parents. And ever since I realized that those gods had to be somewhere in me. Ever since I was thirteen and set out on a quest to find the gods inside.

* * *

Then Ralph came up with another assignment for me. The Apollo Theater, the world's iconic capital of black music. The Apollo had hosted stars like Duke Ellington, Count Basie, Ella Fitzgerald, Sarah Vaughan, Moms Mabley, Nat King Cole, Billie Holiday, James Brown, Aretha Franklin, and Michael Jackson and his brothers, the Jackson Five. But it had gone belly-up financially and had been closed for two years.[64] A friend of Ralph's was reopening the place. This was major news. Ralph wanted me to represent the reopening. He wanted me to help save a sacred site in the collective soul of the black community.

We got a ton of press. Then, on opening night, the lobby of the Apollo was one big party. An elegant party. And Ralph introduced me to the man who was paying our bills. He was tall, black, aristocratic, dressed in a tuxedo, and utterly charming. When we shook hands, his face had a glorious, warm, caring, and joyful smile. His name: Nicky Barnes. He was the head of the black mob that had taken over the Harlem drug trade from a competing gang called the Mafia. In other words, this glorious, welcoming man had ordered many a murder.

Why would quick glimpses of the Mob start appearing in my life?

* * *

I had risked my career at Gulf and Western by championing Stephanie Mills. I had hated it when I discovered at ABC that the West Coast PR staff would not work with black acts and was overlooking Chaka Khan. Ralph MacDonald had given me an education in the history of black music. And I had reopened the Apollo Theater. I was rapidly becoming something utterly unexpected: possibly the best black publicist in the music business. And I'm white. But there would be more.

17

WORKING MIRACLES—
SATURDAY NIGHT FEVER

How I came to the attention of a superstar publicist from London, Annie Ivil, I do not remember. But through Annie Ivil I would learn a tale that would educate me farther in PR.

Hollywood looked down on music-industry people—a booby-trapped barrier we'll see again when we get to Bette Midler. For a music-industry person other than Harry Belafonte to make a film was impossible. But Robert Stigwood, who we will soon see dangled out of a sixth-story window by his ankles, was a miracle-maker. He had come from Australia to England and had gotten started in the music industry in the late 1950s, just a few years before the entry into the business of one of his future friends, Brian Epstein, the manager of the Beatles.

Stigwood had managed the sixties supergroup Cream and had been involved with the stage productions of *Hair* and *Jesus Christ Superstar*. But his core band would be an Australian group, the Bee Gees. The Bee Gees had sent a tape to the Beatles' Epstein, Epstein had passed the tape to Stigwood, and Stigwood had asked the band to audition for him. Under Stigwood's guidance, the Bee Gees had been huge in the late 1960s. Their first album had gone to No. 7 on the pop charts. Now it was the mid-1970s, and Stigwood was going to try to pull off something impossible. He was going to get the Bee Gees to reinvent themselves. And he was going to do it, in part, with something else impossible—two films. What's more, the soundtrack for one of those films would include excerpts from Ralph MacDonald's landmark historical composition, "The Path."

Stigwood started with an unusual seed, what Wikipedia describes as "a 1976 *New York* magazine article by British writer Nik Cohn, 'Tribal Rites of the New Saturday Night.'"[65] Again, for a music-business person to make a film was impossible. But that didn't stop Stigwood.

Reinventing a successful group's music and bringing it back to the very top of the charts was impossible. But Stigwood put the Bee Gees with a new producer, a Turkish producer who had become an integral part of Atlantic Records in New York, Arif Mardin. And, together, Mardin and the Gibb brothers created an entirely new sound. Then came another impossibility, the one I watched carefully for lessons. Stigwood decided to pin his film's fate on a TV star. Yes, he chose a TV star to be the film's star. Why was this impossible? People paid to see movies. They got TV for free. So, in the mid-1970s, whenever a producer tried to hinge a movie on a TV star, the attempt was a failure. People did not want to pay for what they got for nothing.

In other words, picking a TV star was suicide. Especially if you were a music person and already had one foot on the banana peel and your teeth clenched on a cyanide pellet. But Stigwood put another obstacle in his own path. He picked not an A-level TV star but an actor from the B-level. *Welcome Back, Kotter* was a TV comedy about a high-school teacher and his students. The star was comedian Gabe Kaplan, the teacher. The pupils were very much second on the bill. But Stigwood had the unmitigated gall to pick one of those kids. In other words, it was as if Stigwood had methodically stacked every conceivable odd against himself. Now the problem was this. How do you get that B-level TV actor on the cover of every magazine in America? For a film that's still not finished and that could easily flop? A film from a Hollywood pariah, an outsider from the music biz?

The answer was PR. Stigwood did something unprecedented. He did not bring in PR experts three or six months in advance of the film. He brought them in over a year in advance. And he realized something. It's what Paul Simon calls the one-trick pony. Each of us has a specialty, something we are uniquely good at. In other areas, we are weak. So Stigwood brought in not just one but four PR firms. Each of them with its own area of expertise. He brought in the firm of a sleazy guy who was brilliant with trade magazines—Morty Wax. He brought in a publicist who did a very good job with mainstream press—my once-upon-a-very-brief-time boss, Bob Levinson. He brought in Annie Ivil for her close connections with the glamour and fashion magazines. And, if my memory is accurate, he brought in a mainstream film PR firm. Then he motivated this team gloriously. And just before the film hit the theaters, Stigwood's second-tier TV star was on the cover of everything in sight. That B-level TV star, by the way, was named John Travolta.

The name of the film Stigwood put together? *Saturday Night Fever*.

And what was *Saturday Night Fever* all about? The ecstasies drawn out of an ordinary lower-middle-class human by music and dance. A film about the gods inside.

* * *

It pays to have an eye for talent. And to see clearly what an expert can and cannot do. For me, this was a profound lesson in the power of PR. I would try to outdo Stigwood's quartet of PR firms with just one company, the Howard Bloom Organization Ltd.

In fact, I would copy a practice of the trade-press masters—walking press releases from my office on Fifty-Fifth Street near Lexington Avenue over to the trade magazines just north of Times Square and handing them to the trade editors and journalists face-to-face. Thanks to seeing what Stigwood had achieved in the trades by hiring Morty Wax. This would turn out to be a terrific way to build relationships.

It would be one of the reasons I would soon be able to put Ray Caviano in all three trade magazines over and over and over again. And it would be one of the reasons I would get to work with Bob Marley.

18

CHRIS BLACKWELL— THE MAN WHO MADE REGGAE

Ever heard of Cross and Blackwell? Way back in the 1940s and 1950s, Cross and Blackwell sold extremely expensive, high-end canned food specialties—especially gourmet canned fruitcake—at the swankiest department stores in any town worthy of an American with aspirations to a stiff upper lip and a walking stick. Nowadays, Cross and Blackwell is owned by Smucker's and sells chutneys.

Well, Cross and Blackwell was Chris Blackwell. Chris was born in Westminster, London. His father came from a London family that, since 1819, had salted, preserved, and pickled just about anything a human being could eat. Except for insects and small children. But during World War II, Chris's British dad had ended up as a major in a British regiment in the Caribbean—the Jamaica Regiment. Which is probably where he met Chris Blackwell's mom, Blanche Lindo. And Chris's mom was worth a lifetime move to the Caribbean. You'll see why in a minute.

Chris's mother's family, the Lindos, had made their fortune in sugar and rum in the nineteenth century, and had become one of the twenty-one families that ran Jamaica. It was rumored that they had Jewish roots. One way or the other, Blanche Lindo had a good deal more sex appeal than your normal pretty girl. In fact, she was so far outside the norm that the creator of James Bond, former British Naval Intelligence Division[66] agent Ian Fleming, apparently fell for her madly. And Fleming based two of his most impressive superheroines on her, Pussy Galore, and, if I've got this right, Octopussy.

How did the Fleming-Blackwell connection get started? In 1942, when World War II was still raging, Ian Fleming—the future creator of 007—had attended an Anglo-American intelligence conference in Jamaica. While he was there, his boss, the director of the British Naval Intelligence Division, had taught him scuba diving. Ian Fleming loved scuba diving,[67] loved Jamaica, bought a fourteen-acre dream villa there, and named it *Goldeneye*, after a naval operation in which he had helped prevent the Spanish from providing aid to the Nazis. When the war ended, Fleming made his

Jamaican villa, *Goldeneye*, his home. Every morning at breakfast, he had two things on his table, in addition to food. One was a pair of binoculars. The other was a book, *The Birds of the West Indies*. The name of the author of the bird book? James Bond.[68]

Fleming stole the ornithologist's name and wrote fourteen James Bond books on a wooden desk with a fabulous Jamaican view.[69] *Goldeneye* would be the setting for two James Bond movies. And it would provide the title for the seventeenth Bond movie—*Goldeneye*—in 1995. If you were lucky, you may have been awed by Fleming's *Goldeneye* on the silver screen. The first time I saw it in a Bond movie, it utterly floored me. So Ian Fleming was a neighbor of Blackwell's mom. And an admirer. But that's an understatement. Remember the name of the character he based on her—Pussy Galore.

Then there's Noël Coward, writer of more than fifty plays, a songwriter, singer, director, and actor who set the style of what *Time* calls "chic, pose, and poise"[70] in the early and mid-twentieth century. Chris's mom owned thousands of acres. Coward fell so in love with her real estate that he bought two-acres of her property for himself. And he became a family friend.[71]

This is the social circle in which Chris Blackwell grew up in Jamaica. Because he was an aristocrat, Chris lived on the top of the hill. He and his family were the masters of all they surveyed.

Blame any inaccuracies in this portrait on my poor memory, but my impression from talking to Chris is that he preferred downhill to uphill.[72] He liked to go down to the black community of Trenchtown, where the tempos were fast, the life was dangerous, and where there were hints of the gods inside.

* * *

At that point, Jamaica was about to make a major contribution to the theological storehouse of humanity—Rastafarianism. There are many islands in the Caribbean. Many islands in the world. But few have turned out original religions. Religions that stuck. Religions with a global impact. One island managed to pull this off: Jamaica.

But to understand Rastafarianism, you have to understand something that anthropologists discovered in the 1940s, just after World War II: cargo cults.[73] When people on totally isolated islands were visited for the first time by ships from the modern world, the appearance of these vessels challenged previous religious beliefs. First off, the ships came over the horizon as if out of nowhere. And they were propelled by means the islanders had never seen before. They moved without the use of oars or sails. Second, the people who disembarked from those ships were different in skin color, facial bone structure, and costume from anything the islanders had ever seen before.

Third, these strange visitors from an alien world had gadgets and material goods the natives had never imagined, from steel knives and iron axe heads to firearms.

According to Spanish accounts, the Aztecs and Incas of Central America fit this into their religion by imagining that the strangers appearing as if from nowhere were gods long predicted by their religions, saviors come to change the world. Some islanders in the Pacific handled the miracle of the aliens by discarding their old religions and starting new ones. In the new religions, they invented rituals that would bring the steamships of the fabulous goods-givers back someday. And they sometimes imagined that, when these ships came, the vessels would take the native population to the land of the ancestors, to paradise. Each tribe, of course, had a different idea of what that paradise might be. These new religions were called cargo cults. For the cargo of new riches the natives hoped would arrive next.

In the case of one of the most famous cargo cults, the people of Vanuatu in the South Pacific built runways once a year[74] in the hope that their savior, the American pilot John Frum, would land an airplane bringing "jeeps and washing machines, radios and motorcycles, canned meat and candy."[75] Or, as one villager put it, "John promised he'll bring planeloads and shiploads of cargo to us from America if we pray to him. Radios, TVs, trucks, boats, watches, iceboxes, medicine, Coca-Cola and many other wonderful things."[76] Talk about the gods inside.

Rastafarianism began as a classic cargo cult. But the Rasta cult was built around the Bible. The Bible and Haile Selassie. In the Bible, the chosen people, us Jews, live in exile in Babylon. And Babylon becomes the symbol of oppression. In Rastafarianism, Babylon is Jamaica. It is the hell in which Rastafarians are oppressed and enslaved. It is the land from which Rastafarians must escape. The Rastafarians await salvation from a god who will come and take them to their paradise. Who is that god? Ras Tafari—Haile Selassie. Haile Selassie, emperor of Ethiopia from 1930 to 1974. An international figure in the days before World War II, when Italy's Benito Mussolini conquered Ethiopia and made it one of the first colonies of what he hoped would be a new Roman Empire.[77] Selassie became internationally renowned, speaking on behalf of Ethiopian freedom and addressing the League of Nations with what some regarded as one of the most stirring speeches of the twentieth century.[78]

Some Rastas say Selassie is God. Others say that Selassie is merely God's representative on earth. One way or the other, the Rastafarians imagined that Haile Selassie would appear someday off the coasts of Jamaica in a giant ship, and would take all of his believers to paradise. And where is paradise? Where is the one spot in which the black diaspora can be gathered and be free? Ethiopia.

One more thing. In Jamaica, Rastas tended to congregate in gangs. And these gangs of believers in Rastafari frequently killed each other. Shades of the motorcycle gangs versus the marines at a ZZ Top concert. Human groups compete. And sometimes their competition isn't nice.

* * *

Whites in Jamaica in 1958 knew only that Rastas were a wild and primitive tribe. A tribe of people to be avoided at all cost. A tribe too dangerous to approach. When Chris Blackwell was twenty-one years old, he was out sailing. His boat ran aground on mangrove roots. In what seemed like an endless swim, Blackwell headed for the shore. By the time he reached land, he was so exhausted that he collapsed on the beach.

Chris tells the story like this. When he got back the ability to stand, he walked for miles looking for someone, anyone. He was desperate. He says, "I was literally dying of thirst." To his relief, Blackwell reached a clearing, a clearing with what he describes as "a little hut." A man poked his head out of the hut's window. The result should have been joy. Instead, it was terror. The man poking his head out of the window was a Rasta. And white Jamaicans regarded Rastas as murderous barbarians. But Chris's thirst proved stronger than his fear. He asked for water. Recalls Blackwell, "He gave me some water in a gourd and he was as sweet and gentle as any man could be."

Chris laid down to take a nap. He didn't wake up for hours, but when he did he was terrified all over again. Why? He was surrounded by Rastas, supposedly the most dangerous people in Jamaica. But Blackwell's fear subsided rapidly. These Rastas were as kind as the man who had given Chris water. And one of them took Blackwell back to his own neighborhood.

Says Blackwell, "It had a profound impact on me, and changed how I saw Rastafarians."[79] And that change would make a massive difference in Chris Blackwell's life. And in music history.

* * *

Blackwell had gotten something rare for a white man—a full-immersion introduction to the Rastafarian way of life. Meanwhile, the Rasta teens of Trenchtown were inventing their own music, complete with its own unique rhythms. Then they were pressing records of that music and selling them locally. Chris liked the music. He liked it so much that he packed a suitcase full of locally pressed Jamaican records, flew to London, and sold the discs from the back of a car, a Mini Cooper,[80] to London's island black community. Thus was reggae born. And internationalized.

And thus did Chris Blackwell lay the base for his own record company, Island Records (as in the island of Jamaica), the record company he founded when he was twenty-one, the year of his sailing accident.[81] At Island, Blackwell would sign Traffic, Steve Winwood, Cat Stevens, and U2. All future stars. Not to mention Bob Marley, whose tale we will dive into later.

But let's get back to 1978. Blackwell was a restless man. He brought a new president into his record company every year or two, got tired of him (again, it was always a him), then replaced him. Yes, at the end of eighteen months, Blackwell ejected each old president and brought in another. He did the same with PR people.

Blackwell spotted the explosion of the Ray Caviano campaign and told his president of the moment, Marshall Blonstein, to seek out Caviano's publicist and hire that publicist for Island. Blonstein did some research and found me. Then Chris saw another explosive PR campaign. It was a press blitz for a new New York record label backed to the tune of twenty million dollars by one of the most powerful men in the entertainment industry, Sid Sheinberg, head of MCA and of Universal Studios. That campaign had landed three features and a cover in a single issue of *New York* magazine. Plus a feature in the slick, full-color business magazine *Fortune*. A PR miracle. So Chris changed his mind. He ordered Blonstein to hunt down the Sheinberg label's publicist and hire him instead. When Blonstein did a bit of research, he discovered that the publicity miracle-maker behind the cover stories about Infinity Records in *Billboard*, *Record World*, and *Cashbox*, and the coverage of Infinity in *New York* magazine and *Fortune* was, how do I say this without sounding obnoxious? Me.

In the end, Blackwell would keep me in his brain trust for the next twelve years. Not bad for a man who changes personnel the way you change socks. But more on that when we get to Bob Marley. No, we are not at Marley yet.

* * *

Blackwell had more than just a swinging door for personnel. He had an eye for new movements. An eye for cutting-edge talent. And he had an eye for striking women. Supermodel Grace Jones, for example, would be one of his finds. But the female he was focused on when he hired me was Betty Davis. Not Bette Davis the actress. Betty Davis the singer. The one Wikipedia calls "one of the most influential voices of the funk era."[82]

Betty was extremely pretty, spectacularly dressed, and had gotten her last name, Davis, from an august source: Miles Davis. She had been Miles Davis's wife. And Miles credited her with introducing him to Jimi Hendrix and Sly Stone. Betty and

Miles were now divorced, and Betty was on her own. Which meant that she went to an awful lot of parties. And those parties were saturated with superstars.

Meanwhile, a publicist is only as strong as his or her media relationships. And I wanted to build a relationship with *Rolling Stone*. Back in my Cloud Studio days, the art director of the Boy Scout magazine, *Boys' Life*, had taught me that the most-read section of a magazine is the page or two with short bits. Chuck Young—Charles M. Young, Jr.—was the editor of that two-page spread of bits and pieces in *Rolling Stone*: "Random Notes." So I trained Betty Davis in gossip-spotting. Once a week, I'd touch base with Betty, catch up on what parties she'd been to that week, and zero in on the hot superstar stories she'd picked up, steamy tidbits that could be told in 125 words. And, once a week, I'd call *Rolling Stone*'s Chuck Young with Betty's tales of the stars. Tales of big name folks I did not represent, but whose names would make Chuck salivate. And tales that would give juice to his section of the magazine. It worked. I gave Chuck a steady source of luscious info. So Chuck always picked up my calls. And I got a lot of press for Betty Davis. But the Betty Davis trick also helped another of my clients—Michael Henderson.

19

BUDDHA RECORDS—
THE FACE DRAINED BY THE MOB

It was 1976, and I was still working on half of a coffee table in Danny Goldberg's West Seventy-Ninth Street living room. There were no laptops in those days. But I'd reduced my essential work tools to two sheets of paper I could carry in a notebook, so I could work anywhere that I and my notebook happened to find ourselves. Those two sheets were a to-be-done list and a list of the phone numbers of over one hundred press people. When I wasn't doing PR for my clients on Danny's coffee table, I was at Buddha Records. They had extra desks with extra phones, and they didn't mind if I took one of those desks over and worked like a maniac. It set a good example for their own staff.

What was Buddha Records? Buddha Records had been a hit-making company in the late 1960s—a company that had rolled out one hundred singles that had made the charts. It was a company with a magic reputation. It had scored big with Melanie ("Candles in the Rain"), Captain Beefheart, and Gladys Knight and the Pips. And it had handled some of the bands who tried to commercialize the psychedelic revolution—the revolution that I had accidentally helped start on the West Coast fourteen years earlier: the Ohio Express and the 1910 Fruitgum Company, bands whose music was known as bubblegum pop.

The head of the company was Art Kass, a man in trouble. A conglomerate, a corporate gobbler called Viewlex, had bought Buddha. Then, in 1976, Viewlex had gone bankrupt, and Art had bought Buddha back. But it had cost him. Big. The sales price was $2.7 million—nearly $16 million in current dollars. But the amount of the loan was only part of the problem. Interest payments rapidly ballooned the $2.7 million Art had borrowed to $10 million. That's nearly $59 million in today's dollars. To pay off his bank, Art was forced to turn to Morris Levy, the man in the record business who represented the Mafia, the Mob.[83] And my guess is that the interest rates the broken-nose brigade charged doubled and tripled what you owed at a pace that made bank interest rates look philanthropic.

So, whenever you stepped into Art Kass's office, you realized that this was a man undergoing stress levels that could kill. You read it in his body language and in the strange grayish-yellow color and the sickened seriousness of his face.

But Art and his head of publicity, Nancy Lewis, liked my obsessive, totally workaholic dedication to my clients. So they gave me a few of their acts. First, Michael Henderson.

Michael Henderson had gone out on tour with Stevie Wonder as Stevie's bassist. At the time, both Michael and Stevie were in their late teens. That was my hook. The Stevie Wonder connection made Michael a potential story. But his odds of getting into *Rolling Stone* were zero. At least they would have been zero without the steady stream of mind-jolting news coming from Betty Davis. With that stream, I had a foot in the door with Chuck Young. And I got Michael Henderson into *Rolling Stone*.

Meanwhile, I had moved from Danny Goldberg's living room to a two-room office on Manhattan's East Fifty-Fifth Street. The office where the Village People would be born. The first two weeks after the move, my new office wasn't ready. The landlord was still painting. A floor above us was the office of a pair of attorneys—Allen Grubman and Artie Indursky. For reasons utterly beyond my ken, Allen Grubman invited me to use his private office for those two weeks. It was an act of extraordinary kindness from a round, driven little man who would gain a reputation as a terror—a ferocious, unstoppable force who would go on to represent Billy Joel,[84] Madonna, Bruce Springsteen, Elton John, Andrew Lloyd Weber, U2, John Mellencamp, Rod Stewart, and just about every other major superstar in the musical firmament. Not to mention Clive Davis, Calvin Klein, Diane Sawyer, Tommy Hilfiger, Barbara Walters, and Martha Stewart, with whom he would weather a scandal.

Finally, we moved into my new office. I had almost no staff. I'd asked Michael Henderson to come into New York from Detroit to do two days of interviews. That's roughly twelve interviews. I could pull in most of these myself with my one-page list of writers and their phone numbers, but I needed help. Sid Seidenberg, the manager for B.B. King and for Gladys Knight and the Pips, had told me about a black publicist he used. He'd praised her highly. In fact, to his mind, she was a force of nature.

So I hired her to work with me for a few weeks on Michael. There were two desks in my personal office. I gave her one of those desks. Which meant I could watch everything she did. Her work was not as effective as I'd hoped. I still had to pull in all the Henderson interviews. But she taught me a valuable lesson. Nearly every major city in America has at least one black newspaper. White publicists either don't know these papers exist or don't care. But these papers are vital pipelines to the heart of the black community. If you take the time to understand what they need, offer it, and show respect, those papers will reward you richly with coverage. And the black community will reward you, too. Working with the black papers and supplying them with photo-stories—stories that coupled captions with pictures—became a standard practice for the new Howard Bloom Organization Ltd. And it would be essential for Marley and the Jacksons. But, again, I'm getting ahead of myself.

The hard work on Michael Henderson would eventually pay off. He would play with Betty Davis's former husband, Miles Davis. He would also record with Aretha Franklin, Marvin Gaye, and Dr. John. He would put out eight albums. And, in 2018, Wikipedia would dub him "one of the most influential *jazz* and *soul* musicians of the past 40 years."[85]

Then there was Phyllis Hyman.

* * *

Phyllis Hyman was tall, black, and gorgeous. Well, not really black. She was a khaki tan. And she had friends in music's aristocracy. Her best buddy was another tall and gorgeous black woman who just happened to be a personal assistant to Mick Jagger. Phyllis was another of Art Kass's finds. She was a jazz-influenced singer. Phyllis had friends in the fashion world and in the world of fashionable people. That's where she felt comfortable. Being in fashion spreads was what she wanted. And I was determined to get her there. Even though that was not a world where I had connections.

To get Phyllis into the fashion publications, and to get her fashion-ish spreads in general interest magazines and newspapers, we needed to prove that Phyllis was fashion material. In this, we had a problem: Art Kass's financial difficulties. Art was having a very hard time repaying his loan. Things were so tight that I'd get phone calls from Art's office telling me specifically when I could pick up a check. Then I'd get more phone calls telling me exactly when I should cash it. The money was not yet in the account. And if I didn't cash the check at precisely the right instant, the money would no longer be there.

But I put together seven fashion photo shoots for the cost of one. And they showed Phyllis as beautiful and glamorous.

* * *

Meanwhile, Phyllis called one day and said she wanted to take me to a party. Now, look, I'm not a party person. When I was growing up in Buffalo, New York, any kid throwing a party wanted me as far away from it as I could possibly go. Like Indonesia. It took me decades to realize that party is not just a noun, it is a verb. When I threw

a $75,000 party for Ray Caviano at Studio 54—a $265,000 party in today's dollars—
and had guests like 007's Sean Connery, I did it based on watching my fellow humans
from a distance. I knew what elements were necessary to make my lab animals—party
guests—have a good time. A lot of high-quality liquor was high on that list. And food
no one had ever imagined. And a location no one had ever used for a party before but
that stunned the eye. Like the New York Public Library on Fifth Avenue and Forty-
Second Street—the one with the lions flanking the steps and with the three-story high
marble entrance chamber. A site I used to launch a label called Infinity Records. But at
the party itself, I watched from a distance. Sort of like God ordering Adam and Eve to
be fruitful and multiply, but staying in the skies when the actual deeds were going on.
And occasionally shielding his eyes with a cloud. So being invited to a party was new
to me. Especially a party with Phyllis and her friend Alvenia Bridges, the gorgeous
black woman who was Mick Jagger's assistant.

The party was on the top floor of the 101st-tallest hotel in the world, a forty-sev-
en-story building on New York's Avenue of the Americas, a building that spanned the
block between Fifty-Third and Fifty-Fourth Street—the Hilton Hotel. First we went
to the second-highest floor in the hotel. It was devoted entirely to dressing rooms.
Phyllis and Alvenia went into one room together to put on their party clothes. I waited
in the corridor. Near me in the hallway, sitting on a folding chair, was a woman who
looked homeless. She was overweight, listing to one side, and clearly sloshed on either
alcohol or drugs, or both. Her eyes were two-thirds closed. She did not look happy. Far
from it. In fact, you could see at a glance that she was a living, breathing tragedy. Then
I peered more closely. It was Elizabeth Taylor.

From the dressing room floor we went to the floor above, the top floor. The windows looked out on Manhattan from a height you only normally see when you're in a
helicopter. And the tables were laid out with white tablecloths for an intimate dinner
for roughly two hundred people. Phyllis and Alvenia found their spot at a dining table
and sat me next to them. And, from that perch, I would learn a lesson about the entertainment industry—a dark one.

Across from me at the table was the daughter of a man who had been a superstar
when I was a child, Nat King Cole.

Nat King Cole had scored a hundred hits on the music charts. That's a staggering
track record. But his daughter Natalie was even more impressive. She was gorgeous.
She was vivacious. She was articulate and smart. And it felt as if the energy of a thousand laser beams came from the pupils of her eyes. Very much like the eyes of Tina
Turner. I loved Natalie immediately. Sitting a bit further down the table was Chuck

Mangione, the trumpeter, flugelhorn player, and composer who would almost single-handedly carve out the field of fusion jazz—instrumental jazz that could make it to FM rock radio. That's a field that eventually I would help carve out, too. And both Natalie and Mangione would eventually be my clients.

But there was a problem. Periodically, Phyllis, Alvenia, Natalie, and Chuck would get all giddy and giggly about going to the bathroom together. Bathrooms were either male or female in those days. So three women and one man headed to the same bathroom was a bit strange. Now, look, I had helped start the drug revolution in the early 1960s. Yes, I was one of the early adopters of LSD and peyote in 1962. Not to mention Methedrine. But I'd used each chemical twice, learned from the experience, then shunned recreational drugs for the rest of my life. In other words, I am a straight arrow. Rigidly and boringly straight.

When everyone knows you don't do drugs, no drug user talks about his or her high of choice with you. In your world, it's as if drugs don't exist. But slowly it dawned on me why Phyllis, Alvenia, Natalie, and Chuck were sharing a bathroom every forty minutes or so. They were snorting cocaine. In the long run, the results would be deadly.

* * *

Back to Phyllis Hyman. I loved her. And her boyfriend/manager was a man whose smile could light you up on a day when all of your Labrador retrievers had been poisoned. Eventually, Phyllis would come to be known for three songs, "You Know How to Love Me," "Living All Alone," and "Don't Wanna Change the World." And she would have a gold album, the 1991 *Prime of My Life*. More important, she would star in *Sophisticated Ladies*, a Broadway musical based on the music of Duke Ellington. For that role, she would win a Theater World Award and be nominated for a Tony.

But at 2:00 p.m. on June 30, 1995, when she was forty-five years old and due to perform at the Apollo Theater that night, she took a deliberate overdose of pentobarbital and secobarbital and ended her life. The note she left said simply, "I'm tired. I'm tired. Those of you that I love know who you are. May God bless you."[86] What had worn Phyllis Hyman down? I strongly suspect her dependence on cocaine. And the money it took to sustain her habit.

20

THE SECRET POLICEMAN'S BALL—
PLANTING AMNESTY INTERNATIONAL

How would Chris Blackwell and Island Records open a door to torture, political prisoners, and John Cleese?

Amnesty International was a struggling, twenty-year-old UK-based human-rights organization that helped "prisoners of conscience"[87]—political prisoners who were jailed, tortured, and given death sentences for the expression of their beliefs. In 1975, Amnesty's assistant director noticed a name on his list of donors: John Cleese. Yes, John Cleese of Monty Python's Flying Circus and *Fawlty Towers*. Possibly the funniest comic on the face of planet earth in the twentieth century. The Amnesty International assistant director set up a meeting with Cleese, and the two of them cooked up an idea: superstar London comedy performances to raise money for Amnesty. An unusual idea back in the 1970s.

Four years later, Cleese and the Amnesty assistant director brought in a brash American instigator and humorist who ran America's periodic Fests for Beatles Fans, Martin Lewis. Lewis added rockers like Eric Clapton, Phil Collins, Sting, Jeff Beck, and the Who's Pete Townshend to the comedic mix. He organized London concerts with these musical wizards and gave the events an irresistible name: the Secret Policeman's Ball. Those balls, whose later incarnations would also feature Michael Palin, Bono, and Bruce Springsteen, were wildly successful. So were the films of the concerts. "But," explains Lewis, "the films and comedy albums of these shows were not getting exposure in the US. So I made a deal with Chris Blackwell's Island Records to distribute albums of the musical performances."[88] Good idea. So far.

But Lewis knew he needed what he called "smart publicizing" to crack the American coconut. Island's president of the moment sent him to us. My account executive, Joan Tarshis, worked maniacally to publicize the albums. And that publicity, along with a film Lewis put together for American distribution, helped put Amnesty International's North American operation on the map.

Long after the Amnesty campaign was over, Mary Daly, who helped run Amnesty in the USA, would drop over to my office and give me massive sheaves of information on atrocities in Africa. And those sheaves would lead to strange revelations about England's Band Aid and America's "We Are the World." But that's for later. Much, much later.

Meanwhile, Amnesty's head of North American operations, Jack Healey, would be overheard at a dinner party saying that there was only one real publicist in the United States, Howard Bloom. That came to me as a bit of a shock. Joan Tarshis should also have gotten some credit.

What's more, Joan, who had been a child star in Hollywood, told a very strange story. When she was a teen, the comedian Bill Cosby had offered to mentor her. One night, she was alone in a hotel room with the celebrated comedian. He gave her something to drink that he swore would relax her. It did a good deal more than loosen her up: it knocked her out. When she awoke, Cosby was waving his erect penis over her. She blurted out that she had a venereal disease and thus warded him away from her vagina. Instead, she was raped in the mouth. Roughly forty years later, Cosby's habit of using knockout drugs on girls then raping them made the headlines. Joan's story turned out to be true.

21

GENESIS—
THE BAND THAT WOULDN'T TALK

Nancy Lewis, the head of publicity for Buddha, must have liked the work we did for Michael Henderson and Phyllis Hyman.

On the side, she was handling publicity for an odd little British record company called Charisma Records. So she hired us, the Howard Bloom Organization Ltd., to handle Charisma. What acts did Charisma have? Well, Genesis, with Phil Collins. And former Genesis lead singer Peter Gabriel. I had not yet developed the craft I would eventually call "secular shamanism." I had not yet learned the crucial role of imprinting points in soul. A tale we'll soon explore with the help of birds that swim. Instead, I approached clients with the journalistic skills I had developed at *Circus* magazine. Which meant that I needed to research my clients, meet with them, and find the stories that made them unique. But that didn't always work. It certainly didn't with Genesis.

Charisma flew me and one of my account executives to Florida to meet with the band on tour. When we entered the band's presence, it was as if we didn't exist. They were relaxing by splashing in a hotel swimming pool. They never gave us any of their time. And I was not yet strong enough to demand that time or to refuse to work with the band.

But there was a strange twist to this nonevent. Back in my Gulf and Western days, I had worked with a jazz band called Brand X. I'd never met the band. In fact, I'd had a hard time figuring out what made them a story. But I gave what I had to my tour publicist, she worked relentlessly, and we got the band publicity in every city Brand X visited. Remember that hotel swimming pool in which Genesis was splashing around? In it was Genesis's new vocalist, Phil Collins. Turns out that Brand X was Phil Collins's jazz band, and that he'd deliberately kept me and my staff in the dark about his presence in the band. Why? He wanted to tour as an anonymous jazz band and NOT capitalize on his fame in pop. So, when he refused to meet me in Florida, it turns out he'd already worked with me from a distance. And working at a distance, it would later turn out, was something that I would have to be strong enough to outlaw. But first I would have to build my bargaining power.

* * *

The account executive I brought down to Florida with me was one of my male mistakes. He talked as if he was working. He walked as if he was working. He breathed as if he was working. And he said he was working. But he wasn't. I demanded a minimum of sixty press breaks a month per client. The average number of press breaks we got was 120. Yes, every month. And the maximum was 750. But from this account executive I got zero.

Why did I insist on this huge number of stories? I'd come out of neuroscience and psychology, and eventually I'd be a visiting scholar in the graduate psychology department at NYU. Psychological research indicated that if you only saw a name once, you didn't register it. But if you saw it roughly fifteen times, all of a sudden it pierced your perceptual envelope.[89] And strangely, on roughly your fifteenth viewing, you felt as if you were seeing it for the first time. So both quality and quantity counted. I thought of it as the Chinese-water-torture approach to publicity. But more on that later.

To repeat, my male account executive on Genesis delivered nothing. Zero. Nada. One reason that I would soon no longer employ men.

What probably saved us was the press delivered by my tour publicist—the publicist going for newspaper stories and TV interviews as Genesis went from city to city.

But the real Charisma Records treat would be Peter Gabriel.

22

PETER GABRIEL—THE ROCKER WHO GOT COMPUTERS RIGHT

Despite what I considered to be an utter failure on Genesis, Nancy Lewis asked us to work with Genesis's former lead singer, the new solo artist Peter Gabriel. On this, things went very differently.

I looked for Peter's obsessions, his key interests, his central passions. What emerged? Peter was a technology freak. Then I got together with Peter for lunch in Manhattan. We had a wonderful time. And, yes, technology was at Peter's core. If I remember correctly—and there's a good chance that I don't—Gabriel's dad, an electrical engineer, had helped computerize Britain for the Post Office. And the family lust for human-enhancing machines had stuck. In fact, it was so strong that Peter requested something of me. Could I please find the author of a book called *Science and Technology in the Arts*? Yes, I could.

I tracked down the author, Stewart Kranz, a painter, art historian, film art director, and theorist,[90] introduced him to Peter over lunch, and proposed an idea. It was roughly 1979. The 1990s seemed to be way, way off in the future. All three of us at the restaurant table were technology freaks. Peter had entertainment credentials. And the author of *Science and Technology in the Arts* was a Harvard man with advanced degrees from Columbia University and additional studies at the Art Students League. What's more, Kranz worked for Digital Equipment Corporation, one of the biggest computer companies in the world. And his book had been put out by one of the most prestigious publishers in science, Van Nostrand Reinhold.[91] Why not brainstorm ideas, I suggested, for the home entertainment technology of the 1990s? So we did.

I came up with a hodge-podge of wild ideas. A holographic, interactive coffee table that would play you a Rolling Stones concert in 3-D, like the holographic projection of Princess Leia in *Star Wars*. But the projection would be as interactive as the primitive hot new videogame *Pong*. So if you applauded at the end of "Honky Tonk Woman," Mick Jagger would come to the edge of the coffee table and throw rose petals at you. But if you booed, Jagger would turn his back and moon you. Without taking his pants down, of course. This is family entertainment.

Then there was the musical device I sketched out. If you are incapable of carrying a tune, which I am, and if you have a piece of Vivaldi, Fats Waller, or the Beatles going through your brain—a piece of music that Vivaldi, Fats Waller, or the Fab Four never got around to writing—you could hum it into your musical device. The electronics would correct what you'd hummed until your gizmo got the melody right. Then you could tell your gadget to orchestrate that piece of music in the style of Vivaldi, Fats Waller, Fats Domino, or John Lennon, and, voila, the creation that had been dancing in your head but that you were too musically inept to get out of the prison of your thick skull would be there in the real world, where everyone you knew could hear it. And grimace.

Needless to say, none of my great ideas ever came to be.

Peter's idea was simple. Computers had been the size of houses. Back in 1943, John Watson, head of IBM, had reportedly said that computers were so expensive that only five would ever be sold, most of them to giant corporations and the military. Peter foresaw what he called the democratization of the computer. He thought that computers would become so small and inexpensive that you and I would be able to afford them. Ridiculous. Right?

Then there was our academic, a lovely man who would stay in touch with me until he lost his mind to Alzheimer's and died. When it came to ideas, he had none. But we needed his credentials to give us validity.

The pitch on this one was too complex to get across to one of my account executives. So I handled it myself. We got two big, full-color, two-page spreads. One in the LA *Herald Examiner*. The other in *Rolling Stone*.[92] *Omni* wanted to do one, too. But when it saw that it had been scooped by the *Herald Examiner* and *Rolling Stone*, it pulled out.

What did we accomplish? We established Peter Gabriel as a man with an individual identity separate from the band he'd just left—Genesis. And we established him as a man with a brain. Peter would later establish that he was also a man with a heart.

* * *

What happened to our predictions? Mine were easy to sell to journalists but never nosed their way into the real world. But Peter's vision did become a reality. A reality that would change society. In 1983, four years after our speculations, computers would become so small and inexpensive that I could buy seventeen of them for my office. One for every employee. And three for me. Ours were Kaypros. They looked like small suitcases. You laid them flat on a table, pried open a built-in stand, got them up at a thirty-five degree angle, then you pulled at two clasps and the end of the suitcase came down and turned out to be a keyboard. Staring at you was a nine-inch green-and-white screen. One of the most fabulous toys in history.

Then, in 1984, IBM would go mainstream with its second-generation personal computer, and all hell would break lose. Computers would begin their invasion of everyday life. And another ten years down the line, Toshiba would introduce something called the laptop.

* * *

I had been wrong. But Peter Gabriel had been a seer, a visionary, and a prophet.

And I loved working with him. What's more, he planted a seed. One day, he walked into my office and told me I should check out something called the Gaia Hypothesis. I did. I found it wondrous but disagreed with its enthusiasm over a mass die-off of bacteria roughly two billion years ago. Eventually, I would write a book in response to it, *The Lucifer Principle: A Scientific Expedition into the Forces of History*. All thanks to Peter Gabriel.

* * *

Nancy Lewis, the kindly Buddha Records publicist who had pulled me in to work with Peter Gabriel, would go on to greater things. She would become the North American manager for Monty Python's Flying Circus. If Monty Python was before your time and you're not quite sure who they were, here's what the keeper of today's folk wisdom about everything on earth and beyond says:

> The Pythons' influence on comedy has been compared to the Beatles' influence on music. Their sketch show has been referred to as "not only one of the more enduring icons of 1970s British popular culture, but also an important moment in the evolution of television comedy."[93]

Yes, that's Wikipedia speaking. It was Nancy Lewis who got Monty Python on American TV—on PBS, to be specific—in 1974. Nancy would be credited as director of Python's US relations on the 1983 Monty Python film *The Meaning of Life*. She would show up in the playbill for Monty Python's 2005 Broadway hit show, *Spamalot*, which would win three Tony Awards. She would appear in three episodes of Monty Python's 2009 mini-series *Almost the Truth: The Lawyer's Cut*. And she would marry an actor—Simon Jones—she met on the set of Monty Pyhton's *The Meaning of Life* in 1982. Apparently, Nancy took British humor seriously.

23

THE POLICE—PUNK AND
THE DAD WHO CO-FOUNDED THE CIA

Two years later, when things were going very well, I became bored. I needed something new. I'd helped Texas culture and the gay community come out of the closet. Now I ached for a new subculture to champion. A friend of mine at *Billboard*, Roman Kozak, had been writing a series of articles about a club called CBGB's and a new movement: punk.

Remember Miles Copeland? The manager of the Climax Blues Band and Renaissance, two of my very first clients? Miles's company, British Talent Management, had gone belly-up. Bankrupt. Miles had disappeared for roughly two years. And I missed him. Psychologist Howard Rachlin calls it functional bonding. When you've been in the trenches together, working with all your might for a common goal, it glues you together as if you were brothers. So I was very attached to Miles. And I was wounded for him. I imagined that losing his company must have hurt.

Then, one day, I came out of a meeting at A&M Records' New York office on the corner of Fifty-Seventh Street and Madison Avenue, and there, in the waiting room, was Miles Copeland, sitting forlorn, as if he were a cut-rate printer-cartridge salesman whose pitch had just been turned down. We walked out together. Miles's body language was beaten, as if he couldn't imagine that anyone would want to spend time with him. When I pried into what he'd been doing, he reached under his left arm and produced two LPs he'd been carrying pressed between his bicep and his ribs. One was by a group called Squeeze. Another was by a band called the Police. At that moment, no one had heard of either band.

Meanwhile, another Copeland, one of Miles's two younger brothers, had set up a booking agency, FBI. Punk was creeping out of the unknown and was pushing to assert itself. And Ian Copeland, the founder of FBI, was booking nearly every rebellious punk band there was.

As I said, I was bored and needed a new subculture to champion. So I asked for a meeting with Ian Copeland. When I met him in his shabby but spacious office on

Broadway near Fifty-Seventh Street, I told him a simple truth. My company was the most expensive in the business. Either you paid our high fees, or we weren't interested. We had a quality standard to maintain, and we couldn't do it without charging those high rates. But, for Ian, I would do something I never did. I would cut my price. Dramatically. Why? I wanted to climb inside the world he was helping to build. I wanted to enter the world of punk.

But I ended up climbing into a very different world than I'd anticipated.

* * *

Way back in 1974, four years before I started to work for Ian, I'd met a new roadie for the Climax Blues band. He was slim, blond, and very young. He looked fifteen, but he was twenty-two. And he was charming. Turns out that he was Miles and Ian's younger brother, Stewart. And Stewart was more than just a roadie. He was a drummer. In fact, a few years after we met, he would put together a band. That band would record one of the two orphan, unsigned LPs that Miles Copeland was carrying under his arm when we walked out of the A&M Records waiting room together. Ian Copeland's booking agency was called the FBI. Stewart's band was called the Police. See any thread in common? There's a reason. But we'll get to that in a minute.

Miles, Ian, and Stewart had come up with a remarkable idea. Every city had a major concert promoter or two. And these gentlemen controlled every major concert venue in their territory. What's more, every city had its established music clubs. If the club owners and concert bookers did not want to book you, you had no place else to go. Until Miles, Ian, and Stewart Copeland came onto the scene.

Ian Copeland reasoned that every city worth touring also has a university. Every university has a student-activities committee. And every student-activities committee has at least one kid who has become an expert in putting on concerts—in securing the hall, bringing in the equipment, advertising the date, selling the tickets, and settling up with the stars after the show, dividing up the money. So Ian found that student on each campus and made a deal with him or her (in those days, it was all hims). Ian told the student promoter to go out and find a hall, any hall, even an old, cobwebbed movie theater that had been shuttered for years. If you were one of those students, and you found a place that could hold two hundred kids, Ian made a deal with you. He would send you his brother's unknown band, the Police. But he would do more. He would send you fifty other bands in the same genre—punk. And over the course of a year, with those fifty bands, you could establish yourself as THE promoter for the punk movement in your town.

The college student activities promoters went for it. Now all Ian had to do was find another fifty bands, which he did. American and British bands. Thus was punk taken from New York's Bowery and London's Camden[94] to the hinterlands of North America.

* * *

Miles Copeland would do so well with his brother Ian's booking strategy that he would be able to land two deals with A&M Records: one for Squeeze and another for the Police. Then he would be able to go farther. He would be able to establish his own record label, IRS, distributed by A&M. And he would be able to have his own LA management office, LAPD. Again, see any common theme in those names, the Police, FBI, IRS, and LAPD?

Slowly a story emerged from Ian. A story that took me totally by surprise. Remember, at this point I'd been working with Miles Copeland on and off for six years, and I hadn't a clue. The father of the three Copeland brothers was, like his eldest son, named Miles. Miles the elder came from a high-tone Southern family that bragged that it had produced a gang of bank robbers who had once robbed a passel of Atlanta banks by setting a fire on the opposite side of town from the banks and waiting until all the police and firemen ran to the fire and attempted to put it out, and until a massive number of townsmen and women ran to see the blaze. Then the Copeland Gang rode their horses over to the deserted side of town and lifted everything of value from its banks.

Miles the elder was a musician, a trumpeter. But his career was interrupted by an inconvenient incident—World War II. Since Miles was a Southern aristocrat, he was drafted and posted to America's intelligence service, the Office of Strategic Services, the OSS. America's spy agency. A repository for American aristocrats. When the war was over, the OSS became the base for a new intelligence agency, the CIA. Then the top brass at the new agency divvied up the world between them. Miles Copeland the elder got the olive in the martini—he was delegated to start a CIA branch in the Middle East.

But since this was totally hush-hush, he never told his kids. In other words, the Copeland boys had no idea of what their dad did for a living.

Which means that Miles the younger and his two brothers, Ian and Stewart, did not grow up like normal American kids. For one thing, they didn't grow up in America. They grew up in Beirut, Lebanon. In those days, Beirut was known as the Paris of the Middle East. It was a city where the international jet set and diplomatic class congregated, a city where there were dances every weekend on the hotel rooftops—dances

with bands from England, France, or the USA. The Copeland kids were as international as the city they grew up in. Their mom was a British archaeologist who had been a
spy during World War II.

Everything was uneventful until Miles hit roughly the age of seventeen and became dissatisfied with the size of his allowance. Dad only showed up for roughly two
weeks a year. Then he'd be god-knows-where doing god-knows-what for six months.
Miles waited for his dad to return from god-knows-where and raised hell about the in-
adequacy of the funds allotted to him each week. His dad said, "You think you can handle the family finances better than I can? Here's the checkbook. Now you're in charge
of keeping us solvent." And dad flew back to the god-knows-where of the month.

Miles the younger promptly instituted a policy shift. He cut his younger brother
Ian's allowance. Ian objected. But Miles was deaf to Ian's complaints. So Ian ran away
from home. And he did it by holing up in a place where no one on earth could possibly
find him: Beirut's motorcycle gang neighborhood, a location known for its absolute
impenetrability.

Then a strange thing happened. In what felt like only a few hours, dad showed up.
Yes, dad showed up in a neighborhood where criminals on the lam, Middle Eastern
criminals, are able to disappear without a trace. How the heck?

"Look," said Dad, "I think it's time I told you what I do for a living." And Dad
explained that he worked for the CIA. In fact, that he ran the CIA's Middle Eastern
branch. His best friends were people like the first president of Egypt, Gamal Abdal
Nasser, and the president who came after Nasser, Anwar Sadat. "Which means," said
Papa Copeland, "I will buy you an airline ticket to run away from home in London,
New York, LA, or Atlanta. But you can't run away from home in the Middle East.
Here, someone will grab you and use you to compromise me."

This is how the Copeland kids learned their dad's line of business. Hence the
names: the Police, the FBI, IRS, and LAPD. It ran in the family.

I told this story to a sometime-cartoonist, sometime-writer for the *New Yorker*,
Jim Stevenson.[95] And Jim turned it into a feature. One of the few *New Yorker* feature
stories on the rock world in those days. Another was Jim's story on Todd Rundgren
and Rundgren's futuristic, computerized video and audio studio in Woodstock. Todd
was also a client of mine.

From that point on, I'd get periodic phone calls from Courtney Cox, a cousin of
the Copeland brothers who had come to New York to seek her fortune in acting and
was working as FBI's receptionist to make a living. She would eventually become one
of the three female leads in the TV series *Friends*. The brunette. Courtney would say,

"Dad is coming into town and wants to see you tomorrow at 1:00 p.m. at the Palm Court of the Plaza Hotel." I would try to explain that the Palm Court of the Plaza Hotel requires a jacket and tie, and that I don't wear a jacket and tie. Remember my first article for the underground fashion magazine, *Rags*? On the tortures of a suit jacket and of a neck tourniquet? I'd offer to book us a reservation at one of the sixty tie-less restaurants in my seven Rolodexes. "You didn't understand me," Courtney would say. "Dad wants to see you tomorrow at 1:00 p.m. at the Palm Court of the Plaza Hotel." So I would show up. Dad was simply too colorful a character to miss and, frankly, I was fascinated.

Dad would convince the maître d' to let me in without a tie. And he would pepper me with stories. For example, there was the night when he and his associates in the Middle Eastern branch of the CIA got drunk and dared each other to get rid of the king of Iraq. One bragged that he could topple the Iraqi king in twenty-four hours. The others took the bet. And, sure enough, a day later, Iraq's king was out, and the country had a new prime minister.[96] Thus opening the way for a murderous dictator named Saddam Hussein. The man at the center of two American wars, 1990's Gulf War and 2003's Iraq War. All because of a drunken boast.

And there's one more tale, a tale I didn't believe. At least not for the first few years. It went like this. "When Stewart was five years old, I used to take him on trips to Africa with me," said dad. "He'd sit at the feet of the drummers while I went off and bargained with the chiefs. That's what got him into drumming." A ridiculous tale, right? How gullible did he think I was?

* * *

In 1984, I got a call from the Copelands. Stewart had just made a movie. I had to do the publicity. What was that film? It was called *The Rhythmatist*. It was a documentary. A documentary in which Stewart went to Africa, sought out the tribes least touched by Western culture, and listened to their drumming and their music. For what purpose? The promotional materials called the film "a musical odyssey through the heart of Africa in search of the roots of rock and roll." Dad had not been kidding around.

But we'll get to see more of what sitting at the feet of African drummers can do to your brain when we reach the mystery of imprinting. And its relationship to soul.

24

AL GREEN AND CREAM RECORDS—
THE MECCA OF MEMPHIS

Meanwhile, a new record company came to me, Cream Records. Cream had been founded by Alvin Bennett, another Southern aristocrat who, way back in 1956, had been the sales manager for Dot Records, the company I would later work with.[97] Then he had taken over Liberty Records and turned the company into a major success. One of Liberty's artists created a novelty record that became a smash, a disc that was played decade after decade: Alvin and the Chipmunks. You can imagine who the lead chipmunk, Alvin, was named after. Okay, just in case you can't imagine—it was Alvin Bennett.

Cream's real claim to fame was that it had signed Al Green, the musical messiah Bob Small and Ray Caviano had gushed about.

In the seven years since Caviano and Small had pitched Al Green to me across a lunch table at a New York restaurant, Green had become a legend. His music was given the kind of respect that Muhammad Ali, the boxer, received. Al was, as *The All Music Guide to Soul* would put it, "the last of the great soul singers." And *Rolling Stone* would eventually list him as one of the hundred greatest artists of all time. Why? Between 1971 and 1974, Al had put out six gold LPs. And he'd had an extraordinary eight gold singles.

But, in 1975, the string of gold records had come to a stop. Why? Late at night on October 18, 1974, Al got into a strange fight. Eight days earlier, a woman had left her husband and three children, and had insisted on living and sleeping with Al. Al and this peculiarly unstable newcomer, Mary Woodson, got into a fight. Mary wanted to get married. After sharing a bed with Al for only eight nights. Green did not want to commit himself to love, cherish, and obey a woman he scarcely knew. What's worse, there was another woman in the house, a woman Al had brought back from the studio that night. At 1:15 a.m., Al was about to get into the bathtub. Mary was apparently in the kitchen. When the argument about getting married reached its peak, Mary barged into the bathroom and threw a pot of boiling grits on Al, burning his back, his stomach, and his arms. Then Mary died of a gunshot wound from one of the two guns that Al kept in the home.

Rumor said that Al had taken a pistol and killed her. It took a long time to get a different story: that Mary had committed suicide with Green's .38. And that she'd left a suicide note in her purse.[98]

You sing about the pains of love in your songs. But you don't expect the extremes of romantic grief to enter your life in quite this manner.

* * *

So there was a cloud over Al Green's life when I first met him. And his record sales had dropped dramatically.

There was one more reason for the drop in record sales. A battle between subcultures. The battle in the black community between gospel and pop, between religious music and secular soul. Al had gotten his start singing in the Greene Brothers in Dansby, Arkansas, when he was ten. The Greene Brothers toured the gospel circuit. And those who supported gospel music in the black community loathed and despised those among them who started in gospel, then deserted the church and moved over to pop. Sam Cooke was the gospel escapee with the highest profile, and the highest degree of hate. (I would later work with Sam Cooke's daughter, Linda Womack, who would teach me more about this gospel-pop gap. But that's for later.) And Jackie Wilson was also way up there on the list of deplorable gospel escapees. More about Jackie Wilson when we get back to Michael Jackson.

When Al Green was roughly sixteen, his dad caught him listening to Jackie Wilson and threw him out of the house. For good. But as John Mellencamp will explain in a later episode, and as Prince will demonstrate vividly, first you rebel against your father. Then you become him. The call of gospel had been buried inside of Al since his childhood. And, in the face of murder rumors, it came back to life. So Al bought the Full Gospel Tabernacle of Memphis, Tennessee, and became its minister. And he switched his music from pop back to the music of God.

I flew from New York to Memphis in roughly 1979 to meet my new client. I was picked up at the airport by a tall, beautiful black woman dressed in military garb. National liberation movements and guerilla operations were popular at the time. She looked like the sort of underground commando Memphis might have employed if it had decided to liberate itself from the United States and had hired Che Guevara as a consultant. She drove me to a wood-shingled, three-story house in a residential neighborhood, ushered me inside through the kitchen door, and introduced me to her brother, Al Green.

Al had one of those smiles that light you up. He told me he wanted to show me something and popped me into his car. I had no idea of where we were going. I was still a bit disoriented from the airline flight. As we cruised the Memphis streets, Al peppered our conversation with lofty phrases that sounded like they came straight out of the Holy Scriptures. Biblical phrase number one was: "You can't always get what you want, but if you try, sometimes you get what you need." Biblical phrase number two: "Anything you conceive and believe, you can achieve." No, these were not from Matthew, Mark, Luke, or John. The first was from the Rolling Stones. And the second was from Napoleon Hill, the 1930s motivational writer. The august gravity that made these sentences sound biblical came from Al's intonations, his preacher's voice.

But despite their sources, the second motto that Al gave me—"Anything you conceive and believe, you can achieve"—has stuck with me for the rest of my life. If you believe hard enough in one of your ideas and persist in bringing it to life, if you utterly and completely persist, you can turn mere fantasies into realities. But the key is in the word both Al and Napoleon Hill left out: persistence. In other words, Al had cherry-picked bits of enormous wisdom. And, in two minutes, he'd made a difference in my life.

* * *

Meanwhile, as we turned from one residential street to another, I still had no idea of where Al was taking me. Then he came to a stop in front of an eight-foot-tall black wrought-iron fence with spearhead-shaped tops, a fence definitely designed to keep intruders out. Al had taken me to his personal mecca. Or maybe to what he thought was my personal mecca—Elvis Presley's mansion. The gates were closed, the place was still in legal limbo, and it would take time before it would be opened to the public. The person who would save the place would be Priscilla Presley, who would make a crucial phone call from a plane. She would call a bunch of bankers about to sell off everything Elvis owned to pay the King's back taxes. And she would convince the financiers not to sell anything until she met with them. When that meeting took place, she persuaded the bankers to give her a year to show that she could make a profit for them with what Elvis had left behind. The bankers agreed to wait, and Priscilla Presley proceeded to turn Elvis's estate into a multi-million dollar a year business. Or that's the story Priscilla's common-law husband, Marco Garibaldi, would tell me, over twenty years later. But Marco's superstar gossip wouldn't prove its full value until way, way down the line when you try to figure out who is undermining, you guessed it, Michael Jackson.

When Al and I arrived, you could not see the mansion through the trees behind the forbidding fence. All you saw were tree trunks. Still, we were in a holy site. As a consolation for the lack of a view, Al took me to lunch at a restaurant in a tiny strip mall across the street. The food was standard American 1970s strip-mall fare. But the location and the company were not.

* * *

Then I persuaded Al to come up to New York City, the capital of rock and mainstream journalism, for two days of interviews, so I could splash him across the American press. We set up sixteen interviews, sent Al a copy of his itinerary by messenger to his hotel the day before the interviews were due to begin, and I went to the hotel at something like 9:00 a.m. to make sure Al was ready for his 10:00 a.m. interview.

I was too late. Al wasn't there. I was frantic. Outwardly calm and measured, but frantic. Or at least I hoped I was outwardly calm and measured. I used a payphone and a stack of dimes to call every place I could think of where Al might be. Finally, I got WBLS, the biggest R&B radio station—the biggest black music station—in North America. "Is the Reverend Al Green there?" I asked the receptionist. "Yes, I think he is," she answered, then she did a bit of hunting and put him on the phone. I knew from his voice this was not the Reverend Al Green. However, it was a Reverend Al. The Reverend Al Sharpton. That was my first encounter with Sharpton. It wouldn't be my last.

This was also one of my very few encounters with CPT—colored people's time. A cultural characteristic that I suspect has just about ceased to exist. And it meant that Al missed all of his interviews. Every single one of them.

25

SOUL AND PASSION POINTS— MEET THE GEESE WHO FALL IN LOVE WITH, WELL, WITH YOU

I was not yet a master of the star-making machine. I was still just an apprentice. An apprentice who would have to invent the technique he was trying to learn: secular shamanism.

To understand that still-embryonic technique, let's take another detour. Remember, I had spent nine years studying booking strategy and six years developing contacts with booking agents so that I could be a booking strategist myself. And I had learned the nuances of that strategy at the feet of ZZ Top's Bill Ham.

But I had been missing something: soul. And soul, it turns out, is the heart of rock and roll. What is soul? If you are a writer of any kind, including a writer of rock-and-roll lyrics, you sit down at two in the afternoon in front of a blank piece of paper or a blank laptop screen knowing that you have to write a lyric. You are absolutely certain that you can't do it. You have no idea of how you've written lyrics in the past, but you know right down to the hairs on the back of the hands you are resting on the keyboard that you can't do it again. Then, on a good day, by 4:00 p.m., there is a lyric on your screen. On a really, really good day—maybe three times in your life—the lyric is so perfect that you feel like it wrote itself and merely used you as a pipe to make it to the page.

Then you go onstage a few months later. And, if it's a good night, you sense the pupils of the people in the audience dilating—growing wider. You see the faces of your watchers melt. You see these listeners lose the self-consciousness they had when they first took their seats and were trying to look cool to the people behind them and on either side. You see the individuals in the audience losing their individuality and melding into a mass, as if their energy had come together into a single giant amoebic blob. And you feel that blob reach a pseudopod, a giant limb, a giant tunnel, out to, of all people, you. You feel the energy of that audience go through you, as if you were an empty pipe.

You feel it reach something in your head or just above it. You see that energy transmogrified, transmuted, reshaped and reborn as something strange. And you feel that transmogrification flow back through you, out to the audience. You see it open your listeners' pupils even wider, and you see them send their collective energy flowing back to—and through—you. You and the audience are now joined in one giant reverberatory loop. Scientific researchers call this "neural coupling."[99] Your brain and the brains of your audience sync up, they pulse with the same frequency. To put it differently, you and your audience become a part of something bigger than yourselves. You become a collective ball of passion and intensity. You are caught up in the fireball of what one of sociology's founding fathers, Emile Durkheim, called "collective effervescence."

And where is your self when all of this happens? It is conveniently out of the picture. It is parked on the ceiling, watching from a distance of fifteen feet while you are being danced like a puppet on a string, danced by a collective energy. What has taken you over? Your most elemental source of passion. The gods inside. Your soul. And something more: the soul of a group. The collective soul of your audience.

When you get offstage, it takes you time before your everyday self returns. It used to take John Mellencamp an hour to get his self back. An hour he saw as an agony. John would come off the stage with his eye sockets black and empty, like the entrances to caves. His face would look as hollowed out as a skull. For an hour he would hide in a tiny room backstage where no one could see him but his wife and possibly one other close person. Sometimes me. He would wait for his normal, everyday self to return. And when that hour was over, his onstage transformation and his return to normal had been so wrenching that John would swear he would never tour again.

How jolting can that withdrawal from the group soul be? Once upon a time, Peter Townshend, the founder of the Who, and George Harrison were trying to get a friend of theirs, Eric Clapton, off cocaine and heroin.[100] Peter is reported to have said to Clapton something along the following lines. "Look, let me explain to you why you do drugs. You perform in an arena for eighteen thousand people for seventy minutes. For seventy minutes, you are a pipe for eighteen thousand souls. You connect them to the Godhead,[101] and the Godhead uses you to communicate back to them. For seventy minutes you are filled with the energy of eighteen thousand people. And with god. Then you come offstage and you are empty. It hurts. It hurts a lot. So you fill that emptiness with drugs." You use drugs to dampen the torture of withdrawal. Withdrawal from a secular experience of divinity.

In other words, it isn't you who writes the songs and who dances you onstage. It's something within you. Something separate from the nice, polite person who says,

"Hello. How are you?" And separate from the you who answers, "Fine, thank you very much. And how are you?"

It's the gods inside of you. It's your fucking soul.

Why do the faces of the members of your audience lose their individuality? Why do their pupils open so wide? And why does their energy feed you? Because they, too, are losing their normal selves and are opening to the gods inside. They, too, are in the grip of a second self, their soul. Does this have anything in common with the high-tempo dances of the gay community on Fire Island, where cowboys, firemen, and Indian chiefs leaped like flames from the bodies of accountants, clothing designers, and art directors? And does it remind you of dancing onstage at the Park School of Buffalo and being carried out on the shoulders of the audience? Not to mention the way that Mick Fleetwood galvanized an audience at Carnegie Hall? The way he called forth the soul of the group and set it blazing like a bonfire? You bet.

And you, Bloom, have you finally landed in the territory of the Gods Inside? Have you finally discovered the beating heart of soul?

No wonder I'd get periodic calls telling me that John Mellencamp refused to ever tour again, and that I would have to call John immediately, I was the only person he would listen to. The shift from a divine frenzy to a demonic emptiness and back again—150 times on a single tour—was too painful for John to endure. For John, it was a crucifixion.

* * *

Which brings us to one of the keys to my next steps: imprinting points, passion points. We've had the insight of the sheep. Now for a lesson about rock and roll from geese. Yes, from geese. Once upon a time, in Vienna, Austria, there was six-year-old named Konrad Lorenz. Konrad Lorenz's father, an orthopedic surgeon, had become globally famous for inventing a new hip-joint operation.[102] Every summer, the surgeon could now afford to move his family to a fairytale forest in Austria's Altenberg, far from other humans. His little boy, Konrad, loved animals—fish, dogs, cats, rabbits, and monkeys.[103] But he had a particular fondness for birds. When he was six, Konrad Lorenz and a girlfriend found a gaggle of baby geese that had just hatched in the marshes of the Danube River.[104] The baby geese looked on the six-year-old boy as their mother and became inordinately attached to him. It was Konrad Lorenz's first encounter with imprinting.

Later in life, Lorenz bought a jackdaw and put it in an upstairs bedroom from which the bird could make its way through a hole to the attic and out of the attic to the open air. From the jackdaw, Lorenz had his first glimpse of the relationship between imprinting and falling in love. The jackdaw male had a crush on Lorenz and tried to woo him the way male jackdaws woo females—by giving him presents. The present the jackdaw had prepared especially for Lorenz was a pre-chewed worm. When Konrad Lorenz refused to open his mouth to accept the gift, the jackdaw jumped on his shoulder and tried to insert the pellet of worm-mash into the storage tunnel of Konrad's ear.[105]

After a stint in the Nazi army in World War II, Konrad Lorenz returned home. He persuaded the Max Plank Center, Germany's most prestigious scientific organization, to give him a stipend and eventually to let him turn his parents' old summerhouse in the fairytale forest of Altenberg into a research station. There, Lorenz raised ducks and greylag geese. And he let ducks and geese raise their chicks. Konrad Lorenz was one of the founders of ethology—the study of the natural behavior of animals and of human beings. In fact, he would win a Nobel Prize for his work establishing the discipline. Along with his friend Nikko Tinbergen, the father of the supernormal stimulus, the father of the artificial egg more persuasive than a real egg.

Have you ever seen baby ducklings or geese with their mother? When the mother is walking on dry land, her chicks walk on the land behind her, lined up in single file. And when she is in the water, they swim behind her in single file. Just like Thomas Carlisle's single file of sheep. One day, Lorenz bicycled up to his Altenberg research station and walked past all the nests that the ducks and geese had built on the flat of the yard around the house. The tiny, fluffy goslings in one of the nests spotted him and followed him, one chick lined up behind the other. When Lorenz had to step up to get past the kitchen lintel, the goslings had trouble climbing a height that, to them, was like a cliff. But they continued to follow Lorenz. In a neat single file. For days. For months. And for the rest of their lives. Even when Lorenz was seated at his desk, the baby geese crowded around his feet.[106]

What had happened here? Lorenz slowly figured it out. If an object of any kind moves past newly hatched goslings of a certain age—roughly thirteen to sixteen hours old—the goslings will follow it. Since what's walking past the nest at this point in a gosling's life is usually Mom, the instinct works well. But there are slipups. Lorenz was one of the slips. He was a supernormal stimulus. The wrong supernormal stimulus.

Eventually tiny, fluffy goslings grow up. What happened when Konrad Lorenz's goslings got older . . . and bigger? They kept their attachment to Konrad Lorenz. In fact, when they reached adolescence and their hormones flowed, they were mate hungry. Who were their ideal sexual targets? Not other geese. They lusted for creatures who looked just like good old Mom—like Konrad Lorenz. If you'd visited Lorenz at his research station at this point in time, you would almost certainly have found yourself wooed by a sexually ardent goose.

At the end of Konrad Lorenz's landmark book *On Aggression*, there is a series of photos. One shows a flock of geese flying in a perfect V formation. But there are two strange things in this photo. First, the V is flying at an altitude you've never seen— about four feet off the ground, not high in the sky. Second, the point at which the two lines of the V converge is the head of a man riding a bicycle. The name of that man? Konrad Lorenz.

Lorenz called this imprinting. At a certain age, your brain opens a space it seeks to fill. And it finds what it needs, then wraps itself around that thing for the rest of your life. It makes that thing a part of your brain's basic shape, its morphology. Let's call these moments of seizing on things that the brain keeps forever "imprinting points." Or "passion points." And building musical stars, it turns out, is not just a matter of making wonderful music, being a fabulous performer, and touring. Music is an exchange of soul. But what does soul have to do with passion points? Everything.

26

SUPERTRAMP—ESCAPING THE INDUSTRIAL NIGHTMARE

In 1979, A&M Records hit big with a band from England called Supertramp. Like most of the other acts on A&M, Supertramp's music was so utterly unique that it was uncategorizable. Their high-pitched singing, way up in the countertenor range—a range that even canaries have trouble reaching—was unlike anything else in rock or pop. So were their equally high-pitched keyboards. But the result was delicious. So delicious that Supertramp had had a hit in 1977 with the terrific single "Give a Little Bit." Then they'd hit much bigger two years later in 1979 with their album *Breakfast in America*, which had reached No. 1 on the American charts and No. 3 in Britain, and had generated an unbelievable four hit singles. Four hits from just one LP—"The Logical Song," "Take the Long Way Home," "Breakfast in America," and "Goodbye Stranger."

All in all, *Breakfast in America* would sell an astonishing twenty million copies. Part of that success came from a simple fact: Supertramp's manager was one of the few who understood touring strategy. Supertramp had built a solid base of dedicated fans by touring heavily before they had struck with their first hit. In other words, onstage Supertramp had bonded with audiences by giving them ecstasies and exaltations, a sense of being lifted and flown by something bigger than themselves.

By the time A&M Records put me on Supertramp's case, the hubbub about *Breakfast in America* was over. Supertramp was last year's band.

But my growing insights on passion points and the roots of soul were about to change the way I did publicity. Instead of merely interviewing to find a good story, I'd look for imprinting points. Why? Because I suspected that those points are the roots of the human soul. The roots of the passions that drive us. The roots of the passions that make some of us great. The roots of the passions that change the course of history. The roots of the gods inside. And the first hint of those passion points would come with Supertramp.

I had gotten Queen into *Newsweek* magazine without ever meeting the key figure in the band, Freddie Mercury. But I was gaining in credibility and power, and I could now make certain demands. I insisted on two interviews. One each with the band's two leaders—Rick Davies and Roger Hodgson. Alone. No more group interviews like the Genesis talk-session that never took place. And, for the first time, I demanded to see my new clients in their own environment.

So, at A&M's generous expense, I flew out first to LA to meet Rick Davies at his home in Ventura County, then to San Francisco to meet Roger Hodgson in the garden of his house. In LA, I stayed at a hotel near Hollywood's Sunset Boulevard, where the record companies and music managers were centered. Then I drove my rental car the short ride north through the hills to the green suburban sprawl of Thousand Oaks and Rick's home.

When I sat down with Rick Davies in his living room, the furnishings did not give a sense of him at all. He had recently married one of his publicists at A&M. And, like many wives, she had plans for Rick. Those plans included one of the forms of conspicuous consumption with which Hollywood wives try to one-up each other—remodeling. Multimillion-dollar remodeling. It reminded me of how the most infamous rock wife of all time—Yoko Ono—had broken up the Beatles.

And it reminded me of pecking orders. Yes, among chickens. The top bird in the barnyard gets first crack at the food trough. And she gets to peck every other chicken in the flock. The second bird in the pecking order goes second in the lunch line. And she gets to peck everyone else in the passel of poultry, with one exception. She dares not lay a beak on chicken number one. Chicken number three goes third in the food line and gets to peck almost everyone else in sight.[107] Yes, almost. She dares not poke chicken number one or hen number two. And everyone gets to peck on the last chicken in the line. Who ends up embarrassingly naked, with all her feathers pecked out. For women in LA, budget-busting interior decorating is the way to muscle your way up the pecking order.

Another problem was that Rick was filled with resentment. For pecking-order reasons. The year before, when he had walked through the A&M Records lot—the sprawling former Charlie Chaplin film-studio campus riddled with small, one-story buildings—everyone had come out of their bungalows to bow, scrape, and say hello. In other words, Rick had been treated like a rock star. But this year, when he walked through the A&M campus, no one paid attention. Why? Because last year, Supertramp had been on its way to selling twenty million albums. But now, A&M had a new set of rock stars: Simple Minds, a band on its way to selling seventy million albums.

What bothered Rick was that he had worked for seventeen years to get his fingers to make exceptional music on an old-fashioned instrument, the piano. But Rick was convinced that Simple Minds had used computers, synthesizers, and samplers, devices they'd been able to master in a year or two. It wasn't fair. In fact, it was cheating.

Home decorating and resentment against a new musical technology were not Supertramp's real story. And they were not the only manifestation of the pecking order. Rick's half of the Supertramp saga was this. He had grown up in a small industrial town in England, a town that a hundred years earlier had manufactured one of Britain's hottest exports to the world, locomotives. Rick's hometown still made locomotives. But, by now, the rest of the world was about to convert to high-speed rail, and the engines made in Rick's hometown were about to become obsolete.

In the equivalent of sixth grade, all British kids were given a pass-it-or-else test. Those who did well were put on the track to an academic or a white-collar future—going to Oxford, Cambridge, or some other university. They were on their way to the middle class. Or higher. Those who failed would have a blue collar, vocational education. They were on their way to the lower class. Rick failed the test. What's more, the kids who had not done well were taken on a tour of the local railroad-engine factory. It was huge—bigger than a cathedral. And each of the kids on the tour knew he would work in that factory until he hit retirement age. To Rick, that future in the locomotive factory looked like hell. It was an imprinting moment, a passion point. No wonder Rick worked so hard to master the piano. It was his ticket out.

To meet Rick's partner in Supertramp, Roger Hodgson, I flew from LA up to San Francisco. I met Roger in the sunny grounds of his home, a wonderland of flowers and greenery. Roger had never worried about flunking a sixth-grade test that would twist the rest of his life. He was a son of the upper class. He was born near the top of the pecking order.

This was a dynamite story. But early in the Supertramp campaign, in 1980, I was hit with a huge health problem. On Friday evenings I carried a scarlet leather satchel stuffed with roughly thirty pounds of paperwork—a deep file-drawer worth of papers—home so I could continue my work on Saturday and Sunday. Then I carried the leather bag of dead tree pulp back to my office again on Monday morning. One Monday early in the summer of 1980, I was waiting for the elevator to the fifth floor of the wonderfully old Victorian building where, on two floors connected by a circular staircase, the Howard Bloom Organization Ltd. was now housed. This was on Manhattan's Fifty-Fifth Street, between Lexington Avenue and Third Avenue, a few blocks from Bloomingdales. It was a very upscale neighborhood where almost all of the offices were anonymous boxes of plasterboard carved out in featureless high-rise modern office buildings. Our office had character.

When the elevator arrived, I stuck out my right leg like a dancer doing a pirouette, reached with my left hand for the lead-like satchel, picked it up, and felt something in my back snap. Yes, like a breaking rubber band, something literally snapped in my back. It was painful. So, two days later, I went to a chiropractor in the building next door. He made it worse. Then my two-week, end-of-August vacation arrived.

We had made reservations in Maine, a place where I'd never spent any time. I figured I'd get rest and the back problem would go away. But I discovered that I couldn't sit in the car. The back problem produced too much pain. So my wife drove, and I lay down on the back seat. A big mistake. All the bumps and potholes that your body and the shock absorbers of the car normally absorb with ease hit me like hammers. Each one made me worse. By the time we'd traveled the 441 miles to our destination in Maine, I couldn't walk. I don't know how I managed to get out of the car and into our hotel room.

I hobbled around the seaside town in Maine a few hundred feet each day, though I don't know how. And I limped into a bookstore and bought a book on back problems filled with exercises guaranteed to make your back better. They didn't. By the time we returned to Brooklyn, I had to be nearly shoveled into bed.

So we bought one of those rolling dinner trays they use in hospitals that puts a surface big enough for a main course plate, a desert plate, a cup of coffee, and silverware over the torso of a patient prone on a mattress. I had three of my seven Rolodexes brought home to put on the tray, positioned a telephone next to the Rolodexes, and slid the tray over my chest during the day while I lay naked under the sheets. This is how I ran my office from September until December. Yes, there I was in a bed in Park Slope, Brooklyn, putting together projects in which I connected people in London to people in LA. But my staff—a very good staff—was left to do the publicity. And one of my jobs—getting high-level feature coverage by telling compelling stories to my lead-sheep press contacts—slowed down considerably. So I don't remember landing Supertramp the kind of transformative reevaluation of their significance that they deserved.

Then things got worse. The back problem weakened me so much that for three months I couldn't talk. No more setting up conference calls between LA and London. In fact, no more words or sentences at all. Then I started to soak my buttocks in an aluminum turkey pan of DMSO—dimethyl sulfoxide—a miracle liquid that *Sixty Minutes* and *Discover* magazine had touted highly. And the number of pains began to go down. Only by one pain or two a day, but the decline in the number of pains was nonstop. Finally, in March, I was able to walk again. And to talk. But I never got to tell the Supertramp story to the folks who counted most—the rock-crit elite.

My six-month imprisonment in a bed would become important to a protégé of a Minneapolis teenager named Prince. But, once more, I'm getting ahead of myself.

27

SIMON AND GARFUNKEL REUNITE

Meanwhile, Paul Simon's manager chose us for an event that Paul's office and New York's Commissioner of Parks were about to put on—a reunion of Simon and Garfunkel after eleven years apart, a reunion in New York's Central Park.[108] A free concert. Working on that concert would teach me a lesson in how jolts of soul in poetry and song lyrics can sometimes buckle your knees.

I did the initial work on the Simon and Garfunkel reunion when I was still upright—interviewing Art Garfunkel on the history of the band and writing all the press materials. Then I had to supervise the event's publicity from my bed in Brooklyn. But the Howard Bloom Organization was structured to allow my account executives to work on only two-and-a-half clients each, instead of my competitors' sixteen. So I was able to clear one of my account executives, Nancy Ambrosio, of just about everything else so that she could do the reunion concert almost full-time—a luxury none of my competitors could provide. Nancy did an excellent job. So did Simon and Garfunkel. The concert was a huge success. It drew four hundred thousand people. The result: Simon and Garfunkel decided to go out on the road and tour. Again, we were able to put Nancy on this full-time along with the backup of a tour publicist and interns, and this team led by Nancy did a magnificent job.

Art Garfunkel, unfortunately, did not turn out to be one of my favorite people on planet earth. He whined like a baby. It felt as if he'd never advanced past the age of five. But, God, what a voice. And I would be forced to work with Art again a few years later.

Paul Simon was another story. He and the creator and producer of *Saturday Night Live*, Lorne Michaels, had bought a historic building together on Broadway, near Forty-Ninth Street. This was not just any old historic landmark. It was the Brill Building, the capital of Tin Pan Alley, one of the most illustrious sites in the history of popular entertainment. The Brill Building had housed 165 music companies. The songwriters and artists headquartered in its eleven floors and 175,000 square feet had included Carol King, Burt Bacharach, Neil Diamond, Jerry Leiber and Mike Stoller, Neil Sedaka, Barry Mann, Johnny Mercer, Gerry Goffin, Bobby Darin, Hal David, Don Kirshner, Sonny Bono, Tony Orlando, Ellie Greenwich, Artie Kornfeld, Laura

Nyro, the Drifters, Connie Francis, Darlene Love, Liza Minnelli, the Ronettes, the Shangri-Las, the Shirelles, the Sweet Inspirations, Frankie Valli and the Four Seasons, and Dionne Warwick.[109] Give me a minute. Reciting that list has left me out of breath.

Now the Brill Building housed Paul's offices on one floor and Lorne's on another. They rented out its leftover space.

Lorne was looking for a publicist for *Saturday Night Live*. Paul recommended me. I had never really enjoyed *Saturday Night Live*. I'd visited the set a number of times when I'd had clients on the show. Julia Louis-Dreyfus was a sparkling presence, a woman nearly every male in the world would fall in love with. And John Belushi used to pick up the phone when I called in to the set and apparently said nice things about me behind my back. But I didn't care for the sketches. To me, they weren't very funny. Plus I had no idea at all of how to do press for a TV show. People are my specialty. I like to collect souls.

But as a matter of courtesy and curiosity, I went over to Paul and Lorne's building for a meeting. After my session with Lorne, I was in the elevator going back to ground level. Paul got in. He was carrying a piece of paper with type on it. I asked what it was. He said it was the lyrics to his next album. I asked if I could read them as we descended from one floor to another. Remember, poetry had played a crucial role in my life since I'd been fourteen. And I'd edited a college literary magazine that had won two Academy of American Poets prizes.

What I read nearly made my knees buckle. And that is not a figure of speech. It's a muscular reality. Paul's lyrics were some of the most staggering pieces of poetry I had ever seen in my life. I told Paul that. And I asked if I could have a xerox to show a friend at the *New York Times*. So we waited until the elevator arrived at Paul's floor, and Paul made me a copy. I walked as fast as I could back to my office, and made a phone call to the *New York Times'* Stephen Holden. Stephen was one of the lead sheep. But he was less hemmed in by the opinions of those around him than any of the other alpha animals in the rock-crit pack. Why? He was gay in the days before you could say that out loud without losing your career. So Stephen never quite fit in to the group. Which meant I could relate to him. And I could sometimes tempt him to an unconventional opinion. I who liked to work with unconventional artists.

I told Stephen Holden that I'd just read what I thought were the most startling lyrics I'd ever seen in my life. And I explained how they had almost made me lose control of my knees. "If I send them over to you by messenger," I said, "could you please tell me if I'm sane?" Stephen was eager for the lyrics. They arrived in his hands an hour later. He called me. "You are thoroughly sane," he said.

Now I was not just doing this out of generosity and commitment to the truth at any price, including the price of your life. Though Paul's lyrics hit at truths beyond my powers of speech. I knew that seeing Paul's lyrics at such an early stage would give Stephen Holden an ego-stake in Paul Simon's upcoming album. Stephen Holden would champion it. Why? Not just because he believed in it, which he did. But because the more Paul's new album succeeded, the more Stephen Holden succeeded. In what? In demonstrating his power to make a difference. In demonstrating his power to kick off an avalanche. An avalanche of opinions that would ape his own. Championing Paul's album would feed Stephen's ego. And ego is not always the monster we make it out to be. Sometimes ego is like a stallion—it can carry us to accomplishments that improve the quality of life.

I had one more ulterior motive. I admired Paul Simon's talents immensely. I wanted him to become one of my clients. That, alas, did not happen. Warner Bros, Paul's record company, had an insanely good publicist named Liz Rosenberg. And Liz would inspire the utter loyalty of two clients above all others: Paul Simon and Madonna.

My teeth gnashed in envy.

But this left me with another mystery of soul. How can the poetry of mere lyrics, mere words to songs, seize control of your body so deeply that you almost fall to the ground?

28

THE MAN WHO BIT THE HEAD OFF A BAT—OZZY OSBOURNE

Meanwhile, on the trail of soul and imprinting points, there was an encounter with a guy I never worked for, Ozzy Osbourne.

Ozzy Osbourne first came to my attention in 1971, when I was studying rock and roll madly so I could be an effective editor at *Circus*. I was discovering that touring bands meant a heck of a lot more to my audience than singers who had hits. One of those touring bands, one of those bands selling albums but not singles, was Black Sabbath. I'd figure out something else. You don't discover whether or not you like a piece of music until you've heard it roughly fifteen times—the magic number of memory. Plus, I was trying to reinvent the record review. I wanted to use poetic imagery to get across an album's sensory impact, the impact of its rhythms, its melodies, and its sounds. The album I chose to write one of these fifteen-listening, prose-poetry reviews about was, yes, Black Sabbath.

Then, eleven years later, somewhere around 1982, someone I didn't know apparently heard that I was an entertaining novelty. His name was Don Arden. Don Arden was even shorter than I am. And, like many of the characters in this book, he was round. Little and round. In the days when he was still slim, Arden had been a tap dancer and singer who had appeared onstage in music halls with his wife. Then Don had gone into music management. He'd been involved with clients like Jerry Lee Lewis, Little Richard, Air Supply, the Small Faces, the Move, Black Sabbath, and the Electric Light Orchestra. Now he had a mansion in the hills of LA. And he summoned me to meet him there. So, on one of my LA trips, I drove my rental car into the hills and made a discovery. A palatial estate in LA was vastly different from the palatial estates in England that LA mansions try to imitate.

The roads in the hills of Hollywood can be snaky, sneaky, switch-backed, winding, and steep. My rental car zigged back and forth as it tried to climb the horizontal z's of Don Arden's mountain. The road grew more and more narrow and the foliage closed closer and closer around us—around me and the poor, overworked automobile. Finally, we came to a ten-foot-tall iron gate complete with a small building just big enough for a guard to stand up in. But there was no guard. And the gate was very strange. It was barely wedged into a claustrophobic space between the steep hill's shoulders and the greenery. What's worse, the method for entry was very confusing. In those days, with no cellphones, you couldn't simply call your friends inside the estate for instructions. So I puzzled and puzzled and finally realized there was a microphone hidden in the gate, a speaker, and a call button. I managed to reach out of the left-hand window, stretch far enough to hit the call button, and announce myself. The gate—which, as I said, was claustrophobically wedged between the steepnesses—swung open. Automatically. Electrically.

Now if this had been a British country pile, the landscape to which the gate gave entry would have been vast, gardened, and green. But Don Arden's manse in the hills had no luxurious expanse of greenery. In fact, it had no greenery at all. Instead, it had a black asphalt driveway big enough for sixteen cars, and it had three three-car garages. Plus an entrance to the house.

In England, space in the countryside is relatively cheap. In LA, there is no countryside. And every inch of space costs a fortune. So buildings pretend to be huge and imposing. But instead they are palatial homes squeezed into postage stamp sized pieces of property. As I would later discover with Lionel Richie.

I parked my car along with a few others, and could immediately see how badly this place wanted to be a true country pile. How? In one corner of the garage closest to the house there was a corral. And in that corral was the tiniest miniature horse I had ever seen. Yes, a live horse, chewing hay. But shrunken dramatically.

I walked past the horse and the garages to the house's entrance, which was fronted not with green lawn but with the parking area's pavement. The huge wooden door opened. A beautiful young woman greeted me. Arden's mistress. So did two massive dogs, each one bigger than the horse. I love dogs, and they are often kind enough to love me back, so this was a treat. I petted them, they licked my face. Then the woman led me to my first meeting with the man who had summoned me, Don Arden. She, alas, did not lick my face.

Don asked for these visits several times. It appears he got a rise out of me by showing me pornographic movies on the screen in the basement den—films of a kind I had never seen before. Or he amused himself shocking me with stories. Like the tale of the time he'd had a disagreement with the Bee Gees' amazing manager, Robert Stigwood, the man who would make *Saturday Night Fever* and *Grease*. When Stigwood stubbornly refused to see Don's point of view, Don says he grabbed Stigwood by the ankles and held him out the window. As you may recall, they were on the sixth floor, and escape by landing on the sidewalk was not an appealing idea.

My face must have flashed an unusually high degree of emotion when Don told his tales or showed his movies, because he kept inviting me back. What's more, when he rented a $3,200-a-day, two-story suite at the Helmsley Palace Hotel in Manhattan, he wanted me to see it. So he summoned me over, and I got to spend a few minutes just a room or two away from Sharon Osbourne and Ozzy. Sharon was about to bolt from her father, take Ozzy with her, and start her own career as a superstar manager and a reality TV star. To pay me off for my quality of amazement, Don gave me one of his bands to work with, Air Supply. An Australian duo whose vocals were gorgeous.

But my most important experience at Don's LA mansion on its nonexistent piece of property came one day when I was passing through the living room and spotted a figure with an elaborately embroidered, silk English smoking jacket, dozing by the side of the fire. Yes, by the side of a fully flaming fireplace. Like something out of *Masterpiece Theatre*. I went over, took a chance on waking the sleeping figure up, and introduced myself. It was Black Sabbath's lead singer, Ozzy Osbourne, who was just cutting out a solo career for himself.

On January 20, 1982, Ozzy had made headlines by biting off the head of a live bat onstage. Every animal-protection group and committed fruitarian had bitten off Ozzy's head in headlines for this outrageous deed. But when I took the chair at the fire next to Ozzy, he not only woke up, he explained something. "When I got out of school," said Ozzy, "the only job I could get was in a slaughter house. I watched all of these cows going through a narrow passage on their way to being slaughtered. Every night I went home crying. If I'd stayed at that job for the rest of my life, how many animals would I have helped kill? Ten thousand? A hundred thousand? For the sake of my career, I've killed one animal. And I didn't like it. But one animal instead of a hundred thousand? That's a big difference."

How very much like Supertramp's Roger Davies. How very much a passion point and an avenue to the soul. But my hunt for soul would go deeper. Far deeper.

29

JOAN JETT—THE STORY OF THE SINGING FIST

Way back in my ABC days—the days when I'd worked out of a glass-enclosed cubicle on Sixth Avenue and West Fifty-Fourth Street with an indistinct view of windows way off in the distance—there had been a big, corner office with lots of windows not far away. I could easily see its closed door through the clear cubicle walls around my desk. In it was the top ABC talent scout for the East Coast. The East Coast's head of artist and repertoire, the A&R guy.

He was a very sweet man, but he looked like a throwback to the days of artificial pop stars. He'd apparently had something to do with Jay and the Americans. And he looked the part: dyed blond hair, a California tan, a shirt open to the clavicle, white pants, slender, and a good two inches taller than I am, which is not tough. Cocker spaniels standing on their hind legs can be taller than I am. The talent scout's name was Sandy. His last name escapes me. But, periodically, musicians and songwriters would come to visit him and enjoy his view. A view of the walls of other skyscrapers. But to get to his office, they had to thread past mine. And mine, as you know, had glass walls. So I was as visible as a goldfish in a glass bowl. One of Sandy's musical friends always had the courtesy to smile and say hello.

When you've been raised in solitude, every smile and hello means a lot. It means another human is willing to pay attention to you voluntarily. And I don't know about you, but I remain eternally grateful to anyone who has dished out that minuscule degree of interest without being forced into it by his mother. What's more, the person who said hello was as short as I am. Almost. His name was Kenny Laguna.

Kenny was a songwriter, singer, and keyboardist who had been a part of the pop explosion—the explosion that had put Art Kass's Buddha Records on the charts. He had written songs for Tony Orlando, the Ohio Express, and the Lemon Pipers. He had played on Tommy James and the Shondells' "Mony Mony," Crazy Elephant's "Gimme Gimme Good Lovin'," the Lemon Pipers' "Green Tambourine," and Jay and the Americans' "This Magic Moment" and "Walking in the Rain." All songs that had hit between 1968 and 1970. And all props in singles-oriented careers, pop careers—the very opposite of the sort of album careers I insisted on building.

I hadn't seen Kenny for roughly four years, since I'd left ABC. But when he called in 1979 and asked for a favor, I was up for it. To me, it felt as if Kenny had done me the hugest favor in the world. So Kenny came over to my office, entered through the fifth floor, with its woodsy brown-painted, Warner Bros–like walls, its even woodsier clear stained wood baseboards, its tan carpets, and its unusual modern furniture and sunken lighting. Kenny told the receptionist he had a meeting with me, and was guided down the circular staircase to my office on the fourth floor with its two windows, its chrome-and-wood desk the size of the landing platform of an aircraft carrier, and the seven Rolodexes, not to mention the two bentwood guest chairs, and the couch. Kenny chose the couch. Then he explained his problem.

He had been hired to produce an album for a nineteen-year-old named Joan Jett. At the age of fifteen, Joan had been the central member of an LA phenomenon called the Runaways. The Runaways were an all-girl rock band in a day when women were still seldom seen with guitars in their hands. And the Runaways were a deliberate sexual provocation. All of them, it was said, were a mere fifteen. Which made them a band of blatantly underage women using their sexuality along with their musical chops. It was four newly nubile women. Allegedly just a short age jump above kiddy porn. Playing savage, slashing rock. An all-male form of music.

The band had been founded when an LA super-self-promoter named Kim Fowley gave singer/guitarist Joan Jett's phone number to a fifteen-year-old female drummer and guitarist, Sandy West. Joan and Sandy lived four bus rides apart in LA, a murderous distance. But they got together, worked up some songs, and played them for Fowley. Fowley, called "one of the most colorful characters in the annals of rock and roll"[110] by *Dangerous Minds*, must have been impressed. Jett and West added two other female members in their age range—early teens. They were the Runaways. They recorded five albums, including a *Live in Japan* LP that Wikipedia calls "one of the biggest-selling imports in US and UK history." The title of their first single tells you all you need to know about the Runaways' sexual leverage: "Cherry Bomb."

When the band broke up in 1979, Joan went out on her own. Kenny explained to me that Joan couldn't get an American deal. Twenty-three record companies had turned her down. At that point, when small companies were being eaten up or put out of business by conglomerates, it was hard to even find twenty-three record companies. But the Runaways had always been bigger in Europe and Japan than in America. So a Swedish label had given Joan a record deal. And an album budget: $25,000, about one fourth of what it normally cost to produce an album in America in those days. Those days meant 1979.

Kenny Laguna had been hired to produce the Swedish album. Joan was touring Europe. So Kenny flew to Germany to meet her. "It was terrible," he told me. "Joannie was playing in the sort of Berlin clubs where the Beatles got their start. But no one had booked her a hotel room. So she was going onstage, getting all sweated up, then sleeping on the floor of the club after it closed. The problem is that they turn off the heat in these buildings once the last show is over. So there was Joannie trying to sleep on a concrete floor, drenched in sweat, in her leather pants and jacket, with her teeth chattering, freezing all night long." Kenny's mission became bigger than just producing an LP. He wanted to make sure Joan Jett was properly taken care of.

What was the favor Kenny wanted to ask of me? There were three record-industry trade magazines back then—*Billboard*, *Record World*, and *Cashbox*. *Cashbox* was at the bottom of the heap. "Just get Joannie a line in *Cashbox*," Kenny pleaded. "Then a record company will sign her. The record company will make her a star, and I can go back to producing her albums."

Here's where all the years studying artist development and the star-making machine snapped into action. All the years of studying the career paths of album artists, the booking strategies that put album artists on top. Not to mention the insights on booking strategy from ZZ Top's mastermind, Bill Ham. All of it came to a head in a vision.

What's a vision? It's not necessarily a visual panorama like an IMAX movie. In this case, it was a gut-and-muscle sense of what will happen. And of exactly how to make it happen.

I moved out from behind my desk, sat on a guest chair, loomed over Kenny on the low-slung couch, and said, "There's no such thing as being signed by a record company because of fifteen words in *Cashbox*. And there's no such thing as a record company that will make you a star." I explained that, "The day you sign with a record company is the day your troubles begin. The record company will throw every conceivable obstacle in your path. And quite a few you can't conceive of."

"You need," I said, "a panzer-tank strategy. A panzer tank is built to go over every fence, tree, house, and chicken coop in its path. You need a strategy that can go over every obstacle that the record company throws at you." Then I made a very strange statement, a statement of a kind I hadn't made since the afternoon when I'd sat with Rufus's manager in the back of a limo and had promised the manager that if he let me put all of the focus on his lead singer, I'd give him a star. As you know, that lead singer had been Chaka Khan.

"If you work the way I work," I said, "if you put in seventeen-hour days, seven days a week, and if you do everything I tell you to, I guarantee you we will have a star in two years."

The engine I had in mind for the panzer tank was booking. Touring. Getting out on the road and connecting with the audience. I had never seen Joan perform. I had never met her. In fact, I did something very strange. I didn't even ask to meet her. Don't ask me how, but I knew what she could do onstage. Maybe it was from the way Kenny spoke about her.

Kenny agreed to this very strange proposition. As for pay, I believe I said something else very uncharacteristic. Remember, I charged the highest fees in the music industry. And I didn't bargain or offer deals. Except in the case of Ian Copeland's booking agency, FBI. I told Kenny I would work to be paid when the money came in.

When Kenny left, I called Ian Copeland and talked him into signing Joan Jett. A month later, Ian hadn't booked a single date. That's very typical of agents of all kinds. You think they are going to go out and beat the bushes for you. They don't. They wait for calls to come to them. Which is not the way to build careers. So I called Ian and nudged him. Hard. And the dates began to come—club dates.

Then I called Kenny and explained something to him. "I want you to press 350 copies of Joan's Swedish album. You can put any label on it you want. Make up your own record company. If Joan goes into Cleveland and doesn't have a record, my staff can't get press for her. But if she has a record, we can get both daily newspapers to run features." Kenny made up a label—Blackheart Records. For Joan Jett and the Blackhearts. He didn't just press 350 records. He pressed 6,000. He also did something I hadn't thought of. He hired a freelance promotion man, Steve Leeds—a professional dedicated to doing the impossible: getting airplay on the radio for a record from an unknown label.

So Joan Jett went out on the road. She performed the entire Eastern Seaboard from Bangor, Maine, down to the Florida Keys, with Boston, New York, Philadelphia, Washington, and Charleston in between. Thanks to hotel bills, food, and travel, touring is expensive. So is pressing records and paying a promotion man. Where did Kenny get the money? He took it from the kitty he'd been saving to put his eight-month-old daughter through college. A brave move.

Onstage, Joan is explosive. She takes possession of three key things: her guitar, the stage, and you. The owners of the clubs where she'd performed wanted her back. And word of mouth spread from those who had seen her first performance in each town. So she did the Atlantic seaboard strip again. And the audiences were much bigger the second time around.

Once again, the club owners wanted her back. So she did the Atlantic strip a third time. Then Kenny got all excited. If Joan would do a fourth sweep of the eastern strip, the club owners were offering enough money to cover expenses and to pay back some of the money Kenny had stolen from his daughter's kitty. Here's where mastering the nuances of touring strategy kicked in. I tried to explain something difficult to Kenny. Now that they're offering you real money, you have to stop. You have to leave the audience hungry. It's only if people hear from their friends that they missed something that they will hanker after Joan. And it's only if those who have seen Joan before have undergone deprivation that they will value her. Otherwise, they'll get bored. They'll see Joan as a commodity, like hot and cold running water.

Plus, I explained, "We are up against a deadline. We have a hit on this album, 'I Love Rock 'n' Roll.' If that hit breaks through while we've only done one sliver of this country, we are finished. Joan will be a singles artist. A one-hit wonder. She will be over and out. But if we cover the entire country from the Atlantic to the Pacific with three performances per city, Joan will be an album artist. She will be an icon. Her fans will never let her go."

This may seem a strange message to deliver when Joan didn't even have a mainstream record company. But it's that vision thing. The sense of a future you know in your bones. Something you know because you've marinated yourself in your field. You've eaten, breathed, and slept it. It's what my book *The Genius of the Beast* calls saturated intuition. And it's a close cousin of the amazement that made your knees buckle over Paul Simon's poetry. It's a muscular truth.

Meanwhile, Kenny had hired the most powerful attorney in the East Coast record industry, Allen Grubman. The man who had let you, Howard Bloom, use his office when your own had not been painted yet. One of the hottest record executives in the business was Neil Bogart. In 1967, Art Kass had taken a huge chance at Buddha and had hired Bogart, a mere twenty-four-year old, then had put him in charge of Buddha's daily operations. Bogart had played a major role in landing Buddha a hundred hits. In 1973, when he was thirty, Bogart had started his own record company, Casablanca, and had signed KISS, disco queen Donna Summer, and the Village People. He had a magic, a charisma, a cachet. And Bogart had worked on some of the bubblegum-pop singles Kenny Laguna had written and/or played on. Allen Grubman was considered powerful. So was Bogart. Grubman got Bogart to sign Joan to Casablanca.

And, just as predicted, that's when Joan's troubles began. Steve Leeds, the independent promotion man who Kenny had hired to get airplay for Joan's music, was doing a magnificent job. And Joan's songs were proving popular with radio listeners. But every DJ allots a certain amount of airtime to each label. And each record company designates four or five records as the week's priorities, then sends its promotion men out to radio stations to wangle its priority records airplay. Now that Neil Bogart had signed Joan, she was no longer considered a Blackheart artist. She was a Casablanca artist. But she was never on the priority lists of Casablanca's promotion men. So, if you were a DJ, when a Casablanca promotion man showed up in your office and you had been playing Joan's record, the Casablanca guy would make a very strange demand. He'd insist that you take Joan Jett's record off of your turntable to make room for the Casablanca records on the priority list. Think about it: the promotion man was up against a problem. Get airplay for the priority artists, or lose your job. So highly skilled promotion men with very solid relationships at radio were working their balls off to destroy Joan Jett's radio play.

I walked over to meet Kenny Laguna at Allen Grubman's seven-room rabbit warren a block from my HQ on Fifty-Fifth Street. I took the elevator to the fourth-floor office that Allen Grubman had let me use for a week. I barged into Allen's private office. He was trying to go from behind his desk to the door so he could go into the hallway and head for a meeting. But the space between the desk and the wall was only three feet wide. I trapped Allen in that tiny space and did something I'd never done before and have never done since: I put Allen Grubman up against the wall. Yes, for real. "You will not fuck with this artist," I said about Joan. "You will not let Neil Bogart use Joan as a tax write-off." I am small. I'm the guy kids loved to beat up. But when you know a truth, you have the force. Literally. You have an uncanny power. I never laid a finger on Allen. But there was the fury of Jehovah in me. And Grubman got the message.

Bogart's promo men stopped working to take away Joan's airplay.

My statement to Kenny that we'd have a star in two years turned out to be wrong. We finished our three-date-per-city touring from the Atlantic to the Pacific just before "I Love Rock 'n' Roll" went to No. 1 on the charts, stayed there for a phenomenal seven weeks, went platinum, and was named one of the top three singles of 1983. Which meant that, from the day I had made my promise, Joan's album went double-platinum in eighteen months. I had been off by six months.

* * *

Kenny Laguna laid his life, his marriage, and his daughter's future on the line for Joan Jett. Not to mention his time. It's forty years later, and he is still working seventeen-hour days seven days a week for Joan.

And ZZ Top's Bill Ham, the man who taught me the most about tour strategy, had played a major role in the success of an artist he never met.

30

LESSONS FROM JOAN JETT— POWER MOMS

One day, after Joan Jett had broken very big, Joan and Kenny—who travel together, live near each other on Long Island, are like brother and sister, and are inseparable, despite Kenny's wife and daughter—were staying in a bungalow at, where else? The Beverly Hills Hotel. Yes, one of the same bungalows where Howard Hughes would have a piping-hot hamburger deposited every night at precisely 3:00 a.m.

What was a bungalow at the Beverly Hills Hotel? A separate building surrounded by some of the lushest plant life you've ever seen. Huge tropical leaves the size of your torso and the thickness of a rubber gasket. The biggest bird of paradise blossoms you've ever seen. All crowding in from the outside toward the dozen and a half windows. A few separate bedrooms. A kitchen. And a living room so huge that it had not one but two entire sets of furniture. Each set had two couches facing each other around a coffee table, with an armchair at each of the coffee table's ends. Yes, the living room had four couches and four armchairs. With a space that seemed the size of a backyard basketball court in between them. And a fireplace. So this was how Howard Hughes lived when he was in LA! Not to mention Art Ford!

Joan and I were sitting on the bed in one of the bungalow bedrooms. Her bed, I assume.

In the same way that I, a person steeped in science, cannot completely explain where visions come from, there's another strange way the self below the floorboards of your self speaks to you. Or through you. It's captured in a rough paraphrase of a quote from E. M. Forster: "How do I know what I think until I hear what I have to say?"

For reasons utterly unknown, I gave Joan Jett an analysis of her success—one that had never occurred to me before. It went like this.

If you were a little girl in the 1950s, you lived in the suburbs. Your mom made breakfast; your dad came down to the kitchen table wearing his suit and tie, put down his briefcase, gobbled his cereal, picked up his briefcase again, and walked out the door, headed for the train station and for a distant place as alien to you as another planet, the city. Your mom hung around the house, hugging the vacuum cleaner and watching soap operas until you got home from school. Then she fed you milk and cookies.

That was your role model of femininity. So, when you hit puberty and there was a woman onstage, she was allowed to sing—like Grace Slick with the Jefferson Airplane, or Janis Joplin with Big Brother and the Holding Company. But the men had the monopoly on the power instrument, the guitar.

But if you were a little girl in the late 1960s or the 1970s, things were different. Your dad would come down to breakfast dressed in his power suit, gobble down his cereal, pick up his briefcase, and go off to work. And your mom would come down to the breakfast table dressed in her power suit—her pantsuit—eat, pick up her briefcase, and head out to the office where she worked. So, when you hit twelve, you were part of a very new generation of girls with a very new set of imprinting points, a new palette of feelings. Feelings there were no words for. Feelings you thought meant that you were insane.

Then, I said, you, Joan Jett, came along. And you seized the power instrument. You held it in a stance that meant that you were no longer Donna Reed/milk-and-cookies feminine. You were something new. You were a tower of strength. You owned the stage. You shouted with all the force that was in you and you performed with every muscle of your body. You were the rebel, the one who had taken over. You were the one balling your hand up in a fist. You had the sledgehammer of control—your guitar. Your audience could not put what you did for them in words, but they no longer felt insane. They recognized their unspoken feelings in you. They recognized it in your stance, in your possession of the guitar, and in the way that you raised your fist. Yes, they no longer felt insane. They realized that they were a movement.

You became the voice of a generation. You became the crystal dropped into the supersaturated water. You became the tongue of a group soul.

Joan's mother, by the way, had been one of those power moms who go off to work every day. Joan's mother had been a secretary.

* * *

Then there's something I didn't explain to Joan. Joan would periodically do a photo shoot. Thousands of color slides in hundreds of slide sheets would come to my office by messenger. I would take those heaps of slide sheets into an empty room with an overhead lightbulb and a loop—a magnifying glass. And I would look for something very specific. I would look for pictures thirteen-year-old boys would want to jerk off to. Yes, that they would want to masturbate to. Why? Because I wanted twelve- and thirteen-year-olds to hang Joan's pictures on their walls. I wanted her to be an icon.

Again, why? Because Joan represented rebellion. Healthy rebellion. The need of adolescents to claim their right to an individual identity. To claim their right to be the next generation who would remake the world. The right to shout, "Don't give a damn about my bad reputation."

Twenty years later, my second book, *Global Brain: The Evolution of Mass Mind from the Big Bang to the 21st Century*, would be the subject of a one-hour Dutch TV special written by Marcel Roele, a science writer for the second largest newspaper in Holland. Marcel was a lot younger than I am. I told him what I was looking for in Joan Jett slides. He had a very simple comment: "It worked." He had been one of those boys with Joan's poster on his bedroom walls.

* * *

Another tiny Joan Jett detail. Another lesson in soul. One day, I ran into Joan at the office of Aerosmith's managers, David Krebs and Steve Leber, an office just four doors away from mine. Joan was slumped in a chair in the waiting area, almost lifeless. Why? Joan needed the stage and her audience to amp her energy up to megavolt level. She needed the audience to bring life to the gods inside. A few years later, I would see the difference an audience makes once again . . . with Bette Midler.

31

REO SPEEDWAGON—THE HOUSE THAT SLID INTO A BETTER NEIGHBORHOOD

From my work with ZZ Top, one thing became obvious to the denizens of the music industry. Something you already know. I liked to work with bands the critics hated. And Epic Records—a part of the CBS music empire—had a band that no one on the label's staff could stand: REO Speedwagon.

It was the end of the 1978 fiscal year. Glen Brunman headed Epic's PR department. He had a few thousand dollars left in his PR budget. If he didn't spend that money before the fiscal year was up, he'd lose it. So he had a clever idea. Why not hire Bloom to work with the band that no one at Epic could tolerate? Thus did the Howard Bloom Organization Ltd. roll up its sleeves and go to work for REO Speedwagon. And thus did I learn a lesson.

I read everything in Epic's press clipping file on REO. Then I flew out to LA to meet the band. I went notepad in hand. In fact, I went everywhere notepad in hand. A standard practice since my *Rags* magazine days. But I had a purpose with that notepad when I went to see REO Speedwagon. I wanted to get the story of what made REO tick.

And what did I find? First, a tale of imprinting that would have brought a glow to the heart of Konrad Lorenz. Two sights turned Kevin Cronin, REO's lead singer and main songwriter, into a music fanatic: seeing Elvis Presley on *The Ed Sullivan Show* when he was five years old, and seeing the Beatles on *The Ed Sullivan Show* when he was thirteen. The sense of overwhelming attention, sexual attention, focused on just one person—or four—and the sound of girls screaming with desire were supernormal stimuli. Like an oversized, polka-dotted egg. Kevin was hooked. Imprinted.

But there was more. The REO Speedwagon story was riddled with mishaps. Keystone comedy mishaps. Here's roughly how it went.

REO Speedwagon got together in Champaign, Illinois, home of the University of Illinois Urbana-Champaign, in 1967. Meanwhile, a kid in nearby Chicago had a nutty idea for finding a band that could use his vocals and his songs. He would pretend to be a talent scout for unsigned musicians. If you needed a drummer, he would find you one. If you needed a piccolo player, well, that was a little tougher, but he'd try. In reality, he was waiting for the band that would call begging for a singer. Guess who called? The band from Champaign, Illinois. In this manner did Kevin Cronin, the wily kid from Chicago, become REO Speedwagon's lead singer. And lead songwriter.

REO Speedwagon had an ambition. They wanted to be the biggest frat band in Champaign, Illinois. And they achieved it. How? By working their asses off. By playing every frat party they could possibly find. Then they had a new ambition: to become the biggest band of any kind in Illinois. And they achieved it. How? The same thing. They worked their heinies off. They toured. They played every concert they could possibly find. Then they wanted to become the biggest band in the entire Midwest. And they snagged that goal, too. Again, by touring until their tongues hung out. When I met them, REO wanted to be the biggest band in North America. And anyone with brains would tell you this one was impossible. I mean, look at who they were up against in 1978 when I first met them: the Sex Pistols, Elton John, the Bee Gees, the Electric Light Orchestra, Ted Nugent, Van Halen, Aerosmith, Foreigner, Heart, Bob Marley, the Rolling Stones, Rush, Journey, the Doobie Brothers, and the Grateful Dead, to name just a few.

What was REO Speedwagon's secret weapon? A work ethic that wouldn't quit. An absolute insistence on touring. The very same magic ingredient that my correlational studies at *Circus* magazine had revealed as the key to success. The very same magic ingredient whose nuances I was learning from Bill Ham of ZZ Top. In fact, REO Speedwagon were so dedicated to touring that they bought an ancient limousine to carry them from town to town. And, one day, that limousine gave out. An axle snapped. And REO Speedwagon ended up with the nose of their limo plowed into a cornfield and the front windshield providing a detailed view of the cornstalks' roots. When the geographic territory they were touring expanded beyond the range of a used limo, REO chartered a private airplane, and its pilot became like a member of the band. One day, that plane, too, failed them. It skidded off the runway sideways and ended up in a position as ridiculous as the limo's—tilted with one wing resting on the ground. The miracle was that no one was hurt.

Where was the story in all of this? Where was the hook? The element of uniqueness? In the band's insanity. In its sense of humor. Wherever they went, the band members seasoned their boredom with ridiculousness. For example, at one hotel in god knows what major Midwestern city, they went to a Kmart, bought plastic rifles and handguns, and had a mock guerrilla war in the hotel's corridors. Something you could only do in the days before terrorist attacks would make this form of silliness scary. Turns out there was a convention of Sweet Adelines in the hotel. Middle-aged women who sang the female equivalent of barbershop-quartet music. A cappella. These poor women found REO's corridor warfare unsettling. And unsettling the Sweet Adelines was great fun.

Since doing silly things on the road was a weekly occurrence, I trained Kevin Cronin, the lead singer and songwriter, in something neither of us had ever done before: comedy writing. The sort of thing that Woody Allen used to do for one of the kings of 1950s TV comedy, Sid Caesar. I taught Kevin how to spot an anecdote, an interesting tale. And I asked Kevin to call me every Sunday, from whatever city he was in, and tell me whatever ridiculous thing the band had done that week. Turns out that this encouraged the band to do even more ridiculous things than ever before. For example, they were staying at one of Memphis's most aristocratic hotels—the Peabody. The Peabody hotel was famous for the ducks swimming in the pool in the center of the lobby. Yes, live ducks.

So each member of REO Speedwagon stole one of the ducks and used it as a rubber ducky in his hotel bathtub.

But the real secret was something Kevin thought I was teaching him, but in fact that we were teaching each other: writing punch lines. Kevin says that I wrote most of them. But one Sunday, Kevin was back home in Thousand Oaks, California, in the valley just the other side of the Santa Monica Mountains (actually hills pretending to be mountains) from Hollywood. That week, LA—the city of which Hollywood and Thousand Oaks are a part—was making headlines. Why? It was being soaked by rainstorms like the ones that floated Noah's ark. And buildings were losing their moorings on the slopes of the LA hills and land-sliding down into the valleys. When we had our weekly Sunday phone meeting, Kevin reported this: "My house just slid into a better neighborhood."

With our wild tales, we managed to get on Casey Kasem's *Coast to Coast*, the syndicated show that appeared on 520 radio stations and that had helped educate me about popular music, nearly every week.[111] And we hit thousands of other media outlets. Regularly. Over and over again. Remember, we often don't realize we've been exposed to something—something like REO Speedwagon's name and humor—until we've seen it roughly fifteen times. Then the sixteenth time strikes us as the very first time we've seen it. In psychology, it's called "cueing."[112]

Which is why I used the machine-gun approach to exposure with as many of my clients as I could. I used the Chinese-water-torture strategy. My staff and I got each client hundreds of "exposures" a month. Why? I wanted you to remember my acts. Which would prove crucial in building Prince. But that's a tale for later.

Meanwhile, there was more to REO than I realized. It wasn't in their touring, it was in their ability to reach the realm of muscular truths Paul Simon's lyrics had hinted at. There was an emotional substance to REO Speedwagon's music that critics have not acknowledged to this very day. One afternoon, I was in Kevin Cronin's living room in Thousand Oaks—a living room that, it turned out, had not done any sliding. In fact, it was on flat land. Kevin asked, "Can I play you something? Something I just wrote?" He sat down at his big, black grand piano with the curtained windows behind him looking out on a green lawn and a green, tree-lined street, and launched into "Can't Fight This Feeling." Sometimes you hear something and your rational mind crumbles. Your emotions grow soft. They take you over. They open you with awe. And you almost cry. It's that soul-exchange thing. That's what "Can't Fight This Feeling" did to me. Even sung with just one voice and a piano. "Can't Fight This Feeling" grabbed your self below the floorboards of the self the way that Paul Simon's lyrics had. No wonder the song would eventually hold down the No. 1 position on the charts for three solid weeks.[113]

Then, after three years of touring and pounding the press with amusing anecdotes, we hit a treacherous twist of the earth around the sun called 1981. The American economy went into its biggest nosedive since the crash of 1929. That drop began in November 1980 and lasted until August 1982. In the stock market, the S&P 500 dived from 140.52 to 101.44, losing nearly 30 percent of its value.[114] A whopping big loss.

Nineteen eighty-one was so bad for the record industry that it gave rise to a standing joke. To get it, you have to understand what returns are. If I am a record company and you own a record store, I work hard to get you to stock a hundred copies of my latest priority album. But if you only sell fifty of those albums, you ship the unsold fifty back to me. Those fifty you send back are called "returns." The joke in the industry in 1981 was that, "You ship gold, and you get platinum returns." You ship 500,000 records to the stores. And the stores send you back a million.[115]

In other words, records were simply not selling. With one exception: REO Speedwagon. All that touring was paying off. So was all the publicity—the hundreds of stories, the hundreds of "exposures," a month. Not to mention Kevin Cronin's songwriting. And his vocals. In fact, REO Speedwagon sold fifteen million albums in a year when album sales seemed impossible.

Every record company in sight was laying off employees by the hundreds. But not Epic Records . . . or its parent, Columbia Records, CBS Records. Why? REO Speedwagon.

* * *

The week REO Speedwagon went to No. 1 on the charts, they came to New York. They holed up in a luxury hotel on West Fifty-Sixth Street, close to Black Rock, the huge, ultra-modern black building on Sixth Avenue and Fifty-Third Street that housed CBS. I walked over from my office to see the band members. They probably expected flattery. And congratulations. But that is not what I gave them. I told them this was the most dangerous moment of their career.

What in the world was I talking about? I explained it to them like this. First you wanted to be the biggest frat band in Champaign, Illinois, and you achieved your goal. Then you wanted to be the biggest band in Illinois, and you achieved that goal, too. Then you wanted to be the biggest band in the Midwest, and you did it. Your next goal was clear: to be the biggest band in America. But, instead, you skipped over your goal and became something you thought would come later. Far, far later. You became the biggest band in the world. At every step, you had a step beyond—a higher goal that you were going for. Now you are in desperate need of a next step. A next big goal.

If you perceive what you've just achieved as your final goal, the very end of all your ambitions, you are doomed. Instead, you have to see what you've achieved as climbing to the top of a four-thousand-foot-high mountain and discovering the peaks of the seventeen-thousand-foot mountain range beyond.

Remember the grief of Alexander the Great when he thought that he had conquered the entire world? He went to the top of a mountain and wept, because he had no more worlds to conquer. But, in fact, Alexander was not out of worlds. He had failed to conquer India. Yes, he had tried and failed. Then there was China and Japan, not to mention sub-Saharan Africa. The new worlds Alexander ached for were there waiting. Alexander was not out of worlds. He was out of imagination.

You have to find your next goal. And that goal should be to sustain and grow. Yes, sustaining is one of the hardest things in the world.

REO Speedwagon did not listen to me. And they paid mightily. Word had it that they rented luxury hotel suites in Hawaii with floor-to-ceiling sliding glass doors looking out on the beach. And they stayed in those hotel rooms without opening the curtains. They snorted platters of cocaine and chugged bottles of whiskey. And they lay on their beds staring up at the ceiling. Utterly depressed. Or that was the tale that trickled back to me.

Even worse, REO Speedwagon became caricatures of themselves. Nearly forty years later, they were still playing their hits from the early 1980s. They were not catching fire with anything new.

* * *

So I would preach to REO Speedwagon. But I would also learn from them. I'd learn things that would give me new abilities with the clients yet to come. By the way, REO Speedwagon had the biggest-selling album of 1981. The biggest-selling album of the year would soon become normal for the Howard Bloom Organization Ltd.

* * *

We bond with the people we work with and achieve with. Some of them become the people we love. I loved Kevin Cronin like a brother.

Speaking of people we bond with and love, then came Styx.

32

STYX—THE MAN WHO SAW THE FUTURE

Styx would open my eyes in ways I never imagined. To the ways that group souls can make war.

Styx shared a lot in common with REO Speedwagon. Kevin Cronin came from Chicago. Styx was a Chicago band, a band from the Chicago suburbs. Styx was categorized as heavy metal. So was REO Speedwagon. A huge mistake. Styx and REO were richly melodic. And Styx was a huge touring band with eight Top 40 hits under its belt and a highly distinctive vocalist and songwriter, Dennis DeYoung.

But the city of Chicago never had a Bill Ham—a person who could articulate its cultural uniqueness, sum it up, and try to put it on the map. Instead, it had the Darth Vader of the music industry—an absolutely brilliant man who knew how to put bands on the map but who utterly lacked a moral compass. We may see more of him when we get back to Michael Jackson. Or we may not. One of his talents is the ability to remain invisible.

* * *

At heart, Styx was radically different from REO Speedwagon. Very, very different. Why? It was delivering big-picture messages, geopolitical messages, civilizational messages. And even its manager, one of the brightest men in the music industry, Derek Sutton, didn't realize it.

Derek Sutton had called and offered me Styx. Not only was Styx huge and about to get huger, it was on A&M Records, where I knew and loved the staff. What could go wrong? Something that went right.

This was when everything that I'd done to date—from reading William James's *Varieties of the Religious Experience* at fourteen to working with Chaka Khan, the gay community, and punk—began to crystallize. It began to come together in the approach that I would later call "secular shamanism." A very weird name to come from a science-drenched atheist doing fieldwork in the dark underbelly where new myths and movements are made. But I was on a search for soul. And I hadn't quite found it. Yet.

From the successes of ZZ Top, Joan Jett, REO Speedwagon, and Simon and Garfunkel, I had gained in power. So I made demands from Derek Sutton before I'd work with Styx. First off, I let Derek know that we were unlikely to produce any results until we were six weeks into the campaign. Why? Because I needed to research the band, find good stories, and write our press materials. But there was something more. Before I wrote a word, I wanted a month to get everything on the band in the record company's PR file cabinets, every story ever written on the band, every review and interview. I wanted to study this material, put it in chronological order, and to create a preliminary sketch of the band's story and of its sales hooks—the platinum albums, the records it might have broken, and the praise from high-level critics, which in the case of most of my clients was nonexistent. I wanted to read every lyric and see every album cover. Then came the key point, the whopper. I wanted to spend anywhere from one to three days with the key members of the band—like the time I'd spent with Supertramp but even more intense. I wanted that time in the bandleaders' environment, with no wives or managers anywhere in sight. And I wanted these meetings one at a time. No more crowd interviews like my first meeting with REO Speedwagon. One at a time.

Why? I wanted to dig down to the soul that came alive when the client was in front of a blank page or screen, the soul that wrote the lyrics and the melodies. And I wanted to dig down to the soul that danced the performer when he or she had an out of body experience onstage. You guessed it—I wanted to find the gods inside.

* * *

When I read Dennis DeYoung's lyrics and looked at his album covers, I was staggered. Despite the success of the hit romantic ballad "Lady," Dennis was writing geopolitical albums. He was warning that Western civilization had to wake up or be doomed. Not just Western civilization, American civilization.

To see the importance of Dennis's message, you have to understand where America stood in 1981. In the 1940s, World War II wrecked the industrial base of Europe and Japan. Most of the factories of France, Germany, England, and Japan had been bombed into rubble. But America's factories had grown because of World War II. We had produced the ships, the tanks, and the clothing that had kept Europe going and that had armed our military allies England, China, and Russia. So we emerged from World War II in 1945 as the world's industrial powerhouse. For the next thirty years, we were the world's biggest exporting nation. We turned out half of the world's manufactured goods and possessed more than two thirds of the world's gold.[116]

But that lofty state would not last. Why? Europe and Japan rebuilt their factories. What's more, manufacturing technology had advanced since the days when America's factories had been constructed. So the industrial plants of Japan and Germany were more modern than ours. It took time for Germany and Japan's consumer goods—from cars to radios and TVs—to catch up with ours. But, once they did, Japanese cars replaced American cars on the world market. Germany's BMW and Mercedes-Benz took over the luxury car market from Lincoln and Cadillac. And Japan took the electronics business that had started in the USA and ran with it, putting American electronics-factory workers on unemployment.

What's worse, two other things happened.

In 1973, the Arab nations were pissed off with us for supporting Israel and decided to make a point by cutting our access to oil. America, the world's leader, was suddenly reduced to the status of a beggar. Us Americans waited in lines that it was said were miles long for what little gas we could find. We waited for hours just to tank up. One more thing. To repeat, we were the world's leading exporting nation from roughly 1920 to 1970.[117] But in 1971, America experienced its first modern trade deficit. Since then, our trade deficit has grown like a tumor. In other words, by 1981, America was in trouble. And Dennis DeYoung knew it. It was written all over his lyrics and his album covers.

I flew out to god-knows-where to interview the band. It might have been LA. It might have been Chicago. I was blind to the location. My eye was on Dennis DeYoung's amazing concept albums. I sat down with Dennis in a ground-floor motel room for roughly six hours. And, yes, I'd been right. Dennis was writing prophetic warnings that America could easily go the way of the Easter Islanders, who had erected massive stone monuments—giant stones chiseled into the shape of human heads—then had utterly disappeared.

Derek Sutton is certain to this day that I made the stories of these concept albums up. I did not. The concepts were what Styx had been delivering through a string of nine remarkable albums.

Critics write about words, not music. They respond to stories. And they respond to authenticity. Styx had stories and authenticity in spades. With those stories, we landed Styx in *Rolling Stone*. In a giant feature. Why was that one story in *Rolling Stone* so important? Because *Rolling Stone* is a lead sheep. Where it goes, journalists across the country follow. *Rolling Stone* was validation. It was a signal to the nation's critics to go from putting the band down to seeing its merits. And merits Styx had.

Some indications of those merits? The first Styx album we worked on, *Paradise Theater*, went to No. 1 on the charts, went triple-platinum, had four chart singles, and was one of the biggest-selling albums of 1982.

Meanwhile, Derek Sutton was planning one of the biggest tours America had ever seen. Styx had become such a concert monster that Derek was able to summon all the top concert promoters in America to a summit in LA. At that summit, Derek laid out how each concert would have to be promoted if you were going to win the right to present a Styx show in your city. What Derek explained, step by step, was exciting, smart, fair, and ethically amazing. I was awed. Somehow, Derek had captured the first rule of science—the truth at any price, including the price of your life—in a national concert-tour plan.

But that plan was not to last.

* * *

In the middle of the first concert tour I worked on with Styx, I flew down to Washington to be with the band. They were staying at a Four Seasons Hotel in the Washington suburbs. The entire band and I spent an hour staring at a television set in the living room of one member's suite. Why? The Space Shuttle was about to make its first landing on the surface of the earth after its first, historic flight. With a crew of two, the shuttle had been tested to see if all systems worked. It had been in space for two days, doing thirty-seven orbits of the earth. Now, its crew was going to land the shuttle's entire 195,466 pounds, despite the shuttle's preposterously tiny wings and its 21,000 delicate insulation tiles.

Because the shuttle did not have power—the fuel in its rockets was entirely spent—it couldn't make one attempt at a landing, decide things weren't quite right, accelerate, climb, and try again. It got only one shot at landing a stubby vehicle of a kind no human had ever flown into space and landed before. If the shuttle crashed on entry, America would be seriously embarrassed, but if it landed successfully, America would retain its leadership in the eyes of the world. What did Styx write and perform albums about? The rise and fall of American civilization.

We held our breath as the shuttle glided without power through the atmosphere toward its landing strip. When the wheels touched down on the runway of Edwards Air Force Base in California, we cheered. American civilization was safe from obsolescence and disintegration for another day.

Yes, we—Styx and I—cheered like little boys. We were caught up in an exaltation of group soul. The soul of America.

But that sense of triumph would be short-lived.

* * *

Styx put out another of its concept albums on February 22, 1983, *Kilroy Was Here*. And the entire premise looked ridiculous. At least to me.

The religious right was counterattacking against the hippie values I had helped establish in the 1960s—free love, the drug culture, secularism, questioning traditional family structure, and adventuring outside the box. Right-wing preacher Pat Robertson was spreading the religious right's message via a cable TV channel dedicated to saving America. Robertson preached bringing America back to a very right-wing interpretation of Christ. And Robertson offered a sense of purpose and belonging to people who were lost and alone. If you suffered isolation and a lack of meaning, you could join one of Robertson's 700 Clubs and find fellowship and purpose. You could get on a phone in a room with your teammates and try to save souls. And try to bring in money.

Meanwhile, Jerry Falwell was organizing the Moral Majority, another team dedicated to saving America with the cross. And Jimmy Swaggart was preaching on TV[118] that the gospel must rule America. These evangelical preachers were making frightening progress. On October 3, 1980, presidential candidate Ronald Reagan spoke to a conference of religious broadcasters in Lynchburg, Virginia, to ask for their support. A month later, Reagan was voted president. Now, the religious right had a foothold in the White House.

But the story told by Styx's new album, *Kilroy Was Here*, went way beyond this. It predicted that, in the 1990s, the gospel hawks would burn rock-and-roll records in the streets of America's biggest cities. And that enthusiastic audiences would cheer them on.

Okay, look. It's true that in Florence, Italy, in 1497, a Catholic preacher of gospel hysteria—Girolamo Savonarola[119]—had whipped up a frenzy of hatred against the pop culture of his day, and had led the pious citizens in burning major masterpieces of prose, sculpture, and paintings—the pop culture of the day. Not to mention sinful dresses, vanity-inducing mirrors, cosmetics, playing cards, and musical instruments. It was a miracle that the paintings of Botticelli survived. This social epidemic was called the Bonfire of the Vanities. And, in 1987, Tom Wolfe would seize hold of the phrase for a book and a movie. But the idea of book burnings was a science-fiction cliché. I'd read it in Ray Bradbury's 1953 novel *Fahrenheit 451* when I was ten. The idea was trite, banal, and antique.

But, just in case, I had my staff look for the leading anticensorship organization in America—which turned out to be the National Coalition Against Censorship. And I called its head, Leanne Katz. I explained the plot of *Kilroy Was Here* to Leanne. I also let her know that I thought it was absurd. She disagreed. Totally. "There are record burnings taking place just a short cab ride away from where you're sitting," she said. "They're happening on Long Island. Have you ever heard of the Peters Brothers?" No,

I hadn't. "Let me send you some clippings," said Leanne. A few hours later, a stack of clippings three inches high arrived by messenger. I put them in the middle of my desk and read all of them. I was the stupid one. Dennis DeYoung was right. The Peters Brothers were touring America, supervising record burnings.

So I based our press materials for *Kilroy Was Here* on what Leanne Katz had sent me. And I stayed in frequent contact with her. She would be my guide to a world I hadn't known.

A world in which the Varieties of the Religious Experience wage culture wars. A world in which group souls collide.

* * *

Eventually, Leanne would put me in touch with Skipp Porteous, an expert on the evangelical conservative right. Porteous would clue me into the fact that the religious right was doing more than just luring Republican presidential candidates to its conventions. It had a strategy for taking over America's politics. Completely.

The religious right had noticed that no one pays attention to small, local elections. No one knows anything about the people who run for school boards, city councils, and state senates. So the religious right and its organizations—the Moral Majority, the 700 Club, Christian Voice, and Focus on the Family—ran candidates at all these levels, starting with the smallest, the school boards. Then they used America's churches as propaganda centers, getting their candidates inserted into sermons, slipping literature for their candidates under the windshield wipers of the cars parked in the lots of mega- and mini-churches, and using the computerized national mailing lists organized by a behind-the-scenes genius of the conservative and religious right, Richard Viguerie,[120] in a time when computerized mailing lists were a brand new invention. In those days, laptops and personal computers did not exist. To do something by computer, you needed a machine the size of a living room.

Again, Dennis DeYoung had been so right that it was scary.

Meanwhile J.Y., Styx's bassist, was fascinated with a technology on the brighter end of things, a new innovation called solar energy. I was fascinated by solar energy, too. And it gave us another hook with which to snag press for Styx. So, with help from A&M Records and from a key activist on solar energy, Ty Braswell, J.Y. and I put together the very first public-service radio-advertising campaign for solar power.

Then a very strange thing happened. Derek Sutton, Styx's manager, was a man of extraordinary vision. And with the capacity to deliver extraordinary things. He put 80 percent of his work time into Styx. What he delivered for the band was brilliant. So it came as a shock when Styx fired him. And when they did it right before the biggest tour in their history. A tour for an album that was powerfully prophetic. An album whose message had to get out.

What had happened? From the bits and pieces I was able to pick up, something like this. The band had been wooed by another manager. But not just any other manager. A manager who had been a genius at putting bands on the map. That manager had apparently seduced the band with two things: cocaine and flattery. When he had the band in an inebriated state, he had told them they could achieve a greatness far beyond the dreams of a mere Derek Sutton. They could reach heights they had never imagined. But only this new manager could take them to that level of exaltation.

Styx ditched Derek and went to the new manager. I was appalled. This was poor judgment up the kazoo. But the band kept me and my company.

Who was this new manager? Remember Joe Walsh on his hands and knees muttering incoherently in his fourth-floor room at the Warwick Hotel on Manhattan's West Fifty-Fourth Street? Remember the one eye exposed by the two-inch opening of Joe's door, the tiny man who asked that I go away? His name was Irving Azoff. And his track record was spectacular. He had built the careers of the Eagles and Dan Fogelberg. He would go on to work with Harry Styles, Christina Aguilera, Journey, Van Halen, Thirty Seconds to Mars, Steely Dan, Maroon 5, No Doubt, Gwen Stefani, Triumph, Fleetwood Mac, and Bon Jovi. And he would build an empire, controlling the American touring industry by merging his management company, Frontline, first with Ticketmaster, the major seller of concert tickets, then with Live Nation Entertainment, which controlled most of the venues in which artists perform, not to mention owning the promotional apparatus essential to putting on a concert, and owning roughly 140 artist-management companies—companies that managed an astonishing 500 artists.[121]

As a manager, Irving Azoff was one of a kind. Most managers achieve prominence by lucking out and having a band that hits with or without them. David Bowie, in the case of Tony Defries. Hall and Oates, in the case of Tommy Mottola. KISS, in the case of Bill Aucoin, whose strange story we will get to later. That one accidental stroke of lightning gives others in the music industry the impression that these managers are men of genius. (And, yes, once again, almost all were men.) It usually also gives the manager himself the illusion that he knows how to make careers. But most of these managers don't have a clue. They have no idea of how to do it again.

Irving Azoff was one of the very few managers who knew how to make it happen more than once. In fact, Irving was one of the very few managers who knew how to play the instrument I had worked so hard to learn—the star-making machine. He was the only one, aside from ZZ Top's Bill Ham and Prince's Bob Cavallo, whose astonishing tale we will get to in a bit. But, as I mentioned before, Irving had no moral compass. Look how he managed Joe Walsh. And the word that oozed out on the Eagles, the same word that they committed to their lyrics in "Life in the Fast Lane," was that they, too, were part of the cocaine brigade. In other words, for all his brilliance, it appeared that Irving was controlling his acts with drugs.[122]

What did Irving Azoff's peculiar approach do for Styx? *Kilroy Was Here* should have been one of the biggest tours in rock history. Dennis DeYoung and the band had commissioned stage sets to take you through the story of Dennis's dark view of the coming 1990s along with the songs. Dennis's underlying idea was on target. And Dennis, like REO Speedwagon's Kevin Cronin, has a unique voice—a voice that can hit you emotionally even if you think you hate the band. A voice that can summon your invisible self, your gods inside.

But the *Kilroy Was Here* tour and album were failures compared to Styx's previous album and their Paradise Theater tour. *Paradise Theater*, the last album before Irving, was one in a string of four triple-platinum LPs. Yes, four triple-platinum albums in a row. Something few bands ever achieve. But *Kilroy Was Here* sold roughly a third of what the previous albums had. It merely went platinum. Single platinum. And the *Kilroy Was Here* tour was the one that spelled the end of the band. At the Capital Center in Landover, Maryland, guitarist Tommy Shaw smashed his guitar, threw the pieces into the audience, and stomped offstage.[123] Tommy has admitted he was having drug problems. But guess who I suspect uses drugs to control his acts? Irving Azoff.

You could get a sense of why things were collapsing from the way Azoff's office dealt with us. The goal of Irving's staff wasn't to get the maximum press and the maximum respect for Styx on this tour. It wasn't even to sell the maximum number of concert tickets and albums. Azoff's aim had nothing to do with furthering the interests of Styx. His aim was something radically different. It was to cement control over the band. It was to get rid of us. To get the band to fire the Howard Bloom Organization Ltd. Azoff's PR person and personal assistant was Larry Solters, who will become important to this story once again when we get to the crucifixion of Michael Jackson. Solters tried to make sure that we did not receive the schedule of tour dates until it was too late to do anything about them. Then he could go to the band and say, "Look, you've got to fire these bozos. You just had three major dates, and Bloom's office didn't get you a word of press."

We figured out how to get the dates with sufficient lead time, in spite of Irving's office. But it wasn't easy. And building the band to the heights that Irving had apparently promised was never his goal. In fact, he seemed to be aiming at the opposite: splitting the band up. Word was that Azoff's people, using the tools of cocaine and flattery, were swelling guitarist Tommy Shaw's head and convincing him that he was really the backbone of the band, and that Styx would be better off if Dennis DeYoung was ejected from the outfit. Or that's the way it looked from the outside. And, indeed, the band did break up.

So Irving Azoff, the Darth Vader of the music business, destroyed Styx. And *Paradise Theater*, the last Styx album managed by Derek Sutton, was the band's best-selling LP. Ever. Remember, it went triple-platinum. Despite Dennis DeYoung's brilliance, it was all downhill from there.

Yes, Virginia, there are villains. And we'll see more of the villain of the Styx story later.

33

QUEEN, SOUL, SOUTH AMERICA

In 1980, the managers of Queen, the band I'd worked for once but had never met, tracked me down and asked me to handle a whoppingly big project. Queen was at the peak of its success. Five years earlier, in 1975, "Bohemian Rhapsody" had shown that Queen was utterly unique. And the song "Crazy Little Thing Called Love" had just gone to No. 1 in the USA and stayed there for four solid weeks. What's more, Queen was huge all over the world. And I do mean all over. So now Queen was planning something that this planet had never seen: a rock-and-roll stadium tour in South America.

To understand an audacious move like this, it's helpful to understand an article on Queen that my mushy memory says was written by Robert Hilburn, a god of the rock-crit elite and the chief music journalist for the *Los Angeles Times*. Hilburn can't find it in his computer files and doesn't remember it. But whoever wrote it, it was stunningly insightful. The headline was "Pretension." Normally, that's a negative word. Normally it's an accusation and a denunciation. But here the writer turned the meaning upside down and pointed out the word's positives. Pretension is when you aim for something impossibly high. And pretension, said the article, is when you achieve it. Freddy Mercury's "Bohemian Rhapsody," for example, was pretentious. It was an effort to combine the sensibilities of opera and intellect with raw, melodic rock and roll. And guess what? It worked.

A soccer-stadium tour of South America was an even higher impossible goal. Why? To mount stadium tours in the United States or Europe takes an infrastructure. It takes a highly experienced concert promoter in each city that you're going to visit. An expert who knows how to advertise, publicize, and staff a venue with security, ushers, and other skilled personnel. A promoter with a solid track record who knows, most of all, how to sell tickets. And a promoter with a well-established reputation for honestly splitting up the cash at the end of the night. It also takes companies that have been building stages, sound systems, and lighting systems for years, and have the art down pat. Touring stages, sound systems, and lighting systems that you can truck from one city to another, erect in fourteen hours, knock down and pack in trucks in three hours, then take to another city and erect in fourteen hours again. Not to mention the trucks, drivers, and roadies who know exactly how to take these massive systems down, pack them away, and put them up again without a flaw. There was no way of knowing if an infrastructure of this kind existed in South America. And, when push came to shove, it turned out there wasn't. But Queen's managers found that out the hard way.

They researched the South American companies that claimed to have these areas of expertise, set up meetings, and flew down to South America to work out contracts. The South American contractors said they were absolutely capable of achieving what Queen would need. The dominant phrase from the South American contractors was "no problem." Six months passed. Queen's managers went back down to South America to see how things were going. And they made a discovery: nothing was being done. Nothing at all. They discovered South America's *mañana* attitude—we'll do it tomorrow. "No problem." So the managers came back to the Northern Hemisphere, called in experts from the United States and Europe, put them on the case, then rented a Boeing 747 and flew the needed equipment—the modules of a stage, a sound system, scaffolding, and a lighting system—down from North America.

What did Queen's managers want me to do? They would pay all the expenses to fly a dozen key journalists down to the tour date in Buenos Aires, Argentina. And they would pay to fly me down with one of my account executives. The rock-crit elite can't resist free travel. So we got rock writers from the *New York Times*, the *Los Angeles Times*, and *Rolling Stone*. Not to mention Lisa Robinson.

Lisa was the queen of the rock-crit elite. She'd been editor of *Hit Parader*—not a prestige position. Yet she was the one person in New York who could throw a party and be certain that all the rock-crit elite members in town would come. Her summons was like a summons from royalty. And Robinson often dictated which stars should be adored, which should be ignored, and which should be despised. So it was a shock when Lisa Robinson said she'd come, and that she'd bring her right-hand woman, her sister, the hidden heart of her operation.

We all packed ourselves into a plane only to discover that the latest model of supersized Boeing luxury jets looked more like buses when they were headed for South America. The folks crowded into coach seats were hauling TV sets, microwave ovens, and, it seemed, washing machines as carryon luggage. If they could have carried sheep, goats, chickens, and llamas, it looked like they would have. But, frankly, there were better sheep, goats, chickens, and llamas in South America. However, it appears that many South Americans in 1981 looked at the USA as a convenient shopping mall, just a quick eleven-hour jet flight away.

I sat up front. In first class. God knows why. The journalists sat in the back. If I'd had my choice, I would have been back there doing all I could to bond with these thorny clique members I normally despised.

But the real revelations would come when we were comfortably settled in a Buenos Aires hotel, given some rest and relaxation, allowed to walk around in the city, then driven in a bus to the suburban soccer stadium where Queen was playing. First of all, you have to realize something. Football was big in America. In 1981, the NFL teams had stadiums that seated between 55,000 (Shea Stadium in New York City) and 80,000 (Pontiac Silverdome, in Pontiac, Michigan). And when folks are trying to tell you that something is truly huge these days, they tell you that it occupies as much space as a football stadium. But soccer is twice as big in Europe and South America. How can you tell? To repeat, American football and baseball stadiums seated an average of roughly 70,000 in 1981. Those were the stadiums that ZZ Top played. But European and South American soccer stadiums were nearly twice that size. They seated 120,000. Yes, 120,000. More than the entire population of Odessa, Texas; Evansville, Indiana; or Allentown, Pennsylvania. Keep that in mind. You'll need it to understand how I got involved with Bob Marley.

Normally, I had an all-access pass and could go anywhere I wanted in the theater or stadium. Not this time. Argentina had been a violent anarchy and now was under the rule of a military dictatorship. Between 15,000 and 30,000 citizens had been "disappeared." There were uniformed men armed with submachine guns on the streets. Including the suburban streets of peaceful, single-family homes with lawns that our bus cruised through on its way to the stadium. So we press visitors were rigidly confined. We were allocated a row of seats at the very back of the stadium. The nosebleed seats, high in the air, where the humongous stage looked like a shrunken postage stamp. And where the band members looked smaller than bed bugs.

When Queen took to the stage, they were just a tad smaller than the periods on this page. We really could not see them. But when the band got to "We Are the Champions," they taught me a lesson. One hundred and twenty thousand people rose from their seats, stood, lit cigarette lighters, held them high in the air, and sang. Queen had accomplished an extreme feat for the individual and the collective soul. The band had roused the human spirit in ways it's hard to describe in mere typed words. With an audience that didn't even speak the English language. We were all caught up in a sense of being lifted out of our personal predicaments to something higher and more exhilarating than ourselves. In that moment, Queen taught me the power of an anthem. And that power would later save my life, when I would try to kill myself. But that's a subject for another book.

When the show was over, Fred Schruers from *Rolling Stone* somehow managed to get backstage and take pictures with the camera slung around his neck. Turned out that some of the normal-looking civilians around him were plainclothes police. One of them demanded Fred's film. When Fred refused to hand it over, he recalls, "One of the gray-suited evil Argentine cops in their gray Falcons grabbed my hand, held it under my nose with the webbing between thumb and forefinger exposed, and put a nasty little cigar-cutter blade up against that. Made me pull out the film and expose it."[124]

Argentina was not the home of the free and the brave, the home of freedom of the press.

* * *

Did I meet Queen? Well, sort of. The managers set up a meeting for me in our Buenos Aires hotel with lead guitarist Brian May. Brian had done his graduate thesis on the properties of cosmic dust, so I felt at home. And I met with Roger Taylor, the band's drummer, who, with Brian May, had founded Smile, the band that became Queen. But the real story of Queen was Freddie Mercury, a gay man of Iranian descent who had grown up as a part of an oppressed minority, a Zoroastrian, in the Muslim Sultanate of Zanzibar, and in Bombay, India. A man whose real name was Farrokh Bulsara. A man who didn't arrive in England until he was seventeen, and who came with his family fleeing a Zanzibarian revolution in which people like him were being slaughtered. A singer with a four-octave range. A man who dared to be audacious. And, for the second time, Freddie Mercury evaded me. Maybe for the better. It wasn't until seventeen years later that I'd discover the power of an anthem to save lives. Including mine. It wasn't until seventeen years later that I'd discover the power of the music of Queen. The power of what poured from Freddie Mercury's soul.

But the sight of 120,000 raised lighters was burned into my memory.

And I learned two lessons:

1. The importance of anthems to the human spirit.
2. The sheer size of the world's soccer stadiums, a lesson I'd need if I was going to solve a problem that faced Bob Marley.

34

BOB MARLEY—
TURNING DYING INTO LIVING

In 1980, Chris Blackwell, the man who put reggae on the map, had a new assignment for me.

Blackwell's Island Records was bursting with talents. But he had a problem. To see Chris's predicament, let's go back a decade to the 1970s. In 1970, Chris Blackwell had had a vision of how to get Jamaica's music across to a rock-and-roll audience. He had come to know that rock-and-roll audience intimately through his work with the rock acts he had signed to his Island Records label—the Spencer Davis Group, Traffic, Steve Winwood, King Crimson, and Cat Stevens. Blackwell's vision showed a path to get across Jamaica's black music to a white audience. The rock audience.

Blackwell invested in a film to get that idea across. What idea did Chris want to rouse in the hidden heart of Western civilization? An idea of mythic rebellion. But with a black Jamaican as its hero. The film was *The Harder They Come*. And the artist at the center of the film, Jimmy Cliff, was the man Blackwell positioned to embody that rebel image—an image like that of Jimi Hendrix but with a Caribbean twist. However, Jimmy Cliff put Blackwell's plan on hold. He left Island Records to make more money at a bigger label. So Chris was left dangling. He had a plan, but he didn't have a man.

Then a twenty-six-year-old Bob Marley walked into his office and turned out to be the real deal. More than that, Marley would become Blackwell's flagship artist.

When Chris Blackwell began his relationship with Bob Marley, the reggae master was utterly unknown. But thanks in large part to Chris's efforts, that would change. In the beginning, Blackwell advised Marley and his bandmates to become "a tight road band, capable of touring."[125] Like a rock band. Chris knew the secret of artist development, of building album acts. He knew the secret of the star-making machine. He knew the importance of touring. The result: by 1980, Marley was a legend worldwide. And he was a stadium-filler. Which brings us back to the lesson of Queen in South America: most American football and baseball stadiums at that point had roughly 70,000 seats. But European and South American soccer stadiums were nearly twice as big. They had seats for between 80,000 and 120,000.

Here was Chris Blackwell's problem. Bob Marley could sell out any soccer stadium in Europe or Africa. But he could not come anywhere near packing even a measly football stadium in North America. Could I solve the problem, asked Chris?

Yes, of course I could. I explained something simple. In America, Bob had built a fandom of white kids on college campuses—the rock audience that Chris had targeted. But Marley had never built a base of fans in the black community. There were two reasons. One, Marley's previous publicists had done a fantastic job. But they didn't know the black media. It was invisible to them. So they had never worked it. Two, there is a split in the black community that worked against Bob viciously. Island blacks and American blacks hated each other.

How did I, a white man, know this? Back in 1962, when I'd been inadvertently helping kick off the hippie movement, I'd been riding illegally in an empty boxcar from Berkeley to Stockton, California—a hub where freight trains stop, are taken apart, and are reassembled at the far end of the yard, then reshuffled so that the cars going to the same destination are all linked together in a long chain. When we reached Stockton, and I got out of my boxcar, I saw another man getting out of the same train roughly a quarter of a mile behind me. This made us brothers. Functional bonding. So I waited for him to catch up with me, then we took the long walk to the center of the freight yard together. He was black. He had just come from LA. Or, as he saw it, he had just escaped from LA. What was so bad about LA, I wanted to know. "The black people," he said with clenched teeth. "They lie, they cheat, they steal, and if you stick around long enough, they'll kill you." "But," I said, "you're black. How could you say such a thing?" Then he explained that he was from the islands of the Caribbean. And island blacks and American blacks do not like each other.

Bob was an island black. He did not have a natural base in the American black community. But I'd schooled myself to be the leading black publicist in the industry. I felt I knew exactly how to get Marley the black base that would beef up his audience dramatically. The analysis made sense to Chris. So he took me to a meeting.

* * *

At the head of a conference table somewhere a few blocks north of Times Square sat Percy Sutton, former borough president of Manhattan, former attorney for Malcolm X, a civil rights activist who had been jailed with Stokely Carmichael, a confidante of New York mayor David Dinkins and of New York state governor Basil Patterson. Sutton headed the leading black radio chain in North America, Inner City Broadcasting, whose holdings included radio stations in eight cities, two cable joint ventures with Time Warner, and the black station that set national trends, WBLS.[126]

The black station whose receptionist had made a mistake and put me on the phone with the Reverend Al Sharpton.

I was in the middle of the right-hand side of the table. Chris Blackwell was at the table's foot. And directly across from me was a god, a legend . . . Bob Marley.

At the table's head was Percy Sutton. Sutton started the meeting with a long speech about Marley's importance. Bob, he said, had a significance just a tad less than that of Jesus Christ. Well, maybe in reality a tad more. Sutton said this as if Bob were the only audience in the room. How did Sutton know Marley's towering influence? Percy had just come from a trip to Africa. Then Sutton launched into a description of the inefficiencies of African record pressing. Inefficiencies like those Bob had been forced to fight when he and his crew had pressed their own records in Jamaica. But that was not Percy's point. In Africa, Sutton said, Bob was worshipped as a saint. Once the praises and African anecdotes were over, it was time to get down to business.

How could Bob Marley perform a concert in New York that would reflect his global stature? The fact was that Bob could only sell thirty thousand tickets in the Big Apple. That would land him two nights at Madison Square Garden. Two nights that would look pathetic, because the second night would not be sold out. What in the world could be done?

I had an answer. The Beacon Theater. The Beacon Theater is a high-prestige, gorgeous, acoustically perfect theater uptown at Seventy-Fourth Street and Broadway, in the middle of the upscale Upper West Side, a neighborhood in which the black community and the white gentrifiers lived side by side. And the real magic: the Beacon Theater has only 2,894 seats. Bob Marley could sell thirty thousand tickets in New York City. That's ten nights at the Beacon Theater. Ten nights with a hungry audience of those who were not able to buy tickets and were not able to get in. Ten sold-out nights. In the music industry, you have to leave an audience hungry. The more hunger, the higher the word of mouth will be the next time you come back into town. That's one of the most important lessons of touring strategy. A lesson I'd applied with Joan Jett.

Ten sold-out nights in New York is a headline. It's news. And it's growth. In 1976, Marley had played the Beacon, but only for two nights, with two sets per night. Two sets per night was a mistake. It made it look like Marley had only managed two nights. There are times when making yourself look small is valuable. But this was not one of them.

The idea of ten nights at the Beacon was adopted immediately. So I'd had an opportunity to shine in Bob's eyes. And in those of Percy Sutton. Which would come in handy a few years later. With Tommy Mottola, and Hall and Oates. But we'll get to that in a bit.

Next, I did my thing. I spent a month reading every clipping I could find about Bob, every interview and feature story. What struck me the hardest was the gang culture that underlay Rastafarianism.

* * *

In 1976, there had been outright warfare in the Rasta world. Gang warfare. Gang members were murdering their rivals. So Bob Marley planned a Christmas Day concert to pull the rival factions back together: a peace concert, the Smile Jamaica concert. The posters for the concert went up all over Jamaica in October. Then, two days before the December 25 concert, Marley was rehearsing at his home, a home filled with members of his entourage, the home at 56 Hope Road that Bob called Tuff Gong. Bob left the rehearsal room where he'd been practicing with his band members. He was hungry. He moseyed into the crowded kitchen, picked up a grapefruit, and began to peel it.[127] He didn't know it yet, but, according to *Rolling Stone*, "a carload of assassins"[128] had driven up to Tuff Gong. One of the gunmen appeared on the stairs outside the kitchen door, firing fast and wild. Don Taylor, Bob's manager, "took four shots in the groin."

According to Chris Salewicz, the former articles editor of Britain's *New Musical Express* who developed a friendship with Bob, and who was privy to inside information, Bob's wife, Rita, was driving up to the house. She was still outside "the lion-encrusted wrought-iron gate of the property." One of the hail of bullets skimmed across Rita's scalp, leaving her bloody but not seriously damaged. But there was more to come. One of the gunmen ran up to Rita's car to finish her off. She played dead, and the killer ran off to take care of other business.

Meanwhile, four of Bob's entourage ran into the bathroom and piled on top of each other in the metal tub. Bob ran from the kitchen and jumped in on top of them, knocking the faucet knob and pouring water on the five Rastas below him. It was only after the shooters left that his musicians noticed that Bob was rubbing his arm. A bullet had ricocheted off the kitchen wall and had wounded him. Chris Salewicz says, "If he had been inhaling instead of exhaling, the bullet would have gone into his heart."[129]

Then the police showed up at the house, looking for four of Marley's kids. But there's something you need to know about the Jamaican police. They, too, were unpredictable and dangerous gunmen. Especially when they encountered Rastas. This was closer to a visit by a second gang than an outreach from helpers anxious to restore the peace.

Marley was taken to the hospital, where the doctors concluded that his wound was superficial and bandaged him up. But Bob had almost lost his life. The gang after him was still at large. Where could he be safe? Says Salewicz, Bob was driven up "the road of 365 curves that leads to Chris Blackwell's home of Strawberry Hill in the

Blue Mountains, overlooking Kingston," overlooking the city from the lofty altitude of three thousand feet. And "a police guard was mounted around the premises." Reports Salewicz, Marley, like a Lion of Judah, was not frightened, he was furious. He was convinced that fifty-six bullets had been fired at him—the number of his address, 56 Hope Road. And he prophesied. He predicted with holy conviction that the men who had tried to assassinate him would also die in a rain of fifty-six bullets.[130]

But would Bob Marley and the Wailers do the Smile Jamaica concert? The gunmen who'd attacked him were still on the loose. Lord knows what they might do next. Says Salewicz, Rita went home to find one of Jamaica's leading politicians, Tony Spaulding, a man who pork-barreled his base by building housing for the poor. According to CBS news, Spaulding was an "architect of Jamaica's gang system."[131] Adds Salewicz, Spaulding was also the builder of the Tony Spaulding Sports Complex. Spaulding was "speaking on a walkie-talkie to Bob at Strawberry Hill. 'He was telling him he has to do the concert; the people were waiting on him; he had to show them he had overcome this,' said Judy."[132] Judy is Judy Mowatt, a member of Bob's backup singing group, the I-3s.

But Bob was up against a dilemma that I'd soon be schooled about by John Mellencamp. When we build a figure up to mythic proportions, we sometimes expect things that are beyond human powers. You'd think that Bob Marley, the voice of freedom, would have had unalloyed courage about his upcoming concert. Courage without a single doubt. But that's not what Salewicz reports. Bob was as human as you and me. He had second thoughts. Judy Mowatt told Salewicz, "Bob was kind of iffy . . . Bob was asking everybody's opinion. He asked me, 'Judy, wha' ya t'ink?'"[133]

Originally, Bob Marley and his band, the Wailers, had been scheduled to do only one song at the Smile Jamaica concert. Instead, when they hit the stage of the National Heroes Park in Kingston, they played a ninety-minute set. To an audience of eighty thousand.

The concert left its mark. Wikipedia has an entire entry devoted to the event.[134] Jamaican TV would create a morning show called Smile Jamaica, named after the concert. And the courage with which a wounded Bob Marley had risen above his would-be killers would become a part of the Marley legend.

* * *

I was beginning to feel my way toward what would later blossom as secular shamanism. I asked Chris Blackwell to let me meet with Bob Marley for a day alone in Bob's environment. I should have specified Jamaica. But Bob was not in Jamaica at that moment. He was in his home in Miami. So I flew down to Miami to meet the King of Reggae.

Bob's Miami home was a rambling one-story ranch house surrounded by green lawn and foliage. It was three times the size of Bill Ham's one-story house/management office in Houston.[135] But it was nothing special, and it told me nothing about Bob. It was the house any accountant who had moved up to VP would have purchased with pride. I didn't realize it, but meeting with Bob alone took him totally out of his context. He was normally surrounded by a small tribe of roughly twenty-five men of whom he was the chief, the undisputed leader. I would see that later.

I had an intense three-hour interview with Bob. I used both my usual notepad and a cassette recorder to get it all down. And it was all incomprehensible. I couldn't understand Bob's patois. His Jamaican creole. But two clues jumped out of the confusion. Bob told me he'd been in one of the clubs in which Rasta gangs entertain themselves by killing each other. These gang clubs were frequently raided by the police. And, in those raids, people were shot. Shot dead. Bob explained that he was in one of these clubs when he felt a hand on his shoulder. A hand telling him it was time to go. So Bob exited the club. And, a few minutes later, the club was raided. When Bob sang, "I Shot the Sheriff," he wasn't talking about imaginary cowboy movies. He was talking about real confrontations with the police in which real people died.

Clue number two: as I was leaving the living room in which Bob and I had our session, I turned from the door for a second and said, "If you ever need anything in New York, let me know." Bob did, indeed, need something. Haile Selassie had given a speech to the League of Nations in New York in 1936.[136] Bob wanted a copy of the *New York Times* story reporting on the speech. In those pre-Google days, clips like these were hard to find. But I said yes.

What had Bob been hinting at with these two clues?

1. Haile Selassie was God.
2. God himself had tapped Bob on the shoulder in that Jamaican club. In other words, Bob Marley was a prophet of God.

Or that's the message I got.

A few months later, I saw Bob in a milieu that gave away more of who he was. Bob was in New York. He was staying at the Essex House, a hotel we'll see more of in the future. A hotel whose rooms looked out over Central Park. When I entered Bob's suite, the furniture had been cleared out or pushed up against the wall. Six or seven members of Bob's entourage, his tribe, his gang, were doing their various things in the huge living room. It felt as if there were a fire in the middle of the room with a goat being roasted on a spit. There was no fire. And there was no goat. The hotel management would have frowned on such a thing. But the feel of Bob as a leader of his own tiny tribe was so strong that the image of the goat and the fire has lingered in my memory much more vividly than the details of the actual room.

* * *

The first step in our campaign was to establish Bob Marley in the black press and in the black community. As you've seen, there are black weekly papers all over North America, and they are starved for content. They need news. And, even more important, they need photos. Bob had a dedicated tour photographer who traveled with him from one concert to another. So we called her, had her come to our office, and had her bring stacks and stacks of slide sheets, thousands and thousands of photos. Then we went through them looking for photos that could be hooked to news stories. And we began a regular flood of photos with captions that told stories to the black press. Genuine stories.

Six months later, everything was going like clockwork. Slowly but surely, through the Chinese-water-torture method of press visibility, the machine-gun method of PR, we were building a familiarity with Bob in the black community. An ownership of Bob. An ego stake. All the kinds of things that would later be important in maintaining the loyalty of that base for Michael Jackson and his brothers.

Then I got a call. Bob Marley had cancer. It had spread through his body. It was incurable.

* * *

Rastafarians do not believe in Western medicine. Bob had initially had cancer in a toe.[137] But he had refused to go to a Western doctor. Now that cancer had metastasized. Cells from the cancer in his toe had entered his bloodstream and had traveled to distant parts of his body, then had set up shop. It's this metastasization that makes cancer deadly. Now, Bob was holed up in Switzerland near an alternative doctor. His whole crew, the twenty-five people who went with him everywhere, was there. Chris Blackwell had a special assistant delegated solely to Bob. She was British. And she, too, was with Bob. She called me on the phone and explained that, from now on, I had a new job.

Every day, Bob got up, went down to breakfast at his Swiss chalet, and had newspapers from all over the world spread out around his breakfast plate. If any one of those papers said that Bob Marley was dying of cancer, he would leave the table without eating breakfast, go back up to his room, and sit in the darkness all day long. But if not a single paper said a word about his cancer, he would eat his breakfast, then go out on the lawn and play soccer in the sunshine with his retinue.

In other words, I had a new assignment. You and I could die at any minute. We could easily perceive ourselves as having a terminal illness: life. Why? All lives end in death. Including yours and mine. In other words, one way or the other, death is in our future. But we can make a choice. With every minute, we can perceive ourselves as living, or we can perceive ourselves as dying.

My job: make sure that Bob perceived every minute of his last year as living. So I collected anecdotes about what Bob was up to all week long. Then I came in early on Monday mornings to a stack of messages from Italy, Spain, and Sweden. Journalists wanted to know how Bob was. I told them the stories. I only kept two things from them. Bob's location in Switzerland. And cancer.

Why did Bob want to mislead the press about his location? Photos of him sold to tabloid newspapers for a fortune. The paparazzi were hunting Marley like a rare animal. Once, there had been a photographer planted on a Swiss road with a lens the size of a very big backyard telescope hoping Bob would pass. Bob wanted me to insist that he was in Ethiopia. The Rastafarians' paradise.

My goal was to overwhelm journalists with accurate details. Accurate, as you know, minus the location. And minus Bob's prognosis. I hate lying with a passion. My whole life has been dedicated to truth. And I've put myself in the path of death in order to defend veracity. Literally. But Bob's life was far more important than the accuracy of his location.

* * *

After ten months of this, I got a phone call. It came from the assistant Chris Blackwell had provided to Marley. "Bob doesn't need you anymore," she said. The unspoken message was brutal: Bob Marley had given up on living. I came close to tears. In fact, I come close to tears all over again every time I tell this story. I'm close to them right now typing this to you.

How in the world can you come so close to someone you do not feel you understand?

* * *

Three years later, I got a call from Richard Branson's new US music company, Virgin Records. The company's two co-presidents, Jordan Harris and Jeff Ayeroff, were among the best people I'd worked with when they were at A&M Records. You'd think they would have used me often. But, in fact, they used me never. So why was their company calling? They had a new artist. The artist's mother had told Virgin that their family had its own publicist, and that if they wanted to work with her, they were going to have to work with me. That mother was named Rita. Rita Marley, Bob's wife. The woman whose scalp had been skimmed by a bullet. A power in Bob's life. A legend. And a woman I had never met in person or even spoken with on the phone. The son she was launching on a musical career? Ziggy Marley.

So, yes, we launched Ziggy Marley's career. And I will be forever grateful to Rita, a woman I never spoke with even once.

* * *

One more gift that Bob gave me. One of the members of his extended tribe was Danny Sims. In roughly the late 1950s, Danny Sims had started Sapphire,[138] a soul food restaurant just off Times Square that attracted diners like Harry Belafonte, Sidney Poitier, and Ossie Davis. Sims was partnered with one of the very first reggae stars, Johnny Nash, writer and singer of the song "I Can See Clearly Now," which hit No. 1 on the pop charts in 1972. Seven years earlier, in roughly 1965, Sims and Nash had founded the JODA Records label in New York, then had discovered the Cowsills, a family group from Newport, Rhode Island, who would score a three-million-selling single in 1967, with "The Rain, the Park, and Other Things."[139] What's more, though Sims was black, he managed the white pop star Paul Anka, a teen idol and songwriter who had churned out tunes in the Brill Building. The building that would later be bought by Paul Simon and Lorne Michaels. A black manager for a white star was a one-of-a-kind phenomenon.

As if that weren't enough, Sims and Nash put together concerts in the Caribbean and South America. But the real topper would flick to the surface in Jamaica. Sims and Nash discovered they could record albums for surprisingly low cost in the island of Rasta. But one more thing drove Sims to set up a home in Jamaica—the FBI.

It was the middle of the 1960s, and black riots were erupting in Harlem, Chicago, Washington, Detroit, Baltimore, Cleveland, Rochester, Newark, and Los Angeles.[140] Those riots had major consequences for Danny Sims. Here's how Sims tells the tale in Chris Salewicz's *Bob Marley: The Untold Story*.

Sims convinced his partner, singer Johnny Nash, to make an R&B record, a rhythm and blues record, a song aimed at the black charts. It was called "Let's Move and Groove Together," and, Sims says, it went to No. 1 on the R&B chart. Sims decided to make a commercial for the record to push its sales even farther. But, without Sims's knowledge, the maker of the commercial put these words into the ad: "Burn, baby, burn."

It was not a good time in which to use that line. Blacks were torching neighborhoods in Chicago, Detroit, and Watts. And the residents of other cities were afraid that they would be next. Sims swears that the FBI phoned, concerned that he was calling for more riots of fire. "Danny," Sims says the FBI told him, "we finally got you." Explains Sims, "We thought we were going to get killed by the CIA and the FBI, for 'inciting a riot.'" So Sims and his partner, Johnny Nash, moved to Jamaica. Says Sims, "Jamaica was a place to get away from the shooting."

But Danny Sims had one more claim to fame, and it was a big one. He'd discovered Bob Marley. Well, actually, Sims's partner, Johnny Nash, had discovered Bob Marley. Nash was religious tourist-ing. He was curious about the Rasta religion. So he took his girlfriend "to west Kingston on 7 January 1968, the Ethiopian Christmas Day; taking place there was a ceremony at which the Nyabinghi rituals of drumming and chanting were enacted—a groun-ation."[141] A groun-ation is a religious dance-and-trance ritual of the sort that summoned the god of thunder, Chango, into the bodies of men and women in Africa. Like something out of *The Varieties of the Religious Experience*, it was a deliberate summoning of the gods inside.

Bob and Rita Marley were present, sharing the "chalice" of marijuana that made the rounds of the participants. Says Chris Salewicz, "Nash couldn't believe the number of beautiful, clearly commercial songs Bob Marley sang and had also written."[142]

But when Marley bicycled up the hill for his first meeting at Sims and Nash's posh Jamaican home in Russell Heights, Salewicz writes, "the maid refused to serve Bob food," the neighbors complained, and the snooty uptown girls hanging out retreated to the rear of the house. Why? Rastas were as downscale as the untouchables in India. Maybe just a bit more downscale.

Most Rastas lived a subsistence lifestyle, eating what they raised in their own gardens and going out to sea to bring home fish for dinner. So Danny Sims signed Bob Marley for management and publishing and paid Bob, his wife Rita, and one of Bob's musicians, Peter Tosh, one hundred dollars a week apiece—a fortune to a Rasta. Over the course of time, Bob would record 211 songs for Sims. Then, when Chris Blackwell came along, Blackwell would be forced to buy Marley out of his contract with Sims, and out of a deal that Sims had obtained for Marley with CBS. But Sims would retain that magic way of making money without working: publishing. And he would get two percent of every album Marley sold. Easy money.

Danny adopted me. He had me up to his apartment on Fifth Avenue and 105th Street near Harlem several times. You removed your shoes at the door. Then you stepped into what looked like a fifteen-room apartment, an apartment that was huge. Huge and overrun with a tribe, like Marley's, but a tribe where goats and fires would have been completely inappropriate. This was more like a well-behaved Harlem gang.

When Danny was out in LA and I was out there, too, Danny invited me to visit him. He was at the posh Beverly Wilshire Hotel. It was eleven in the morning. I was ushered into the bedroom. Danny was naked in the bed, covered by a sheet. Next to him, also naked beneath the sheets, was his girlfriend, Beverly Johnson, the first black model to ever appear on the cover of *Vogue*. The two of them were holding court. Danny was sunny and extremely good-looking. So was Beverly, a warm and open woman. With their stunningly erect postures and their welcoming smiles, Danny and Beverley looked like an African king and queen.

When we were both back in New York, Danny told me he wanted to introduce me to someone and booked a lunchtime meeting. I walked from Fifty-Fifth Street over to Second Avenue near Sixtieth Street. The location was an Italian restaurant. But when I walked in, the place was empty. At the height of lunchtime. A very good way to throw out ten thousand dollars in revenue. The place had been cleared specifically for us. Danny took me to a table at the very back. Waiting for us in a padded booth was a gnarled little old man. Danny introduced us. Our elderly host had an Italian name. He was the restaurant's owner. He revealed nothing about himself during the course of the lunch. I wondered why Danny had invited me.

My guess is that I was an amusing exhibition. An entertainment. Like I'd been for Don Arden. And I was being vetted. By whom? Probably by one of the few figures who would loan money to Art Kass at Buddha and to black artists. Artists like Sylvia Robinson, who we will get to when she helps introduce the world to a new music, rap.

Apparently, even to be successful as a Mafia loan shark, you have to scan the horizon for talent.

35

EARTH, WIND, AND FIRE— THE PATH TO PRINCE

In the 1970s, the Howard Bloom Organization Ltd. had a West Coast office for a few years. But by 1980, for reasons I utterly forget, I gave up on the LA office. Instead, I worked with Bobbi Cowan. Remember Bobbi? She was the publicist at Gibson and Stromberg who worked with Jethro Tull in the days when I was covering Tull for *Circus*. Her job had included setting me up for transoceanic phone meetings with Jethro Tull's manager, Derek Sutton, the future manager of Styx. Since then, Bobbi had been a consultant on the film *Spinal Tap*. So had Derek Sutton. So I hired Bobbi when we had projects that needed West Coast help.

One day, Bobbi called me. She had a potential client—Earth, Wind, and Fire. Would I Like to work on the band with her? Heck, yes. Earth, Wind, and Fire were giants. Says Wikipedia, they sold over 90 million records, "making them one of the world's biggest selling bands of all time."[143] They'd been nominated for an unbelievable twenty Grammys. And *Rolling Stone* declared that they'd "changed the sound of black pop." What's more, there were things we could do for them. For one thing, we could keep them close to their black audience via our network of black newspapers. And we might be able to find hooks for the white press—hooks that others had missed.

I was on the lip of inventing secular shamanism. On the cusp. So I put in a month reading everything ever written on Earth, Wind, and Fire. I read their lyrics and studied their album covers. And, as in the case of Styx, the real clues to the band's essence were in their album art. Earth, Wind, and Fire's mastermind was Maurice White. I couldn't see him in his own environment, and I did not yet know that I should make that demand. But Maurice was coming into New York and staying at the Essex House hotel, where you just saw Bob Marley and his merry tribe. And where you would eventually have a crucial breakfast with Billy Joel. Would I like to have lunch with Maurice? Hell yes. It was essential.

So I sat opposite Maurice at a small table with a white tablecloth hovered over by punctilious waiters and said something simple. "Maurice, I get the impression from your album covers that you believe that a civilization from a distant solar system or galaxy came to earth roughly eleven thousand years ago and planted the wisdom that led to modern culture, science, and technology. In fact, I get the impression that you feel these seeds of wisdom were left in the pyramids. Am I crazy?" Maurice grinned. I'd hit it on the head. So I explained something to him. There was an astronomer at Cornell University. He'd just appeared in his own thirteen-part TV series on PBS. It had been the most-watched series in PBS's history. And he was trying to set up an organization to scan the stars and planets for signals—signals from extraterrestrial civilizations. What the astronomer needed more than anything else right now was money. If I put Maurice together with the astronomer, would Maurice be interested in doing a benefit concert? Maurice said an absolute yes. The astronomer's project was called SETI, the Search for Extra-Terrestrial Intelligence. His TV series was called *Cosmos*. And his name was Carl Sagan.

So my staff and I went to work to track Sagan down. Again, there was no Google in 1980. Lord knows how my staff did it. But Earth, Wind, and Fire's name carried some weight. Finally, we got the phone number for Sagan's summer cottage. My staff set up a conference call. But before I tell you how that went, you have to remember how delicate Carl Sagan's position was in 1981.

Sagan was a scientist in danger of losing his credibility in the scientific community. First he'd done that TV series that had been the most-watched program in PBS's history—*Cosmos*. And his academic colleagues hated him for it. Why was he getting all this attention and not them? Surely they were far more brilliant than he was. We humans use a good many ruses to climb the pecking order. One of those scams with which we deceive ourselves is tearing down someone above us. The farther the top person descends, the higher we rise. Or so instinct tells us. Meanwhile, that instinct disguises itself as righteous indignation, justified anger.

Sagan, the story went, had abandoned serious science when he went on TV. Now he was no longer a member of the scientific tribe. He was something petty and contemptible. He was a mere popularizer. So Sagan already had a target painted on his forehead. Now he was asking his fellow scientists to take seriously something they'd always scoffed at—flying-saucer stuff, the idea of intelligent beings on other heavenly bodies. Which meant that, in addition to the target painted on his forehead, Sagan had now painted one on his back. His standing in his field was frighteningly precarious.

So, when my staff tracked down the phone number of Sagan's summer home, and I introduced Carl Sagan to Maurice White on the phone, Sagan was guarded and cautious. Two minutes into the conversation, the astronomical maverick caught a whiff of where Maurice was coming from, and it was all over. The call ended. Sagan couldn't get anywhere near this pseudoscience, even if it meant visibility and money.

So I was forced to take a different approach. I hooked Earth, Wind, and Fire up with the Black United Fund, and we promoted the Fund's existence.

We were back to making sure a black act with a huge crossover success didn't lose its black base. And that skill would come in handy farther down the line. As you suspected, with the Jacksons.

But first, another story: how Earth, Wind, and Fire led to Prince.

36

PRINCE

It was 1980, and I was trying to get up the gumption to do something mean: to part with Bobbi Cowan. She wasn't pulling her weight.

Meanwhile, five years earlier, in 1976, Bob Small and Ray Caviano had insisted I embark on a ritual: reading all three music-industry trade magazines the minute I got into the office on Monday mornings. And in 1980, in those trade magazines, I spotted something strange. There was an act I knew nothing about moving up the R&B charts, the charts to which white music-industry execs paid almost no attention. Not only did his album go to No. 3, it turned platinum. And I'd never heard of the singer before. He was getting zero press. Something strange was happening here.

Then Bobbi Cowan called. Earth, Wind, and Fire's manager, Bob Cavallo, had another act for us: the unknown black artist whose mysterious chart success I'd been tracking. But I was not willing to work with Bobbi Cowan anymore. I insisted that my staff produce a minimum of sixty stories per client a month. Bobbi produced six. And much as I begged, I was totally unable to get her to live up to our standards. In fact, we'd landed more than 120 stories a month for Earth, Wind, and Fire. And Bob Cavallo wanted what he'd gotten on Earth, Wind, and Fire. Including my staff's 120 stories a month.

So I called Bob Cavallo and explained that he'd have to pick, alas, between Bobbi and us. I trotted out every sales point for Bobbi. She had years of experience. She had excellent press contacts. Superb, in fact. And I recommended that he go with her. Instead, he chose to go with us.

The name of the new client? Prince.

And, with Prince, secular shamanism finally came to full bloom. If you'll kindly allow me to get away with that verb.

* * *

I demanded from Bob Cavallo what I had demanded from Derek Sutton, Styx's manager—that I be given a month to study Prince intensely. To read every article ever written about him, every lyric he'd ever written, every album cover, and to sift through whatever other clues to his inner fire I could find. I insisted on a month to list his awards and achievements and to produce a first draft of a chronology of his life. Then I demanded that I be allowed to see Prince in his own environment, alone, with no managers, wives, or intercessors. I demanded between one and three days of face-to-face and eyeball-to-eyeball contact. Bob said yes. Which means that Bob's boss, Prince, said yes.

This, at last, was full-blown secular shamanism. Why? Because on top of all of my demands, I was zeroing in on a new way to dig down to the bedrock of soul: looking for imprinting moments, looking for passion points.

The fact is that there were no clippings on Prince to be found. He hadn't been written up. It was the first time I'd ever encountered such utter press anonymity. So I turned to Prince's lyrics for clues. While I was studying, I got a call from one of Warner Bros' West Coast publicists. One of their black publicists. A few things to remember before you hear the substance of her warning. As you know, in those days, black artists were ghettoized in their record companies. Remember how the white staff at ABC Records had turned their noses up at Rufus, the band whose lead singer was Chaka Khan, back in 1975? Big labels employed black staffers to handle black acts. And because the companies looked down on their black artists, the quality of black staffers wasn't high. That wasn't true at Warner Bros.

Yes, black artists were still ghettoized at Warners. There was still a wall separating black artists from the white staff. True to the norm, only black staffers worked on black acts. But the quality of those staffers at Warners was exquisitely high. So the call I received was from a black staffer with a Harvard level of intelligence and articulation. "You're going to have a problem with Prince," she said. "He's incapable of doing interviews. We set up two interviews for him out here. He wouldn't talk to the first interviewer. And he tried to strangle the second. Prince is impossible." I'd never heard a warning like this. And I'd never hear anything like it again. Was it true?

I finished my month of study. The album Prince was about to put out was *Dirty Mind*. It had the most audaciously sexual lyrics I'd ever seen. But you have to understand where I was coming from. In my days accidentally starting the sixties, I'd been a participant in the first flowering of the sexual revolution. Okay, I'd had a lot less sex than you'd expect from a revolutionary. But in 1962, when I was a catalyst for that tiny movement on the West Coast, we believed that sex played a central role in a healthy life. And Prince's openness about sexuality was totally in tune with what we pre-hippies had preached back in 1962.

So I'm not normal. But by any normal standards—even by the standards of the sexual revolution—Prince's *Dirty Mind* was shocking. Its song "Head" talks about meeting a woman on her way to her wedding. The wedding-gowned bride gets all excited about the singer, he's "such a hunk" that she can't contain her lust. To retain her virginity for her groom, she volunteers to give the singer oral sex—head. In a limousine on the way to the ceremony that will bind her to another man 'til death do you part. But the oral sex turns out to be so arousing that she wants to get in bed. And to give oral sex morning, noon, and night. Writes Prince, "I came on your wedding gown." Finally, the bride marries the singer instead of her fiancé. But not necessarily legally. Only in the sense that she can't stop sucking his sexual organ.

A few years later, a group of would-be rock censors would complain about sexually explicit lyrics hidden in rock albums. We'll get to these censors in a few minutes. But there was nothing hidden about the sex in *Dirty Mind*. Prince's lyrics did not sneak. They crowed. Yes, about sexuality. And more. They bragged about incest, one of the most despised of society's sexual sins. In "Sister," Prince is sixteen and his sister is thirty-two, luscious, and loose, so loose that she doesn't wear underwear. She initiates Prince in oral sex. And Prince is staggered by the whole new meaning she teaches him of the phrase "blow job." In eighteen states, oral sex is called sodomy and is against the law. But not on Prince's *Dirty Mind*, where it shows up all over the place.

What's more, Prince exclaims that he's the only one his sister has ever made love to and that she's the reason for his sexuality. And Prince's sex with his sister gets a lot stranger than that. His sister takes a whip to him, apparently with sexual intent. And the sensation is so rousing that it makes Prince shout "motherfucker," a curse word that's straight-up incest.

You may have noticed that this is not the traditional language that had been used for 1940s and 1950s pop songs about moon, spoon, and June. But Prince delivers the verdict that "incest is everything it's said to be."

Oh, two more things. Incest is illegal in forty-eight states out of fifty.

And these lyrics were not black. They were not what you'd expect from an R&B singer. They were a declaration of independence from race. By breaking all the rules in one sex-packed album, Prince was making the statement that he refused to abide by the walls between black and white. He was neither. He was beyond crossover. He was universal.

* * *

So I had done step one of my new approach, secular shamanism—study the hell out of the new client. Immerse yourself in him for a month. Now for part two: seeing the artist in his own environment with no managers, wives, or intercessors.

Prince was rehearsing for his *Dirty Mind* tour. Bringing me to a rehearsal was bringing me to his environment. The odd thing was the place that Prince had chosen for rehearsals. It was my place, not his. Prince wasn't rehearsing in the city where he'd been born and raised: Minneapolis. He was rehearsing in the town where I'd been born and raised: Buffalo, New York. In a theater where I'd gone to see a movie when I was eleven years old: Shea's Theater.

But the Buffalo, New York, I saw when I flew up to see Prince was far more Prince's than mine. Why? Buffalo had built a new downtown since I'd left there, twenty years earlier, at the age of eighteen. It was a downtown with massive, modern hotels unlike anything the city had possessed in my youth. Prince was staying at a Hyatt on a big new central plaza. So that's where Bob Cavallo's staff put me. When I checked in and headed for the elevator, someone I knew from New York—and from Argentina—was already in the elevator cab, Fred Schruers from *Rolling Stone*. The same Fred Schruers I'd taken to see Queen in Buenos Aires. Fred is only an inch taller than I am. With him was another five-foot-nine man. Fred introduced me. It was Bruce Springsteen. No, this was not the Buffalo of my youth.

Once my lone bag was in my room, I drove to Shea's Theater, a dozen blocks or so away on Main Street. It was roughly ten o'clock at night. I was scheduled to meet one-on-one with Prince when the rehearsals ended. I watched the band work on their music until 1:00 a.m. Then Prince and I found an empty room backstage, a room with a sturdy door, and locked ourselves in. How was this opening interview with a person Warners was convinced wouldn't and couldn't do interviews? We didn't finish until 6:00 a.m. That's a measure of how much we explored. And Prince did not try to strangle me.

* * *

What did I discover? A story. A remarkable story.

Prince grew up in Minneapolis in an integrated neighborhood. He went to school with white and black kids. That may be why his band was such an anomaly. Many are the white artists who've had black rhythm sections. Rhythm, in fact, has traditionally been a much more dominant component of black music than of white music. White music tends to stress melody. But Prince reversed the racial order. He was a black singer with a white rhythm section. In fact, a middle-class Jewish white rhythm section. Or that's the way it looked to my untrained eyes. In fact, Prince's band had three white members, two of whom were Jewish—Bobby Z. on drums, and Dr. Fink, Matt Fink, on keyboards. The band's third white member was keyboardist Lisa Coleman, who would become more important as time went on. Then there were the two black members—André Cymone on bass, and Dez Dickerson on guitar.

What was Prince's story? Where were his inner gods, his soul? Remember Konrad Lorenz and the geese that flew behind him in a V formation as he rode his bicycle down a rural German road? Remember the geese that used the scientist's head as the tip of the V, the point where the two wings of their flying V met? And remember how fixing on Konrad Lorenz as Mom froze these birds' sexual preferences? In other words, remember imprinting? Remember passion points? My suspicion was that's where soul is rooted. That, I guessed, is the point from which soul grows. To get at those imprinting points, I had a ridiculously simple question: when was the first time you remember being interested in music. Stupidly simple, right?

Prince's answer was fascinating. Five is a normal imprinting age for musicians. Five, says Sigmund Freud, is an age bursting with sexuality. It's five-year-olds who you find naked in closets in boy-girl pairs comparing their sexual equipment. Or playing house or doctor with body exploration in mind. Then there's something else—attention. Attention is the oxygen of the human soul. Musical imprinting frequently happens at the intersection where sex and attention meet.

Here's how it worked with Prince. Prince was five years old—that magical age. His father was a musician—a jazz pianist and composer.[144] Prince's mom took him to see his father rehearse at a theater very similar to the Shea's Theater we were sitting in. Prince's father was center stage at his piano. In the spotlight. Aimed at him was all the implied attention of five hundred empty seats, all pointed at the spot where his dad sat. And behind his father, said Prince, were five of the most beautiful women he had ever seen. Attention, sexuality, and music. Supernormal stimuli. Prince was hooked.

Sex continued to play a key role in Prince's further imprinting points. Prince had a friend, André Cymone. Yes, the same André Cymone playing bass on the Shea's Theater stage an hour before. And André Cymone's mother had a basement. It was an unused room, and as long as the kids were off the street and were diligent about school, she didn't care what they did down there. So Prince gathered a tribe. A tribe with a very different rule than the ones they teach you in junior high school. That rule was absolute sexual freedom. And that absolute freedom melded with an idea left over from the movement I'd helped start in 1962, an idea summed up in the hippie slogan "make love, not war." Uninhibited sexual freedom would turn earth into a peaceful paradise. Oh, and one more thing that Prince did in that basement. He had a band. A band with André Cymone, and with one of Prince's cousins.

Was the sex real, or was it merely a fantasy? Matt Thorne, in his book *Prince*, quotes Pepé Willie, an adult busy studying music management when Prince was a kid, explaining, "I went to pick Prince up one time, and Prince had this girl downstairs that he was getting busy with, and he had done his business, and [André Cymone's mother] Bernadette walks in the door from work and asks Prince, 'Did you go to school today?' And Prince goes, 'No, I didn't.' And immediately she started whipping his butt, right there in front of me, in front of the girl, everything. She busted him up. That was great, man."[145] Could this have produced yet another sexual thrill? A sexual imprinting point? Could it have been behind Prince's excitement with his sister when "she took a whip to me until I shout"?

But note that this whipping was not for sex. It was for skipping school. And skipping school is not something Prince did regularly. He told me that he had very high grades: A's. He may have been exaggerating. But even B's would have been a miracle, considering what else he was up to.

By the time he was in high school, Prince said that he had a band that went out on tour every weekend, playing dates all over Minnesota.

Meanwhile, Prince was teaching himself to play just about every instrument used in Western rock and pop. And not just passably. Brilliantly. So brilliantly that he told me he was able to work out a deal with a recording studio. Studio time was hideously expensive in those days. It could be as high as $2,500 an hour—$9,000 an hour in today's dollars. No kid could afford it. But Prince said that he went to one of the biggest studios in Minneapolis and proposed a deal. Studios spend a fortune hiring musicians to play drums, guitar, and all the other instruments needed to make musical soundtracks for local radio and TV advertisements. Studio owners could spend thousands of dollars a day on studio musicians.[146] Prince made an unbelievable claim. He said he could play all the instruments the studio needed. Not just a few, but all. And he must have proved it. Why? Because the studio agreed that if Prince would do all the instrumentals on their work, they would turn over the keys to the studio when they left at night and let Prince record anything he wanted on their forty-eight-track, multimillion-dollar equipment. Or that's the way Prince told the tale.

So Prince recorded an album. Then he went to New York City to visit his half-sister, Sharon. Prince was fifteen years old. Yet, he says, he went around to record companies and production companies, trying to get a deal. His gumption was astonishing. In fact, he said, two production companies offered him a contract. Any other fifteen-year-old would have jumped at the chance and signed on the dotted line. But, said Prince, the two production companies wanted to tell him what to record, tell him how to record it, and tell him how to dress and what his press photos and album covers should look like. Prince said no. He wanted total control. An astonishing demand from a fifteen-year-old.

So Prince went back to Minneapolis. Did anything sexual happen with his sister while he was in New York, or was that just fantasy? We will never know.

Four years later, the head of a small Minneapolis ad agency, Owen Husney, flew out to LA and pulled off a miracle.[147] He got Prince a deal with one of the two biggest and best companies in the music biz—Warner Bros. But the deal was highly unusual. It gave Prince total control. Total control of his music, total control of the production of that music, and total control of every photo and album cover Prince would ever put out. How old was Prince when Husney got him this highly unusual contract? There's been some dispute about that, but Prince said he was nineteen.

I flew back to New York. It was just before the personal computer would enter the scene. I had taken notes on everything Prince had said. When he went too fast for me, I told him, "What you just said was very interesting. But I write slowly. Could you say it again?" And I'd hunted for details like what André Cymone's basement looked like, what sort of neighborhood it had been in. Fly-on-the-wall details that would help me tell Prince's story vividly. The sort of details that had driven Steve Marriot wild. The details that I hoped would make you, a reader, feel as if you'd been in the room. Then I typed my notes up, used scissors and Scotch tape, took the notes apart, and rearranged them in chronological order so they told the story you just read. And so they focused on the passion points, the imprinting moments.

The next step? I sent the rearranged transcript to Prince. And I schooled him in doing interviews. Something I had not realized was necessary in the days when I had let a record-company head, a client, blow an interview with *Fortune*. By telling irrelevant tales.

"These are your best stories," I told Prince. "They explain who you are. I'm going to have my staff set up interviews for you. There will be a lot of them. When we bring you into New York, we'll have you do eight interviews a day. Three days in a row. We'll do the same thing in LA. At each interview, you have to tell the stories you told me. The stories in the transcript I just gave you. You'll feel awkward about repeating what you just said to another interviewer. You'll want to apologize for repeating yourself. You'll want to say, 'As I just told the previous reporter.' Never say that. Tell the stories as if you've never told them to a soul before. Make the interviewer feel as he's the only person you've ever told your story to. Look at it the way you look at your concert set. You play your best songs over and over again. And, each time, you try to play them as if you've never played them for anyone else before in your life.

"Here's the deal. A reporter will walk into the room and ask you really stupid questions. Questions like, 'How do you categorize your music?' Your job is to turn every question, no matter how dumb, into an opportunity to tell your story. If you do that well, no matter how irrelevant what you've said is to the interviewer's first question, that man will go back to his wife that night and say, 'Honey, you wouldn't believe how brilliant I am. I asked this amazing question, "How do you categorize your music?" and I got this astonishing story out of this kid called Prince.'"

Yes, in those days all the interviewers were still men.

Why tell the stories that reveal who you are? I tried to explain, "Ultimately, you are not talking to the interviewer. He is a megaphone. A megaphone through whom you are talking to the kids you want to reach. He is the microphone through whom you are speaking to your audience."

Prince listened well. You'll see how well in a few minutes. And he did roughly a hundred interviews over the next two years. What's more, he never choked up. And he never tried to strangle an interviewer.

37

PRINCE'S PUPPETS

Prince was a person who ate, breathed, and slept music. Writing songs and recording them was as essential to him as oxygen. He did it every day. But, in the beginning, he could only put out one album every six months. Then, when he got big, things became worse. He could only put out one album each year. He had to keep his audience hungry. What was he going to do with all the extra music he made? Prince began to spawn sock-puppet acts, protégés, people who would use his songs, use some of their own, let Prince produce them, and let Prince direct their careers. And protégés who would be managed by Prince's managers, Bob Cavallo and one of Cavallo's two partners, Steve Fargnoli.

The first act Prince used to get more of his music out was Vanity Six. Vanity was born Denise Matthews in Niagara Falls, Ontario. She competed in beauty pageants and modeled in New York. She was startlingly gorgeous. Prince renamed her and managed her identity. The speech I'd given him on how to handle the press—and the script that I'd handed him—the transcript of his own words put in chronological order so it told a story, a story built around imprinting points—was, to Prince, a vital part of star-making. So he flew me out to Minneapolis to meet with Vanity at his spacious new studio complex, Paisley Park. Prince wanted me to get Vanity's story from her, and to do what I'd done for him.

Yes, I extracted Vanity's story from her. But I could not get to the root of her passions about music. Possibly because Prince had worked with her to get the good stuff out of the tale of her life, and to give her a Prince-conceived, artificial biography. Nonetheless, I turned what she said into a script and gave her the talk about how to do interviews. And we had her interviewed by journalists up the kazoo.

Then I came down with the back problem that interfered with my campaign for Supertramp. Eventually, as you know, I was reduced to laying in a bed naked with just a sheet and working on a wheeled tray table hovering above my abdomen equipped with three Rolodexes and a phone. Then I got a call from LA. It was Jamie Shoop from Bob Cavallo's management company. "Prince has a new act," she said, "Morris Day and the Time. And Prince says that you have to give Morris your training." "But Jaime," I said,

"I can't. I have a back problem and I'm lying here naked under a sheet." "Give me your address," said Jamie, "we'll be there at eleven o'clock tomorrow morning."

My brownstone in Park Slope was on a block that, way back in 1981, was a slum. Today, my block is one of the hottest pieces of real estate in America. It pays to be fascinated by trends and mass emotional mood swings. You can find a neighborhood that will improve around you. But back then, my block was treeless, and the Italians and Puerto Ricans on the block had actually made war with each other for a week using Molotov cocktails and guns. Until the Italians went down to the Italian social club at the corner, begged for help, and the Colombo crime family—the family that controlled our neighborhood—put out the word that if tomorrow there was still Puerto Rican–Italian warfare on the street, there would be no more Puerto Ricans.

What's more, my apartment was a well-kept secret. Five days a week, I dressed to be ready for an unscheduled meeting with a record company president at any minute. Black velvet jeans I had custom made by a Trinidadian tailor, black turtlenecks of which I'd bought the last twenty when Calvin Klein stopped making them, belts from Bloomingdale's, and a gold digital watch the thickness of a dime with a gold LED background—a watch of a kind I'd never seen before and have never seen again since. And I had my clothes dry-cleaned and pressed, then only wore them for a day and put on a new change of clothes the next morning so that my shirt was unrumpled and my pants were meticulously creased. But no one in the music industry was ever supposed to see the place I lived, my apartment in my Park Slope brownstone. Why?

I knew that, in my forties, my body would no longer be able to take the nonstop stress, the seventeen-hour days, and the seven-day workweeks of the music industry. Look, I love stress. I eat it up. But bodies under constant stress wear out. In the back of my head was the notion that fighter pilots in combat are periodically given a week or two of rest and relaxation.[148] Without it, the high stress of dogfights in the sky would burn them out. I was getting zero rest and relaxation.

So my wife and I lived like church mice. We lived as inexpensively as possible, so we could save our pennies and invest in real estate. If I was right and my body gave out in my forties, I would need the real estate income to keep me alive. And, in fact, my body would break down when I was forty-five. And my brownstone would save me. But that's for later.

This meant that we had no normal furniture in the house, with the exception of brand new work desks and desk chairs. All of our leisure chairs had been dragged in from the streets. What's worse, my wife had been obsessed with saving feral mother cats just after they'd had their kittens. Yes, she saved the kittens, too. She would keep track of pregnant cats by peering out of the back window with binoculars. When the cats suddenly slimmed down, she would knock on doors until she found the backyard where the new mother felines had dropped their kittens. Then she would bring the kittens and their wild mothers into our house, have the moms spayed, and send my blonde, beautiful stepdaughter out on the street to give the kittens away. Which meant that eighty cats had cycled through our house at one time or another. And each one had sharpened her claws on the stuffed chairs that we'd found abandoned on the sidewalk.

The result was simple. All of our chairs had been shredded. What remained of them was wooden frames with naked springs. That, along with the fact that we'd renovated the three apartments we rented out but had never finished the renovation of our own apartment. There was coaxial cable dangling from the ceiling. The walls of our apartment hadn't been painted since 1965. The plaster on the walls of the bathroom had buckled and crumpled, and now looked like a dinosaur's scales. And the dust bunnies were all over the place. Not to mention the two dogs. Big dogs. This was not what I wanted to show to the stars and record-company presidents I worked with. Even though the dogs were friendly.

But the next morning at eleven o'clock, the neighbors must have been startled. A long, black Cadillac limo came around the treeless, slum corner of President Street, headed downhill roughly sixteen houses, pulled over to the right-hand side of the road, and stopped. Where? At the Bloom Brownstone. Out of the left-hand side came a gorgeous, young, vivacious California blonde—Jamie Shoop. And out of the right came a black man in an astonishing zoot suit, one so crisply pressed that it looked as if he'd had a stylist in the backseat of the car ironing the creases to a razor sharpness. This was Morris Day. Morris Day of the Time.

Dodging the carnivorous dust bunnies, Jamie and Morris climbed the three flights of wooden stairs to our fourth-floor apartment. They knocked on the door. My wife, Linda, opened it. Morris stepped in. One dog goosed him from the front. The other dog goosed him from the rear. A friendly gesture among dogs. Then he was guided to the bedroom, where I was laid out in the bed under a sheet. Yes, I'd put on clothes.

The one positive of the room was its view. Three windows overlooking the Manhattan skyline—from the Empire State Building to the World Trade Center. Plus something I'd seen at the Beverly Wilshire hotel and had stolen. A way to make a room seem more spacious. A sliding mirrored door on the ten-foot-wide closet at the back of the room, opposite the windows. A ten-foot-wide mirrored sliding door that reflected the view from the windows. The result was a sense of living in the sky. With three real windows at one end of the room and the reflection of those three windows at the other. But that didn't compensate for the furnishings. Linda had thrown a sheet over one of the wood and spring armchairs, the chairs denuded by the claws of cats. Not a nice place to sit. But that was it. There was no more comfortable furniture in the apartment.

So Morris Day sat for three hours on springs covered with a thin cotton sheet while I dragged his story out of him, furiously taking notes and asking him to stop and repeat when I couldn't keep up.

It was like my session with Vanity. I didn't get anything memorable. Morris had played drums with Prince's band—Grand Central Corporation—when they were in high school. But I'm not even sure that he told me that. I fished it out of Matt Thorne's 2016 book on Prince. I would later come to feel that Prince may have schooled Vanity and Morris in what to tell me and what to not tell me. Neither gave me stories that I can remember.

Why would Prince shape the biographies of Vanity and Morris Day? Because anything said about them would influence the public perception of him. And Prince may have wanted a control over that perception as absolute as the control he'd insisted on over his music, his photos, and his album covers. But that's just a guess.

And remember, Vanity and Morris Day were not vigorously independent artists. They were pipelines through which Prince channeled his overabundance of music without saturating his public. So it may be that their passions about music were not as unique . . . or as deep as their puppet master's.

* * *

Two more aspects of my newly developing secular shamanism would be crucial to understanding my relationship with Prince. As I was pulling the tale of your passion points out of you, I would try to find anchoring points inside of me that resonated to your frequency. Yes, anchoring points inside of me. Why?

Hermann Hesse, the legendary German novelist whose influence permeated the spirit of the sixties, says that we all have a secret closet deep inside of us, hidden way down in the darkness. Inside that closet are ten thousand personalities. Those are identities we could have had if the one identity that we think is us hadn't fought its way to the top of the pack and taken over. These are the identities that seize a novelist or a screenwriter when she sits down to a blank computer screen and forty characters come tumbling out of her, forty vivid people with vivid personalities, each with a will of its own. Each able to object when she writes a scene they don't feel fits them.

The theory of secular shamanism says that those ten thousand personalities are hidden in your empathic center. Where is that center? Today, we'd guess it's in the mirror neurons spread across four different areas of your brain. And that it's in a feel for others that yanks together brain parts as different as the amygdala and the right supramarginal gyrus. Back in the early 1980s, I imagined that the empathic center is in your heart and in your gut. How did your empathic centers make Prince a permanent part of you? How did your mirror neurons find a common frequency and swallow Prince whole?

Remember, you had accidentally become the catalyst, the center, of a tribe of people in Berkeley and San Francisco in 1962 when you were seeking Zen Buddhist enlightenment—satori. Since no clique or tribe would accept you, you'd been forced to assemble your own. And your own tribe had possessed its own worldview and its own norms. For example, when you were indoors, you didn't wear clothes. None. You were naked. All half-dozen of you. Naked became such a norm that it was hard to remind yourself to put on clothes to go to the supermarket. It was hard to believe that normal people would find your 360-degree skin exposure shocking. What's more, you were all after some form of radical change in your emotional state, whether that change is called satori or not.

Add in Sigmund Freud. You'd read Freud's *Moses and Monotheism* in 1963. It's an amazing book. In 1902, Freud was putting together a tribe of his own in Vienna. He wanted his tribe—the tribe of physicians he gathered every Wednesday evening[149] in his apartment at Berggasse 19—to become as permanent as possible. And he wanted his ideas to sustain long into the future, long after he was gone. So he went to Rome to see Michelangelo's *Moses*—the big, powerful marble figure with the controversial horns. In fact, Freud reports that he once spent three entire weeks sitting at that statue's base, pondering. It makes sense. Moses had pieced together a tribe of people that Freud imagined had scarcely existed before. Moses had given that tribe a new worldview, a new set of rules, and ten commandments. Plus a simple slogan: "Hear, oh Israel, the Lord thy God, the Lord is one." Listen up, you Jews. There is only one God. And he is your boss, your commander, and your master. Moses ordered his newly gathered people to put this slogan on their doorposts and to bind it to their foreheads and wrists so they would see it whenever they walked in or out and so they'd dwell on the slogan morning, noon and night. Marketing. Then to brand his new vision into the very souls of his people, Moses took them out to the desert and made them trudge around for forty years. Long enough for the generation that remembered Egypt to die, and for a new generation to arise who had known nothing but Moses's commandments from birth. Or that's how Sigmund Freud saw what Moses had done. How do we know? It's in Freud's *Moses and Monotheism*. At least, it's in the way you perceived the book. And that perception would prove crucial in understanding Prince.

As you saw it, in André Cymone's mother's basement, Prince had done what you'd done on the West Coast with a movement that would not get a name until after you left it: the hippie movement. Prince had done what Sigmund Freud wanted so badly to do. Prince had built a tribe of his own, a tribe with a new basic rule: sex is salvation.

That phrase, "sex is salvation," is how you summed up the philosophy of Prince's personal flock, his people. Bob Cavallo is convinced that you made it up. Maybe that's so, but it is an accurate summation of a philosophy Prince put across in his albums back in the early 1980s. And Cavallo says that after you made it up, he started to see it everywhere in the press. Yes, that's possible. But it was a distillation of Prince, not of you.

Both you and Prince had compensated for your outsider status by creating your own inside groups. So had Moses and Sigmund Freud.

The bottom line: one of secular shamanism's goals is to find another person within you. The hidden personality inside of you that resonates to your client's frequency. We'll get back to the impact of this on your work with Prince in a minute.

* * *

One other aspect of secular shamanism. We are all like the caterpillar that goes through a radical transformation and becomes a butterfly. We age. And, as we age, we change. We change from a baby to a toddler to a child to a teenager to an adult and finally to a shrunken little gray person. These are profoundly physical metamorphoses. But even the way we feel and the way we see changes. If you were my client, I told you that my first step would be to find the inner you who writes your music and who dances you onstage. My next step would be to introduce that inner self to the self that knows how to say, "Hello, how are you?" and "Fine, thank you very much." Then I would help you stay true to the self that made your music. To the gods inside. But every year you would change. The way you once changed from a baby to a toddler. And your inner gods would change, too.

But there's more. By expressing the gods inside of you through your music and your performance, you speak for your audience. You validate feelings they were sure were their own personal insanities. Once you express those feelings, even if you do it only in the way that you stand and dance onstage, you help your fans see that they are not alone, they are a movement. But every year, as your audience members go from teenagers to twentysomethings to middle age, they have new strangenesses bubbling inside of them . . . new feelings that they think are insane. If you allow your music to come from the changing and maturing gods inside of you, from your soul, you will validate those new insanities. You will turn those desperately wordless feelings into the visions of the sane. Which meant I intended to come back out to see you every time you released a new album. I would study your lyrics and probe for the shifts of your gods within. Those gods would change in Prince in ways that would surprise even me. But we'll get to that in a minute.

Prince let me come out to Minneapolis to see him again a year after *Dirty Mind*. He had another album, *Controversy*. This time, I watched him rehearse in an indoor arena in his hometown. When the rehearsal was over, I went backstage and interviewed Prince. A year after our first interview. Prince was grappling in this album with the controversies he'd stirred with *Dirty Mind*. He was in rebellion. Rebellion about sexuality, Rebellion about religion. Rebellion about politics and history. The press found it fascinating.

So, when year three arrived, I was eager to go out to Minneapolis to delve into Prince's soul once again. Especially because his albums were increasingly reaching back to the philosophies of the psychedelic sixties—my sixties. Paisley was the hippie fabric of the sixties, and the fantasy of a Paisley Park was inching toward birth. Remember, I'd had a five-dollar used fox-fur coat lined with a red paisley fabric in roughly 1969. What's more, underlying the lyrics of songs like "Ronnie Talk to Russia" was the imperative to make love, not war. A sixties slogan. A slogan of the movement I'd helped found. I flew out to Minneapolis, sat through rehearsals, and discovered that Prince was having a hard time backstage making up his mind about whether or not to see me. Why?

Here's a guess. Prince was five foot two. It took me three years to realize that. Because of his giant personality, he seemed beyond size. But imagine being black and five foot two in grammar school and high school. Both the white kids and the black kids would pick on you. Your only defense? Withdraw into a world of your own. A world where you can establish control. And where you can build a chosen people of your own.

So Prince was afraid of men. Not women. Especially not gorgeous women. But, yes, he was afraid of men. Whenever Liz Smith, the syndicated columnist, found one of the rumors that came from this shyness, she would pounce on it and it would show up in seventy newspapers, not to mention on TV and radio.[150]

So Prince wouldn't see me. I went all the way to Minneapolis, and no Prince. Apparently, Prince was doing the same thing to his managers, Bob Cavallo and Cavallo's partner, Steve Fargnoli. Because one day I got a call from Bob. "You're not supposed to know this, but I have the lyrics to Prince's next album," said Bob. "You're not supposed to see them. But if they somehow show up in your office tomorrow morning at 10:30 a.m., can you tell me what Prince is thinking?" The answer was yes. And that's what I did the following morning, an hour after the Federal Express envelope arrived—I told Bob Cavallo what was on Prince's mind. How could I know? Because I had hauled one of the ten thousand personalities out of the dark closet of my possible selves. And because I'd used that hidden personality, and the experiences I shared in common with Prince, to install a mini-Prince, a simulation of Prince, deep inside of me. Presumably in my empathic core. And Prince's lyrics brought that emotional simulation up to date. Or at least that's how what I was doing looked to me.

Then came a shock. A film.

* * *

Steve Fargnoli was having difficulties. Remember the wall that separates the black staff and the white staff at record companies? Remember how black acts like Chaka Khan are tossed over to the black staffers—if there are any—and are kept from the white staffers by habit, prejudice, taste, fashion, or deliberate policy? Steve had run into that race barrier at Warner Bros. Could I write a memo Fargnoli could use to crack the color barrier at WB? So I did. In essence, it said that the natural home for Prince's music was not on solid black stations like New York's WBLS, or KGFJ in Los Angeles. It was at progressive rock radio stations like WNEW-FM in New York and KLOS in LA. The stations whose format I'd played a microscopic part in establishing for ABC in my Cloud Studio days.

I don't know whether the memo helped or not. Because everything we were doing was about to be eclipsed by something far bigger.

* * *

Bob Cavallo explains in Matt Thorne's book that Cavallo, Ruffalo, and Fargnoli, Bob's management company, was coming to the end of its first five-year contract with Prince.[151] Bob was confident his firm had done a brilliant job, and that Prince would renew. Bob wanted a renewal for another five years. Prince said yes to the five years. Which in itself is astonishing. But yes on one condition—that his management company get him a feature film. And not a feature film from some "jeweler or drug dealer."[152] Not from some narcotics peddler or some Jewish diamond merchant. A film from a major studio.

Bob must have been aghast. What Prince was asking was impossible. Yes, Elvis Presley and the Beatles had made films. But that was the 1950s and 1960s. In the 1980s, it was undoable. The film community in Hollywood looked down on music people as if they were homeless lepers. Despite the success of Robert Stigwood's *Saturday Night Fever* and *Grease*.

Why do I love Bob Cavallo? Because the vast majority of humans on this planet talk of big things they would like to do. But there is only a tiny palmful of people on this earth who can make impossible things happen. Bob Cavallo is one of that tiny palmful.

Somehow, Bob managed to pull together almost nine million dollars. That's $25.5 million in today's money. Not a lot for a film, but still . . .

38

PURPLE RAIN

For roughly a year, something was going on in Minnesota. I wasn't quite sure what it was. Then I got a call from Bob. They were filming on the set in Minneapolis. They wanted me out there. I was never quite sure why. Yes, Prince had some new protégés. Jill Jones and Susan, for example. And Wendy and Lisa. And, yes, Prince wanted me to put them through the interview training I'd given to him, to Vanity, and to Morris Day. But something else on the set bothered me.

Hollywood rules require that you have a "unit publicist" on the set. And, in my view, a unit publicist should be snooping around the set every day like a cross between a bloodhound and an investigative journalist. Looking for interesting anecdotes and good stories. Good stories for people like Liz Smith, who ate up Prince anecdotes like chocolate-covered cherries. Good stories that would get the film talked about for a year before it hit the theaters. Good stories that would make the film's name a household word.

That wasn't happening with Prince's movie. So I planted myself in a motel room adjacent to the set for a week. And I never got out of that motel room except to walk down the corridor to the diner-like hotel restaurant. Why? One by one, Prince's protégés paraded to my room, and I interviewed them to get their stories. And I looked for anecdotes about the film. The result was eighty pages of material—a complete press kit for the movie.

Then I headed back to New York, to my office. By now, in addition to a couch, a few designer bentwood chairs, and my burl-wood-and-chrome desk with my seven Rolodexes, I had one more thing. Behind my big, brown, super expensive, super-comfy office chair, propped up against the chocolate-painted wall with the stained natural wood baseboard, was a small red nylon backpack I'd gotten at a bargain store half a block from Times Square for $19.95. In it was a spare shirt, a toothbrush, a razor, and a device you'll later see more of—a TRS 100, the very first laptop computer ever made.

Why the red nylon backpack? Because I'd begun to get calls from California, Michigan, Georgia, and other spots where my clients rehearsed or performed, or where their managers had their offices. The calls usually came in at four in the afternoon. And the gist was always this: "You've got to be out here by eleven o'clock tonight. There's been a crisis. You're the only one who can handle it." I was like Red Adair, the fireman you called when you had a massive oil-field explosion. But I was there for career and PR disasters.

Sure enough, at 4:00 p.m. one day I got a call from Bob Cavallo. He sounded desperate. "You've got to be out here at 11:00 a.m. tomorrow morning," he said, "we're screening the film for Warner Bros, and I need you." But there was more. "I've been in the editing room for weeks," said Bob, "and I just can't make this a movie.

"Please see the film tomorrow morning with us when we show it to Warner Bros' executive team and tell me what you think."

By then, I'd had twelve years of film experience. I'd done statistical analyses of the film audience at Paramount Pictures. I'd been there with the Paramount Pictures staff when they had watched one of Burt Reynolds's first movies—*The Longest Yard*. They hated it. I loved it. It went on to win an Academy Award. I'd been there when a Manhattan publicist friend ran a screening for New York's snootiest cinema critics and had asked me to come along to hold her hand. The reel of celluloid she handed to the man in the projection booth featured a German bodybuilder who had the audacity to think he could act. The movie's name was *Pumping Iron*. My publicist friend hated it. So did the critics from the *New York Times* and the *Village Voice* who sat in the room with us. I loved it. There was something about the German weightlifter-plus-actor-wannabe you couldn't resist. His name was Arnold Schwarzenegger.

All of these experiences had wetted my feet in film. I'd soon gain an additional edge thanks to a scheduling accident. Instead of the usual 6:00 p.m. flight to LA, I had the leisure of taking a plane at 9:00 a.m. the next morning. When the stewardess walked up and down the aisles, offering headphones to watch the movie, I don't know why, but I took one. I normally work on planes—that's why the TRS 100 laptop was in the knapsack. And I've never felt like watching films early in the morning. But this was an exception—again, I didn't really quite know why.

On paper, the movie the flight attendants were about to roll should have been sensational. A powerful new audience had emerged in the mid-1980s—single, white, middle-class working mothers, the products of premature divorce . . . or, in some daring cases, of women aware that their fertility clock was running down and determined to have a kid with or without the benefit of a wedding ceremony and a live-in man. The airplane film that morning was about this target demographic—it zeroed in on a single, white, middle-class mom's romantic trials and tribulations. A woman living on her own with her child who meets her son's school truant officer, then falls in love with him. The female star was very hot—Susan Sarandon. The male star had come off huge successes in George Lucas's *American Graffiti* and Stephen Spielberg's *Close Encounters of the Third Kind*—Richard Dreyfuss. From the very first instant, I could feel the position papers that I'd have written to promote this film within a company like Paramount Pictures. I could feel the way I'd have pitched the film at a meeting of the marketing, promotion, and publicity teams.

I wanted to like it. I *knew* I'd like it. But I didn't. The movie—*The Buddy System*—lacked something critical . . . soul. It lacked a factor I suddenly realized isn't spoken of in the sciences or in the entertainment industry. It failed to make my throat clench. It failed to bring a tear to a corner of my eye. It failed to sweep me into that very private realm of feeling whose aftermath leaves you wishing that the lights wouldn't go up in the theater and that you wouldn't have to march up the aisles and out the door with other people who could catch a glimpse of your face. After a really good film, you don't want anyone to see you because you are as emotionally open and vulnerable as a clam without a shell.

After *The Buddy System*, I was in perfect control of my emotions. Why? The movie had flunked the lump-in-the-throat and tear-in-the-eye test. Which means that by the time the plane landed at LAX, I'd learned a new lesson in movie measurement.

So, when my cab pulled into the gate of the Warners lot and I found my way to the building in whose screening room Cavallo was waiting with a crowd of roughly forty other people, I declined Bob's invitation to sit with him and one of his partners. The screening room had one hundred seats. Sixty of them were empty. I found my way to a seat at the back of the screening room, far from anyone else. There was a solid reason for this anti-sociality. If Prince's movie was going to score on the clenched-throat-and-tear-duct meter, I didn't want my business associates to see me. I didn't want to be embarrassed.

What's more, I didn't want to feel inhibited. I didn't want to be aware of the image I projected to Bob and to the Warners executives. I wanted my emotions to make the judgment. Those intimate feelings might have stayed in hiding if I'd sensed that my reactions were on review.

One hour and fifty-one minutes later, I knew we had a movie, a film I'd be willing to fight for, no matter what. *Purple Rain* worked my emotional core into exquisite twists. I had never, ever seen a film like this—a movie with a rock soundtrack that did for me what I suspect the Broadway musicals of Lerner and Loewe had done for my parents—delivered its emotional punches and its uplifting feelings through the power of its music. The music literally made the plot of the film.

When the film was over and we'd had a solid five minutes to recompose ourselves, we—the Warner VPs and department heads, and the producers, Bob Cavallo and his partner Joe Ruffalo—marched into a large but strangely arranged conference room next door. What was strange? The conference table's head was to our left and its foot off to our right. Normally, a door looks out over the table's tail or head. But this conference room's entrance was aimed smack at the broad, anonymous middle of the conference table. The part of the table relegated to unimportant people. And your positioning at a conference table can be crucial.

The mood once we all trooped in and found places to sit was funereal. I was seated at the table's center, facing the door. Officially, the folks at the table's head and foot should have been the focus of attention and authority. But the spot that faces the door has an unconscious power, no matter where the head may be. I was in the unseen sweet spot, the secret power spot.

The meeting started with the official film publicists Bob Cavallo had hired. They looked as if they were experiencing severe stomach cramps. Or as if their cat had just come down with cancer. The words didn't matter. Their faces and body posture said that this film was an embarrassment, a failure. Then came the official Warner Bros position. "We have a plan for this film," a Warners exec said. "We're going to roll it out in six theaters in Arizona and see how it does before we take it national." Those words were not what they seemed. They were a secret cinema-world cliché, a ritual death sentence. Warner Bros had just said that it was going to can the film, chuck it, and abort it. That's what the "six theaters in Arizona" speech means. I had learned this in my days working films. I was furious. This was literally one of the best films I'd ever seen.

So I took over and gave a speech that in a sense I didn't give at all. It was a lecture that spoke itself through me. Even the demeanor with which it delivered itself came from a place that isn't normal—it came from a place of Charlton-Heston-as-Moses-parting-the-Red-Sea intensity. An intensity we'll see again later.

"You cannot kill this film," I said. "If you try, you will kill a piece of cinema history. This film hits you where it counts—in the gut, in the throat, and in the corner of your eye. It says something with emotional power, something so charged and potent that there's no way to sum up its message in words.

"This film," I explained, "can be a watershed in pop culture. Until 1965, songwriters in Tin Pan Alley wrote the hits. Singers were just puppets who put those songs across. It took the Beatles in the 1960s to set singers free so they could do something outrageous, write their own songs and sing them. Now Prince has taken that a step further. He's the first musician to write not just his own songs, but his own film."

That speech, in its own small way, helped save *Purple Rain* from the coffins of film-dom. That, plus a series of miracles wrought by Bob Cavallo. Not to mention one more tiny act of subversion that Cavallo used to do the trick. Warners ran a sneak preview of *Purple Rain* in San Diego. I wasn't supposed to know about it. Cavallo slipped me the word. If I sent press down to see it, Warners would be furious. Warners had threatened to put me out of business once before—a story we'll get to when we reach the tale of John Mellencamp—and it could easily try it again.

But when you're on a crusade, barriers are invitations to breakthroughs. I had my staff call three key critics in LA—Mikal Gilmore from *Rolling Stone*, Robert Hilburn from the *Los Angeles Times*, and David Ansen from *Newsweek*. Each went down to San Diego knowing he absolutely wasn't supposed to be there. This gave each of these writers something vital, an ego stake. Before Warners could make its final marketing decisions, *Rolling Stone*, the *Los Angeles Times*, and *Newsweek* all broke with reviews riddled with quotes like this one from David Ansen's *Newsweek* piece:

> As a movie star, he's unprecedented. Prince may find himself anointed as the screen's newest and most singular idol. Prince is one of the handful of performers who've restored the urgency and danger—and the beat—to the rock scene. And *PURPLE RAIN* gets that excitement on the screen.[153]

Warners changed its attitude. The film was rolled out nationally in one hundred theaters. It was rolled out in a promotion that tied the movie to MTV . . . the first film-tied promotion in MTV's then-brief history. Roughly six months later, *Purple Rain*, the movie that had cost less than nine million dollars to make, had grossed eighty million dollars—almost ten times its production budget.[154]

In other words, *Purple Rain* grossed roughly $188 million in today's dollars. Close to a fifth of a billion dollars.

But had *Purple Rain* really made film history?

* * *

In 2003, when I finally beat an illness that kept me imprisoned in my bedroom for fifteen years—a tale for later—I settled myself into a café a few blocks away from the Bloom Brownstone to write. I had been out of the world like Rip Van Winkle for nearly an entire human generation. I wondered if kids still remembered the musicians I'd helped implant in the public memory. When I mentioned Prince, a twenty-year-old went slack jawed. "You worked with Prince?" he asked. I was curious to see whether he remembered the film that Bob Cavallo and I had fought so hard for. "*Purple Rain*," he said, "are you kidding? It's the ultimate make-out movie."

Why was that a more powerful statement than he imagined? Because making transitions from one stage of life to another is rough. That's why we have ceremonies, to help us over the chasm from one state to another. That's why we have bar mitzvahs, confirmations, graduations, weddings, and funerals. But there's one huge jump across a chasm for which we have no rituals: the transition from childhood to sexuality.

I'm talking about the terror of a first date. Do I dare to take her hand? Can I work up the gumption to put my hand on her left shoulder? Will she loathe and reject me if I put my arm behind her head and move my hand over to her right shoulder? And will I be cast in hell if I move my hands down her torso? For the leap across that gap, we have no official ceremonies.

Purple Rain had become a rite of passage.

* * *

Sometimes your self below the floorboards of the self knows things your conscious mind is oblivious to. And, sometimes, it's crucial to let the voices of that hidden self speak through you. It's crucial to be a mouthpiece for the gods inside.

One day in 1984, pretty much out of nowhere, I tried to issue a wake-up call to Bob Cavallo and Steve Fargnoli. I told them that we were about to go through a shift so radical that it would feel as if the laws of physics had changed. What was I talking about? It felt as if we'd been rolling a stone up a mountain for three years with Prince, generating those 160 stories and more a month to make his name a household word. But if you are successful at what you're doing, there comes a time when you reach the peak of the mountain. And, all of a sudden, you're in an entirely different game. The stone you've been rolling uphill escapes your fingers and rolls down the mountain's other side, gathering speed. Now the problem is no longer to push it. The problem is to keep up with it. The problem is to guide it.

In the early days of the star-building process, I tried to explain to Bob Cavallo and Steve Fargnoli, you usually have two weeks after you see a problem in which to ponder the dilemma, make a decision about how to confront it, then to execute your solution. But the time would soon arrive when we'd only have twenty minutes. If we had a warning of a problem at 10:00 a.m., when we got into our offices, we'd have to re-solve it by 10:20 a.m. Why? Because the wire-service writers would file their stories at 10:30 a.m. If we hadn't fixed inaccurate and negative stories by then, those wire service stories would appear in a thousand newspapers. And journalists doing articles on your client—on Prince—would carry files of all of those clippings around with them on planes when they were putting together in-depth features on Prince. If you explained to them that the stories in their folder were false, they would simply point at the stack of clippings next to them on an empty airplane seat. Who were they indicating they believed—you or the stack of stories? The stack of stories! It's the tale of the sheep. But in overdrive.

So you had twenty minutes to catch a false story—or to correct the facts. The moment when the laws of physics changed came with "We Are the World."

* * *

Innocent children had been starving to death in Bangladesh in 1971, when George Harrison had thrown his Madison Square Garden concert with Eric Clapton. Now, in 1984, children were starving to death again, this time in Ethiopia. We'll see the hidden reason why in a bit. But in England, Bob Geldof, the Irish lead singer of the punk band the Boomtown Rats, decided to do something about Ethiopian starvation. He co-wrote a song, "Do They Know It's Christmas?" Then he recorded it with a group called Band Aid—Bono, Phil Collins, Sting, David Bowie, Paul McCartney, Boy George, Robert Kool Bell, members of Spandau Ballet, Simon Le Bon of Duran Duran, George Michael, and roughly ten others. Phil Collins, Kool and the Gang, Spandau Ballet, and George Michael were or would soon be my clients.

In response, Harry Belafonte—the man we saw shaping Martin Luther King and my client, Ralph MacDonald, in a previous episode—got together with a remarkable music-industry manager named Ken Kragen and planned a similar project in the United States.

Thanks to Ken, two of my future clients—Lionel Richie and Michael Jackson—got together to write a song called "We Are the World." As Lionel described it to me, "We were in Michael's bedroom. We were lying on the floor writing. We were passing ideas for words back and forth. And, all of a sudden, on my right, I felt something looking at me. Remember, we were laying on the floor. But whatever it was was staring at me from eye level." Lionel turned his head slowly. Very slowly. And whose eyes were focused on his with laser precision? Said Lionel, "Michael's boa constrictor, Muscles."[155] Lionel hoped that Muscles wasn't hungry.

Kragen worked to get every star he could to come to the studio to sing the song Michael and Lionel wrote, the way the superstars in Band Aid had gotten together in the UK and had made entertainment history. Because he is so good at what he does, and because he had a superb team, Ken was able to get thirty-seven stars in one room at one time. They included: Bob Dylan, Bruce Springsteen, Paul Simon, Billy Joel, Bette Midler, Ray Charles, Stevie Wonder, Diana Ross, Smokey Robinson, Tina Turner, Quincy Jones, Dionne Warwick, Bob Geldof, Kenny Loggins, Dan Aykroyd (of *Saturday Night Live* and the Blues Brothers), Sheila E., La Toya Jackson, the Pointer Sisters, Steve Perry (of Aerosmith), Lindsey Buckingham (of Fleetwood Mac), Huey Lewis, Harry Belafonte, John Oates (of Hall and Oates), Kenny Rogers, Waylon Jennings, Willie Nelson, and Cyndi Lauper. Of those, nine were my clients. Or eventually would be.

But back to Prince and the change in the laws of physics. When Kragen was putting "We Are the World" together, I got a call asking if any of my clients would participate. I suggested Kenny Loggins, who has one of the sweetest voices on earth. Then someone in Prince's management team got the same call. And that's where the trouble began.

Prince was not comfortable around men. That's why he eventually fled from me. And he was not comfortable being swallowed by someone else's clique. He was not comfortable as just another face in someone else's crowd. That's why Prince had assembled his own chosen people in André Cymone's basement. And that's why he continued assembling his own communities, his own teams, tribes, utopias, and mini-societies. So Prince offered to go into the studio on his own and record a track for the *We Are the World* album. This should have been a gift. Instead, it was a problem.

At 9:30 a.m. one morning, the press was preparing to write up Prince's move. With a negative spin. According to that spin, Prince was selfish, difficult, and refusing to contribute to a project in which every other big name artist was participating. As if the offer of an entire album track meant nothing. I wanted to counter this with a more accurate spin. Immediately. Remember, we only had between 9:30 a.m. and 10:15 a.m. in which to change the press's perception. Forty-five minutes. I called Bob Cavallo and Steve Fargnoli. I'd tried to warn them earlier that the day would come when they'd no longer have the luxury of deliberating for two weeks. That moment had come. But Bob and Steve hadn't yet understood the shift in urgency. They dithered. I didn't get to call the press to explain. The result made Prince look selfish and uncharitable.

In fact, Prince was anything but uncharitable. He'd seen a TV episode about a Chicago educator named Marva Collins who took black kids off the street, fed them a curriculum rich in challenging material like Shakespeare, and turned them into super-students. We'll see the irony of feeding kids Shakespeare in a few minutes. Prince asked me to track Marva down. And he began donating large amounts of money to her organization. I was his liaison to Marva for the next five years. And I was supposed to stay absolutely silent about this philanthropy. I did. Until this paragraph.

But there was more trouble to come. And who would the next big obstacle come from? God.

* * *

Two years after *Purple Rain*, I got another call from Bob Cavallo about another Prince movie Bob was insecure about—*Under the Cherry Moon*. But to get to *Under the Cherry Moon* and why it failed, we need a few crucial details.

First, a story we haven't gotten to yet: John Mellencamp. One day, I was at John Mellencamp's house in Seymour, Indiana, the town where John had grown up. It was a house whose entrance looks like a tiny tool shed with a full-sized door on the top of a woodsy hill. You step through the door and discover that it contains the top of a staircase. A staircase leading down into the interior of a house. A house that spills down the hill. You walk down one flight of stairs and you are on the third floor. You go down another flight of stairs and you are on the second floor. One more floor down and you're on floor one. Each floor has windows facing out through the tree trunks of a thick forest that also spills down the hillside like a cataract, a falls. A green falls. John and I were in the living room. Alone. In front of the house's biggest TV. In the days of picture-tube televisions and VHS tape machines. John had two films he wanted to show me on VHS. Two Paul Newman films that had shaped him when he was in high school. Two imprinting-point films. Two passion points.

One of those films was *Hud*. Hud is the son of a wealthy rancher in someplace like Texas. He owns a big, white Cadillac convertible in the days when Cadillacs were the ultimate luxury car. And when Cadillacs were twice as long as any car should ever be. Every day, Hud drives into town, goes to the local bar, and looks for lonely housewives whose husbands are away at work until evening, housewives who are bored with their lives. Bored, but gorgeous. And what do you imagine Hud does with these women? Yes, you got it.

Then, one day, the federal agricultural authorities come to Hud's dad with bad news. There is hoof-and-mouth disease in the neighborhood. To keep it from spreading clear across the continent, the feds are going to have to kill every cow and bull surrounding the area of the outbreak. That includes the cattle of Hud's dad. To cattlemen, your herd is your 401k. It's your entire life savings. Put your herd to sleep, and you've just kissed your bank account goodbye. You've just tossed away the small fortune that supports Hud in his Cadillac-convertible-and-housewife lifestyle.

Hud does not want to go from the son of a rich man to the son of a poor man. He plots to steal his dad's cattle in the middle of the night and sell them before the Feds can appear with their herd extermination equipment. If he succeeds, there's a good chance he will spread the hoof-and-mouth disease to the entire state and beyond. Then something his father said hits Hud. It more than hits him. It seizes him. It takes him over. You owe an obligation to your fellow human beings. And living up to that obligation is more important than life itself. So Hud stops himself and abandons the cattle-rustling plan.

When the film was over, Mellencamp, a brilliant explainer, gave the message of the film to me. "First," said John, "you rebel against your father. Then you become your father."

That's what was happening with Prince. One day, Prince's tour of the moment was playing at a location only forty miles from the Bloom Brownstone in Brooklyn. Prince was appearing at Nassau Coliseum on Long Island. Remember, Prince was one of the most astonishing performers you'll ever see in your life. He, John Mellencamp, and Michael Jackson—two others we'll get to later. So I needed to go to the Nassau Coliseum show to demonstrate my support. But I also needed to go to see what Prince was up to. And to retune my empathic center to Prince. I needed to update the emotional simulation of Prince in my gut.

The performance, as always with Prince, was flat-out stunning. The lighting was gorgeous—with its colors and its changes. But there was a moment when Prince was humping the stage. Then, suddenly, his body grew still, and he lay there flat on the floor of the stage. None of us were concerned. We all knew it was part of the act. But he stayed still, not even breathing so far as those of us in the audience could see. And he lay, and lay, and lay. We eighteen thousand in the audience began to panic. What if Prince had just had a heart attack? Shouldn't we rush up to the stage to save him before it was too late? The magic of the concert started to evaporate. Instead of losing our self-consciousness and melting into a tongue that licked the stage and ate Prince up like a candy, we were aware of our individual identities again. Aware of how we looked to those around us. Then, suddenly, a voice came from the peak of the arena's ceiling, sixty feet up in the air. It talked to Prince. It was the voice of God. God, the ultimate father.

It was an early sign that Prince was going through the *Hud* metamorphosis. First you rebel against your father. Then you become him. Prince may not have seen it this way, but the voice of God in the ceiling was the voice of Prince's dad.

The next sign came two years after *Purple Rain*, when I got another call from Bob Cavallo. Prince had disappeared for a year. To get to the Purple One or to Steve Fargnoli, the Cavallo partner who worked with Prince on a twenty-four-hour-a-day basis, we had to call France. Prince had moved his entire tribe to the land of *parlez vous* to make a new film. Now, Bob said, "We're screening Prince's new film, *Under the Cherry Moon*, tomorrow. It's going to be at one of those theaters where you test the movie on six hundred kids, and each one has a dial they twist to the right to show they like what they are watching or to the left if they dislike it. You have to be here." So I had my staff book a flight and a hotel and get a car service to pick me up. I put my $19.95 red nylon knapsack on my back, and I headed for the airport.

The next afternoon was sunny when we entered the dark of the theater. I watched *Under the Cherry Moon* and loved it. It wasn't a classic like *Purple Rain*. But it was light, entertaining, and it absolutely worked. When we, the six hundred in the theater, spilled out onto the sunlit, broad sidewalk of Sunset Boulevard and I found Bob in the crowd, I told him proudly that he had another genuine, fully functioning film. I was proud of him. And proud of Prince.

Two weeks later, I got another call from Bob. There was trouble. Could I please come out as rapidly as possible? When I arrived in Hollywood, Prince had a new protégé for me to train in interviews, Kristin Scott Thomas. The female star of *Under the Cherry Moon*. The actress who would go on to give stunning lead performances in *The English Patient*, *The Horse Whisperer*, *Salmon Fishing in the Yemen*, and *The Darkest Hour*. Performances that would be nominated for at least one Academy Award, five British BAFTA Awards, and five Olivier Awards, and that would win a BAFTA for "Best Actress in a Supporting Role" and an Olivier for "Best Actress."[156] At the moment, Thomas was utterly unknown. But that wasn't the problem. Prince had changed the ending of the movie. As usual, it was a secret. I wasn't supposed to see it. But if Cavallo's staff set the newly altered film up on a VCR machine in a utility closet with a tiny TV, could I please stay after the building shut down for the night and render an opinion?

Why do utility closets keep showing up in my life? But I digress.

I spent the afternoon in a conference room at Cavallo, Ruffalo, and Fargnoli's office, pulling passion points and life stories out of Kristin Scott Thomas. Prince had discovered her in France. And what an astonishing discovery she'd turned out to be. Kristin was tall, slender, elegant, with high cheekbones and a presence it's hard to compare with that of any other woman on the planet. She had an air of command, of aristocracy, and of warmth all at once. And her accomplishments were huge. She was from England but had made her acting career in France. Which is almost impossible. The French hate the English, and vice versa. Plus, France has institutions of a kind we never imagine in the USA. France sees itself the leading culture on planet earth, the one culture that all peoples would aspire to if only they knew the secrets of *liberté*, *égalité*, and *fraternité*, the trio of principles underlying the French Revolution, the revolution that shaped modern France. Not to mention the modern world.

Since France has the globe's only perfect culture, French men and women have the obligation to establish strict systems to maintain their culture's flawlessness. Not to mention its supremacy. The Académie Française presides over the French language, keeping it pure. So important is this Académie that its forty members are called *Les immortels*, the immortals. Under the Institut Français are eight other academies designed to make the diamond-like facets of French culture sparkle with star-like clarity: an Academy of the Humanities, an Academy of Sciences, an Academy of Fine Arts, an Academy of Painting and Sculpture, an Academy of Music, an Academy of Architecture, and an Academy of Moral and Political Sciences. Then there is the organization that filters out the dross and maintains the absolute perfection of a key column supporting the overarching ceiling of French culture: it's known sometimes as the Comédie-Française, and at others as the Théâtre-Français. The French Theater. Those who are not native French speakers are banished from working in the place. In theory, they should not even be allowed to scrub the floors.

What's more, the French hate their high-culture competitors, the English. Yet Kristin Scott Thomas, an English woman, was a member of the Comédie-Française. A full member. An impossible proposition. Which meant that both her acting and her pronunciation of the French language were so exquisite that France's leading authorities, France's culture-definers, were willing to exalt her as an archetype of French culture—a picture of the perfection toward which all Frenchmen and women should aspire.

Discovering Kristin Scott Thomas's story was a privilege. But that was not the real mission. Six o'clock rolled around, the office closed, and everyone left. Everyone, that is, but me. I was scrunched on the floor of the utility closet whose bottom shelf had the VHS player and the ten-inch-screen mini-TV. Not a good way to see a film. And, alas, the film simply did not work.

Why? In the first version of *Under the Cherry Moon*, the version with the happy ending that I'd seen on Sunset Boulevard, Prince is a scamp. He and his best friend, another scamp—Jerome Benton of the Time—are on the Riviera, France's southern beaches where the rich go to sunbathe, gamble, and play. But they have a problem. They've run out of money. To replenish their empty wallets, they set their sights on a rich French girl Prince can seduce and fleece. The rich French girl they set their sights on is Kristin Scott Thomas. And, despite complications and the revelation that Prince and his pal are con men, Prince reforms and gets the girl. Nice, happy ending.

But remember the concert at Nassau Coliseum? Prince had begun talking to God. And listening to him. Or, to put it in John Cougar Mellencamp terms, the voice of his father had come alive in Prince's head.

Way back in the days of one of the very first novels ever written in the English language, *Moll Flanders*, the author, Daniel Defoe, tantalized you by taking you into the scandalous life of a woman from the seamier side of the cultural divide—a woman from Britain's criminal underclass. Defoe gave you 186 pages in which to wallow vicariously in Moll's sins—from crime to sexuality. But this left Defoe with a problem. How could he titillate you without giving you the feeling that you were morally corrupt? Easy. In his last chapter, he killed Moll off. Moll was bad. Now she'd gotten her punishment. Your morality as a reader, and Defoe's as an author, was restored.

The voice of God had come to the same conclusion about Prince's scamp. The Prince of *Under the Cherry Moon* had been up to criminal misdeeds. In a God-shaped universe, criminality could not be allowed to succeed. In fact, it had to be punished. So, in the new version of the film, Prince killed off his main character. Leaving you, the viewer, bereft. Where there had previously been emotional warmth, now there was a cold place in your heart. You, the viewer, had invested yourself in Prince's main character for an hour. Then Prince had kicked you in the teeth.

First Prince rebelled against his father. Then he became his father. Prince the scamp was turning into Prince the enforcer of morality.

This time, when I delivered the conclusion of my lump-in-the-throat and tear-in-the-corner-of-the-eye meter to Bob, the news was not good. Remember, over the long run, *Purple Rain* would gross a world total of $80 million[157]—$188 million in today's money. *Under the Cherry Moon* would cost $12 million to make. And it would gross $12.5 million.[158] A pathetic waste of everyone's time, energy, and momentum.

Getting to the top is hard. Staying there is even harder.

* * *

Bob Cavallo and I were on the case until 1988—seven years—building Prince from an unknown to a superstar. Then Bob called with bad news. "The Kid," Prince, was severing ties with me. And he was severing ties with Bob. I felt this was a huge mistake. Bob Cavallo was not your ordinary manager. He had one of the rarest talents on earth—the ability to turn fantasies into realities. Cavallo would go on to produce nine films, including Terry Gilliam's *Twelve Monkeys* with Bruce Willis, Brad Pitt, and Madeleine Stowe. *Twelve Monkeys* would gross $168 million. That's $275 million in today's dollars. The film would win two Academy Award nominations, a Golden Globe, an award at the Berlin International Film Festival, a Hugo Award, and the Academy of Science Fiction, Fantasy, and Horror Film's Saturn Award. Then Cavallo would head Disney's music operation for thirteen years.

When Bob Cavallo took the Disney Music Group over in 1998, the record industry had plunged into the toilet. You couldn't sell records anymore. They'd been replaced by downloads. Record companies were drowning in red ink. Bob became chairman of what was then called the Buena Vista Music Group,[159] an operation that was losing

Disney roughly $250 million a year. Disney wanted to sell it. Bob went to the heads of Disney and begged them to give him a year. He brought the company from a $250 million loss to a loss of zero in twelve months. Then, each year thereafter, he doubled the music operation's profits. An absolutely impossible accomplishment. *Variety* put it like this: "Under his aegis, the Disney Music Group . . . evolved from a moribund operation [as in dead, totally dead] into one grossing nearly $500 million in revenues."[160] When Cavallo retired from Disney after thirteen years, Rich Ross, chairman of the Walt Disney Studios, said, "Bob Cavallo is nothing less than a legend in the music industry."[161]

And this is the sort of one-of-a-kind people-power that Prince threw away. Superstardom is not just the achievement of the star himself. It's the achievement of a team. And the genius of Prince's team would be irreplaceable.

Alas, the result was that, in many ways, Prince's career peaked. Yes, his audiences grew in Europe and Japan. Yes, he made history with twenty-one sold-out concerts in a row at London's O2 Arena in 2007.[162] Yes, his legend grew. And, yes, he continued to remain a vital part of the lives of millions of fans in the USA. A vital part of those fans' identities. But he never reached the kind of explosive success he'd had in the days of *Purple Rain*.

When Prince died on April 21, 2016, it was a blow. He should have lived into his nineties.

But Prince had helped transform the Howard Bloom Organization Ltd. Radically.

* * *

Once upon a time, a road manager I vaguely knew called and asked for help. His name was Joe Dera. He wanted to switch from road managing to publicity. I called a friend at another PR firm, Levenson and Associates, and got Joe Dera a job. Joe was a hard worker and moved up. In 1976, he became the head of the East Coast music operation and executive vice president for the biggest of my competitors, Rogers and Cowan, a Hollywood-based firm that had started in film in 1950, then had grown huge and diversified.

Joe had a sales pitch for new clients. It went something like this: "Don't go with Bloom. He's second rate. He's never delivered a magazine cover in his life. Look at all the magazine covers we've gotten." Then Joe would mention the coups Rogers and Cowan had achieved for Paul McCartney, Mick Jagger, and David Bowie. What Joe didn't tell his prospective clients was that McCartney, Jagger, and Bowie had already become cover material long before Rogers and Cowan entered the scene. But someone other than Rogers and Cowan had gotten them up to cover stature. And that ability to engineer the big lift from anonymity to stardom is the real talent you want to have in your corner. That ability is where the magic lies.

What did the Joe Dera speech mean? It was time for the Howard Bloom Organization to get covers. And it was time to do it with musicians whose fame we had built from the bottom up, not acts others had taken from the valley to the peak.

Prince was the first of these cover musicians. He would be on the cover of *Rolling Stone* four times. And there would be more covers from the Howard Bloom Organization Ltd. in the future. Many more.

39

RAP—SHIT ALL OVER YOUR FACE

Before we get to John Mellencamp, Billy Idol, Billy Joel, Bette Midler, and Michael Jackson, let's go back to another new subculture that used music as its voice. Let's go back to another group soul.

In 1981, I got a call from Sylvia Robinson, asking for a meeting. I was excited. Why? Back in 1956, when I was thirteen and listening to classical music, a pop song had caught my attention. It was too yummy to ignore. It was "Love Is Strange" by Mickey and Sylvia. Then, when I was working with Art Kass at Buddha Records, Art had put out two albums by an artist I'd never heard of: Sylvia. Yes, just Sylvia. She was middle-aged—a kiss of death in the music business for a new artist. Yet both her Buddha albums went platinum. I wanted to know how and why. Turns out that Sylvia was not as unknown as I thought. She was the Sylvia of Mickey and Sylvia. Sylvia Robinson.

We set up the meeting Sylvia requested. Sylvia had her driver bring her from New Jersey to Manhattan in her Rolls-Royce. And she told me a story. Sylvia had been cruising the streets of the South Bronx in her Rolls. Something new was happening. Kids were blocking off the side streets for block parties, setting up a stage at one end of the street, packing it with a sound system and turntables, and making a new form of music—a form of music somewhat like the calypso of Trinidad, where the words were the meat of the matter. Calypso's words had spread the news. But in this new musical form, the vocalists bragged about their prowess and their success. They did it with poetry. They did it with rhyme. And they didn't sing their songs. They spoke them. There was one more secret to this new style. The performers recited their lyrics with a snapping, amphetamine-arousing beat. Sylvia listened to this street music, then hustled back to New Jersey. Why?

Turns out that when Sylvia was twenty-one, way back in 1956, two sorts of people were not allowed in the control room of a recording studio where the mixing and production are done. They were not allowed near the control boards where raw vocals and instrumentals are turned into luscious music. Those two forbidden categories of humans were women and blacks. Sylvia was both. But she got into a studio anyway.

She created Mickey and Sylvia as a studio group. She produced the record herself—an absolute no in those days. And she had a hit. At the age of twenty-one. Then she built her own record company. She named it after the swankiest neighborhood in the ghetto where she'd grown up—the Sugar Hill neighborhood in Harlem. She called it Sugar Hill Records.

Eventually, Sylvia worked her way up to ownership of a small, white, self-standing former dry-cleaning building in Englewood, New Jersey. A building shaped like a rail-road boxcar. It was just four rooms, but it housed her office and her studio.

After hearing the new music on the streets of the South Bronx, Sylvia found a song in the street style, recruited a group of studio musicians, and recorded it. She named her studio group the Sugar Hill Gang. After her company, Sugar Hill Records. Then she did something audacious. Disco DJs were all over the place by 1981. The DJs Ray Caviano had helped cultivate. There were disco dance clubs in every major city. They needed fresh music. One kind of record was easiest for them to play—the 12-inch single. But very few record companies put out discs in this format. Sylvia issued her new, South Bronx–style song as a 12-inch single. It became the first 12-inch single to go platinum. It was called "Rapper's Delight." And it introduced a new musical form to a national audience. You guessed it: rap.

After the success of "Rapper's Delight," Sylvia went back to the streets of the South Bronx to look for the best group she could find doing the new style. The group she found was Grandmaster Flash and the Furious Five. Sylvia told me the story and asked if I would help her with her next step, putting rap and Grandmaster Flash and the Furious Five on the map. What a wonderful idea, giving another subculture a voice and a right to be. That was one of the privileges I loved the most. I said yes.

Grandmaster Flash—Joseph Saddler—had invented something very new. He'd set up two turntables side by side. He'd pick up the needle and skip around on the records, something we now do with electronic devices and computers and call "sampling." Flash had switched from one turntable to another. He had changed discs with an astonishing precision. And his fingers had been stunningly skilled in finding the exact groove with the musical phrase he was seeking. Flash had reinvented the turntable as a musical instrument. The way Trinidadians had reinvented the oil drum.

We had a stroke of luck with Grandmaster Flash and the Furious Five. The ogre of the rock press, the man who had invented the phrase "a rock-critic establishment," and who had long ago declared himself the pope of the rock journalists, Bob Christgau at the *Village Voice*, loved the group. He loved the music. And he loved the lyrics. Grandmaster Flash and the Furious Five's words were not about bragging, sex, and bling. They were socially conscious descriptions of the community from which Grandmaster Flash and the Furious Five had come.

Christgau's approval made getting press for Grandmaster Flash and the Furious Five easy. Remember, once the lead sheep jumps over your cane, the thousand other sheep behind it will follow. Even if you withdraw the cane.

We did the usual for Grandmaster Flash and the Furious Five and for the entire field of rap—a minimum of 120 stories a month. Enough stories to get you to recognize the group and to insert it into your musical vocabulary. Not to mention enough stories to bring your attention to the genre—rap.

Then, one day, I was at Chrysalis Records discussing Billy Idol—whose story and near-death experience we will get to in a little bit. A few years earlier, while I'd been working with REO Speedwagon, I'd met a new executive at Epic Records—Rick Dobbis. He was straight out of college and dressed like a hippie—long hair and jeans. And I liked him. But somewhere along the line, Dobbis had noticed something. There are two ways of dressing in the music industry. If you dress in jeans and long hair, you muddle your way up the job ladder and stop at a middling level of authority. But if you wear a suit and tie and have your hair cut in a more upscale manner, you can be a record-company president. Rick had switched to suit, tie, and power haircut, and carried himself as if he were already a record-company president. I still liked him.

Rick saw me coming out of an office at Chrysalis, took me to an empty corridor, and said something strange. "Look," he told me, "you've worked very hard for years to establish your credibility in this industry. And you've done it. But you are involved with a form of music that's shit. You know it's shit. I know it's shit. In six months, it's going to be all over. It's going to blow up. And, when it blows up, it's going to leave shit all over your face."

Rick's speech made one thing glaringly apparent. Giving dignity to the despised was a necessity. I absolutely had to work with rap.

* * *

Meanwhile, I wasn't alone in rap. Tom Silverman had founded Tommy Boy Records to put out rap music. Russell Simmons and his team had been working on Kurtis Blow.

But now something new was happening. Russell Simmons was moving from edgy outsider to the mainstream. He managed a rap group formed around his brother, Run. The group was Run-DMC. And Run-DMC would be the crew with which we would go a step beyond Sylvia Robinson and Grandmaster Flash and the Furious Five. We would mainstream rap. But more on that in a minute.

* * *

The mainstreaming of rap would produce a problem for Sylvia Robinson. The major record labels had no feel for rap or its audience. They shared Rick Dobbis's opinion that rap was shit. But they could see that it was making money. And they wanted to get in on the cash. So the majors offered large amounts of moolah to Grandmaster Flash and the Furious Five. Remember, these were kids from the South Bronx. A number with four figures sounded big to them. Now they were being offered millions. They jumped at one of the offers—from Elektra Records, the company that had put the Doors, the Cars, Metallica, and Teddy Pendergrass on the map.

Then the members of Grandmaster Flash and the Furious Five told the press they had left Sugar Hill because Sylvia wasn't paying them. Meanwhile, they regarded me as a father figure and came to my office to get guidance and to have a shoulder to cry on. I deeply appreciated this trust. To me, it was precious. But so was my relationship with Sylvia. And my respect for her accomplishments. What's more, I didn't believe that Sylvia Robinson was not paying the band.

Sylvia was upset by the charges being made against her. I don't blame her. She called and asked if I could help her. Question number one was, what was true? Did or did not Sylvia Robinson pay Grandmaster Flash and the Furious Five? Sylvia swore that, yes, she had paid the band. So I asked her to xerox every check Sugar Hill Records or Sylvia Robinson personally had ever turned over to the band. And to xerox the backs to show that the checks had been cashed. Sylvia had her staff put in a few days at the xerox machine. There were a lot of checks. Then I asked her to get all the xeroxes to me. In a brown paper shopping bag.

I stashed the shopping bag behind my desk, next to the red nylon knapsack. And I started to call the black shows that I suspected Grandmaster Flash and the Furious Five had made their accusations on. Like Gil Noble's WABC-TV New York show *Like It Is*. Normally, Gil did not cover music. He did not want to give credence to the idea that the only thing blacks can do is sing and dance. But he'd had Stephanie Mills, my artist, on in spite of this rule. Gil agreed to an interview with me and my shopping bag full of checks.

But what was really happening? First off, a small label like Sugar Hill is forced to pay a lower royalty rate than the majors. A small label has a harder time surviving. And a small black label has one more problem that drives up its costs. Major labels like CBS and Warner Bros are parts of big, stable conglomerates. They can borrow money from banks. And they can get that money at relatively low rates of interest. A small, black label does not have that luxury. In the 1980s, the banks were deeply suspicious of the entertainment industry. It was too volatile for them. Too much a matter of hit and miss. And if you were black the suspicion tripled. So you had recourse to only one lending institution, the Mob. And, as you've seen with Art Kass, the interest rates the Mob charges are extortionate.

Nonetheless, the Mob kept one of its representatives in the record industry at all times, prepared to bail out small record-company presidents of talent when they hit trouble. His name was Morris Levi. I never met him. Which is probably for the best. However, I did meet Danny Sims's Italian godfather. A man who I suspect supplied more than just lunch. And Nicky Barnes, the man who drove the Mafia out of Harlem and took over the territory's drug business.

But there was one more difficulty. Sylvia explained that she had paid Grandmaster Flash and the Furious Five a lot of money in cash. The band members would run out of pocket change, come to Sylvia's kitchen door at night, and beg for money, and Sylvia would empty her purse and her wallet and give them all that she had.

There was a reason the band members ran out of money frequently: cocaine. It is said that the band, in fact, had their own coke dealer traveling on their tour bus with them. Cocaine messes up lives. And it's expensive. Remember how Phyllis Hyman ran out of the will to live and killed herself? As you know, I suspect the cost of cocaine had something to do with it.

Which means I was not very tolerant of the idea that Grandmaster Flash and the Furious Five were cocaining.

* * *

Then I got a call from Profile Records. They wanted us to work with Run-DMC. Meaning that Run-DMC's manager, Russell Simmons, wanted us to work with Run-DMC.

We did our usual job with Run-DMC. I wrote the press materials, looking for strong hooks. The account executive on the case, Susan Crane, went after national publicity with fervor. And our touring publicists delivered the goods.

But Run-DMC puzzled me. Sylvia Robinson had found rap bubbling up in the South Bronx. The South Bronx had a reputation as the most violent neighborhood in New York.[163] In 1977, just three years before Sylvia's trip to the South Bronx, network TV sportscaster Howard Cosell had told America, "The Bronx is burning."[164] Some sections of the Bronx had lost 97 percent of their buildings to arson. Sociologist Randol Contreras, who grew up in the South Bronx during what he calls "the crack era," says, "The South Bronx was an urban inferno, with thieves, drug pushers, and vandals roaming its abandoned streets."[165] The police called the central police station in the

South Bronx "Fort Apache," after the Arizona Fort that had been under furious siege in the Apache Wars of 1881. For decades, Harlem had been the heart of the black underclass. But that heart—and its high crime statistics—had moved to the South Bronx.

As you know, there is a magic to the black underclass. Yes, its murder rates and gang wars are intolerable. But it is incredibly inventive. It invented tap-dancing, Double Dutch jump-roping, break dancing, beatboxing, and rap. In fact, it invented so many forms of street dance and street athletics that I tried to talk Miles Copeland into starting an annual Olympics of black street arts.

But a strange thing had happened with black neighborhoods since the civil rights movement of the 1960s. Until then, blacks were penned up in inner-city ghettos. If they tried to rent an apartment or buy a house outside a black ghetto like Harlem, they were turned away. Turning down black applicants for a mortgage if they got uppity and applied for funds to buy a house outside of their allotted slum was called redlining. Something I'd been schooled on when I was sixteen and was named the head of the social-action committee for Buffalo's Unitarian youth group. How a Jewish atheist became committee head for a group sponsored by the Unitarian church is a story for another time. Redlining means blacks were caged in the neighborhood set aside for them. Then the civil rights movement put an end to redlining and made discrimination in renting illegal. Suddenly, the rising black middle class could flee the ghetto. It could isolate itself and leave the underclass behind.

Russell Simmons, the man who would become the most successful manager in rap, and one of the most successful figures in the music industry, and his brother Run, of Run-DMC, came from that black exodus, the flight of the middle class from the inner city. Their parents were professionals. Their father was a public school administrator and their mom was a city park administrator. They grew up in a neighborhood far from the violence of Harlem or the South Bronx. They were raised in the calm of the New York borough called Queens.

The puzzle was this. Russell and Run's parents had worked hard to flee the ghetto. Now Russell and Run wanted to go back into it. At least they wanted to go back to its music. Russell, in fact, got his start throwing parties in Harlem.

Why did these sons of the black middle class want to go back to the ghetto that their parents had escaped? I could only guess. But in the 1960s and 1970s, white kids fled the suburban paradise where their parents had bought homes. They went backward in search of an escape. An escape from what? From their parents and from the authority figures of their parents' generation—the Establishment. Young white suburban kids rebelled by going back to the earth, and to skills that didn't require a college degree—carpentry, leather crafting, and farming. In England, lower-middle-class kids escaped their parents and society's mainstream by glomming on to obscure records from black Americans like Muddy Waters, Howlin' Wolf, and Robert Johnson. Going backward . . . and down . . . can give kids excitement.

Why the excitement? Why were black middle-class kids attracted to the subculture of the underclass? The subculture their parents had worked so hard to avoid? The whisperings of roots. And individuation—using a return to roots to rebel against your parents. Using the culture that your mom and dad loathed, and from which they had fled, to set yourself apart from your parents. Using music to give a big fuck-you to the soporific comfort in which you were raised. Like ZZ Top's Billy Gibbons escaping his parents by listening to the forbidden race music of Wolfman Jack. And imprinting on it.

But there was more than that at work in rap's appeal to the kids of the black—and white—middle class. When I took the bus to the all-white neighborhoods of a small Republican city, my wife's hometown of Kingston, New York, in 1982 and 1983, I headed out on long walks through the 100 percent white neighborhoods of big white houses with even bigger front and back lawns, and was surprised to hear rap music—the music I was championing—coming from the backyards. Some affluent white kids found rap to be just as effective a screw-you to their parents as Alice Cooper had once been. Rap appeared to be a tool for giving parental society the finger—the way the music of sperm, jazz, had given parents the finger in the 1920s.

In my days at *Circus* in 1971–1973, white suburban kids had loathed the music of the inner city—black music. But ten years later, in 1981, America's racial attitudes were changing. And that change showed up in music.

It would also show up in a song called "Little Pink Houses."

40

JOHN MELLENCAMP—HURT SO GOOD

I now had secular shamanism down to a formula. If I worked with you, I was after the gods inside of you. I was after the soul that wrote your songs and danced you onstage. I was after your passion points. Your imprinting points.

To pull that involuntary, invisible, muscular self to the surface, where you and I could see it, I made demands. You already know the drill. I would need a month to study you. Then I'd need a one-to-three-day meeting with you in your own environment, with no handlers, wives, or managers in sight. If you came to me to do your publicity, these became nonnegotiable demands.

One sunny day in 1982, I was driving a rental car east on Sunset Boulevard in Hollywood, past the offices of many of the managers I worked with. A song came on the radio that riveted me. I couldn't drive. I found a place to park and pulled over to keep myself and other drivers out of danger. The song coming from the car's quad speaker system had grabbed my muscular self, the self beneath the floorboards of the self. It had set the gods inside in motion. As I said, I literally could not continue driving. It was like feeling my knees buckle when I'd read the lyrics of Paul Simon.

No song had ever done this to me before. And no song would ever do it again.

The song was "Hurts So Good" by John Mellencamp. Or John Cougar, as he was known in those days.

Back in New York, I got a call from a person I'd never heard of, Russell Shaw. John Cougar wanted to work with me. Yes, the same John Cougar who had sung "Hurts So Good." I have no clue to how I'd caught John's attention.

Russell Shaw was a one of a kind in the music industry. Well, actually, he was very much like ZZ Top's Bob Small. On paper, John Cougar was managed by Billy Gaff, the man who had built the career of Rod Stewart and had been involved with Cream, the Bee Gees, Peter Frampton, Status Quo, and the Clash. Billy had probably thrown his weight around to get John a record deal. But when it came to the day-to-day, Billy was off managing his racehorses. If he did anything for John Cougar more than once every two years, I never saw it. But Russell Shaw was another matter. He was Gaff's arms, eyes, and ears. He worked all his waking hours on John Cougar, seven days a week, without vacations. He was, to use a word you've seen before in these pages, a kamikaze. John's life came before Russell's own. Russell would do anything necessary to serve or build John, including laying down his life. Which is ultimately what he would do.

I'd been following John Cougar's career from a distance. Yes, I loved his "Hurts So Good" intensely. But I followed all the successful careers in the record industry. I studied the strategies that succeeded and those that failed. And I came up with ways to overcome the weaknesses and to emulate or better the strengths. Or, at least, I did it to the best of my ability. I analyzed careers and loved doing it. My greatest love, as you've seen, was one of the things I'd used to build Joan Jett—tour strategy. Panzer-tank career-building strategy.

There were two careers in 1982 that were heading for trouble—Billy Idol's and John Cougar's. Why? Because they were headed for a category without a future. They were about to become two-hit wonders.

As you already know, a two-hit wonder is what Joan Jett could have easily become if we hadn't blanketed the country with three tour dates per town before her song "I Love Rock 'n' Roll" was released as a single. A two-hit wonder has no tour base. No base of loyal fans—fans with a gut-deep commitment—to sustain him or her. The two-hit wonder has two hits. Those hits soar up the charts. But without a base of fans and a base in the press, the audience members—you and me—feel these singers have been shoved down our throats. We have no ownership of these hit makers. We have no ego stake in them. They did not come to us via word of mouth from our friends. We have not gone to a concert and been seized by the forces that yank us out of ourselves through the star's frenzies. We haven't been melted and lifted by the star into ecstasies. So we reject these hit makers. And we forget them. They are cursed by the success of their songs. They are cursed because their groundwork has not been done properly. Because they haven't toured in the keep-'em-hungry manner. John Cougar was headed for the two-hit-wonder trap.

I ran my conditions past Russell Shaw on the phone. My month of study, and at least a day with John Cougar in his own environment. Alone. He said absolutely not. Two days later, he called again. He'd discussed it with John. And John had said, "If that's the way he does things, then let's try it." Bless John.

So I studied John Cougar for a month and discovered that he had a huge obstacle in his path. The press hated him. The entire rock-crit elite. If you were a member of the rock-crit aristocracy having lunch with your fellow rock critics and you even mentioned merely listening to Johnny Cougar, you'd be mocked and shunned. There was a prescribed way of treating a John Cougar LP. A ritual. A way to demonstrate your taste and discernment. You set the Cougar album on the reject pile, and you wrote your review without listening. Then you sold the unopened album. What did this ritual insist you write? That John Cougar's music was shit, and that his personality was even shittier. How had this come about? Through an overdose of cleverness.

John had driven his Pontiac from Indiana to New York in 1975 with one goal in mind. David Bowie had become a huge star. Bowie's manager, Tony Defries, took the credit for that career explosion. Remember, it was an attractive and gorgeously dressed young woman from Defries's office who had come to you once a month at *Circus* magazine with a huge heap of slide sheets—photos of Bowie's newest moves. And Defries had two other claims to fame. He managed Lou Reed and Iggy Pop.[166] Two musicians who had become legends long before Defries met them.

So John had driven to New York with the goal of convincing Tony Defries to manage him. John spent several days in Defries's waiting room, hoping to get the super-manager's attention. He failed. So he left a tape. And he had a bit of luck. The receptionist he gave the tape to was from John's home state, Indiana. Tapes usually go into the slush pile, never to be heard. But this tape was an exception. John went home to Seymour, Indiana, where he got an unexpected phone call. Defries had heard his tape and wanted to meet. In fact, Defries sent John a plane ticket to New York.[167] And Defries finally agreed to manage him. At that moment in time, John's last name was Mellencamp. Defries was convinced that he had made David Robert Jones a star by changing his last name to Bowie. So Defries came up with another of what he regarded as his strokes of genius. He renamed John Mellencamp Johnny Cougar. Wow. What brilliance. Right?

Then Defries and the people around him came up with a one-of-a-kind grand idea for driving Johnny Cougar into the rock crits' collective heart. Defries's team worked with the well-connected head of *Radio and Records*, a massively hip, underground-ish music trade magazine. That head identified all the key critics in America. Then, in John Cougar's name, Defries put together a coffee-table art book with a page on each critic, a photo, and a bio. And he sent a copy to *every one of them*.

Defries had radically misunderstood the psychology of the rock writers. Yes, they operate like a herd of sheep. But they are addicted to power. To their own power. They like to believe that they are singlehandedly making the careers of the musicians whom they have discovered. They hate having musicians shoved down their throats. If they can build a musician they feel that they have discovered, that's power. If a musician becomes a star without them, they display their power by tearing him down. By destroying him. The way Robert Christgau had tried to destroy ZZ Top.

What's more, the critics regard themselves as the archetypes of rectitude. In other words, they believe they can't be bought. Lumping them together in an expensive art book designed to promote a musician they had never heard of meant that they had not discovered Cougar, Cougar was being shoveled past their clenched teeth into their esophagus. That made them victims, not power brokers. And it violated their sense of unbribable virtue in the most heavy-handed way imaginable, short of sending each one a thousand-dollar bill.

So they hated John Cougar. On principle. They wouldn't even listen to him. And, worse, they were convinced that he had an outrageous and appalling personality. I'd seen this collective perception at work with a friend and neighbor, Ken Emerson. Ken came from an august Boston family. And he lived a few blocks from me in Park Slope, Brooklyn. He was the record-review editor at *Rolling Stone*. He'd taken over that position from one of the gods of the rock-crit elite, John Landau.

Who was John Landau? Beginning in 1974, Landau had orchestrated a press frenzy for a musician the rock critics were convinced they had discovered and had lifted to stardom. Landau was in a lofty position at *Rolling Stone*. As you've seen, he was the magazine's review editor. Every major critic in the USA had to come to him, begging to be published. And Landau was this New Jersey musician's praiser-in-chief. It was Landau who kept the top critics convinced that they were personally responsible for the artist's roaring rise. Then Landau left the writing business and became the artist's manager. The artist Landau had built by giving the rock-crit elite a nonstop sense of control was Bruce Springsteen.[168]

Now Ken Emerson was in Landau's lofty perch at *Rolling Stone* as record-review editor. I liked Ken. Twice when I walked down the central business street of Park Slope, Seventh Avenue, on my way to the subway, I passed Ken, who was six feet tall, reading a book while he walked and looking like Ichabod Crane. How Ken avoided injuring himself, I do not know. But I was raised by books the way Mowgli in *The Jungle Book* was raised by wolves. Anyone this devoted to reading was on my wavelength. So I began to take Ken to lunch in Manhattan. Our one o'clock lunches would last until three or four. How did Ken feel about John Cougar when Cougar's name first came up in conversation? If I understood correctly, Ken wrote negative reviews of Cougar LPs without ever slitting the shrink-wrap. And he tossed in a line or two about Cougar's appalling personality.

This was a prejudice we would have to undo. But first, I needed to see into John's soul. I had to see if there was an authentic god inside. So I flew out to Indiana. John's brother Ted met me at the airport and drove me through two hours of the greenest countryside I'd ever seen—green farms and green forests—to the woods outside of John's hometown, Seymour, Indiana. We pulled up to a driveway and garage in an asphalt-paved circular clearing on the top of a short, blunt hill, a hilltop smothered by the trees of a forest. There was no house in sight. We parked. I was led to a structure you've already glimpsed—what looked like a tool shed just big enough to have that full-sized door I told you about. Ted opened the door, and I discovered we were in the attic, in the entrance to a house that spilled down the side of a steep hill. I walked down the stairs, met John and his wife, and was given a bedroom in which to spend the night. Before bedtime, I suspect they fed me dinner, but I honestly don't remember. Why? Because our big interview would be the next day.

My bedroom had a full wall of glass looking out at the thick, black trunks of the trees that rose on the steep hill around us. When I woke up in the morning, I felt as if I were in Africa. There was a black beetle on the window twice the size of your thumb. And it had horns of immense size. Those horns made it look dangerous. It sat in one spot, unmoving but threatening. Ten times the size of a New York City cockroach. So Indiana was not exactly Brooklyn.

I put on my clothes, went to the kitchen, and had breakfast served by John's blonde, slender wife, Vicki. Vicki was the daughter of a stuntman in Hollywood. One day, when she was roughly sixteen or seventeen, she'd been on the set of a film. The stunt driver who was supposed to flip a car 360 degrees and get it to land on its tires again for a chase scene had not shown up. Vicki volunteered to do the stunt. She had balls. And, as I'd discover further down the line, she had a heart.

At 9:00 a.m., John and I settled in the living room. Alone. No handlers, managers, or wives. We sat in normal living-room chairs, stuffed, comfy. I took the one across from the wall of windows looking at the tree trunks and leaves of the forest. John took a seat facing the door. At a ninety-degree angle from me. The power seat. And I probed for his imprinting points.

Here were the key elements. The life that counted for John, the life that conjured up the gods inside him, came from his days in high school. As you know, John grew up in Seymour, Indiana. His parents were normal middle-class folks. Well, maybe not entirely normal. His father had worked his way up in an electrical contracting company—Robbins Electric—from an entry-level job in the field pulling double shifts and seven-day workweeks to an executive vice president and member of the board overseeing big projects, including the wiring of a nuclear power plant.[169] John's dad, like me, was a workaholic. But John's family was not like any I'd ever seen. John's great grandfather was a plowman-for-hire who had come from Germany to America, bought his own piece of land, and had started his own farm. Said John, his great grandfather had been a silent man. When he settled a disagreement, he did it with his fists. And John identified strongly with that approach. It was one of his imprinting points.

According to one of his biographers, Heather Johnson, in her book *Born in a Small Town*, John picked up on that tradition from the time he was a child. Kids living near him had to run an obstacle course when leaving their houses to get to the school bus. The kid next door, John Mellencamp, was pelting them with stones. Meanly. Viciously.

In high school, John and his friends cruised the streets in their cars looking for girls. They drove to nearby towns, visited the bars, and got into fights. They joked about gross details like "dingle berries"—little bits of shit still clinging to the pubic hair of girls they picked up. But there was a hidden drama underlying these teen activities. In addition to his fist-fighting grandfather, John had imprinted on two Paul Newman movies. One was *Hud*, the film that taught John the lesson that would illuminate Prince. First we rebel against our father. Then we become him. The second film was Paul Newman's *Cool Hand Luke*.

To show me *Cool Hand Luke*, John sat me on the living-room rug just a few feet from the TV, sat himself two feet away from me, and showed me *Hud* and *Cool Hand Luke* back to back. He explained the lesson of *Hud* brilliantly. Next, he gave me the lesson of *Cool Hand Luke*. Cool Hand Luke—Paul Newman—is a former war hero who got drunk one night and cut the heads off of a few parking meters. He's in a Florida jail that specializes in forcing chain gangs to break rocks. Luke attempts to escape. Twice. Once to attend his mother's funeral. The prison warden is pissed off and delivers the famous line, "What we have here is a failure to communicate." But there is a price for Luke's courage. The warden has him thrown in "the box," a tin shed the size of an upright coffin. During the day, the sun heats the shed like a vertical frying pan and makes it unendurably stifling inside. So, when Luke comes out of the box twenty-four hours later, he can barely stand. Luke takes this punishment like a man. What's more, he's fitted with double leg irons and is forced to dig a grave every day and fill it in again. But almost nothing wears down his astonishing defiance.[170]

The other prisoners idolize him. He becomes their hero, their spokesman, and their savior. He becomes the tongue of the group. Which is where Luke's problems begin. His fellow prisoners expect things from him that are superhuman. There's no way he can live up to their image of him. Like the other prisoners, he has weaknesses and limits. Like Bob Marley asking one of his backup singers, "Wha' ya t'ink?" Ultimately, trying live up to his fellow prisoners' fantasies about his powers kills him. Luke is like Christ, assuming all the aspirations, sins, and burdens of mankind, and being crucified for it. In other words, even in high school, John saw himself as a potential leader, and foresaw the dangers of leadership. Or, to put it differently, he had a sense that he could be an icon, a legend. And he foresaw that that legendary status sometimes comes at a price. That price would indeed arrive . . . when John Mellencamp performed onstage. Something you've already glimpsed. But let's not sprint ahead of ourselves.

What impact did the Newman films have on John's high-school life? John saw himself in the Newman role in every barroom fight, every encounter with his school's authorities, and every battle with his parents. He and his friends were also influenced by David Bowie and Iggy Pop. John grew his hair long and fought with his parents and the school authorities over its length. But with every battle and sexual conquest—or imagined sexual conquest—John saw himself as Newman. He saw himself as a very big presence on a cinemascope screen. In fact, he saw himself as the film's lead.

Then John graduated high school, and everything changed. By then, he had gotten his girlfriend pregnant. So he had an unplanned wife and a baby daughter. He had not learned any particular skills. He had not hankered after any particular goals. He had not yet even become serious about music. He grew depressed. So depressed that when he woke up in the morning he had a hard time getting the motivation to pick up his socks and put them on. Suddenly, he'd gone from a very big figure filling a Cinemascope screen to a single pixel on an infinite screen. He'd gone from the star of a film to a speck of dust. Or less.

John got a job as a lineman for his wife's employer, the phone company. His dad had started as a lineman and had worked his way up to vice president. But not John. He screwed up most of his assignments. And he was nasty to the customers. He lost the job.

Going from a big deal in high school to a nonentity in the real world was at the heart of John's story. It's at the heart of songs like "Small Town" and "Jack and Diane." And other gut-level aspects of the human experience were behind songs like "Hurts So Good" and "Hand to Hold On To." In other words, John was authentic. He had a powerful story. And that story had reams to say about the uniqueness of the culture of small-town Indiana.

John had sung in bars on and off since high school, but unlike Prince, who ate, breathed, and slept music, John hadn't been that serious about it. Despite that, he'd made a demo tape with just two songs.

Then John had set out on a quest to take over the center of the screen again. First, he drove to New York and visited every record company he could think of. The few who paid any attention to him listened to the tape and told him it was raw sewage.

The demo was two meager cover tunes. It was amateur. The idea that he would have to write songs came to John as a shock. He later explained that, "When I first started making records, the idea of writing songs never really occurred to me, because I was in a bar band in Indiana and I was a singer. We did other people's material, so when I got a record deal, it was like, 'Oh, you have to write your own songs? I don't know how to do that.'"[171]

But John demoed more songs by Bob Dylan and Woody Guthrie, drove back to New York, and landed Defries.

In fact, Mellencamp didn't record songs of his own until his second album, *A Biography*, in 1978—an album that wasn't even released in the United States.[172] But that album contained a Mellencamp-written hit: "I Need a Lover Who Won't Drive Me Crazy," which reached the Top 40 in John's version, and nabbed heavy airplay on America's progressive rock radio stations in a rendering by Pat Benatar.

* * *

By the time 4:00 p.m. rolled around and our interview was finished, John looked hollowed out. There were caverns of darkness where his eyes should have been. He was limp and weakened. This would not be the first time I'd see him in this state.

But I was exultant. On my notepad with the Howard Bloom Organization logo and the butterfly clip to keep the fat wad of pages from falling apart was a story. Complete with things that came as revelations to me. Particularly the shift from the very finite film screen of high school to the endless screen of adulthood. That was something I could identify with completely. Something of the sort had once happened to me. But that's not a story for this book.

I flew back to New York, sat on my Park Slope brownstone's front stoop in the summer weather with scissors and Scotch tape, fought the wind that threatened to blow away the strips of paper into which I was scissoring John's story, put the ribbons of Mellencamp's tale in chronological order so I could see the underlying story—the drama that John had given me—and, when Monday came, I had the result typed up. Then I sent it to John and explained the rules of interviews, the same rules I'd given to Prince.

I hadn't yet learned that I needed to write all of our bios and press materials myself. So I had our writer, Martin Torgoff, turn John's story into an official biography, and I radically rewrote what poor Martin turned in. John's tale must have hit home with Torgoff. His first two books had been about Elvis Presley. But, in 1986, he would write his third book, *American Fool: The Roots and Improbable Rise of John Cougar Mellencamp*. And he'd win the ASCAP Deems Taylor Award for excellence in music journalism for his Mellencamp book.

I began taking key members of the rock-crit elite to lunch. I had a simple mission: explain John Cougar. Tell his story. Open the writers' eyes to a Middle America they didn't know. And to a person whose life had been a journey with passion and authenticity. I had two things going for me:

1. Even though songwriting had come late to John, the songs he was creating were often staggering. Like "Hurt So Good," the song that had stopped me dead in my tracks in a rented car on Sunset Boulevard. Or "Hand to Hold On To," whose lyrics captured something deep in your life and mine, and in the life of anyone who has ever felt alone. "Everyone needs a hand to hold on to."
2. John's stage performance. It made your jaw drop. The god that came out of John and danced him onstage rendered you speechless. To repeat, of the performers I've worked with, the three most amazing were Michael Jackson, Prince, and John Cougar. And you could easily reshuffle that list any way you want, because all three were equally astonishing. Equally awe-making.

My role was to make sure that, when John toured, he never oversaturated a city. And that he did not leave any sections of the USA uncovered. In other words, like any good seduction, the art was to make sure that John was a presence in your life but that his touring left you hungry.

Meanwhile, telling John's tale and changing the rock-crit perception would be very, very hard. I took critic after critic to lunch. I told John's story. I tried to explain what John accomplished onstage. Was it paying off? No, not for the first year or two. But, when in doubt, persist. In the third year, the critical perception of John shifted dramatically. The lead sheep slowly but surely changed their minds. We had finally supersaturated our solution. And we had finally hit the tipping point, the moment when a crystal hits the water. John had a New York date at Radio City Music Hall—a prestige location all the New York critics could get to with ease. Sherry Ring, the publicist at John's record company, my Mellencamp account executive, and I got on the phone like maniacs. We did our best to make sure that every critic who mattered came to see the show. Every critic whose ear I had talked off over lunch. In three years of lunches.

I don't have words for what John did onstage. He'd come late to performance. He didn't really start performing regularly until he met Defries and went out on tour. But talk about being seized by the gods inside and puppeteered as if you were a marionette. Remember, whenever John came offstage, he didn't want anyone to see him. He'd been a pipe for the souls of eighteen thousand people, and for something transcendent inside of himself. Now he was empty, a husk. His eye sockets were caverns. He hid in a tiny room off the dressing room for an hour. He only saw his wife and, once, me. Why? It took an hour for John's normal self to come back to life. That's the power of his gods inside.

So, when John Mellencamp stepped onstage, he was a force of nature. He cleaved the very stone of your soul. When the Radio City Music Hall concert ended, his record company, Polygram, had a reception at a posh, huge, lower-level Radio City Music Hall room lined with red velvet. All the critics were there. First Tim White, a superstar writer from the Associated Press and *Rolling Stone*, came up to me, glowing. He took my biceps in his hands, held on tight, and said, "You were right. You were right. You were right." It wasn't just the words that conveyed his feelings, it was that flush in his face. Then Vic Garbarini, the super-snooty editor of the high-prestige *Musician* magazine, sought me out in the crowd. He did what Timothy White had just done. He took my biceps in his hands and with his face just a foot from mine said almost the same words Tim had used. John's performance was a revelation. Or, to use a phrase from my book *The Genius of the Beast: A Radical Re-Vision of Capitalism*, John's performance was an act of secular salvation. No evangelical preacher from Indiana could have wrought a conversion this profound with a single performance.

One proof: Timothy White would later be listed in Heather Johnson's *Born in a Small Town* as one of John Mellencamp's best friends. Timothy had been a skeptic. It had taken three years to win him over. This was a friendship I would nurture long after the Radio City Music Hall epiphany. And there was another.

* * *

Back in the days when I had co-founded an art studio to escape the Auschwitz of the mind called grad school, and when I had entered a field I knew nothing about, popular culture, I'd visited every art director I could find in New York City with Cloud Studio's portfolio. At *Penthouse* magazine, I'd met a nineteen-year-old with a British accent and dark hair who was putting together fan magazines of a kind that were normal in England, but that had never been seen in the States. They looked like a normal magazine on the newsstands—with glossy paper and vivid color printing. But when you got them home, they unfolded more like a highway map. On the back side, each folded page had a new photo of whatever star the issue featured. But the front side unfolded as an enormous color poster. The entrepreneur behind this unusual magazine approach, the editor and art-director all rolled up in one, was Bob Guccione Jr. The nineteen-year-old son of the man who had created *Penthouse*, then founded *Omni*— Bob Guccione Sr. I liked Bob the Younger a lot. And he apparently liked me.

Founding new magazines ran in the family. Roughly fifteen years after we first met, Bob Guccione Jr. showed up in the music industry. He created a new rock publication, a big format, gorgeous, full-color magazine called *Spin*. The year was 1985. *Rolling Stone* was THE music magazine. Yet *Spin*, in its own way, became hipper than *Rolling Stone*. It had a finer feel for the cutting edge, with bands like the Jesus and Mary Chain on the cover.

But *Spin* rapidly became notorious among publicists. In fact, the major publicists in the industry hated *Spin*. For a reason. No one could get its editor and chief, the man who made the final decisions, on the phone. Bob Guccione Jr. didn't feel that taking calls from publicists was worth his time. I was wildly excited to see Bob reappear in my world. I called him. He took the call. Then he invited me to dinner and promised he would cook for me himself. Which he did. Several times. Over the course of the years, he and I would become brothers in spirit. I admired his ability to turn magazines into art forms. But there was more. We were both seekers after the gods inside. We were both on a quest for soul.

So when I told Bob the stories of this new soul I had found, this new blowtorch of the human spirit, John Cougar Mellencamp, Bob believed me. And when John's coups on the charts added to the flame, Bob said he'd give John a cover if he could do what I'd done: if he could fly out to Seymour and spend at least a day with the rocker from Indiana. Digging for John's soul. That started another long-term Mellencamp friendship. And it kicked off what *Spin* writer Jim Greer, in the pages of the April 1995 *Spin*, called "too many John Mellencamp covers"—by my count, four.

Meanwhile, John's success on the charts was enormous. In 1982, John would have two hits in the Top 10 at the same time, "Hurts So Good" and "Jack and Diane." In fact, "Jack and Diane" would be the most-added record in the history of Polygram Records up to that time. "Hurts So Good" would be No. 1 on the Mainstream Rock charts for twelve straight weeks—three months. All of this made Mellencamp what biographer Heather Johnson says was "the first male artist to have two Top 10 singles and a No. 1 album simultaneously."[173]

But John's press coronation came when I called Jann Wenner, the founder and publisher of *Rolling Stone*, one of the most powerful people in the music industry—someone I'd never met or talked to before. By now, I was working with Prince, Bob Marley, Michael Jackson, John Mellencamp, and Billy Joel, some of whose stories are yet to come. I had been working with the top critics in the business for ten years. What's more, Ken Emerson—who was now an editor at the *New York Times Magazine*, one of the most influential publications in the world—had told another publicist that,

"Every publicist should be like Howard Bloom. He knows how to tell a story." In other words, I had clout. Nonetheless, I had to screw up my courage to call Wenner. What was I offering him? The chance to meet John Cougar Mellencamp. Formerly the most hated rocker in the United States. At a moment when John Cougar was the hottest phenomenon on the charts. And at a moment when press belief in him had gone from minus 1,000 to plus 90. Maybe a bit higher.

Wenner said yes. So when John was in New York, I took him over to 745 Fifth Avenue at Fifty-Eighth Street, up the elevator, and to Jann's office, with its astonishing view of Central Park from its private roof terrace. And, yes, Jann did put John Cougar on *Rolling Stone*'s cover. On January 30 of 1986.

So much for Joe Dera's claim that we couldn't deliver covers. We just did it a bit differently than Dera. We built the visibility of the stars who landed those covers ourselves.

                                    * * *

I also set John up for a private meeting with Billy Joel. But that's a story for another time.

                                    * * *

If I worked for you, my job was to find your soul, then to keep you true to it. When push came to shove, my job was to remind you of who you were. In other words, my job was to find your self below the floorboards of the self—the gods that danced you like a puppet. My job was to put those gods in words. One day in roughly 1983, John called. Heinz wanted to use "Hurts So Good" in its ketchup campaign. This was the campaign that had used Carly Simon's hit "Anticipation" to make a virtue out of Heinz ketchup's most irritating property in the days before squeeze bottles—the fact that no matter how much you curse, shake, and slap the darned glass bottle, the red stuff simply refuses to come out.

Heinz had offered John $1.25 million. That's close to $3 million in today's money.

I asked a question: in fifteen years, which would you rather do, make money off of your investments or be onstage making music? John's answer was making music.

"Then you have to turn down the Heinz money," I said, and I explained why. "You speak for your audience," I said. "When they feel worn down by the system, you give them strength and courage. More important, you give them the right to be. You are a rock prophet. Like a prophet, you stand outside the closed gates of the city, you raise your fist in the air, and you proclaim that you and all those like you have a right to exist. Heinz ketchup and other commercial sponsors are the keepers of the very gates that you challenge. Sign up for corporate sponsorship, and you cease to be the voice of the outsider. You become an insider. You become one of the powerful elders against whom you've been rebelling."

John turned down the ketchup ad. And he turned totally against corporate sponsorship. Heather Johnson, in her book *Born in a Small Town*, says this issue tore the relationship between John and his manager, Billy Gaff, apart. She may have been right. One day, I got another call from John. Who would I recommend as a new manager? I recommended Tommy Mottola.

* * *

Who was Tommy Mottola? One of the most famous forces in the record industry. *New York* magazine called him "the industry's most flamboyant mogul, and one of its most powerful."[174] Tommy had been in music publishing at Chappell Music when he'd heard the music of Daryl Hall and John Oates—Hall and Oates. Mottola switched sides from publishing to the side of the artist and became Hall and Oates's manager. Then he famously negotiated Hall and Oates a roughly five-million-dollar deal with RCA Records . . . after first insisting on thirteen million.[175] He was proud of his ability to negotiate unbelievable amounts of money.

In fact, Mottola was engaged in a rivalry with another music industry titan, the president of CBS Records, Walter Yetnikoff. If Yetnikoff pulled in seven million dollars, Tommy had to one-up him by making ten million. If Yetnikoff made seventeen million, Tommy had to one-up him by making twenty million. It wasn't greed. It was a game. It was something totally immaterial—status. It was a competition to see who could come out on top of the pecking order.

Why did I recommend Tommy Mottola for John Mellencamp?

1. He was powerful.
2. In reality, Tommy had no idea of how to build a career. But he was terrific at pulling smart people into his team and motivating them. He'd pulled me in on Hall and Oates.

Meeting with Tommy and his team in their office on West Fifty-Seventh Street across the hall from Woody Allen's office was a treat. If you came up with a good idea, Tommy recognized it immediately and started the process of execution on the spot.

One day, I was in Tommy's office and I came up with one of those good ideas. Tommy had hired me to represent Hall and Oates, which, as you've seen, was the pillar of his business at the time. In searching for Hall and Oates's passion points, one thing had become obvious. As kids growing up in Philadelphia, Daryl Hall and John Oates had shared one overarching ambition: to be the Temptations. The Temptations were one of Motown's most iconic and influential acts. Says Wikipedia, the fivesome were "one of the most successful groups in music history."[176] The Temptations had been, for John Hall and Daryl Oates, a supernormal stimulus. An imprinting point.

Daryl and John would go to every Temptations show in Philly and would hang around the backstage entrance, hoping to meet the group's members. Their own songs and vocals would owe a huge debt to the Temptations' influence. Their style would be a monument to their ache to be the Temptations. The Temptations would be, for them, what Les Paul had been for Bill Chinnock—a trellis to climb on. The Temptations revealed one the roles of an icon. There would be more.

The Apollo Theater, the mecca of black music, was about to reopen once again. The man opening the place this time was Percy Sutton, former borough president of Manhattan, owner of WBLS, the leading black station in New York City, and owner of a chain of twenty-six other successful black stations across America. As you remember, I had met Sutton at a conference table with Bob Marley. Sutton was famous for not taking calls from white people.

I suggested to Tommy Mottola that we put Hall and Oates together with the Temptations and make Hall and Oates the act that reopens the Apollo. An enormous coup for a duo with their roots in R&B. Especially a white duo. And I suggested that we film the event and put it out as something new that was selling like hotcakes—a VHS tape. Tommy liked the idea. If he got the Temptations, I said, I would get Percy Sutton. Why would Percy Sutton take my call? Because of the impression I hoped I'd made on Percy when we had had our Marley meeting. I got Percy. And Tommy got the Temptations. The opening night at the Apollo was already booked. So we got the second night. And the VHS tape was a huge seller.

John Mellencamp liked to pilot his own career. He liked to make the key decisions. And I liked piloting strategy, too. Especially when it came to booking strategy for John—an area that John had let me step into whenever it looked like something crucial needed addressing. In other words, Tommy Mottola appreciated quality input. So I enjoyed working with Tommy. And I suspected John would enjoy it, too. John did indeed hire Tommy as his manager. And Tommy would later say that Mellencamp was the worst hell he would ever be forced to live through.[177] But, hell or not, bigger things were to come.

* * *

In 1985, I was acting as temporary manager for Lionel Richie. I worked in Lionel's dining room in LA two days a week and worked in New York the other five. More about that in a minute. But the weight of the Howard Bloom Organization's success was crushing me. So I hired a vice president with a lot of publicity experience. I made her a deal. In addition to a salary, she'd get 50 percent of any money we pulled in in excess of what we'd made the year before she joined the company. And, with my new freedom, we pulled in a lot. My new VP's name was Victoria Rose. And she was a hard and effective worker.

While I was out in LA with Lionel Richie, Vicki got a call. America's small family farmers were in trouble. Seymour, Indiana, was in the middle of farm country. John's friends, neighbors, and relatives were farmers. His great-grandfather and grandfather had been farmers. John was acutely aware of the trouble family farmers were in. Bob Dylan had suggested that someone from the rock world jump in to save these sinking plowmen. Remember, Mellencamp's grandfather had been a plowman. So John, Willie Nelson, and Neil Young had decided to put together a concert to raise money for family farmers—a concert to draw attention to the farmers' plight. They would call it Farm Aid. Vicki Rose handled this all on her own. With massive help from the rest of my staff.

The concert was a huge success. And it did what it was supposed to do—it put a spotlight on the problems of family farmers. During one of my yearly checkups on the state of John's soul, he drove me very early one morning from his house to a naked cinder-block gray building surrounded by farm fields that stretched as far as the eye could see. There was a parking lot on two sides of the place big enough for roughly a dozen vehicles. And a dozen vehicles there were. But none of them were cars. They were tractors. Big, praying mantis–like tractors. This is where the neighborhood's farmers came to eat breakfast and trade gossip before doing the morning's seeding and planting. John wasn't kidding around when he said he lived among small family farmers.

John did something more. He gave me the names and phone numbers of two lobbyists who worked in Washington, D.C., representing the interests of small family farmers. The lobbyists, two friendly little round guys, schooled me on the farm situation the way that ZZ Top had schooled me on Texas culture, the way that Ray Caviano had schooled me on the gay community, and the way that Leanne Katz had schooled me on censorship for Styx. Six months into a working relationship with the lobbyists, they called with an urgent dilemma. In Chillicothe, Missouri, a dozen farmers had been protesting in front of the Livingston County Farmers Home Administration office for eight solid weeks.[178] Their mortgages were about to be foreclosed. The FHA was about to throw them out of their homes and was about to seize their farms. Their situation was urgent. The farms would be foreclosed in the next two weeks. And they couldn't get any attention. They couldn't get a stitch of press.

John had mentioned that he wanted to do an acoustic performance of his songs someday but had never had the chance. I called him, explained the predicament of the Chillicothe farmers, and urged him to use this chance to perform his acoustic set. I imagined him doing it simply, with a chair, a guitar, and a microphone. John picked up the idea and ran with it. He brought in his entire concert team and had a superb stage, lighting, and sound system set up. Normally, the three big TV networks—networks that monopolized your television in 1986—would not have covered John Cougar— now known by his real name, John Mellencamp. And as for farm stories, the press had been tapped out. A farm crisis was old news. But put two and two together and you can sometimes get eight.

The Chillicothe event was explosive. It attracted ten thousand fans, some of whom UPI said had driven in from as far away as Michigan.[179] More important, it pulled in all three of the TV networks. You could tell. Each network had set up a huge parabolic antenna a few hundred yards away from the stage. A sight you very rarely see.

Johnnie Cougar, the rocker the press hated, had taken another step as John Mellencamp, the rocker the press loved. The Chillicothe event drove home two messages: it drove home who John was. It drove home his authenticity. And it saved a handful of family farmers.

It also helped express the soul of a once-silent group. It added a tiny current to the forces of history.

* * *

When I'd preached that we'd have to do a checkup every year to find out what direction your mutating soul was taking in the latest loop of the earth around the sun, John Mellencamp had understood better than anyone else I ever worked with what I was talking about. He also understood one more thing I preached. An insight even I didn't entirely understand at the time. One of those things your self below the floorboards of the self knows is true but that your verbal mind can't explain. You don't just owe your audience your songs. You owe your audience your life. If we succeed in making you an icon, you will be what Les Paul and the Temptations had been—a trellis on which a new generation of adolescents will grow. So I went out to Seymour in 1987 for the annual soul-dive. I pulled up on the tarmac road through the woods to the asphalt circle by the garage and the tiny structure that led down into the attic of John's house, and John was barbecuing hamburgers with one of his friends from high school. They were using the sort of tiny charcoal grill on a short tripod you can get at Walmart for fifteen dollars. John was, indeed, staying true to his roots. But his next album, *The Lonesome Jubilee*, was about the strange twist he was afraid his roots would take next.

John had an uncle. That uncle had spent his whole life boozing, smoking, and sleeping with as many women as he could lay his hands—and other body parts—on. The result was tragic. When John's uncle had hit middle age, he'd discovered that he had no friends and no close ties with his family. He was bitterly, brokenly, painfully alone. Then he died of cancer at the age of fifty-seven. Alone. That is not what John wanted for his own future. The example of Uncle John haunted Mellencamp's new LP.

Meanwhile, John would divorce Vicki in 1989. He would eventually marry a model, Elaine Irwin. His marriages tended to break up because of other women. And, frankly, one of the reasons most young men go into rock is for the sake of easy access to those other women. Or, as John put it, "How many guys you know in rock bands that have been divorced? There's a reason for that. I don't care who you are or who you think you are, you're gonna fall into the pitfalls of that sooner or later. It's rock and roll. I mean, what other reason would a guy ever pick up a guitar as a teenager?"[180] John's marriage with Elaine would eventually break up, too. But John would keep his family close to him. His brother Ted—who'd picked me up at the airport on my first trip to Seymour—would continue to be his road manager on and off. And his dad would become a key factor in his management. More important, his dad would run Belmont Mall, the studio John built for himself in Belmont, Indiana, and rented out to others, like R.E.M. What's more, when John went into painting in 1988, I suspect it drew him closer to his mother, who had also been an amateur painter. So, despite the fact that John had yielded to sexual temptation during his marriages, he is the big man in his own tribe. His family.

John has saved himself from his uncle John's isolation. He has hands to hold on to. The next move with John Mellencamp would be a nail-biter.

* * *

It was early 1983. I pulled together the sales figures on all of the biggest artists on the charts for 1982. And I encountered a surprise. John Mellencamp had had the biggest-selling album of the year. I double-checked and triple-checked the figures. Yes, hard as it was to believe, the "artificial pop star" destined to be a two-hit wonder, then disappear, had sold more LPs than any of his competitors. So I wrote up a press release on John's achievement and sent it out.

Then I got a call from the VP of public relations at Warner Bros Records, Bob Merlis. The man who I suspect had gotten me fired from ZZ Top. "Your press release says that John Cougar Mellencamp has the biggest selling album of 1982," said Bob. "He doesn't. Asia does." Asia was a very un-Warner-Bros-like band. It was an artificial rock group. It was a band that seemed to have been cobbled together by cagey A&R men, sneaky talent scouts, to capitalize on the success of bands like Rush and Boston. It wasn't real. And part of Warners strategy, judging from this phone call, was to hype it with phony achievements. Like having the biggest-selling album of 1982.

"But John Cougar Mellencamp has the biggest-selling album of 1982," I said. "I've gone over the sales figures, and John is it." "You don't understand me," said Bob, a person I still regarded as a nice guy. "Asia has the biggest-selling album of the year." Then Bob reminded me that Warners controlled one third of the music business. CBS controlled another third. That's 66 percent. The folks at CBS were close friends of Bob's. And if Asia didn't have the biggest-selling album of the year, I would never get another client from CBS or Warners again. I'd be out of business.

"Bob," I said, "John Cougar Mellencamp has the biggest-selling album of 1982. If you send me numbers proving otherwise, I will personally put out a press release saying that Asia has the biggest-selling album of the year. But until you produce those figures, John Cougar Mellencamp has the biggest selling album of 1982." Then we said goodbye. Or maybe we simply hung up. But I doubt it. Not a word had been spoken in anger.

As if he were a mind reader, ten minutes later, John Cougar Mellencamp called. John only called me maybe three times in my life, so this was a surprise. I told John what had just happened. I thought he'd be proud. After all, I'm the wimp who never lasted more than fifteen seconds in a boxing match, and he's the Little Bastard, the tough guy. But as I told the tale, I could hear John turning as yellow as a medical sample cup filling with urine. You could hear his quaking in the way he breathed. "You shouldn't have done that," he said.

So even heroes can be undertowed by fear. Again, like Bob Marley rattled by gunmen. Roughly ten years later, John would thank me for what this standoff had added to his career. And for the tens of millions of dollars it had made him. He and Joan Jett were the only two who ever thanked me. At least as far as I can remember.

* * *

Long after I would leave the music industry, in the 2000s, I would hear that John Mellencamp was developing a project called *Riding the Cage*. It sounded familiar. When I looked into it, it was the story of building a spherical cage out of steel struts, welding in a bucket seat and safety harness, packing a kid into it, taking it to the highway by truck, then releasing it from the back of the truck when the vehicle had reached top speed. John had apparently forgotten where he had gotten that story. In fact, he had incorporated it into his personal mythology, his story of his own rebellion, and was telling it to journalists as something he and his high-school buddies had done.[181] Its actual source? ZZ Top. And who had told it to John one day in his living room? His publicist. His secular shaman.

41

BOB GUCCIONE JR—THE SLAUGHTER OF THE HUTU AND THE TUTSIS

Now for the real story behind "We Are the World" and its starving African kids.

In the 1980s, South Africa's rigid separation between blacks and whites was shoving blacks down to a position as a permanent underclass—a class that lived in shanties and earned their wages by slaving for the folks in elegant homes, South Africa's whites. It was called apartheid. And, every day, when I walked from the subway to my office, I passed the South African embassy. In front of that embassy, every single work day, there were picketers demanding an end to apartheid.

But I was upset. Upset because the protesters opposed apartheid but ignored something more urgent: a mass murder in the works. Remember, groups have souls. And sometimes those souls' exaltation of you and me into something greater than our selves has brutal consequences. Groups switch to battle songs. Groups make war. Two tribes in Central Africa were at each other's throats, and worse. They were murdering each other. And the murder showed signs of getting worse.

I hoped that by making headlines we could stop a mass murder before it happened. So I pitched the story to Bob Guccione Jr. Well, I didn't really pitch him. By that time, we'd become good friends. Bob's venture, *Spin* magazine, had been wildly successful. It had set the standard for what was hip. It had hit hot-button investigative topics that no one else would cover. And it was drop-dead gorgeous. Bob's gift for art-direction was astonishing. The magazine did so well that Bob's father, Bob Guccione Sr., the creator of *Penthouse* and *Omni*, was ticked off. His son was overshadowing him. It's that pecking-order and langur-monkey thing. So Bob Sr. embarked on a vicious battle to take *Spin* away from his son. Because both Guccione's were media celebrities, this battle made headlines.

Remember how Bob had dodged phone calls from publicists? Remember how that had made him unpopular? This meant that when his dad threatened Bob Jr.'s very existence as a publisher, no one came to his aid. All the publicists turned up their noses and hoped that this would be Bob Jr.'s end. All the publicists but me. I gave Bob daily consolation, energy, and guidance. Then, when Bob threw a press conference to give his side of the story, I literally stood by him. I stood next to him on his left. We were literally shoulder-to-shoulder as he took on one of the greatest crises of his life.

So, when I say I pitched Bob, I mean I ranted about mass murder in central Africa to a friend. Bob said, "Why don't you write a story about it?"

In my first eight years in music publicity, I'd taken no vacations. Then, back in the days before my staff went all-female, one of my few male account executives walked up to my desk and said, "You need a vacation." His publicity instincts were abysmal, but on this one, I believed him. So I started taking an annual two-week vacation in August. Usually ending up in LA, so I could do business the minute I stopped relaxing.

In 1985, when Bob Jr. asked me to write a story on mass murder in Central Africa, I planned to take my vacation in my hometown, Buffalo, New York. I'd become aware of the fact that I wouldn't have my parents forever. Yes, they were perfectly healthy and playing golf several times a week. But we are all mortal. Remember, one lesson from Bob Marley: life is a fatal disease. So I'd mapped out two weeks in late August in my dad and mom's territory, seeing them as often as I could. And I'd spent the remaining time on that vacation in Buffalo's central library—where I'd researched my high-school senior thesis on Jesus and Saint Paul. Yes, a high-school dive into the gods within. But this time, in 1985, I was researching a clash between the tribes of Central Africa.

When vacation ended and I was back in my office, I sent Bob the article. It was too historical, he said. He needed something more topical, something with a current hook. Then he found that hook: Live Aid and "We Are the World."

* * *

One afternoon, Bob Guccione Jr. called to invite me to dinner at his dad's house. Why? His dad was having a guest who might interest me. So I showed up at Bob's dad's house at 7:00 p.m.

This was no ordinary house. Buildings in the East Sixties in Manhattan a short walk from Central Park cost a fortune. But Bob Guccione Sr. had two of them. Two right next to each other. And he'd joined them together into one single super-mansion. The wooden doors I knocked on to announce my presence were huge. With good reason. They were antiques shipped in from an Italian castle. The doors were cracked opened by a butler. Possibly the only real, live butler I have ever seen. Beyond those massive wooden doors was a marble-floored entrance hall straight out of *Gone with the Wind*. It was two stories high, with a double staircase of marble under a ceiling imported from yet another classic Italian palace.

Doberman Pinschers were dogs with a very special reputation in those days. They were noted for their ferocity. If you wanted someone torn apart, you turned the job over to your Dobermans. When the wooden doors opened, four Dobermans charged down the two curving staircases. Two per staircase. You could hear the clatter of their claws on the marble of the stairs. What treat were they rushing down to sample? You. Or, in this case, me. Fortunately, as you remember from the visit to Don Arden's mansion in the Hollywood Hills, big dogs tend to like me. And I adore them. So a whole lot of petting took place. And face licking.

My winter coat was taken, and I was ushered into a dining room with a massive antique table that could seat twenty. The table, too, came from a palace in Italy. Bob and I were there. So was Bob's dad. In a smoking robe like the one Ozzy Osbourne had worn sitting in front of Don Arden's fireplace. But the poor man had obviously knocked himself out at work that day. He was scarcely awake. And who else was at the table? An Ethiopian general. A general who wanted to topple the existing Ethiopian regime. A general who was applying to Bob Guccione Sr. for the funds with which to stage a coup.

Alas, Bob Sr. nodded off during the general's plea. But that plea provided a clue. A clue to what? To a problem behind Live Aid and "We Are the World."

* * *

The team behind Live Aid and "We Are the World's" two massive, superstar-studded events said that the mass death of Ethiopians was caused by drought. One of *Spin*'s editors, Robert Keating, a brilliant investigative journalist, said that was false. Keating dug down to the bedrock and discovered that the ghastly starvation killing at least a hundred thousand Ethiopians was no fluke of the weather.[182] It was part of a deliberate government policy. It was part of a deliberate Stalinist policy. In Ethiopia. A policy inflicted by the Marxist-Leninist government that our general wanted to topple.

To understand that policy, you have to understand a trick invented by Joseph Stalin.

To get the peasant population under his control in the Russia of 1929, Stalin attacked Russia's successful, entrepreneurial peasants, the kulaks. Stalin rounded them up like cattle. He deliberately starved them to death. In the middle of this mass murder, the Soviets put together a giant press junket for America's journalists. A press trip to demonstrate that Russia was a Marxist utopia. The sort of junket that would inspire the legendary journalist Lincoln Steffens to write, "I have seen the future and it works." The press tour was a trip by train. Remember the lesson of Queen in South America: journalists are suckers for travel. All of the journalists on this train trip were true believers in the transformational power of Soviet Communism. But writers like the brilliant Arthur Koestler saw starving peasants on the platforms of Russia's railroad stations. Kulaks. The American scribes oohed and ahhhhed that they were witnessing the birth of tomorrow, the birth of a new paradise. The starving kulaks were, they said, the remnants of the old order. "I was told," said Koestler, "that these were kulaks who had resisted the collectivization of the land and I accepted the explanation; they were enemies of the people who preferred begging to work."[183]

Not true. These were people Stalin was deliberately starving. People he was killing off so that he could strip the peasants of their land and place the duller agriculturists in communes where they would be docile prisoners under his control. Stalin did not want those with initiative, discipline, and vision. They would get in the way of his plans. So he was murdering them with the weapon of deliberate famine. Thanks to Stalin's collectivization, fifteen million peasants died. Aleksandr M. Nekrich, a longtime member of Russia's USSR Academy of Sciences Institute of History, calls the result "the first socialist genocide."[184]

But that was the distant past. What did it have to do with starvation in Africa, Live Aid, and "We Are the World"? Everything.

In 1977, Ethiopia had been taken over by a new ruler, Mengistu Haile Mariam, a Marxist determined to use Stalin's methods. Miriam deliberately imposed mass starvation on his land-holding farmers. Why? To herd them into cargo airplanes where many couldn't breathe. Stuffing people in with blows of rifle butts like passengers in a subway car at rush hour in Tokyo. Suffocating some. Crushing others. Asphyxiating babies in their mothers' arms. Then transporting those who survived to "resettlement centers" where they could be as rigidly controlled as military recruits during basic training.

Reported Keating:

> Soviet Antonov planes, designed to carry 50 paratroopers, were put into duty moving 350 to 400 people more than 500 miles to the camps in the south. People were crushed to death on the impact of takeoff and landing. . . . They were suffocating, throwing up on each other, literally being asphyxiated. One woman was standing on a body that she didn't know if it was dead or alive— but she couldn't move. Children had to be held over people's heads so they wouldn't be smashed. Women miscarried and bled. And then the army would come in with a hose, wash the plane out, and go back and do it again.[185]

Meanwhile, *Spin* discovered that Mengistu Haile Mariam was using money from Band Aid, Live Aid, and "We Are the World" to buy "sophisticated weapons from the Russians."[186] And "We Are the World" and Band Aid were helping the Stalinists even farther. How? By sending them food that the Stalinists could use to lure the people they were deliberately starving into the prisons of their "resettlement centers."

The good-hearted celebrities trying to save Ethiopian lives were financing mass murder. And many of these generous philanthropists were my clients and my friends.

Talk about the forces of history!

But that wasn't the only African mass murder in the works.

* * *

One day, I got a call from a member of Bruce Springsteen's E-Street Band and from a TV producer who was working with him, ABC's Danny Schechter. They wanted to do an event like Farm Aid, Live Aid, and "We Are the World." An event designed to help bring down apartheid. My company had done the Secret Policeman's Ball LPs for Amnesty International, and we had done Farm Aid. Would we be willing to publicize Artists United Against Apartheid? I was still urgently trying to do something about the Central Africans killing each other. I felt that if we could focus a media spotlight on their killing, we could stop it before it got worse.

So I proposed that we spend 50 percent of our time publicizing apartheid and 50 percent publicizing the tribal violence in Central Africa. In other words, that we spend 50 percent working to end apartheid, a hideous disgrace. And 50 percent of our time trying to stop something far more permanent than an attack on human dignity—mass murder. It was no-go. Schechter and Little Steven came from a segment of the left that toes the party line. And the party line was that publicizing what was called "black-on-black violence" was racist. It burnished the image of blacks as violent. So, discussing black-on-black violence in any way, shape or form was taboo, forbidden. No matter how real.

We didn't work with Artists United Against Apartheid.

* * *

There were consequences to toeing the party line. In 1994, the conflict between the Central Africans erupted in genocide. Between 500,000 and a million people were killed. Brutally. Burned alive in their homes and churches.[187] Hacked apart with machetes. And we could have stopped it. Instead, the journalists of the obedient left waited until it was over. Then they lamented the genocide in articles and films with which they won prizes. They made an unprecedented eight films about the topic. After it was too late. In other words, the left—my side—was an accomplice to the crime. And worse. They were disaster exploiters, not disaster stoppers. They made money and milked fame from a genocide. They were what they despised: war profiteers.

The name of the two tribes I'd been trying to warn about? The Hutus and the Tutsis. And the nation in which this all took place? Rwanda.

* * *

If you see a mass murder coming and you fail to speak out against it, you are an accomplice to the deed. Especially if you are a celebrity.

42

HOW MTV CAME TO BE

Meanwhile, there was another manager I'd wanted to work with, Bud Prager. Bud had an impish arch to his eyebrows whenever we talked. He listened to my explanation of what I did for a living and for a life—collecting human souls. And helping those souls feed the souls of others. He listened to how I did it. Secular shamanism, a month of study then an intense all-day session to get to a client's passion points. He didn't believe it.

Bud had taken a radically different approach. He had put two longtime British musicians—Spooky Tooth's Mick Jones and King Crimson's Ian MacDonald—together with one of the most astonishing American rock singers you have ever heard in your life, Rochester, New York's Lou Gramm. Then, Bud said, he had helped the resulting band write its songs. And the result was one of the best-selling bands of all time—Foreigner. A band that has sold the whoppingly huge figure of eighty million albums.

Bud challenged me. He said he bet I couldn't find the soul—or the story—in Foreigner. Indeed, I couldn't find the hint of a story in their past press clippings and interviews. But that was common. When it came to the big, soul-diving interview with Mick Jones, the hub of the band, it never happened. So, yes, I failed. I was never allowed to actually do my thing. All I know is that Lou Gramm, like Paul Simon, is even shorter than I am. That he started out playing in bars so tough that the stages had a wall of chicken wire in front of the stage to protect musicians from the audience's favorite form of criticism: throwing beer bottles. And that Lou reads history novels for fun. Nearly thirty-five years later, Gramm's vocals and Foreigner's songs still knock me out. And, yes, we did a good and thorough job for the band when they toured. But, no, I never got to do the hunt for soul.

Meanwhile, Bud had a publicity liaison named Sue Steinberg. Sue left Bud to take a job with a cutting-edge company that had been moving into the bold and experimental world of interactive TV, Time Warner. And Time Warner had a new idea. Rock stars were making videos of their songs. But there was almost no place to show those videos. One or two cafés on the North American continent had video jukeboxes, but that was about it. Time Warner had a bright idea. Cable TV was the hot new thing. Why not form an entire cable channel based on showing these music videos? Sue asked if we could have lunch every week to bounce ideas around. My big idea was to turn Kevin Cronin of REO Speedwagon, the funniest man in rock and roll, into a video jockey, a VJ. But that was impossible. Kevin needed to stay out on the road touring. So god knows if I was of any earthly value to Sue . . . or to Time Warner.

Which means I was a mere crease between the bubbles in the pot that was boiling up MTV. But MTV would be crucial to REO Speedwagon, John Mellencamp, Prince, Michael Jackson, and more. A heck of a lot more.

Including Billy Idol . . .

43

BILLY IDOL—THE CLIENT
WHO ALMOST DIED

You recall that back in 1981 and 1982, I'd been tracking the careers of two artists on the skids, two rockers on their way to becoming two-hit wonders. One was John Cougar. The other was Billy Idol.

Billy Idol had just put out two dance-club hits—"Dancing with Myself" and a song that went to the Top 10 on the dance charts, "Mony, Mony." But he hadn't toured the USA.[188] He hadn't bonded with, or built, a die-hard fan base. And the rock-crit elite regarded him as silly. Yes, he had been a genuine pioneer of Britain's punk explosion. In England, where he'd grown up. Along with his friends, Siouxsie and the Banshees. But on his own, the critics believed, he was all visual gimmickry and pop. Pop to the rock-crit elite was meaningless, consumerist crap.

There are two artists I didn't have to do secular shamanism with. One was Joan Jett. The other was Billy Idol. Brace yourself for a very strange claim. I got Joan and Billy, I understood their soul, their essence, simply from their body posture, their stance, the way they carried themselves. John Mellencamp raised a fist against the establishment when he got out of high school, and when he had become just a dot on a huge film screen. But Billy Idol and Joan Jett WERE that fist.

Yes, I did my research on Billy. I got his history, his role in the British punk movement as it frothed forth in London. But what counted was his attitude. Billy had moved from London to Manhattan. Instead of allowing me to come downtown to his place, Billy came up to my place, to my office on West Fifty-Fifth Street near Lexington Avenue. The only other rocker who had done that was Peter Gabriel. Billy was a highly articulate, intelligent person whose way with words was scrambled by drugs. He could be hard to understand. But you could sense the smarts inside of him. More important, he came into my office dressed the way he always dresses. A leather vest. Chains. Crosses. Bare shoulders. And on those bare shoulders was a clue to Billy's hidden selves, his gods inside, his soul. On his right shoulder was a tattoo of a luscious sixteen-year-old superheroine. Her attitude, her stance, like Billy's, was spectacular. It was sheer rebellion. Who was she, I asked? A Russian underground comic figure,

Octobriana, the original spirit of the Russian Revolution of October 1917. The spirit that had been lost in the crushing, bureaucratic dictatorships of Lenin and Stalin. The spirit of the hope and freedom that the Russian people had ached for but had never achieved. The spirit of rebellion against the establishment. The Russian establishment. The Soviet establishment.

There was no long narrative to yank out of Billy. The statement of who and what he was was in that tattoo. And it was bristlingly, boldly authentic. It was what Billy ate, slept, and breathed. Like Joan Jett and John Mellencamp, Billy Idol was an attitude.

By now, I'd learned that to get what I saw in my clients across, I was going to have to write my own press materials—my own bios and press releases. That's highly unusual in rock-and-roll PR. Especially since I was now running the biggest PR firm in the music industry, with a total of fifteen employees. The president of the company does not write the materials for a campaign. But there were visions implicit in my artists—like the visions of Dennis DeYoung. And there were muscular statements, like the raised fists of Joan Jett, John Mellencamp, and Billy Idol. The message in each muscular stance was the heart of a campaign. And our press materials needed to get across not just good stories but muscular statements. Attitude. Stance.

So, with Billy Idol, we had not just a story but a message to get across to the rock press. But the messenger was in danger.

* * *

Billy was recording an album at Electric Lady Studio. Electric Lady was legendary. It had been founded by Jimi Hendrix in 1970. Explains the studio's website, "On August 26th, 1970, Hendrix hosted the grand opening of his psychedelic studio lair to fellow musicians and friends. Guests included Steve Winwood, Eric Clapton, Ron Wood, and Patti Smith."[189] Twenty-three days later, on September 18, Hendrix would die of an overdose of barbiturates—sleeping pills and Vesparax—choking in his own vomit in the apartment of a girlfriend in London. This may have been an omen.

Electric Lady was smack in the heart of the global capital of bohemianism and rebellion, Greenwich Village, in the spot where the East Village and the West Village meet and on the Village's central spine—Eighth Street. What's more, Electric Lady was just a short subway ride away from my office. So I went downtown to check up on Billy.

To understand what comes next, you have to understand how recording studios are built. They are made to be soundproof. No sound at all is allowed to leak in from the street. Or from anywhere outside the studio. The result is that no sound can leak out. Which is perfect. Because every room in a sound studio has to be acoustically separated from every other room. With no exceptions. Not even the slightest wisp of sound leakage is allowed. The walls are roughly two feet thick and stuffed with layer after layer of acoustic insulation, of soundproofing materials.[190]

But when I walked into the narrow entrance passage to Electric Lady, I could hear Billy Idol inside one of the studios. Through the soundproof walls. I could hear Billy raving. Look, *rave* is a word we hear all the time. It's one of those words whose meaning you think you know. You don't until you hear it for the first time. It is a rush of crazed, high-speed, incomprehensible noise. It's a screaming, shouting, keening, and threatening all mixed up in one. It is the sound of raw and frustrated fury. A fury with no words. The desire for words, perhaps. But no words you can understand. I heard the raving when I walked in through the door. And I heard it all the way down the corridor to the reception desk. I don't believe they actually let me in to see Billy in this state.

But the ranting, shrieking incoherence was deeply disturbing. How can you make music in that state? How can you retain the loyalty of the people you work with, the people who are vital to you, like Steve Stevens, Billy's guitarist; and Keith Forsey, his producer? And how can you stay alive?

I was concerned. And that's an understatement. But things were even worse than they appeared.

* * *

Billy Idol's manager was one of the most enjoyable people on the planet, Bill Aucoin.

In Billy's extraordinary book, *Dancing with Myself*, Idol enthuses that Bill Aucoin was "a wild man of rock 'n' roll. He was a force of nature." Like Joan Jett, Bill Aucoin would come to life in front of an audience, in front of a record company president or a marketing meeting. Idol says, "He loved the selling part of the job." Aucoin would step into a conference of record-company executives with the zeal of an evangelical preacher. And he'd revel in making converts. Especially from deep-dyed unbelievers. He'd turn these skeptics around by showing them a whole new vision of the future of pop culture, then painting the way that Billy Idol would be central in turning that vision into a reality. Explains Idol, "Then he would tell them how to use their standing in the industry to contribute to or even change popular culture in a positive way." By the time Aucoin was finished, says Billy, he'd have half a dozen executives "lit up like Christmas trees" and "eating out of his hand . . . . The execs in the room ended up raving too." Concludes Idol, "That was Bill Aucoin—from zero to a hundred miles per hour in the span of a pitch meeting." What's more, Billy Idol says that he learned from Aucoin's performances. He was challenged by them. "I would have to go some distance to beat his energy in the boardroom with my own actions onstage."[191]

By the time Bill Aucoin began to work with Billy Idol, Aucoin had made a fortune from KISS. There was a building in New York where even the vast majority of the wealthy could not afford to live: the fifty-one-story Olympic Tower on New York's prized Fifth Avenue, between Fifty-First and Fifty-Second Street. Bill Aucoin lived on roughly the twenty-fourth floor. His corner apartment was all windows. Floor-to-ceiling windows on two sides. It was filled with the round and flowing shapes of chrome modern sculptures—all original works, all hideously expensive. The views were amazing, if the sculptures didn't block your line of sight. And they usually did.

But, as you've witnessed before, very few managers in the music business actually know how to play the most important instrument in music—the star-making machine. Most have one accidental success, think they've been responsible for it, then sign other acts with the promise that they can do it again. And inadvertently they keep those other acts in a state of obscurity. Tommy Mottola's big accident was Hall and Oates. Bill Aucoin's big accident was KISS.

In reality, KISS managed themselves. When no one had ever heard of them, KISS would rent the Crystal Ballroom at the Hotel Diplomat near Times Square and schedule their own shows.[192] Then they would have thousands of 8 ½" x 11" fliers printed in just one-color ink, black. They'd pile these cheap fliers into a van. And, late at night, when there were no authorities around to stop them, they would go methodically through New York's five boroughs, slapping those posters up on every telephone pole, lamppost, and wall they could find. This was not Bill Aucoin's work. It was the work of Gene Simmons and Paul Stanley, KISS's two masterminds.

My job was to spot a manager's strengths and weaknesses, then to invisibly fill in for the deficiencies. And to let the manager take the credit. I loved working for Bill Aucoin, not just because he continually brought me joy. But because he let me play the star-making machine. And he made me feel rewarded. Not with money. But with his delight. The missing piece of the Idol puzzle was touring. So I took over the dictation of touring strategy, using what I'd learned from ZZ Top's Bill Ham and had executed with Joan Jett. And Billy delivered onstage. Powerfully.

But Bill Aucoin had a problem. A big one. Cocaine. And not just any cocaine. Freebasing cocaine. Freebasing crack. Smoking it to get it to the brain ultra-fast. With ultra-risk. Remember, in 1980, the comedy superstar Richard Pryor had nearly burned himself alive freebasing.[193] Aucoin, as Billy Idol says in his book, was extremely good at motivating talented people—a gift he shared with Tommy Mottola. So he had five attractive young women working for him. All of them were Ivy League–level minds and Ivy League–level achievers. It was a pleasure to work with them. But one afternoon, one of them called. There was trouble.

Bill hadn't been to the office in a month. He was freebasing crack in his Olympic Towers apartment. He had locked himself in his huge bathroom and wouldn't come out. There was a phone in the bathroom. Could I please call him? I was the only one he would listen to. I called Bill. He was his normal, affable self. Which means he was covering up. I was unsuccessful in persuading him to stop his drug use. Or even in convincing him to come out of the bathroom.

Meanwhile, my main concern was Billy. Both Billy Idol and Bill Aucoin seemed just an inch away from a drug overdose. Then Billy's parents flew from England to New York City for a visit. We were two years or more into our campaign, and Billy's career was becoming huge. To his team, Billy represented money, power, and prestige. Nobody wanted to lose these privileges. Billy's parents called each of us into a private room, one at a time, to see how Billy was doing. Everyone who went into that room assured the parents that everything was peachy keen, just fine. Then I went in. "Your son is killing himself with drugs," I said, "and if we don't do something fast, we could easily lose him."

Billy's parents yanked him away from Bill Aucoin. They asked me to manage him. I love career strategy, but I hate dealing with money, so I said no. First Billy went with Madonna's manager, Freddy DeMann. Then he switched to Tom Petty's manager, Tony Dimitriades. But Billy weaned himself off heavy drug use. Decades later, when his book *Dancing with Myself* came out, I'd discover that Billy hadn't just been freebasing crack like Bill Aucoin. He had also been overindulging in alcohol. And heroin. The news of that combination was spine-shuddering.

Meanwhile, we raised Billy Idol's credibility and his visibility so dramatically that, with a lot of help from his music, the touring that I helped shape, and his record company, Chrysalis—a company deeply committed to its artists—on January 31, 1985, we got Billy Idol, the man about to become a two-hit wonder, on the cover of *Rolling Stone*. One more disproof of Joe Dera's claim that we couldn't get covers.

* * *

Because we were getting magazine covers one after another, we put out each cover on glossy, thick paper as a micro-poster, a bookmark-sized image in full color with our logo. These slender mini-posters were like trading cards, but twice as tall and a little bit wider. They were gorgeous. We mailed them out to managers and record-company people. Secretaries of several company presidents collected the full set and put them up on their bulletin boards. So the chief honchos at the big companies walked into their offices every day past a bulletin board that kept the Howard Bloom Organization Ltd. in their minds.

The Chinese-water-torture approach to publicity. For a publicity firm.

* * *

Whatever happened to Bill Aucoin? I wanted Billy Idol to follow in the path of Prince. I wanted him to make a film that was as much a personal expression as his music. Billy wanted that, too. So did Bill Aucoin. But according to Billy's brilliant and insight-riddled *Dancing with Myself*, when the two flew out to Hollywood to sort through a small slew of film offers, Aucoin lost it. He went wild with drugs. Something he'd already been doing when his staff had begged me to call him in his New York luxury highrise bathroom. Oh, and he went wild with gorgeous young boys. Bill Aucoin was gay. The result: Aucoin lost his shot at a Billy Idol movie. He lost his apartment at the Olympic Tower. He lost his sculptures and his artworks. He lost his company. And he disappeared.

He reappeared in the music industry in roughly 2005, when I had gone back to my science. And he tried to revive his momentum. But it was utterly and completely lost. He died in 2010.

Goddamn fucking cocaine.

44

BILLY JOEL—DUMBED DOWN BY LOVE . . . AND BY CHRISTIE BRINKLEY

Drugs are not the only source of dependence.

It was 1982, and Billy Joel was about to put out his album *Nylon Curtain*. Billy had a problem. The same problem Mellencamp had. The press hated him. Robert Hilburn, one of the gods of the rock-crit elite—had run a huge story in the *Los Angeles Times* comparing Billy Joel to Bob Seger. Hilburn's point was that Seger's lyrics were masterworks and Joel's lyrics were trash.

Now, look, I love Bob Seger's music. I adore it. But the lyrics are, well, normal. And, in fact, the Joel lyrics that Hilburn quoted made a mockery of his argument. They were clearly better than those of Seger.

Let's put this differently. And let me repeat. I'd been kidnapped into editing a literary magazine at NYU, and that magazine had won two Academy of American Poets prizes. There were two people whose lyrics I was certain would be printed in the poetry anthologies of the 2000s: Paul Simon's and . . . Billy Joel's. And I was certain of this long before I met either one of them.

What's more, Billy Joel's albums had the controlled anger that makes rock explosive. I loved his music.

God knows who, how, and why, but someone from Billy Joel's office called me and asked if I'd like to work with Billy Joel. Like to? Hell, I'd love to.

Billy's was one of those careers I'd been analyzing from a distance for years. So I knew his problem. I rented a car and drove out to his house on Oyster Bay—the bay where Teddy Roosevelt used to live—and explained it to him. This time I was taking the trip so Billy could audition me, not so that I could interview him. Here's what I explained. When Billy had first started out with his debut album, *Cold Spring Harbor*, in 1971, on Family Productions, my impression was that Family's publicist—Harriet Vidal—had done an excellent job.[194] The rock-crit elite loved him. Why? In part because they felt they were making his career with their ten tiny typing fingers. Then something happened. Billy lost that connection with the critics. And he started to have hits. To the rock writers, each hit felt like something that had happened not because of them but in spite of them. The press had lost their ego stake. And, as you know, what the press can't build, they destroy.

I told the story of Thomas Carlyle's sheep to Billy. And I explained that the best way around this sheepishness was to first be able to make a strong and totally valid argument for the authenticity of his lyrics. An argument that his lyrics merited in spades. Then to make that case with some of the people at the head of the rock-crit flock who could occasionally be convinced to bolt from the rest of the lead sheep and make up their own minds. Billy Joel is an extremely intelligent guy. He reads books. Lots of them. He was amused. He dubbed this strategy "guerrilla publicity." And he said yes.

Now I had a problem. Which account executive should I assign to Billy Joel? He needed someone who could give him lots of time and attention. My other account executives were tied up with Prince, John Mellencamp, REO Speedwagon, Styx, Billy Idol, Joan Jett, and Bob Marley. I had a neighbor who was the music editor at *Rolling Stone*—Jim Henke.[195] Yes, *the* music editor. And, yes, Jim lived out here in Park Slope, Brooklyn. Jim was a shy man, a person I enjoyed getting together with for dinner. His girlfriend was a publicist. He asked if I'd interview her for a job. Her name was Elaine Cooper.

* * *

The Howard Bloom Organization Ltd. was a very strange place. We had an approach to publicity unlike that of any other music-industry PR firm. And we trained our people in our unusual approach, starting them as receptionists then moving them up, step by step, for at least two years. Hiring people who'd been schooled in any other way of doing things backfired. People not trained in our office could not accustom themselves to campaigns with an average of 120 press breaks per month. In fact, one fashionable, intelligent, highly experienced publicist I hired from the world of corporate PR produced no results at all.

So I was reluctant to hire Elaine. But she had incredible connections. She was close to Robert Hilburn, the pope of West Coast rock critics—the one who had compared Billy Joel to Bob Seger, and had found Joel wanting. And the one who I credited with spotting the positives in the pretentiousness of Queen. Elaine was also close to the music editor of *Rolling Stone*, who she lived with. And she knew most of the other rock-crit aristocrats. She was also intelligent, articulate, and attractive. So I hired her.

Elaine was the person with the most spare time, so I wanted to put her on the case of Billy Joel. She would be one high-quality person representing another. But there was a problem. A big one. Most publicists feel it's their job to hang with the rock-crit elite and to become popular with these aristocratic writers. To be liked, they worship what the rock-crit pack loves, and they detest what the rock-crit elite loathes. They become members of the herd of sheep, not people who can turn the flock in a new direction. This was Elaine's approach to publicity. Which meant that because the press hated Billy Joel, she hated Billy Joel. She refused to work on the case.

Somehow I got her into a rental car on the way out to Joel's house on Long Island. And I propagandized her for an hour and a half as I drove the car. *Propagandize* is a harsh word. The fact is that Billy Joel is a treasure, and the press attitude was blatantly false. But I had to browbeat and brainwash poor Elaine into seeing that. I had to argue like a defense attorney trying to save an innocent man. I had to trot out example after example of Billy's passion, uniqueness, and insight. By the time we got to Long Island, Elaine had agreed to work with Billy Joel, the client she had hated. In the long run, Elaine left Jim Henke, married one of Billy Joel's managers, and, I believe, is still working with Billy Joel, over thirty years later. A little persuasion can go a long way. Especially when what you are selling is the truth.

* * *

Our task was to show the press Billy's authenticity and his gifts. Once Elaine became a convert, she was very good at turning the key writers in Billy's favor. And when Billy's next album came out, I got an early pressing, a pressing two months ahead of release. I called Ken Tucker in Boston—the record reviewer for *Newsweek*, back in the days when *Time* and *Newsweek* ruled the newsstands. One of the lead sheep. I told Ken that I'd personally deliver this top-secret advance copy of Billy's LP if he'd promise to listen to it. I wanted to give him an ego stake. Ken said yes. I flew up to Boston, drove to Ken's part of town, met him in the restaurant he'd asked for, and handed him the white-sleeved, label-less LP over the luncheon table.

In other words, we did what I'd promised Billy. We turned the press around. Which was ironic. Because just as we were turning the press around, the authenticity of Billy's lyrics started to fade. Billy wrote a protest song about the layoffs in the steel industry—layoffs that punched America like a lead fist in the late 1970s and early 1980s. Billy focused his lyrics on one town in particular that had been gutted by the closure of Bethlehem Steel—Allentown, Pennsylvania. He wrote another song about what it was like to be a foot soldier in the jungles of Vietnam—something he had never been through. He was writing songs derived from headlines, not from personal experience.

Then something horrible happened: Billy Joel fell in love.

* * *

I hadn't seen Billy in a while, and I called him up one day to do something I really don't know how to do—to socialize. To hang out. I needed to bring myself up to date on the state of his soul. We scheduled a breakfast at the restaurant on the ground floor of the place where Billy maintained a Manhattan apartment—the Essex House. The same place where Chris Blackwell had an apartment in the sky. Where I'd lunched with Earth, Wind, and Fire's Maurice White. And where Bob Marley's tribe had Jamaicanized an entire suite.

Billy took the elevator down from his apartment and met me at the elevator door on the ground floor. In his right hand was something very strange. It was a notebook with a black cardboard cover marbled in white. The kind your mother probably bought for you when you were about to start second grade. It was the first day of genuine spring, the first day when women who have been cloaked in winter coats and scarves all winter long walk the streets with just blouses and skirts or pants. The first day when you get to see the necks, legs, and arms of young women after a long beauty-drought. So we took a table outside. I don't know about Billy, but the corners of my eyes were girl watching frantically.

You know how it works. Your eye spots an attractive woman and imagines what she'd be like in bed, what she'd be like in an argument, what she'd be like in a long-term relationship, and what she'd be like when you both were in your sixties. All in the flash of a second. Then your eye moves on to another woman and does it again. All while you do your best to pay attention to the matter at hand.

Which just happened to be the perception of women. "When I was a teenager," Billy said, "we'd hang out on corners watching the girls go by. A bunch of us guys." But, said Billy, that bunch of guys had a very strange idea of what girls were. "They were another species," said Billy, "a whole different kind of animal. I mean you could talk to other guys. But you couldn't talk to a girl. If you wanted an intelligent conversation, you had to have it with your friends." Friends who were male.

"But a strange thing happened last night," Billy continued. "I met a woman you can talk to. I met a woman who is as bright as any guy." That had astonished him. Said Billy, the two had talked from roughly midnight until three in the morning. Then something even stranger had happened. But to understand its strangeness, you have to understand Billy Joel's creative process.

Out at his home on Oyster Bay, Billy Joel has a music room. In it is a grand piano. Songs come to Billy with extreme difficulty. Whenever a melody does occur to him, he gets self-conscious and throws it away. He believes that each tune and lyric, if it comes from him, is trite, hackneyed, derivative, and clichéd. So he spends more time pacing back and forth and raging at the piano. In fact, he calls the piano "the beast with eighty-eight teeth." It can take him three entire months wrestling with that beast to write a single song.

But when Billy left his three hours with the amazing, intelligent woman of seven hours ago, the woman who thought like a man, an utterly non-Billy-Joel-ish thing happened to him. He sat down and wrote an entire album full of songs, twelve songs, in two hours. Those songs were in the marbled children's notebook he'd carried to the table in his right hand.

The woman who had entranced Billy with her intelligence was one of the most visible and gorgeous models in North America in 1982. Christie Brinkley. And, eventually, Christie would begin to take over Billy's life.

* * *

I got a call one day asking me to have lunch with Christie's publicist. It sounded like a good idea. So we had lunch at the restaurant I regarded as the Howard Bloom Organization Ltd.'s company cafeteria. It was an elegant Italian place on the ground floor of our Victorian building, a place owned by our office landlord, the man who rented us our two floors. He was a tall, sixty-ish Italian who treated me as if I was his son. And he let me continue to host lunch guests long after lunchtime had ended and all the other guests had left. Among those guests at a three-hour conversation had been the aforementioned *New York Times* Sunday magazine's Ken Emerson, *Rolling Stone*'s Timothy White, and the extraordinarily dressed model, singer, and personality Grace Jones.

The place was called Hyperbole. An ironic name for the haunt of a publicist who tried to avoid overstatement.

Christie Brinkley's publicist and I sat down for lunch, and I tried to describe the philosophy behind what we were doing. I explained, among other things, that a rock star has to appear to have superhuman powers. That is, the wires with which he or she flies have to be invisible. Those wires are the human beings behind the scenes. People like her or like me. Which is why I never allowed photos to be taken with me and any of my clients. The goal, as you saw many chapters ago, was to publicize the client. Not to publicize me.

The next day, an item appeared in the *New York Post*'s "Page Six" announcing that I, Billy Joel's publicist, had said something demeaning about the rock audience. It was a twisted version of what I'd said. Christie Brinkley had set me up. She wanted total control over Billy's team. The next day, on the basis of that item, we were fired.

But we'd had two years with Billy. And in that time we'd done what I'd said we were going to do. We'd established Billy's credibility with the rock-crit elite. We'd gotten the critics to see Billy's genuine genius.

But there was a strange twist. An irony.

* * *

Billy Joel was right when he said he had an entire album of songs in the notebook he'd slaved over in the hours after he met Christie Brinkley. It would be called *An Innocent Man*. *An Innocent Man* would be riddled with hits like the No. 1 "Tell Her About It" and the No. 3 "Uptown Girl," which became the biggest-selling single of 1983 in Britain. In fact, *An Innocent Man* would spawn six Top 30 hits—more than any other Billy Joel album. But Billy had feared being trite, stale, and derivative his whole career. This was the most derivative album he had ever made. Possibly the only derivative album. It was an homage to the music of his roots—the doo-wop of the 1950s and 1960s. Which meant it was the least Billy Joel-ish of his LPs. It was the least of his artistic contributions. And, for reasons I will never understand, it sold seven million copies. Yes, it went seven times platinum.

But I felt fortunate that I didn't have to work with it. Strange, no?

45

LIONEL RICHIE—I FAILED

I failed Lionel Richie.

What happened? Lionel always wanted the best of everything. And the most expensive. The Howard Bloom Organization Ltd. qualified. I was the publicist for Prince, Michael Jackson (a tale we'll get back to in a bit), John Mellencamp, Joan Jett, Billy Idol, Styx, and REO Speedwagon. My company and I had publicized the biggest-selling albums of the year, over and over again. Our name, by now, was everywhere.

A few months into the campaign with Lionel, he did something unfathomable. His manager was Ken Kragen, the man who put together Hands Across America and "We Are the World." A man who, like Prince's Bob Cavallo, was a miracle-maker. Lionel fired Ken and asked me to act as his manager until he could find someone new.

That's when I figured Lionel would take half of every workweek, calculated how much I'd normally have to bring in in half a week to keep my office going, and charged him that whoppingly huge amount. Which meant starting a new work routine. Every Wednesday night I caught a 9:00 p.m. flight to LA. At 11:00 p.m. LA time, I settled into a nice hotel in Westwood, a walking distance from UCLA, one of the few places in LA where pedestrians are welcomed.

On Thursday morning, I showed up bright and early at Lionel's house, and worked in his kitchen or his dining room. When I got back to my hotel room on Thursday night, I'd get a call from Sheila E. She was madly in love with Prince and wanted to marry him and bear his children. The fact that he rejected her in this role but mated with her in the music they made together tore her apart. Romantic pain is one of the most horrible pains in the world. Ironically, it's the pain from which song lyrics are made. All I could do was listen and try to soothe her.

If there was something happening Thursday night and I wanted a companion, I called Ronnie Dashev, an attractive and bright female attorney who worked on Lionel and would soon become president of Madonna's record company, Maverick Records. Ronnie was married, but her husband would kindly let her go out with me. I apparently come across as harmless.

Then, Friday morning, I'd be back at Lionel's house, working. And Friday night I'd catch the overnight at 10:30 p.m., the redeye back to New York. I'd do my best to get sleep in my seat. An impossible task. And Saturday morning at 9:00 a.m. I'd be back at work in my own Brooklyn apartment, which by now had been turned into a big office with a private bedroom on the side and had been written up in *Stereo Review* magazine as the electronic apartment of the future.

I worked very hard for Lionel. But, in the end, I felt I accomplished absolutely nothing for him. I kept him calm and grounded while he went through a career change. And my staff got him a slew of press. But, frankly, I never found Lionel's soul. There may be a reason. I was in Lionel's kitchen and living room. I was in his den talking to Chita Rivera. I was in the world Lionel shared with his wife. But Lionel had two lives. His home life. And his nightlife. At night he would prowl the clubs and apparently pick up girls. That was a life I could not be allowed to see. Or his wife might catch wind of his nightlife and stop it. Even worse. She might leave him. That nightlife may have been where Lionel's soul came alive.

But I learned something interesting from the Lionel Richie experience. Something about eyes.

* * *

One day, I got the message that Lionel was going to be in New York and wanted to do a photo session. Terrific. I had relationships with a dozen talented photographers who would do a shoot for $3,500—that's roughly $8,500 in today's dollars. But that's not what Lionel wanted. He wanted the man who shot nearly every *Cosmopolitan* cover of the era, Francesco Scavullo. And how much would Scavullo charge? I had one of my staff call his studio and ask. Seventeen thousand dollars—roughly $41,000 in today's dollars. A big difference.

But if Lionel wanted Scavullo, it was Scavullo he would have. So we booked a date with Scavullo. If you go to Google Images and look at Scavullo's shots, you'll see that his photos do, in fact, have something unique. Every one of his photo subjects stares at you with a glowing focus, with a spark of soul that ignites you. I set aside my day and accompanied Lionel to the studio. In the process, I learned Scavullo's secret.

It was a secret that helps explain how an audience melts and its energy surges through you when you're onstage.

* * *

Scavullo had a standard setup he always worked with. He had a seamless backdrop—a long, broad sheet of paper the width of a narrow room. A sheet of paper on a giant roll, like a paper towel. That roll was nine feet in the air. The paper sheet plunged straight down, then hit the floor with a gentle curve and covered ten feet of the floorboards. This gave the picture a uniform background, with no corners or shadows to distract the eye. On the horizontal surface of the seamless backdrop was a stool. Pointed at the stool were two giant pieces of lighting equipment with reflective umbrellas at their rear. These umbrellas helped diffuse the light. And five feet further from the backdrop, pointed at the stool, was a rare and expensive Hasselblad big-format, single-lens reflex camera.

When the time for the photo shoot neared, three of Scavullo's assistants readied the apparatus. One sat on the stool. Another went behind the camera. And a third adjusted the lights. At the orders of the assistant behind the camera, the lighting assistant moved the lighting tripods that held the umbrellas slightly this way and that. Until the three assistants finally got what they wanted. But what in the world were they looking for? What did they want to achieve with all these micro-adjustments?

Finally, Scavullo descended from his room and made his grand appearance. He assumed his position behind the camera. The assistants ushered Lionel to the stool. Then, with Scavullo directing, the assistants made final adjustments to the position of the lighting umbrellas. Scavullo shot fifty photos. He shot another fifty. And the session was over.

What was Scavullo looking for? What gave his pictures their magic, their sense of intensity, their sense of focused life force? Scavullo's secret was in the eyes of his subjects. It was a reflection. The reflection of his bright lighting fixtures. Where? In the very center of the pupil. A bright spark of light.

And why did this work? Because we humans judge the interest in each other's eyes by the dilation—the opening of the pupils. If someone's pupils stay small while we are talking to her, deep down inside of us we know she is not all that interested. If her pupils open wide, we know we have excited her. And our invisible self, the self below the floorboards of our self, lights up. We are happier. We are energized. Attention is the oxygen of the human soul. And we read attention in each other's eyes.

Remember what dilated pupils in the audience did to you when you danced onstage at the Park School of Buffalo? And what dilated pupils do to power rock stars onstage? They generate ecstasies. And ecstasies are at the heart of stardom.

By putting a bright light in the center of each pupil of his subjects' eyes, Scavullo was making you feel that his photo subject was intensely interested in just one person—you. That was Scavullo's magic. That was his trick. That was why his pictures were so vital to the covers of *Cosmopolitan* magazine. He made cover girls look like they were personally entranced by, yes, you. Those glints in the centers of eyes made you want to buy the magazine. This is why Scavullo was able to charge seventeen thousand dollars per session.

It's a trick I've been teaching to photographers ever since. Then there's another trick of emotionally focused attention. I had glimpsed it with Joan Jett. And I would learn more about it from Bette Midler.

46

BETTE MIDLER AND THE TALKING DOG

In roughly 1984, I started getting calls from Bette Midler's office, asking me to handle Bette's publicity. The calls came from Bette's right-hand person, the woman who would later co-produce a brilliant film with Bette, *Beaches*. That woman was Bonnie Bruckheimer. Why did I resist working with the Divine Miss M? She didn't need me. I told the same thing to Bonnie every time she called, the same thing I'd told the manager of the Jacksons: you could train a talking dog to say "Bette Midler" on the phone and any magazine editor in the country would give her a cover in exchange for an interview.

Any publicist in America, no matter how untalented, could do a fabulous job for Bette Midler. Turns out I was wrong.

One afternoon, I got my usual call from Bonnie. But she didn't make the usual request. She said, "I'm not asking you this time. I'm telling you. You are Bette Midler's publicist. And it would be wise for you to be out here tomorrow morning at 10:30 to meet your client." Out here was Beverly Hills.

So I shouldered my little red nylon knapsack and flew out to LA, to meet with Bette at her home. A lovely three-story, off-white building with the sort of architecture you'd see in the houses of the medium upper crust in places like my hometown, Buffalo. I mean, the house actually had a lawn. Bette's block was lined with trees. And riddled with traditional architecture. But in Hollywood, that sort of architecture doesn't come naturally. It costs a fortune.

From my first meeting with Bette, I realized that she had grown up as a bookworm, something I could relate to. Bette had a copy of Oliver Sacks's *The Man Who Mistook His Wife for a Hat* on her coffee table. It was the hippest thing you could read if you liked to keep your intellect sharp in 1985.

But there was more. I had watched Bette's career advance for years, from her beginning as an unknown to the gay bathhouses of New York, where she had been accepted as an incarnation of the extreme flamboyance at the core of many a gay soul. I had continued to watch her all the way up to the film *The Rose*, in which she played a Janis Joplin–like singer. *The Rose* had been flat-out amazing. One of the most fabulous performances I'd ever seen in my life. And it had amazed for one more reason.

Bette originally broke through as a singer. You recall that music people were looked down on as pee-ons in the film industry. Not peons, pee-ons. People beneath contempt. Despite the success of *Saturday Night Fever*, *Purple Rain*, and Talking Heads' *Stop Making Sense*—another movie we would work on. But Bette had crossed over to film. And not in some minor role. *The Rose* was Bette and Bette was *The Rose*. She WAS the film.

I thought it had been all smooth sailing for her from there. I was wrong. Stupidly wrong. The success of *The Rose* had brought Bette another starring part. In a film called *Jinxed*. *Jinxed* had made headlines in Hollywood. It had made big news when it was being made. And it had made even bigger news when it had been a hideously embarrassing flop.[196] In fact, *Jinxed*'s failure had given Bette a nervous breakdown. For three years.[197] She had felt her film career was over, and her resulting depression was more than she could take.

Then something miraculous had happened. But to understand the miracle, you have to understand another entity in deep trouble, a film studio.

* * *

Bette is Jewish. I'm Jewish. Ever since the 1930s, there had been one film studio in Hollywood that refused to hire Jews. That studio had experienced tremendous success in the 1930s and 1940s. In the early 1950s, it had built its visibility even farther by having two successful TV shows, shows that starred the company name and image. And by creating two wildly successful theme parks. Then came the 1960s and 1970s, and the company's film operation tanked. It went tail-up like a Cadillac convertible driven into a swimming pool. No, it hadn't gone out of business. But it had made film after film, and hadn't been able to lure genuine ticket-buying humans into the theaters. It was no longer a real film studio.

Then the powers that be at the company grew desperate. They decided on a risky move. The company would hire two Jews. Those two were Jeffrey Katzenberg and Michael Eisner. And it was the responsibility of these two to turn a failing studio around. Not an easy job.

Katzenberg and Eisner made a bold decision on how to give the company a U-turn. They would place their bets on a film star who had also tanked. A film star who was also Jewish: Bette Midler. Surely this was an utterly insane move. Even more dangerous, Eisner and Katzenberg would bet on scripts very different from the traditional fare of the company that had employed them. That company, that whale of a film studio hoping to be given mouth-to-mouth or blowhole-to-blowhole resuscitation, was Disney. The Walt Disney Company.

I thought a talking dog could handle Bette Midler. I was plumb out of my skull. This was one of the most delicate periods of Bette's career. And, more, it was one of the trickiest passages in the careers of Katzenberg, Eisner, and an entire studio.

I can't say that I added a lot. Bette's position was the opposite of that of most of my clients. Remember, I went for between 120 and 750 press breaks a month for my normal clients. Yes, we hit 750 a month and more with ZZ Top and Prince. But Bette was in danger of overexposure. My job was, of all things, to say no. My job was to look for the one or two very big things that would advance Bette's career, and to keep those one or two big things spaced far apart. My job had something in common with building Joan Jett and recommending the Beacon Theater for Bob Marley. My task was to keep the public hungry.

As you know, I like to make things happen that wouldn't have happened without me. But, this time, the things happening without me were fascinating. Disney's intention was to do something I'd never heard of before or since. They would break "the new Disney" by putting the same star in a series of four unconnected films. Those films would be *Down and Out in Beverly Hills*, *Outrageous Fortune*, *Ruthless People*, and *Big Business*. Then Disney would let Bette put together a film of her own—the aforementioned *Beaches*. But just to make sure these films would be blockbusters, Eisner and Katzenberg packed the pictures with some of the most amazing comic talents of the 1980s. Bette's co-stars included Danny DeVito, Lily Tomlin, and *Cheers'* Shelly Long.

The films were hits. They packed theaters. They were outrageously funny. They were, in fact, some of the funniest, smartest films I've ever seen. And they brought two things back to life: Disney and Bette Midler.

* * *

What was working with Bette Midler like? One day, I was in Bette's living room in Beverly Hills, explaining an idea from evolutionary biology—the Coolidge effect. When Calvin Coolidge was president back in the 1920s, he and his wife were taken on a tour of a model farm designed to help advance agricultural science and the productivity of American farmers. Mrs. Coolidge was shown a rooster. A hen was placed in the rooster's cage. The rooster went through its courtship rituals, then mounted the hen. The hen was taken away, and another hen was placed in the rooster's cage. The rooster got all puffed up and paraded himself around again, strutting his stuff to woo the new female. Then, when he had impressed her with enough foreplay to gain her consent, he got on her back and performed his sexual services all over again. And, said the guide, the rooster managed this puffery followed by pokery as many as twenty times a day. Mrs. Coolidge was impressed. She turned around to Cal and told him to pay attention to the rooster. The bird was demonstrating something that Cal should try to equal in the presidential bedroom. Yes, said her husband. But you failed to notice something. Each time the rooster performs, it's with a different hen.[198]

The Coolidge effect. It works with roosters and hens. It works with guinea pigs. And it works with just about any other sexual animal you can name. The male gets all excited. He does his best to win the female. He mounts her with eagerness. Then he does the rooster or guinea pig equivalent of laying back on the couch, watching a football game, and smoking a cigar. He seems sexually exhausted. But take out the previous female, put a new female in the cage, and what have we here? Another bout of eagerness and the urge to strut, show off, woo, and make love, or the animal equivalent thereof.

It's why rock stars on the road, no matter how much they love their wives, are tempted to take new groupies to bed whenever they can get their hands or various other body parts on them. Or in them. Males produce 150 million to 350 million[199] sperm per ejaculation—525 billion sperm in a lifetime.[200] Enough to impregnate every female on earth 150 times. Men are built to bed as many females as they can. It isn't just their infidelity, it's their biology. The Coolidge effect.

And the Coolidge effect is at the heart of courtship rituals. It's at the heart of love and mating—the very things that just happen to be the subject of pop, rock, and soul songs. Like a song that REO Speedwagon never wrote: "I Can't Get That Feeling Anymore."

Bette had just married Martin Von Haselberg, a performance artist and stock trader whose stage name was Harry Kipper.[201] Harry was taking care of something—receiving a package from a deliveryman—in the next room. "Harry, Harry, come here," Bette said. When Harry entered the living room, Bette said, "Howard, tell that story again."

* * *

But that's a revealing story about me. A more revealing tale about Bette happened when I went to visit her on the set of the film *Big Business*, the film she made with Lily Tomlin.[202] Bette was in New York, my home base. In fact, she was shooting at the Plaza Hotel, just a few blocks from my office. The place where Stephanie Mills got her start. I hadn't seen Bette in a while, and decided to pay her a visit. I walked over to the Plaza, where a 150-person film crew was preparing several huge cameras and a lot of lighting apparatus, all of it focused on one doormat-sized spot at the bottom of the sparkling white-painted stairs of the Plaza's eastern entrance. Only fifty feet from that spot was a dressing trailer—a trailer set up with all the amenities of a dressing room. That was Bette's trailer. I knocked and walked in. The section of the trailer nearest the door had banquettes—padded benches with padded backs—on each of the trailer's sides. Bette sat on the banquette closest to the door. Not the power seat opposite the door. And she didn't really sit. She slumped. She lay against the back of the bench like an animal we've seen before in this book: a jellyfish. She looked drained. The sight reminded me of the day I'd gone to visit her at her new duplex apartment in a dumpy, treeless, industrial, abandoned, concrete-dominated Manhattan neighborhood that was just beginning to rise in prestige—Tribeca. On that occasion, I'd realized that Bette is not really good-looking. She sparkles entirely because of the energy of her personality. When she's not performing, she is likely to wear the kind of dress you'd see on a cleaning woman. And because Bette can schlump along when she's not performing, you could easily mistake her for a bag lady.

Okay, so there was Bette on the banquette of her movie dressing room trailer, flumped back with only her shoulders touching the banquette's back. She was curved like a spoon, limp as a boiled leaf of lettuce, drained, without energy, and, yes, jellyfished. I said, "Hi, Bette, how are you?" Wrong question. Bette's answer? "I feel terrible. I had the flu. It was killing me. Now I've got a cold." And she proceeded to recite a string of symptoms. To rattle them off, sluggishly. No wonder she was as lifeless as a dishrag and her face seemed slightly gray. Then a voice outside the trailer door gave her her call to go on camera. As Bette got to her feet, she transformed. An energy filled her. Her face became ruddy and flush. Her back straightened. Her step gained in energy. By the time she got to the top of the three stairs that led from the trailer to the sidewalk, she was giving off the rays of a thousand galactic blazars. And, as she paraded to the spot in front of the Plaza's steps where all the cameras and lights were focused, she became the Divine Miss M. A blast of energy as intense as a supernova.

Imagine a charcoal briquette. Unappealing, black, and shedding unsightly dust. Douse it with lighter fluid. Apply a match. And what do you have? The glory of a flame. The performer is the briquette. Her passion points are the lighter fluid. And the attention of an audience is the match that brings the flame to life.

Attention is the oxygen of the human soul. And performance brings something transformative to the surface. It rouses the gods inside.

* * *

Thanks to *Down and Out in Beverly Hills*, *Outrageous Fortune*, *Ruthless People*, and *Big Business*, Disney was back in the film business. And something bigger was born—a new Disney.

While the new Disney was relishing its reborn vigor, Jane Rosenthal, the tall, slender woman who acted as Jeffrey Katzenberg's right hand—the one I had gotten to know on a plane from New York to LA for a ZZ Top meeting at Warner Bros—took me under her wing. I thought the story of how the Copelands had grown up in Beirut and had found out what their dad did for a living was film material. I wrote up the idea, and Jane schooled me on what a film pitch should be. I never got takers on the concept. I still think it's a good idea. After all, it explains the birth of the Police, the band that gave Sting his start. And the birth of America's role in the Middle East. But Jane Rosenthal took very good care of me.

Then, one day, Jane said over the phone that she was going to leave Disney with an actor, and the two were going to start a film company in New York. This sounded insane. New York hadn't been a center of film since the founders of the film industry had pioneered the studio culture in the New York City boroughs of the Bronx and Queens from 1894 to 1918, then had moved the whole thing to Hollywood.[203]

And actors did not have a good track record as film producers, much less as company heads. Or at least they hadn't had a track record since the days when Charlie Chaplin, Mary Pickford, and Douglas Fairbanks had joined forces with D. W. Griffith, stomped out of the traditional film companies, and set up United Artists in 1919.[204]

But Jane picked up stakes, threw her lot in with Robert De Niro, and founded a company in the same gritty, treeless, industrial but promising lower Manhattan neighborhood where Bette had just bought an apartment—Tribeca. Rosenthal, De Niro and Rosenthal's husband, real-estate investor Craig Hatkoff, would go on to create the Tribeca Film Festival, one of the most prestigious film festivals in the world.[205] And Tribeca would produce over thirty-five films.

When I thought Jane Rosenthal was crazy, I was wrong. But that's not all I would be wrong about.

47

THE STARS I COULD NOT GROK

Grokking is a word from a Robert Heinlein novel, *Stranger in a Strange Land*. It means comprehending something from guzzle to zatch, understanding it in your heart, your brain, your gut, your muscles, and your bones. Building a simulation of it in your empathic core.

My technique, secular shamanism, worked for many acts. In some cases, it was essential to their stardom. But, sometimes, it didn't work at all. Yes, we did a spectacular job of generating media coverage in mass quantities for 95 percent of our clients. But that's just providing a megaphone. At its best, it's a megaphone for soul. But sometimes the soul slipped past me. A megaphone is meaningless when you have nothing to say.

Billy Squier was one of the most powerful vocalists in rock and roll. I loved his music. And I loved him. He was bright and personable. I promised him that I could find the soul inside of him, the god who made his music. I couldn't. I found the son of a very successful marketing man. But I never found the roar and soar inside, the force that made Billy Squier tick. And I regret that to this day. Had we found that essence, that spontaneous flame of passion, we might have been able to ensure that Billy would be remembered beyond his brief period of fame from 1981 to 1984.

Toto was a band whose music I continue to hear on the sound system of the café where I write and where I run my scientific groups. I studied Toto intensely. Then I flew out to LA to interview them. They were very, very LA. That's where they had grown up. The sons of professional musicians. And there was something in that LA studio-musician culture that I simply couldn't understand. I also made a foolish error. I interviewed them as a group. Which is a great way to find out nothing.

Peter Cetera, the former vocalist for Chicago, who went out on his own and made magnificent music, was another one whose essence I couldn't grok. That might be because he kept his wife at his side when he talked to me, pretty much like Lionel Richie. And the side of yourself that you show to your wife is seldom the side of you that makes your music. Music comes from the side of you that puffs and struts hoping to impress the next lady down the road. Music comes from the Coolidge effect.

Natalie Cole's manager came to me when I was in bed with my six-month-long back problem. I had loved Natalie when she had sat across from me at a table on the top floor of the Hilton Hotel in Manhattan and her eyes had danced with light. And I'd wondered why she, Chuck Mangione, Mick Jagger's assistant Alvenia Bridges, and my friend and client Phyllis Hyman had made so many giggling trips to the bathroom together. Now, roughly three years later, those trips to the bathroom had taken their toll. When I called Natalie at her hotel room in Manhattan, she couldn't even mumble. The noise she made was incoherent. The light in her eyes three years earlier had apparently been powered by cocaine. And now the drug was destroying her.

Then Chuck Mangione's managers brought him to me. But he wouldn't talk to me on the phone. I suspect he, too, was coked-up.

I'd been hired at the same time to work with Peter, Paul, and Mary. Because I was in bed, that also had to depend on a phone call to get to know each other. Mary Travers was wonderful. She caught wind of my scientific side and recommended a book called *The Panda's Thumb*. I read it, and it introduced me to the work of evolutionary biologist Stephen Jay Gould, whose thinking would play an important role in my later life.

* * *

But one of the most unusual failures of all came when I was hired by George Michael's manager for a very strange purpose. I had turned down George Michael's group Wham! in 1983. Why? I was on this planet to get to the roots of soul. Wham! was all surface glitz—all white shorts and suntan—with its soul so carefully hidden that it was invisible. Wham! was what I loathed—empty image.

Now, in the late 1980s, there were rumors that George Michael was gay. And rumors of that sort back in the 1980s could destroy your career. So Michael's managers sent me a videotape of an extremely pretty woman in her early twenties, explaining that George Michael was her boyfriend and that there was nothing gay about him. I studied George and paid special attention to the lyrics of his first solo album, *Faith*. To me, the entire LP sounded like a love letter to another singer who was gay but hiding it—Elton John.

Yet I naively believed the videotape of the girlfriend. Then I flew to London to meet with George. Somehow I got my driving instructions wrong. George had booked me into the most fashionable, ultra-modern hotel in London. I flew in late at night and drove to the wrong hotel. When I arrived, the clerk behind the counter could find no record of my reservation. But he dug up a room for me anyway. The hotel was a dump. Very accommodating, but a dump. And, frankly, I can't remember the meeting with George.

Needless to say, I'd made a fool of myself, and I'd found no great and blazing soul. Which was my mistake, not George's. In listening to his music in the three decades since, I've heard massive flares of soul. In fact, George Michael's music is friggin' gorgeous. But apparently his managers had hired me because I "reeked of integrity." And I was being used to tell a lie. That George was straight. He wasn't.

George would eventually be arrested in the public men's room of a Beverly Hills park for a "lewd act."[206] And he would finally come out of the closet in a CNN interview.[207] But that would be eleven years later, in 1998. In a very different era. When the public had finally accepted same-sex preferences. George Michael would die at the age of fifty-three. And the loss would be huge.

Alas, I was never able to explore his real soul. If I had, could I have helped him hold on to his reason for living? We will never know.

* * *

Twice, when I did succeed in groking someone down to the marrow, showing that marrow to the public was the worst thing I could have done.

First, there was the real story of Chaka Khan. Chaka was in high school in the sixties in Chicago. Student protests were fashionable in those days, and the students in Chaka's school mounted a protest against the cafeteria food. Yes, against the low quality of the cuisine. But the school was largely black. Policemen are willing to regard student protests among white kids as a form of political expression. But they look at black protests as riots. It appears that the police managed to turn this particular protest into what they thought it was by physically assaulting the kids. One policeman had Chaka's best friend on the ground and was bent over, pummeling her. Chaka swung her heavy book bag at the gendarme's head with all her might and knocked him out. And her friend was able to escape. In 1974, this tale would not have gone over well.

More important, when Chaka got out of high school, she hung around with a group that used its women—Chaka among them—as lures. These girls went to upscale clubs, met women wearing masses of jewelry, befriended them, then put LSD in their drinks and took them to the mini-gang's apartment. While their victims were totally zoned out, Chaka's crew stripped them of their jewelry, then put them on a bus and let them ride to the end of the line and back as many times as it took these jewel-stripped ladies to come down and get their bearings.

This was not a story with which to establish Chaka Khan as what she was: one of the most powerful singers of her generation.

But an even stranger failure of my approach would come in 1985, with Kenny Loggins. Kenny has one of the most delicious, most emotion-grabbing voices I have ever heard. I did my usual month of preparation and was utterly baffled. I had the lyrics to Kenny's upcoming album, and for the first three weeks reading them, I could make no sense of them whatsoever. Then, like jigsaw-puzzle pieces, they all fell into place. The album was about a woman in Kenny's life who towered over him, squashing him, taking all the air out of his lungs. What did he need more than anything else? To flee her. Driving the fastest car available at the time, preferably a Lamborghini.

The trip out to Santa Barbara to meet Kenny in person was a bit strange. I had acquired John Denver as a client. Denver was not taken seriously back then. And his biggest hits were way behind him. He had become a has-been. A has-been and a joke. But he was a phenomenon onstage. My job was to rescue him from his status as an unwelcome musical zombie. After I'd been fired from ABC Records, I'd been unemployed for two weeks and had written an article about John for *Scholastic* magazine. Even then, his essence had been clear. John Denver grew up in a military family. His father and mother stayed in a town for a year or two, then were assigned to another base and another city. Which meant that John was always the stranger, always the person in school everyone turns their back on. To get a squeak of attention and warmth, John would go into the school cafeteria and play guitar. But his isolation stayed with him all his life.

The one thing that gave him warmth and connection was his marriage to his wife, Annie. Then Annie went to a local psychiatrist in Aspen, Colorado, who, over the course of roughly two years, convinced Annie to divorce John. When Annie left, John was devastated. Once again, he was utterly alone.

First, I met with John and the president of his record company, Jose Menendez, in an executive dining room on one of the top floors of RCA Records' headquarters on Manhattan's Sixth Avenue, a short walk east from Times Square. Which means we sat in a dining room with one table big enough for four people and were served by a waiter totally dedicated just to us, a waiter who brought us food crafted by a chef, who, like the waiter, was working just for us three. Menendez was a man of total self-control. He was politely charming, but never revealed a true emotion.

Five years later, Menendez's two sons—Lyle, twenty-one, and Erik, nineteen—walked into the den of one of the family homes, the one in Beverly Hills, where their dad and mom were dozing. The brothers carried shotguns. They blasted their father in the back of the head. The noise woke their mother, who was sleeping on the couch. The brothers wounded her in the leg while she ran for the hallway, where she slipped on her own blood. The boys finished her off with shots to her face, her arm, and her chest. To make the murders look like a mob hit job, they also shot their parents' kneecaps.

Then they called 911 and pretended that, to their horror, they'd just walked in and had discovered the bodies of their murdered parents.

The boys restrained themselves for months, going about as normal a life as you can have when you have just executed your parents in one of your family homes. Then they began to spend money, buying a Rolex and a Porsche. When they'd spent $700,000 of their inheritance, Erik confessed what he'd done to his psychologist. The psychologist told the story to his girlfriend. Ten months after the murder, the Menendez brothers were arrested, and the story made headlines. This sort of coldness seemed to dog poor John Denver wherever he went.

After the dinner in the private RCA dining room, I studied John, and I flew out to meet him again at his house in Aspen. John was extremely proud of that house. It was in a Le Corbusier, cube-dominated, geometric, Bauhaus style. One of the coldest architectural styles ever inflicted on humanity. John proudly rattled off all the ecologically friendly systems the house possessed—solar electricity, solar water heating, passive heating and cooling, and every other technology available for an enormously expensive, environmentally conscious domicile in 1985. What John didn't seem to see was how emotionally frigid and empty the house was. The floors were tile and wood, without a stitch of carpeting to give them warmth. The white furniture was achingly unused. The views out of the huge walls of windows showed mountains. Stone and snow, but no life. None. The house trumpeted the fact that John Denver was completely abandoned, completely bereft of human company, achingly on his own. It was the loneliest place I'd ever seen.

But John had something going on the night of my visit. He was hosting a charity Trivial Pursuit contest at a bar in the center of town. Now, I can't help it, and please forgive me in advance for it, but when I open my mouth I sound like a walking encyclopedia. Growing up reading two books a day will do that to you. Not to mention going through the *Scientific American* from cover to cover as a kid. John got all excited. With me on his team, he thought he couldn't lose. So he recruited me as a ringer. Little did he realize that Trivial Pursuit contests hinge on a knowledge of TV shows. I knew my fields—science, history, music, and film. But aside from in-depth news shows, I didn't watch TV.

This was a problem. And there was another. I had an evening flight booked from Aspen to LA. I was due to meet the next morning with Kenny Loggins at his home in Santa Barbara for brunch. I would be in the air by the time John's Trivial Pursuit contest began.

John must have been very persuasive. He got me to book a 6:00 a.m. flight on a small plane to LA. Thanks to the rescheduled flight, I was John Denver's ringer in the Trivial Pursuit contest. In a jovial, cheery bar filled with people, all of whom were watching our every move. And we lost. Humiliatingly. For a simple reason. As I said, try me on history, science, or politics, and you'd be surprised. But on the subject of TV personalities and the dates when key episodes were first aired, I am witless.

Seven hours after losing the Trivial Pursuit contest for John, I flew out to LA at the godforsaken hour of 6:00 a.m.—which means getting up at four in the morning, one of my least favorite things to do, and being bounced up and down at dawn as we flew over and under clouds. With a great view over the right shoulder of the pilot through the windshield. Sometimes a frightening view, as the clouds rear up above you like solid cliffs and make it very clear that your plane is tiny and vulnerable. When we landed, I picked up my rental car at the airport and drove south on the Pacific Coast Highway, the highway I'd hitchhiked in 1962 when I was accidentally helping to start the hippie movement. The Pacific Ocean was visible to the left. And I arrived at a big, modern, airy house in the greenery of the hills. It was Kenny in his own environment. Or was it? When we sat down, I gave the singer my interpretation of his album and intended to ask if it was accurate. But I didn't get to the end. Kenny stopped me abruptly and angrily. "Who's been telling you about my relationship with my wife?" he spat. Well, really, only one person. Kenny Loggins. Through his lyrics.

Even with his wife out of the room, she hovered over the conversation. She was a five feet eight-and-a-half inches tall, impressive, blonde.[208] No, this was not Kenny's environment, it was hers.

The story behind Kenny's new music was one I couldn't reveal to the public.

So, secular shamanism was limited by the limits of my understanding. And it was sometimes limited by the nature of the truths it found.

48

THE PMRC—THE WITCHES
OF WASHINGTON

When it came to popular culture, I was not the only sage to occasionally miss the mark.

In roughly 370 BC, in Athens, Plato decried a new information technology. Yes, Plato, the founder of Western philosophy. This newfangled tech, he said, would destroy the minds of kids. Why? Up until then, children had been required to memorize the two foundational books of Greek culture: the *Iliad* and the *Odyssey*. They had to commit every single word of those two books to the storage space in their brains. This, said Plato, was the discipline that gave rigor to the Greek mind. But Plato was convinced that the new data tech would reduce children and adolescents to slackers. Why? Because they would no longer have to memorize. What was the new information tool Plato deplored? Writing.

What Plato failed to realize was that, in the days of committing the *Iliad* and the *Odyssey* to memory, most people were only familiar with two books. Now, thanks to writing, they could dive into a hundred. Or, in the case of the soon-to-be-built library at Alexandria, Egypt, between forty thousand and four hundred thousand.[209]

Then there were the city fathers of London in 1574 and 1597.[210] There was a new form of entertainment that was wildly popular with London's youth. But the town fathers could see clearly that it was going to saw away the morals of the young, leading them down the primrose path to sex and violence. So the city fathers passed an ordinance banning the new entertainment. What they failed to account for was the monarch in Richmond Palace.[211] She loved the new art form. She loved it so much that she had it staged in the very heart of her castle. Because she was a fan, she overrode the town fathers' ban and kept the new amusement going. What was this insidious recreation about to destroy the minds of the young? Theater. Who was the ruler in Westminster Castle who saved the day? Queen Elizabeth. And who was one of the leaders in the new form of theater? William Shakespeare. Today, educators like Prince's favorite, Marva Collins, force-feed teenagers Shakespeare. They think it will make teenagers smart.

So much for the panics of adults over the new technologies and entertainments of the young. But another of these panics was about to arrive. Just as Dennis DeYoung of Styx had predicted.

* * *

Remember the manila envelope that Chet Flippo, the editor who founded *Rolling Stone* magazine's East Coast office, sent you one afternoon by messenger? The one with six pages accusing you of founding a new magazine genre, the heavy-metal magazine? And remember how *Circus*'s publisher, Gerald Rothberg, eventually chucked the formula you'd labored on from dawn to dusk and on weekends? The formula to make *Circus* everything Gerry wanted it to be—America's *Time* magazine for music. Not to mention America's *Bravo* and *Salut les copains*. And remember how Gerry's singularly blockheaded misjudgment forced *Circus* into chapter 11 bankruptcy?

Remember how you'd felt miffed and rejected, and had then given your secret formula to the key figures at two other music magazines—*Creem* and *Hit Parader*? Thus boosting their sales and making them newsstand forces to be reckoned with? In other words, remember how much blood, sweat, tears, neuronal juice, and soul you had invested in creating the genre of the heavy-metal magazine?

Well, in 1985, someone started fucking with my baby. Someone was working behind the scenes to get certain magazines banished from newsstands in major periodical-selling parlors like 7-11 and Walmart. Working behind the scenes and succeeding. In the name of defending the youth of America from sex, violence, and barbarity. And it wasn't just us rock-and-roll folks they were sabotaging. These anonymous morality police were freezing two enormously successful publications out of respectability, *Playboy* and *Penthouse*. Not to mention freezing them out of 7-11 and Walmart.

In a nation that demands monogamy, and in a civilization whose wives lose interest in sex after the first two years of marriage, how are men who can't afford mistresses going to function without *Playboy* and *Penthouse*? Our society handles this problem by providing a harmless outlet for the Coolidge effect, porn. In fact, soft porn may be one of the most brilliant escape valves for the animals in the brain that Western civilization has ever invented. Porn allows a society bursting with unmet male sexual needs to keep it together. Without violence.

Let's be honest, solitary masturbation may be embarrassing, but it does a hell of a lot less harm than rape. Or than the sexual outlet the Greeks, the Romans, and the early Muslims favored—sacking cities, burning down buildings, killing men and children, and making off with the girls as sex slaves. Yes, this is what even the ancient Greeks did to the city of Troy. They laid siege to the city for ten years. When they overcame the town with a giant party favor, the Trojan horse, they did what testosterone-filled langur monkeys do when they knock an elder off his throne. They slaughtered the men and the children so they could get at the town's girls and turn them into sex slaves. In other words, soft porn is better than mass murder and rape. Hell, even hard porn is better than mass murder and rape.

But back to the point. Someone was assaulting rock and roll. Who? At first it was a loose coalition of right wing organizations. Organizations who said they were engaged in a culture war against, well, against the movement in which I'd played a seminal role back in 1962, a culture war against those goddamned hippies. In this cabal—this loose coalition—was Pat Robertson's 700 Club, Jerry Falwell's Moral Majority, and James Dodson's Focus on the Family. This was a conspiracy straight out of the nightmares of Styx's *Kilroy Was Here* and Leanne Katz's National Coalition Against Censorship.

Then a front group emerged. It called itself the Parents Music Resource Center. It pretended to be mainstream. And it used women of power as its focal figures: Tipper Gore, wife of senator, future vice president, and future Democratic presidential candidate Al Gore; Susan Baker, wife of a backstage superhero of Republican presidential politics who cycled from Secretary of State to head of the Treasury, James Baker; and two lesser-known women, Sally Nevius, the wife of ex-Washington Council Chairman John Nevius, and Pam Howar, a super-high-society Washington hostess and wife of a realtor.[212] As Wikipedia will tell you, this little coven of political witches were known as the Washington Wives.[213]

The Washington Wives—the Witches of Washington—campaigned to label rock records that contained sexually explicit lyrics or violence. Sounds reasonable, right? We all have a right to know what's in the fancy packages we buy. If it's food and it has peanut oil, you don't want to lose a perfectly good seven-year-old daughter to anaphylactic shock. A daughter who has a peanut allergy. Full disclosure on a label can save lives. But in rock and roll, labeling wasn't as reasonable as it sounded. Why? Records were sold in record stores. Most record stores were in malls. And malls did not want pornography. They did not want the downscale grime and grunge that goes with triple-x-rated slime. That slime would have torpedoed their property value.

Which meant that if you wanted to start a record store in a mall, you had to sign a contract. A contract enforcing that mall's standards. And that contract said that you wouldn't sell smut. If you did, you'd be kicked out. So what looked like a label proclaiming sexually explicit and violent material was a "please kick me out" sign in disguise. It meant most record stores would not be able to stock and sell a labeled album. The goal of the PMRC wasn't just an honest description of what you were about to buy. It was censorship. In other words, the PMRC lied about its intentions.

And that wasn't all that the Washington Wives lied about. Their executive director, Jennifer Norwood, and their members were doing interviews in every media outlet they could find, from *The Today Show* and *Good Morning America* to *People* and *Time*.[214] And they continually presented themselves as just a normal, middle-of-the-road, secular bunch. But they distributed a press kit to every media decision maker they could reach. That press kit was an inch and a half thick. Impressive, but much too thick for any writer or producer to read.

If you did find the time to read what was in that whonking stack of tree pulp, if you read it carefully, you might have had your socks shocked off. Paper after paper purported to be from solid academic sources. But they weren't. They were whacko claims from right-wing religious crazies. Papers purporting to come from experts that were the work, in fact, of raving lunatics. Papers without the slightest semblance of fact-checking. One standout press-kit-stuffer buried in the stack was an article from a man who pretended to be a high-placed academic. How did he demonstrate his credentials? His name was followed by roughly seventeen highfalutin acronyms—GEC, ACC, UTC, HBF, etc. All of these acronyms were phony. They were not legitimate degrees from legitimate institutions. In the first paragraphs of his detailed "study" of rock-and-roll music, this "expert" claimed that all rock bands are active Satanists, that they sacrifice babies and small children before each concert, and that you could see the proof of their Satanism in their names. I am not exaggerating. KISS stood for Knights in Service to Satan. AC/DC stood for Anti-Christ/Devil's Children. Styx was named for a river in hell—a clear tipoff to Satanism. And a whole string of more. Now, look, I knew KISS, and I would eventually work with them. Gene Simmons and Paul Stanley are two normal kids of Jewish descent who always dreamed of being rock stars. They would have found Satanism a ludicrous waste of their precious time. I also worked with AC/DC. Anti-Christ/Devil's Children? Are you kidding? AC/DC got its name from a bit of stamped metal on the back of a vacuum cleaner—AC/DC, alternating current/direct current. Then there was Styx, a band writing about the future of Western civilization. As for kidnapping nice, fat Christian babies for sacrificial purposes? Please. Give me a break.

In other words, these Washington women had put their names on materials in which right-wing religious extremists lied their asses off. Lied or fantasized. And the Washington Wives had been so careless that they'd allowed this provably false material to go out under their names. Remember, this was before the age of Trump. It was before lies in politics became hourly fare. And, to repeat, it was straight out of the darkest visions of Styx's Dennis DeYoung.

Let's go back to one other basic fact. I can't throw or catch a ball. I can't do normal things. Heck, I don't even know how to neck in the back seat of a car. The one thing I can do is use words. I can speak and write. Which means that freedom of speech is way up there for me with the first two rules of science. It's sacred. It's what makes America America. It's what allows me to be me.

So, when I saw the move to censor magazines, and when I realized it was choking off two of the most important magazine outlets in North America, 7/11 and Walmart, I was outraged.

I called two friends and asked them to get together with me for lunch. One was Bob Guccione Jr., a man you've met before with the Hutus and the Tutsis—the founder of *Spin* magazine and the son of Bob Guccione Sr., founder of *Penthouse*. The other was David Krebs, the manager who put Aerosmith, AC/DC, and Ted Nugent on the map. Both had intellects focused on much more than just rock and roll. I laid out the forces of evil we were up against. I explained the details of the rabid religious right that I'd learned from my Styx campaign and had kept an eye on ever since. I explained how the religious right was manipulating Gore and Baker. And what this could mean in the long run—music censorship. If these women could, they would take us back to the meaningless blather of moon, June, and spoon lyrics. They would return us to the idiocy of artificial rock stars. Stars with nothing to say. They would return us to the days when popular music could not help us find our identities. When music could not help us speak the passions for which we have no words. When music could not be the articulator of group soul.

The three of us decided to form an organization—Music in Action, MIA—a name Bob Guccione Jr. invented. We would all chip in money to fund the thing. But the person who would do the work, who would track the PMRC's moves, and who would go on radio and TV to counter the PMRC, would be me. Unless it was something huge, in which case Bob would be the one before the camera. He had a much higher public profile than I did. This meant that I henceforth made a regular practice of confronting the false statements of the PMRC in the media. And, when it could be arranged, I'd debate one-on-one on TV with the woman who ran the day-to-day affairs of the PMRC—Jennifer Norwood.

Meanwhile, we wrote a petition and gathered signatures—fifty thousand of them, not a lot. But this was before email, Change.org, and Facebook made this kind of thing easy. Then we had our petitions delivered to Congress.

The Washington Wives posed a greater threat to the music industry than you might think. These were not just any old women raising a stink. They were women plugged in at the highest level of government. And government can choke the music industry to death. How? Remember the 240 or so record companies I'd pursued back in my days at Cloud Studio? And remember how they'd boiled themselves down to six? That six were the properties of conglomerates. Many of these conglomerates owned radio and TV stations. Radio and TV stations operate with licenses from the FCC. Take those licenses away, and very rich companies become paupers overnight.

Just to show its power, in 1985 the government had gone after a company called RKO, an entertainment giant formed in 1928 as one of the pioneering firms in "talkies"—talking pictures. The builders of the companies RKO had bought included Howard Hughes and President John F. Kennedy's father, Joseph Kennedy. Among the most powerful men on earth, right? What's more, RKO Pictures had made the Fred Astaire and Ginger Rogers movies. Not to mention *King Kong* and *Citizen Kane*. Yet in roughly 1985, just as the PMRC was being founded, the FCC was able to revoke RKO's licenses for all its TV and radio stations, thus shutting what little was left of RKO out of the entertainment industry. Completely. And, for all practical purposes, reducing the company from an elephant to a flea.

Would the Washington Wives use this power? Well, they sure as hell tried to use it on me. One Wednesday evening, I took the car service out to JFK, New York's biggest airport, to pay a visit to my only client in Hannover, Germany, the Scorpions. I had a wonderful time in Germany, and I gathered a little bit more of what made the band tick. As a bonus, one of the business managers for the band took me for a ride on the Autobahn and showed me why those who can afford them buy Porsches. He accelerated from a standstill to eighty miles per hour in what felt like two seconds and plastered me so far into the back of my bucket seat that you could have mistaken me for a cushion. Then I headed for the Hannover Airport on Friday morning, hopped a plane, and was back in my office in Manhattan by 5:00 p.m. Ready to work. When I arrived at my desk, there was a copy of the *Hollywood Reporter*, a big-format trade magazine that takes up a lot of space, splayed across my desk, where its headline blared directly at my eyeballs the minute I sat down. That headline announced that the PMRC had attempted to put me out of business.

Said the story, the gentle ladies of the PMRC had sent a secret letter to the heads of the six big record companies. The message? There was an irritant making their lives miserable. If the big six valued their FCC licenses, they would remove this pest and eject him from the entertainment industry. His name was Howard Bloom.

Someone had gotten a copy of this letter and had leaked it to the press, thus saving my tiny tailbone. Who might have done such a thing? Probably the Darth Vader of the music industry. What clue did I have? Don Henley of the Eagles had joined Music in Action. And Don Henley was managed by Irving Azoff.

I owe Irving a favor. But the Azoff technique—leaking inside materials to key press people—would soon drive a nail through the wrist of Michael Jackson.

49

WHO KILLED MICHAEL JACKSON?

Everything I'd done in my years of immersion in pop, rock, and the dark underbelly where new myths and mass passions are made came to a head in Michael Jackson. In fact, everything I am came to a head.

I've told you the story of my first meeting with Michael Jackson at his brother Marlon's pool house in Encino, California. Michael stunned me. I had never met anyone like him. His quality of awe, wonder, and surprise was the closest I'd ever witnessed to a living incarnation of William Blake's order to see the infinite in the tiniest of things. And that wonder was clear when we'd gone through the portfolios of illustrators and Michael's knees had buckled and his throat had erupted in soft, orgasmic "oooohhhhhs."

What's more, Michael and his brothers had let me help art-direct their album cover. I suggested we go with Michael Whelan, a fantasy illustrator from Connecticut whose visions boggle the mind. I turned the pages of Whelan's portfolio to show Michael and his brothers a picture of strange, fuzzy, koala-like creatures coming to the crest of a forested hill and seeing a paradise in the valley below. I suggested that we replace the fuzzy fantasy creatures with the Jacksons and replace the lush, green paradise in the valley with LA. LA as you see it from the homes up in the Hollywood Hills—laid out at night in a gleaming, glowing, flat, map-like grid. The Jacksons loved the idea, and the CBS art director was given the task of rounding up Whelan and turning the concept into a reality. Ultimately, though, the concept was dumbed down. There was no hill, no moment of discovery, just the Jacksons with the gleaming grid of nighttime LA laid out in the background. The Whelan magic was gone. So was Michael Jackson's. The result was very un-Jackson. It was boring.

My next encounter with Michael Jackson came over his black base. He'd become huge. He'd sold thirty-two million copies of just one LP—*Thriller*—in just a little bit more than a year, something no one had ever done before . . . or since. Something not even the Beatles or Elvis Presley had achieved. *Thriller* went thirty-three times platinum, won eight Grammys, and spawned an unprecedented seven Top 10 singles.[215] All of its songs but two became major hits. Said *Rolling Stone*, "Michael is now, quite simply, the biggest star in the pop-cultural universe." Bigger, said *Rolling Stone*, than the Beatles, and just possibly bigger than Jesus.[216]

Or, as *Rolling Stone* put it, "How big is Michael Jackson? . . . Add up all the copies of David Bowie's *Let's Dance*, the Police's *Synchronicity*, the Rolling Stones' *Undercover*, Culture Club's *Colour by Numbers*, Quiet Riot's *Metal Health*, and Duran Duran's *Seven and the Ragged Tiger* that have been sold in the US. A lot of records, right? Now double that figure. That's how big Michael Jackson is."[217] Confirming that stature were *Guinness Book of World Records* citations for "most Top 10 singles off one LP," most singles sold by a solo artist, and "most records ever sold."[218] Period!

When you succeed on that level, you have a serious danger. It has to do with an ego stake. As long as your fans feel that they are building your career, as long as they feel that recruiting their friends to your music makes all the difference in the world to your rise, those fans will stick with you. But when those fans feel that you have left them behind, turned your back on them, and ignored them, they will turn on you. And they will show their power in a new way—by tearing you apart.

The black base was particularly sensitive to giving a start to artists who then turned their backs and left the black community behind. So making sure the black base felt like a part of the engine of your success, not a victim of the white machine, was important.

Ever since the achievements of the civil rights movement in the 1960s, the National Association for the Advancement of Colored People and other organizations had worked their butts off to get blacks to vote. In 1983, the NAACP proposed putting a voter-registration booth at every one of the Jacksons' fifty-five concerts. I was all for it. But there was an obstacle: Michael's religion. Michael was a Jehovah's Witness.[219] A religion instilled in him by his mother. And the Jehovah's Witnesses forbade any involvement with voting.[220] When I lobbied hard to go with the NAACP's idea of voter-registration booths, all of the members of the Victory Tour's inner team said no. There was no way Michael would allow it. But Michael said yes. It was the beginning of my reputation as someone Michael would listen to. Little did I know it, but that reputation would soon turn from a tool into a time bomb.

The NAACP was having an annual convention in LA. It was going to be chaired by Benjamin Hooks, a legend in black history and a man who would go on to be awarded the Presidential Medal of Freedom by George W. Bush.[221] The NAACP wanted Michael to put in an appearance at the LA event. They wanted him to pop in, meet Benjamin Hooks onstage, and just say a few words. Since Michael was one of the biggest headline-generators in the world in 1984, this would draw attention. I wanted to do it. It would show a commitment to the black audience. Again, the core team said it was impossible. But Michael said yes.

So, when the date was coming for the NAACP appearance, I flew out to LA to supervise the NAACP pop-in. Which means that Michael and I sat together in the back of a black van driven by security guards as we headed through LA streets toward the site of the conference. And Michael explained something to me. "Here's why I have security guards," he said. "When you're in my position and you get out of a van like this, the sidewalk crowds up with people who love you. Because they love you, they want to get just a hair of your head or a thread from your coat. But your flesh is weaker than you think. In fact, it's as weak as an overcooked noodle. So, when a big crowd reaches out to touch you, they can tear you apart. All because they love you."

Very much like John Mellencamp's interpretation of *Cool Hand Luke*. Very much like Jesus Christ. And an insight that would prove to have a darker side than even Michael Jackson imagined.

I flew back to New York. To understand my next encounter with Michael, my most important encounter, you have to understand something else.

* * *

When I said yes to the Jacksons at their suite at the Helmsley Palace Hotel in December of 1983, there was a reason. The Jackson Victory Tour was in trouble. The press was about to descend like a flock of harpies and try to tear the tour apart. Not to mention ripping at the Jacksons, and Michael. And this was not because of love. Far from it. First came the stories from the pages of one of the lead sheep in the music world—*Rolling Stone*—about Don King's involvement as a promoter of the tour and about his conviction for manslaughter.[222] Remember, he had punched a man to the ground, then kicked him to death over a debt of six hundred dollars.

Then a new perception of the tour emerged, again from *Rolling Stone*. *Rolling Stone*'s West Coast investigative journalist, Michael Goldberg, had been given copies of the drafts of the Jacksons' contracts with potential tour promoters, and Goldberg claimed those contracts were predatory.

More important, whoever slipped Goldberg those contracts had also given him a vicious new narrative frame. An evil spin. Ticket prices for normal concerts were as low as $11.50 per ticket in those dim and distant days of the mid-1980s.[223] But the Jacksons were going to charge $30. Why, asked Michael Goldberg's source. The anonymous source apparently had an answer. The Jacksons were desperate for money. The brothers had expensive lifestyles, but they had lost their income since Michael had stopped recording with them. This was their last chance to cash in on their little brother's phenomenal success. They were sinking their teeth into the jugular of Michael's audience and sucking as much blood as possible, before it was too late.[224] There was only one problem. So far as I could see, this wasn't true.

Then another damaging idea arose in the rock-crit elite. Its main promoter was Bruce Springsteen's biographer, Dave Marsh. If Bob Christgau was the pope of the rock-crit elite, Dave Marsh was a cardinal. Dave wrote the following in every media outlet he could reach: We, the rock-crit elite, know everyone of any consequence in the music industry. A tour of the magnitude the Jacksons are planning will require hiring the best in the business. And no one we know, Marsh said, has been hired to work the Jackson tour. Marsh predicted that this would have serious consequences. Amateur lighting rigs would topple over on the audience, killing hundreds. A poorly built stage would collapse in mid-performance. A clumsily rigged sound system would electrocute the performers. And unprofessional security people at the concerts would leave the place open to gang fights. Parents would want to take their kids to a Jackson concert but wouldn't be able to. The threat of stabbings and flying bullets would be too great.

Marsh promoted this idea wherever he could. He was using Michael Jackson's visibility to get visibility for himself. He'd even publish a book on Jackson a year later, in 1985: *Trapped: Michael Jackson and the Crossover Dream*.[225] One day in the spring of 1984, the *CBS Morning News* called. They were going to have Dave Marsh on network TV, reciting his litany of catastrophes. Could I come on immediately afterward and refute his arguments? I sure could, and I did.

Remember something. When ABC Records had fired Jay Lasker and brought in a lawyer as a president because Clive Davis was a lawyer, that lawyer had installed a new head of publicity in LA, and the new head of publicity had fired me. Why? So he could replace me with a member of his social circle, a buddy's girlfriend. That buddy with the girlfriend was Dave Marsh. And Dave Marsh had played a role in my firing. More important, Dave Marsh and his girlfriend had played a tiny role in the utter destruction of ABC Records. So listening to Dave Marsh's advice could be poisonous to your health. And, when it came to the Jacksons, Dave Marsh had all of America listening.

So I went on the *CBS Morning News* immediately after Marsh and debunked every false word he had said. But even I didn't entirely understand why the Victory Tour was fertile ground for such rumors. I wouldn't understand that until I would have my most important encounter with Michael Jackson.

* * *

The press was in a frenzy over Michael Jackson and the Jacksons' Victory Tour. I usually avoided convening press conferences like the plague. But for the Jacksons, press conferences were essential. You couldn't sit down with journalists one at a time and tell them the real story. There were too many journalists on the case. When we had our first press conferences to announce tour details, 3,500 reporters showed up in New York, and another 3,500 showed up in LA. That, frankly, is an unbelievable number.

Why did so many flock to these press events? Boston had two major daily newspapers: the *Boston Globe* and the *Boston Herald*. The *Globe*, a nationally respected paper with twenty-nine Pulitzer Prizes under its belt—a paper now owned by the *New York Times*—outsold the *Herald* by twenty thousand to thirty thousand copies a day. Then, one morning, the publisher of the *Herald* did something unheard of. He came down to the newsroom where thirty reporters sat at their typewriters and announced that, the next day, the paper would have a cover on Michael Jackson. He ordered his reporters to come up with an angle, a topical hook—something newsworthy. The reporters were outraged. "We are not a tabloid. We are not a supermarket celebrity rag," they said. "We've won eight Pulitzers. We are a newspaper. We print news." "Sorry," said the publisher, "tomorrow we are doing a Michael Jackson cover." And he left to go back upstairs to his office.

The *Herald* had a Michael Jackson cover the next day. And, instead of lagging behind the *Globe* by thirty thousand copies, the *Herald* outsold the *Globe* by twenty thousand. The next day, the publisher showed up in the *Herald*'s newsroom again. He pointed to the paper's music critic and said, "You. I'm giving you your own office with your own secretary. From now on, I want a Michael Jackson story every day." And the publisher of the *Boston Globe* did the same.

The message wasn't lost on the publishing community of America. Michael Jackson stories made money. Why? First, there was a public romance with Michael that had gone on since he was six years old. But, more important, there was something phenomenally real about Michael that no one else I've ever met in my life had. In other words, the public sensed something in Michael for which there are few words. Something that, in my humble opinion, has still never been adequately expressed. Or adequately turned into headlines. Michael's goodness, his quality of wonder, and his generosity. But we'll see that in the flesh in a few minutes, and you can judge for yourself.

The press learned another, darker lesson. When you couldn't find a positive story about Michael Jackson, you could always concoct a negative one. You could always find someone with a complaint. And the negative stories outsold the positive stories. To cook them up, all you had to do was follow the path of the lead sheep, *Rolling Stone*'s Michael Goldberg and Bruce Springsteen's biographer, Dave Marsh.

For example, it became popular to print stories saying that the Jacksons or their bodyguards had abused someone—had manhandled some poor innocent. On the weekend of July 29, 1984, the Jacksons' Victory Tour came to play three concerts in New York City. The concerts were scheduled for Sunday, Monday, and Tuesday night at Giants Stadium, an 80,242-seat sports stadium across the river from New York City in New Jersey.[226] The setup of the stage made 44,000 seats available per night, and all 132,000 of those seats were sold out. An utter astonishment. That's more people than the entire population of New Haven, Connecticut.

The Jacksons were staying at the Helmsley Palace Hotel, as usual. It was a Sunday, the day of the first concert, and I subwayed into Manhattan to see the brothers. The minute I showed up in the hotel lobby, one of the Jacksons' road team grabbed me and asked me to handle a crisis. A reporter and a photographer for the *New York Post* had filed a story saying that the Jacksons' bodyguards had threatened them with a tire iron. It would appear in roughly two hours. Could I do something about it?

The story would fit the Jacksons-as-bad-guys narrative that Michael Goldberg and Dave Marsh had set up perfectly. And it would fulfill the first imperative of Jacksons journalism: if you can't find a positive story, invent a negative one. Negative stories outsell positive stories.

The first step in crisis management is to dig up the facts. And to be as good a journalist as the journalists you serve. I interviewed as many people as I could find who had been at the confrontation. A disturbing tale emerged. The Jacksons were being hunted for photos by the paparazzi the way Bob Marley had been hunted in Switzerland. And the family members were being trailed by journalists. There were crowds of reporters and photographers at the entrances to all of their hotels waiting for the Jacksons to emerge. In those days, stars traveled in long stretch limousines. Usually black Cadillacs or Lincolns. So the Jacksons had a decoy stretch limousine leave the hotel entrance at the critical moment. Then the Jacksons would exit from the cargo garage in what looked like laundry vans.

The *New York Post*'s photographer and writer had figured out the trick. They had ignored the decoys and planted themselves at the cargo garage. Then, when the Jacksons' van emerged, the *Post* duo had followed the brothers west on New York's clogged crosstown streets until the Jackson van made a left turn on Eleventh Avenue, a four-lane highway with a big concrete divider separating the northbound traffic from the southbound. Then the *Post* pair had pulled off a chase scene. They had jockeyed their car into a lane adjoining the Jacksons and had tried over and over again to nose ahead of the Jacksons van and get pictures. The Jacksons' drivers were from the LAPD and well practiced in this kind of stunt driving. And the avenue was clogged with traffic. So the *Post* pair could not manage to nudge ahead of the Jacksons' van.

Finally, in desperation, the *Post* newshounds had done something potentially murderous. They'd jumped the concrete divider, taken a chance on a head-on collision, and had sped through traffic going in the opposite direction. They had gotten ahead of the Jacksons' van, jumped the divider again, and planted themselves at a ninety-degree angle to the Jacksons' van, setting up a roadblock and stopping traffic. Then they'd jumped out of their car prepared to get photos.

Michael's security guards explained to me that Michael received roughly three hundred letters a day with death threats. His security people had to go through them all to see if any might turn into real assassination attempts. And the *Post* news-gatherers' car was not marked. So Michael's security people had no idea of who the people were who had just threatened the lives of families on a Sunday outing traveling in the northbound lane with a head-on collision. When two of the Jacksons' security detail got out of their van, one of them carried a tire iron. Seeing the iron, one *Post* employee opened the door of the car and got out a gun. It was a tense standoff. But the Jacksons got to the stadium on time for their sound check.

Then the *Post* people had written up a story claiming that for absolutely no reason whatsoever, the Jacksons' security guys had threatened them with a tire iron. Typical of the employees of the vampire Jackson brothers. But I had the real story, and it didn't make the *Post* look good.

Don't ask me how, but I got the phone number of the country club where the *Post*'s owner was playing golf that Sunday afternoon. I asked him to kill the false story about the Jacksons' security guys as attackers. Alas, if he didn't, I'd be forced to put out the real story. Including the fact that one of the *Post*'s employees had been arrested for using a gun in a threatening manner in the past.

The *Post* killed the story. But there were lots of others.

* * *

Meanwhile, other forms of hell were breaking loose. The Reverend Al Sharpton had trained in civil-rights activism with Jesse Jackson. What Al had learned from Jesse wasn't pretty. Find a big name, headline-generating company or person. Then picket it and boycott it. Make nasty headlines that won't go away. Stop only when the organization or person you are picketing caves in and gives you what you demand. And remember when you are making your demands to demand money.

Jesse Jackson had focused this procedure on companies like Coca-Cola and the beer giant Anheuser-Busch.[227] Among the perks these protests produced, fourteen years later Anheuser-Busch would agree to sell its Chicago beer distributorship to two of Jackson's sons.[228] Sharpton came up with a new variation on Jackson's technique. Focus your protests and boycotts on superstars. His first choice was a woman who had briefly been a client of mine—Diana Ross. Sharpton claimed that Diana was a racist—she wasn't employing enough blacks. We were the obvious next target. By we, I mean the Jacksons' Victory Tour.

After considering dozens of offers from folks who wanted to promote the Victory Tour, the Jacksons had made a decision. The Sullivan family owned Fox Stadium in Boston and the Boston Patriots.[229] The Sullivan's apparently felt involvement with the Jacksons would burnish their reputation and bring in a profit. And they were super-rich. They had the money to finance a superior tour. Or so it seemed. In reality, they were drowning in debt.[230] But they hid it well. So I got in touch with the Reverend Al Sharpton, to see what it would take to keep him from disrupting our tour. The answer: $35,000—$85,000 in today's dollars. I went to the Sullivans, explained the problem to them, and hired the Reverend Al as a consultant for, guess what amount? Thirty-five thousand dollars. Which would mean that during the tour, when I flew out to each concert, I would take the Reverend Al Sharpton with me. Like a guard handcuffed to a prisoner on a plane. Al dressed in brand-new red gym clothes for these trips. With spotless red-and-white gym shoes and a gold chain. He looked fabulously, rappishly hip. And he looked rich. Periodically, Al would come up with an idea—like getting gangs together for a peace conference. His ideas, each one of them, would have damaged the reputation of the tour. When I said no, Al was very nice about it. In fact, he was charming.

When it comes to negatives from the press, I had a very strange stroke of luck. My office got roughly 350 calls a day from press people wanting the Jacksons. Not just ordinary press people. Calls from people like Don Hewitt, the founding producer of *60 Minutes*, who called me one day begging for concert tickets and promising he would owe me for the rest of his life. But our press tickets were limited to a few hundred. What's more, we could only do a small number of interviews.

One day, my receptionist got a call from a reporter at *People* magazine, a publication you remember that I'd been getting clients into since its inception in 1974. I was grabbing my little red nylon knapsack and heading downstairs to the car-service auto that would take me to the airport to be with the Jacksons in LA. Today, you'd handle an important call like this on your cellphone and take care of business while putting your arms through the straps of your backpack and while going down the stairs. Then you'd take more calls in the cab. But in those days we had no cell phones. A telephone was wired to a wall. Leave the vicinity of the wall and you left the ability to take the call.

My receptionist told the *People* journalist that I wasn't available. I was on my way to the airport to fly to LA. The journalist, Jim McBride, had spunk. He called every major airline with flights to LA, said he was me, and told them he needed to confirm the details of his flight to LA. When he hit American Airlines, he was told precisely what flight I was on and its departure time. Then he went to his editor and asked what he should do next. "Get on that flight with Bloom," said the editor. "But I'm not packed," said Jim. "Doesn't matter," said his editor, "we have a company bungalow in LA where you can stay. When you get there, you'll find a new toothbrush and a fresh razor. If you need anything else—a change of your shirt or pants—put it on the *People* magazine credit card."

So, when I got to the airport and checked in, the woman behind the American Airlines counter said, "Oh, your traveling companion is already here." Traveling companion? When I sat down there was this thin, five foot ten, half-black, half-Jewish person with a wonderful smile seated to my right. It was Jim McBride from *People* magazine.

* * *

Remember how I did my best work at three-hour lunches, telling the tales that proved that people like John Mellencamp were authentic? A five-and-half-hour flight was even better. The tales of the Jacksons' authenticity—not to mention honesty and commitment to the poor and the oppressed—took at least three hours to tell in detail. By the time we reached LA, Jim's perception of the Jackson tour had been turned on its head. He saw the good. And he saw the evil of the story that this was a vampirical tour. But even I didn't understand just how deeply the Jacksons were the opposite of vampirical. Yet.

* * *

My job was to track down the source of the Jacksons Victory Tour's monstrous attacks and to stop them. One source of continuing embarrassment was Don King. Every time he opened his mouth, he discredited the tour. And he discredited the Jacksons. Yes, Don was a flamboyant and fabulous showman. A genius in his field. He was also charming. But he stood for the very opposite of the Jacksons' values. As to those values, I had sat with Marlon and Tito when they'd reviewed the terms of contracts with potential promoters. They'd pointed out every single clause they felt was unfair to the promoters. And they'd had those clauses rewritten. But the first drafts with the unfair passages will turn out to have more importance than you imagine in a minute. Meanwhile, the Jacksons insisted that roughly three hundred seats per concert be set aside for inner-city kids who couldn't afford the ticket price. And they wondered how they could use the tour to feed starving kids in Africa.

I campaigned to get Don King muzzled. Yes, I was going up against someone who had killed. But the truth at any price, including the price of your life. Right? Muzzling King took three months. But finally he was given a gag order. And then it became obvious that someone else was causing problems.

Don King created difficulties loudly and dramatically. But this mysterious someone else was working to sabotage the tour invisibly. Who could that someone be?

* * *

Not all trouble comes from villains. Rock and R&B performers are athletes. The best of them do extraordinary acts of physical strength onstage. And many athletes and rockers suffer the consequences. The big medical issue of 1984 was bone chips in the knee. Billy Squier had been hit by them. They stopped your walking. But they could be removed arthroscopically. That is, instead of cutting open your knee and doing serious damage, a doctor could make a small incision and feed in a fiber-optic cable with a tiny TV camera, and could use a long, thin instrument with a blade at its end. The doctor could thread the instrument into the tiny hole in the skin of your knee and remove the bone chip.[231]

Jackie Jackson was hit by one of these bone chips in his knee. The press was tracking the Jacksons breathlessly, following the *Boston Herald* imperative—a Jackson story every day. A Jackson story, good or bad. But preferably bad.

So I flew out to LA, accompanied Jackie to the hospital, and supervised a press conference in which the doctors explained Jackie's condition and his prognosis. These medics hoped Jackie would be functioning normally again by the time of the tour. Then I flew back to Manhattan.

One afternoon at four, I was sitting at my broad chrome-and-burl desk on East Fifty-Fifth Street in Manhattan when a call came in. "You've got to be out here at eleven o'clock tonight. Michael is canceling his tour, and you're the only one he'll listen to." I told my receptionist to call the car service and get me a flight to LA. Then I grabbed my little red nylon knapsack and headed down the five flights of stairs.

I arrived in LA at roughly 10:00 p.m., grabbed a rental car, and headed to the address I'd been given. The destination was the lot of one of the top film studios ... something on a par with Paramount. A film studio lot at night is a dark and heart-crushing sight. It consists of roughly a dozen aircraft hangar–sized buildings. Huge, high, open-space, arched structures big enough to house at least one Boeing 747 each. Most are eerily dark and silent. And, even when they are lit, they seem to swallow all joy and transform it into gloom. I was ushered into the only lit, arched hangar on the lot. At one end of this enormous building, The Jacksons were rehearsing on a huge stage that had been designed for the tour.

Outside the studio were the usual trailers set up as dressing rooms. Like the one in which Bette Midler had slumped outside the Plaza Hotel. I waited while the Jacksons finished their rehearsal. Then Michael, his brothers, and I all filed into one of the darkened trailers. I'm not sure we even bothered to turn on the lights. The trailer had long, maroon, padded-vinyl banquets on each side, and one short banquet next to the entrance facing the trailer's rear. That short banquet was the power seat, the throne. Michael took it. I took the corner of the banquet at his left hand. His nonthreatening side. Michael explained what was going on. "Jackie," he said, "is the best dancer I've ever seen. He choreographs all our shows. And he's amazing onstage. But the bone-chip surgery isn't healing as fast as we thought. I can't go onstage without Jackie. So I want to postpone the tour until Jackie is better."

Why not just use the rest of the brothers and go out on schedule? "Jackie is the best dancer I've ever seen," repeated Michael. "I owe my kids the best." Without Jackie, Michael explained, he could not overwhelm his kids with amazement. "So I have to wait for Jackie to heal." Why? To give his kids the highest grade of astonishment he possibly could.

This is where Michael's qualities of awe, wonder, and surprise came in. In Michael's opinion, God had given him his ability to see the infinite in the tiniest of things. And Michael felt he owed that experience to his audience. God had given him an exuberantly supercharged sense of the world, and it was Michael's obligation to give that bowled-over bliss to others—specifically to his kids. When Michael spoke of his absolute obligation to those kids, I had a vision—whatever-the-hell a vision is. I saw Michael's ribs as golden gates. I saw them open. And I saw tens of thousands of kids, Michael's kids, beyond those gates. The tens of thousands alive at all times in Michael's chest. Michael felt it was his job on planet earth to love, protect, and amaze those kids. To surprise them. To open their eyes with awe and wonder.

Then Michael finally revealed why the tour had been so vulnerable to accusations that everything was going to fall apart and kill audience members because "nobody we know has been hired to handle this tour. No one truly professional is working on it"—the Dave Marsh argument.

A square inch of an artist's illustration had made Michael's knees buckle. It had lit him with a sense of awe and surprise. Michael wanted to give that gob smacking, de-light-walloping sense of surprise to his kids. To do it, he'd started working on the stage, the lighting, and the humdingers, lollapaloozas, and eyeball-stunners from magicians and costumers over a year in advance. He'd looked for the top talent he could find. Then he'd made everyone he hired sign an NDA—a nondisclosure agreement. He wanted every detail of the tour to be a secret. He wanted to spring a total wonder, a brain-flummoxer. He wanted to spring the ultimate surprise. The people Michael had hired were not amateurs. Far from it. They were the crème de la crème. But the utter secrecy had opened Michael to accusations from folks like Dave Marsh. Michael was vulnerable because of his total commitment to his kids, his total commitment to his audience's almost supernatural astonishment.

This also explained the high ticket price—thirty dollars—the price that outraged the press. The ticket price was high because Michael was intent on giving a show on a level that no one had ever seen. A tour that would cost a fortune to mount. A tour that would carry more equipment than any previous tour in history, according to a much later story by UPI, "more than 365 tons" of theatrical gear.[232]

Again, Jackie was the best dancer Michael had ever seen. And Michael had seen and studied every major pop-culture dancer of the twentieth century, from James Brown and Jackie Wilson to Fred Astaire. There was no way he'd allow his kids to be cheated by not seeing the best.

There was an army of kids in Michael's chest. And there was an arsenal of truths in mine. Harsh truths. I explained how the press was making a mockery of the Jacksons, seeing negatives wherever they could. I explained the Dave Marsh–led misperception that the entire tour was being handled by amateurs and that its equipment would collapse, killing Michael's kids. I told Michael that postponing the tour would make all these predictions of catastrophe look as if they were about to come true. Postponing the tour would destroy Michael's credibility. It would convince the parents of Michael's fans that the tour was not being handled by professionals. It would convince those parents not to buy tickets. And if Michael postponed, his kids would never get the stunning surprises he had planned.

Michael and I shared one thing in common: we believed in our truths down to the very core. And, when we explained ourselves, we could come across with the force of prophets. Both of us. It was two Charlton Hestons parting the Red Sea going head-to-head.

Michael understood what I was saying. More important, he saw the need to be on time with the tour. He changed his mind. Bless him. And he taught me one more lesson about who and what he was.

I've worked with many extraordinary people. From Prince to the eleventh president of India, Dr. APJ Kalam, and the astronaut Buzz Aldrin. But Michael stands so far above them that he's an entirely different kind of human being. He's the closest to a saint that I will ever meet. He redefines the nature of the possible. He is the living embodiment of the first two rules of science:

1. The truth at any price, including the price of your life. The law of courage.
2. Look at things right under your nose as if you've never seen them before. Then proceed from there. The law of wonder and awe.

Michael carried within him something that I, an atheist, can only call divine. But divinity is not just the quality of a god in heaven. It is an emotional potential inside of all of us. It is an exuberant ignition of the gods inside. And Michael Jackson dedicated all that he was to a simple goal: bringing those gods to life.

* * *

When the Jacksons' Victory Tour actually began, in Kansas City's Arrowhead Stadium on July 6, 1984, I adjusted my work schedule.[233] I spent three days a week on the road with the Jacksons and four days working in my Manhattan office. At each date, I'd roam backstage while Michael performed. With notepad in hand, I'd look for every detail that made the night unique. Michael was a very different performer than any I'd ever seen. He was as powerful as Prince, John Mellencamp, Billy Idol, and Joan Jett. Every one of these was a performer who connected with the secular equivalent of divinity onstage, taking it in from the audience, godifying it, and lashing it back out again. But Michael was very different from these. Prince and Mellencamp were different at each performance. The gods inside seized them and made them do things you'd never seen them do before. But Michael was disciplined and consistent. He'd spent his lifetime working out his basic approach. And he'd spent a year working out this tour's every move. Once he found the ultimate in what he was trying to achieve, he locked it in. And he did it every night. Perfectly. Scrupulously. With joy and ferocity. As if he'd never done it before in his life.

One detail about Michael's moves onstage. In the 1930s, black tap dancers first appeared in films.[234] But blacks were an underclass who showed up in white films only with permission from the masters, the whites. To signal that they meant no harm, the black tap dancers did something strange with their hands. They went limp at the wrist. They let their hands dangle uselessly and, with their eyes, they focused all attention on their feet. They used what evolutionary biologists call submission gestures. Gestures that say, "I'm not a threat. I'll blend into the background and be passive. Don't attack me."

When Fred Astaire picked up tap dancing from its black inventors, he was so busy paying attention to his feet that he failed to choreograph another key part of his body, his hands. He used the same limp wrists and dangling hands that blacks had used. Which made him seem totally ridiculous as a suitor to Ginger Rogers. At least to me. I mean, if you are a man and you woo a woman, you do not do it using submission gestures. You do it using dominance gestures.

Michael studied James Brown and Jackie Wilson—two bombshells onstage. James Brown's dancing was so intense that he was able to call himself "the hardest-working man in show business." And Jackie Wilson was such a tornado onstage that he was known as "Mr. Excitement." When he was nine years old, Michael stood backstage just behind the curtain at New York's Apollo Theater, Chicago's Regal Theater, and Kansas City's Uptown Theater, watching his heroes perform, noting every detail, learning how to connect with his audience like a lightning bolt, and learning to connect with the bonfires of his own emotional core.[235]

"I knew every step, every grunt, every spin and turn," Michael writes in *Moonwalk*. But there was more to James Brown's performance than his moves. There was his superhuman energy. Remember, James Brown billed himself as "the hardest-working man in show business." And *Billboard* magazine wrote that Brown "would routinely lose two or three pounds each time he performed."[236] Says Michael, with his astonishment at James Brown clear in his prose, "He would give a performance that would exhaust you, just wear you out emotionally." Jackson was stunned by "the fire coming out of his pores" and "every bead of sweat on his face." And Michael's empathic centers, his emotional core, tracked Brown as intensely as you had tracked Prince. From Brown's moves, his superhuman energy, and his beads of sweat, says Michael, "You'd know what he was going through." In watching the hardest-working man in show business, Michael became him. He felt Brown's moves and emotions in his very sinews. Concludes Jackson, "I've never seen anybody perform like him."[237] Michael's qualities of awe and amazement may have grokked James Brown with more intensity than any other concertgoer on earth.

But Michael did more than learn from the greats. He tried to top them. And he succeeded. He perfected maneuvers like the moonwalk that nudged into the realm of the impossible. Why? Because the impossible grabs us by the gut. It awes and fascinates us. And awing, fascinating, and gripping was Michael's mission in life.

One of Michael's most important inventions was his use of his hands when he was dancing. Instead of limp wrists and useless hands, Michael pointed. He pointed at the floor, he pointed straight out. He pointed straight up. He took over the stage with something new to black dance—dominance gestures. Seeing that fierce and total dominance erupt from a gentle person for fifty-five nights was an astonishment.

So the surprises of the night were not in Michael's stage show. That was always ferocious. And it was always the same. The newsworthy stuff was in the things going on backstage. Every night, for roughly two hours, I roamed the stadium looking for those things and writing them down in my trusty pad.

And every night, when the performance was over, two hundred reporters would gather in the stadium's press box, and I'd give an hour-long press conference going over everything in my notes. Among those two hundred reporters were the writers that the *Boston Herald* and the *Boston Globe* had made full-time Michael Jackson specialists way back when the *Herald* outsold the *Globe* by putting Michael Jackson on its cover.

* * *

When we were on the road, we took over the top two floors of the best hotel in town. The top floor would have the rooms of Michael's brothers, Michael's room, and the adjacent room of his traveling companion, a beautiful woman in her forties, a mother of three kids who had permission from her husband to travel with Michael. There were no groupies . . . and no little kids. And that top floor would have one more amenity. Its own organic chef, cooking food in the hallway. Sounds like a frivolous luxury, doesn't it? It wasn't. It was essential. The Jacksons would leave the stadium and get back to the hotel long after room service had folded up for the night. Without the private chef, they'd have had nothing to eat. For me, it was worse. I'd arrive at the hotel two hours after the Jacksons, thanks to the nightly news conferences. So the food from the private chef was crucial.

My impression was that Michael sometimes had horrible taste in business people. His focus was so intent on the creative end that he was, alas, occasionally blind to talent on the managerial side of things. On the Victory Tour, Michael had a former promotion man—a bag man—from Epic Records as his manager, Frank DiLeo. Michael writes in *Moonwalk* that DiLeo's "understanding of the recording industry" was "brilliant."[238] Alas, I didn't see it that way. I thought Frank DiLeo was literally the dumbest person I'd ever met in the music industry. Perhaps the only dumb person I'd ever encountered in the biz. Frank was a little, round, red-faced man who literally was convinced that I wrote every news story that appeared on Michael. Mind you, there were hundreds each day. That's a lot of writing. So Frank would ball me out about sentences he didn't like.

But, one night, Frank DiLeo told me something profoundly important. Prepping to go onstage in front of forty-eight thousand people is hard. People like John

Mellencamp would psych themselves up completely in private. But Michael had been going onstage in front of audiences since his father first entered the Jackson Five in talent contests in Indiana and Chicago when Michael was six.[239] Going onstage was as natural as breathing.

Nonetheless, Michael did have one preparatory ritual. In each town he entered, Michael ordered his manager, Frank DiLeo, to find two kids dying of cancer, two kids who wanted more than anything else in the world to meet Michael Jackson. And it was those kids with whom Michael spent the hour before he went onstage. I suspect it was part of his mission—to give to others what God had given to him. But Michael made DiLeo keep it utterly secret.

I also suspect that meeting with those kids reminded Michael of how incredibly important he was in the eyes of his fans. Look, we all become insecure and wonder if we're of any value to anyone at all. Michael had his kids to validate him, to buck him up before he went onstage. He had these kids to rev and prime him.

But the biggest question of all lurked in the background. Who was the invisible villain behind the very first negative press on the Jacksons? Who would eventually kill Michael Jackson?

* * *

As we went from city to city, and as I put out press fires, I got closer and closer to a guess, a hypothesis, about who was undermining the Jacksons and why. I got closer and closer to what I'd been hired for, in my opinion, sniffing out the evil and stopping it. And saving the soul of Michael Jackson.

Here's what I think happened.

Someone had deliberately leaked early drafts of unsigned Jackson contracts in roughly October and November of 1983 to *Rolling Stone*'s Michael Goldberg. Someone who knew what I knew, the nature of journalists as sheep in single file. Someone who had a close relationship with at least two lead sheep in the rock-crit elite—Dave Marsh and *Rolling Stone*'s Michael Goldberg. And that someone knew how to play these journalists to trigger a domino effect—a cascade of negativity that crossed the nation and would even be picked up by the Japanese and the European press. Who could that hidden person be?

Remember the Darth Vader of the music industry, the man you met in 1975 with only one of his eyes peeking out from a slit in a barely opened Manhattan hotel-room door? The man trying to keep you from Joe Walsh? Yes, Joe Walsh on his hands and knees, muttering incoherently on the floor behind him? And remember how Styx was broken to pieces? Destroyed by a new manager? Remember who I suspect saved me from the witches of Washington? And how he did it—by leaking a secret document? Remember the man about whom Randy Newman would allegedly write the song "Short People"?[240] A song about tiny little people with tiny little hands and tiny little eyes who walk around telling great big lies?

Remember the man one of his employees called "the poison dwarf?"

Remember Irving Azoff? Azoff insinuated himself into the Jackson tour early, at a price of $500,000.[241] My memory says that Azoff received $750,000 from the Jacksons. But *Rolling Stone*'s Steve Knopper, in his book *The Genius of Michael Jackson*, asserts that Irving was hired for $500,000. Half a million dollars. Over $1.2 million in today's money. Azoff's job? Tour consulting. But the odds were that Irving caused some of the trouble he had been hired to stop. What's the evidence?

In my opinion, the best PR firm in the entertainment industry when I started at *Circus* magazine in 1971 was Solters and Roskin. Lee Solters was a PR genius. Reading his press releases at *Circus*, and observing how he sent them—devoid of fancy art direction, just typewritten and printed in black-and-white, looking like raw news, not like prepackaged hype—had given me an education. Lee Solters, I suspect, knew better than just about anyone else on earth how the lead sheep could be used to turn the entire herd around. And he passed that knowledge—and the connections it took to act on it—down to his son. That son was Larry Solters.

Larry Solters just happened to be the right-hand man to a music-industry manager with gigantic ambitions. A manager with an uncommon genius. And a manager with no moral compass. Who could that manager have been? Irving Azoff.[242]

Years later, a group of German Michael Jackson fans I'd rendezvoused with in LA after Michael died sent me a few pages from the music-biz book *Hit Men*. Those pages described Irving Azoff's modus operandi. When Irving wanted in on a whirlwind phenomenon like Michael Jackson, he'd start trouble. To quote *Hit Men*, "He was a master at creating a problem and then riding in on a white horse . . . . He would agree on something, let it go forward, and after it was done, call the artists and scream and yell that the record label had fucked it up. Then he'd ride in and solve the problem. Irving could do that all day long. He had total retention on every level and could tap dance and maneuver his way out of the tightest corners."[243] Sometimes Azoff would stir up a shitstorm having no idea of where it would lead. But he knew that it would provide an opening to insert himself. As it did with the Jacksons.

Remember, the Jacksons' troubles all started in roughly November 1983, when someone leaked unsigned drafts of contracts to *Rolling Stone*'s Michael Goldberg. To understand the significance of that leak, there's something you have to know about the

first draft of contracts. Let's say you make a deal with me. The two of us get along fabulously over lunch. You and I agree about everything. We really look forward to working
together. So you ask your lawyer to draw up a contract. She does. And what she sends
you shocks you. It is a vicious document. It treats me, your new business partner, as
an enemy. It inflicts punishments on me. It could destroy your relationship with me,
no matter how much you'd love to work with me. So you go over it, line by line, and
you demand rewrites. Which is exactly what the Jacksons did to their contracts with
potential promoters. Tito and Marlon, in particular, changed everything that had to
be changed.

But if the first drafts are leaked out, you look like a monster. And it was first drafts
that Larry Solters was apparently handing to *Rolling Stone*. Along with the narrative
frame in which Michael's brothers were Draculas, drinking the blood of their brother's
audience. And my guess was that these leaks were all on behalf of an invisible trouble-
maker, Irving Azoff.

What would Irving's motivation for spreading negative publicity have been? Why
would he have deliberately poisoned the well?

* * *

In 1983, Michael Jackson was the biggest phenomenon in pop history. His success
eclipsed that of Elvis and competed with that of the Beatles. Irving Azoff was drawn
to two things, money and power. As one music industry insider put it in *Hit Men*,
"Michael Jackson is the biggest star in the world, and Irving knows the simple rule of
the power junkie: If there is something that has power, acquire it."[244] One more crucial
detail: to repeat, Irving had no moral compass. None. To him, all was fair in love, war,
and the entertainment industry.

More than ten years after the events in this book ended, a friend came out to
Park Slope to visit me in the bedroom where I was trapped by illness for fifteen years.
His name was Marco Garibaldi. He was Priscilla Presley's common-law husband, the
father of Priscilla Presley's nineteen-year-old son. With Priscilla, he'd flown around
in the private jets of men of wealth and power, men like Steve Wynn, the Las Vegas
casino magnate who would later head the Republican National Committee, the group
gathering hundreds of millions for the candidates of Donald Trump's Republican
Party.[245] So Marco literally flew in high circles.

When I asked Marco what Irving Azoff could have been after, his answer was
simple: the Beatles' publishing. Remember publishing, the business George Pincus
explained to you over lunch? Where you do almost no work but you sit back and collect carloads of money when the songs you own are played? Now imagine how much

money the Beatles' song catalogue brings in every year. Said Marco, the Beatles would block any attempts to buy their song catalogue. Any attempts but one—a bid from Michael Jackson, an artist with whom they felt a kinship. An artist who was a personal friend of Paul McCartney.[246] So you could control the biggest goldmine in the entertainment industry, the Beatles' publishing, if you could accomplish one simple thing: turning Michael Jackson into a finger-puppet.[247]

But was Irving ever able to turn Michael Jackson into a puppet?

* * *

Marco Garibaldi was right about Irving Azoff's interest in acquiring the Beatles catalogue. To do it, Irving would have to buy a publishing company called ATV.[248] ATV owned 250 Beatles songs, plus 3,750 songs from others, including Bruce Springsteen, the Rolling Stones, and Elvis Presley.[249] In September 1984, while the Jacksons' Victory Tour was hitting cities on the East Coast, John Branca—Michael Jackson's attorney—let Michael know that the Beatles catalogue was available.[250] According to Michael's definitive biographer, J. Randy Taraborrelli, "Michael skipped about the room, whooping and hollering. Branca explained that Michael was up against heavy duty competition. 'I don't care,' Michael declared. 'I want those songs. Get me those songs.'"[251]

In fact, the heavy-duty competition would be Irving Azoff. Azoff headed MCA Records at the time. In the spring of 1985, Azoff was using MCA's deep pockets to bankroll two publishing wizards, Martin Bandier and Charles Koppelman, in a bid to buy ATV. Bandier and Koppelman were about to board a plane to England to complete the deal. But because Michael Jackson wanted the ATV catalogue, his lawyer, John Branca, reportedly called Irving, told him that Michael was interested in ATV, and asked Azoff to yank his funding for the Bandier-Koppelman deal.

A small pack of investigative journalists have relied on an account of that phone call from J. Randy Taraborrelli's book *Michael Jackson: The Magic, the Madness, the Whole Story, 1958–2009*. John Branca, writes Taraborrelli, said, "Man, you can't give these guys money to buy this catalogue." Why? Because Michael Jackson wanted it. And Branca reminded Azoff that the Jacksons had paid Irving handsomely to consult on the Victory Tour. Azoff's reported response? "Johnny, don't worry about it, I'll take care of it."[252]

Azoff then pulled the rug out from under Koppelman and Bandier by refusing to finance their offer.

Yes, Irving Azoff pulled the funding from Bandier and Koppelman.[253] Just as they were about to board a plane to England to consummate the deal for the Beatles' publishing. But why did Azoff do it? What favor did he want in return? Did that favor involve owning a piece of Michael Jackson? And did it involve carving out a piece of ATV? Branca managed to get himself a 5 percent slice of the ATV deal. Did some of that slice go to Irving?

Or was there some other form of quid quo pro?

* * *

David Geffen, a music industry giant, was the man who once employed Irving Azoff in his office and put him together with the Eagles, the band that became the cornerstone of Azoff's career. Geffen says about Azoff, "I don't wish to have him in my life, even for a second." Why? He's "done so many bad things to so many people, including me." Says Geffen, Irving is "devilish." And that can be interesting, says Geffen, when it's accompanied by "intelligence, or charm, or wit, or real, true ability." But, in Geffen's opinion, Irving Azoff has none of those qualities. Instead, "he thinks that in order to be powerful or important, you have to fuck with people. Or frighten them, or be awful to them, which I find unacceptable behavior."[254]

I disagree with Geffen on one point. Azoff does have "true ability." Astonishing ability. However, he sometimes uses it for purposes that would make Geffen, you, and me shudder.

Walter Yetnikoff, former president of CBS Records, wants you to know one more thing about Irving Azoff.[255] Says Yetnikoff, Azoff lies. Unstoppably. Unbelievably. Swears Yetnikoff, "It's not a character flaw, it's a genetic defect. Irving lies when it's to his advantage to tell the truth. He just can't help it."[256]

* * *

By the midpoint of the Jacksons' Victory Tour, I felt I was on to Irving. But I failed to realize something. Irving was also on to me.

As I got closer and closer to uncovering Irving Azoff, someone worked harder and harder to get me out of Michael's life.

For example, at one point the Jacksons were in New York, having a meeting at CBS Records. Michael and his brothers were allowed to take over an entire conference room at Black Rock, CBS's imposing Sixth Avenue headquarters. Something that had never happened before in my time in the music biz. And someone walked into that Jackson family meeting to try to convince the Jacksons that I was a spy from Prince. Sorry, Prince had his own unique genius, and he wasn't the least bit interested in spying on the Jacksons. But someone was using any argument he or she could concoct to cut my connection with the Jacksons. And, in particular, with Michael. But who was doing this?

Finally, it worked. I got the message that I had been banished from the tour. I never saw Michael again. It was one of the greatest losses of my life. But Michael was one of the greatest gifts.

* * *

Despite all the negative press, was the Jacksons' Victory Tour a success? Here was UPI's conclusion: "The 2.5 million people attending the concerts surpassed by 500,000 the record set by the Rolling Stones on their 1981 tour." What's more, according to UPI, "The Jacksons gave away nearly $1 million worth of tickets to the disadvantaged and the disabled."[257] In other words, the Victory Tour made music history. And it lived up to the Jacksons' ethic—uplift the poor and the oppressed.

What's more, the definitive music journalist, Jon Pareles of the *New York Times*, who had come out to my threadbare Park Slope brownstone apartment when he first moved to New York from Boston, then had become godlike and unapproachable, concluded:

> The stage show by Michael Jackson and his four brothers—Jermaine, Randy, Marlon, and Tito—was designed to dazzle the eye as movies and rock-video clips do. At that, it succeeded. Lasers beamed into the air, fireworks flamed, spotlights shone in blinding white.... But the most spectacular special effect was the most basic one—Michael Jackson's fancy footwork and high, heartfelt singing. Mr. Jackson sang hits from *Thriller*, the Jacksons' album *Triumph*, and his earlier album *Off the Wall*, demonstrating that all the stamina and energy of his five-minute video clips can be sustained onstage. It is no illusion.[258]

Michael set out to amaze. And he succeeded. Every single night. Why? Because he was the real thing.

50

MICHAEL JACKSON'S SEXUAL CRUCIFIXION

Lies run sprints, but the truth runs marathons.

—Quote attributed to Michael Jackson

To understand what I think happened next, I need to tell you a Billy Joel story. Billy loved motorcycling. Remember his lyrics about riding a motorcycle in the rain? A suicidal thing to do, but a thrill.

One afternoon, we set Billy Joel up for a photo shoot, to get across who and what he was. We took a few of Billy's motorcycles, and, working with a towering figure of twentieth-century rock photography, Annie Leibovitz, we set those motorcycles up at the end of Billy's road on Oyster Bay, overlooking the water and the sky. Annie waited until 5:30 p.m., when the sun was low and reddening, and the colors of the sky were reflected by the vast expanse of water. The golden hour. Then she shot roughly sixty rolls of film. It's called bracketing your shots. By the way, Annie was wonderful to work with.

Billy was particularly proud of his bikes from BMW. He told me to get one. They are absolutely silent and free of the shocks and vibrations that shake you to the bone on lesser bikes—like the ancient 1973 Honda 550 cc motorcycle on which I now commuted from Park Slope to my office in Manhattan. But on April 15, 1982, Billy was motorcycling on the roads of Huntington, Long Island, four miles from his home, on his 1978 Harley Davidson. He was about to reach the intersection of New York Avenue and West Ninth Street. He saw a stoplight ahead. It was green. So Billy approached the coming intersection at a normal cruising speed. The cars on the roadway that crossed the intersection had a red light. That means stop, right? But a driver motoring on the perpendicular road did not stop. Instead, she went through the red light, and started to make a left turn.[259] Said Joel, "I hit the brakes as hard as I could, but it was too close. So I ran into the side of her car. . . . This [left] thumb got crushed and this [right] wrist got pulled out of the socket. And I flipped over the car and landed on my back."[260]

The offending driver was hysterical. She was afraid she had killed this poor motor-cyclist she'd just cut off. She rushed over to the motorcycle to offer help. Billy was heli-coptered to Manhattan's Columbia Presbyterian Hospital. The fear was that he would lose the use of his right hand and of his left thumb. Remember something. One of Billy's first hits was "Piano Man." Billy is most alive when he is on the piano, pounding it in front of an audience. "I practice," he said when he was recuperating, "but there's no substitute for going on a stage. You can bang as hard as you want at your house . . . but when you go out on stage and there's twenty thousand people going [makes roaring crowd noise], that's when you really pound."[261] You smash the keys in ways beyond your control when your audience rouses the gods inside.

Billy Joel's right hand would be a serious loss to all of us. It took two hours of surgery to restore his wrist and thumb. In fact, his thumb is permanently missing the bone that used to support its tip. And his recuperation took an entire month in the hospital.[262]

From the version of the story I got, it appears that the motorist who nearly killed Billy went to her attorney. And it appears that the attorney said something like this:

You've just had an accident with a superstar. So I have news for you. You didn't cut him off. He hit you. And if you sue him, he will be forced to hush you up so he doesn't damage his reputation. He will offer you a settlement to keep you quiet. You can walk away from this with a cool quarter of a million dollars.

That's $604,000 in modern money. So the twenty-seven-year-old woman who almost killed Billy Joel apparently let her lawyer threaten to sue, and walked away with a settlement.

What does this have to do with Michael Jackson? Everything. A superstar is a money bag. A superstar is a target.

* * *

One more story to understand how the avalanche of sexual accusations may have begun.

One day we—the Jacksons and I—were doing a photo shoot on a beach overlook-ing the Pacific. To find an empty stretch of sand, we'd gone about sixty miles north of LA. It was a small public park with a grassy lawn adjacent to the sand. We'd had five dream cars trucked in for the shoot—a Maserati, a Lamborghini, a Lotus, etc. The sort of cars Kenny Loggins fantasized about using to escape his wife. There were the usual trailers set up as dressing rooms. One housed Jermaine, who was trying to start a separate solo career with Arista Records. The others were for all the brothers. And on either side of this two-hundred-foot-wide park were long, thick tree branches stripped of bark and assembled in ranch-like fences.

It took hours for the photographer to set up the shoot. Hours of waiting. The brothers spent those hours inside their trailers. But not Michael. Kids had gathered at one of the wooden ranch fences. Maybe twenty of them. And Michael spent his time with those kids. His kids.

Why children, not teenagers or adults? Michael Jackson began a life of disciplined rehearsals with his brothers when he was five years old.[263] He was a professional, as were his brothers. Their father was a musician. Dad's band was the Falcons. Joe Jackson kept his guitar in a closet. And he ordered that his kids never touch it. But touch it they did. In fact, when their dad was at work, they practiced on it. They wanted to be musicians like their pop. And their mom, a lifelong singer, thought they had talent. So, when Joe Jackson discovered that his kids had been hauling his guitar out of the closet and using it, all hell should have broken loose. But instead, their mom stood up for them. And Joe saw possibilities. He became their music trainer, promoter, and manager.

In other words, from the time he was five years old, Michael was a professional. He was a miniature adult. He didn't have a childhood.

The work of evolutionary psychologist Jaak Panksepp, a colleague of mine who would visit me later, when I was in bed, proved something about mice. Young mice play with each other. If you take that opportunity to play away from them, they suffer play deprivation.[264] They still need to get in their biologically fixed amount of goofing around. So they do their playing when they are adults.

I suffered from adolescence deprivation. That's one of the reasons I was able to put everything I am into *Circus* magazine and into my readers. Through those readers, I got the adolescence I never had. Michael suffered from childhood deprivation. He apparently filled that deprivation with his love of his kids.

Another bit of speculation. One of the most exciting things kids do is sleepovers with each other. Sleepovers are exhilarating. You can stay up until dawn, jabbering. So Michael had kids over for sleepovers. But you have to understand something else. Wherever he goes, Michael's bedroom is not the private place you and I have. It's a public place. Michael's bedroom on tour was smack dab in the middle of the top floor of a hotel, surrounded by the bedrooms of his brothers and key members of his professional team. I was on the floor below. But the doors of most of those bedrooms were open most of the time. And at home, when Michael and Lionel Richie decided to write "We Are the World," they did it in Michael's bedroom. That's where Lionel felt the probing eyes of Michael's snake.

So, for Michael, inviting kids over for the night was not a private event where secret sexual things could be done. It was a public event.

Put all this together and what do you get? In 1993, one father—Evan Chandler, a dentist who owed $68,400 in child support—apparently realized that he, like Billy Joel's near-killer, could extract hush money and threatened to go public with sexual claims.[265] Chandler got $23 million, and the accusations made Michael so sick that he had to cancel the Asian leg of his Dangerous World Tour. But the incident did more than poison the life of Michael Jackson. It was not helpful to the life of the father who had extracted the $23 million payoff. His relationship with his son broke down. That son, Jordan Chandler, filed for and got emancipation from his parents. He didn't talk to his mom for eleven years. And the father, Evan Chandler, was accused of choking his son and attacking him with a barbell and a mace. That father committed suicide six years after the settlement. So who really abused Evan Chandler, Michael Jackson or his gold-digging father?

According to Michael's definitive biographer, J. Randy Taraborrelli, two grand juries would later question "more than two hundred witnesses, including thirty children who had been friends of Michael's over the years." Not a single one of these friends of Michael had been molested or had seen signs of Michael molesting others.[266] Let me repeat. Not a single one of them. According to the testimony of these two hundred witnesses, the sexual accusations were false. But manufacturing sexual allegations against Michael Jackson became a cottage industry. Parents, attorneys, former employees and one prosecutor—Santa Barbara County district attorney Tom Sneddon—made their fame and fortune off of Michael Jackson's sexual crucifixion.[267] A crucifixion that destroyed Michael's health, crippled his career, turned him into a prescription-drug addict, and ultimately snuffed out one of the brightest lights this planet has ever seen.

But who really killed Michael Jackson? Could it have been a press corps that learned its lesson the day the *Boston Herald* ran its first Jackson cover and boosted sales by roughly forty thousand copies? Could it have been the publishers who learned that negative stories on Michael Jackson sold more copies than positive stories? And could Michael's killers have been you and me, the public who lapped up those negative stories? Could Michael's killers have been we the public, who lapped up these stories out of sheer prurient interest? Did we all kill Michael Jackson?

But where did the perceptual frame that generated the negative stories begin? It began with whoever leaked contracts to Michael Goldberg.

Whoever leaked those contracts helped kill Michael Jackson. And so, in our own way, did you and I.

There are moments in writing this book that have brought me close to tears, and this is one of them.

* * *

You know what happened from there. The negative press that had been deliberately triggered at *Rolling Stone* became an avalanche. Negative stories about Michael goosed sales for media outlets so much that, in the 1990s, stories began to appear that Michael was sexually abusing children. And those turned into a torrent. Michael spent fifty years on this earth. He was the closest person to the godhead I've ever met. He had more to give to his fellow humans than anyone you or I have ever imagined. And his gift was buried by sexual allegations. Michael Jackson spent fifty years among us. And, for twenty-five of those years, he was crucified.

51

PERCEPTUAL IMPRISONMENT

One more story to understand Michael's plight after he rocketed beyond any form of superstardom that pop culture had ever known. One day, Peter Frampton and his girlfriend dropped in to see me at my mocha-painted, two-story Manhattan office on East Fifty-Fifth Street. And Peter told me one of the darkest stories I had ever heard.

Peter had been a member of Steve Marriott's Humble Pie. Marriott is the singer who invented the vocal style that would put AC/DC on top. Marriott is also the one who was furious with you for writing a story that made it seem like you had been in his home. But it was not Marriott who would experience tremendous success. It was the member of Marriott's band who had made it on the cover of the British music papers for having the prettiest male face of 1968: Peter Frampton.

Frampton introduced a new guitar technique, speaking through a tube to shape the guitar sounds. He wrote some very good songs. And he toured his ass off. The result was *Frampton Comes Alive*, the biggest selling album of 1976, an album that *Rolling Stone* says was briefly "the biggest-selling album of all time, until the *Saturday Night Fever* soundtrack topped it."[268]

Which brings us back to Dee Anthony. Remember Dee? He's the manager who offered to send his Rolls Royce down to Thirty-Fourth Street to get you a slice of the best pizza in New York. A sweet, if gruff, little round man. A character. But that character had a dark side.

When Frampton's career soared and he represented money and power, Dee explained to Peter what Michael Jackson explained to me in the back of a van headed for an NAACP conference in LA. Dee told Frampton that his fans would mob him if he went outdoors. That because they loved him, all they'd want from him is a hair from his head or a thread from his jacket. But because human flesh, as Michael Jackson put it, is as fragile as an overcooked noodle, Peter's fans would tear him apart. Literally.

So Dee Anthony offered Peter Frampton a luxury suite at the hotel of his choice. Plus at least one twenty-four-hour bodyguard to protect Peter in his room. And bodyguards to protect him if he went out. But Dee advised not going out. It was too dangerous. "Look," said Dee, according to Peter's retelling, "I'll make sure you get anything you need sent up. If you need girls, just let us know what you want—blondes, Asians, Black girls, we'll get them for you. And if you need drugs, hey, we deliver." Now, Peter explained, Dee had Peter as a virtual prisoner.

But Dee did not want to imprison just Peter's body. He wanted to imprison Peter's mind. How did he do it? Peter explained that he got a call one day from Dee saying something like this:

> Peter, I know you've had your road manager for years. I know you love him dearly. I know you rely on him for everything. But I have to tell you honestly that he's just not cutting it anymore. He was good for you when you were un-known. He was good for you when you went gold. He was good for you when you went platinum. But now you are eight times platinum.[269] You are on a whole new level. A level very few stars have ever achieved. You need someone who is able to handle that level. With your permission, please let me find a road manager who can handle megastardom.

A few months later, Dee made the same speech about Peter's accountant. Then Peter's lawyer.

So, Peter said, "If Dee wanted me to believe that NASA just discovered the moon is made of goat cheese, he'd have my road manager tell me that he'd just seen the head-line in the *New York Times*. So I'd ask my accountant if that was true, and he'd say yes. Then I'd ask my lawyer, and he'd say yes, too. By the end of the day, I'd believe them. The moon was made of goat cheese. All because that's what Dee wanted me to believe." In those days, there was no Google with which to do a quick fact-check.

Did anyone attempt this with Michael Jackson? Did anyone use the sort of drug dependence that Irving Azoff seems to have used on rockers like Joe Walsh on Michael? But this time with prescription drugs? And, if so, who?

* * *

Four years after Michael's death, as Britain's *Daily Mail* reported, "John Branca, co-ex-ecutor of the Michael Jackson estate, admitted to journalist Robin Leach in June 2013 that Michael was now worth much more than he was when alive. 'He's made more money in the four years since his death than he made during his lifetime,' Branca said. Since he died, he's sold 50 million albums and is still the biggest-selling artist on iTunes.'" What's more, said the *Daily Mail*, "When he died on June 25, 2009, the singer was $500 million in debt. But his estate turned its fortunes around, bringing him $1.5bn in the black."[270]

Billboard, the leading music-industry trade magazine, quoted "a source close to the estate" who called this "a billion-dollar turnaround."[271] And *Billboard* outlined a series of "blockbuster moves that last year pushed Jackson to the top of *Forbes*'s list of Top-Earning Dead Celebrities with a reported $115 million, ahead of Elvis Presley, Bob Marley, and Marilyn Monroe."[272]

Remember a high-placed art dealer's advice to Peter Bogdanovich on how his painter father could achieve success? By dying? In other words, to people like his attorney, John Branca, Michael Jackson was worth far more dead than alive. At least a billion dollars more.

Does Irving Azoff have a piece of this postmortem Michael Jackson pie?

* * *

To me, my entire Voyage of the Beagle from science into a field where I did not belong—rock and roll—was a journey in search of soul. Those who undid Michael Jackson helped kill the most astonishing soul that I have ever known.

52

SICKNESS—THE BLADE OF CFS

Then came my crash.

The year was 1988. I was forty-five years old. And Chris Blackwell had a new assignment for me. He conveyed it through the latest in his line of eighteen-month Island record-company presidents, Lou Maglia. The clients were called Womack and Womack—the Womacks. And they were not your ordinary new duo.

Linda Womack was the daughter of Sam Cooke, the man *Rolling Stone* says "helped invent soul music."[273] Cooke influenced Michael Jackson, Rod Stewart, Otis Redding, Justin Timberlake, and your client, Al Greene. And his song "A Change Is Gonna Come" became an anthem of the civil rights movement.

Linda's husband, Cecil Womack, had written with his brother Bobby the Rolling Stones' first hit, "It's All Over Now." What's more, the Womack Brothers had been discovered by Sam Cooke. And Cecil's brother, "soul music genius" Bobby Womack, had married Sam Cooke's widow.[274]

Linda and Cecil were show-business aristocrats . . . and show-business veterans. They'd prepared a thirty-two-page marketing plan for their first album. And they were dictatorial about its implementation. They had boxed poor Lou Maglia into a corner. Demanding that he follow their plan down to the last jot and tittle. I did my usual month of research. Then I went over their marketing plan. I sat down with them in a meeting at Island's New York office on Fourth Street and Broadway in the East Village and gave them a very different marketing plan. Including a new pick for a first single. A song I was convinced could be a hit. In Lou Maglia's office, I explained it. It made sense to them. They wanted me to become their manager.

But I still hadn't done my secular shamanism, my great soul hunt. Linda and Cecil lived in the territory where West Virginia and Kentucky converge. On a farm deep in the countryside. To get there, I flew down to an airport I forget—possibly in Richmond, Virginia. A jeep picked me up at the airport and drove me five hours into the countryside. Deep, deep into the countryside. I forget who was doing the driving.

When we arrived, there was a hill with sheep grazing. On top of that hill was a house very much like the Hollywood studio where I had met the Jacksons. But a bit smaller. It was built like an aircraft hangar with a curved roof arched over it. And it was still under construction. It was a cold spring day, March 10, 1988. There was no heat. And no furniture. Linda, Cecil, and I sat on the unfinished wood floor with no support for our backs. For five hours. And I discovered an entire culture I didn't know existed.

Linda and Cecil both came from families of black coalminers. Most of us don't know that black coalminers even existed. To make their lives hacking black stuff in dark caves beneath the ground bearable, the miners sang. They sang spiritual songs, godly stuff. Then, on the weekends, they sang in church. And more. The best of them got into buses and traveled to distant churches. To sing.

This was music to the lord, and the coalminers' singing culture was strict about this. They didn't tolerate pop. And they despised anyone who might want to leave the church world and go into the world of earthly sin, the world of popular music. Remember how Al Green's father had kicked him out of the house permanently for listening to Jackie Wilson?

Sam Cooke was one of the renegades these church singers hated most. He had bolted from the world of God's music and gone over to the side of sin—popular music. He had gone from singing the Holy Spirit to singing to impress women.

I took five hours of furiously fevered notes, despite freezing on the floorboards of the house. I was fascinated. Here was one of the roots of the soul I'd been seeking since I was fourteen, hunting down a copy of William James's *The Varieties of the Religious Experience*. Then we took the five-hour Jeep ride back to the airport. And I organized my notes on the plane, putting the incidents in chronological order to find the drama, to find the story. But, by now, I was doing this rearrangement on my Radio Shack TRS 100, an inch-thick, three-pound device smaller and lighter than a modern laptop. The TRS 100 had a full keyboard on its upper surface and a narrow, ribbon-like, liquid-crystal display laid flat above the keys—a gray screen that showed you a crawl of words, like the words scrolling on a teleprompter. Yes, just one line of words at a time. Cutting and pasting on the TRS 100 was a heck of a lot easier than the scissors-and-Scotch-tape method I'd used sitting on my front stoop to organize my John Mellencamp notes back in 1982.

When I left the plane and headed for the Bloom Brownstone, forty minutes from LaGuardia Airport by cab, I discovered I'd done something stupid. I'd left my TRS 100 behind on the plane. When we called the airline, no one had found it. It was an irresistible gadget. Someone must have made off with it. Fortunately, I had another TRS 100 at home. And I had three Kaypro computers in my apartment—the apartment that was a big office attached to a three-window bedroom overlooking the Manhattan skyline. The apartment where my two dogs had greeted Morris Day of Prince's the Time by poking their noses into his richest-smelling zones. So I was able to consult my handwritten notes and reassemble the story I had lost.

I'd made the trip to see the Womacks on a Friday. Saturday I felt a cold coming on. But I had a way of dealing with colds. Work your ass off. Take your normal long walks. Power through it. That usually worked. This time, it didn't. Sunday I was worse. But I worked all my waking hours as usual and took my long walk in the 526-acre park three blocks up the hill—Prospect Park.

Monday I was a basket case. I made it to the office. But I can't remember the day at all. I was seriously dysfunctional. Then came Tuesday. I made it to the office once more. But, around 11:00 a.m., I started losing strength. Fast. So fast that I asked my staff to call me a car service before I could become too weak to walk. When the car arrived, one staff member got under my right armpit and another under my left. They helped me get to the elevator, descend to the ground floor, and they slung me like a bag of onions into the rear of the waiting car. I have no idea of how I got up the stairs of the Bloom Brownstone to my apartment in the sky, my apartment on the fourth floor.

I thought I knew what was going on. Back in 1981, I'd had the back problem that had eventually made me so weak I couldn't speak for three months. The back problem that meant I'd been forced to interview Morris Day from my mattress. In 1982, I'd been out on the West Coast handling things for legendary A&M Records jazz producer Tommy LiPuma. I went to interview the world's most extraordinary mandolinist, David Grisman, in Marin County, just across the Golden Gate Bridge from San Francisco, but I hadn't accounted for the severe drop in temperature in the California night. I'd dressed with just a shirt open at the neck for the daytime weather, a nice, tropical eighty degrees. When it dropped to closer to fifty degrees after sundown, I was still out on the streets of San Francisco, headed for a club where Tommy LiPuma had a performer he wanted me to see, and I froze. I flew to LA the next day for meetings, then, at the Hyatt Hotel on Sunset Boulevard, the hotel known in the music industry as the Riot Hyatt, I felt my strength dwindling fast. I grabbed my luggage, struggled down five flights of stairs because the elevator was broken, checked out, rushed to the airport by cab, and got myself home as rapidly as possible. I did not want to be bedridden or hospitalized 2,500 miles away from my home.

Normally, colds did not stop me. This, whatever it was, did. It kept me home and in bed for two days—an eternity when you are accustomed to working seven-day weeks and packing the maximum amount of work into every second. Nothing like it had ever happened to me in my adult life.

Then, in roughly 1984, I had this weird virus again. This time, it kept me in bed not for two days but for two weeks. Its power over me was growing.

Now, after the Womack trip, I figured the power of the killer virus had grown even stronger. I was zonked in bed for three months. And I do mean zonked. It felt as if the power to my brain had been cut. I could lay on the bed, stare at the ceiling, and be perfectly content. I didn't have enough brainpower to be bored. There wasn't even enough energy to fire up my nearly perpetual depression. So I lay and watched movies on the TV. With a babysitter to make sure I didn't fall off the bed.

At the end of three months, I seemed to be fine. One day, I had meetings at CBS's Black Rock over on Sixth Avenue, then at Atlantic Records near Columbus Circle. By the end of the day, my pedometer told me I had walked seven miles. I was delighted. I had my health back.

The next day, one of my bands, the Scorpions, were playing at the Meadowlands, opening for Metallica. It was an outdoor stadium. And the entire audience was on its feet for the whole performance. So I had to stand, too. In the cold. Then I took a cab to Madison Square Garden, where John Mellencamp was playing. I hate watching from backstage, but I did that for twenty minutes, just to show John I was there to support him. Then I cabbed out to Queens. I had a new client, Cyndi Lauper. I hadn't met her yet. But she had dropped out of high school. Her school was so impressed with what she'd achieved since then that they'd decided to give her an honorary diploma. So I was headed for Cyndi Lauper's high-school graduation.

I would not recover from that day for fifteen years.

* * *

Cyndi Lauper had a new film coming out, *Vibes*. It was a comedy with Jeff Goldblum, and it was hilarious. Lauper was one of the most expressive actresses I'd ever seen. When I'd worked with Paramount, I'd gone to see three staff screenings of a new movie that amazed me—*Chinatown*—just to examine the craft with which the film was built. The female star, Faye Dunaway, only had three facial expressions. Her "acting" was created in the editing room. It was produced by splicing the right expression in at the right moment. But Cyndi Lauper could show seven emotions crossing her face, and conflicting with each other, in a second. An amazing ability I'd only seen in one other actress, Meg Ryan. I knew that if I'd been brought in six months earlier, I could have worked to save that film the way I'd helped save *Purple Rain*. But it was too late. The studio was already implementing the six-theaters-in-Arizona strategy. The official kiss of death. Then I met with David Wolf, Cyndi's boyfriend and manager, at his West

Fifty-Eighth Street Manhattan office. But I didn't have the strength to sit up. I took the entire meeting in David's office laying on a couch.

The next day, I went downtown and met with Lou Maglia and the Womacks in the same condition, laying on a couch in Lou's office.

Fortunately, my brain still worked.

* * *

My family physician had no idea of what was wrong with me. He offered no solutions. I went to a super-expensive doctor in Manhattan. He gave me a diagnosis that sounded very highfalutin but was utter nonsense. An obscure illness for which modern medicine had no treatments.

Meanwhile, the mystery illness was producing bizarre symptoms. I wore a Thinsulate winter vest in the middle of a hot New York summer. Why? When the temperature was ninety-five degrees, I was freezing. Not just cold, but shivering. And when the temperature was down to fifty, I was overheated. And perspiring. What's more, I was as weak as a starved puppy. And getting weaker.

One day, I came into the office, gathered my staff, told them I'd be out in two weeks, that I didn't know what I had, that I might easily be dying, and that I was giving them the business, the entire Howard Bloom Organization Ltd. They believed that they were what made the HBO run and that I was unnecessary, so that sounded good to them. As Peter Gabriel once explained to me, "In any collaboration, each collaborator overvalues his contribution." The next day, one of my competitors called and offered me a huge, honking amount of money for the business. I explained that it was too late. I had given the business to my staff.

Two weeks later, I was gone. Imprisoned in a bedroom for fifteen years. The company went belly up in a year. The staff had been right. They were an essential core of the business. But so was I. It wasn't either or, it was both.

The song I'd insisted that Island release as the first single from Womack and Womack—"Teardrops"—did nothing in the United States. But it became one of the top ten hits of the year in Europe. And Wikipedia reports that the album, *Conscience*, went "gold in ten countries and platinum in three."[275]

* * *

When I left the music industry, soul left with me. I insisted that terms like *image, marketing*, and *product* were false. They dehumanized one of the most human exchanges on the face of the planet. Music, I preached, is an exchange of soul. But another new term joined *marketing* and *product*—*branding*. All terms that sucked the soul out of the music industry. Powerful new singers like Maroon Five and Ben Harper were sold as platforms for corporate sponsors. The emotional reality at the heart of music was lost.

I've often wished I could wade in and preach soul all over again. But, instead, I've gone back to my science. I've written seven books. The office of the Secretary of Defense has thrown a forum based on one of my books and has brought in representatives from the State Department, the Energy Department, DARPA, IBM, and MIT. I've co-designed a multi-planetary project at Caltech. In 1995, I founded and ran the group that validated the use of the term "group selection" in evolutionary biology—the Group Selection Squad. I run another group I was asked to found by the astronaut Buzz Aldrin, the second man on the moon, the Space Development Steering Committee. That group has included Buzz Aldrin and Edgar Mitchell, the sixth man on the moon. Plus members of the National Science Foundation, NASA, and the National Space Society. The Sheikh who runs Dubai and made it what it is today has named a racehorse after one of my books. The eleventh president of India has called my work "a visionary creation" and partnered with me for four years on a nonprofit energy project. I've debated one-on-one with senior figures from Hamas and the Muslim Brotherhood on Iranian TV. I've appeared over 300 times on the highest-rated overnight talk-radio show in North America, a show that runs on 545 radio stations: *Coast to Coast AM*. Dissecting issues from the biome, the community of bacteria in your gut, to America's diplomatic dance with North Korea.

Oh, and I escaped my bedroom after fifteen years, and have been out in the world since 2003, walking five miles a day and starting the day with between 600 and 1,200 pushups in a row without stopping. Not to mention being flown to lecture in Moscow, Amsterdam, Paris, Vienna, Kuala Lumpur, Seoul, Kobe, and Chengdu, on subjects from theoretical physics, information science, geopolitics, and neurobiology to governance and harvesting solar power in space and transmitting it to earth.

And I still have come nowhere near processing all of my adventures in rock and roll, my Voyage of the Beagle in the dark underbelly where new myths and movements are made, my search for soul in the power pits of rock and roll. But have I learned more than I would have if I'd taken up my fellowship at Columbia University and gone to grad school? Have I learned more about the mass passions that power the forces of history than if I'd become a college professor? Have I learned more about the gods inside? You bet your tailbone.

* * *

What did I learn? First, I had to become a good publicist. I figured out the basics when publicists swamped me with press material at *Circus* magazine. I applied those basics in my days at Gulf and Western. Then I had to build my press relationships. That got a boost from the superstar stories of Betty Davis. Next I had to invent a whole new way to do publicity. I based that on the standard of excellence set by Frank Yablans, the president of Paramount Pictures.

Finally, I could get down to the real mystery—your soul and mine. The sort of soul that ached to express itself in ZZ Top, and in disco, the music of the gay community. The soul that comes alive in ecstatic moments, then becomes the tongue of a group. To get at that soul, I would have to work out what I called secular shamanism.

One clue to soul would be imprinting. Another would be the supernormal stimulus, the super-egg. What do you hear in music? Screams, pleas, cries, pain, and rage—the supernormal stimuli of raw emotion. Like the sound of Billy Idol ranting in a studio. Like the sounds you make when you're having sex. In music you hear tones, timbers, and textures that, like the polka-dotted super-egg, are releasers of raw passion. Releasers of raw soul. And all of this would become clear in Prince's story of how he imprinted on music.

As Prince would show in *Dirty Mind*, music is about sex. Think of Jelly Roll Morton, named after the taste of a woman's vagina; jazz, named after sperm; rock and roll, a term for fucking; and the terrors of the episcopal bishop of New York and the Archbishop of Dubuque over the sexuality of swing music. Sex is one of the few experiences in which some of us go ecstatic. It's one of the few experiences in which our normal self steps aside, and selves we do not know come to life inside of us, making noises we do not recognize. Sex is the epitome of emotionally charged attention. If we are making love, my attention is riveted on you, and your attention is riveted on me. Attention is the oxygen of the human soul. Look how attention energized Bette Midler. Look how it brought Joan Jett to life.

Sex can trigger war. Look at the Mycenaean's and the Trojans, making war over Helen of Troy. Look at the violence of langur monkeys, knocking elders of their perch and killing babies to gain harems, clusters of females they could rape. Where does music fit into this? It's the anthem of a generation seizing control from its elders. It's the supercharger of fighters united, motivated, and coordinated by their war songs. Warriors fight for glory the way singers compete to be superstars. What does winning bring? You've got it, and John Mellencamp explained it—sex.

But the rock and pop music of the last hundred years is a secular miracle. It drains the lust for blood, the craving for war. It rouses the animals of sex and violence nonviolently.

* * *

So what in the world is soul? It's the most deeply personal thing you and I have got. But it is also the most social. Soul comes alive when you are on a stage, taking in the energy of a crowd, transforming it, and sending it back to the folks with amazed eyes in the audience. Soul comes alive when you are in the audience, when you lose your sense of individual identity, when you melt into the collective energy of the crowd, and when you send that energy through the empty pipe of a superstar to what Peter Townshend called the godhead. Soul is most alive when the ritual of the concert lifts you and me out of our selves and gives us an emotion you might call divine. No wonder the force of our collective soul gives the singer onstage an out-of-body experience, a transcendent experience, an ecstasy. That ecstasy is intensely personal. Yet it is the highest expression of the group. Weird, right?

Music does more than melt an audience and drive a performer into frenzies. It does more than produce what Émile Durkheim called "collective effervescence," and what group psychologist Jonathan Haidt and his writing partner Greg Lukianoff call "a charge of social electricity."[276] Groups have a collective soul. Music and its stars catch fire and become that collective soul's living incarnation. Stars are the vocal chords of a group just beginning to find its voice. You would learn that through Joan Jett, power moms, country-and-western music, ZZ Top, disco, and rap.

Music is also the badge of identity of a crowd, a subculture, or a nation. When you and I meet for the first time, we compare our musical tastes. Why? To see if we share the same likes and aspirations. To see if we are part of the same subculture. That would become vividly apparent with disco, punk, and rap.

What's more, as you know, unlike the exaltations of Hitler's torchlight parades, the ecstasies of popular culture fuel fantasies of sex and violence safely, in a vacuum, where they can harm no one. That's the lesson of Alice Cooper axing baby dolls onstage, Ozzy Osbourne biting the head off of a live bat, and the plunge of violence in the real world between Alice's prime, Ozzy's outrageous deed, and today.

Then there's the lesson of tuned empathy. Understand others by digging through the hidden personalities in your self and finding the inner you that resonates to another's frequency. The way you channeled teenagers in your days at *Circus*. The way you channeled Prince when he refused to talk to his managers. The way that Michael Jackson channeled his kids.

Sometimes, you have to listen to the selves below the floorboards of your self. And sometimes you have to let the gods within you speak. When they and only they can speak the truth.

Where are the forces of history in all of this? Music plucks history's harp strings. In fact, music acts as one of history's galvanizers. Music is a bonding mechanism—it helps pull together movements. Look what Woody Guthrie's "This Land Is Your Land" did to pull together the left in the 1950s, the 1960s, and beyond. NPR says that the song became "an alternative national anthem."[277] Look what "We Shall Overcome" did for the civil rights movement in the 1960s. Look what music did in 1971 for the starving children of Bangladesh, thanks to George Harrison and Eric Clapton. Look at the achievements of Farm Aid, Band Aid, and "We Are the World" in 1984 and 1985.

But musicians can be misled. And, in turn, they can mislead you and me. Look at the Ethiopian genocide that Band Aid and "We Are the World" unknowingly helped finance. Look at Little Steven's refusal to try to stop another genocide, the one between the Hutus and the Tutsis in Rwanda—a conflict that took between 500,000 and a million lives.

Then there's the lesson of the icons, the lesson of Les Paul and Bill Chinnock. You owe your audience more than your songs. You owe your audience your life. Why? Because you are the trellis on which others will climb. You are the highest stair step on which others will stand. You are the platform from which others will build the next stair step up. One star's ceiling is the next star's floor. The most astonishing upward-stair step-builder I would ever see? Michael Jackson. A man whose legacy challenges us to new heights of awe, wonder, surprise, and ecstasy. A man with the potential to expand the perceptual envelope of all humankind. If only we can grok the truth of who and what he truly was.

* * *

In the end, it all comes down to an evolutionary trinity explained in my first book, *The Lucifer Principle: A Scientific Expedition into the Forces of History.* That trinity? Superorganisms, memes, and the pecking order.

Music is a meme. A meme that pulls you and me together into a superorganism, a group, a gang, a clique, a subculture, a nation, or a civilization. A superorganism is a larger being in which you and I are mere cells. But superorganisms compete. They compete with the memes at their core.

What do superorganisms—social groups, cliques, subcultures, tribes, nations, and civilizations—compete for? Status. Top position in the pecking order. What does status get you? Sex. And what does sex get you? The ability to reproduce. The ability to make a new generation carrying your genes. A new generation who will someday try to toss you off your throne. Why? To get sex.

And where does music fit into this? Everywhere. Like the salt crystal in the super-saturated solution, it pulls groups together. It uses ecstasies to give a new generation a sense of a collective identity. It uses musicians to express inner emotions that most of us thought made us insane. It uses music to put you and me on the same page, and to help us march to the beat of the same drummer. It uses music as our group's badge of identity. And it uses music to help our group climb the pecking order. In other words, music is the groin-deep voice of two things—the group . . . and sex. Two creations of the gods inside. And two of the sources of the fire with which those gods sometimes come to life.

Who taught me these lessons? Teachers like Prince, Bob Marley, Bette Midler, Billy Joel, Billy Idol, Joan Jett, Ralph MacDonald, and my ultimate educator, Michael Jackson.

We are powered by myth and driven by ecstasies. Superstars are the mythic figures of modernity. And superstars are driven by the gods inside.

* * *

A huge thanks for letting me tell you this story. Let me close with an epigram I wrote way back in 2001. An epigram that, strange as it sounds, gets to the heart of my seventeen-year quest in the music industry:

> Since there is no God, it is our job to do His work. God is not a being, He is an aspiration, a gift, a vision, a goal to seek. Ours is the responsibility of making a cruel universe turn just, of turning pains to understandings and new insights into joy, of creating ways to soar the skies for generations yet to come, of fashioning wings with which our children's children shall overcome, of making worlds of fantasy materialize as reality, of mining and transforming our greatest gifts—our passions, our imaginings, our pains, our insecurities, and our lusts. This is the work of deity, and deity is a power that resides in us.

NOTES

1. Graham Betts, *Motown Encyclopedia* (AC Publishing, 2014).

2. Phillip Morris, "Don King Stomped a Man to Death 50 Years Ago on Cedar Ave., Now Cleveland City Council Wants to Get in on the Act," *Cleveland Plain Dealer*, September 16, 2016, http://www.cleveland.com/morris/index. ssf/2016/09/don_king_stomped_a_man_to_deat.html.

3. William James, *The Varieties of Religious Experience: A Study in Human Nature: Being the Gifford Lectures on Natural Religion, Delivered at Edinburgh in 1901–1902* (Longmans, Green, 1923), 414.

4. Dale Ted Watkins, "The Crew Cut Men's Hair Cut History by Dale Ted Watkins," June 27, 2016, https://myhairdressers.com/blog/crew-cut-history/.

5. Arlo Guthrie, "Alice's Restaurant."

6. John Kuehl, "Threnody Is My Name," *VQR*, Spring 1994, http://www.vqronline. org/threnody-my-name.

7. "Ten Things You Didn't Know About 17-11-70," April 19, 2017, https://www. eltonjohn.com/stories/ten-things-you-didnt-know-about-17-11-70.

8. "Cleve Backster," Wikipedia, https://en.wikipedia.org/wiki/Cleve_Backster.

9. "The Secret Life of Plants," Wikipedia, https://en.wikipedia.org/wiki/ The_Secret_Life_of_Plants.

10. Jim Caroompas, "Evil Swing Music, Largest Naval Battle in History, Nelson Mandala Sentenced to Prison," *Patch*, October 25, 2011, https://patch.com/california/martinez/ evil-swing-music-largest-naval-battle-in-history-nelsb135a8e0b8.

11. Melissa A. Schilling, *Quirky: The Remarkable Story of the Traits, Foibles, and Genius of Breakthrough Innovators Who Changed the World* (Public Affairs, 2018), 205.

12. Jack Doyle, "The Sinatra Riots, 1942–1944," *Pop History Dig*, March 18, 2008, http://www.pophistorydig.com/topics/sinatra-riots-1942-1944/. "Paramount Theater (New York City)," Wikipedia, https://en.wikipedia.org/wiki/ Paramount_Theatre_(New_York_City).

13. Jack Doyle, "The Sinatra Riots, 1942–1944," *Pop History Dig*, March 18, 2008, http://www.pophistorydig.com/topics/sinatra-riots-1942-1944/.

14. Niko Tinbergen, *Curious Naturalists* (University of Massachusetts Press, 1984), 253.

15. Niko Tinbergen et al., "On the Stimulus Situation Releasing the Begging Response in the Newly Hatched Herring Gull Chick," *Studies in Animal and Human Behavior* (Havard University Press, 1974 edition). See also: Deirdre Barrett, *Supernormal Stimuli: How Primal Urges Overran Their Evolutionary Purpose* (W.W. Norton and Company, 2010), 13; Marianne Taylor, *RSPB Seabirds* (Bloomsbury Publishing, 2016), 154; Zdeněk Veselovský, *Animal Consciousness and Animal Ethics: Perspectives from the Netherlands* (Methuen, 1973), 14.

16. Ben Cosgrove, "The Invention of Teenagers: LIFE and the Triumph of Youth Culture," *Time*, September 28, 2013, http://time.com/3639041/the-invention-of-teenagers-life-and-the-triumph-of-youth-culture/. "The Invention of the Teenager, U.S History: Pre-Columbian to the New Millennium," http://www.ushistory.org/us/46c.asp.

17. "Fabian Forte," *Playgirl* (September 1973), reprinted on the blog *Welcome to My World*, http://welclometomyworld0426.blogspot.com/2013/09/fabian-forte-playgirl-september-1973.html.

18. Jeff Slate, "The Beatles: Inspirations," Tidal, January 16, 2016, http://read.tidal.com/article/the-beatles-inspirations. Jann S. Wenner, "John Lennon: The Rolling Stone Interview Part Two," *Rolling Stone*, February 4, 1971, https://www.rollingstone.com/music/music-news/john-lennon-the-rolling-stone-interview-part-two-160932/.

19. Joshua Wolf Shenk, *Powers of Two: How Relationships Drive Creativity* (Houghton Mifflin Harcourt, 2014), 11.

20. Garry Berman, *"We're Going to See the Beatles!": An Oral History of Beatlemania as Told by the Fans Who Were There* (Santa Monica Press, 2008).

21. John Rockwell, *The New York Times, The Times of the Sixties: The Culture, Politics, and Personalities That Shaped the Decade* (Running Press, 2014).

22. "50 Years Ago Today The Rolling Stones Came to America," *The Future Heart*, June 1, 2014, https://thefutureheart.com/2014/06/01/rolling-stones-america/.

23. "Art Ford: A Swing to Jazz," WNEW 1130, https://www.wnew1130.com/music-2/staff/e-f-g-h/522-2/.

24. "The Great Atlantic & Pacific Tea Company," Wikipedia, https://en.wikipedia.org/wiki/The_Great_Atlantic_%26_Pacific_Tea_Company. See also: Avis H. Anderson, *The Story of the Great Atlantic and Pacific Tea Company* (Arcadia Publishing, 2002); Juliet Hartford, *Huntington Hartford* (Gerhard Steidl

Druckerei und Verlag, 2020); Marc Levinson, *The Great A&P and the Struggle for Small Business in America* (Hill and Wang, 2011).

25. Daniel Lewis, "Huntington Hartford, A&P Heir, Dies at 97," *New York Times*, May 20, 2008, http://www.nytimes.com/2008/05/20/arts/design/20hartford. html.

26. Mary Manning, "Howard Hughes: A Revolutionary Recluse," *Las Vegas Sun*, May 15, 2008, https://lasvegassun.com/news/2008/may/15/ how-vegas-went-mob-corporate/.

27. William Grimes, "Clifford Irving, Author of a Notorious Literary Hoax, Dies at 87," *New York Times*, December 17, 2017, https://www.nytimes. com/2017/12/20/obituaries/clifford-irving-author-of-a-notorious-literary-hoax-dies-at-87.html.

28. Mary Dellas, "Dressing David Bowie as 'Ziggy Stardust,'" *The Cut*, February 27, 2018, https://www.thecut.com/2018/02/kansai-yamamoto-on-dressing-david-bowie-as-ziggy-stardust.html. Tessa Wong et al., "David Bowie's Love Affair with Japanese Style," BBC, January 12, 2016, http://www.bbc.com/news/ world-asia-35278488.

29. Sheryl Garrett, "David Bowie's Style Legacy: 'He Stole Ideas from Everywhere,'" *Guardian*, January 11, 2016, https://www.theguardian.com/music/2016/jan/11/ david-bowie-style-icon-fashion-legacy-aladdin-sane.

30. Carol Devine, "Station to Station: David Bowie on the Trans-Siberian Railway," *Calvert Journal*, January 18, 2016, https://www.calvertjournal.com/photography/ show/5291/bowie-trans-siberian-moscow-red-square-iggy-pop.

31. John Gramlich, "5 Facts About Crime in the US," Pew Research Center, January 30, 2018, http://www.pewresearch.org/ fact-tank/2018/01/30/5-facts-about-crime-in-the-u-s/.

32. "Art Nouveau (c. 1880 to 1910)," *BBC Homes*, http://www.bbc.co.uk/homes/ design/period_artnouveau.shtml. Tim Wu, *The Attention Merchants: The Epic Struggle to Get Inside Our Heads* (Knopf, 2016). "Jules Cheret," https://www. britannica.com/biography/Jules-Cheret.

33. Karl Taro Greenfeld, "Voracious Inc. Conglomerates Roamed the Earth During the '60s," *Time*, December 7, 1998.

34. John Snelson et al., *Andrew Lloyd Webber* (Yale University Press, 2004).

35. Andrew Lloyd Webber, "Jesus Christ Superstar," Andrew Lloyd Webber's own thoughts on *Jesus Christ Superstar*, http://www.andrewlloydwebber.com/theatre/ jcs.php.

36. Sonny Carson, "Koreans and Racism," *New York Times*, May 8, 1990. Tamar Jacoby, "Sonny Carson and the Politics of Protest," *City Journal*, Summer 1991. "Thugs Don't Deserve Honors," *New York Post*, April 14, 2007. Mark Santora, "Sonny Carson, 66, Figure in '60s Battle for Schools," *New York Times*, December 23, 2002.

37. "Roger Bannister," *Encyclopedia Britannica*, https://www.britannica.com/biography/Roger-Bannister.

38. "Four-Minute Mile," Wikipedia, https://en.wikipedia.org/wiki/Four-minute_mile.

39. Dr. Bruce R. Magee, "Evangeline Lecture," Louisiana Tech University, http://www2.latech.edu/~bmagee/475-575_epics/lectures/Week_09b_Evangeline.html. "The French and Indian War: British Expulsion of the Acadians (1755)," *Children in History*, http://histclo.com/essay/war/swc/18/7yw/fiw-aca.html.

40. Richard Hooker, "The Jewish Temples: The Babylonian Exile (597–538 BCE)," Jewish Virtual Library, http://www.jewishvirtuallibrary.org/the-babylonian-exile.

41. "Sidney Seidenberg," *Variety*, May 8, 2006, https://variety.com/2006/scene/people-news/sidney-seidenberg-1200505608/.

42. James Bates et al., "Jerry Rubinstein Has Drawn Static in a Varied Business Career. Now, with a Cable Music System, He's Hoping for a Clear Channel to Profits," *Los Angeles Times*, February 7, 1993, http://articles.latimes.com/1993-02-07/business/fi-1420_1_clear-channel.

43. Myrna Oliver, "John Strauss, 88; Veteran Publicist for Production Firms, Actors," *Los Angeles Times*, September 26, 2001, http://articles.latimes.com/2001/sep/26/local/me-50018. "About Rene A. Henry," http://www.renehenry.com/AboutReneAHenry.html.

44. "About Bob," http://www.robertslevinson.com/bio_2016_03.htm.

45. "The Beatles' Decca Audition," Wikipedia, https://en.wikipedia.org/wiki/The_Beatles%27_Decca_audition.

46. Robert Christgau, "Yes, There Is a Rock-Critic Establishment (But Is That Bad for Rock?)," *Village Voice*, January 26, 1976, https://www.robertchristgau.com/xg/rock/critics-76.php.

47. "Susan Rogers Is Wed on L.I.," New York Times, April 24, 1972, http://www.nytimes.com/1972/04/24/archives/susan-rogers-is-wed-on-li.html. http://garygiddins.com/biography/.

48. "John R. Brinkley," Wikipedia, https://en.wikipedia.org/wiki/John_R._Brinkley.

49. "People Just Don't Understand About X Stations," Ominous Valve, http://www.ominous-valve.com/xerf.html.

50. Thomas Carlyle, *Thomas Carlyle's Works: Critical and Miscellaneous Essays* (Chapman and Hall, 1887), 283–284.

51. Clement Shorter, "On Criticism," *The Idler*, February 1900, 949.

52. Thomas Carlyle, *Essays: Burns, Boswell's Life of Johnson, Sir Walter Scott, The Diamond Necklace* (Chapman and Hall, 1883), 20.

53. Robert Christgau, "Yes, There Is a Rock-Critic Establishment (But Is That Bad for Rock?)," *Village Voice*, January 26, 1976, https://www.robertchristgau.com/xg/rock/critics-76.php.

54. Scott Mervis, "ZZ Top-Aerosmith Concert at Three Rivers Stadium was One Crazy Day," *Pittsburgh Post-Gazette*, June 21, 2009, http://www.post-gazette.com/ae/music/2009/06/21/ZZ-Top-Aerosmith-concert-at-Three-Rivers-Stadium-was-one-crazy-day/stories/200906210207.

55. "Warner Bros. Records Building," Los Angeles Conservancy, https://www.laconservancy.org/locations/warner-bros-records-building.

56. Bob Grossweiner and Jane Cohen, "Industry Profile: Bob Merlis," Celebrity Access, http://members.celebrityaccess.com/news/profile.html?id=180.

57. "George McCrae—Rock Your Baby," Discogs, https://www.discogs.com/George-McCrae-Rock-Your-Baby/release/580306.

58. "George Pincus & Sons Music Corp.," Discogs, https://www.discogs.com/label/271917-George-Pincus-Sons-Music-Corp.

59. Bilal Kaiser, "Royalties for Cover Songs," Legal Zoom, www.legalzoom.com/articles/royalties-for-cover-songs.

60. "RHM Acquires Rights in Six Early Beatles Songs Along with the Entire GIL Music and George Pincus and Sons Music Catalogs," Round Hill Music, December 31, 2011, https://roundhillmusic.com/rhm-acquires-rights-in-six-early-beatles-songs-along-with-the-entire-gil-music-and-george-pincus-and-sons-music-catalogs/.

61. Bob Cromwell, "Wards Island Wastewater Treatment Plant," Toilet Guru, https://toilet-guru.com/nyc-sewer-wards-island.php.

62. David J. Garrow, "The FBI and Martin Luther King," *The Atlantic*, July/August 2002, https://www.theatlantic.com/magazine/archive/2002/07/the-fbi-and-martin-luther-king/302537/. Ben Kamin, *Dangerous Friendship: Stanley Levison,*

Martin Luther King Jr., and the Kennedy Brothers (Michigan State University Press, 2014).

63. Laird Scranton, "Shango," *Encyclopaedia Britannica*, https://www.britannica.com/topic/Shango.

64. "May Reopening Set for Apollo Theater," *New York Times*, April 28, 1978, https://www.nytimes.com/1978/04/28/archives/may-reopening-set-for-apollo-theater.html.

65. "Saturday Night Fever," Wikipedia, https://en.wikipedia.org/wiki/Saturday_Night_Fever.

66. "The Story of Goldeneye," https://www.goldeneye.com/the-story-of-goldeneye/.

67. David Leigh, "Essential Skills for 00 Agents—Scuba Diving," James Bond Dossier, February 22, 2010, https://www.thejamesbonddossier.com/content/essential-skills-for-00-agents-scuba-diving.htm.

68. Susan Ward, "Special Assignment: Ian Fleming's Jamaica," *Caribbean Beat* (issue 16), November/December 1995, http://www.caribbean-beat.com/issue-16/special-assignment-ian-flemings-jamaica#axzz58qXotUa8.

69. "The History: The Fleming Villa," *Island Outpost*, http://www.theflemingvilla.com/the-history/.

70. "Noël Coward," Wikipedia, https://en.wikipedia.org/wiki/No%C3%ABl_Coward.

71. "Chris Blackwell's Mom, Blanche Passes at 104," *Jamaica Observer*, August 13, 2017, http://www.jamaicaobserver.com/news/chris-blackwell-8217-s-mom-blanche-passes-at-104_107614.

72. Meanwhile, here are other sources for the facts: "Chris Blackwell," Wikipedia, https://en.wikipedia.org/wiki/Chris_Blackwell. "Crosse & Blackwell," Wikipedia, https://en.wikipedia.org/wiki/Crosse_%26_Blackwell. Andy Serwer, "Chris Blackwell Is the Most Interesting Man in the World," *Jamaica Observer*, December 21, 2016, http://www.jamaicaobserver.com/news/Chris-Blackwell-is-the-most-interesting-man-in-the-world_85200. Edward Helmore, "Chris Blackwell: The Original Trustafarian," *Telegraph*, May 8, 2012, http://www.telegraph.co.uk/culture/music/rockandpopfeatures/9243693/Chris-Blackwell-the-original-trustafarian.html.

73. "Cargo Cult," Wikipedia, https://en.wikipedia.org/wiki/Cargo_cult.

74. Thayer Watkins, "The Cargo Cults of the South Pacific," San Jose State University, http://www.sjsu.edu/faculty/watkins/cargocult.htm.

75. Paul Raffaele, "In John They Trust," *Smithsonian*, February 2006, https://www. smithsonianmag.com/history/in-john-they-trust-109294882/.

76. Paul Raffaele, "In John They Trust," *Smithsonian*, February 2006, https://www. smithsonianmag.com/history/in-john-they-trust-109294882/.

77. "Benito Mussolini," History, http://www.history.com/topics/world-war-ii/ benito-mussolini.

78. "Haile Selassie," Wikipedia, https://en.wikipedia.org/wiki/ Haile_Selassie#Exile_debate.

79. John Clarke, "Q&A: Chris Blackwell on Anniversary of Bob Marley 'Catch a Fire,'" *Rolling Stone*, April 22, 2013, https://www.rollingstone.com/music/news/ q-a-bob-marley-producer-chris-blackwell-on-the-40th-anniversary-of-catch-a-fire-20130422.

80. John Clarke, "Q&A: Chris Blackwell on Anniversary of Bob Marley 'Catch a Fire,'" *Rolling Stone*, April 22, 2013, https://www.rollingstone.com/music/news/ q-a-bob-marley-producer-chris-blackwell-on-the-40th-anniversary-of-catch-a-fire-20130422.

81. Pierre Perrone, "Island: The Record Label That Changed the World," *Independent*, May 1, 2009, https://www.independent.co.uk/arts-entertainment/ music/features/island-the-record-label-that-changed-the-world-1676691.html.

82. "Betty Davis," Wikipedia, https://en.wikipedia.org/wiki/Betty_Davis.

83. Frederic Dannen, *Hit Men: Power Brokers and Fast Money Inside the Music Business* (Knopf Doubleday Publishing Group, 1990), 165–167.

84. Geraldine Fabrikant, "Billy Joel Takes His Lawyers to Court," *New York Times*, September 24, 1992, http://www.nytimes.com/1992/09/24/business/billy-joel-takes-his-lawyers-to-court.html.

85. "Michael Henderson," Wikipedia, https://en.wikipedia.org/wiki/ Michael_Henderson.

86. Carletta Smith, "June 30, 1995: Phyllis Hyman Committed Suicide by Overdosing," *Black Then*, February 10, 2017, https://blackthen.com/june-30-1995-phyllis-hyman-committed-suicide-overdosing/. Shantel Noel, "A New Musical Will Highlight the Life of Phyllis Hyman," November 5, 2016, http:// saintheron.com/news/a-new-musical-will-highlight-the-life-of-phyllis-hyman/.

87. Amnesty International, https://www.amnestyusa.org/.

88. Martin Lewis, personal correspondence, February 26, 2018.

89. Hermann Ebbinghaus, *Memory: A Contribution to Experimental Psychology (1885)*, *Annals of Neuroscience*, October 2013, 155–156. Mark A. Gluck et al.,

"In Memory and Mind: A Festschrift for Gordon H. Bower," *Psychology Press*, September 10, 2012. James Playsted Wood, *Advertising and the Soul's Belly: Repetition and Memory in Advertising*, (University of Georgia Press, 1961). Scott A. Hawkins et al., "Low-Involvement Learning: Memory without Evaluation," *Journal of Consumer Research* (vol. 19, issue 2), September 1, 1992, 212–225.

90. "Stewart Kranz, Winthrop Art Winner, Opens First Hub Exhibit with 17 Watercolors in Copley Gallery Today," *Harvard Crimson*, February 17, 1947, http://www.thecrimson.com/article/1947/2/17/stewart-kranz-winthrop-art-winner-opens/.

91. "Stewart Kranz," AskArt, http://www.askart.com/artist_bio/Stewart_Kranz/11268682/Stewart_Kranz.aspx.

92. Mikal Gilmore, "Rock and Roll Fantasies," *Rolling Stone*, February 22, 1979, https://www.rollingstone.com/music/features/rock-roll-fantasies-19790222

93. "Monty Python," Wikipedia, https://en.wikipedia.org/wiki/Monty_Python.

94. "Camden Town's Punk Story," Camden Market, July 7, 2016, https://www.camdenmarket.com/journal/camden-towns-punk-story.

95. Richard Sandimor, "James Stevenson, Longtime New Yorker Cartoonist, Dies at 87," *New York Times*, February 23, 2017, https://www.nytimes.com/2017/02/23/arts/james-stevenson-dead-new-yorker-cartoonist.html.

96. Richard Sale, "Exclusive: Saddam key in early CIA plot," *UPI Intelligence Correspondent*, April 10, 2003, https://www.upi.com/Exclusive-Saddam-key-in-early-CIA-plot/65571050017416/.

97. Toney Butler Schlesinger, "Alvin Silas (Al) Bennett (1926–1989)," *Encyclopedia of Arkansas History and Culture*, http://www.encyclopediaofarkansas.net/encyclopedia/entry-detail.aspx?entryID=7366.

98. George F. Brown, "The Inside Story of Fatal Shooting in Al Green's Home," *Jet*, November 7, 1974, 13.

99. Yichuan Liu et al., "Measuring Speaker–Listener Neural Coupling with Functional Near Infrared Spectroscopy," *Nature*, February 27, 2017, https://www.nature.com/articles/srep43293. Po-He Tseng et al., "Interbrain Cortical Synchronization Encodes Multiple Aspects of Social Interactions in Monkey Pairs," *Scientific Reports*, 2018. "Monkeys' Brains Synchronize as They Collaborate to Perform a Motor Task: Levels of Synchronicity in Motor Cortex Are Influenced by Proximity, Social Status," *Science Daily*, March 29, 2018, https://www.sciencedaily.com/releases/2018/03/180329095444.htm.

100. "Sex, Drugs and Rock 'N' Roll: Clapton After 'Cocaine'," *All Things Considered*, October 18, 2007, https://www.npr.org/templates/story/story.php?storyId=15412830.

101. "Shri Meher Baba," *Back to Godhead* (vol. 3), 1956, 8, http://back2godhead.com/shri-meher-baba/.

102. Leslie Mertz, "Konrad Lorenz," *Psychology Encyclopedia*, http://psychology.jrank.org/pages/390/Konrad-Lorenz.html.

103. Eckhard H. Hess, "Konrad Lorenz Austrian Zoologist," *Encyclopedia Britannica*, https://www.britannica.com/biography/Konrad-Lorenz.

104. Dale Peterson, *Jane Goodall: The Woman Who Redefined Man* (Houghton Mifflin Harcourt, 2014), 266.

105. Konrad Lorenz, *King Solomon's Ring* (Methuen, 1952), 129–130.

106. Dale Peterson, *Jane Goodall: The Woman Who Redefined Man* (Houghton Mifflin Harcourt, 2014), 266.

107. Thorleif Schjelderup-Ebbe, "Beiträge zur Sozialpsychologie des Haushuhns," Z. Psychol. 88 (1922), 225–252. John Sparks, *The Discovery of Animal Behaviour* (Little, Brown and Company, 1982), 226–230. Joseph Altman, *Organic Foundations of Animal Behavior* (Holt Rinehart and Winston, 1966), 454. David McFarland (ed.), *The Oxford Companion to Animal Behavior* (Oxford University Press, 1982), 139–140.

108. Dave Lifton, "Revisiting Simon and Garfunkel's 'Concert in Central Park' Reunion," *Ultimate Classic Rock*, September 19, 2015, http://ultimateclassicrock.com/simon-and-garfunkel-reunite-for-the-concert-in-central-park-september-19-1981/.

109. "Brill Building," Wikipedia, https://en.wikipedia.org/wiki/Brill_Building#Brill_Building_composers_and_lyricists_included.

110. Richard Metzger, "Outrageous: Kim Fowley Part 2," *Dangerous Minds*, September 16, 2011, https://dangerousminds.net/comments/outrageoous_kim_fowley_part_2.

111. "American Top 40," Wikipedia, https://en.wikipedia.org/wiki/American_Top_40.

112. John Bargh, *Before You Know It: The Unconscious Reasons We Do What We Do* (Touchstone, 2017). John Bargh et al., "The Unbearable Automaticity of Being," *American Psychologist* (vol. 54, issue 7), July 1999, 462–479.

113. "Can't Fight This Feeling," Wikipedia, https://en.wikipedia.org/wiki/Can%27t_Fight_This_Feeling.

114. "11 Historic Bear Markets: From the Great Depression to the Great Recession," NBC News, http://www.nbcnews.com/id/37740147/ns/business-stocks_and_economy/t/historic-bear-markets/.

115. "In 1981, 55 million fewer singles and albums were sold than in 1980." Deena Weinstein, *Rock 'n America: A Social and Cultural History* (University of Toronto Press, 2015), 185.

116. Paul Kennedy, *The Rise and Fall of the Great Powers: Economic Change and Military Conflict from 1500 to 2000* (Random House, 1987).

117. Paul Kennedy, *The Rise and Fall of the Great Powers: Economic Change and Military Conflict from 1500 to 2000* (Random House, 1987).

118. "A Brief Biography of Jimmy Swaggart," Jimmy Swaggart Ministries, http://www.jsm.org/jimmy-swaggart.html.

119. "Bonfire of the Vanities," Wikipedia, https://en.wikipedia.org/wiki/Bonfire_of_the_vanities.

120. Michael Thompson, *Confronting the New Conservatism: The Rise of the Right in America*, (NYU Press, 2007), 83.

121. Tim Ingham, "Live Nation Companies Now Manage Over 500 Artists Worldwide," *Music Business Worldwide*, February 27, 2017, https://www.musicbusinessworldwide.com/live-nation-companies-now-manage-500-artists-worldwide/. Steve Knopper, "Irving Azoff's Live Nation Exit Leaves Many Questions Unanswered," *Rolling Stone*, January 4, 2013, https://www.rollingstone.com/music/news/irving-izoffs-live-nation-exit-leaves-many-questions-unanswered-20130104.

122. For Irving Azoff's reputation as a monster, a real life Darth Vader, see: "Azoff's reputation for ill-tempered dealings rivaled my own. Some called him an even bigger prick than me." Walter Yetnikoff and David Ritz, *Howling at the Moon* (Broadway Books, 2004). "Joe Smith, an executive at Elektra, once described Irving humorously at a roast as 'a little bundle of hate.'" Don Felder and Wendy Holden, *Heaven and Hell: My Life in the Eagles (1974–2001)* (Wiley, 2008), 159. "People that aren't close to me would think I kill for sport . . . you gotta kill sometimes." Cameron Crowe, *Rolling Stone*, June 15, 1978, excerpted in http://www.theuncool.com/journalism/rs267-irving-azoff/. See also: "Irving Azoff, Manager of the Eagles," in Michael Heatley, *Sex 'n' Drugs 'n' Strong Opinions: The Book of Rock Quotes* (Omnibus Books, 2008); Steve Eng, *Jimmy Buffett: The Man from Margaritaville* (St. Martin's Griffin, 1996); Scott Faragher, *Music City Babylon: Inside the World of Country Music* (Carol Publishing, 1992).

123. Sterling Whitaker, "How 'Kilroy Was Here' Tore Styx Apart," *Ultimate Classic Rock*, February 28, 2015, http://ultimateclassicrock.com/styx-kilroy-was-here/.

124. Fred Schruers, personal communication, January 28, 2019.

125. Chris Salewicz, *Bob Marley: The Untold Story* (Farrar, Straus, and Giroux, 2014).

126. "In the 1970s, WBLS Was Nothing Short of a Miracle." Dan Charnas, "Long Kiss Goodbye: Fear of a Black Planet Killed A Black Radio Station," NewsOne. com, May 2, 2012, https://newsone.com/2005493/long-kiss-goodbye-charnas-987-kiss-fm-wbls/ 7-30-2018.

127. Chris Salewicz, *Bob Marley: The Untold Story* (Farrar, Straus, and Giroux, 2014).

128. Roger Steffens, "The Night Bob Marley Got Shot," *Rolling Stone*, July 7, 2017.

129. Chris Salewicz, *Bob Marley: The Untold Story* (Farrar, Straus, and Giroux, 2014).

130. Chris Salewicz, *Bob Marley: The Untold Story* (Farrar, Straus, and Giroux, 2014).

131. "Jamaica Struggles to Cut Government-Gang Ties," AP/ CBS News, June 3, 2010, https://www.cbsnews.com/news/ jamaica-struggles-to-cut-government-gang-ties/.

132. Chris Salewicz, *Bob Marley: The Untold Story* (Farrar, Straus, and Giroux, 2014).

133. Chris Salewicz, *Bob Marley: The Untold Story* (Farrar, Straus, and Giroux, 2014).

134. "Smile Jamaica Concert," Wikipedia, https://en.wikipedia.org/wiki/ Smile_Jamaica_Concert.

135. Lone Wolf, http://www.lone-wolf.com/.

136. Haile Selassie, "Speech of Haile Selassie Before League of Nations Assembly, June 30, 1936," https://www.mtholyoke.edu/acad/intrel/selassie.htm. Peter Schwab, *Haile Selassie I: Ethiopia's Lion of Judah* (Nelson-Hall, 1979).

137. Kat Arney, "Bob Marley, Genomics, and a Rare Form of Melanoma," Cancer Research UK, August 24, 2014, http://scienceblog.cancerresearchuk. org/2014/08/20/bob-marley-genomics-and-a-rare-form-of-melanoma/.

138. Rob Kenner, "Danny Sims, Producer Who Signed Bob Marley, Dies at 75," *New York Times*, October 30, 2012, https://www.nytimes.com/2012/10/31/arts/music/ danny-sims-producer-of-bob-marley-dies-at-75.html.

139. "Johnny Nash," Wikipedia, https://en.wikipedia.org/wiki/Johnny_Nash. "The Rain, the Park & Other Things," Wikipedia, https://en.wikipedia.org/wiki/ The_Rain,_the_Park_%26_Other_Things. "The Cowsills," Wikipedia, https:// en.wikipedia.org/wiki/The_Cowsills.

140. "Urban Riots," Wikipedia, https://en.wikipedia.org/wiki/Urban_riots#1960s.

141. William Grant, "Rastafari Culture," Roots Reggae Rock Dread Library, https:// debate.uvm.edu/dreadlibrary/grant02.htm.

142 Chris Salewicz, *Bob Marley: The Untold Story* (Farrar, Straus, and Giroux, 2014).

143 "Earth, Wind & Fire," Wikipedia, https://en.wikipedia.org/wiki/
Earth,_Wind_%26_Fire.

144 Max Savage Levenson, "A Jazz Album Written by Prince's Father Finally Sees
the Light of Day," March 6, 2018, https://daily.bandcamp.com/2018/03/05/
princes-father-jazz-album-interview/.

145 Matt Thorne, *Prince* (Faber and Faber, 2012).

146 "Session Musicians—Know Your Rights," Music Industry Inside Out, April 18,
2015, https://musicindustryinsideout.com.au/session-musicians-know-rights/.

147 Matt Thorne, *Prince* (Faber and Faber, 2012).

148 Norman Ferguson, "German Military Doctors Would Diagnose Appendicitis
for Fighter Pilots to Give the Men Two Weeks of Rest and Recreation," *Battle of
Britain: A Miscellany* (Summersdale Publishers Ltd., 2015).

149 Pamela Cooper-White, "'Old and Dirty Gods': Religion and Freud's Wednesday
Night Psychological Society—from Habsburg Vienna, to the Holocaust," *Journal
of Pastoral Theology* (vol. 27, issue 1), 2017, 3–16, https://www.tandfonline.com/
doi/abs/10.1080/10649867.2017.1361700.

150 Katharine Q. Seelye, "In the Blog Era, Liz Smith Wonders if There's
Room for the Pro," *New York Times*, March 28, 2005, http://www.nytimes.
com/2005/03/28/business/media/in-the-blog-era-liz-smith-wonders-if-theres-
room-for-the-pro.html.

151 Matt Thorne, *Prince* (Faber and Faber, 2012).

152 Matt Thorne, *Prince* (Faber and Faber, 2012). Brian Raftery, "Prince: The
Oral History of 'Purple Rain': A Look Back at the Making of Prince's
1984 Masterpiece," *Spin*, April 22, 2016, https://www.spin.com/2016/04/
prince-the-oral-history-of-purple-rain-brian-raftery/.

153 David Ansen, review of *Purple Rain* in *Newsweek*, reprinted in *Daily News*,
August 3, 1984, 429.

154 "Purple Rain," Wikipedia, https://en.wikipedia.org/wiki/Purple_Rain_(film).
Howard Bloom, *The Genius of the Beast: A Radical Re-Vision of Capitalism*
(Prometheus Books, 2009).

155 Rachel, "Michael Jackson Owned a Snake," Michael Jackson Museum,
May 11, 2013, http://www.michaeljacksonsmuseum.com/facts/
michael-jackson-owned-a-snake/.

156 "Kristin Scott Thomas," Wikipedia, https://en.wikipedia.org/wiki/
Kristin_Scott_Thomas.

157 "Purple Rain," IMDb, http://www.imdb.com/title/tt0087957/.

158 "Under the Cherry Moon," the Movie Wiki, http://themoviesgamelionhead. wikia.com/wiki/Under_the_Cherry_Moon.

159 "Bob Cavallo," Wikipedia, https://en.wikipedia.org/wiki/Bob_Cavallo.

160 Adam Sandler, "Bob Cavallo," *Variety*, October 4, 2007, http://variety. com/2007/music/markets-festivals/bob-cavallo-1117973380/.

161 "Chairman of Disney Music Group Announces Retirement," *Hollywood Reporter*, June 11, 2011, https://www.hollywoodreporter.com/news/ chairman-disney-music-group-announces-193904.

162 Matt Thorne, "Prince Makes History with O2 Shows," *Telegraph*, September 22, 2007, https://www.telegraph.co.uk/culture/music/3668073/Prince-makes-history-with-O2-shows.html.

163 Gene Weingarten, "East Bronx Story—Return of the Street Gangs," *New York*, March 27, 1972, http://nymag.com/news/features/crime/48271/.

164 "South Bronx," Wikipedia, https://en.wikipedia.org/wiki/ South_Bronx#1970s:_"The_Bronx_is_burning".

165 Randol Contreras, *The Stickup Kids: Race, Drugs, Violence, and the American Dream* (University of California Press, 2013).

166 Bryan Wawzenek, "The Story of John Mellencamp's Long Battle to Escape 'Johnny Cougar,'" *Ultimate Classic Rock*, October 3, 2016, http:// ultimateclassicrock.com/john-cougar-john-mellencamp-name-change/.

167 Heather Johnson, *Born in a Small Town—John Mellencamp, The Story* (Omnibus Press, 2007).

168 Dave Lifton, "'I Saw Rock 'n' Roll Future': The History of Bruce Springsteen and Jon Landau," *Ultimate Classic Rock*, May 9, 2014, http://ultimateclassicrock. com/bruce-springsteen-jon-landau/. Andy Greene, "Rolling Stone at 50: Inside Bruce Springsteen's Long History with the Magazine," *Rolling Stone*, October 9, 2017, https://www.rollingstone.com/music/news/ inside-bruce-springsteens-long-history-with-rolling-stone-w507443.

169 Heather Johnson, *Born in a Small Town—John Mellencamp, The Story* (Omnibus Press, 2007).

170 "Cool Hand Luke," Wikipedia, https://en.wikipedia.org/wiki/ Cool_Hand_Luke.

171 Heather Johnson, *Born in a Small Town—John Mellencamp, The Story* (Omnibus Press, 2007).

172. Paul Zollo, "John Mellencamp," *American Songwriter*, January 1, 2005, http://americansongwriter.com/2005/01/john-mellencamp/.

173. Heather Johnson, *Born in a Small Town—John Mellencamp, The Story* (Omnibus Press, 2007).

174. Phoebe Eaton, "Tommy Mottola Faces the Music," *New York*, February 21, 2003, http://nymag.com/nymetro/news/features/n_8387/.

175. Lynn Hirschberg, "For Daryl Hall and John Oates, Life as Pop Music's Biggest Duo Is Not Good Enough," *Rolling Stone*, January 17, 1985, https://www.rollingstone.com/music/news/hall-and-oates-the-self-righteous-brothers-19850117.

176. "The Temptations," Wikipedia, https://en.wikipedia.org/wiki/The_Temptations.

177. Kevin Fallon, "Speed Read: Juiciest Bits from the Tommy Mottola Memoir 'Hitmaker'," *Daily Beast*, January 31, 2013, https://www.thedailybeast.com/speed-read-juiciest-bits-from-the-tommy-mottola-memoir-hitmaker.

178. Connie Bramstedt, "Mellencamp Sings at Farmers' Protest," UPI, May 8, 1986, https://www.upi.com/Archives/1986/05/08/Mellencamp-sings-at-farmers-protest/9465515908800/.

179. Connie Bramstedt, "Mellencamp Sings at Farmers' Protest," UPI, May 8, 1986, https://www.upi.com/Archives/1986/05/08/Mellencamp-sings-at-farmers-protest/9465515908800/.

180. Seth Eisenberg, "John Mellencamp—Another Void in My Heart," Fatherhood Channel, https://fatherhoodchannel.com/2011/01/02/john-mellencamp-another-void-in-my-heart-002/.

181. Chet Flippo, "Nashville Skyline: John Mellencamp Rides Freedom's Road. New CD Explores His Roots Rock Approach to American Values," CMT, January 11, 2007, http://www.cmt.com/news/1549816/nashville-skyline-john-mellencamp-rides-freedoms-road/.

182. Robert Keating, "Live Aid: The Terrible Truth," *Spin*, July 1986, https://www.spin.com/featured/live-aid-the-terrible-truth-ethiopia-bob-geldof-feature/.

183. Arthur Koestler, *The God That Failed* (Columbia University Press, 1950), 60. Timothy Snyder, *Bloodlands: Europe Between Hitler and Stalin* (Basic Books, 2012), 54.

184. Mikhail Heller et al., *Utopia in Power: The History of the Soviet Union from 1917 to the Present* (Summit Books, 1982), 235.

185. Iosif G. Dyadkin, *Unnatural Deaths in the USSR, 1928–1954* (Transaction Books, 1983), 25.

186. Bob Guccione Jr., "Live Aid: The Terrible Truth," *Spin*, July 13, 2015, https://www.spin.com/featured/live-aid-the-terrible-truth-ethiopia-bob-geldof-feature/.

187. Susan Dominus, "Portraits of Reconciliation: 20 Years After the Genocide in Rwanda, Reconciliation Still Happens One Encounter at a Time," *New York Times Magazine*, April 6, 2014, https://www.nytimes.com/interactive/2014/04/06/magazine/06-pieter-hugo-rwanda-portraits.html. Deborah Bloom et al., "Rwanda's Catholic Church says Sorry for Its Role in 1994 Genocide," CNN, November 21, 2016, https://www.cnn.com/2016/11/21/africa/rwanda-catholic-church-apology/index.html.

188. Billy Idol, *Dancing with Myself* (Touchstone, 2014), 173.

189. "Electric Lady: A Brief History," http://electricladystudios.com/studios/.

190. Blair Jackson, "Eddie Kramer and the Early Days of Electric Lady," *Mix*, October 1, 2013, https://www.mixonline.com/recording/eddie-kramer-and-early-days-electric-lady-366450.

191. Billy Idol, *Dancing with Myself* (Touchstone, 2014), 138.

192. Leon Zephyr, "New York City Music Trip/From the Life of Original Kiss Members, #5 of 5: From the Birth of KISS to Their Golden Era in NYC," TripMuze, August 3, 2016, http://tripmuze.com/2016/08/03/new-york-city-music-tripfrom-the-life-of-original-kiss-members-part-5-from-the-birth-of-kiss-to-their-golden-era-in-nyc/.

193. Scott McCabe, "Crime History: Richard Pryor Sets Self on Fire," *Washington Examiner*, June 8, 2011, https://www.washingtonexaminer.com/crime-history-richard-pryor-sets-self-on-fire.

194. Bryan Wawzenek, "45 Years Ago: Billy Joel Releases His First Album, 'Cold Spring Harbor'," *Ultimate Classic Rock*, March 31, 2018, http://ultimateclassicrock.com/billy-joel-cold-spring-harbor/.

195. Chuck Yarborough, "Jim Henke, Rock Hall's Chief Curator, Leaves 'to Focus on Collecting and Writing as a Consultant,'" *Cleveland Plain Dealer*, October 22, 2012, http://www.cleveland.com/entertainment/index.ssf/2012/10/jim_henke_rock_halls_chief_cur.html.

196. "Jinxed!," Wikipedia, https://en.wikipedia.org/wiki/Jinxed!_(1982_film)#Reception.

197. Leslie Rubinstein, "A Sure Bette: Midler Charges Full-Tilt Into Her Latest Role," *Los Angeles Times*, June 5, 1988, http://articles.chicagotribune.com/1988-06-05/entertainment/8801050590_1_harry-kipper-martin-von-haselberg-bette-midler.

198. Hal Belch, *What Is Psychology? Motivation and Emotion* (Social Studies School Service, 2004), 34. David P. Barash et al., *Gender Gap: The Biology of Male-Female Differences* (Routledge, 2017).

199. Meredith F. Small, *What's Love Got to Do with It?: The Evolution of Human Mating* (Anchor Books, 1995), 111.

200. Eric R. Olson, "Why Are 250 Million Sperm Cells Released During Sex?," *Live Science*, January 24, 2013, https://www.livescience.com/32437-why-are-250-million-sperm-cells-released-during-sex.html.

201. "Martin von Haselberg," IMDb, http://www.imdb.com/name/nm0902393/bio.

202. "Big Business," IMDb, http://www.imdb.com/title/tt0094739/.

203. "New York City and the Birth of the Film Industry 1894–1918," Bowery Boys History, February 18, 2011, http://www.boweryboyshistory.com/2011/02/new-york-city-and-birth-of-film.html. Andrew A. Erish, *Col. William N. Selig, the Man Who Invented Hollywood* (University of Texas Press, 2012), 10. "Marcus Loew," Wikipedia, https://en.wikipedia.org/wiki/Marcus_Loew.

204. "United Artists," Wikipedia, https://en.wikipedia.org/wiki/United_Artists.

205. "Tribeca Film Festival," Wikipedia, https://en.wikipedia.org/wiki/Tribeca_Film_Festival#History.

206. Tim Cornwell, "George Michael Arrested Over 'Lewd Act'," *Independent*, April 8, 1998, https://www.independent.co.uk/news/george-michael-arrested-over-lewd-act-1155246.html.

207. Kara Fox, "1998: George Michael Comes Out in CNN Interview," CNN, December 26, 2016, https://www.cnn.com/2016/12/26/entertainment/george-michael-cnn-interview-1998/index.html.

208. "Eva Ein," IMDb, http://www.imdb.com/name/nm1223777/.

209. Seneca, De Tranquillitate Animi (On Tranquility of Mind), cited at Wikipedia, https://en.wikipedia.org/wiki/Destruction_of_the_Library_of_Alexandria. See also: Ismail Serageldin, Mostafa El-Abbadi, Omnia Mounir Fathallah (eds.), *What Happened to the Ancient Library of Alexandria?* (Brill, 2008), 72.

210. Louise Nicholson, *National Geographic Traveler: London* (National Geographic Books, 2016), 44. Louise McConnell, *Dictionary of Shakespeare* (Taylor and Francis, 2000), 48.

211. "Elizabeth I: Her Life in Buildings," *Discover Britain*, http://www.discoverbritainmag.com/elizabeth-i/.

212. Elisabeth Bumiller, "The Case of the Missing Hostess," *Washington Post*, October 14, 1980, https://www.washingtonpost.com/archive/lifestyle/1980/10/14/the-case-of-the-missing-hostess/.

213. "Parents Music Resource Center," Wikipedia, https://en.wikipedia.org/wiki/Parents_Music_Resource_Center.

214. Richard Harrington, "W.A.S.P., Lewd and Clear," *Washington Post*, February 8, 1987, https://www.washingtonpost.com/archive/lifestyle/style/1987/02/08/wasp-lewd-and-clear/8f34fa3d-11e4-42c8-b2ba-38798817293e/?utm_term=.bfa55344916d.

215. Keith Caulfield, "Michael Jackson's 'Thriller' Extends Reign as Highest Certified Album in US History," *Billboard*, February 16, 2017, https://www.billboard.com/articles/news/7693419/michael-jackson-thriller-highest-certified-album.

216. Michael Goldberg and Christopher Connelly, "Michael Jackson: Trouble in Paradise," *Rolling Stone*, March 15, 1984, https://www.rollingstone.com/music/news/trouble-in-paradise-19840315.

217. Michael Goldberg and Christopher Connelly, "Michael Jackson: Trouble in Paradise," *Rolling Stone*, March 15, 1984, https://www.rollingstone.com/music/news/trouble-in-paradise-19840315.

218. "Best Selling Album," Guinness World Records, http://www.guinnessworldrecords.com/world-records/70133-best-selling-album. Michael Goldberg and Christopher Connelly, "Michael Jackson: Trouble in Paradise," *Rolling Stone*, March 15, 1984, https://www.rollingstone.com/music/news/trouble-in-paradise-19840315.

219. "Michael Jackson's Life as a Jehovah's Witness," Facts About Jehovah's Witnesses, http://jwfacts.com/watchtower/experiences/michael-jackson-jehovah.php. "John Branca: 'Charming, Ruthless, Asshole,'" MUZIKfactory2, August 4, 2011, http://muzikfactorytwo.blogspot.com/2011/08/john-branca-charming-ruthless-asshole.html.

220. Jacob Leibenluft, "Why Don't Jehovah's Witnesses Vote? Because They're Representatives of God's Heavenly Kingdom," *Slate*, June 2008, http://www.slate.com/articles/news_and_politics/explainer/2008/06/why_dont_jehovahs_witnesses_vote.html.

221. "About Dr. Benjamin L. Hooks: Civil Rights Activist, Minister, Veteran and Philanthropist," University of Memphis, http://www.memphis.edu/benhooks/about/about-benjamin-hooks.php.

222. Phillip Morris, "Don King Stomped a Man to Death 50 Years Ago on Cedar Ave., Now Cleveland City Council Wants to Get in on the Act," *Cleveland Plain Dealer*, September 16, 2016, http://www.cleveland.com/morris/index. ssf/2016/09/don_king_stomped_a_man_to_deat.html.

223. "1984 Concert Ticket Stubs," Rocksandy.com, October 15, 2016, https:// rocksandy.rocks/2016/10/15/my-1984-concert-ticket-stubs/.

224. Michael Goldberg and Christopher Connelly, "Michael Jackson: Trouble in Paradise," *Rolling Stone*, March 15, 1984, https://www.rollingstone.com/music/ news/trouble-in-paradise-19840315.

225. Dave Marsh, *Trapped: Michael Jackson and the Crossover Dream* (Bantam, 1985).

226. Jon Pareles, "Concert: Jacksons at Giants Stadium," *New York Times*, July 30, 1984, https://www.nytimes.com/1984/07/30/arts/concert-jacksons-at-giants-stadium.html. "Giants Stadium," Wikipedia, https://en.wikipedia.org/wiki/ Giants_Stadium.

227. "Accord Ends Coke Boycott," *New York Times*, August 11, 1981, https://www. nytimes.com/1981/08/11/business/accord-ends-coke-boycott.html. "Rainbow/ PUSH," Wikipedia, https://en.wikipedia.org/wiki/Rainbow/PUSH. Ronald Smothers, "After Year of Boycott, Push Endorses Anheuser-Busch Plans," *New York Times*, September 10, 1983, https://www.nytimes.com/1983/09/10/us/after-year-of-boycott-push-endorses-anheuser-busch-plans.html 4-3-2018.

228. "Jesse Jackson's Sons to Buy Beer Distributor," *Los Angeles Times*, November 21, 1998, http://articles.latimes.com/1998/nov/21/news/nc-46240.

229. J. Randy Taraborrelli, *Michael Jackson: The Magic, the Madness, the Whole Story, 1958–2009* (Grand Central Publishing, 2010). John Steinbreder, "The $126 Million Fumble: How Billy Sullivan and His Son Chuck Turned a $25,000 Investment in the Patriots into a Financial Disaster," *Sports Illustrated*, March 14, 1988, https://www.si.com/vault/1988/03/14/117304/the-126-million-fumble-how-billy-sullivan-and-his-son-chuck-turned-a-25000-investment-in-the-patriots-into-a-financial-disaster.

230. John Steinbreder, "The $126 Million Fumble: How Billy Sullivan and His Son Chuck Turned a $25,000 Investment in the Patriots into a Financial Disaster," *Sports Illustrated*, March 14, 1988, https://www.si.com/vault/1988/03/14/117304/the-126-million-fumble-how-billy-sullivan-and-his-son-chuck-turned-a-25000-investment-in-the-patriots-into-a-financial-disaster.

231. Stacey Oke, DVM, MSc, "Bone Chips in Horses: Why, Where, and What to Do," *Horse*, October 7, 2015, https://thehorse.com/113210/bone-chips-in-horses-why-where-and-what-to-do/.
232. Jeff Wilson, "Jackson's Victory Tour a Draw," UPI, December 9, 1984, https://www.upi.com/Archives/1984/12/09/Jacksons-victory-tour-a-draw/2586471416400/.
233. "Victory Tour," Wikipedia, https://en.wikipedia.org/wiki/Victory_Tour_(The_Jacksons_tour)#Tour_dates.
234. "Bill Robinson," Wikipedia, https://en.wikipedia.org/wiki/Bill_Robinson. To see the Little Colonel Bojangles dance: https://www.youtube.com/watch?v=wtHvetGnOdM.
235. Michael Jackson, *Moonwalk* (Crown/Archetype, 2009), Kindle location 489.
236. "'Godfather Of Soul' James Brown Dies at 73," *Billboard*, December 25, 2006, https://www.billboard.com/articles/news/56366/godfather-of-soul-james-brown-dies-at-73.
237. Michael Jackson, *Moonwalk* (Crown/Archetype, 2009), Kindle location 473.
238. Michael Jackson, *Moonwalk* (Crown/Archetype, 2009), Kindle location 1810.
239. Michael Jackson, *Moonwalk* (Crown/Archetype, 2009), Kindle location 331.
240. See also: Jerry Heller, Gil Reavill, *Ruthless: A Memoir* (Simon and Schuster, 2007), 60.
241. J. Randy Taraborrelli, *Michael Jackson: The Magic, the Madness, the Whole Story, 1958-2009* (Grand Central Publishing, 2010). "John Branca: 'Charming, Ruthless, Asshole,'" *MUZIKfactory2*, August 4, 2011, http://muzikfactorytwo.blogspot.com/2011/08/john-branca-charming-ruthless-asshole.html. Steve Knopper, *MJ: The Genius of Michael Jackson* (Simon and Schuster, 2016), 144. Michael Goldberg, "Behind-the-Scenes Confusion Causing Various Delays: Wheeling and Dealing Continues as Jacksons Tour Approaches," *Rolling Stone*, June 21, 1984, 51.
242. Irving Azoff and cocaine abuse seemed to go hand in hand. Azoff's key acts included the band he started his career with, the Eagles, plus Fleetwood Mac, Steely Dan, Jimmy Buffett, and, as you've seen, Joe Walsh. All were drowning themselves in cocaine. I also suspect that Azoff and his employees used cocaine to become cozy with members of the press. For references to Azoff's perpetual proximity to snowstorms of cocaine, see: Barney Hoskyns, *Waiting for the Sun:*

A Rock 'n' Roll History of Los Angeles (St. Martin's Press, 1996); Jim Beviglia, *Playing Back the 80s: A Decade of Unstoppable Hits* (Rowman & Littlefield, 2018); Carol Ann Harris, *Storms: My Life with Lindsey Buckingham and Fleetwood Mac* (Chicago Review Press, 2007); Stephen Davis, *Gold Dust Woman: The Biography of Stevie Nicks* (St Martin's Press, 2017); Steve Eng, *Jimmy Buffett: The Man from Margaritaville* (St. Martin's Griffin, 1996); Michael Sarno, "Gaucho: The Near Implosion of Steely Dan's Yacht Rock Masterpiece," Yacht Rock, November 20, 2017, http://www.yachtrock.com/captainsblog/2017/11/9/gaucho-how-steely-dans-highly-anticipated-yacht-rock-masterpiece-wasdestined-to-implode; Michael Heaton, "David Spiro, Artist Manager, Talks About What Went On Behind the Scenes with the Eagles—Exclusive Interview," *Plain Dealer*, July 7, 2013, https://www.cleveland.com/popmusic/2013/07/david-spero artist-manager tal.html.

243. Frederic Dannen, *Hit Men: Power Brokers and Fast Money Inside the Music Business* (Knopf Doubleday Publishing Group, 1990), 135.

244. Frederic Dannen, *Hit Men: Power Brokers and Fast Money Inside the Music Business* (Knopf Doubleday Publishing Group, 1990), 232.

245. Alex Isenstadt, "RNC Finance Chair Steve Wynn Resigns After Sexual Harassment Allegations," *Politico*, January 27, 2018, https://www.politico.com/story/2018/01/27/steve-wynn-resign-rnc-finance-chair-sexual-misconduct-accusations-373768.

246. Michael Jackson, *Moonwalk* (Crown/Archetype, 2009), Kindle locations 1412–14.

247. For the story of how Michael bought the ATV catalogue riddled with Beatles songs and John Branca's role in that purchase, see Zack O'Malley Greenburg, "Media and Entertainment: Buying The Beatles: Inside Michael Jackson's Best Business Bet," *Forbes*, June 2, 2014, https://www.forbes.com/sites/zackomalleygreenburg/2014/06/02/buying-the-beatles-inside-michael-jacksons-best-business-bet/2/#5a5628da62de 4-6-2018. See also: Zack O'Malley Greenburg, *Michael Jackson, Inc.: The Rise, Fall, and Rebirth of a Billion-Dollar Empire* (Atria Books, June 3, 2014).

248. Johnnie L. Roberts, "How Michael Jackson Nearly Lost His Prized Music Catalog," the *Wrap*, May 5, 2011, https://www.thewrap.com/michael-jackson-1-can-john-branca-save-jackson-again-22420/.

249. Dan Rys, "A Brief History of the Ownership of the Beatles Catalog," *Billboard*, January 20, 2017, https://www.billboard.com/articles/columns/rock/7662519/beatles-catalog-paul-mccartney-brief-history-ownership.

250. Johnnie L. Roberts, "How Michael Jackson Nearly Lost His Prized Music Catalog," the *Wrap*, May 5, 2011, https://www.thewrap.com/michael-jackson-1-can-john-branca-save-jackson-again-22420/.

251. J. Randy Taraborrelli, *Michael Jackson: The Magic, the Madness, the Whole Story, 1958-2009* (Grand Central Publishing, 2010).

252. J. Randy Taraborrelli, *Michael Jackson: The Magic, the Madness, the Whole Story, 1958-2009* (Grand Central Publishing, 2010).

253. J. Randy Taraborrelli, *Michael Jackson: The Magic, the Madness, the Whole Story, 1958-2009* (Grand Central Publishing, 2010).

254. Frederic Dannen, *Hit Men: Power Brokers and Fast Money Inside the Music Business* (Knopf Doubleday Publishing Group, 1990), 137–138.

255. Sandra Salmans, "The King of Records at CBS," *New York Times*, January 22, 1984, https://www.nytimes.com/1984/01/22/business/the-king-of-records-at-cbs.html.

256. Frederic Dannen, *Hit Men: Power Brokers and Fast Money Inside the Music Business* (Knopf Doubleday Publishing Group, 1990), 138.

257. Jeff Wilson, "Jackson's Victory Tour a Draw," UPI, December 9, 1984, https://www.upi.com/Archives/1984/12/09/Jacksons-victory-tour-a-draw/2586471416400/.

258. Jon Pareles, "Concert: Jacksons at Giants Stadium," *New York Times*, July 30, 1984, https://www.nytimes.com/1984/07/30/arts/concert-jacksons-at-giants-stadium.html.

259. Ellan Cates, "Piano-Playing Rock Superstar Billy Joel Suffered a Fractured Right," UPI, April 16, 1982, https://www.upi.com/Archives/1982/04/16/Piano-playing-rock-superstar-Billy-Joel-suffered-a-fractured-right/9931387781200/.

260. Bryan Wawzenek, "35 Years Ago: Billy Joel Injures Both Hands in Motorcycle Accident," *Ultimate Classic Rock*, April 15, 2017, http://ultimateclassicrock.com/billy-joel-motorcycle-accident/.

261. Bryan Wawzenek, "35 Years Ago: Billy Joel Injures Both Hands in Motorcycle Accident," *Ultimate Classic Rock*, April 15, 2017, http://ultimateclassicrock.com/billy-joel-motorcycle-accident/.

262. Bryan Wawzenek, "35 Years Ago: Billy Joel Injures Both Hands in Motorcycle Accident," *Ultimate Classic Rock*, April 15, 2017, http://ultimateclassicrock.com/billy-joel-motorcycle-accident/.

263. Michael Jackson, *Moonwalk* (Crown/Archetype, 2009).

264. Kenneth L. Davis et al., *The Emotional Foundations of Personality: A Neurobiological and Evolutionary Approach* (W. W. Norton and Company, 2018).

265. "Child Sexual Abuse Accusations Against Michael Jackson," Wikipedia, https://en.wikipedia.org/wiki/1993_child_sexual_abuse_accusations_against_Michael_Jackson.

266. J. Randy Taraborrelli, *Michael Jackson: The Magic, the Madness, the Whole Story, 1958-2009* (Grand Central Publishing, 2010).

267. "Thomas W. Sneddon Jr.," Wikipedia, https://en.wikipedia.org/wiki/Thomas_W._Sneddon_Jr.

268. David Menconi, "Peter Frampton, 'Frampton Comes Alive!' (1976), in 50 Greatest Live Albums of All Time," *Rolling Stone*, April 29, 2015, https://www.rollingstone.com/music/lists/50-greatest-live-albums-of-all-time-20150429/peter-frampton-frampton-comes-alive-1976-20150427 4-7-2018.

269. "Frampton Comes Alive!," Wikipedia, https://en.wikipedia.org/wiki/Frampton_Comes_Alive!.

270. Ian Halperin, "How the King of Pop Made $1.5 billion . . . Over His Dead Body: Five Years on, Michael Jackson's Posthumous Fortune Has Broken All Records. Now This Brilliant Report Asks, Who Is Making a Mint from His Death?," *Daily Mail*, June 7, 2014, http://www.dailymail.co.uk/news/article-2651584/How-king-pop-1-5billion-dead-body-Five-years-Michael-Jacksons-posthumous-fortune-broken-records-Now-brilliant-report-asks-IS-making-mint-death.html.

271. Gil Kaufman, "The Michael Jackson Estate's Billion-Dollar Turnaround: From $500 Million in Debt to $500 Million in Cash," *Billboard*, March 15, 2016, https://www.billboard.com/articles/business/7262698/michael-jackson-estate-billion-dollar-turnaround-sony-atv.

272. Gil Kaufman, "The Michael Jackson Estate's Billion-Dollar Turnaround: From $500 Million in Debt to $500 Million in Cash," *Billboard*, March 15, 2016, https://www.billboard.com/articles/business/7262698/michael-jackson-estate-billion-dollar-turnaround-sony-atv.

273. Mark Kemp, "Sam Cooke," RollingStone.com, https://www.rollingstone.com/music/artists/sam-cooke/biography.

274. Gavin Edwards, "Bobby Womack (1944–2014)," *Rolling Stone*, June 28, 2014, https://www.rollingstone.com/music/news/bobby-womack-1944-2014-20140628.

275. "Womack & Womack," Wikipedia, https://en.wikipedia.org/wiki/Womack_%26_Womack.

276. Greg Lukianoff and Jonathan Haidt, *The Coddling of the American Mind* (Penguin, 2018), 103.

277. Nick Spitzer, "The Story of Woody Guthrie's 'This Land Is Your Land,'" NPR Music, February 15, 2012, https://www.npr.org/2000/07/03/1076186/this-land-is-your-land.

INDEX

ABC Radio: advertising for, 27–28; *Jesus Christ Superstar* debut on, 74–75

ABC Records: artist ambassador work for, 97; black music/artists snub from, 95–96, 131, 234; dissolution of, 100–101; firing from, 100–101, 328, 342; G&W music acquisition by, 93–95; leadership change in, 100–101; offices at, 95, 187; publicity work with, x, 95–100, 102–3, 187; talent scout for, 187

AC/DC, 59–60, 334, 335, 367

adolescence. *See* childhood and adolescence

Aerosmith, 111–12, 195, 335

African benefits. *See* Band Aid; Live Aid; "We Are the World"

African music: Stewart Copeland influenced by, 161; trance rituals history in, 130–31

African starvation and violence. *See* Ethiopia; Hutu-Tutsi violence

Air Supply, 183, 185

Aldrin, Buzz, 6, 350–51, 376

Alvin and the Chipmunks, 163

Ambrosio, Nancy, 179

Amnesty International, 2, 149–50, 299

A&M Records, 157–59, 173, 174

androgyny, 49–50, 63

Ansen, David, 255

anthems, 43, 122, 215–16, 371, 377, 379

Anthony, Dee, 59–60, 367–68

A&P. *See* Great Atlantic and Pacific Tea Company

Apollo Theater, 124, 131, 288, 352

Arden, Don, 183–85

Argentina, 215–16

art direction: for *Circus*, 50; for Jacksons, 5–6, 339; magazine industry notice of early, 24, 27; Victory Tour, 5–6

Art Direction (magazine), 6, 27

Artists United Against Apartheid, 299

art nouveau, 39–70

art studio. *See* Cloud Studio

Asia, 292

astronauts, 6, 350–51, 376

atheism, 12, 380

Atlantic Records, 73, 133–34, 374

attorneys: CBS Records president background as, 100; for Michael Jackson, 357–58, 368–69; Michael Jackson sexual crucifixion profiting, 364; moral depravity of, 362; music industry, 120, 144, 191, 357–58, 368–69

ATV publishing, 357–58

Aucoin, Bill: cocaine problem for, 306–7, 308; Billy Idol management by, 305–6; KISS management by, 209, 306

audience: aging of, 246–47; black artists loyalty to black, 340–41; *Circus*, 35–36, 66, 104, 273; female, behavior of, 42–44, 45, 71, 116; Great Sex Switch with, 45–47; Michael Jackson commitment to, 349–50, 354; loyal, impact of, 276; magazine, study of, 35–36; male magazine, 36; for Bob Marley, 218; for Bette Midler, 195; motivation and dynamics with, 168, 195; 1960s music and male, 45–46, 47; rap, 271–73; of Rolling Stones relation to gender, 45–47, 71; sex and violence attracting magazine, 33, 35–36, 66; ZZ Top, size, 107, 112; ZZ Top female, 116

Avalon, Frankie, 44

Azoff, Irving: aggressive competition from, 210–11; concert circuit control of, 209; drugs used in artist control tactics of, 209, 210–11, 368; information leaks to press tactic of, 337, 355–56; Michael Jackson manipulation by, 356–59; moral depravity of, 210, 355, 356, 358–59; star-making power of, 206, 209–10, 356, 358; Styx management by, 209–11, 354; Victory Tour involvement of, 354–56, 357, 358–59

Badfinger, 38

Bailey, Jerry, 90

Baker, Susan, 333, 335

Baldwin, James, 97–98

Band Aid, 150, 257, 298–99, 379

Bangladesh, concert for, 37–38, 379

Bannister, Roger, 85

Barnes, Nicky, 131, 271

Baxter, Cleve, 31–32

Bay of Pigs, 58

Beard, Frank, 107, 110, 112. *See also* ZZ Top

Beard, Henry, 29

Beatles, 17; black music inspiration for, 44–45, 96; Capitol Records success with, 73; catalogue, Michael Jackson acquisition of, 357–58; Decca Records rejection of, 104; early pop music of, 18, 47; female audience behavior with, 45; male audience needs with, 46–47; manager of, 133; publisher royalties from songs of, 126; subculture voice with, 18–19

Beck, Jeff, 149

Bee Gees, 133–34, 184–85, 198, 275

Belafonte, Harry, 128–29, 133, 225, 257

benefit concerts: Amnesty International, 149; Band Aid, 150, 257, 298–99, 379; Bangladesh, 37–38, 379; Farm Aid, 289, 299, 379; Live Aid, 296, 297–99; John Cougar Mellencamp, 289–90; Secret Policeman's Ball, 149, 299; "We Are the World," 150, 184, 257–58, 295–99, 379

Bennett, Alvin, 163

Beverly Hills Hotel, 57, 58, 193

Big Business (film), 321, 322–23

Bill Haley and the Comets, 104

birthday (of Bloom, H.), 1

black mob/mafia, 131, 271

black music/artists: ABC Records snub of, 95–96, 131, 234; bank lending for, 270–71; Beatles inspired by, 44–45, 96; black audience loyalty from, 340–41; black newspaper publicity for, 144–45; black staffers for handling, 234; *Circus* audience and, 104, 273; coalminers singing culture and, 372; crossover success with, 231, 235; evolution in attitudes on, 273; gods inside and, 45, 125, 130–31; jazz and history of, 39–40, 41; origins, study of, 130–31; Elvis Presley influenced by, 43, 44–45, 96; publicity success with, 131, 144–45; radio stations focusing on, 218–19, 248, 288; rap appeal and audience and, 271–73; Rastafarianism influence for, 140; Rolling Stones inspired by, 44–45, 96; segregation encountered with, 129; Danny Sims management of, 225–26; soul and, 39–40, 45; subcultures, battle between, 164, 218; time management of, 127, 166; Warner

Bros Records handling of, 234, 248; whites adoption of, 40–41; Wolfman Jack playing of, 108, 273; ZZ Top influenced by, 109. *See also specific artists*

Black Orpheus (film), 98

black riots (1960s), 225–26

Black Sabbath, 183, 185

black underclass and ghettos, 271–72

Black United Fund, 231

Blackwell, Chris: background of, 137–38, 140; Island Records founding and leadership of, 141, 149; Bob Marley management by, 217–21, 223, 224, 226; publicity work with, 141, 149, 371; Rastafarian immersion for, 140; reggae beginnings and, 140, 217; talent scout ability of, 141–42

Blake, William, 6

Blonstein, Marshall, 141

Bloom, Howard. *See specific topics*

Bloom, Linda (wife), 30–31, 33, 69, 105, 119; cat rescues of, 242–43; graduate school threat to relationship with, 24–25; hometown, 273

blues music, 97

Bogart, Neil, 191–92

Bogdanovich, Peter, 82–83, 123, 369

"Bohemian Rhapsody," 213

booking strategies: control over, 288; of Ian Copeland, 157–59; Bill Ham lessons in, 107, 167, 189, 192, 306

books (by Bloom, H.): *The Genius of the Beast*, 65, 73, 77, 93, 191, 284; *God Problem*, 12, 34; *How I Accidentally Started the Sixties*, 14, 17; *The Lucifer Principle*, 155, 379

Boston Globe (newspaper), 343, 353

Boston Herald (newspaper), 343, 348, 353

Bowie, David, 209, 257, 265; androgyny appeal of, 49; *Circus* covering, 50; fashion/fashion designers for, 64

Boy Scouts of America, 26, 142

Bramley, Peter, 23, 25–29

Branca, John, 357–58, 368–69

Brand X, 151

Braswell, Ty, 208

Bravo (magazine), 34–35, 332

Breakfast in America (album), 173

Bridges, Alvenia, 146, 326

Brill Building, 179–80, 225

Brinkley, Christie, 313–14

Brinkley, John, 108

TRAC
FAMILY

CH00661403

L. G. Pine is an internationally recognized authority on
genealogy, a former editor of *Burke's Peerage* and
Burke's Landed Gentry, and the author of more than
thirty books, including *The Genealogist's Encyclopaedia*
and works on Norman ancestry, heraldry and the
Scottish clans. A professional researcher, he has traced
almost one thousand years of his own family history, to
Cornish, Welsh, French and ultimately Spanish origins.

TEACH YOURSELF BOOKS

Also by L. G. Pine

TRACE YOUR FAMILY HISTORY

L. G. Pine

TEACH YOURSELF BOOKS

Hodder and Stoughton

For Vanessa Edith Marjorie Pine

First published 1984
Second impression 1986

British Library Cataloguing in Publication Data

Pine, L. G.
Trace your family history.—(Teach
yourself books)
1. Great Britain—Genealogy
I. Title
929'.1'0941   CS414

ISBN 0 340 35654 5

Printed and bound in Great Britain for
Hodder and Stoughton Educational,
a division of Hodder and Stoughton Ltd,
Mill Road, Dunton Green, Sevenoaks, Kent,
by Richard Clay (The Chaucer Press) Ltd,
Bungay, Suffolk.

Contents

Illustrations

1

How to Begin

Introduction

Perhaps you have often wished that you knew more about your ancestors – where your family originated, how you acquired the mental and physical characteristics which mark you as different from your fellows. It is a natural desire, yet you may have done nothing about it, probably for one or both of two reasons – the question of expense or the idea that pedigrees are the concern of high and mighty folk.

As to expense, this depends very much upon your method of working: whether you do the work yourself or employ someone else to do it. In the latter case, the professional worker, like all other workers, has to be paid for his labour. It should be realised, too, that his labour may result in nothing, if the records are either deficient or not available. For instance, in one case of a man whose grandfather was abandoned as an infant, an exhaustive inquiry ended with the fact that the records of the Foundling Hospital in question had been destroyed by bombing during the Second World War. A hard fact of genealogical research.

If, on the other hand, you are carrying out the research yourself, then you supply the time and labour. The expenses will be those of any other hobby which you pursue because you are interested in it. There are official fees and charges. Owing to inflation these have risen steeply, but this is simply in keeping with all other expenses.

The other deterrent to research – the belief that it is only people like kings, dukes and earls who possess pedigrees – is completely wrong. A former Garter King of Arms once said that pedigrees are not for nobs or snobs but for *people*. Remember the remarks about the Browns at the beginning of *Tom Brown's Schooldays*: that the story is not about the St Maurs or De Veres who led armies or made laws, but about the ordinary folk, the Browns, who have served their country and their kin. In fact, as we shall see, there *are* no ordinary people, for the lines of ancestry are so criss-crossed that ordinary and out-of-the-ordinary folk are very much connected. One instance can suffice for the present. In the maternal ancestry of Queen Elizabeth II, there are a large number of kinsfolk who are plain misters and misses, as well as peers and ultimately royal descent from the kings of Scotland.

A moment's consideration will show that the expression 'an old family' is meaningless. All families must necessarily be of the same longevity. A correct phrasing is 'an old recorded family', since some families are able to trace their lines of descent further than others. All of us are descendants from Adam or, if they are preferred, from some of Dr Leakey's fabulous anthropological discoveries. There is an amusing and historically true incident when James VI of Scotland, on his way to become James I of England, was shown by his host the enormous Lumley pedigree. 'Mon', James exclaimed, 'now I know that Adam's surname was Lumley.'

We come then from the same progenitors, and to work backwards we begin with our parents. A word of warning: always work backwards, never the reverse. Many people find someone of the same surname living some 400 years ago. They assume that they must descend from him, and then work forwards trying to establish a link with themselves. It might work by accident in a very few cases, but in the vast majority it means labour in vain.

Suppose, for example, that your name is Buckmaster and that you know a little about your family – the name of your great-grandfather but nothing beyond that. You find that about 1650 there lived a celebrated man, Sir Henry Buckmaster. You decide that he must have been your ancestor and you work forward from him. He had six sons, so you have to follow up all their lines of descent, and then those of their children. After you have worked on this for a time you will probably find not the slightest sign that you are going to meet the progenitor of your great-grandfather. After all your labour you may be left high and dry, your only reward perhaps being the thanks of someone whose ancestry you have unwittingly uncovered. There may be no relationship between you and the seventeenth-century Buckmaster.

A recent instance which has come to my notice is that of an American family of Andrews which migrated from East Anglia in the seventeenth century. This family believed itself to be connected with the celebrated Anglican bishop, Lancelot Andrewes, who died in 1627. When it was pointed out that the Bishop was a bachelor, the inquirer suggested a possible descent from one of his brothers. Even so, among the recorded East Anglian families of Andrews, none shows a connection with the seventeenth-century emigrant, so all the work may have been done in vain.

Genealogical evidence

One little-discussed aspect of research concerns evidence. Evidence which is valid in genealogical research is of the same nature as that which is accepted in a court of law. In court, a child born in wedlock is *ipso facto* presumed to be the child of the husband of the marriage. Yet every genealogist must have thought, in looking at a long pedigree, did feminine frailty never occur? However, we have to accept the official evidence and allow a woman what Samuel Butler in *Hudibras* calls 'the clergy of her belly'. The only alternative is to copy the ancient German practice, and trace through the mother only.

We must stick to the principles of the law courts: documents which are official. Birth certificates, wills and entries from parish registers are records which have either been ordered to be kept by law or, in the case of wills, have been kept by private volition and have afterwards been hallowed by the law's acceptance.

Social class

Every searcher into his family history must dismiss modern prejudices against class. Equality is one of the slogans of the twentieth century but it has no relevance in history, nor indeed today, for as one class declines or disappears, another takes its place. Thus the tracing of your ancestry depends on the period to be examined.

When Lord Macaulay began his *History of England*, he had to cope with the problem of population in the England of Charles II. He relied largely on the researches of Gregory King (1648–1712), who estimated that the population of England and Wales approached 5,200,000. King considered that one-tenth of the population was made up of servants. Nor were these the dear old retainers so beloved of romantic writers, but people engaged by the year at fairs and markets, and therefore moving about frequently.

Two useful sources of help for the beginner are (*a*) a family Bible, which can save the search for some certificates, and (*b*) any elderly member of the family, whose knowledge of it should be tapped before it is too late. But you must begin with your parents. I cannot better the sound advice given in an official leaflet issued from the General Register Office at St Catherine's House in Kingsway, London: '. . . if a person wishes to trace the record of his father's birth but does not know where he was born, it may be necessary first to search for the record of the father's marriage. . . . A certificate of the marriage should give the bridegroom's age and the name of his father, and so will give the starting point for tracing . . .'. Therefore, if you do not already possess your parents' marriage certificate, you should obtain it.

The General Registers

Since 1 July 1837 all births, marriages and deaths in England and Wales have been by law registered. Thus, for the great majority of people now living in England and Wales, it is possible through the registers at St Catherine's House to get back to the marriage of their great-grandparents or, in the case of people born since 1940, to their great-great-grandparents. Four or five generations forms a very respectable beginning to a pedigree.

St Catherine's House is the repository of the registers of births and marriages. These records were formerly kept at Somerset House, in the Strand, London: references to Somerset House in older works must now be translated as pertaining to St Catherine's.

The records of deaths from 1 July 1837, formerly at Alexandra House, are now also kept at St Catherine's.

These changes are only two of the many alterations in reference to records made by successive British governments in recent years. Most of these changes are not to the advantage of the inquirer, but

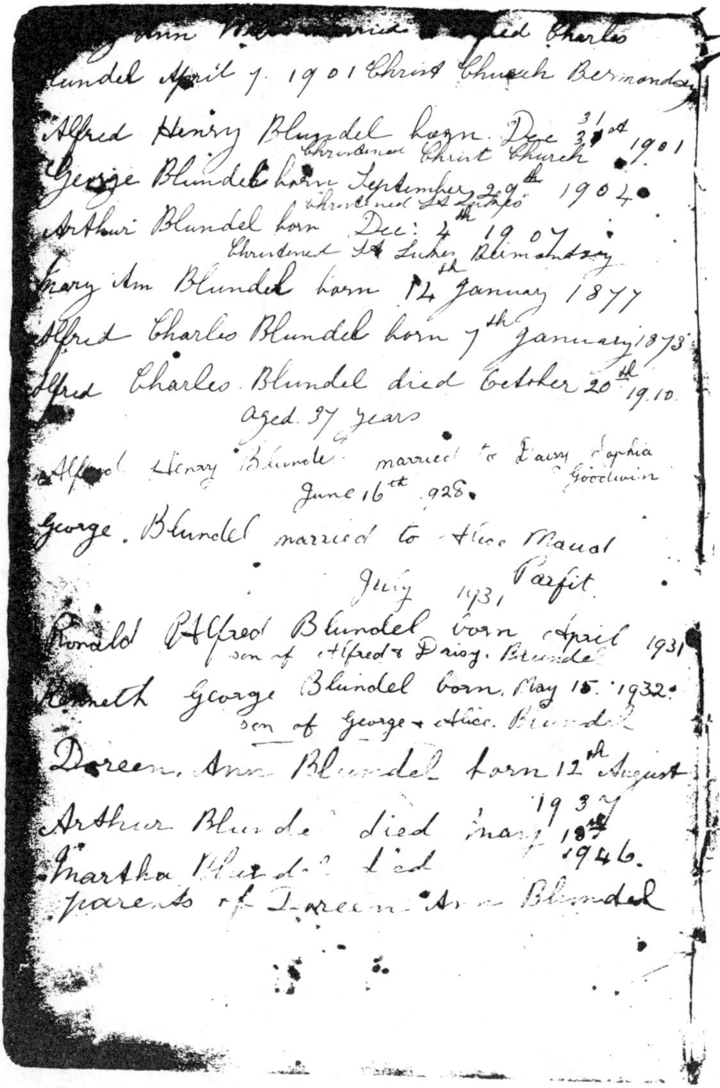
[illegible] Ann [illegible] married Charles
Blundel April 7. 1901 Christ Church Bermondsey
Alfred Henry Blundel born Dec 31st 1901
christened Christ Church
George Blundel born September 29th 1904
christened St Lukes
Arthur Blundel born Dec: 4th 1907
christened St Lukes Bermondsey
Mary Ann Blundel born 14th January 1877
Alfred Charles Blundel born 7th January 1873
Alfred Charles Blundel died October 20th 1910
Aged 37 years
Alfred Henry Blundel married to Daisy Sophia Goodwin
June 16th 1928.
George Blundel married to Alice Maud Parfit
July 1931
Ronald Alfred Blundel born April 1931
son of Alfred & Daisy Blundel
Kenneth George Blundel born May 15 1932
son of George & Alice Blundel
Doreen Ann Blundel born 12th August 1937
Arthur Blundel died May 18th 1946.
Martha Blundel died
parents of Doreen Ann Blundel

An extract from a Family Bible

Certificate of Marriage.

Registration District *Manor*

192__. Marriage solemnized at *St. Paul's Church*
of *Roath* in the County of *Middlesbar* in the Parish of *Middlesbar*

Columns:—							
No.	When Married.	Name and Surname.	Age.	Condition.	Rank or Profession.	Residence at the time of Marriage.	Father's Name and Surname.	Rank or Profession of Father.
1	June 12th 192_	Joseph Thomas Buchanan	24	Bachelor	Tiler	12 Tennant Place, West Bromwich	Joseph Buchanan	Tiler
	1921	Elsie Kate Brakes	23	Spinster		8 Pulfriction Road, West Roath	William Brakes	Labourer

Married in the *Parish Church* according to the Rites and Ceremonies of the *Established Church* by *Banns* by me,

| This marriage was solemnized between us, | Joseph Thomas Buchanan Elsie Kate Brakes | in the presence of us, | William Brakes Dorothy Brakes |

	A. W. W. Nicholson Vicar

I, *A. W. W. Nicholson, Vicar* of *Roath* in the County of *Middlesbar* do hereby certify that this is a true Copy of the Entry No. — 21 — in the Marriage Register Books of the said *Parish*

Witness my Hand this — 12 — day of — June — 192_

A. W. W. Nicholson Vicar

An original Marriage Certificate, 1921

the present arrangements at St Catherine's House are an improvement on those formerly available at Somerset House.

The separate records of births, marriages and deaths are kept in huge volumes, in alphabetical order, quarter by quarter (by date of registration). It is now much easier to manipulate them than it was on the narrow antiquated ledges at Somerset House. This is not to say that the visitor to St Catherine's House will find the task easy. There has been an enormous increase in interest in genealogy in recent years, and it is sometimes necessary to queue to get into St Catherine's.

Even so, you will find it much cheaper to conduct your inquiries in person than to write for a particular certificate. You can put in an application while you are visiting St Catherine's and return in a few days to collect the copy document, or you can arrange for it to be posted to you. Here, too, the increase in the number of inquiries has resulted in inevitable delays in sending certificates through the post.

The increase in fees charged for certificates can make research an expensive business. Families in the nineteenth century were much larger than those of today: a fully worked out pedigree, with birth certificates for each son and daughter in a family, could easily amount to £60–£100 in one generation, according to whether application is made through the post or in person.

Still, for pedigree purposes, it is essential that you should obtain (*a*) your parents' marriage certificate, (*b*) your father's birth certificate, (*c*) the marriage certificate of your grandparents and the birth and death certificates of your grandfather, and (*d*) similar details for your great-grandparents or – as indicated above – your great-great-grandparents.

I have assumed that you are beginning your research with a knowledge of your parents and some rudimentary details of your grandparents. Details of this nature can often be obtained through contact with an older relative, from family Bibles and from letters and documents of various kinds.

I have also been referring to tracing the male line. You, of course, may prefer to follow up your mother's family or other female lines of ancestry; or you may wish to trace all lines of ancestry on both male and female sides. If the latter course is followed, the size of pedigree laterally will be greater than longitudinally. It is entirely a matter of personal choice.

CERTIFIED COPY OF AN ENTRY OF BIRTH

GIVEN AT THE GENERAL REGISTER OFFICE, LONDON

Application Number BB57

BIRTH in the Sub-district of St Paul Hammersmith in the County of Middlesex

REGISTRATION DISTRICT Fulham

1876.

No.	When and where born	Name, if any	Sex	Name and surname of father	Name, surname and maiden surname of mother	Occupation of father	Signature, description and residence of informant	When registered	Signature of registrar	Name entered after registration
Columns:—	1	2	3	4	5	6	7	8	9	10*
30	Sixth February 1876 Kilmaine Road, Mead, Noth	Joseph Buchanan	Boy	William George Buchanan	Emma Elizabeth Buchanan formerly Williams	Carpenter	H. G. Buchanan father & Linns, Clothes Kilmaine Road, Noth Hammersmith	Eighteenth March 1876	William A. Cff Registrar	

CERTIFIED to be a true copy of an entry in the certified copy of a Register of Births in the District above mentioned.
Given at the GENERAL REGISTER OFFICE, LONDON, under the Seal of the said Office, the 25th day of April 19 84

BXA 942693

This certificate is issued in pursuance of the Births and Deaths Registration Act 1953. Section 34 provides that any certified copy of an entry purporting to be sealed or stamped with the seal of the General Register Office shall be received as evidence of the birth or death to which it relates without any further or other proof of the entry, and no certified copy purporting to have been given in the said Office shall be of any force or effect unless it is sealed or stamped as aforesaid.

CAUTION:—It is an offence to falsify a certificate or to make or knowingly use a false certificate or a copy of a false certificate intending it to be accepted as genuine to the prejudice of any person or to possess a certificate knowing it to be false without lawful authority.

*See note overleaf

Form A502M Dd 8264376 100M 6/83 Mcr (301297)

A copy Birth Certificate, 1876

(In this case the child was born illegitimate but took his father's surname.)

CERTIFIED COPY OF AN ENTRY OF MARRIAGE

GIVEN AT THE GENERAL REGISTER OFFICE, LONDON

Application Number. B6659

1894. Marriage solemnized at St Cloud Ongworts in the Parish of St Marylebone in the County of London

No.	When Married.	Name and Surname.	Age.	Condition.	Rank or Profession.	Residence at the time of Marriage.	Father's Name and Surname.	Rank or Profession of Father.
281	Eighth July 184	Joseph Buchanan	20	Bachelor	Tiler	7 Crawford St	William Buchanan	Carpenter
		Julia Elizabeth Russell	19	Spinster	Servant	9 Crawford St	Alfred Russell	Tiler

Married in the White Church according to the Rites and Ceremonies of the Established Church, by or after Banns by me,

This Marriage was solemnized between us,

{ Joseph Buchanan
{ Julia Elizabeth Russell

in the Presence of us,

H Brugge
R J A Smith

H Brugge
Edith L Brugge

CERTIFIED to be a true copy of an entry in the certified copy of a register of Marriages in the Registration District of Marylebone

Given at the GENERAL REGISTER OFFICE, LONDON, under the Seal of the said Office, the 25th day of April 19 . 89

MX 835726

This certificate is issued in pursuance of section 65 of the Marriage Act 1949. Sub-section 3 of that section provides that any certified copy of an entry purporting to be sealed or stamped with the seal of the General Register Office shall be received as evidence of the marriage to which it relates without any further or other proof of the entry, and no certified copy purporting to have been given in the said Office shall be of any force or effect unless it is sealed or stamped as aforesaid.

CAUTION:— It is an offence to falsify a certificate or to make or knowingly use a false certificate or a copy of a false certificate intending it to be accepted as genuine to the prejudice of any person, or to possess a certificate knowing it to be false without lawful authority.

Form A513MX   DM 8264404   65M   1/83   Mcr(300528)

A copy Marriage Certificate, 1894

(The birth and death certificates show that the bridegroom's age was in fact 18, not 20 as stated.)

CERTIFIED COPY OF AN ENTRY OF DEATH

Given at the GENERAL REGISTER OFFICE, LONDON.

Application Number. 8657

REGISTRATION DISTRICT Croydon

1960 DEATH in the Sub-district of Croydon South in the County Borough of Croydon

No.	When and where died	Name and surname	Sex	Age	Occupation	Cause of death	Signature, description, and residence of informant	When registered	Signature of registrar
Columns:—	1	2	3	4	5	6	7	8	9
7	second September 1960 Purley and District War Memorial Hospital Purley Croydon	Joseph Buchanan	Male	84 years	of 12 Tamworth Place Croydon, Surrey Retired File Fixer	Pulmonary Embolism Thrombo phlebitis of veins of left leg following fracture of left ankle caused by a fall Verdict Misadventure P.M.	Certificate received from J.W.Bennett Coroner for County Borough of Croydon Inquest held 8 September 1960	Ninth September 1960	J.H.Sturdee Registrar

CERTIFIED to be a true copy of an entry in the certified copy of a Register of Deaths in the District above mentioned.
Given at the GENERAL REGISTER OFFICE, LONDON, under the Seal of the said Office, the 25th day of April 1984—

DA 773626

This certificate is issued in pursuance of the Births and Deaths Registration Act 1953.
Section 34 provides that any certified copy of an entry purporting to be sealed or stamped with the seal of the General Register Office shall be received as evidence of the birth or death to which it relates without any further or other proof of the entry, and no certified copy purporting to have been given in the said Office shall be of any force or effect unless it is sealed or stamped as aforesaid.
CAUTION:—Any person who (1) falsifies any of the particulars on this certificate, or (2) uses a falsified certificate as true, knowing it to be false, is liable to prosecution.

Form A504 Dd. 8264355 20m 10/81 Mc(3160)

A copy Death Certificate, 1960

Pedigrees begin at St Catherine's House. A leaflet is available for visitors to the General Register Office entitled 'Brief Notes for Visitors'. After some preliminary remarks there is a section headed 'Family Trees'. The purpose of the leaflet is to point out what I have outlined above – that pedigrees begin with one's parents and therefore must start with the Registers at St Catherine's.

Registration in Scotland and Ireland

Registration of births, marriages and deaths began in Scotland in 1855. Application should be made to the Registrar General, New Register House, Edinburgh EH1 3YT (see Chapter 10).

In Ireland, registration began in 1864. Application should be made to the Registrar General, Custom House, Dublin 1, or, for Northern Ireland, to the Registrar General, Oxford House, 49–55 Chichester Street, Belfast BT1 4HL (see Chapter 12).

Surnames

Before going on, a word of caution should be given on the subject of surnames. Identity of surname does not necessarily denote identity of family.

There are two principles to be observed.

First, the very existence and usage of surnames is a western and European phenomenon.

The surname was not much used among the Greeks – though we do find such clan forms as Peistradae – nor among the Hebrews, as is quite clear from the Bible. In the second century BC, among the Jews, we have reference to the Maccabees or the Hasmoneans, who were descended from Hasmon, the ancestor of Judas Maccabeus, but as a rule the surname is not found in antiquity apart from the Roman usage.

A Roman normally had three names. Thus Caius Julius Caesar consists of the *praenomen*, corresponding to our Christian or forename; this was followed by the clan name, and last came the *cognomen* or surname.

In Britain, after the fall of the Roman Empire, surnames fell into disuse. By the time of the Norman Conquest (1066–73) there were no surnames in England.

Three prominent men bore the Christian name of Harold. They

were distinguished by sobriquets in two cases: Harold Hardrada (Hard Counsel) and Harold Harefoot. In the third case, King Harold II who was killed at Hastings, we have an incipient surname as he was referred to as Harold Godwinson.

Some surnames were brought into England by the Norman invaders and some of these have lasted, for example Curzon from Courson in Normandy. Otherwise it was only very gradually that surnames were adopted in England and in Europe generally until, by the thirteenth century, the practice had become fairly common.

The second principle regarding surnames is their variation. This is easily understood. Scribes – in this context usually clerics – were required to take down names from people who were for the most part illiterate. The names were very often written in Latin. As the men concerned could not spell, the scribe had to write according to the man's pronunciation of his name. This fact accounts for the large number of variations in the spelling of surnames over several centuries, until at least the eighteenth, and is of practical importance to the genealogist. We have only to read a seventeenth-century work to see the variations of spelling of even ordinary words. All works from Chaucer and Langland up to Shakespeare and Spenser have their spelling modernised in the current editions. In fact, it was due to Dr Johnson's famous *Dictionary*, published in 1755, that English spelling became standardised.

As surnames were not necessarily fixed, they were subject to change. The term *alias* now has a pejorative meaning, associated with persons brought before the criminal courts. Yet in the sixteenth and seventeenth centuries men of the highest integrity often used aliases. An interesting example is given in Keble's edition of Hooker's *Ecclesiastical Polity* (6th edition, 1874) which shows a short pedigree of the Hookers alias Vowel. Similar, too, is the signature of Oliver Williams or Cromwell in writing to his kinsman, the Archbishop of York. The real name of the Cromwell family in the male line was Williams: after the execution of Thomas Cromwell, Henry VIII suggested that Sir Richard Williams, the brother-in-law of the deceased, should assume the name of Cromwell. It was from this Sir Richard Cromwell (alias Williams) that Oliver Cromwell descended, being thus only a collateral descendant of Thomas Cromwell.

Surnames, then, are a very unreliable guide to family connections. To take an extreme example: of the 200,000 families of Smith in England only two take their name from the place of Smeeth in Kent. The remainder bear a surname of occupation, hence with small likelihood of genealogical identity.

In fiction, there is the example of Mr Stokes who had purchased some property with the name of D'Urberville. 'He considered', wrote Thomas Hardy, 'that D'Urberville looked and sounded well and D'Urberville accordingly was annexed to his own name for himself and his heirs eternally.' The pages of *Burke's Landed Gentry* and *Burke's Peerage* contain many instances of hyphenated names whose origin resembles that described in Hardy's novel.

Surnames are divisible into four classes:

1 Place names These have come into existence because the original bearer has left his birthplace. To distinguish him from the other innumerable Johns, Williams and Thomases, he was called John of Lavenham or Sudbury or Morden, etc. This habit was passed on and used by his descendants in many cases.

The opposite habit, of the place being called after the family – *vide* the Psalmist's remark 'they called the land after their own name' – is comparatively rare. It does occur in the west of England on a large scale; much less in other parts (one instance is the village of Thorpe Morieux in Suffolk). Thus in the counties of Devon and Somerset we get examples such as Curry Malet or Upton Pyne. In all these cases the first name is that of the original place, the second that of the foreign immigrant who settled there. Of course, in such cases the newcomer from France or Normandy did possess the surname which he gave to his land holding before he arrived in England. Most of the old county families in England or Scotland, however, took their surnames from their ancestral lands, as the Okeovers of Okeover in Staffordshire or the Swintons of Swinton in Berwickshire.

Many place names – such as Attlee (by the meadow) or Atwood – cannot now be identified because the exact place which bestowed the designation is lost.

2 Patronymics The second class of surnames is that of patronymics, of which there are an enormous number. They indicate whose son a man was, as in Watson, Wilson, Hopkinson, Hodgkinson,

Anderson, Thompson – a few specimens from a legion. The patronymic is the common form among the natives of the British Isles. The Highlanders have *Mac* = son of; the Irish, too, have *Mac* and the familiar *O'*; among the Welsh, *ap* meant 'son of' and has been merged so that it has become Parry, Plews, Price, etc.

3   Occupations   Here again is a huge collection such as Taylor, Glover, Cook, Butler, Butcher, Sadler, Baker. Names of this type sometimes belong to a high class of persons, like Despencer, the high steward of a great family. The name was originally spelt or pronounced *Del spens* or *atte Spence* (= larder). Names of this class come in a few instances from great feudal dignitaries like the Butlers, the Dukes of Ormond who were the chief Butlers of Ireland. Their duty was to hand the Sovereign his cup of wine; such menial services were regarded as privileges by the proudest nobles.

4   Nicknames   Nicknames form the fourth class of surnames. These were common in medieval times and some of these nicknames continued as surnames. For many centuries, even the kings of England were known by their nicknames. William the Conqueror was also known as William Bastard. William II was Rufus for his red hair. Henry I was called Beau Clerk because he had acquired some formal education. John was Lackland – as a younger son he had little land. Richard Coeur de Lion's sobriquet came from his undoubted bravery as a warrior. Edward I was Longshanks owing to his height. None of these nicknames has continued to the posterity of the bearers, but the name of one very notable family has lasted to our time: Scrope means crab, and the remote ancestor of this distinguished Norman house had a crablike walk.

Our ancestors were far from kindly in their bestowal of nicknames. Severe physical defects were made the subject of unpleasant nicknames, most of which probably died out because the unfortunate bearer did not propagate. But Foljambe has survived: it came from an ancestor who had a silly or useless leg. 'Old cripple foot' was the way in which our forthright and brutal ancestors stigmatised some poor fellow whose leg had been badly injured or who had been born a cripple.

Records from the Middle Ages feature names like Crypling, Handless, Onehand, Head, Neck, Mouth, Blind, Daft, Mutter and

Stutter. It is fortunate – at least for the happiness of the owners – that such nicknames have not survived.

Still other names point to some physical quality – Swift, Lightfoot, Strong, Strongitharm, Little, Lowe, Thin and Stout. Here, though, you should remember the vicissitudes of our spelling in past centuries. Coward has nothing to do with moral defects, but is a variant of 'cowherd'. Thynne, the surname of the Marquess of Bath, does not refer to any slenderness of body, but means simply 'at the inn'. My *Dictionary of Nicknames* (Routledge and Kegan Paul, 1984) is a useful reference guide.

The above comments are included simply as a warning to beginners to genealogical research. I have treated this subject in detail in my book *The Story of Surnames* (Country Life), now out of print but accessible in libraries.

English surnames

With English surnames the position is difficult owing to their great number. The best authority is P. H. Reaney's *A Dictionary of British Surnames* (Routledge and Kegan Paul), which deals very thoroughly with English names and is based throughout on Old English and medieval English scholarship. About 35,000 names are explained, but as there are possibly as many as 100,000 English surnames it is obvious that many have been omitted. Statements as to the meanings of names in older works are often quite inaccurate, since the correct etymology of names did not begin until the nineteenth century.

C. W. Bardsley's *English Surnames* (David and Charles Reprints) is another useful work.

Scottish and Irish surnames

Caution is also needed from the genealogical viewpoint in dealing with Highland Scottish and Irish surnames. I say advisedly Highland Scottish, because there is a great cleavage between Highland and Lowland people in Scotland. As we shall see in Chapter 10, what was known as the Highland Line stretched diagonally from the Perthshire hills to the Clyde. North of this line were the clans. To the south, the Lowlanders were closely akin to the English. Along the borders with England there were no clans, but families of the same name, like the Johnstons. It is only in the present century that clans have been discovered all over Scotland. As late as 1826, Sir Walter Scott stated that he did not know of clans outside the Highlands. In Frank Adams' book *The Clans, Septs and Regiments of the Scottish Highlands*, the clan map covers only the Highlands and leaves the Lowlands blank. The book was published in 1908. When the sixth edition was revised by Sir Thomas Innes of Learney in 1960 the clan map had advanced into the Lowlands which, instead of being left blank, were covered with the names of families. The more popular Scottish map-makers lost no time in colouring the whole of Scotland with clan divisions.

For this reason, there are thousands of people who bear names like MacMillan, Macintyre, Mackenzie, Macfarlane, etc., who would be hard put to show their ancestry beyond three or four generations. A case in point is that of former Prime Minister Harold Macmillan, descended from a Highland crofter but not a member of the clan chief's family.

The same consideration applies to such familiar Highland names as Mackintosh and Macpherson. THE MacKintosh and THE Mac-Pherson (note the capitals for the article) have their pedigrees recorded in *Burke's Landed Gentry*. But beside the Chief's family is gathered a multitude who took their surname, as they took their land and protection, from the Chief: they are by no means genealogically connected with his family, but have come at some past period under the umbrella of his protection.

The same principle applies to the Irish. Not every O'Con(n)or is connected by blood with the O'Conor Don (or Chief). The tribal principle has applied among these two Celtic peoples and the researcher must be on his guard not to assume that a line of family bearing a chief's name is allied to him by blood.

The clan system – and this applies to families of the name in the Scottish Lowlands – has resulted in comparatively few Highland surnames. All Scots surnames, Highland and Lowland, are listed and explained in Dr George Black's *The Surnames of Scotland* (published by New York Public Library), an invaluable work. For Irish surnames, the work to consult is Dr Edward MacLysaght's *The Surnames of Ireland* (Irish Universities Press). No Scots or Irish names are omitted from the two books.

Welsh surnames

Dealing with Welsh surnames, too, can be difficult. Right until the reign of Henry VIII, when by statutes in 1542 and 1547 Wales was united with England administratively, Wales was governed by its own old Celtic law. This included an equal distribution of property among a man's sons. Surnames were not used, but a Welshman would have on his lips 150–180 years of his pedigree. He was Rhys ap Morgan, ap Evan, ap Caradoc, ap Bleddin, ap Griffith ('ap' meaning 'son of'). When Henry VIII applied English laws and usage to Wales, the Welshman found that he had to have a surname and in most cases he made it a patronymic, using his father's Christian name. Hence the multitude of Evans, Jones and Williams in the Principality.

Those who are unfamiliar with old Welsh practice are often puzzled to note that some of the noblest families in Wales bear common surnames just like their servants or tenants. A short study of their pedigrees shows the assumption of the particular surname in the sixteenth or seventeenth century. But this historical accident has made the task of the searcher very difficult. Everyone in a village can be named Jones.

Changes of surname

A surname can be changed at the owner's pleasure. Sometimes a notice may be put in a newspaper to the effect that, for example, Mr William Smith intends in future to be known as William Addison. If, however, anyone wishes to register a change of name, this is done by deed poll, before a Commissioner for Oaths who is usually a solicitor. The deed poll may be enrolled in the Filing Department of the Central Office of the Supreme Court and must be advertised in the *London Gazette*.

Other ways of changing a surname are much more expensive than the above. Change can be made by Act of Parliament or by Royal Licence. The latter must be made through the College of Arms. This form of change arises through what is known as the name and arms clause in a will. Such a clause arises when a testator leaves his property (usually to a relative in the female line) on condition that the beneficiary is to assume the name and arms of the testator. The High Court requires proof that the change has been effected through the College of Arms.

Adopted children

At St Catherine's House, there is a register of adoptions which records the date of birth, the parents who adopted, the court which granted the adoption and the adoption order date. For further particulars of the real parentage, application can be made to the Court, but permission for the release of the information may not be granted. For obvious reasons, the position of those involved has been safeguarded by legislation.

Christian names

Owing to the presence in Britain of large numbers of non-Christians – Moslems, Jews, Hindus, etc. – the term *forename* is now common-ly used in official documents. In searching the records of former centuries great caution must be observed regarding unusual Christ-ian names. They may be a guide to identity of pedigree, but equally may have been bestowed for quite different reasons.

A source of frequent confusion in previous generations is the use of the same Christian name by more than one child in the same generation in the same family. The reason is the melancholy fact of the considerable infant mortality in the past. Two or even three Edwards in the same generation were so named because a child or children had died young.

A useful book is *The Oxford Dictionary of English Christian Names* compiled by E. G. Withycombe (Oxford, The Clarendon Press).

Having given this digression as a help to the inquirer, I would add the encouraging considerations briefly mentioned earlier: that many of the lines of ancestry in Britain do not run parallel but criss-cross. Otherwise it is obvious that in 1066 there would have been not one million, but hundreds of millions of people in Britain.

In conclusion, it should be noted that a number of records earlier than 1 July 1837 are held at the Public Record Office. After mentioning the parish registers (which we consider in Chapter 2) the official notice states: 'Records and registers of births, baptisms, deaths, burials and marriages were also kept by denominations other than the Church of England. These records are in the custody of the Keeper of Public Records, Public Record Office' (see Chap-ter 5). There are also other records in St Catherine's House, as we shall see in Chapter 9.

2

The Parish Registers and the Census

The parish registers

The next important stage in investigation is in the parish registers. They existed for 300 years before the General Registration in 1837. A certain amount of interest in the doings of its citizens was manifested in the Europe of the sixteenth and seventeenth centuries. Even earlier are the Spanish parish registers, the oldest of which date from the fourteenth century.

In England, the origin of the parish registers is interesting. In 1538, each parish was ordered to keep records of all baptisms, marriages and burials which occurred within its boundaries. Three years earlier, in 1535, Henry VIII by virtue of the Act of Supremacy had made himself the head on earth of the Church of England, thus displacing the Pope. Henry's chief minister had been Cardinal Wolsey and on the latter's fall, one of his closest assistants, Thomas Cromwell, was appointed by Henry to the perilous position of principal minister. Henry made Cromwell his Vicar General, mainly because he offered to the King an unscrupulous financial policy. It was Thomas Cromwell who ordered the keeping of the parish registers. His motives were much suspected by contemporaries, but would appear to have reflected the general trend in sixteenth- and seventeenth-century Europe to maintain national records.

The parish registers were not popular in country districts and considerable difficulty was experienced in getting them kept. Very few of the surviving parish registers begin in 1538: the majority date from the seventeenth century. Some are much better kept than others. Many have been lost through negligence, damp, fire and other accidents. But they are always a most valuable source of information.

Once you have discovered the birthplace of an ancestor, the parish registers can be consulted. Here the latest generation of inquirers have an advantage over their predecessors. Since the Second World War there has been a great development in County Record Offices (see Appendix 1). Very often the parish registers of the county have been deposited there. This, of course, spares the inquirer much tedious correspondence. It should be understood that the staff of the County Record Office cannot undertake research, but they do possess indices which will yield much valuable information. For instance, an inquiry at a County Record Office will often yield an extract from a parish register or from a census (see page 28) or it may provide pointers to other sources.

However, if the parish register is still in the possession of the incumbent of the parish, you must be prepared for what may be a protracted correspondence. The incumbent is a priest of the Church of England and as such has many duties which take precedence over genealogical inquiries.

A few practical hints based on long experience may be helpful. Address your letter to The Rector or The Vicar. His address can be obtained from *Crockford's Clerical Directory* which lists all Church of England parishes, with the incumbent's name. It is not advisable to write to the reverend gentleman whose name is given, as the entry may be out of date. Always include a stamped and addressed envelope for a reply. Some incumbents charge a fee, some do not, but it is always a good idea to make a small donation to church funds once you have received the information requested.

A few further points should be mentioned regarding the parish registers. The records can be difficult to decipher owing to the different style of writing in former times. This applies also, of course, to other documents which will be considered later. There are, however, guides to the handwriting of the sixteenth and seventeenth centuries. Some are published by the Essex Record Office. In cases of extreme difficulty, the County Record Offices usually keep lists of people who are searchers and who can assist in deciphering scripts. After 1650, the writing is often easier to read.

Also, in the early 1750s, the English calendar changed from the

BAPTISM CERTIFICATE.

Page 40

Baptism solemnized in the Parish of *Ashwick* in the Diocese of *Bath & Wells* and County of *Somerset.* in the Year 1828

| Alleged date of Birth. | When Baptised. | Child's Christian Name. | Parents' Names. | | Abode. | Quality, Trade, or Profession. | God-Parents' Names. | By whom the Sacrament was administered. |
			Christian.	Surname.				
—	1828 Aug 29	Elizabeth Dr. of	George + Elizabeth	Pine	Ashwick	Statherate	—	W. H. Quicke

I Certify, that the foregoing is a true Copy of the entry of the Baptism of *Elizabeth Pine* in the Register of Baptisms for the said

Parish of *Ashwick*

Dated this *29th* day of *January* 19 50

Signed *M. F. Ralph Bonner.*

A copy Baptism Certificate, 1828

Printed by J. B. SHEARS & SONS, 44 Sydney Street, Chelsea, S.W.1.

MARRIAGES SOLEMNISED IN THE PARISH OF HUNTSHAM
IN THE COUNTY OF   DEVON   IN THE YEAR   1824

DANIEL SAYER (BACHELOR)   OF THIS PARISH
      YEOMAN
AND ELIZABETH PINE   OF THE PARISH
      OF HOCKWORTHY,   SPINSTER
WERE MARRIED IN THIS CHURCH BY LICENCE WITH CONSENT OF
   PARENTS   THIS   FOURTH   DAY   OF   NOVEMBER
IN THE YEAR ONE THOUSAND, EIGHT HUNDRED AND TWENTY FOUR
   BY ME   HENRY BARKER   MINISTER   DANIEL SAYER
THIS MARRIAGE WAS SOLEMNISED BETWEEN US   ELIZABETH PINE
                        GEORGE PINE
IN THE PRESENCE OF   MARY T. PINE

NO. 19

This is a correct copy of the marriage register of the parish of
Huntsham, Devon for entry No. 19.

         (*signed*)
              Rector of Huntsham
                 (*date*)

An extract (transcript) from a parish register of marriages (1824)

I declare that the following is a true copy of the entry in the records of Ashbrittle Church in the county of Somerset.

(*signed*) Rector   (*date*)

Name	Abode	When buried	Age	By whom
NO. 189. ELIZABETH PINE	ASHBRITTLE	NOV 28 1834	6	JOHN TURNER

An extract (transcript) from a parish register of burials (1834)

(Old Style) Julian system – which started the year on 25 March – to the (New Style) Gregorian calendar, adopted in Scotland in 1660. The adjustment included the 'loss' of eleven days in September 1752; and some registers from this period have dates recorded in both forms.

Deficiency in parish registers 1645–60
While many parish registers begin later than 1538, there is one serious gap during the Civil War and the Commonwealth period. Between 1645 and 1660 there was almost complete cessation of entries. The national Church was in a depressed state as the Puritans were opposed to the Episcopal system and the Book of Common Prayer. In many cases, clergymen were driven out of their parishes, simply because they adhered to the Church of England. They were replaced by Puritan ministers who had their own system which did not include the maintenance of proper registers. John Walker's book *The Sufferings of the Clergy who were sequestered in the Grand Rebellion* gives a good account of church affairs in this period; so also does Scott's novel *Woodstock*. If you trace an ancestor born in this period, you are unlikely to find the record of his baptism. This is the reason for the statement in many otherwise well documented pedigrees that a person of some local importance was born 'about' a date in the mid-seventeenth century. In most cases, the parentage of the parties of a marriage – the most vital item of information for the genealogist – was omitted. How one is inclined to curse the negligence of the parson!

Having established the parish in which your ancestor was born, you may be fortunate enough to be able to trace his forbears for several generations. But what if you do not know his place of birth?

Suppose a couple married in Bristol in 1852. Will both bride and bridegroom have been born in that city? As the groom usually goes to the bride's parish for the marriage, there may be a presumption that he originated elsewhere. But where was he born?

Genealogy illuminates national history just as national history can and does condition genealogy. Before the Industrial Revolution from 1770 and the greater influence of the rapid development of railways from 1830, perhaps the majority of British people lived out their lives in the places where they were born. It follows, then, that many men who were active in a city in the 1850s and 1860s had in fact been born in some village or small hamlet. So, with our couple married in Bristol in 1852, the groom's birthplace may not be known. Fortunately, there is a means of bridging the gap between the General Registers and the parish registers. This is provided by the census returns (see page 28).

Population migration

I do not want to overstress the comparative immovability of our ancestors. There was a certain amount of movement from one part of the country to another and from one village to the next. But there are numerous instances in which a family's history can be traced for centuries in one place. Nothing could be more illuminating than the ancestry of the late Viscount Nuffield where the antecedents of the peer can be traced for 400 years from 1586 in a small area of Oxfordshire. Here the members of the Morris family were born, lived and died: we have records of their baptism, marriage and burial. As the *Complete Peerage* remarked: 'The pedigree is a good example of the value of public records as the source of information for the history of a typical yeoman family who were tenants and not landowners' (Vol. 13).

Other well known and similar cases are those of the Burbidges (the family who ruled Harrods for three generations) who can trace their yeoman ancestors to the reign of Henry VII; and the Wills, the great tobacco kings, whose ancestry has been traced to the seventeenth century. Or what of the great dynasty of the Harmsworths, who revolutionised the newspaper industry and whose ancestry can be traced through a succession of undistinguished Harmsworths in Hampshire to 1540? After ten generations 'each in his narrow niche forever laid' one of them went to London and begat a son, Alfred, who became a barrister. In the course of his career, he visited Dublin where he married Miss Geraldine Mary Maffet and brought a new strain into the family with the results that everyone knows.

There is, however, one important caution which must be observed by all genealogical researchers. It used to be frequently stated that before the Industrial Revolution, in the latter part of the eighteenth century, there was little movement of people in England

and that multitudes in the rural areas were born, lived and died in the same parish. Yet records show that there was movement within the area, though it might be for only a few miles. Also the pull of London was great.

James I thought London was too big, 'the great wen' as it was called. An examination of some of the notable writers of the Elizabethan/Jacobean era shows the flow of men of talent and ambition to London, and in many cases out of it again. After many years in London, Shakespeare still maintained his connection with his birthplace and returned there to die. In the case of Richard Hooker, we have a man born at Heavitree, near Exeter, living in London from 1585 to 1595 and dying at Bishopsbourne in Kent. Sir Walter Raleigh was another Devonian, with estates there, but he died in London after spending many years in the capital. Fulke Greville and Sir Philip Sidney came to London from Shrewsbury. Francis Bacon was a countryman and returned to the country after his disgrace. Edmund Spenser and Ben Jonson were born in London, but their parents came respectively from Lancashire and the Scottish border. Many other instances of literary men who found their way to London can be gleaned from George Saintsbury's *A Short History of English Literature*.

If great men found their way to the capital, so too did many lesser people. London grew and grew, absorbing large numbers and, be it added, killing them off. Edouard Perroy (*La Guerre de Cent Annes*) contemptuously dismissed London's 50,000 population in 1350 when contrasted with Paris' 150,000. When James VI of Scotland became James I of England, the population of London has been estimated at 200,000 although it had still not caught up with Paris. But by 1700 the population of London had soared to nearly 600,000. This despite a terrible mortality rate – 69,000 died in the Plague year of 1665 alone. But always there was an influx of new people to replace, and more than replace, the deaths and withdrawals to the country. Where did they come from? The answer, so far as studies show, is from all over England. It must be remembered, too, that there were also foreign immigrants.

An even greater draw than that of the theatres and literature was the vast growth in importance of the City of London. Sir Thomas Gresham, the great finance minister to Elizabeth I, not only restored English finances: he wrested from Antwerp the position of

London as the financial capital of Europe. Thereafter he built the Royal Exchange and from that were hived off the various Exchanges which still operate in the City. To feed this ever waxing mighty metropolis required a yearly average on balance of 8,000 persons – representing, so it has been estimated, the difference between immigration into London and emigration from it.

One last attraction of London was as a centre of pleasure. Oswald Barron, in one of his delightful essays in *The Ancestor* (12 volumes, 1902–5), remarked how few families of long standing were to be found in counties such as Surrey, adjacent to London. The Brays of Shere were one of the very few. Whereas an indiscretion by the son of the family in a rural setting could easily be overcome, it was very different when he indulged in the delights of the metropolis, like the Angry Boy in Jonson's *Alchemist*.

Remembering that, in the sixteenth to early nineteenth centuries, transport was dependent either on a person's own legs or those of a horse, the movement towards London represents a considerable slice of the population. What of other cities?

Bristol, the second city in the kingdom, and Norwich both claimed some immigrants and emigrants. Research has shown some cases of people coming to Norwich from as much as fifty miles away. As to Bristol, an interesting case can be cited from the first half of the nineteenth century. A man born in 1827 in Porlock, Somerset, and brought up in a village in the same county, made his way to London. Then in 1850 he established himself in Bristol where his descendants lived for a century. His birthplace was traced via the census of 1851, but his father's birthplace was traced only through the County Record Office. Before that, the family was found to have resided for a century in a village in Devon.

Leaving out movement into the few cities, what of migrations in the rural areas themselves? Dr Peter Spufford has described several surveys made in different parts of England. From these it can be seen that many families, perhaps a majority, did *not* remain in the parish of birth. Yet after all this research, Dr Spufford's conclusion is that movement was often, or even as a rule, determined by ten or twenty miles' walking, half a day or a day's journey (*Genealogists' Magazine* 1973–74).

Census records

The first census was made in 1801, when for the first time it was possible to know accurately how many people there were in England and Wales – then 12 million. Regular censuses have been held every ten years since – except in 1941 – but the results only were kept, not the actual papers, until 1841. Since then the papers of the enumeration have been kept and now the records for 1841, 1851, 1861, 1871 and 1881 are available to the researcher at the Public Record Office in Portugal Street, London, only a few minutes' walk from St Catherine's House.

An unknown genius in the Civil Service must have suggested the preservation of the 1841 returns. They shed a great deal of light on the families recorded, but there is a serious flaw. One question asked was ambiguous: was the person concerned born in the county where he or she lived at the time of the census. A negative reply to this question does not advance research very much. Another difficulty is that ages given in this 1841 census are misleading, as they are 'rounded'. For example, if at the time of the census a person's age was 21 it would be shown as 20, and if it was 23 or 24 it would be shown as 25.

But in 1851 another unknown benefactor to genealogy altered the question to 'Where were you born?'

From 1851, then, the census returns give the location of the household, the relationship of each person present to the head of the household and, for each, their sex, matrimonial status, age, rank, profession or occupation, and birthplace.

In the age of the Industrial Revolution, as we have seen, multitudes flocked to the rapidly growing cities, like Sheffield, Liverpool, Leeds and Birmingham, which had previously been little more than villages. The existing cities like London and Bristol became greatly enlarged. The 1851 census then showed many of these new city dwellers as having come from small, often tiny, places in rural districts. The census of 1851 often provides the link between a great-grandfather in St Catherine's registers and the parish registers of the place where he was born and baptised.

Census returns are made accessible to the public when it is considered unlikely that any person recorded will be inconvenienced by the search. Hence returns later than 1881 (1891 in

1841 Census

Kerswell, Honiton, Devon

1 Edward Derby   25   farmer
2 Jane Derby   wife   25
3 Loveday   18
4 George Pine   12   Born in same county
5 John Needs   15
6 Thomas Tottle   20
7 William Jaat   12
8 Harriet Vicary   15
9 Anne Hawking   13

(Some of these particulars are incorrect. For example, George
Pine – who was being brought up by step in-laws – was actually
14. He was also born in Porlock, Somerset, as appears below.)

1851 Census

---

5 Christmas Street, Bristol

George Pine	Head	Unm.	23	Grocer	Somerset, Porlock
Henry Geoman	Servant	Unm.	23	Grocer	Somerset, Bath
Mary Ann Tulford	Servant	M.	30	House-keeper	Dorset, Salisbury

---

1881 Census

High Street (not numbered), Glastonbury, Somerset

John Beswetherick	Head	M.	48	Draper & Tailor	Cornwall, Bodmin
Lavina	,,	Wife	M.	48	—	London
James P.	,,	Son	Unm.	19	Draper's Assistant	Cornwall, Bodmin
Courtney	,,	,,	Unm.	17	,, ,,	,, ,,
Henry C.	,,	,,	—	11	Scholar	,, ,,
Mabel	,,	Dau.	—	8	,,	,, ,,

**The information supplied in response to three census inquiries
(1841, 1851, 1881)**

Scotland) are not yet accessible to the public, but information can in some cases be obtained by writing to the General Register Office giving the name and precise address of the person sought, together with written permission from that person or a direct descendant.

It will be appreciated that the venerable documents of 1841 and 1851 were suffering from constant handling and the census books are no longer put into inquirers' hands. All records of the five censuses available are now on microfilm: this does not make for easy reading but there is no alternative. One good result is that a microfilm of a particular county is now often found in that County Record Office.

Attendance at Portugal Street, as with all other genealogical sources, is now much greater than a few years ago. You will have to wait your turn to obtain a seat and access to the microfilm. If application is made in writing the expense is considerable and this will necessarily increase. There will also be a considerable delay as the establishment at Portugal Street is small.

Obviously, you will have to expend much effort on the tracing of your ancestors. If one of them, having been baptised in a parish, omits to be buried there, you must search in gradually widening circles. A map is essential and you can but hope that the ten or twenty miles 'limit' will apply.

Having dealt with these matters of population movement, we can apply the census of 1851 as a means of discovering the birthplace origins of our couple who were married in Bristol in 1852. We assume that the addresses for the bride and bridegroom were the same in 1851 as in 1852. Looking in the returns for 1851, we find that the bride was born in Bristol, the bridegroom in a small country place, Porlock in Somerset. The parish registers at Porlock give the date of the bridegroom's baptism and particulars of his parentage, or at least of his father.

Thus the General Registers at St Catherine's House have been connected with the parish registers, via the census.

Pedigrees

The word pedigree derives from two Latin words – *pes* (foot) and *grus* (crane), because the sign formerly used to indicate descent was in the shape of a crane's foot.

In printed pedigrees it is conventional to use abbreviations, of which the most common are:

b.	born	d.s.p.	*decessit sine prole*, died without issue
bach.	bachelor		
bapt.	baptised	m.	married
bur.	buried	MI	monumental inscription
c.	*circa*, about	PCC	Prerogative Court of Canterbury
d.	died	PCY	Prerogative Court of York
dau.	daughter	unm.	unmarried

Another convention in line and sketch pedigrees (see below) is that the male offspring are given before the female, regardless of the birth order.

In the sample pedigrees which follow, the first is a brief pedigree illustrating particulars of (*a*) birth, marriage and death from St Catherine's, (*b*) census returns, (*c*) parish registers, and (*d*) other sources such as monumental inscriptions (see Chapter 3) and university records (see Chapter 9). It is a skeleton outline, but it covers seven generations spanning 200 years.

The second example is a pedigree sketch in narrative form, which is the method more generally used because it allows much more room for detail. It must be remembered, however, that the filling out of collateral details can be costly.

An Outline Pedigree

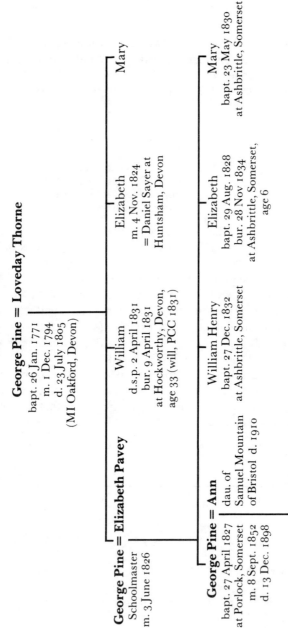

George Pine = **Loveday Thorne**
bapt. 26 Jan. 1771
m. 1 Dec. 1794
d. 23 July 1805
(MI Oakford, Devon)

Mary

Elizabeth
m. 4 Nov. 1824
= Daniel Sayer at
Huntsham, Devon

William
d.s.p. 2 April 1831
bur. 9 April 1831
at Hockworthy, Devon,
age 33 (will, PCC 1831)

George Pine = **Elizabeth Pavey**
Schoolmaster
m. 3 June 1826

Mary
bapt. 23 May 1830
at Ashbrittle, Somerset

Elizabeth
bapt. 29 Aug. 1828
bur. 28 Nov 1834
at Ashbrittle, Somerset,
age 6

William Henry
bapt. 27 Dec. 1832
at Ashbrittle, Somerset

George Pine = **Ann**
bapt. 27 April 1827   dau. of
at Porlock, Somerset   Samuel Mountain
m. 8 Sept. 1852   of Bristol d. 1910
d. 13 Dec. 1898

George Pine = **Elizabeth**
b. 29 July 1853   dau. of
m. 1880   John Moorshead
d. 29 Dec. 1890

George   **Henry Moorshead Pine** = **Lilian Grace**   Arthur Stanley   Alice Mary

Henry Moorshead Pine
b. 17 Nov. 1882
m. 10 Sept. 1906
d. 27 June 1960

Lilian Grace
dau. of James
Phillips Beswetherick
d. 1957

Leslie Gilbert Pine = **Grace Violet**
b. 22 Dec. 1907
BA, London
Barrister, Inner Temple
m. 7 Aug. 1948

Grace Violet
dau. of
Albert James Griffin

Richard Leslie Pine = **Melanie Ann**
b. 21 Aug. 1949
MA, Trinity Coll., Dublin
m. 28 Oct. 1972

Melanie Ann
dau. of Eric Creagan
(BLG, Ireland 1958,*
under Wynnes)

Emily Ruth Alice Pine
b. 22 Jan. 1977

Vanessa Edith Marjorie Pine
b. 25 Nov. 1982

* BLG, *Burke's Landed Gentry*

A Modern Pedigree Sketch

The word 'modern' used here is perhaps a little arbitrary, but to a genealogist an English pedigree of some 250 years, back to 1700 or so, is viewed as comparatively modern, in contrast to those which can be traced before 1600. For the overwhelming majority of English people whose forbears have been living in England for any length of time, the tracing of a pedigree for 250–300 years does not normally present any insuperable difficulties. Before that time, i.e. before the reign of Charles II (1660–85), the tracing of a pedigree depends largely upon records of ownership of land, and it is in the period previous to 1660 that the Visitation-type pedigree (see page 159), comes into existence.

William Orme married at St Michael's Church, Stone, Staffordshire on 31 December 1734. William Orme was of the parish of Stone, where record of his baptism is not available in the period 1700 –1720. There are, however, to be found two small areas in the registers which have been damp for some time, and which are now quite illegible. It could be that William Orme's baptism was recorded on the unreadable pages. This is mentioned only as an example of some of the difficulties encountered in searching the parish records.

William Orme's bride, Mary Emery, was of the parish of Stoke-upon-Trent. There is no indication of the parentage or ages of the parties – information which should have been, but is not, given. According to some old family papers, Mary was the daughter of John Emery, and she and William Orme had seven children, of whom six are recorded in the baptismal registers of Stone.

They were:

1   A dau., baptised 19 Feb. 1735.
2   Mary, bapt. 7 May 1738.
3   Cecilia, bapt. 9 Nov. 1740.
4   Thomas, bapt. 18 Aug. 1745.
5   Francis, bapt. 10 April 1748.
6   Robert, bapt. 10 June 1750.

The fifth of these children,
Francis Orme, bapt. 10 April 1748, m. 15 July 1771, Anne Timmis,

at Bucknall Church, Staffs and had issue (his will is dated 24 Feb. 1821),

1 Josiah, b. 19 April, bapt. 10 May 1772.
2 Anne, b. 7 Feb., bapt. 6 Mar. 1774.
3 Hannah, b. 14 April, bapt. 10 May 1778.
4 Elizabeth, b. 20 July, bapt. 17 Sept. 1780, m. Geo. Silcock.
5 Anne, (Nanny), b. 10 July, bapt. 3 Aug. 1783, m. Job Bagnall and had issue.
6 Mary, b. 19 June, bapt. 10 July 1785, m. William Griffin.
7 John, b. 4 Oct. bapt. 2 Dec. 1787, (?) had a son, John.
8 Michael, b. 10 July, bapt. 1 Aug. 1790.

The youngest of the above eight children,
Michael Orme, is mentioned in the 1841 census as of Burslem, Dale Hall, (New Church Lane). His age is there given as 49 (discrepancies in exact age are of frequent occurrence in the records), and he is described as a botanist. In the same census, the other members of his family are given as Francis, age 14, a botanist, Michael, age 20, a botanist, and Jane, age 20. In the 1851 census his wife's name is given as Mary, age 70, b. May Bank, Staffs, and he is there described as having a granddau., Ellen, aged 8. It would seem that some mistake occurred, and Ellen his granddau. was aged 5, not 8 (see below). It appears that he died in 1870, being buried at Dale Hall Church, Burslem. From the 1871 census further details are available about members of Michael Orme's family, as follows:

1 Michael, age 20 in 1841, a joiner, (according to 1871 census, this occupation being apparently concurrent with the earlier mentioned botanist) residing in 1871 at 63 Howard Street, Burslem, Stoke-upon-Trent, b. at Tittensor, 1819, (age 52 in 1871). His wife, Jane, age 50, born at Leek; his six daus., all b. at Burslem, were:

    1 Elizabeth, 17, warehouse woman, pottery.
    2 Marian, 15, painter (pottery).
    3 Mary, 15, painter (pottery).
    4 Martha, 11, pottery at home.
    5 Agnes, 9, scholar.
    6 Sarah J., 7, scholar.

Also residing with him was a granddau., Agnes J. Beech. Michael d. 6 Jan. 1872, and was bur. in Dale Hall Church.

2   Francis, a botanist (in 1841 census) and a joiner, on his marriage certificate, b. 1827, m. 29 Dec. 1845, Tamar, dau. of John Oakes, of George Street, Newcastle-under-Lyme, a collier, and d. 30 July 1849, being bur. at sea on his way to America, having had issue,

Ellen, b. 11 Mar. 1846. m. William Cooke, and grandmother of present living descendant, to whom I am obliged for permission to include the above account.

Thus a pedigree of seven generations can be constructed by the combined use of parochial records, St Catherine's House registers, census returns, and family papers. It is quite possible that earlier generations of this family will be found in the same area in Staffordshire. A former vicar of Tittensor made notes that, in 1597, Sir Gilbert Gerrard rebuilt a manor house at Tittensor, and that William Orme occupied the manor (the Ormes, it is added, were a yeoman family from Hanch (?) Hall, Longsden). In 1643 the manor house was destroyed and after 1660 it was rebuilt by William Orme and Sir Charles Gerrard. It appears reasonable to conclude that further research will indicate a connection between William Orme of 1660 and William Orme of 1734 (born probably 1700–14). Moreover, there was a Visitation family of Orme in Staffordshire.

3

Other Denominational Records

The Bishops' Transcripts

It must not be thought that after 1538 no more attention was given to the keeping of the parish registers. In 1563 Parliament wished 'to erect an office of registership of all the church books to be kept in every diocese', which could have meant the creation of the Registrar General three centuries earlier. This proposal was defeated by clerical opposition, as was the suggestion of Lord Burghley for an annual summary of the returns for England and Wales. In 1597, however, it was the clergy of the province of Canterbury who ordered that copies of the registers should be sent each year to the Registrar of each diocese. These are the Bishops' Transcripts. Although the transcripts are often defective, they are still frequently useful where the original records have perished. They can be consulted at the various diocesan centres and application should be made to the Diocesan Registrar. A fee is chargeable.

Parliament passed several Acts to regularise the maintenance of the registers, and eventually on the report of a Select Committee in 1836 the Act was passed to establish the present registration system.

The allegations of marriage

Other documents which are useful in seeking records of marriages are the *allegations*. These are copies of applications to the local Bishop to grant a licence for a marriage. In olden times marriage did not take place so much by the calling of banns as by the granting of licences, the latter method being much in use among the better social classes. When a licence was required, application had to be made to the Bishop of the Diocese, or in some cases to the Archbishop or to a Dean of what was known as a Peculiar, the term applied to a particular type of ecclesiastical administrative unit. The licence when granted went to the person who had sought it, but the original application, or allegation, as it was called, was preserved. A most interesting case of the use of allegation occurred in the marriage of William Shakespeare and Ann Hathaway. The full story is in Sir Sidney Lee's *Life of Shakespeare*. The entry of this marriage had never been found until in the early nineteenth century, in the archives of the Diocese of Worcester, the allegation for the marriage was discovered. Shakespeare married his bride when she was three months pregnant, a fact appearing from the birth date of his eldest child.

When the bride was a minor the allegation should give the parents' names and their formal consent. In many cases, this and other vital information is missing, but ideally the allegation should give the names of the prospective husband and wife, their position in life, age, parish and the place intended for the ceremony.

Records in Lambeth Palace Library

On the subject of marriage allegations some very useful material for genealogists exists in the Library of Lambeth Palace, the London home of the Archbishop of Canterbury. The allegations for the grant of a common licence, and to a lesser degree of a special licence, since 1660 are found here. Of the common licences, there are at Lambeth (*a*) those issued by the Archbishop for people who lived in or wished to marry in his diocese of Canterbury, (*b*) requests which the Archbishop received as having under his jurisdiction the Peculiars of Canterbury (which were at Shoreham, Croydon, Bocking and the Court of Arches), (*c*) where one of the partners to the licence came from the province of York. The Archbishop also received requests for common licences from people living in a diocese of the province of Canterbury.

Vicar General's Office   *17th February 1840*

Appeared personally Henry Edward Parker of the parish of St George, Southwark in the County of Surrey, a Bachelor aged twenty one years and upwards and prayed a licence for the solemnisation of matrimony in the parish church of St George's, Southwark, aforesaid between him and Martha Knightley of the same parish spinster aged also 21 years and upwards and made oath that he believeth that there is no impediment of kindred or alliance or of any other lawful cause nor any suit commenced in any ecclesiastical court to bar or hinder the proceedings of the said matrimony according to the tenor of such licence. And he further maketh oath that he the said appearer hath had his usual place of abode within the said parish of St George, Southwark for the space of 15 days last past.

*(*signed*) H.E. Parker*

Sworn before me
*(*signed*) Thomas Blake, Surrog.*

Transcript of a marriage allegation, 1840

*William Pine of the Parish of Oakford
in the County of Devon, Yeoman Widower
appeared Personally and made Oath that the said
William Pine is above the Age of Twenty one Years
and not related to Elizabeth Limebear of the Parish of
Barnstaple in the said County Spinster (for the Marriage
of whom Licence is prayed) within the degrees
prohibited and the said William Pine on his Oath saith
that the said Elizabeth Limebear is likewise above the
Age of Twenty one Years and that the said Elizabeth
Limebear hath had her usual abode in the Parish of
Barnstaple aforesaid for four Weeks and afterwards
immediately proceeding the date hereof*

*Sworn before me this
6th day of August 1786*

*Witness (*signed*) John Roding*

> (signed) *William Pine*
> (signed) *William Cooke, Surrogate*

Transcript of a marriage bond, 1786

The Court of Arches

In all these classes of application for common licences, many species of information of use to genealogists can be found. Among these in the records of the Court of Arches are applications for divorce (see below). The Arches was the Court of Appeal to the Archbishop for the southern Province of Canterbury. It derived its name from the Church of St Mary at Bow, whose Latin name was *de Arcubus*. There anciently the Court of Arches sat. ('Arches' slurred in English from 'archers' or 'bows'.) Morals were of old the province of the ancient Church of England and consequently all sorts of matrimonial sins and failings are to be found in its archives.

We must first define *divortia* (divorce) as understood in these transactions. Broadly, as throughout all Christian Europe until the late eighteenth or mid-nineteenth century, divorce did not mean that two persons, after a decree from an ecclesiastical court, were free to marry other partners. In many cases, the ecclesiastical definition of divorce was what we should now understand as a legal separation – *a thora, a mensa*, from bed and board, with no longer any requirement for cohabitation. Classic cases from history may make this clear.

The Queen of Henry II of England had been married previously to the King of France, by whom she had two children. When she tired of her first husband and was attracted by the much younger Henry II she obtained a divorce – that is, her first marriage was in effect pronounced invalid on grounds of consanguinity. In fact, her first marriage was annulled, but the children of that marriage remained legitimate.

Consider, too, the famous 'divorce' of Henry VIII. He had sought an annulment of his first marriage to Catherine of Aragon. When he could not obtain this from Pope Clement VII, he achieved it by the appointment of Thomas Cranmer as his Archbishop of Canterbury, who then in his court pronounced Henry's first marriage null and void.

So then among the records of the Court of Arches will be found divorces which equal our decrees of annulment, though the majority of the cases equal our legal separations.

In passing, it is of interest to describe Henry VIII's other marriage terminations. His second wife, Anne Boleyn, was accused of adultery, judged guilty of high treason (petit treason for an ordinary wife not a queen) and beheaded. The third wife, Jane Seymour, died as a result of childbirth. Henry's fourth marriage to Anne of Cleves ended not in divorce but an annulment, as Henry seems never to have had carnal knowledge of 'the Flanders Mare'. Wife number five, Catherine Howard, like Anne Boleyn, was accused of adultery and executed for high treason. Number six, Catherine Parr, succeeded in outliving Henry and even married again. Thus, strictly speaking, there is no divorce of Henry VIII.

Divorce by Act of Parliament
But did all the couples who sought a divorce in the Court of Arches remain in a state of separation? They had a remedy if they were determined to marry again. In the period from roughly 1680 to 1858 there were 317 Acts of Parliament passed for the movers to obtain a divorce in the modern sense, and so to make a second legal marriage. Readers of Dr Johnson's 'Life of Richard Savage' in his *Lives of the Poets* will recollect that Earl Rivers doubted that he was the father of Richard and obtained a divorce from his countess by Act of Parliament.

This was possible because of the parliamentary principle (set forth by John Louis De Lolme, d. 1807) that Parliament can do anything except make a man a woman or a woman a man.

Among the applicants for a licence it is interesting to find John Milton on 11 February 1663. This was the poet's third marriage. When his first marriage, contracted in 1643, had nearly foundered, the time was one of confusion in Church and State, probably making it impossible to apply to Parliament for a divorce. This perhaps explains why Milton does not appear to have thought of this remedy in his *Doctrine and Discipline of Divorce*. In the latter, he succeeded in proving to his own satisfaction that Christ's prohibition of divorce meant that He approved of it. In the event, Milton's first wife came back to him but died, in childbed, a few years later.

The above details about divorce are only a selection of what may be gained from the treasures of the Lambeth Library. There are also wills and probate records from the Archbishop's Peculiars mentioned above, those of Croydon and the Court of Arches. Those of the Shoreham Peculiar are with the Kent County Record Office at Maidstone (see a careful account of the archives of the Lambeth

Palace Library by Miss Melanie Barber, *Genealogists' Magazine*, December 1973 and December 1980).

Nonconformist records

With regard to registers other than those of the Church of England, some are kept at St Catherine's House. Others are retained by the particular body: for example, the Society of Friends (commonly called the Quakers), the Roman Catholics and the Huguenots have well-preserved records (see Chapter 9).

There have been many variations in Dissent over the past 350 years so that guidance is needed to be able to distinguish the different bodies. As they have not been restrained by authority as in our episcopal church, all sorts of small bodies have arisen, lived for a time and then died. Then there is the twentieth-century movement for the reunion of Christians. Of this an important development is the United Reform Church, which is the union of the Presbyterians and Congregationalists.

A useful guide to these intricacies is provided in *Sources for Nonconformist Genealogy and Family History* by D. J. Steel and others.

Monumental inscriptions

These are often very informative, apart from the enlightenment (and amusement) afforded by the inscriptions. Some memorials are quite touching, as with a woman who was a servant at the Hall of the local gentry. She had worked there from her girlhood and her death had occurred suddenly in the park. She merited a large tombstone recording her history, which might otherwise have been forgotten.

In country churchyards the tombstones are generally safe from everything destructive except weather. In towns there are other dangers. Some burial grounds are a nuisance to local authorities and are closed. If those authorities obtain a private bill in Parliament to close and remove the burial ground, there is usually a clause to the effect that a copy of the inscriptions must be made and lodged with the Registrar General.

The Women's Institute has carried out a project in which a record was made of the memorials in many village churchyards. The results have been lodged with the County Record Offices.

It is an emotional experience to stand in a churchyard in the depths of the English countryside and to see the lines of tombstones, some of them fallen. It is also a heartening reminder that pedigrees are for all.

One may recall Gray's *Elegy in a Country Churchyard*:

> 'Some mute inglorious Milton here may rest,
> Some Cromwell guiltless of his country's blood,
> Some village Hampden who with dauntless breast
> The petty tyrant of his fields withstood.'

Monumental inscriptions are by no means limited to tombstones in churchyards. Numerous memorials exist inside churches. These include memorial slates, often carrying Latin inscriptions. There may be a history of the church which will contain particulars of such inscriptions, including exact translations. Many churches do have leaflets on the history of the church and some reference to the monuments. It is a good idea to ask at the local County Record Office, or to ask the incumbent if a full history of the church exists.

Another source of information in a church is in the stained glass windows, which have usually been put in as a memorial. It is very desirable that details of inscriptions on windows should be copied and preserved. Many churches have become redundant: eventually the church authorities can order the destruction of the stained glass windows and the memorial inscriptions can be lost forever.

Many objects of church furniture carry notices giving the names of the donors.

Other memorials
Apart from the monumental inscriptions to be found in churches and churchyards, there are many public memorials in various buildings and these can be a valuable source of information about someone's life. For example, on a swimming bath in Fulham there is a reference to a Member of Parliament of many years back who was ultimately created a peer.

War memorials list names which may not be recorded elsewhere.

4

Wills

The importance of wills

By working through the public registers and the parish records (with the aid of the censuses), you will probably be able to establish a genealogical tree of perhaps ten to twelve generations: but it will be a mere record of birth (baptism), marriage and death (burial). The details of the census returns from 1841 to 1881 will give information for the mid-nineteenth century which, by contrast, will make the ancestral picture of the sixteenth to eighteenth centuries look bare, unless it is possible to light up the lines of the forbears by find-ing other sources of information. Of these, the most important are wills, and English wills since 1858 are kept at Somerset House, London, where a fee is charged for examination and for copies.

Wills before 1858

There are, however, rich repositories of earlier wills which yield a great deal of information. For most of England's history, wills came under ecclesiastical jurisdiction, which was not surprising as for some centuries the Christian Church contained the most literate and educated class in the land. In addition, it was the responsibility of priests and monks to put the dying in mind of their duty – that is, to make their peace with God, be at charity with their kinsfolk and neighbours, and to make disposition of their goods.

Some of the wills of which fragments at least remain go back to Anglo-Saxon times. Among the most important wills before 1066 is that of King Alfred the Great. This is written in Old English and dates from 873 to 888. A notable feature of the will is Alfred's reference to his father, King Ethelwulf, to his two brothers, Ethelbald and Ethelred, then on to Edward, his elder son and to his younger son. Alfred also mentions his eldest daughter, middle daughter, youngest daughter and his nephews. A three-generation pedigree can be constructed from this regal will (for a full translation see *English Historical Documents*, Vol. 1, *c.* 500–1042, pp. 492–5).

The proving of wills by Church courts went on until January 1858 when the Principal Probate Registry was established. Before that date, a will could be proved in one of some 300 courts, the location of the court depending upon that of the estate of the deceased.

Will and testament

Distinctions between will and testament have been made in the past, as of a will being limited to land and testament to personal estate. This distinction, if it ever existed, is now quite obsolete, and there are in any event differences between English and Scots usage. The Wills Act 1837 permits of the disposition by will of 'every kind of interest in real and personal estate' (Mozley and Whiteley's *Law Dictionary*, Butterworth, 9th edition 1977).

The history of will-making has considerable relevance the further we go back in our genealogical researches. The forms of will-making which existed before the Norman Conquest were retained and extended afterwards. The ecclesiastical courts had sole jurisdiction over personal property as freeholds could not be bequeathed. (Here it should be remembered that property is divided into *real estate* or *real property* – houses, land, immovables – and *personalty* – money, furniture, chattels.)

In 1857, the Court of Probate Act established the Probate Court to which was transferred the testamentary jurisdiction which had, until then, been administered by ecclesiastical courts. The jurisdiction of the Probate Court is now exercised by the Chancery Division (in contentious cases) or by the Family Division (non-contentious) of the Supreme Court.

. . . Upon trust to pay the rents issues and profits thereof unto my granddaughter Alice Mary Pine for and during the term of her natural life for her own separate use and benefit free from the control of any husband with whom she might intermarry and from and after her death I devise the same dwelling houses Unto and to the use of her children in equal shares if more than one as tenants in common but if the said Alice Mary Pine shall be without issue but leaving a husband her surviving I devise the same dwellinghouses or the rents, issues or profits thereof unto her said husband for and during his life and from and after his decease or in case the said Alice Mary Pine shall die without leaving a husband then I devise the same dwellinghouses unto and to the use of her three brothers in equal shares as tenants in common and as to my freehold dwelling house number 19 West Street St Philips Bristol afore said upon trust to pay the rents issues and profits thereby unto my grandson Henry Moorshead Pine until he shall attain the age of Twenty five years. And from and after his attaining that age I devise the said dwellinghouse unto and to the use of the said Henry Moorshead Pine absolutely and in the event of my said grandson Henry Moorshead Pine dying under the age of Twenty five years without leaving issue but leaving a wife him surviving I devise the same dwelling house or the rents issues and profits thereof unto his said wife for and during her life and from and after her decease or in case the said Henry Moorshead Pine shall so die without leaving a wife then I devise the same dwellinghouse unto and to the use of his brothers and sister in equal shares as tenants in common. . . .

An extract (transcript) from a will, 1898

The system of uses (modern trusts)
A bequest of land had to be made through the medium of the Chancery Court, which led to the practice of uses, as they were called, which was the foundation of our law of trusts.

Gradually the extensive employment of the device of the use forced the authorities to agree to the willing of real property (houses, lands, immovables – see above). In 1540, in the reign of Henry VIII, the Statute of Wills allowed that a written will should pass up to two-thirds at least of land which was held under the feudal system on what was known as 'knight service'. The latter was one of the dissensions which brought about the war between Charles I and his Parliament. When Charles II was restored, the loyal Parliament, while voting him a large sum, was careful to abolish knight service! From then on, all land could be bequeathed by will.

Property in more than one ecclesiastical jurisdiction
The Reformation made no difference to the jurisdiction of the ecclesiastical courts. If a man had property in one area only, his will came into the Archdeacon's Court of the neighbourhood. If he possessed property in more than one jurisdiction, then the will had to be proved in the Prerogative Court of Canterbury. This was, and is, the southern province of the Church of England. The northern province is that of the Archbishop of York. Wills which were proved in the Prerogative Court of York are now in the Borthwick Institute of Historical Research at the University of York, St Anthony's Hall, York YO1 2PW.

The records of the Prerogative Court of Canterbury were transferred from Somerset House in 1962 to the Public Records Office (Chancery Lane).

Location of courts of ecclesiastical jurisdiction
With regard to wills which were not proved in the Prerogative Court of Canterbury or of York, the problem is to find the court in which the grant was made, and then to discover where the records of that court are kept. The location of wills can be found in either of two books – *Wills and Where to Find Them* by J. S. W. Gibson (Phillimore, 1974) and *Wills and Their Whereabouts* by A. J. Camp (1974), both now out of print but available in libraries. Much useful detail is given in the PRO publication *The Prerogative Court of*

Canterbury (1980) and in J. S. W. Gibson's *A Simplified Guide to Probate Jurisdictions* (Gulliver Press, 1980).

It is impossible to over-value wills. While one does not get many cases like that of King Alfred, in which he referred to his predecessors, nearly all wills refer to the testator's successors or contemporaries in his family.

In a case which I was investigating, I decided to look in the PCC wills in the first quarter of the nineteenth century. I found a will of a junior member of this particular family which supplied not only the names of two members of whose existence I had known nothing, but also gave indications of a certain amount of ill feeling in the family. The testator gave some of his property to his only sister, but with the strict proviso that her husband was to have nothing to do with it. He did not explain how this was to be done, seeing that the Married Women's Property Act was fifty years away. The testator's mother was a widow who had married again. Apparently the stepfather was *persona grata* to the testator, as he appointed him his executor. To his mother he left only a clock, and that in a codicil. A picture of a certain amount of family friction emerges.

The evidential value of a will

I was tracing a family called Matthews. They bore the arms of an extinct baronet of the same name. Apparently, the family had a tradition of connection with the baronet's line.

The founder of the baronet's family was one Joachim Matthews of London, a wealthy merchant whose son was the first baronet. I already knew the names of Joachim's sons, because he and they were entered in the Heralds' Visitations of London 1633 (see Chapter 15), but I could not tell whether the one child who became a baronet was the eldest son. To check the possible connection of my inquirer with the baronetcy, I went to Somerset House (at that time the repository of PCC wills) to examine the will of Joachim Matthews. It gave details of all the testator's children. There were two daughters, Sarah and Isabella, who received portions of £2,000 each, and five sons, all under age at the time of the will. The eldest was Philip (the future first Baronet, created in 1662), aged 17. The other boys were Mark Anthony, apprenticed in Lombard Street; Joachim, who was at school and intended for the Inns of Court or

University; James, not yet at school, but to be bound apprentice to a draper, and Francis, who probably died young, since he does not appear in later pedigrees of the family. Each son was to receive a small present on his birthday – the dates were given – to remind him of his father, and a substantial sum when he came of age.

The bearing of the will was this. I had traced the inquirer's family for eight generations to a carpenter in Norwich who was married in 1686. The date of the will was 1659. Now that I had got the relative ages of the five sons, it seemed very unlikely that one of the lads should be predecessor of the Norwich carpenter, who must have been at least twenty years of age in 1686. Any connection of the Matthews whom I was investigating with the baronet's family must have come via Joachim's brother, if he had one.

In this instance, the inquirer was a civic dignitary who in a forthcoming mayoral year wanted to use the arms of the Matthews baronets of Great Gobbions in Essex, where there are Matthews charities to this day. I was sorry to disappoint my inquirer, but the truth must prevail and the evidence of the will was negative.

Again, I was asked to make some researches into the American family of Howe, who originated in Essex. The main object of the inquiry was to discover their possible connection with the ancestry of the Earls Howe. In *Burke's Peerage*, this begins with one Henry Howe, who in the time of Henry VIII held the manor of Compton in Gloucestershire. Much American research had been made in the early years of the present century to connect the Essex line with Henry Howe. This was the origin of the Howe pedigree in *Burke's American Families with British Ancestry*. There are numerous wills of the Essex Howes in the Essex Record Office at Chelmsford. So far their evidence does not bear out a connection between the Essex family and Henry Howe.

In yet another instance, the wills did provide substantiation of a family's ancestry for two or more generations. The Blacker family of Carrickblacker in Ireland derived their origins from Yorkshire. Examination of wills showed that this belief was correct. Valentine Blacker, the soldier adventurer who founded the Irish family, was a scion of an old recorded Yorkshire family, traceable perhaps to the twelfth century, and this was proved from the wills in the Yorkshire archives.

In Scotland, wills were proved before the Commissariat Courts such as that in Edinburgh, where the date of the earliest entry is 1514. These wills have been calendared (indexed) and copies of the indices are on the shelves of the Society of Genealogists in London. The inquirer should approach HM Registrar General, General Register Office at Edinburgh for information.

Most Irish wills were destroyed in the troubles in 1922 (see page 126). Some are still in existence at Dublin Castle, but not many.

While on the subject of loss of wills, a very serious destruction was that of Devon and Cornwall wills at Exeter in 1942, by enemy bombing. On this, J. S. W. Gibson writes:

'All probate records for the diocese of Exeter deposited in the probate registry there were destroyed by enemy action in 1942. These included the episcopal consistory, principal registry and archdeaconry of Exeter records, the consistory court of the Dean and Chapter of Exeter, the peculiar courts of the Dean of Exeter and of the custos of the cathedral and the college of vicars choral and the consistory courts of the archdeacons of Barnstaple and Totnes.'

A melancholy list, is it not? And to make things worse the printed indices to 1799 of the Archdeaconry of Exeter still exist, so that we can realise the documents we have lost (Gibson, *Wills and Where to Find Them*, p. 31).

There is one slight consolation. Some of the Devon wills were copied by the early Inland Revenue and these have been preserved.

Intestacy

What of intestacy? What of those who died without making a will? It has been remarked that before the fairly recent past few people had anything to leave. Very few, comparatively, owned their own houses and therefore all that was left by the deceased was his personalty – his furniture, clothes and money. These possessions were divided by the near relatives and no further action was taken, nor were the ecclesiastical or legal authorities troubled.

It was only when someone who possessed property died intestate, or where a creditor of the deceased was involved, that a grant of letters of administration had to be obtained. Someone – often the surviving spouse – was appointed administrator of the estate. The legal authorities were then approached and an inventory of the goods and chattels of the intestate was lodged with them.

In some instances, however, a late disposition was made (perhaps during the final illness) and in such cases letters of administration or bonds were made. These appear in the probate records after the wills under the particular surname.

Searching in probate registers

In searching the probate registers at Somerset House (Strand, London WC2), of course, it is most helpful to know the date of death of the testator: if this is not known, the fee allows a search through five years. When found, notice of the will has been entered in large handwritten record volumes and then the actual will can be requested and inspected. The wills are bound in books and in some cases the writing has faded.

With regard to wills before 1858 the same difficulty prevails as with other old documents and the help of an expert may be needed. From about 1660, the main trouble is not with the handwriting itself but with its fading.

At the Probate Registry, copying of an entire will is not allowed, though notes can be taken. Photostat copies of wills are supplied at a charge.

In the High Court of Justice

The Principal Probate Registry

BE IT KNOWN that HENRY MOORSHEAD PINE of 42 Bramley Hill South Croydon Surrey

died there on the 27th day of June 19 60

intestate a widower

AND BE IT FURTHER KNOWN that at the date hereunder written Letters of Administration of all the Estate which by law devolves to and vests in the personal representative of the said intestate were granted by the High Court of Justice at the Principal Probate Registry thereof to

LESLIE GILBERT PINE of 42 Bramley Hill aforesaid Managing editor the lawful son and only person entitled to the estate of the said intestate

And it is hereby certified that an Inland Revenue affidavit has been delivered wherein it is shown that the gross value of the said estate in Great Britain (exclusive of what the said deceased may have been possessed of or entitled to as a trustee and not beneficially) amounts to £ 264 - 0 - 10 and that the net value of the estate amounts to £

Dated the 26th day of July 1960

Registrar.

Extracted by the administrator   7A

A Grant of Probate

5

The Public Record Office

However good the County Record Offices are, the genealogist searcher who traces his family beyond 1800 must sooner or later consult the Public Record Office (PRO), the repository for legal and political documents. In view of the importance of this repository and because of the changes which have taken place in it, it is advisable to know how the PRO originated.

The history of English record-keeping

So far as the maintenance of records is concerned, England is probably the richest country in Europe. There are several reasons for this happy state of affairs.

In 1066–73, the Normans conquered a country which already possessed a literature and the rudiments of a civil service. The office of Chancellor existed under Edward the Confessor, and the Conqueror took over an administrative system with a staff composed of clerics who were accustomed to the use of Latin, as well as their own language, even in official documents. The first charter confirmed by the Conqueror, to the citizens of London, was in English, but thereafter all such documents were in Latin. *The Anglo-Saxon Chronicle*, which owed its origins to encouragement from Alfred the Great, continued in English at Peterborough right up to 1153.

It is understandable that the Norman conquerors could not at first lower themselves to learn the language of the conquered English. They themselves were illiterate. Whereas among the Anglo-Saxons it had been possible for a layman to write a Chronicle in Latin (not good Latin, but still Latin) in the eleventh century, the invaders had to leave any written material to their priests, who used Latin. The laity used Norman French as their spoken language, but as they were greatly outnumbered by the English they had gradually to acquire a rudimentary knowledge of the native language. Intermarriage took place and so there arose a mixed language, basically English but with a huge importation of French words, the latter including many derived from Latin, though often strangely altered from the classical forms.

One of the most ill-founded ideas ever put forward by a man of genius was Hilaire Belloc's contention, in his *History of England*, that a new language began in England after the Norman Conquest. Any history of English literature would have shown him how wrong he was. Of course, the passage of a thousand years makes it necessary for the modern Englishman to learn Anglo-Saxon, just as a modern Frenchman finds it necessary to have Rabelais translated.

The significance of the history of English literature is that the Old English civilisation provided the basis for record-keeping. The Domesday Book, although written in Latin, is certainly not a Norman French achievement. It is an Anglo-Saxon compilation and must have been the occasion of a great deal of sadness to the English people who supplied the information. Of the pre-1066 landowners, only eight per cent were still English when Domesday was compiled in 1086.

From Domesday Book to the Great Survey
Domesday is the beginning of English land records and Europe cannot show its like. From then on we have a great deal of information about land. It should be noted, however, that there is a gap after Domesday of some eighty years until the Great Survey held by Henry II in 1166. It is important to stress this fact for it is often fatal to claims of Norman ancestry or, at least, to the statement that someone's ancestors 'came over with the Conqueror'. Oswald Barron, in the twelve volumes of *The Ancestor*, gave studies under the heading of 'Our Oldest Families': none began earlier than the twelfth century. Quite a large number of county families can be traced to that period, but as most members bore French or foreign baptismal names it is impossible to say whether they descended from a Norman conqueror or someone else.

Generally, the claim to Norman ancestry is best forgotten. It rarely exists and I have exhaustively analysed the possible claims in my book *Sons of the Conqueror* (published by Charles Tuttle Inc.).

The wealth of English records

Given this basis of record-keeping in 1086 and to a considerable extent after 1166, it is not surprising that England should have a wealth of records. In addition, the country has been free from invasion for many centuries and, for the past 300 years, from civil war. The worst disaster for English records was in the Dissolution of the Monasteries in 1536. Very little was done to preserve the monastic libraries and there were many cases of wanton destruction of valuable manuscripts. Judging by what was saved, our loss of literary heritage must have been colossal.

The other cause of record destruction was enemy action in the Second World War, which has already been mentioned.

The establishment of the PRO

Granted that English records were extensive, how were they kept? They were dispersed in various places, such as the Chapel of the White Tower in the Tower of London, the Rolls Chapel (on the site of the present Record Office), in the Chapter House of Westminster Abbey, and so on. These former repositories were often damp and dirty: the records were dumped down in any fashion. Very little care was taken of the records and their preservation was more a matter of accident than design. In 1800 there was appointed a Records Commission, as a result of which there began the printing and publication of our ancient documents. This was valuable, but did not allow for the disappearance of documents by human or climatic agency, long before the Commission could succeed in publishing them.

Accordingly, demand grew for the establishment of a safe central place for storing the historical archives of the country. Hence came about the Public Record Office, which was established by Act of Parliament in 1838 and placed under the control of the Master of the Rolls.

This Act rehearsed the unsatisfactory nature of the places in which the public records were kept and directed that they should be stored in one central place and that proper premises and staff should be appointed to hold and deal with them. Within twenty years after 1838 arose the sham Gothic but imposing building in Chancery Lane.

Council on Public Records
Under section 1 of the Public Records Act 1958 the direction of the PRO was transferred from the Master of the Rolls to the Lord Chancellor. It also set up an Advisory Council on Public Records to advise the Lord Chancellor in particular on those aspects of the work of the PRO which affect members of the public who make use of its facilities. The Master of the Rolls is the Chairman of the Council. The remaining members are appointed by the Lord Chancellor: the latter lays before both Houses of Parliament in every year a report on the work of the PRO, which includes any report made to him by the Advisory Council on Public Records. The manorial documents (see Chapter 6) remain in the charge of the Master of the Rolls.

Under the Public Records Act 1958, the Lord Chancellor can appoint places outside the PRO for the safe keeping and preservation of records and their inspection by the public (section 4). Persons who are responsible for public records of any description, not in the PRO or other place appointed by the Lord Chancellor, have the duty to arrange for the selection and safe keeping of records which should be preserved (section 3). All public records up to 1660 are listed for permanent preservation.

In London, approved places for the keeping of records include the British Library (British Museum Library), the Guildhall Library and the Society of Genealogists (see Chapter 7).

The Public Record Office now

As ever-increasing records came to be deposited in the PRO, overcrowding resulted. Consequently, it was decided to set up an entirely new building at Kew. This building is far from attractive externally, but with considerable modern facilities inside. Records are on the upper floor where accommodation is easy. Computers are used for finding the records, and the staff are courteous and helpful in explaining the use of these to the visitor.

The building contains a restaurant which is of practical importance as facilities for refreshment are very limited in the immediate
neighbourhood. There is also a large car park.

In order to study at the PRO a ticket is required, but no difficulty
need be experienced in obtaining one. A useful leaflet is available to
deal with this and other necessary matters.

The main disadvantage of the PRO at Kew is its distance from
central London. Previously the searcher had the various places of
inquiry within easy reach of each other.

Distribution of records: at Kew and at Chancery Lane
It is important to know which records are kept at Kew and which
remain at Chancery Lane. (The PRO census records at Portugal
Street have already been referred to in Chapter 2.) Full lists are
issued (see Appendix 2), but it must be understood that these are
constantly being revised and extended.

To give one instance: the records of the Board of Customs and
Excise are at Kew. Occasionally I have inquired for the records of
people who worked for that Board. In one instance, I wanted the
details of a member of the Moorshead family. There were several
documentary references to this John Moorshead but I had not
discovered his parentage. He had been described as an Inland
Revenue Officer. As a matter of course, I expected to obtain details
of his career from the Inland Revenue. To my surprise, their
representative informed me that after some thirty years no particulars of officers of that service were preserved. The apology for this
deficiency was almost abject. Then I recollected that John Moorshead had in his earlier life been termed an Excise Officer. Accordingly I wrote to the Board of Customs and Excise and, almost by
return of post, was supplied with the full particulars of his career,
including his father's name and his birthplace.

Some years later, in another case, I wrote for particulars to the
Customs and Excise Board only to be informed that the records had
been deposited at Kew. From the PRO at Kew I received a formal
acknowledgement of the inquiry but no information about the
person named was supplied.

It must be admitted that the staff at Kew do not have the time to
deal with a postal inquiry regarding an individual, but I cite it only as
an example of the way in which research has been made far more

arduous by governmental arrangements within the past twenty years.

It is a simple fact that the genealogist must accept. To some extent, as with the large numbers of searchers at St Catherine's House and Portugal Street, the difficulties are due to the huge increase in genealogical inquiries. But in the PRO the need for another office was caused by the enormous increase in the State's concern with the lives of citizens. One has only to examine the list of records at Kew to see how much paper has accumulated in government departments since 1945. Taken at random from the list, we find – for example – Channel Tunnel Advisory Groups, Royal Commission on Distribution and Wealth, or Ministry of Power. While such items are of great value to the historian or the sociologist, they are unlikely to serve the genealogist. He therefore requires as much guidance as possible on the records which will assist him.

Genealogical sources in the PRO

The records of the PRO are predominantly legal or political in content. The Calendars of the PRO, for example, contain the Chancery Records. These concern matters in which the King was approached through the Lord Chancellor. The documents give the royal replies.

English law is peculiar in that for many centuries two systems operated side by side. The Common Law was used through the courts which were, of course, the King's Courts, but very often they could not deal with a complaint because no course of action existed at Common Law. The seeker after justice had therefore to petition the Sovereign via the Lord Chancellor. The matter was then dealt with in the latter's court. Hence the growth of Chancery jurisdiction in what is called Equity. It was not until 1876 that the two systems of Common Law and Equity were fused. It was then laid down that in any case of conflict the rules of Equity were to prevail. Instead of two Lords Chief Justice of Common Pleas and of King's Bench, one only was retained, with the Lord Chancellor as the head of the entire legal profession.

Close Rolls, Fine Rolls, Exchequer records

The *Close Rolls* are those which were sealed when they were sent out to the recipients; the *Fine Rolls* are returns of transactions regarding land. The *Exchequer records* include such items as the record of the holdings of land by the lesser tenants who held their property on the understanding that they gave military service to the King. The *Inquisitiones post mortem* were a form of medieval estate duty and are very important in the case of the land-owning families. Under the Inquisitions, the heir had to prove his right of inheritance and could not enter into possession of his father's land until the feudal dues were paid. We often find the *Inquisitiones* useful in discovering the approximate age of the heir, since if he or she were under age (21) the estates were under Crown administration.

In considering the above it must be remembered that the type of records described apply almost entirely to the landed families. Only rarely is there mention of lower-class men and women, but occasionally – from the thirteenth century onward – it has been possible to make pedigrees even of the villeins (those persons, the serfs, who were bound to an estate which they could not leave without the lord's permission). These short pedigrees sometimes run from 100 to 150 years. They are constructed mainly from the records of the court of the lord of the manor, often because the villein in question tried to show that he was free and therefore could move from the estate, and that he was not compelled to give so many days' labour on the lord's land.

Norman pedigrees

As shown in Chapter 1, many quite ordinary families can be traced to the sixteenth century with the aid of parish and later records. Before that age, a pedigree of any length can normally be constructed only for the land-owning class, with the aid of the records in the PRO mentioned above. To reach the eleventh century is very rare, due to the fact that we do not have a contemporary account of the Conquest. From the sources available, it has been possible for scholars to discover some forty-four names of those who were present on the Norman side at Hastings. Very few English names are known. The number of families who can trace a pre-Conquest descent is limited to three – the Ardens, the Swintons (in Scotland, but from an English root), and the Berkeleys. These are the limits of the proven. Tall stories of ancestry from Hastings or earlier can be discounted. They usually contain an impossibility, such as the use in England long before the Conquest of foreign Christian names. Guy of Warwick, that glittering hero of medieval folklore, was even set down in *Burke's Commoners* as the ancestor of the Ardens. There it was stated that a tournament was held at the Court of King Athelstan (*c.* 937) at which Guy vanquished the knights of France and Germany.

Battle Abbey Roll   Statements of Norman, descent are frequently made on the strength of the Battle Abbey Roll, a most unreliable source. Six copies of the Roll are in existence, made by researchers like John Leland (1506–52) who set out to describe England as it was in the later years of Henry VIII. It is well known that William the Conqueror vowed to build an Abbey on the ground where King Harold's standard had floated. He kept his word. Battle Abbey was never one of the great medieval monasteries, but the idea was that the monks should pray for the souls of the fallen. Whatever list may have been kept, it was without doubt interpolated to include the names of subsequent benefactors. No reliance can be placed upon the Roll as to the presence on it of any name as being that of a person present at Hastings. The best book on the subject is the Duchess of Cleveland's *Battle Abbey Roll*. Although she was mistaken in accepting the validity of the Roll, her analyses of the names contain much good genealogy.

Guides to the PRO

The PRO will issue to the inquirer much useful information as to what he should search: for instance, the subject of emigration to Australia is not easy, but five multigraph pages of sources issued by the PRO are of immense help.

A new Guide to the PRO is being compiled 'in which descriptions of the contents of classes with an index will be produced and printed by the PROPEC system from a computer held database. As present, only an interim computer printout is available, giving descriptions of classes of State Papers and departmental records. It does not as yet cover classes of records included in the first volume of the published *Guide*' (PRO Information for Readers).

The Guide mentioned above was that issued in 1963 by HMSO *Guide to the Contents of the Public Record Office*. It revised the guide to the records by M. S. Guiseppi (1923). Whether the new work will enable one to find particular items in the PRO I do not know, but the older guides limited themselves to the type and class of records. This type of information is very useful in setting out the contents of the records, and it is to be hoped that this will be done again.

Some sections of the Public Record Office are at Kew and some at Chancery Lane, so it is essential to have exact information about the classes of records and where they are held (see Appendix 2).

Records at Hayes   There is one other matter of importance. Under the list of material at Chancery Lane is the note 'Some classes to be seen at Chancery Lane are housed at Hayes, Middlesex, and notice of several working days is required'.

Dormant funds

It is frequently stated by many people that there are large sums held in Chancery, usually in connection with an estate and a title. It is not only Americans who cherish such delusions. Some people spend a lot of time endeavouring to trace sums of money and the titles which are supposed to go with them. All who think this should consult an official document reference S.C. Pay Office No. 161, which deals with dormant funds in court. This is issued from the Supreme Court Pay Office, Royal Courts of Justice, London WC2. Very strong warnings are issued in this leaflet. Amounts of money held in Chancery are very small; there are no millions there.

A book of great value is Professor Galbraith's *An Introduction to the Use of the Public Records* (Oxford, 1934). Some older reference works, though completely out of date as regards places of deposit, do give useful information as to the nature of the records – for example, *A Manual for the Genealogist, Topographer, Antiquary*, etc., by Richard Sims of the British Museum (1888).

Those interested in the early history of the English language are referred to Professor Saintsbury's *A Short History of English Literature*, Basil Cottle's *The Triumph of English 1350–1400* and the Longman *Handbook of English Literature*.

6

Land Records

The manor

One cannot go far in English medieval history, or for that matter in later centuries, without coming across mention of the manor. The term is post-Conquest and is simply defined as a district or piece of ground held under the feudal system by a lord or other great personage. The manors were the means of sustenance and the wealth of the holders. In cases where the same person held a number of manors, the custom was to spend some time at one manor, moving on to another when fresh supplies were needed. The King, of course, possessed more manors than anyone else; indeed, after the Conquest he could be regarded as owning the whole of England. Domesday Book (1086) provides the records of the King's demesne and of what he had allotted to the 'King's Men' – that is, to the barons, of whom there were about 180. These in turn let out parts of their lands to tenants.

The lord of the manor kept part of the land, known as the *demesne*, for his own use and support, and let out the rest to freehold tenants. On the demesne there was serfdom (villeinage) which meant that the land was worked by men who were bound to live on the particular estate: they could not leave without their lord's permission. They were required to do a certain amount of work on his land and on their allotted portions, and their lot was hard indeed. Villeinage eventually passed away about 1500.

Each lord or holder of a manor was empowered to hold a domestic court known as the court baron (manors sometimes being known as baronies) in which he was able to redress anything which was wrong and to settle disputes about property among the tenants.

Modern lordship of a manor
It need hardly be noted that by an Act of 1867 the jurisdiction of the manorial courts was abolished. The term 'lord of the manor' still exists, however. Lordships of manors are sold: not only the honorific distinction remains, but certain rights – mineral, sporting, etc. – still exist.

The court baron, which was held by the steward of the manor, gradually fell into abeyance after the Middle Ages until its jurisdiction was formally abolished in 1867. The records of these manorial courts are of great value in tracing individuals or families.

The Court Rolls
These Court Rolls are sometimes held among family papers belonging to those who formerly owned the manor, or by solicitors who have acted for the families. The Law of Property Act 1922 provided that 'all manorial documents shall be under the charge and superintendence of the Master of the Rolls'. This did not mean that all manorial records were immediately removed from the custody of the lord of the manor, but that the Master of the Rolls had the power to inquire into the keeping of such records, and to direct that those which in his view were not being properly maintained should be transferred to the Public Record Office. Under this Act, manorial documents are defined as court rolls, surveys, maps, terrier documents (see below) and books of every description relating to the boundaries, franchises, wastes, customs or courts of a manor, but they do not include the deeds and other instruments required for evidencing the title of a manor.

(In parenthesis, we may define the term terrier, which is from the Latin *terrarium*, a piece of land, as 'A land roll or survey of lands, containing the quantity of acres, tenants' names, and suchlike and in the Exchequer there is a terrier of all the glebe lands in England made in 1338' – Mozley and Whiteley's *Law Dictionary*, 9th edition, 1977).

Local records

The Local Government (Records) Act 1962 gave power to the local authorities to take steps to set up what in effect are archive services – to enable adequate use to be made of records under their control, to purchase by agreement records of local interest, to accept the gift of records of local interest and the deposit of records which appear to be of local or general interest, and to make grants to any person for expenses incurred in connection with records.

There is a steadily growing volume of records, including manorial documents, in local offices. Should a County Record Office not have been established (see Appendix 1), the relevant documents are to be found in the care of the Clerk of the particular county council.

Tithe records

From very early times, tithes were paid in money instead of actual produce. The object of the tithe was to support the clergy of the Established Church. One of the objects of the enclosure movement in the eighteenth and nineteenth centuries was to get rid of tithes, but by 1836 they were paid in most parishes in England and Wales. By the Tithe Act 1836, three Tithe Commissioners were appointed and the process of commutation of tithes began. Under the Act, every instrument of Apportionment of Tithes had to be recorded in an original document and two copies. The originals are in the PRO, copies went to the registrar of the diocese and to the incumbent and churchwardens of the parish.

In 1936 all tithe rent charges were extinguished, but up to and after that date annotations of the Apportionment were recorded. The Apportionments contain the name of the landowner and of the occupier (who was responsible for paying the tithe rent charge until the Tithe Act 1891) and the names of the tithe owners.

The genealogical content may not be great, but the PRO accounts state: 'Such interest as the preliminary documents afford lies only in such point as whether the parties acted by themselves or by attorney and the signatures of the parties, the kind of material in fact that may interest the family historian.'

Taxation revenues

Through the centuries of English history, the records of taxation provide much information of use to the genealogist. At first, and for some centuries, taxation records concern mainly the upper classes or the wealthier sections of the community. The Great Roll of the Pipe extends from 1155 to 1833. A Great Survey was taken by Henry II in 1166 in order to assess the changes which had occurred among the landowners after eighty years (Domesday was in 1086). The object, of course, was to ascertain what were the dues which the great feudatories owed to the Crown. The records of the Survey were given in the Black Book of the Exchequer – *Liber Niger Scacarii*.

Then later comes the *Liber Rubeus* or Red Book, which records serjeantries, knights' fees and *prima scutagia* of the reigns from Henry II to Henry III.

The *Testa de Nevill sive Liber Feodorum in Curia Scacarii* accounts for knights' fees and serjeantries up to the reign of Edward II (1307–27).

The Close Rolls are royal letters which, because of their private nature, were sealed. They extend from the reign of John up to quite modern times. Many volumes of the Close Rolls have been published by HMSO.

Other medieval sources

There are many other medieval sources such as abbey cartularies (where these have been saved), Escheat Rolls, Fine Rolls and *Inquisitiones post mortem* (see page 60).

Two classes of names appear in these valuable documents. There are names which are mentioned only in passing and whose brief appearance makes us long to know more. Names in the second class are genealogically the mainstay of the great baronial families who are still with us, either in the male or (more probably) the female line.

Details of all these manorial records are contained in an essay which I wrote as the leading introductory article in the 1952 edition of *Burke's Landed Gentry*.

I there pointed out that after 1660 many changes occurred in taxation records. The ancient feudal dues of the Crown, ostensibly the reason for the Civil War, were abolished after the Restoration of

Charles II. There had to be other ways to raise the money for the Sovereign, who was still supposed to be meeting public expenditure. One of these was the Hearth Tax, which lasted only for six years but gives useful information to anyone who can trace his ancestry to 1662, when the tax began. The number of hearths which a taxpayer had was a sure guide to his social standing – for example, the Earl of Clarendon had forty-three hearths in his mansion at Cornbury and Lord Anglesey had thirty. Anyone who had ten hearths would be at least in a good middling position.

Knights' fees
This term often occurs in family histories which go back into medieval land-owning. *Feudum militare* was a quantity of land sufficient to maintain a knight, in order that he could carry out the obligations on which he was allowed to hold the land – that is, to serve the overlord in war. In the reign of Henry III (1216–72) it was £15 per annum, but in the next reign it was estimated at twelve ploughlands, and under Edward II (1307–27) it was held to be £20 per annum.

In the Domesday settlement, there were 5,000 such fees, which would give the Conqueror some 20,000 armed men, counting the personal followers of each knight. But by the time of the Great Survey already mentioned, scutage (i.e. payment in lieu of service) gave the Sovereign the means to hire professional soldiers.

Serjeantry
Serjeantry is divided into *petty* and *grand*. The former consists of holding lands on condition of rendering some service to the Crown, as of presenting a rose at Christmas. Grand serjeantry is a tenure held by virtue of some special service to the Crown – to be the Chief Butler or the Queen's Champion, for example. At the beginning of a reign, a Special Court of Privileges is held at which the various claims to Grand Serjeantry are examined and approved or otherwise. For example, the head of the Dymoke family holds the office of Queen's Champion.

Poll books
Far into the nineteenth century, voting at elections was open and many poll books still remain which are useful in proving where an

ancestor lived at a particular time. From these books may be obtained the names, residences and descriptions of persons having freehold property. The poll books may not contain the names of all freeholders of the county, the lists being only of those who voted.

Union records
From the sixteenth century, it became necessary in England for the government to take measures to deal with vagrants, the homeless or destitute. The Dissolution of the Monasteries in 1536–39 had caused numerous persons to be without sustenance or shelter: previously, those who had no fixed address could seek shelter and food in a monastery. Whatever the faults of the monastic system in the sixteenth century, it did not fail to carry out the charitable work with which it had always been associated.

When the great system disintegrated, most of the abbey lands went to keen men of business who were seldom inspired by motives of charity. Something had to be done, though, about the indigent wanderers and the legal remedy was to confine them to the care of a particular parish. If they moved away, they could not obtain relief from the new parish, but had to return to their original place of sojourn. This kind of treatment went on until 1834, when the Poor Law grouped parishes together into Unions, the workhouses. The records of the Unions are valuable, and not only in the annals of the poor. The workhouse had to be managed and required staff. The Guardians of the Poor were responsible for the management of the workhouses and the Unions. The existing Poor Law was abolished by the National Assistance Act 1948, and in its place was set up the National Assistance Board, with the duty to assist persons who were without resources.

During the century or so that the Unions existed, a great deal of information was recorded concerning workhouse inmates. These records may be held in the county record offices or sometimes in solicitors' offices or in local government offices.

Anyone wishing to study the medieval records referred to in this chapter would gain much useful background information from F. W. Maitland's *Domesday Book and After* and his *Constitutional History of England*, and from J. H. Round's *Feudal England*.

7

Printed Books

Introduction

Mention has been made hitherto of records which are in manuscript (although it should be remembered that many of the parish registers have been printed) and I refer here to the research value of other printed books.

Printing in England has a history of over 500 years. William Caxton set up his printing press in Westminster in 1476. The first dated book printed in England was *The Dictes of the Philosophers* by Lord Rivers, a copy of which he presented to King Edward IV. It then became the habit and pleasure of men of means to collect libraries. The appalling destruction of records in the Dissolution of the Monasteries caused some of the more cultured and public-spirited to form collections, some of which contained savings from the monastic libraries. One of these benefactors was Sir Hans Sloane (1660–1753), a physician and scholar. He bequeathed his library to the nation in consideration of a payment of £20,000. This collection was then housed in Montague House, the nucleus of the British Museum.

Libraries

The British (Museum) Library

From the beginning, the Library was regulated by Act of Parliament under which it was ordained that a copy of every book published in Britain was to be sent to the British Museum Library. This rule was at first frequently ignored, but under the energetic librarianship of Sir Anthony Panizzi, publishers learned to obey. Panizzi (1797–1879) was of Italian origin, one of those adopted sons of England who have done so much for her. As a consequence, the collection of printed books in the British Museum became, by the twentieth century, the largest library in the world. It is now third, after the Central Library in Moscow and the Library of Congress in Washington. Nonetheless, the sight of the Central Reading Room of the British Library, and the awareness of its millions of books, is enough to daunt the most aspiring writer, for in the longest of lifetimes he cannot hope to compass more than a tiny fraction of the wealth of human knowledge and literary creation here collected.

Fortunately, the user of the Library can recover from this depressing reminder of the brevity of human life and the deficiencies which this imposes on our learning. The first step is to master the catalogue, which takes a number of visits. The staff of the Library are always helpful and inevitably they face many inquiries. Apart from the immense quantity of printed books housed in the Library, the number of manuscripts is very considerable, though not to be compared with those in the PRO. Then there are a great number of books which have been privately printed: many family histories fall into this category. These are not required by law to be deposited in the Library, but many writers of privately printed books have the good sense to deposit a copy. These are always welcomed, as are manuscripts, of which again a copy should always be deposited. I mean by this such productions as a parish history. Any author of works which have been privately printed, no matter what the subject, is wise to ensure that copies are sent to the Library. Otherwise, they can easily be lost to general knowledge and posterity.

Owing to the enormous size of the collection, considerable delay can arise in obtaining books, two hours being a fair period between sending in one's application and receiving the book.

Very rarely it happens that a book cannot be obtained at all. This is usually due to the loss of some 240,000 volumes during the German bombing of London. In such a case, we usually have to conclude that the book is unobtainable from any source.

If one knows the publisher of the missing book, it is possible to inquire from that source: but one is usually unlucky. Many publishers have ceased to exist, and even where they still function they are unlikely to possess a spare copy of a book which was published in, say, 1890. Some very well regulated publishing houses may retain a file copy, but that is all. The book having passed out of print, they are also unlikely to possess any details of the author. On the other hand, luck may be with you. I know of one case concerning a book published in 1953, of which 50,000 copies were printed: after a fortnight's search, the publisher found a copy in his company's library.

Around the huge Reading Room of the British Library are many important works of reference on open shelves. These, of course, can be consulted without putting in an application and one soon learns to anchor oneself at the particular spot where one's special subject is located. That is, to get as close as possible for, with the Reading Room as elsewhere in research, there is severe pressure on space. Consequently, it is not always easy to acquire a reader's ticket, though a serious applicant is unlikely to be turned away.

The authorities have done their best to accommodate searchers. Some particularly valuable books have to be consulted in special rooms; it is possible to use the galleries in some cases, which is a great help. For example, in locating Italian nobility, many volumes may have to be consulted. Then, too, on some days there is an extension of closing hours into the evening.

To conclude, a note on the British Library as presently constituted is appropriate. It was established on 1 July 1973 by the British Library Act of 1972. It was designed to bring together (*a*) the Reference Division which comprised the British Museum Library, the Newspaper Library at Colindale, the Science Reference Library and the Library Association Library; (*b*) the Lending Division which comprises the National Lending Library of Science and Technology and the former National Central Library; and (*c*) the Research and Development Department. According to figures given in 1982, the Reference Division contains more than ten million printed books, some 83,000 volumes of Western manuscripts and over 37,000 volumes of Oriental manuscripts.

Other copyright libraries
It is important to remember that other libraries in the British Isles have the right to receive a copy of each work published in Britain.

These libraries are the Bodleian at Oxford, the University Library at Cambridge, the National Library of Wales, the Scottish National Library, and that of Trinity College, Dublin. How far this entitlement (under the Copyright Act 1911) has been enforced, I do not know. In using Cambridge University Library, I have found gaps in an author's works, but at Cambridge, a quarter of an hour is the longest time one is likely to wait for a book. Therefore, anyone living within reasonable distance of one of these five other copyright libraries can find (as at Cambridge) easier conditions of working.

Other London libraries

There are some five hundred libraries in London, most of which are specialised, such as the libraries of the Royal Geographical Society or the Royal Asiatic Society. The Royal Geographical Society's library contains many biographies of noted and less well-known explorers from which copious family information can be gleaned. The library of the Royal Asiatic Society also has much information, including family origins of the British orientalists, as well as details concerning oriental potentates.

All libraries will yield genealogical information if used intelligently, but gaps will certainly be found, requiring some books to be sought in the British Library.

The Society of Genealogists The Society of Genealogists has what is probably the largest collection of genealogical books in Britain. The Society can be consulted by non-members, for a fee, but clearly in a lengthy inquiry it is best to become a member. The best course, then, is to consult the Society's archives to discover how much information the library contains on an individual, a family or a group of people. Having ransacked the collections of the Society, any gaps can then be filled in the British Library. As an example, the Society does not possess complete series of books like *Burke's Peerage*, but if one particular edition is wanted it will be available in the British Library.

The Society also possesses a large card index of various individuals and families, which often provides a vital clue. In addition, there are some manuscripts and a large collection of private family histories. There are said to be some 10,000 family histories in Britain, and the Society is the first place to search for copies. The

Society also holds a microfiche index of the Mormon genealogical records (see page 98).

The Guildhall Library   Also of great importance for the genealogist is the Guildhall Library. This was moved fairly recently and the new premises, if not as picturesque as the old library, are certainly commodious and comfortable. The same arrangement is followed as at the British Library, with useful reference works on open shelves and the rest of the huge collection available via requisition slips. The delay in obtaining a requested book is seldom more than half an hour.

At the Guildhall, the vast collection of books may even make it unnecessary to visit the British Library. In addition, there is the Manuscript Department and the Corporation Record Office. The latter is in the North Office Block behind Guildhall, having its entrance in Basinghall Street. In the Corporation Record Office, as one would expect, there is an immense amount of information about the affairs of the City of London, going back many centuries. Much of the material may lack interest for the genealogist, but anyone who is making research into City families would find it invaluable. There are records of property, citizenship, inhabitants and occupations.

Having obtained some guidance to the London libraries of most value to the searcher, the next important consideration concerns the type of publication likely to be of service.

Types of printed works

Directories
Having traced an ancestor to approximately 1760–80, town and country directories are helpful. Many were published about that period. One of the most celebrated survivals is the series of Kelly's postal and county directories. Over the door of this business house was the proud sign 'Published in three centuries' and the date 1799. There were many other such books but they have not stayed the course. Where they have been preserved, they are most useful. Let us suppose that you have traced an ancestor to a parish, but his date of death is not known. If his occupation is known, you may trace him

through a directory of the locality. Through the various issues, a clue may be obtained as to his date of arrival in the town and even a hint of his place of origin.

Poll books
These were compiled in the eighteenth and early nineteenth centuries to show the number of voters in a place and how they voted. The secret ballot is a modern invention: whatever we may think of the advisability of open ballots, we can be thankful that such things were recorded. In the case of the Matthews family (see page 49) poll books and directories enabled me to trace their progress in Norwich, whereas the registers of the local church helped me but little. The property qualification counted for a good deal in the eighteenth-century franchise, and poll books may thus render information on the status of an ancestor.

Individual families
It is essential to know what material may be in print regarding individual families. *The Genealogists' Guide* by George W. Marshall was reprinted in 1967, though its last edition was in 1903. Obviously, a work which was last published in a new edition so long ago would lack a large quantity of references which have been made regarding pedigrees since then. In 1953 there was published *A Genealogical Guide*, subtitled *An Index to British Pedigrees in continuation of Marshall's Genealogists' Guide (1903)*. Compiled by J. B. Whitmore, this gives us another half-century of pedigree references. Since then, a further volume has appeared: *The Genealogists' Guide* (1977), a supplement to Marshall and Whitmore, by G. B. Barrow. Unless civilisation collapses, these records will continue indefinitely, so that no list of pedigrees can ever be complete. But these books are invaluable to the searcher: if you have not yet formulated your own pedigree, you will want to know what, if anything, has already appeared in print.

These books should be used in conjunction with the works on surnames mentioned in Chapter 1, since the beginner must realise how changes in the spelling of names do not necessarily denote a difference in family relationships. Also of use in connection with the genealogical guides is *Burke's General Armory* which contains entries for some 100,000 coats of arms (see also Chapter 15).

The books mentioned so far should ideally be in the possession of the searcher, since you will make frequent reference to them, especially if you search into female lines. With other volumes, you may not find it necessary to purchase them. Much depends upon the nature of your inquiries. You are likely to need one or other of the books on wills; and it will be hard for the inquirer into family history to proceed far without a peerage reference book. Many peers take a title different from their surname – or at least they did until quite recently. Since 1964, with very few, recent exceptions, only *life* peerages have been created and in the great majority of cases, the new peer has used his surname as his title. However, this applies only in a limited degree to the older titles, especially to those which are hereditary.

'Ordinary' and 'extraordinary' families

No family is 'ordinary' – at least, not to the person who belongs to it. Moreover, as mentioned in Chapter 1, the lines of descent of English people are not parallel but intermingled. It was Augustine Birrell who said 'scratch the peer and you find the peasant' and the opposite is equally true. Huge numbers of 'ordinary' families have traditions of connection with a lord or a knight. Half the population of England and of Scotland is connected with the peerage – hence, perhaps, our blessed freedom from violent revolutions.

Then, too, there are individuals who achieved distinction and who may appear, with biographical information, in *Who Was Who*.

Guides to recorded families

As half the upper classes are not peers, but untitled people, a recent edition of *Burke's Landed Gentry* is useful. As with all publications, the prices of genealogical books have increased enormously in recent years, but sometimes volumes of Burke or Debrett can be obtained in secondhand shops at reasonable prices.

The Burke volumes

Although I have mentioned Debrett along with Burke, the former will not very much assist the genealogist. Debrett is frequently referred to as the great authority on the aristocracy but, in fact, it is not a genealogical work, since it does not contain pedigrees. For these, one must consult Burke. There have been over one hundred editions of *Burke's Peerage* and eighteen of *Burke's Landed Gentry*. The distinction between these two works is simply the absence of hereditary titles from the *Landed Gentry*; otherwise the social classes are the same. The untitled aristocracy sometimes have longer pedigrees than do the peers and baronets. With so many volumes, a huge number of individuals, past and present, are mentioned and often the families recorded have branches which are not covered.

It is a common desire to be connected with 'the right people' or 'the upper ten', to use a colloquialism. Therefore a word of warning is necessary in using Burke. The scientific study of genealogy did not begin until the last quarter of the nineteenth century. It then proceeded with speed in the works of J. H. Round, Oswald Barron, Sir Henry Maxwell Lyte, Professor Freeman and others, but it was a long time before it caught up with the pedigrees in Burke.

Sir Bernard Burke (who was for many years Ulster King of Arms) was engaged almost from boyhood in assisting his father, John Burke, in producing the various Burke volumes. They covered not only *Peerage* and *Gentry* but, in addition, *Extinct Peerage* and *Extinct Baronetcies*, together with many lesser volumes. They began with the first volume of the *Peerage* in 1826. From then on, right through the nineteenth century, a large amount of fabulous material appeared in the Burke volumes. To give one example, the second edition of the *Landed Gentry* appeared in 1842 in two volumes. Many of the families are described as of Norman origin, and some of pre-Conquest date. Although the majority of these stories had been shown to be without foundation by the end of the century, such pedigrees continued to appear, even after Sir Bernard's death in 1982.

The publications were continued by his sons. A. C. Fox-Davies succeeded in clearing up the position of coats of arms in the *Landed Gentry of Ireland* in 1912, and in the main *Landed Gentry* in 1914, but he was unable to deal with the genealogical problems.

At last, in the 1937 edition of the *Landed Gentry*, the Editor was a scholar, Harry Pirie Gordon. He cleared up the pedigrees of the Scots families and the edition was definitely better than its predecessors. However, it was not until after the Second World War that a complete overhaul of the two Burke volumes was undertaken. The idea of this overhaul was mine, and it became possible because the original typesetting of the *Peerage* was dissolved and it had to be completely reset. Thus, in the first post-War edition of the *Peerage* (1949), there was an opportunity which would not occur again – at least in the twentieth century. I enlisted the help of many scholars, including the officers of the College of Arms, especially Michael Trappes Lomax who became our official adviser. Sir Thomas Innes of Learney, the then Lord Lyon, rendered invaluable assistance, as did many others. The volumes of *The Ancestor* and the works of J. H. Round were carefully studied.

The results of this intensive effort were seen in the 1949, 1953, 1956 and 1959 editions of *Burke's Peerage*: not only were legends and myths replaced by facts, but larger pedigrees were included. The position now is that Burke is taken seriously by students and scholars alike.

The same principles were applied to the first post-War *Landed Gentry* in 1952. Here I had expected an easier task and was surprised to find so much effort necessary in weeding out genealogical statements which could not be justified. The 1952 was the last definitive, one-volume, edition of the *Landed Gentry*. Here, too, the whole was overhauled; while some pedigrees still require careful attention (there are 3,000 pages in each of the *Peerage* and *Gentry*) the principles have been set out.

From the general public, I received much publicity and appreciation; from genealogical circles came little but abuse. A. H. Mitten, a distinguished genealogist and one of the best of his generation, told me that though my work was sound I had made many enemies because of the removal of myth and legend.

Works of massive scholarship

There are several reference works which are usually consulted in libraries, though copies are obtainable at a high price. The great scholarship of the late Victorian period was shown in at least three productions: *The Complete Peerage*, the *Dictionary of National Biography* and the *Victoria History of the Counties of England*.

The Complete Peerage, a monumental work in fourteen volumes, is now available (for £300) in a smaller sized printing. It is written without fear or favour, and contains every fact which labour has been able to unearth about each peer. The histories are those of the successors of the peerages, but considerations of size prevent the inclusion of the style of pedigree found in Burke. When succession of a peerage has gone to a distant relative, the genealogy is given in parenthetic form. There could conceivably be an incorrect statement in *The Complete Peerage*, but it is most unlikely.

Its second great merit is in the inclusion of many historical essays – such as one on the Battle of Bannockburn – which are deeply interesting.

The *Dictionary of National Biography* is naturally uneven, as the articles have been contributed by many hands. Still, it is a treasure-house of information on every Briton of distinction. In addition, two volumes give the most important details, with dates, in an abbreviated form. These are the *Concise Dictionary of National Biography*, up to 1900, and a similar volume to 1950. There are also full-size continuation volumes for more recent decades.

The *Victoria History of the Counties of England* deals with every department of knowledge about the county – geological, topographical, etc. Of necessity, there is genealogical information, but it has to be sought out. It is sometimes very extensive: for example, in a volume of the *History* dealing with Essex, there is a translation of the Domesday portion dealing with that county.

Another peerage work of the highest scholarship is *The Scots Peerage*, in eight volumes, by the former Lord Lyon Sir James Balfour Paul.

There is also much useful information to be gleaned from William Anderson's *Antiquity of the Scottish Nation*. Why this should be so often disregarded, I do not know. No doubt it contains legends and perhaps the occasional myth, yet Anderson does give details of all Scots folk up to his time (1840). There is much sober fact and his accounts can always be compared with later histories. (For further information see Chapter 10.)

Valuable periodicals
A publication not likely to be owned by the average searcher is *The Gentleman's Magazine*, which is available in the libraries previously mentioned. This publication was started by Edward Cave in January 1731. The magazine lasted until 1910 and consists of hundreds of volumes. There are index volumes covering several periods; and there are indices to obituaries, marriages, births, etc. The publica-

tion is not easy to use, but provided one has a fairly good notion of the date of an event, the rewards of a search can be great.

Gazetteers

In conjunction with the genealogical guides mentioned here, a gazetteer is essential. *Bartholomew's Gazetteer* covers every place, however small, which is still extant in the British Isles. The older editions contained a series of maps covering the whole of these islands, but when one is studying a particular area nothing can be better than the Ordnance Survey maps.

This is particularly important when seeking for a family background and having no clue other than that the family may have lived in a certain place. For instance, a family lived for perhaps a century in Porlock in Somerset, but the earliest member to live there is shown as having been baptised in 1760. There is no mention of the parents' marriage or residence before Porlock. Bearing in mind that in those days people did not move as much as they have since the Industrial Revolution, it is advisable to search the areas adjacent to Porlock, within a distance of five or ten miles. A map, and a good one, is essential.

Again, you may find a record of death but no trace of a burial. The funeral probably took place where the parents were buried – and the cortege would not be likely to proceed at a fast pace with swiftly galloping horses! It follows that the place of interment is unlikely to have been many miles away, and a careful search within a radius of a few miles should solve the problem.

Loss of reference works

The cessation of many periodicals, such as *Walford's County Families* or *Whitaker's Peerage*, has been a great loss. These annual works carried many biographies of people not always found in Burke or Debrett. In the case of the *Landed Gentry*, which was always of irregular date, a biographical entry could be picked up in Walford or Whitaker. The former ended in 1920 and the latter was a casualty of the Second World War.

It would seem that the time is fast approaching when information about the marriages, children and divorces of what are known vulgarly as 'the upper ten' will either not be published in book form or will be found (and then only for some of the members) only in *Who's Who*.

Use of reprints
One redeeming feature of the situation for genealogical and heraldic works is the large number of reprints of useful books now available. In some cases, new editions have been published and reprints have been made of many others. Even so, under modern conditions price is a serious consideration and many searchers will have to rely on library copies.

Cautions

When using the various works listed in this chapter, one caution must be borne in mind. There is an unconscious supposition that, because something appears in print, it is correct. Put like this, the idea is patently absurd, but it exists nonetheless, and underlies many of the unshakeable prejudices one encounters in genealogical study. Even when a statement has appeared in print, there is still the need to examine carefully the authority behind it.

Similar caution is to be used with the expression, often found in the older genealogical works, 'it is said that'. This expression should never be used without information as to the person or authority who made the statement.

A consideration of an opposite nature also needs to be remembered. Some written sources are so much depreciated that they are passed over and not used at all.

Some sources may be misunderstood. No human work is infallible, but perhaps *The Complete Peerage* is the nearest approach to an infallible authority. This is due to the absence of commercial bias on the part of the compilers (Lord Nuffield made himself financially responsible for the later volumes of this work) and, of course, also to the high scholarship of the authors, like Geoffrey White. Common sense, that rarest of gifts, was used along with the most involved sources of learning. As an example, the surnames of peers are always included. Why they should ever have been omitted from any peerage accounts is inexplicable and Mr White always poured scorn on peers 'losing their surnames'.

8

Newspapers

Introduction

Newspapers are a source of immense value to the genealogist. *The Gentleman's Magazine* was mentioned in Chapter 7, but there are vast realms of information in the extensive newspapers of this country. Everyone, of course, knows about the columns of *The Times* and the *Daily Telegraph* which record births, marriages and deaths, sources which are most useful in checking a family history. There are also the obituary notices which are an important feature of *The Times* and, to a lesser extent, of the *Daily Telegraph*. In either case, the notices deal only with persons who are deemed to be of sufficient importance to warrant a special entry.

The London Gazette

The official publication *The London Gazette* appears four times a week. To the genealogist, it is extremely valuable in giving changes of name and the naturalisation of aliens. With regard to the latter, I can foresee some interesting revelations being made by the professional genealogist a century from now. He who hopes to reap a rich reward from the wealthy patron of AD 2084 will have a shock when, for example, his researches end in *The London Gazette* for 1952 with the name of a Polish, Czech or German refugee who 'intends to be known henceforth as John Robinson'.

The London Gazette is also of prime importance as regards the nomenclature of new peers and the occasional Royal Warrants which give the Queen's directions as to the surname of her family, or the style of the wives and children of the life peers.

Provincial papers
Valuable as the above mentioned sources may be, even more rewarding are the local or provincial papers. I have accumulated whole dossiers on families, which I have obtained from this source. Cregoe Nicholson, a prominent member of the Society of Genealogists, particularly developed this branch of research. As he pointed out, a man who was in business or in trade had to advertise if he was to earn more than a meagre living. Therefore, the newspapers in the district where he lived were likely to contain information about him. One of the best examples of this occurs in the pedigree of the Lords Baillieu, where some two hundred years ago the ancestors were teachers of dancing in Bath. A good deal of information about them was obtained from the contemporary local newspapers.

In England, newspapers go back some two hundred years and there have been a large number of them. There are still many provincial newspapers, although rising costs are frequently forcing their closure.

Where to study newspapers

Colindale
To inspect these useful sources, the first place to call is the Newspaper Library at Colindale, London NW9, some one and a half miles from Hendon. This is part of the British Library, from which it is separated fro the obvious reason of shortage of space. A ticket for the British Library admits the bearer to Colindale. Here, as at Kew, you should devote the day to a visit, as this important office is away from other places of research.

Over the past twenty years or so, conditions at Colindale have varied a great deal. At one period, a visit to the Newspaper Library was a pleasant variation; one could secure a seat without trouble and the required newspaper file was quickly forthcoming. By the 1970s, many more people had discovered the virtues of Colindale and it was often difficult to obtain a seat. In recent years, I have always sent a written request, in advance, for the papers I wish to see. This saves time on arrival and, in fact, on one occasion it was only by this expedient that I obtained admittance. I was told that every seat was taken, but when I explained that the librarian had telephoned me to say that the required newspapers would be available, I was admitted and given a seat among the files themselves. When I emerged some hours later, after peering at the small print of a provincial paper, I could hardly see – but I had gained some valuable and relevant material.

I do not want to deter would-be inquirers. The authorities at Colindale have certainly endeavoured to meet demands, by making more seats available. The offices are comfortable to work in and the required material is brought with admirable alacrity. The staff are most helpful.

Other sources

There are other ways of studying newspapers. With *The Times*, you can go and study their files: the further back one goes, the more extraordinary and unexpected are the entries. One client was interested in a Lord Mayor of London in the early nineteenth century. I traced this man through various means – the Guildhall Library for one – and then found in *The Times* a notice of his death, which had taken place in a lunatic asylum. The issues of *The Times* have been microfilmed and so are available at many large libraries.

The task of searching the files of a local paper is simplified (*a*) if it still exists or (*b*) if the back numbers are kept in some repository. If possible, the best way is to make an appointment to visit the newspaper office and go through the files. If the office is in a distant part of the country, the editor will usually supply, without charge, a particular item of information such as a local obituary notice or an account of a marriage. However, he cannot be expected to detail one of his staff to go through the files of perhaps twenty years picking out items of interest to a searcher.

There are many local societies in the country which, for various reasons, like to keep copies of the local newspapers.

I was making inquiries into a Cornish family, the Beswethericks of Bodmin. One of them, John Beswetherick, was a successful draper at Bodmin and then decided to open a larger business at Glastonbury. There he lived and worked for sixteen years, from 1879 to 1895. From the files of the *Central Somerset Gazette*, I obtained a large body of information. Much of this was in the form of advertising of the drapery, when the owner had obtained someone's stock, or the latest fashions from London. There was also a lot of information about his religious and political affiliations and masonic activities, together with details of his second marriage and the marriages of his children. But then came one of the irritating snags which afflict all researchers: I could not find the volume of the *Central Somerset Gazette* for 1888, not even at Colindale. The editor of the paper was most helpful, but he thought that the volume had been destroyed 'in the war'. At least it was missing, though how enemy action had removed the volume from both Colindale and Bodmin remains a mystery. We have to reconcile ourselves to an element of luck in genealogical research.

The papers to which I have referred differ very considerably from *The Gentleman's Magazine*: this is concerned with the doings of the gentry, landowners and professional people, whereas the local newspapers deal with news of any and every kind, including criminal matters. But each, in its own way, is a valuable source of information and it is well worthwhile to study the old newspapers, which can provide the most important clues.

9

Other Useful Sources

Mention has been made in Chapter 7 of several printed books which are the tools of the researcher. Other printed works can be summarised here.

Educational records

To begin with, there are the records of schools and universities. Any school which has a respectable age – Eton, Harrow, Winchester, Shrewsbury, etc. – will have annals and records of those admitted to it. These usually contain details of the entrants, including their age, place of residence and parentage. Many of these registers have been maintained after the pupil left the school, so that something of his subsequent life has been recorded. Many of the pupils of public and grammar schools went on to Oxford and Cambridge. In the records of the Colleges of the two ancient universities much information is recorded, again of parentage etc., then on to the undergraduate's subsequent career, the degree or degrees which he took, and very often something about his career after leaving the university. To give one instance: when I was studying the Beswetherick family, I knew that one of them (John) had graduated at Keble College, Oxford, but was surprised when, in the College records, I learned that he had died of malaria as a soldier in the East African campaign of 1915.

It is not always easy to get a sight of these school reference works. The best collection which I know is at the Society of Genealogists, but if the particular volume required is not there, application can always be made to the headmaster of the school.

Oxford and Cambridge records
For the University of Cambridge, there are the useful ten volumes of J. A. Venn's (1922–54) *Alumni Cantabrigienses*: for Oxford, J. Foster's (1887–92) *Alumni Oxonienses*.

Other universities
Similar records have been kept of other British universities, the four in Scotland and Trinity College, Dublin. Then, in 1964, P. M. Jacobs proposed a complete list or *Register of the Universities, Colleges and Schools of Great Britain and Ireland*, a gigantic undertaking.

The many new universities of the twentieth century naturally keep records of their undergraduates.

The Inns of Court
It must be remembered that in the sixteenth and seventeenth centuries, many notable men did not go to the universities but resided instead at an Inn of Court. At these institutions they may have acquired some tincture of law, but in many cases they were admitted in order to partake of a liberal education. This was imparted in the Inns (including even tuition in dancing) so that the student received a great deal of the advantage which he would have obtained at Oxford or Cambridge. The records of the four Inns – Inner and Middle Temple, Gray's and Lincoln's – begin as a rule in the sixteenth century, but from then on they illuminate not a little of an entrant's career. The records of the Middle Temple were published in the 1950s in three large volumes.

Of course, many who entered at the Inns did not go on to the Bar. For more modern references to the legal profession we have the annual *Law List*, available in all libraries. Two snags need to be borne in mind when consulting it. Barristers who are not in practice may be dropped from the List unless they pay a small annual fee. Then, as regards solicitors, it may be that a solicitor has been slow in renewing his certificate and consequently his name is not entered. A barrister's entry should mention his degrees.

Records of the clergy

Professional information comes in many volumes. *Crockford's Clerical Directory*, still published, deals with the clergy of the Church of England, and incorporates the older *Clergy List*. This useful work is strictly professional: that is, it gives no details of parentage or of schooling. The ordinand's professional training at university and/or theological college is detailed, as are his ordination as deacon and priest, his clerical appointments and preferments, and books which he has written.

There are also some reference works for clergy of other denominations. *Who's Who in the Free Churches*, published in 1950, was the only work ever to attempt to deal with the Nonconformist bodies. Included in this were the Society of Friends and the Salvation Army, though permission had to be obtained from the Free Church Federal Council to include the Quakers and the Salvationists, as neither organisation is technically a Church. The value of this book is limited to the period around 1950 but, like all reference works which contain biographies, it has its value.

Free Church records

Elaborate records are kept by several Dissenting bodies, so that application to the Baptist, Methodist or Congregational headquarters will often yield required information on ministers and also on laymen who have taken official positions in their respective denominations. Thus, the well-known Fellow of the Royal College of Surgeons, Dr Fletcher Moorshead, who was Secretary of the Baptist Missionary Society, had a biography published by the Baptists which contains some details of his family history, his birth, education and marriage.

Roman Catholics

There are some useful books concerning the Roman Catholics (at one time termed the Papists). *The Catholic Directory* gives the professional positions of priests in Great Britain. *The Catholic Who's Who* appeared in its 35th edition in 1952, edited by Sir Harold Hood, himself a convert to the Roman Church. This work gives a wealth of useful information about affairs not usually mentioned in the general run of reference books. For details of earlier Roman Catholics, the volumes of the Catholic Record Society are useful. These volumes are sometimes found in libraries; otherwise inquiries should be sent to The Catholic Record Society, c/o Archbishop's House, Westminster, London SW1.

The Society of Friends

The Quakers have always kept most careful records and in America these have assumed huge proportions. The Library of the Society of Friends at Friends House, Euston Road, London NW1, has many records.

The Huguenots

After the Revocation of the Edict of Nantes by Louis XIV in 1685, there was an influx of Huguenots into England. These immigrants contributed much of value to their adopted country. Many distinguished families still retain memory of their French origin, and inquiries can be made of the Huguenot Society of London at 54 Knatchbull Road, London SE5. Application should be made to the Hon. Secretary. There is also the Huguenot Library at University College, Gower Street, London W1.

The Jews

Jewish information falls into two classes.

The Jews were banished from England by King Edward I in 1290. Oliver Cromwell allowed them to return in 1655, though Jews did occasionally live in England during the intervening centuries. Queen Elizabeth I is said to have had a Jewish physician.

There are, therefore, some Jewish families of quite long standing in England, such as the Ricardos (in *Landed Gentry*) or the famous Rothschilds. In these instances, there are pedigrees of several generations. A useful work on British Jewry is *The Rise of Provincial Jewry* by Professor Cecil Roth. The subtitle explains the value of the work: 'The early history of the Jewish Community in the English countryside 1740–1840'. It gives details of the Jewish presence in the different cities, as a result of the research by this distinguished scholar who wrote many other books on the history of the Jews in England. The index of the book covers fifteen pages, and is composed mostly of names of individuals.

The second class among the Jewish population is much larger and is composed of the many refugees from Continental tyranny since 1930. These do not possess much in the way of pedigree, but inquirers should contact the Board of Deputies of British Jews, Woburn House, Upper Woburn Place, London WC1. Much valuable information can also be found at the Jewish Museum at the same address.

For a lengthy discussion of the whole subject of Jewish records in European countries see *The Genealogists' Encyclopedia* by L. G. Pine (pages 151–70): this account is derived from the Jewish Historical Archives in Jerusalem and is therefore completely official.

Masonic records

Masonic sources are easily available. The headquarters of the Masonic organisation in England is in Freemasons' Hall, Great Queen Street, London WC2. There are approximately 700,000 Masons in England, and naturally there are Masonic traditions in their families. Anyone who seeks information about a Masonic forbear is advised to write to the Grand Secretary at Freemasons' Hall.

Here is an instance of the speed with which information is supplied. A letter of 11 March was answered on 16 March, with the following helpful details:

'John Beswetherick was Initiated 29 March 1858 in the One and All Lodge, No. 413 (now No. 330) Bodmin, described as aged 26, of Bodmin, Draper. He was Passed 31 May and Raised 27 September and was Master of the Lodge in 1865. He was appointed Provincial Grand Superintendent of Works (Cornwall) 1865. He joined the Pilgrims Lodge, No. 772, 11 October 1879, described as of Glastonbury, Draper.'

This information shed much light on John Beswetherick's early life. I had already gained many details of his life at Glastonbury, but clearly he had been successful in Bodmin at an earlier date. Nor had

I known that he had held Provincial Grand rank. Subsequently, correspondence with the Librarian at Freemasons' Hall enabled me to correct a loosely worded account in the *Central Somerset Gazette*, where he had been mentioned as a Past Master in an account of a function of Pilgrims Lodge. He was never Master of the latter, and the reference in the newspaper was to his original Cornish lodge.

Having got this far, I then sought more information, this time about John Beswetherick's son, James Phillips Beswetherick. He was initiated in the Powell Lodge, No. 2257, Bristol, on 22 September 1902, and is described in the Register as age 41, Buyer, Coronation Road. He resigned from the Lodge in 1908.

City of London records

Records of Freemen and apprentices in connection with the City of London are useful. The Livery Companies of today were formerly the trade guilds. Their freedom records are in the Guildhall Library in London or in the keeping of the clerks of the respective companies. Applications to work in the City of London required the freedom of the City and membership of a trade guild. Apprenticeship records are available for nearly two hundred years, but must be sought in the office of the Chamberlain of London at Guildhall. They are not open to the public, but inquiries can be answered on payment of a fee.

Many of those whose names occur in these records did not actually live in the City, but in adjacent districts such as Bermondsey or Southwark.

Military records

Records of military service are of considerable importance, to both the historian and the genealogist.

Military records in St Catherine's House
Some Army records at St Catherine's date back to 1761, and RAF returns begin in 1920. Also at St Catherine's House are the following:

Index to Consular Births 1849–1965;
Deaths of South African Field Force 1899–1902 (Boer War);

Service Departments: births 1906–65, deaths abroad 1899–1980;
Deaths in the First World War 1914–21, Other Ranks;
Deaths in the Second World War, Other Ranks;
Miscellaneous foreign births, deaths and marriages from 1961;
Marine deaths;
Index Regimental Registers – births and baptisms.

The Foreign Miscellaneous Records were transferred to the PRO in 1977.

The huge volumes of Other Ranks at St Catherine's House prompted me to inquire of the Ministry of Defence for details of the deaths of officers. I received the following information, which I think it advisable to give in full. This came from the Head of Cs(R)2, Ministry of Defence (January 1983):

'Casualty lists for both World Wars have been published and are available at the British Library, Great Russell Street, or by appointment at the Imperial War Museum. A separate Service list was published for the British Army for the First World War. This is entitled (*a*) Officers died in the Great War 1914–19, printed by HMSO in 1919 in one book and (*b*) soldiers died in the Great War 1914–19 printed by HMSO in 1921 in 80 books by Regiment and Corps. Both of these publications may be available at the institutions referred to above.

'In the case of an individual wishing to know more of a relative's life and death whilst serving in the British Army or Royal Navy details may be obtained from this department provided the request is accompanied by written authority from the next of kin of the subject of the inquiry, if the information still exists.

'Furthermore whilst assistance would undoubtedly be given to inquirers making use of the Casualty Lists, the Lists are complicated to operate. This department maintains records for both World Wars and the actions between and since. Whilst these records are not open to public scrutiny, written requests for information will be considered within the rule of the department.'

There was also included an index of Regiments and Corps which were employed in the First World War.

Army records
The regular Army dates officially from 1660 when Charles II, at his Restoration, was permitted to have a permanent force of 5,000 men. The New Model Army of 1645, however, was the basis of the regular army; one unit of the New Model, the Coldstream Guards, was incorporated in the royal army. At a picturesque ceremony, the Coldstreams laid down their arms for the Commonwealth and took them up for King Charles II.

Some details of military personnel before 1660 can be gleaned from such records as the Calendar of State Papers during the Commonwealth (1649–60). After 1660 the records of officers can be traced, but until the late eighteenth century family details and birthplaces are seldom given. The systematic records of Officers' Services begin in 1829. They are arranged by regiments, but some regimental records have not been transferred to the PRO, and are feared lost.

The classes of Officers' Services are:

(*a*) without personal details;
(*b*) from 1828 of officers retired on full or half pay, with age on commissioning, date of marriage and births of children;
(*c*) officers on the active list 1829–1919, with date and place of birth, and particulars of marriage and children.

The Army Records Centre, Bourne Avenue, Hayes, Middlesex, will give details of fairly recent service, but personal material in respect of a deceased ex-officer is not given to a third party without the written consent of his next of kin.

With Other Ranks, the particulars are arranged by regiments. Station Returns may yield the name of the regiment, if the place where the soldier served is known.

Regular soldiers are documented from 1756, and these papers include Discharge Certificates, although records of soldiers who died on service or were not pensioned have been destroyed by fire. Marriage Rolls are found with the Muster Rolls and Pay Lists.

Militia Records are preserved in a few instances where the soldier qualified for a pension in the period 1792–1815. The records of volunteers in the South African (Boer) War of 1899–1902 have been kept: those of the City Imperial Volunteers are at Guildhall. The records of regular soldiers in the South African War were mostly destroyed by bombing during the Second World War, but fragmentary information may be found in the Army Records Centre at Hayes.

Medal Rolls from 1793 to 1904 sometimes give a few details about recipients.

Records of the American War of Independence (1776–83) give, through Muster Rolls and Pay Lists, details of regiments which served in that war. The name, rank and date of discharge of a soldier may appear. For the Muster Rolls of Loyal Americans, of whom 60,000 emigrated to Canada, inquiries should be made to the Public Archives of Canada, in Ottawa.

Records of service in India occur in some sources mentioned above. For details about European officers and Other Ranks in the Honorable East India Company's Service (HEICS) and the Indian (Imperial) Army, inquirers should consult the India Office Library and Records (Foreign and Commonwealth Office), 197 Blackfriars Road, London SE1. At this office there is also an immense amount of information about the Indian States and their coats of arms (see *International Heraldry* by L. G. Pine).

It is essential for an inquirer to know the regiment in which his subject served. Otherwise, he will have an arduous task to trace his quarry and may not succeed. An example of the difficulties encountered in such a case is given in an article 'In search of a soldier ancestor' in *Genealogists' Magazine* (December 1977) where only the fact that the ancestor's widow was described as a pensioner enabled the soldier to be traced.

It must be remembered, when studying the records of private soldiers, that the recruit often gave a false age in order to enlist. For example, in Bristol in 1914, a volunteer would be told that he was too young, but that if he walked round the Centre in Bristol, he would be older. On his return, the volunteer would give a higher age.

In the case of modern military records, the Ministry of Defence can and will supply a résumé of a soldier's career. Here is an example where, in the case of the Cornish family of Beswetherick, I gathered an interesting account of seven years in a soldier's life:

Major Walter James Beswetherick

Enlisted The Gloucestershire Regiment,	
Regular Army	11.9.1914
Discharged on appointment to a Commission	21.6.1915
Appointed to a Temporary Commission as 2nd	
Lieutenant The Gloucestershire Regiment	22.6.1915
Promoted Lieutenant	1.7.1917
Promoted Captain	18.5.1919
Appointed Temporary Major whilst employed	
as Embarkation Staff Officer, Bashrah from	31.3.1920
to	4.10.1921
Relinquished commission and granted rank	
of Major	5.10.1921

The above gives the bare bones of seven years' service, but in cases of soldiers in peacetime a great amount of information is forthcoming. As an example:

A soldier named Ambrose Stowers, from an Essex village, enlisted in the 56th Foot on 2 October 1858, aged 18. (He is listed as Recruit No. 293, enlisted at Braintree, Essex, receiving a bounty of £2.17s.6d.) He served for fifteen years and in that period it was possible to glean a short biography of the man. He was 5 ft 7 ins in height, his hair was light brown. He served in Ireland and twice in India. He married his village sweetheart at her village church: six weeks later, he married her again in the Methodist Church in Aldershot. (Why this repetition of the marriage occurred is not explained: there are simply two certificates.) There were three children, two of whom died during their father's overseas service. One was buried, as was their mother, at Poona. The good conduct of the soldier was marked by his steadily gaining proficiency at musketry tests. In short, he was one of those stalwart redcoats who policed the British Empire. Of his two voyages to India, one was the long haul round Africa but the second, after 1870, was through the Mediterranean and the Red Sea. At last, his duty done, he returned with his surviving child to his native village in Essex.

Many such fascinating accounts of military life can be obtained back even beyond the Napoleonic Wars. In the case of the Birch family in America, I was able to obtain details of a British officer who had served in the Revolutionary War against the rebellious Americans.

Naval records
Naval records cover the period from the seventeenth century. It is essential to know a sailor's ship in order to trace him. Subject to this proviso, the records of naval personnel are numerous. They include:

Yard Pay Books 1660–1857;
Treasurer's Service Series, Ships Musters in four series 1667–1862;
Ticket Office 1669–1832;
Controller 1692–1856;
Various Ships' Pay Books 1691–1710;
Hired Armed Vessels 1794–1815.
Log Books:
  Captains' Logs 1669–1852;
  Masters' Logs 1672–1840;
  Admirals' Logs 1702–1911;
  Ships' Logs 1799–1845;
  Supplementary Series I:
  Masters' Logs 1837–71;
  Supplementary Series II:
  Exploration Logs 1766–1861.

The Royal Marines are documented from 1806 to 1922 in several categories under Woolwich, Chatham, Royal Marine Artillery, Gosport, Plymouth and Deal.

There is also the Register of Seamen's Services 1873–95, and the Court Martial Registers 1834–1916. There are Records of Officers' Services 1777–1915.

Among the miscellaneous records, the following are clearly of great service in genealogical research:

Head Money Vouchers 1716–1833;
Seamen's Effects Papers 1800–1860;
Officers' and Civilians Effects Papers 1830–1860;
Seamen's Wills 1786–1882;
Admiralty Orders 1832–1856 and Record Books 1832–1856;
Greenwich Hospital In-Letters 1702–1869
                Out-Letters 1685–1881;
Marine Pay Office Records 1688–1837;

Medical Department In-Letters 1702–1862
                Out-Letters 1742–1833;
Navy Board Records 1658–1837;
Passing Certificates 1691–1848;
Admiralty Seniority Lists 1717–1850.

Ships Musters cover:

Coastguard and Revenue Cruisers 1824–1857;
Coastguards and Reserves 1875–1914;
Royal Marine Attestation Forms 1790–1883;
Description Books 1750–1888;
Register of Service 1842–1905.

Merchant seamen: press gangs Merchant seamen have always been of great importance to the Royal Navy. Most people know of the old press-gang system, but it is not general knowledge that, in the late eighteenth and early nineteenth centuries, Americans were press-ganged into the Royal Navy. This, of course, did not occur on the mainland, but many American ships were captured in the Napoleonic wars and some of the best seamen were then impressed into the British Navy. As far back as the reign of Richard II, impressment is mentioned as being of ancient practice. The first known commission for it dates from 1355, when Edward III had found it necessary to have a fleet for his wars with France. In 1835, when William IV was king, the practice still persisted, for the term of impressment was then limited to five years.

All sorts of apparently undesirable characters were impressed – vagabonds and criminals, men without fixed homes – and naturally most of these were found in the ports, seamen being obviously regarded as most suitable for the Navy. The practice gradually died out as pay for the Navy improved, and it is noted that press gangs were not used in the Crimean War (1854–6).

It was probably the waning of the practice in the twenty years before the Crimean War which led to the passing of a Merchant Shipping Act in 1835, by which the Masters of merchant ships were required to register with the Register Office of Merchant Seamen details of agreements and Crew Lists. This Act was deliberately intended to create a reserve of seamen to man the Royal Navy in time of war. The authorities had to have particulars of seamen, though the details supplied were often very poor, owing to ignorance and bad writing. Even before this, as far back as 1747, Masters of merchant ships were ordered by Act of Parliament to keep Muster Rolls giving details of the members of the crew and of the ship's voyages. The ostensible reason was the relief of disabled seamen, but it also served as a means of identifying potential recruits for the Navy. These records can be consulted at the PRO (Kew).

Air Force records

Some RAF records are in the PRO under the heading Air Ministry (AIR). With reference to commissioned personnel of the Royal Air Force and those of the Fleet Air Arm Squadrons, application should be made to the Ministry of Defence (RAF), Adastral House, Theobalds Road, London WC1. This also applies to inquiries about officers of the Royal Naval Air Service and the Royal Flying Corps. The Royal Air Force was formed from the combination of these two services on 1 April 1918. The records date from 1913 to the present.

Records of airmen and non-commissioned officers of the Royal Naval Air Service, the Royal Flying Corps and the Royal Air Force from 1913 to date are to be sought from Royal Air Force, Personnel Management Centre, Admin. 2 (RAF), Barnwood, Gloucester. Inquirers should give all the information in their possession when requesting details of RAF personnel. The Ministry of Defence makes this point and adds that the most important clue to personal identity is the individual's service number.

The Mormons

An important genealogical source has come about in the period since the Second World War. This has occurred through the agency of the body called the Church of Jesus Christ of Latter Day Saints, commonly known as the Mormons. This church originates in America and derives its popular name from the Book of Mormon, which it believes to be an inspired revelation. Its members believe in the practice of being baptised for the dead. (This practice is alluded to in St Paul's First Epistle to the Corinthians 15:29: 'Else what shall they do which are baptised for the dead, if the dead rise not at all? Why are they then baptised for the dead?') In accordance with this tenet it is necessary to know who are the dead – the ancestors – for whom baptism is taking place.

This has led the Mormons to seek genealogical records through-out Europe. When I first met one of their representatives, they were engaged in making copies of the births, marriages and deaths records in Somerset House. The Mormon practice is to make microfilm copies of records.

This genealogical work has enormously increased and one result has been to make the Mormon capital, Salt Lake City in Utah, the genealogical centre of the world. The records which are kept there are in bombproof rock chambers.

The Mormon organisation in England is quite large. Among the departments is the London Genealogical Library, 64 Exhibition Road, London SW7. The following information has been provided by the Library.

The International Genealogical Index (IGI), formerly known as the Computer File Index (CFI), is the largest and most accessible list of genealogical information in existence. It contains over 66 million names from the early 1500s, to about 1870, arranged in alphabetical order of surname. The English and American indices are subdivided into counties and states respectively. Other areas covered include Scotland, Wales, Ireland, Scandinavian and European countries, and over seventy other countries. The index for England contains over 47 per cent of existing parish register entries (marriages and christenings) as well as information from many other sources. The index is periodically brought up to date, and the Library holds the latest edition.

Prints of specific surnames can be purchased at a nominal cost per page (about fifty entries to a page) plus postage, by completing an application form at the Library. The prints will be sent to the patron.

Access is available to over one million microfilms (from the main library in Salt Lake City, the largest genealogical library in the world) of original documents, including parish registers (62 per cent of English registers have been filmed), wills, census returns, passenger lists, pedigrees, etc. These are available for a modest fee to cover postage and handling. Indices to the films may be consulted at the Library. Microfilms so ordered may be viewed only at the Library and remain the property of the Mormon organisation.

The London Branch at Exhibition Road has a selection of basic research and reference books and guides. It can arrange genealogical workshops, seminars and films. There are also branch libraries in Bristol, Huddersfield, Loughborough, Merthyr Tydfil, Southampton and Sunderland.

Postal inquiries of a general nature will be answered but no research can be undertaken. A stamped addressed envelope must be enclosed and a telephone number may help in dealing with an inquiry more efficiently.

Members of the public may personally use any of the Mormon library facilities. No fees are charged, but contributions to the upkeep of the library, which is funded only out of voluntary donations, are greatly appreciated.

The IGI is normally available for purchase by *bona fide* libraries, record societies and other repositories. The Guildhall Library holds a copy of the British Isles Index, and the Society of Genealogists has a complete worldwide set. Local public libraries and bodies such as family history societies often hold sections of the Index relevant to their district, and occasionally more complete sets.

10

Genealogy in Scotland

The Scottish clan system

As noted in Chapter 1, few people realise that Scotland is a land of two nations, a fact which has an important bearing on Scottish genealogy. The Lowland Scot is close to the Englishman, just as his language is a dialect of English (once one has mastered Chaucer's archaisms, it is not difficult to read Scots). There is a strong admixture of the Celt in the western shires, but the language has been Scots for centuries.

From the map on page 103 it will be observed that the greater part of Scotland was occupied by Highland clans, this being, however, the most sparsely populated section of the country.

The more populated part of Scotland – the 'waist' of Scotland and the Lowlands generally, including the Border counties – did not have clans. The names which appear in this section are termed *families* of the name, such as the Lindsays and Johnstons. The Scotts, for instance, included the Scotts of Harden, to which branch Sir Walter Scott belonged.

Modern advertising, in the cause of whisky sales or tourism, now covers the whole of Scotland with clans. Any idea that the great house of Douglas was like the Mackintoshes or Macmillans is patently absurd.

The Highland Scot is of the Gaelic race and speech, and often Catholic in religion. He dwelt north and west of the Highland Line, as it was termed, which ran from the estuary of the Clyde up into the Perthshire Highlands. During medieval times, the control of the Scots Kings over the Highlands was often sketchy. As late as 1411, the battle of Harlaw was a contest for mastery between Highland and Lowland.

The feudal spirit has never died out completely in Lowland Scotland. There are many traces of feudalism in Scots law, especially as to titles. But in the Highlands, a feudal system was in operation right up to the 1745 Rebellion. When a chief decided for Prince Charles Edward, he simply called on his clansmen, who held land from him, to follow him to the war.

One of the consequences of the Highland clan system which has a genealogical bearing, was the common use of the chief's surname by his clansmen. The MacKintosh or The MacPherson and the other chiefs had their genealogies which showed their descent over generations and over centuries.

But what of the clansmen who bore the surname of their chief? Were they of his blood? In the majority of cases, no. Their ancestors had come under the protection of the chief, hence their names (see Chapter 1).

The meaning of the word 'clan' is 'children' and it was used in the patriarchal sense, as it is in Genesis and Exodus. Even in that context, there is an express statement that, when the Israelites left Egypt, they were accompanied by a mixed multitude. When circumcision was instituted under Abraham, all who were in his household underwent the rite, and the majority of these dependants were not his kinsfolk. Purity of racial blood did not exist among the Israelites, nor did it among the Highlanders, though in both cases the original system was patriarchal. Gradually over the centuries in the Scottish Highlands, the patriarchal system was transformed into the feudal, and by the seventeenth century the majority of clansmen held land under a species of feudal tenure. This enabled the chiefs to 'call out' their clansmen to follow them to war. This system was outlawed by the Hereditable Jurisdiction Act 1747, which abolished the old feudal powers of the chiefs.

The modern clan system, which has worldwide connections, is a matter of sentiment alone. Chiefs exist. Claims of chiefship are seriously considered by Lyon Court, but the respect and affection shown to chiefs by their clansmen has no legal basis. Owing to the worldwide diffusion of Highlanders, it often happens that the chief of a clan lives abroad – perhaps in the West Indies or Australia – nor does he necessarily own any land in Scotland.

Clan map of Scotland

The bearing of these changes on genealogical research in the Macs is considerable. In most cases, as mentioned above, we can read the genealogies of the chiefs of the greater clans, like MacKintosh or MacPherson, in one or other of the Burke volumes, the *Peerage* or *Landed Gentry*: but does anyone really think that all Macphersons or all Mackintoshes are related to one another, let alone to the chief? Such a belief may exist, but the facts do not bear it out.

The clan system is really a grouping around a central family of persons who, for various reasons, want to gain the protection of that family's name. It happened in times past that there was a great need for this. As we look over the records of the clans – and how imperfect these records often are – we find many examples of what were known as 'broken' men (that is, impoverished or outlawed men) coming under the protection of the chief of some clan who was able to look after them. In this way, many persons who had no blood connection with the original head family of the clan, came to be incorporated and united with it. This phenomenon of people who were strangers coming under the chief's umbrella of protection is not by any means new, as is shown by the famous Combat of the Sixty in 1396 on the North Inch at Perth.

The affair is described with some necessarily fictitious additions in Sir Walter Scott's *Fair Maid of Perth*. Scott himself understood very little Gaelic and, at the distance of 600 years, our Scottish historians differ considerably as to the identity of the combatants, thirty on either side. What is clear, though, is that there were two associations of clans which had disturbed the Highlands. The Scots government decided that a combat would settle the differences which agitated the country. One side obtained a hard-won triumph, all the other side being killed, after which the losers' association disintegrated. What, then, happened to the broken remnants? Obviously, they had to obtain protection somewhere, and may even have submitted to their opponents.

Thus, purity of clan blood was quite unsure 600 years ago. If we ask any Macpherson, Macfarlane or Macvitie, say, how far he can trace his ancestry, the answer will show the artificial nature of most clanship. Normally, he will be able to trace his ancestry for three or four generations, like most people who have not taken the trouble to go further into the matter. For the rest, they are likely to take what is a vicarious pride in the exploits of the chiefs of the clan, with whom in most cases there is no blood connection. For the majority of those who bear the name, the clan is something artificial, but it enables the average Scot to be proud of an ancestry which he has not proved and which is generally unprovable.

At Culloden, in 1745, the Macdonalds of Keppoch were supposed to have hung back because they were affronted by being placed on the left wing of the Prince's army, instead of the right. In all probability, this is a myth: so may be the story that their chief exclaimed angrily 'Have my children deserted me?'. If he used the word 'children' for his clansmen, this was a serious anachronism – or perhaps it would be better to term it atavistic.

As the matter is of moment in tracing Highland genealogy, two examples may be given, one concerning former Prime Minister Harold Macmillan, who was created Earl of Stockton in 1984. It is well known that he is descended from a Highland tacksman, but his ancestry cannot be taken back for more than five generations. This line is supposed to derive from the Macmillans of Lochrazza, but no connection with a chiefship can be shown.

There is a mystery over the Macmillan clan. It is not mentioned in Sir Thomas Innes of Learney's 1960 edition of Frank Adams' book, nor is there any mention in Anderson's *Antiquity of the Scottish Nation*. It is true that in *Burke's Peerage* (1970) there is an entry in the knightage section for General Sir Gordon Macmillan of Macmillan of Krap as chief of the clan Macmillan, but it does not say that this has been accepted in Lyon Court.

Consider, too, the family of Maclaine of Lochbuie: more often spelt as Maclean, this ancient line goes back to the thirteenth century. 'Mac' of course means 'son of' and in this family history the great man was one Gillean. The name was originally spelt as MacGillean, the son of Gillean. The latter was noted as the wielder of the famous battle axe which is the crest of his descendants. The branches of this great family are shown in the pages of *Burke's Peerage* and *Burke's Landed Gentry* and they are carefully connected. But what of the numerous Macleans, Maclanes or Maclaines whom one meets in everyday life? Are they clansmen true? In the growth of modern clan associations, they can be roped in, and that is all.

It is unlikely that the majority of Highland families can trace their ancestry very far. Sources which may supply material are published by various bodies such as the Scottish History Society or the Inverness Field Club, but these appear to relate mainly to the land-owning families. An article in the *Genealogists' Magazine* of March 1982 – 'Source Material for the Scottish Highlands and Islands', by Donald Whyte – gives some useful hints, but these apply to the greater families.

The General Registers

As noted earlier, civil registration of births, marriages and deaths in Scotland began in 1855. These records are kept by the Registrar General, the General Register Office for Scotland, New Register House, Edinburgh EH1 3YT. In the same place are to be found the parish registers before 1855 and the census returns.

The records of the vital statistics are compiled by district registrars and the returns for the year are sent to the General Register Office. There, copies are prepared for district use and separate national indices made for each of the three categories of events.

Other classes of records preserved are:

1   Registers of still births from 1939 (not available for public inspection, and extracts can be issued only in exceptional circumstances).
2   Registers of adopted children from 1930.
3   Marine Register of births and deaths from 1855: these are certified returns received from the Registrar General for Shipping and Seamen in respect of births and deaths on British-registered vessels at sea, if the child's father or the deceased person was a Scottish subject (an expression used in notes supplied by the Registrar General).
4   Air Register of births and deaths from 1948: a record of these events in any part of the world in aircraft registered in the UK, where it appears that the child's father or the deceased person was usually resident in Scotland.
5   Service records from 1881: these include the Army returns for births, marriages and deaths of Scots at military stations abroad, from 1881 to 1959; and the Service Departmental Register from 1 April 1959, which records births, marriages and deaths

outside the UK relating to persons ordinarily resident in Scotland who are serving in or employed by HM Forces.

Under the heading of Service Records, too, are entries of marriages conducted by Army Chaplains outside the UK since 1892, where one party of the marriage is described as Scottish and at least one party is in HM Forces.

6   War Registers from 1899: these are for the South African War 1899–1902, and record deaths of Scottish soldiers in the First World War, 1914–18. Also on record are deaths of Scots serving as Warrant Officers, NCOs or privates in the Army, or as Petty Officers or seamen in the Royal Navy, in the Second World War, 1939–45. There are incomplete returns of deaths of Scottish members of the Armed Forces.

7   Consular returns of births and deaths from 1914 and of marriages from 1917 of persons of Scottish descent or birth.

8   Returns of births and deaths before 1964, supplied by High Commissioners, for persons of Scottish descent or birth from some Commonwealth countries. There are also some returns before 1964 from India, Pakistan, Ceylon and Ghana, with some returns of marriages in certain countries.

9   Registers of births, marriages and deaths in foreign countries from 1860 to 1965, relating to births of children of Scottish parents and the marriages and deaths of Scottish subjects. The record is compiled by the General Register Office.

10   Certificates of foreign marriages (with translation of documents) from 1947, relating to marriages of people from Scotland in some foreign countries, according to the laws of those countries and without the presence of a British Consular Officer.

The parish registers

In Edinburgh, as in Dublin, records are centralised so that inquirers can proceed directly to the study of the old parish registers. These extend from 1553 to 1854. They were kept by parish ministers or sessions clerks before the introduction of compulsory civil registration in 1855. Exactly how they began to be kept we do not know, but it may be that the fashion spread from England. For all the violent extremes of nationalism and the animosities engendered by 300 battles, many English habits and productions have been adopted North of the Tweed, including, for instance, the English Authorised Version of the Bible.

These registers give births and baptisms, proclamations of banns, marriages, deaths and burials. There are 4,000 volumes of the registers covering more than 900 parishes: few are indexed, though a list of indexed material is available in the library of the General Register Office. The registers, like their counterparts in England, are often incomplete and vary considerably from parish to parish.

The fact that the parish registers are all stored in the same place and can be examined with the civil registers is enormously helpful to the inquirer. The only drawback to this central storage of records is that a disaster could destroy so much history, as happened in the loss of the Irish records in 1922.

Research in Scotland is thus assisted by this preservation under one roof of the country's records, although they are not so numerous or as rich as those in England. As Scotland is also a much smaller country, the number of parishes is less. (There is an excellent article on Scottish parish registers in the *Genealogists' Magazine*, March 1951, by Gerald Hamilton-Edwards.)

Census and other records

Census records of the population of Scotland from 1841 and up to and including 1891 are open to the public. The same method in searching must be used as in England: the clearer the knowledge of a person's whereabouts at any of the census dates, the easier it will be to find him or her in the records. If only the town is known, a lengthy search may be involved.

There is also in the Register Office a *Register of Neglected Entries* for the period 1801–54. This has records of births, marriages and deaths that have been proved to have occurred in Scotland between those dates, but were not entered in the parish registers.

Wills and other deeds and documents are held by the Scottish Record Office, which is also in New Register House, Edinburgh. It need hardly be said that wills are as important in the study of Scottish genealogy as they are in England. Once the inquirer has located the parish where his ancestors lived, it is advisable for him to check for the existence of wills in the family. Before 1831, wills were proved before a Commissary, an ecclesiastical judge who had jurisdiction in such matters as legitimacy, succession and declaration of marriage. The place of the Commissary Courts was taken partly by the Sheriff's Court and partly by the Court of Session. The records of the Commissary Courts are naturally of great importance and go back in some cases to the sixteenth century; in most cases they go back to the seventeenth century. Inquiries should be addressed to the Scottish Record Office, as above.

The Lyon Office

Scottish genealogy is closely linked with Scots heraldry. In Chapter 15 I shall consider in detail the connection of heraldry and genealogy, but I would here emphasise the scientific nature of Scots heraldry and its firm legal basis. No Scot is ever at a loss to know whether he possesses a coat of arms. Has he or his father matriculated arms in the Court of the Lord Lyon? The answer decides whether he has armorial bearings. The Lord Lyon is the head of the heraldic establishment in Scotland. He is a judge, his court is a reality and his decisions can be appealed only in the House of Lords.

The importance of the Lyon Office (at New Register House, Edinburgh) to the study of Scottish genealogy cannot be overestimated. It is probable that every person who traces Scottish forbears for more than the past 200 years will consult the records of the Lyon Office. In Scotland the feeling of family consciousness overcomes the English habit of snobbery, so that an ancestor engaged in trade or manual work may yet be regarded as a scion of a landed family. The official guide to Scottish records advises on matters relating to coats of arms, clans, insignia and tartans that recourse should be had to the Lyon Office. I have earlier referred to the works of Sir Thomas Innes of Learney, formerly Lord Lyon. Consideration of chiefship often arises in Scottish genealogy, which makes it as well for the searcher to understand that the rules laid down by Sir Thomas Innes and other Lords Lyon are supported by legal decisions in the Courts up to and including the House of Lords, and that they have never been reversed or reduced.

The Register of Sasines

Scotland has had the advantages of registration of title of land since 1618, whereas in England it has been done only since 1925, and then for the most part voluntarily, though it is now being rapidly extended throughout all areas.

The Register of Sasines came into existence in 1618. The word *sasine* is merely the Scots form of 'seisin' or 'taking, literally by hand or stone' and (later) 'registration of the sasine or of the conveyance itself'. From 1618, the 'registration of all writs relating to land was made obligatory if a good title was to be secured, and the purchaser could then assure himself of the position by "searching" the records which disclose the seller's title and most, if not all, of the securities and encumbrances which might affect it' (*Chambers' Encyclopedia*, article on Scots law by Professor A. D. Gibb).

Quite apart from the obvious legal advantages, the Scots system gives a clear account of the descent of the land for more than 350 years, a great help to genealogical research.

Searches in Edinburgh

Comparatively few people outside Scotland can readily visit the office at New Register House but, on written application to the Registrar General, searches are made for entries in the appropriate statutory register or the old parish registers, subject to the provision of enough information about the individual concerned.

When the person has a fairly common name, some other identifying details, such as parentage, are necessary. In tracing events which occurred before 1 January 1855, much more difficulty arises. It is essential to have accurate information about the place or parish in which the event occurred. The earliest register in the Registrar General's custody relates to baptism and proclamation of banns of marriages in the parish of Errol in Perthshire from 1553, though the records are not complete. For some parishes they do not begin until the early nineteenth century and for others there are no registers at all. An official note adds the caution: 'Moreover, such registers as are available relate only to families associated with the parish church and the standards of record-keeping varied considerably from parish to parish and from year to year. The tracing of lines of descent in these registers may therefore prove to be a very difficult task, and to get started it is essential to have some idea of where the events occurred, i.e. which parish registers are likely to record the events.'

Inquiries about the services of the Office should be addressed to the Registrar General, Search Unit, New Register House, Edinburgh EH1 3YT. If the search for a particular event is likely to take some time, if the Office cannot undertake it or if the search is part of an effort to trace a family tree, you must either conduct the search personally or arrange for a genealogist to do so on your behalf.

Other sources

Kirk Session records
Kirk Session records give information as to the date and reason for a person leaving a parish. For a directory of the ministers of the Kirk, the established (Presbyterian) Church of Scotland, *Fasti Ecclesiae Scoticanae*, a valuable work in seven volumes (1866–71) by Rev. Hew Scott, should be consulted.

University registers
University registers are printed for the ancient Scottish universities of Edinburgh, Glasgow, Aberdeen and St Andrews. If the volumes are not accessible, information as to members of the university may be sought from the Chancellor of the particular university concerned. The records usually show the name of the undergraduate's father.

Reference works and printed books
In addition to the works already mentioned:

Scottish Family History, with a preface by a former Lord Lyon Sir James Balfour Paul, and written by Margaret Stuart, is best described as 'a guide to works of reference on the history and genealogy of Scottish families'.
A Guide to the Public Records in New Register House, Edinburgh, by M. Livingstone, is of great value.
The Scots Peerage, edited by Sir James Balfour Paul, is in eight volumes. Apart from *The Complete Peerage*, it is probably the

best peerage work in Britain. It has an advantage over the latter in that it includes pedigrees which show those junior persons who did not succeed to a peerage.

As many Scottish records were taken to England, the work by Joseph Bain, *Calendar of Scottish Documents deposited in H.M. Public Record Office in London*, is very useful.

I would recommend as a very helpful guide to Scottish history, Andrew Lang's *History of Scotland*, in four volumes. It traces the story up to the Hereditable Jurisdiction Act of 1747 (and gives the sums paid in compensation for loss of feudal dues). It is well written and the four volumes give more detail than, say, Eric Linklater's sprightly one volume on the same theme.

Besides these books, there are others which are useful, if not essential. Genealogy sheds light on history and history sets the scene for genealogical study. For sheer brilliance of writing, Lord Macaulay's account of the clans and of the battle of Killiecrankie (in his *History of England*) cannot be bettered, but it needs to be read in conjunction with other accounts. A very useful work, almost essential to anyone involved in the intricacies of Scottish affairs, is *A Dictionary of Scottish History* by Gordon Donaldson and Robert Morpeth (1977). Also *The Highland Clans: their Origins and History* by L. G. Pine (1972).

Societies

The Scots Ancestry Research Society is of great assistance to the inquirer. It is a non-profit-making organisation established in 1945 to assist persons of Scottish blood to trace facts about their ancestors in Scotland. During the time of its existence, the Society has investigated more than 50,000 inquiries from people of Scottish descent, both at home and abroad. Anyone who desires help in tracing Scottish ancestry would do well to obtain and complete the registration form which the Society requires.

The work done by the Society commonly involves preliminary reference to printed books on surnames and place names, consultation of any indices to records, the actual search of the records, the preparation of notes and the compilation of a final report with, where appropriate, a simple genealogical table. There is a fee for registration, which is payable only once. The search fee is additional and payable on completion of the report, but it should be noted that the fee covers the cost of investigating one ancestral line only – the paternal, unless otherwise instructed – and each additional line to be traced involves payment of a separate search fee. The Society requests inquirers to enclose a stamped addressed envelope for the UK and an International Reply Coupon if writing from overseas. The address of the Society is 3 Albany Street, Edinburgh EH1 3PY.

The Scottish Genealogy Society is also to be found in Edinburgh. This is an important society which you would be well advised to join if you are interested in Scottish records. The aims of the Society are thus stated:

'The Scottish Genealogy Society was founded in Edinburgh on 30 May 1953, by a group of historians and genealogists. The aims of the Society are to promote research into Scottish family history, and to undertake the collection, exchange and publication of material relating to genealogy. In accordance with the wishes of the original members, the Society remains academic and consultative and does not engage itself professionally in record searching. The Hon. Secretary can supply a list of members who are professional researchers, but any commission of this kind must be carried out independently of the Society.'

Since the Society does not engage itself professionally in record-searching, the council has instituted a library service for members residing in the UK. At present, printed books and manuscripts are being collected and foreign periodicals are received in exchange for *The Scottish Genealogist*, the journal of the Society. Inquiries, gifts of books and exchange periodicals should be addressed to the Hon. Librarian, 89 Craigleith Road, Edinburgh EH4 2EH. The Library at 9 Union Strèet, Edinburgh, is open on Wednesdays from 3.30 to 6.30 pm.

The Society continues to collect information for deposit in the Library on pre-1853 Scottish emigrants. A volume dealing with emigrants to the USA, compiled and edited by D. Whyte, was published in 1972.

The Society publishes County lists of pre-1855 tombstone inscriptions, most of which have been compiled by Mr and Mrs J. F. Mitchell. Details can be obtained from the Hon. Secretary at 1 Howard Place, Edinburgh EH3 5JY.

Complete sets of *The Scottish Genealogist* are available. Also available are the monumental inscriptions of the burial ground in the island of Loch Leven pre-1855, and of Speyside and of Angus. The Society also publishes *Introducing Scottish Genealogical Research* by D. Whyte (1982), a comprehensive guide for the beginner on how to get started and the main sources of information in Scotland.

The Society of Antiquaries of Scotland, though primarily concerned with archaeology, does from time to time include in its volumes of Proceedings articles of the greatest value on pedigrees. The Society's address is The National Museum, Queen Street, Edinburgh.

Irregular unions

This may be a good place to mention the marriages, irregular but not invalid in Scots law, which many of the gentry and nobility of Britain contracted in the eighteenth and early nineteenth centuries at Gretna Green, Coldstream or Lamberton Toll. The first of these is in Dumfriesshire, the other two in Berwickshire. With regard to Gretna Green, there is an account by R. C. Reid – *The Register of Irregular Marriages at Gretna Hall 1829–55* – which is held by the Ewart Public Library, Dumfries.

A most interesting instance of one of these marriages occurred in connection with the Earldom of Traquair which was recorded in *Burke's Extinct Peerage* as dormant in 1861. The same view, more or less, was expressed by George Edward Cokayne, the author of the original *Complete Peerage*. However, in the 1937–40 period, a document was brought forward which certified that the last (eighth) Earl of Traquair, when Charles Stuart, Lord Linton (the latter a courtesy title), and Elizabeth Mary Johnston had been lawfully married at Coldstream on 28 April 1818. The marriage was performed by Jock or John Armstrong, a well known but illiterate 'priest', who is said to have performed in 1821 a similar ceremony for the statesman Lord Brougham and Vaux. The certificate, written in a beautifully formed hand, is drawn up by one of the witnesses, William Brigger, who described himself as scribe and witness.

It was during the preparation of the 1939 edition of the *Landed*

Gentry (containing what was later published separately as *Burke's American Families*) that I met in London Charles Edward Traquair Stuart-Linton, who was the great-grandson of the eighth Earl of Traquair, mentioned above as having been married at Coldstream in 1818. I prepared for him an article for the American book which appeared under the heading of Stuart-Linton. For some personal reasons, the article was not completely satisfactory to Mr Stuart-Linton and eventually I suggested that he should have a private family history prepared; I explained to him that this was a procedure common enough, since there were even then at least 8,000 such histories in existence. The result was the very first book by myself to appear in print. This was produced in July 1940, privately printed in America where Stuart-Linton lived.

I did my best to present a worthwhile account in support of my friend's claim to the Earldom of Traquair, but I was hardly prepared for the acclaim which it received and continues to receive. My friend sent a copy to the Lord Lyon, then Sir Francis Grant. He advised Stuart-Linton to file a claim to the Earldom, no mean appreciation. On page 17, I had quoted George Edward Cockayne's view as to the end of the Earldom in 1861 and had asked what he would have made of the Coldstream certificate. The answer is given with the unquestionable authority of the later (now current) edition of *The Complete Peerage*. In the 1959 volume covering the Traquair peerage, there is a reference in some detail to a claim being prepared by C. E. T. Stuart-Linton in 1949, and my book is referred to. The pedigree on which C. E. T. Stuart-Linton's claim was based was given in full in the 1952 edition of *Burke's Landed Gentry*. Stuart-Linton died in New York in 1963. He had always retained his British citizenship. I gave the final coverage to this history in my *New Extinct Peerage* (1972). I have often wondered if this case of an irregular but valid marriage is unique in that it could have provided the succession to a dormant peerage. I am sorry it was never put to the test. Inquiries for my small booklet still come from different parts of the world, thus proving the romantic appeal of this line of Stuart.

11

Welsh Genealogy

Introduction

England and Wales were united administratively by the 1542 and 1547 Acts of Parliament of Henry VIII. Previously, from 1284 (the date of the Edwardian conquest) Wales had been administered under its old Celtic law. From the time of the union, it might be thought that Welsh genealogy would be much the same as English, and indeed it was, as regards the parish registers ordained in 1538, and the institution of statutory records in 1837. The study of Welsh genealogy far antedates 1538, however, and there are a fair number of Welsh genealogies which extend to a millennium. They are constructed quite differently from their counterparts in England. In addition, since the establishment of the National Library of Wales in 1907, a centre for documentary records has existed, which the student of Welsh genealogy cannot overlook.

The best way to begin the study of Welsh pedigrees is to read the leading article on the subject in the 1952 edition of *Burke's Landed Gentry*. This was written by Major Francis Jones, County Archivist for Carmarthen. The article runs to eight closely printed pages and should be consulted by all who wish to understand the apparently complex nature of Welsh pedigrees. They have some elements which they share with those of the Highland chiefs of Scotland and of the great Irish princely lines. They belong to the same Celtic fringe of Britain and the British Isles which has for fifteen centuries been subjected to English influence.

'Welsh genealogy differs radically from its English counterpart, and it is impossible and totally undesirable to apply to Welsh pedigrees the same principles of criticism as are applied to English pedigrees' (F. Jones, *op. cit.*).

There is also the problem of language. Welsh is one of the Celtic tongues and is still a spoken language within the Principality. This does affect a Welsh genealogy which is pre-1500. Translation is then necessary.

Land tenure

The foundation of Welsh genealogy is land tenure, the holding of land by persons on the strength of their relationships in family groups. These were the princes, lords, noblemen and simple gentlemen (the last being known as *bonheddig*, meaning men of pedigree – see page 119). Clearly the majority of the population of ancient Wales would be of the *bonheddig* classification. The word 'class' is inadmissible because there was a real equality between the different persons listed above: they were all freemen. Below them was a section of unfree people, but it was not large. The concept of the clan prevailed in Wales, as in the Scottish Highlands, but with the difference that in Wales the members of the clan were relations. Right up to the conquest by Edward I in 1282–4, the rights and privileges of the landowners, often of very small properties, depended upon the knowledge of their blood relationship. Nor did the Edwardian conquest upset the practice of gavelkind in Wales. This practice (which also prevailed in Kent) involved the equal division of a man's property among his sons.

The ensuing poverty after a few generations can be imagined, with poor but proud gentry possessing perhaps only a few acres, just enough to maintain themselves from the produce of their own land. On a much larger scale, this practice prevented the development of Wales into a kingdom similar to Scotland. More than once, a forceful prince united Wales under his sway. Rhodi Mawr the Great, who died in AD 878, ruled all Wales, but on his death the country was divided among his sons. These divisions facilitated the English Conquest, which really began at the time of the Norman Conquest when the Conqueror allowed his barons to overrun a large part of South Wales.

Dynastic pedigrees

Bad as it was politically and economically, the equalitarian system favoured the growth of genealogical records. What of the dynastic pedigrees? They were kept mainly by the bards, who held an important and official position in the families and households of the princes. Skeleton pedigrees of the principal dynasties are given in Sir Edward Lloyd's *History of Wales from the earliest times to the Edwardian Conquest* (two vols, 1948). This work is essential to an understanding of the ancient families in Wales. The author refers to one of the consequences of the Welsh interest in pedigree: '. . . the free born fearless Welshman who spoke his mind unabashed in the presence of kings' (p. 555).

The dynastic pedigrees correspond very closely to those of the same type in Celtic Ireland (see Chapter 12). This species of family tree would have existed in England, but for the Norman Conquest. The remains of the pre-Conquest Old English pedigrees can be seen in Dr W. G. Searle's compilation *Anglo-Saxon Bishops, Kings and Nobles* (1899). As regards the bishops, the lists are those of succession to the episcopal sees. The royal lines correspond to the Welsh and Irish royal lines, in other words preserved by tradition. On the genealogies of noble families, Dr Searle said that they were mostly very short and fragmentary: 'That they are not more complete is due to the circumstance that no history of any of these families exists' (p. xi). He inserted a pedigree of Hereward the Wake, mainly because of the interest aroused by Charles Kingsley's novel of that name, in which Kingsley had argued strongly in favour of Hereward being a Leofricson.

The reason for the absence of pedigrees for the Old English families was simply that the names of the ancestors were recited by the bards just as among the Celts. The Norman Conquest substituted a new ruling class, so that the bardic pedigrees disappeared. The only true dynastic pedigree to survive was that of Queen Elizabeth II. This was because in the second Norman generation, the King – Henry I – married the heiress of the Old English line, Matilda, the great-grand-daughter of King Edmund Ironside. Her mother, Margaret, was Queen of Scotland, so that her royal descent was well known.

In the case of this regal line who were kings of Wessex – Egbert (*c.* AD 825) became Bretwalda or ruler of the Britons and was grandfather of Alfred the Great – the monkish chronicles followed their usual practice and linked the line of their kings to the Scriptural genealogies in Genesis. They showed considerable ingenuity in finding an ancestor, one Sceaf, a son of Noah, 'born in the Ark'. An interesting feature of this pedigree is Egbert's descent from Woden, who was worshipped as a god among the pagan Anglo-Saxons. Here again was a feature in common with the Celtic genealogies. It was softened by the later Christian chroniclers as with Snoro Sturleson in his *Heimskingle* or *The Norse Sagas*. Here Woden (or Odin in the Scandinavian form) is described as a man and a great leader who brought his people from Asia into Europe. When he died and went to Drontheim (the pagan Paradise) he was divinised, an apotheosis like that of Romulus (in Livy) who became the god Quirinus.

Ancient Welsh law
This digression will help to explain the survival of the Welsh pedigrees, because the Edwardian Conquest of Wales, unlike the Norman Conquest, left the old native law and customs intact.

The Welsh dynastic pedigrees often contain the names of Roman rulers in the earlier portions. In some cases, this also brought in one of the classical deities. After all, Julius Caesar claimed descent from Venus, and his line was not unique in this respect.

According to Francis Jones (*op. cit.*): 'The names that appear in the period from the fifth to the ninth centuries are in all probability based on truth and represent trustworthy tradition, while from the ninth century until 1282 these dynastic trees may be accepted as accurate.'

The *bonheddig* section
On these dynastic trees, many minor persons are found in the period AD 900 to AD 1200. This is the *bonheddig* section and it acquires great importance from the time of the Edwardian Conquest because the ruling dynastic houses then came to an end, but the Welsh land-owning families carried on. As some of these pedigrees went back to the tenth century, this allows for those Welsh genealogies that can show a thousand years of descent. To quote Francis Jones again: 'It is from this ancestral section that the great Welsh aristocratic families trace their descent, and the pedigrees from this

period to modern times need present no difficulties of acceptance.'

Many Welsh surnames are very common, as we saw in Chapter 1. This has given rise to the impression that families bearing such names cannot be of high aristocratic origin. The average Welsh surname was adopted in the sixteenth and seventeenth centuries, following the administrative union of 1542–47. The English rule of primogeniture was then introduced in place of the practice of gavelkind. English law superseded Welsh law and custom. The leading families in Wales then adopted English habits, including the English style in surnames. For ages, the Welsh custom has been to use 'ap' meaning 'son of' which corresponded to the Irish 'O', the Highland 'Mac' and the Norman 'Fitz'. By the use of 'ap' a Welshman could recite half a dozen generations of his pedigree, covering 150 years; he was Ievan, ap Morgan, ap Caradoc, ap Llewelyn, ap David, ap Howell. This showed the line of his descent and the property which he possessed by hereditary right.

Unfortunately, the English lawyers and adminstrators not only failed to understand the Welsh practice, they did not want to know about it. They ridiculed a string of names, asking how many persons had come into court. It provoked the mirth of Scots as well, as in Sir Walter Scott's verses in *Ivanhoe*: 'one widow for so many was too few'. In self defence, the Welshman generally used a patronymic, so that Ievan became Jones, meaning son of Ievan or John. Among the generality of the population, a whole village could be peopled by Joneses, and the various individuals can be distinguished only by their occupations, as Jones the Post or Jones the Grocer.

These concessions to the English did not involve a decline in interest in genealogy. That came about only with the development of the coal mining industry in South Wales. Also there was involved a great decline in Welsh speaking so that now only a quarter of the inhabitants of Wales speak Welsh. In the present century there have been two great Welsh politicians – Lloyd George and Aneurin Bevan. The former was bilingual and a fluent Welsh speaker, whereas Bevan could not learn to speak Welsh.

Manuscripts in Welsh

From the Middle Ages, there exists a large store of manuscripts in Welsh, dealing with genealogy. Much of this material consists of the bardic pedigrees. Sometimes the asinine criticism is raised that the

Welsh family tree is only a list of wild unpronounceable names. But who would invent a string of names? The very sparseness of the medieval pedigrees, having few or no dates, few place names, no details of a grandiloquent nature, is a powerful argument for their authenticity. Such lists look what they are – recited lines of ancestry.

The National Library of Wales

How is the searcher who has gone through the usual sources common to England and Wales, and traced an ancestor to the seventeenth or sixteenth century, to proceed?

There are many Welsh documents at Heralds' College, London, but these are not open to public inspection. The first, and for many the only, source is the National Library of Wales which was established in 1907–9 and which by 1911 had become one of the six libraries in the British Isles possessing the privilege under the Copyright Acts of receiving a copy of every book published in Britain. Many reprints of older genealogical works have been made, which has helped to enrich all the main libraries.

The National Library at Aberystwyth was to ensure the conservation of manuscripts, books and other materials relating to the history of the Welsh people. This was an assistance to higher education, and to literary and scientific research.

The Library soon became, as it were, a combination of Heralds' College and the PRO. In 1913 a Royal Commission on the state of the public records, recommended the establishment of a PRO for Wales, but this was not carried out. It happened that Welsh documents, including court records, began to be sent to the National Library, and it was provided by the Act of 1914, which was to disestablish the Welsh Church, that many of the ecclesiastical records also should go to the Library. Disestablishment took effect in 1920, and the records in question were transferred in 1947.

Many families too have deposited their muniments in the Library.

Genealogical contents of the National Library
Among the contents of a genealogical nature are the following:

1   Bishops' transcripts and marriage licence bonds, dating mostly from the seventeenth century.

2   Parish registers in some cases.
3   Ecclesiastical probate records previous to 1858, deposited from the district probate registers. Most of this class date from the sixteenth century, the rest from the seventeenth century.
4   Nonconformist registers or copies of originals.
5   Quarter sessions records for some Welsh counties.
6   All the records of the Court of Great Sessions of Wales from 1542 to 1830 have been moved from the PR repository at Ashridge. Francis Jones described these papers as containing a number of challenged pedigrees which came into litigation when a party to a suit wished to prove relationship between another party and an official of the court. Such pedigrees, which had to be sworn on oath and examined in court, sometimes contain as many as ten generations with details of collaterals also.
7   Other records of genealogical value include nominal rolls, fines and recoveries and enrolled deeds.

This account of sections of genealogical interest in the National Library was given by Dr E. D. Jones in the *Genealogists' Magazine*, vol. 14, no. 10 (June 1964), pp. 313–21. When I inquired of the Library as to any subsequent changes, the Assistant Keeper, Department of Manuscripts and Records (letter 1 March 1983) thus reassured me:

> 'The article by Dr E. D. Jones in the *Genealogists' Magazine* is still as valuable as it was in 1964, and any minor changes would be confined to pages 314–15. These are an increase in the rate of the deposit of original parish registers, particularly for mid-Wales. This is largely due to the absence of a county record office in Powys, as incumbents are at liberty to send their registers to this library or to the record offices. Both types of institutions, however, co-operate amicably in this matter as is shown by the preparation for publication of a complete list of Welsh parish registers and bishops' transcripts jointly by this library and the Welsh record offices. Another way in which considerable progress has been made is in indexing.'

The last reference is to a pamphlet headed 'Indices of the Department of Manuscripts and Records'. This pamphlet is extremely useful and copies are available for inquirers. In addition, the Library has produced *A Guide to Genealogical Sources at the National Library*:

'This is meant for the amateur genealogist researching modern records, and so the approach is the opposite to that in Dr Jones' article. The most important recent development has been the deposit of *The Calendars of Grants of Probate* in this library, although they were already available in most county record offices.

'One important event has occurred in the field of medieval Welsh genealogy – the publication by the University of Wales Press in 1974 in nine volumes of C. Bartrum: *Welsh Genealogies A.D. 300–1400*. I am also proud to be able to state that his continuation of this work for the following century – in even more volumes – will be published by this library quite soon.'

The *Guide* mentioned above contains much very practical advice, such as the necessity for obtaining as much information as possible from family sources before beginning research in the Library. There are useful headings about Nonconformist records, for example, which are very important in Wales, and helpful explanations of the difficulties which can attend Welsh surnames.

The above, which is concerned mainly with post-fifteenth century pedigrees, does not exhaust the treasures of the National Library. If the family in question can go back to the sixteenth or seventeenth century, and was then possessed of some land, there is the possibility of linking with earlier manuscript pedigrees. There are deeds and manorial records as far back as the thirteenth century, plus the bardic material already mentioned.

Welsh poetry

Welsh poetry forms a large body, including the work of an official royal bard, Gruffydd ap Cynan, who died in 1137, and Llywelyn ap Gruffydd, who died in 1282. All works of this nature contain much genealogical material. As the poetical ability declined, the genealogical content of the poems increased. Thus we have the works of Lewis Dwnn (Lewys ap Rhys ap Owain) who died in 1616. In addition to being a bard, he was also a deputy herald in 1586. His collection of pedigrees, interspersed with his poems, was edited by

Sir Samuel Rush Meyrick in 1846 and published at Llandovery as *Heralds' Visitations*. Transcripts by Dwnn of bardic verses are among the Penarth manuscripts. These latter, with the Mostyn, Panton and Llanstephans collections, are in the National Library.

The Golden Grove manuscript was placed in the London PRO in 1870. A transcript is in the National Library. It is in three volumes, with an index, and gives a careful account of the descent of the great Welsh families, with female and cadet lines from early times to the mid-eighteenth century.

References to the Five Royal Tribes and the Fifteen Noble Tribes occur in Welsh genealogy. The former were the princely dynastic houses of Gwyned and Powys (North Wales) and of Deheubarth (South Wales) and the lines of Elystan Glodrydd on the English border, and of Jestyn ap Gwrgant in Glamorganshire. The Fifteen Tribes were of North Wales and, together with a Sixteenth Tribe (of Tudor Trevor) in the Marches of Wales, came into the schematisation later. This scheme (of the Fifteen Tribes) is not mentioned before the end of the fifteenth century, and is an artificial arrangement not now favoured by genealogists. It depended on a clan grouping with descent from an eponym or prototype which cannot generally be proved.

Two works which are of interest to all who study the history of Wales are by George Borrow, a great linguist who included Welsh among the tongues which he had mastered. In his book *Wild Wales*, written in 1854 and dealing with the north of the country, Borrow relates how often he met natives who evidently 'had no Saxon'. Had all Wales remained rural or pastoral land, it is possible that the whole people might have retained their language.

Borrow's other book, *Celtic Bards, Chiefs and Kings*, was left in manuscript (the author died in 1882) and was not published until 1928. It contains accounts of many of the Welsh bardic genealogists by one who had read and appreciated their works in the original.

12

Irish Genealogy

Introduction

Ireland is divided genealogically as the country is politically, into the Republic of Ireland and Northern Ireland, which remains part of the UK. Northern Ireland consists of six counties – Antrim, Armagh, Down, Fermanagh, Londonderry and Tyrone. The remaining twenty-six counties of Ireland constitute the Republic, which is completely independent of the UK.

From 1169 – when, at the invitation of an Irish king, Strongbow, Earl of Pembroke, invaded Ireland – the country was ruled from England, until 1921 when the British government agreed to the independence of Ireland. The six counties of Northern Ireland – Ulster, as it is often called – elected to remain part of the UK. This establishment was effected in 1922, when the twenty-six counties became Eire, technically a British Dominion. When Eamon de Valera became premier of Eire, he worked for the replacement of Dominion status by a Republic which is now the form of government in the twenty-six counties. There are, therefore, two separate countries in the island of Ireland.

The Republic of Ireland

In Ireland, registration of births, marriages and deaths did not begin until 1864, though records of Protestant marriages were kept from 1845. The parish records which still exist are necessarily few, because of the burning of the Four Courts in Dublin in 1922. This occurred during the Irish Civil War, after the withdrawal of the British in 1921.

In the 1952 edition of *Burke's Landed Gentry*, one of the introductory articles was 'The Study of Genealogy in Ireland', by Anthony Crofton. The dismal catalogue of documentary losses can be summarised as follows. Of the wills, only eleven from the Prerogative Court and one from the Dublin Consistorial Court were saved. The Patent Rolls were lost, but Lodge's manuscripts were salvaged, which means that epitomes of many of the Rolls exist. Also lost was the series of the Pipe Rolls which ended in 1818. Of the parish registers which had been lodged in the PRO, 817 were destroyed, though in some instances whole or partial transcripts have turned up.

Subsequent researches into Irish records have shown that a fair number of parish records have not been destroyed, presumably because they were not then lodged in the PRO, and these are now housed at Oifig An Ard-Chlaraitheora, Custom House, Dublin 1.

As may be understood, the destruction of so much of the history of Ireland's past has brought about a great increase of genealogical interest among Irish people. Sources other than the official records are brought forward as of great service. Among these are tombstones and newspapers. As we have seen, these sources exist in England, too, strange as it may seem to those who assert that Irish records are different from those in England. Of course, tombstones with inscriptions are particularly important when the registers of the place have been destroyed. But it would be strange indeed if they were not noted in England, where the term MI (monumental inscription) is frequent in pedigrees.

As to Irish newspapers, it is worth noting that three were published in Dublin from about 1750 to 1800, and many of the smaller Irish towns had their local newspapers. A great deal of information – birth and marriage announcements, etc. – can be culled from this source.

Finally, a few words from the great authority, T. Ulick Sadlier, who was Deputy Ulster for many years, as to what was saved:

'Fortunately, the strong room resisted the fire, and so its contents were preserved. It had inside it all the Chancery and Exchequer Bill Books, the Judgment Books of Common Law Courts, Bankruptcy Petition Registers, and what documents were being inspected when the disaster took place, including the Religious Census of Castletown Rockes, Co. Cork of 1766, the Census of Killeshandra, Co. Cavan of 1841 and some of the County Antrim Census Returns of 1851. Some further bulky volumes containing the County Antrim Census Returns in 1821 were used to barricade the front windows of the Four Courts during the siege, and as a strong wind was blowing inwards, they mostly escaped destruction. Over and above this, a few odd documents caught in the wind were afterwards picked up in the vicinity.'

By contrast, some interesting details of registers which were not destroyed are given in an article in the Society of Genealogists' magazine for March 1973, but the fact remains that Irish genealogy was dealt a colossal blow when, as it has been said, 'the history of Ireland went up in smoke'.

The mention of Ulster King of Arms above refers to the past heraldic establishment of Ireland, which still subsists under another name (see page 129 and Chapter 15).

Printed works

I was responsible for the compilation of the fourth edition of *Burke's Landed Gentry of Ireland* (1958). Preparing this work between 1956 and 1958 gave me an understanding of the gaps in Irish records which no amount of listing could have done.

Until 1899, Irish families appeared in the *Landed Gentry* in the same volume or volumes as those of Great Britain. The work had become very unwieldy and in 1899 the *Landed Gentry of Ireland* appeared as a separate volume. This was followed in 1904 by a second edition, and in 1912 by a third, this being edited by A. C. Fox-Davies, which ensured heraldic validity. No attempt was made to evaluate the authenticity of the ancient princely family histories.

It seemed unlikely that there would be another Irish edition, considering the enormous changes – political, social and economic – since 1921. In the 1937 *Burke's Landed Gentry* there was an Irish Supplement of some 200 pages which pleased few people. At last it became apparent that there would be sufficient support for a fourth edition. I went to Dublin and found assistance from all sections of the community who had any interest in genealogy. The result was the fourth edition in 1958, running to 800 pages, the same size as its 1912 predecessor.

Since then there has been published *Burke's Irish Family Records*. In addition, of course, the editions of *Burke's Peerage* always contain the histories of the Irish peers.

In 1958, a definite attempt was made to deal with the ancient Celtic families, like the O'Kellys and O'Conor Don. This was done by first obtaining a masterly opening article on 'The Irish Genealogies' by Professor David Greene of Trinity College, Dublin. This gave the evaluation of the traditional lines on the basis that they could be accepted to the time of St Patrick or a generation or two before that. On this rational principle I acted, and with the ancient princely families I experienced no trouble at all. With the later arrivals under the Stuarts, Cromwell or William of Orange, numerous genealogical squabbles occurred. There was a simple explanation: in the sixteenth or seventeenth century, when huge confiscations of Irish land occurred, many a younger son from an old English county family was packed off to Ireland. He retained – or rather, his descendants did – a memory of his ancestry. Very rarely were they able to *prove* their affiliation to the English or Scottish family, however.

A famous instance is that of Viscount Montgomery. He often referred to his Norman ancestry, but the pedigree cannot be demonstrated beyond 1629 in the plantation of Ulster.

Behind the modern works mentioned, there is John O'Hart's (or Hart's) *Irish Pedigrees, the Origin and Stem of the Irish Nation* (1875). In this work, there are the famous Hibernian or Noachian pedigrees, giving some 140 generations of descent from Biblical personages. As mentioned in the chapter on Welsh genealogy, this linking of ancient pedigrees with Old Testament genealogies is a feature common in medieval Europe. Whatever may be thought of these far-flung histories, Hart's collection gives a mass of later information of a more reliable character.

Other sources

Do not overlook the resources of the library of Trinity College: because it is a copyright library under the British system, it is one of the world's greatest libraries. Over the last four centuries the alumni of Trinity College, Dublin, have included many distinguished men.

Their records are available. Similarly with members of the Irish Bar, whose records can be found in the King's Inns, corresponding to the four Inns of Court in London.

The National Library of Ireland in Kildare Street, Dublin, contains some 14,000 manuscript volumes, many of genealogical interest. As in many other libraries, many of the Library's newspaper holdings have been converted into microfilm, including the *Freemans' Journal* for the period 1763 to 1924.

The Public Record Office is at the Four Courts, Dublin 7. The Dublin City Archives are also very important, at City Hall, Dublin 2. The Registry of Deeds is in Henrietta Street, Dublin.

The Masonic body has a small number of adherents in Ireland, and these are usually among the families of the old ascendancy, i.e. the landed class. The Grand Secretary's office is at Freemasons' Hall, Molesworth Street, Dublin. References to Freemasonry occur in the article on the Sirr family, for instance, in the 1958 Burke volume.

The Religious Society of Friends (the Quakers) has excellent records of members of the Society from its beginnings in Ireland. The curator is at 6 Eustace Street, Dublin 2.

Heraldic Office

I have referred to the Genealogical Office, Office of Arms, in Dublin Castle. The origin of the heraldic establishment is as follows.

After de Valera had requested the removal of the office of Ulster King of Arms, and after this had been agreed by the British government, a formal direction was given by the Irish government allocating the administration of the Genealogical Office to the Department of Education. The office is under the immediate direction of the Director of the National Library. The Chief Herald of Ireland has his office on the first floor of the Bedford Tower in Dublin Castle. His work includes the power to design and grant coats of arms on request, and his staff includes genealogical searchers and heraldic artists. In a patent of arms there are two texts, one in Irish and one in English.

The arms of the Genealogical Office consist of those of the four provinces of Ireland, quarterly – Leinster, Connaught, Ulster and Munster – together with a chief which is charged with a portcullis between two scrolls. The portcullis was a prominent charge in the arms of Ulster King of Arms and so serves to indicate continuity with Ulster's Office.

In fact, the Chief Herald carries out the same duties as his British-appointed predecessor. It has been stated by the Genealogical Office that 'due to the destruction of valuable records at various times, as a result of wars and disturbances, genealogical research in Ireland has been rendered difficult'. Thousands of inquiries are handled each year by the office, many requiring prolonged research through the office records, official papers, parish registers or even on-the-spot investigations in remote towns or villages. Another responsibility of the Chief Herald is the care of the Heraldic Museum, located on the ground floor. This is a collection, unique of its kind, where can be seen grants of arms dating back to the seventeenth century, manuscript volumes of ancient pedigrees, and jewellery, plates and glass ornaments with armorial bearings. This museum was largely the work of Sir Neville Wilkinson (the last Ulster King of Arms to live in Dublin, and who died in 1940) and was opened in 1908. Its success and value is proof that in matters pertaining to heraldry the 'Emerald Isle' may have much to teach the United Kingdom and the British dominions.

New Zealand residents of Irish descent have both in the last and the present centuries received grants of arms from Ireland and a study of these is of interest.

When the Ulster Office was resumed by the Crown, it was united with the office of the Norroy King of Arms, with jurisdiction as mentioned above over the six counties of Northern Ireland.

Fees are, of course, charged by the Dublin Office, but as a rule they are lower than those in England. As to the value of searches by Dublin, there is no question; my personal experience with Dublin over many years has been most valuable. It may be thought that perhaps only distinguished families can find help there. If so, one must bear in mind the difficulties attending searches for the rank and file of Irish families. A good illustration occurred in the case of President Nixon, for whose ancestor interment in *two* graveyards was made available by the Irish government.

Northern Ireland

The General Register Office is situated at Oxford House, 49-56 Chichester Street, Belfast BT1 4HL, and is responsible for (*a*) the registration of births and still births, deaths, marriages and adoptions; (*b*) the preliminaries to all marriages other than those celebrated according to the rites of the Roman Catholic Church; and (*c*) the collection and publication of vital statistics. The work at (*a*) and (*b*) is carried out through local Registrars of Births, Marriages and Deaths whose districts are coterminous with the local government districts.

District registrars are concerned with the current registration of births, deaths and marriages occurring in their districts. They also have duties relating to the civil preliminaries to certain marriages including the solemnisation of civil marriages.

District registrars retain original records of marriages which took place on or after 1 April 1845, other than Roman Catholic marriages, the civil registration of which did not commence until 1 January 1864. Marriage records are available in the General Register Office from 1922 only.

Original registrations of births, still births and deaths are forwarded by district registrars to the General Register Office on a weekly basis, although the registrars retain a copy for one year only for certificate production purposes. Birth, death and still-birth records held in the General Register Office relate mainly to those registered since 1 January 1864 in that part of Ireland which is now Northern Ireland.

Church records in many instances commenced earlier than civil registration. If you know the name of the church with which your ancestor was associated, a letter should be sent to the clergyman presently in charge, as he may be able to provide some useful information.

Emigration records

The General Register Office states:

'It is understood that passenger lists and ships' manifests were at one time held in London at the offices of the British Board of Trade, but that these records were not preserved. It is believed that some records regarding immigrants from Ireland who landed at ports on the eastern shore of USA between 1820 and 1865, are held in the National Archives, Washington DC.'

The General Register Office also states:

'It is understood that there has been good preservation of ships' passenger lists for arrival in Australian Colonies, particularly assisted migrants – the majority of Irish migrants to Australia were assisted. These lists are, from the nineteenth century, held in the State Archives of several States [Australian States]. Information varies from a bare record in Queensland to that of considerable detail in New South Wales. The Archives staff do not undertake searches, but access to lists is normally available without charge.'

The Ulster Historical Foundation

This organisation was formerly known as the Ulster Scot Historical Foundation. It is situated at 66 Balmoral Avenue, Belfast BT9 6NY. The Foundation is a non-profit-making organisation set up in 1957 to promote knowledge of and interest in Ulster genealogy and history, and to make more readily available information about the sources for research in this field.

Publications are the Foundation's principal means of disseminating information. It publishes a genealogical series consisting of volumes recording gravestone inscriptions on a geographical basis. Such inscriptions are an important, often unique source for the genealogist. In general, church registers in Ireland have been so poorly kept that an inscription on a gravestone may well be the only record of a person's existence, before civil registration began in 1864. Eighteen volumes have been published for graveyards in Co. Down and a further eight or nine volumes will be required to complete recording of all pre-1900 inscriptions in that county. Two volumes have been published for Co. Antrim and a new series has been started for the City of Belfast. Transcription of inscriptions and surveying of graveyards have recently been greatly extended.

In addition to this graveyard inscription series, the Foundation publishes an historical series which comprises five volumes: R. J. Dickson's *Ulster Emigration to Colonial America 1718-1775*; a volume of essays on eighteenth century Irish history *Penal Era and Golden Age*, edited by T. Bartlett and D. W. Hayton; and David

Stevenson's *Scottish Covenanters and Irish Confederates: Scottish Irish Relations in the mid 17th century*. The other two volumes in this series – M. Perceval-Maxwell's *The Scottish Migration to Ulster in the Reign of James I* and *Essays in Scotch-Irish History* (which includes an essay on Ulster Emigration 1785–1815) – are out of print, but are readily available in most reference libraries.

Ulster Genealogical and Historical Guild   This was established by the Foundation in 1978 in order to bring together people with similar research interests in a kind of book club, and to prevent duplication of research effort. The annual subscription is modest, and subscribers receive a number of benefits. The Guild publishes an annual 36-page *Newsletter*, containing articles about Ulster and Irish genealogy and history, together with news about the work of the Guild and the Foundation. The Guild also publishes an annual *Guild Subscribers Interest List*. This contains an alphabetical list of families being researched by subscribers, with particulars of birth, marriage and/or burial dates and possible places of origin. This list is perhaps the most complete record that exists of Ulster genealogical research in progress, and it enables subscribers to discover others working in the same or related fields. Guild subscribers are also entitled to discount on the Foundation's publications and on any genealogical researches undertaken for them by the Foundation.

Genealogical Searching Service   The Foundation also assists people who have specific inquiries about their own particular Ulster ancestry by offering a genealogical searching service. It can only offer this service on a fee-paying basis, starting with a registration fee which is the administrative charge and non-returnable. A search and report fee is also quoted and will not be exceeded without prior consultation: those wishing to have searches made should be prepared to pay an amount approaching that sum.

A genealogical search can be only as good as the information provided, and as the information obtained from the sources relevant to the search area. The fees charged to inquirers are based on those charged to the Foundation by its searchers for the time involved, and not according to results. Success cannot be guaranteed in any search and an unsuccessful search is usually more time-consuming than a successful one. It is the Foundation's policy not to recommend a search unless there is a reasonable prospect of success.

General information
There are many inquirers whom the Foundation has been unable to help and many searches have proved less successful than could have been wished, for two principal reasons. The first is the destruction of a great number of Irish (including Ulster) records by fire in the Public Record Office, Dublin, in 1922: generally speaking, this makes searching in Ulster more difficult than in the rest of the United Kingdom. The second reason for failure is lack of knowledge on the part of the inquirer. The comparatively late dates of civil registration have already been given. Previous to these, such events were recorded voluntarily in local church or parish registers, the condition and accuracy of which depended entirely upon the interest of the clergyman concerned. So unless the inquirer can give a precise location, such as village, town, townland or parish (county is not sufficient), it is virtually impossible to locate records relating to the particular family, prior to civil registration.

The rest of the advice given by the Foundation to inquirers is very much the same as that given in the first chapter of this book, this being sound advice for anyone in the USA or elsewhere overseas who is seeking his family history. A distinctive feature for the Irish inquirer is that the Foundation requests particulars of the ancestor's religion for, it adds, this is a vital entry point in church registers detailing baptisms, marriages and deaths.

13

The Channel Islands and Isle of Man

The Channel Islands

In considering genealogical factors in the Channel Islands, it has to be remembered that geographically they are not part of the British Isles. They belong physically to France and are the sole remnant of the Duchy of Normandy, which was lost by King John in 1204.

For a long time (up to the reign of George II, according to Dean Stanley) two men, both lay figures, took a high place in the English Coronation procession, as being representatives of the Duke of Normandy and the Duke of Aquitaine. These two territories were anciently held by the English Crown, and the nominal representatives at coronations were reminders of those old possessions. Both territories were feudal holdings from the King of France so that after William, Duke of Normandy, made himself King William I of England, the somewhat ludicrous situation existed whereby a monarch, in his other capacity as Duke of Normandy, had to render homage to his suzerain, the King of France.

The Duchy of Aquitaine became connected with the English Crown on the marriage of Henry II of England to Eleanor, heiress of Aquitaine, in 1154. She had been previously married to the King of France, but they had been divorced (see page 41 on the significance of divorce in the Middle Ages). Her dowry was the huge area of Aquitaine, in south-west France, which reverted to her (and so to her second husband) when the marriage to the French King was declared a nullity. As a result, Henry II had possession of France from the English Channel to the Pyrenees. The Duchy of Aquitaine was lost in 1453. Its possession was the curse of English medieval history. The true line of development for England lay in the unification of the British Isles, but only two English medieval kings, Edward I and Richard II, realised this.

These historical reminders are important in considering the Channel Islands. They are Crown territory, but not part of the United Kingdom. They have their own parliaments. The Channel Islands consist of Jersey and Guernsey. With the latter are grouped the remainder: Alderney, Sark, Herm, Jethou and Brechou. Despite the figure in coronation processions, claim to the Duchy of Normandy was formally renounced in 1259. Henry V, it is true, conquered Normandy after Agincourt (1415) but all the French possessions of the English Crown, except Calais, had been regained by the French by 1453. Extraordinary as it may seem, as late as 1953 a long-standing dispute between France and England existed as to the possession of two uninhabited rocky islets, Les Ecrehous and Les Minquiers. The matter was referred to the International Court of Justice at the Hague; all manner of historical facts and arguments were put forward and the Court gave a decision in Britain's favour.

Jersey and Guernsey

The two islands of Jersey and Guernsey each have their own States, or parliaments. The old Norman connection is still remembered, not only in terms and customs, but also in the existence of a patois which is a species of French.

There is a Lieutenant Governor of Jersey, who is Commander-in-Chief. The other official appointments are those of Secretary, Bailiff of Jersey, Dean of Jersey, Attorney General and Receiver General, Solicitor General and State Treasurer. The Lieutenant Governor is the channel of communication between the British government and the local government. The Bailiff of Jersey is appointed by the Crown and he is both President of the States of Jersey (i.e. the legislature) and of the Royal Courts of Justice.

Ecclesiastically, the Channel Islands since the Reformation have formed part of the diocese of Winchester.

The arrangements for Guernsey and its dependencies (as the smaller islands are called) parallel those of Jersey, but the Lieutenant Governor is a different officer and there are some additional officials – an Assistant Secretary, a States Supervisor and Receiver

General. The Bailiff of Guernsey is a Crown appointee, and as in Jersey he is President of the States and the Royal Courts. The latter consist of twelve jurats, laymen.

For Jersey, records of births, marriages and deaths from April 1842 are kept by the Superintendent Registrar, States Building, St Helier, Jersey. Details of baptisms, marriages and burials before that date can be obtained from the rectors or vicars of the Church of England parishes concerned (see *Crockford's Clerical Directory* for the parishes). Census records are kept with those taken in England.

Regarding wills, those of real estate from 1660 to the present are registered in the Royal Court of the island. Wills of personalty are in the Probate Division. Copies of all wills may be inspected on application to the Judicial Greffier, States Building, St Helier.

For Guernsey, The Registrar General's Office, Greffe, Guernsey, has the record of births and deaths since 1919, and of non-Church of England marriages since 1840. For baptisms, marriages and burials before 1840, application must be made to the incumbents concerned (see *Crockford's* as above). Two of the dependencies, Sark and Alderney, have their own officials. Alderney even has its own parliament, from which it sends representatives to the States of Guernsey. For Alderney and the other dependencies of Guernsey, application should be made to the Registrar General of Guernsey and for inquiries about wills of realty. Copies of wills of personalty are kept by the Registrar to the Ecclesiastical Court, 9 Lefebvre Street, St Peter Port, Guernsey.

Useful societies
There are societies in the Islands which are likely to be helpful to inquirers. La Société Jersiaise, 9 Pier Road, St Helier, Jersey, has a library and a museum. Also in Jersey is the Channel Island Family History Society, 16 La Cloture, Maufant, St Saviour, Jersey. Inquiries should be addressed to the Hon. Secretary at that address.

Language
English is now admitted as an official language, but a knowledge of French is certainly useful, if not essential in genealogical researches in the Islands. A reinforcement of the French element came after the French Revolution, when exiles came to the Islands. This brought an influx of Catholicism. I was informed by the Greffier that

Roman Catholic family records were first held at the Cathedral Church of St Joseph, situated at La Coupderie, St Peter Port, in 1851 when the church was built. Prior to 1851 records commencing in the year 1802 were kept at the French Catholic Church, Notre Dame du Rosaire, Burnt Lane, St Peter Port, Guernsey.

Considerable pitfalls can arise when trying to trace some of these Guernseymen or other Channel Islanders. While they may have been settled in Guernsey or Jersey for over 150–180 years, the ancestor possibly came from France, and further information may not be at all easy to trace.

I remember a case which concerned a family of De Garie. They were Catholics, and on searching for their local background in Guernsey, I found that De Garie is a common name there. No less than forty were listed in the telephone directory, though my informant, a Catholic priest, did not know any of them to be Catholics.

Sark

With regard to Sark, a useful book is *The Story of Sark* by A. R. de Carteret, published in 1956 and obtainable locally, which gives the names of the original settlers in that island. Also of interest for the period 1940-45, the time of the German occupation, is *Islands in Danger* by Alan and Mary Wood (1955).

The loss of some of the Alderney registers is due to the German occupation.

The Isle of Man

The Isle of Man is subject to the British Crown but has its own parliament. There is a Lieutenant Governor and the legislature is called the Tynwald. It consists of two branches, the Legislative Council and the House of Keys. The Council consists of the Lieutenant Governor, the Bishop of Sodar and Man, the Attorney General, and eight members appointed by the House of Keys. In the promulgation of laws on the Tynwald Hill, the announcement is made in English and in Manx, though the latter is now extinct as a native tongue. The title of the Bishop means simply 'South and Man' and is a reference to the ancient Norse possession of the island, when the Norse kings claimed lordship over all islands from the Shetlands southward.

Records
The Isle of Man has the following records in the General Register in Douglas:

Statutory records of births registered in Man from 1878;
Records of the Church of England (baptisms only are held before 1878, the earliest record being of 1611);
Statutory records of marriages registered since 1884;
Church of England and Dissenter marriage records from 1849 to 1883, and Church of England marriages only before 1849 (earliest record 1629);
Statutory records of death from 1878;
Records of Church of England burials only before 1878 (earliest 1610).

There is also an Adopted Children Register giving legal adoptions registered in Man from 1928 (under the Adoption Acts 1928 and 1962).

For forms of application for the above, write to the Registrar, General Registry, Douglas, Isle of Man. The office does not undertake genealogical researches as such. Certified copies of entries of births, baptism, etc. can be issued, however, provided that the applicant can supply sufficient information to locate the required entries.

Census records
In Man, census records are held from 1821 to 1871 (at the usual ten years intervals) at the Manx Museum, Douglas. Census records for 1841 are not complete; the Museum has those of a few parishes but not of the whole island. After 1871, the census returns are kept by the PRO in London. Manx wills dating from 1628 to 1846 are kept at the Manx Museum, Douglas, and wills from 1847 to date are at the Deeds Registry, General Registry.

Deeds to property in the Isle of Man from 1600 approximately to 1846 are kept at the Manx Museum, Douglas, and from 1847 to date in the Deeds Registry, General Registry.

Family History Society
In 1979 the Isle of Man Family History Society was formed. Its object is to study genealogy and family history, particularly within

Man. The Society is a member of the Federation of Family History Societies. The Society, which publishes a quarterly journal, is of benefit to all who are making researches into their families. The Secretary is Mrs Mona Christian of 5 Willow Terrace, Douglas.

In *Burke's Landed Gentry* (1952) there is a long pedigree of the Manx family of Christian. This begins in 1368 with John McCrystyn, Deemster. It includes an entry for Fletcher Christian, RN, Master's Mate and Acting Lieutenant on HMS *Bounty* 1787, leader of the mutiny on that vessel, bapt. 25 September 1764, educated Cockermouth Grammar School, believed to have died on Pitcairn Island *c.* 1795.

14

The Overseas Inquirer

As a general observation, the overseas inquirer seeking to trace his ancestors should follow the lines indicated for UK inquirers. There is one important proviso: he must know not only the name of his first ancestor to come from Britain, but also where he came from. In some cases, the port of embarkation of the immigrant ancestor has been preserved but that, of course, was not his habitat. There is also the very pertinent consideration that the visitor, whose stay in London is limited, should make early application for tickets to the British Library and PRO.

The USA

In the United States the study of genealogy has been carried far. One has only to consider the names of some of the honourable societies in America to realise that a study of the past has been made a matter of most earnest attention. The Society of Colonial Wars, the Society of the Cincinatti, the Sons (and Daughters) of the Revolution, the English Speaking Union, the Descendants of the Noble Knights and Dames of the Order of the Garter, the Sureties of the Magna Carta – these are only a few of the associations which require prospective members to provide careful documentation of their forbears. In addition, in many of the states there is a genealogical society, as in Texas and in California and, of course, in New England, the area of the first settlement. Jamestown in Virginia was begun in 1607.

Records were sedulously kept by the early settlers, so that the various local offices which they filled are described and dated along with the important statistics of birth, marriage and death. It is strange that often only a traditional memory about the parentage of the first immigrant has been preserved. This tradition may not be contemporary with the immigrant, but a conclusion drawn some generations later, owing to the identity of surname of the first arrival with that of a family in England.

Americans often refer to themselves as tenth generation Americans or so on, and this means that they can trace their ancestry to the immigrant ancestor who went to New England from the old country. There are thousands of such pedigrees which bear the stamp of authenticity. The records of the American line, when traced for ten or eleven generations, bear a remarkable resemblance to their English counterparts. Birth, marriage, children, local offices held in church or townships, wills, oaths, legal cases, wartime service, are all a clear indication that when the settlers came to New England they had every intention of keeping up their pedigrees. In a new world, they felt that this was a link with the past. Even those who, like the Pilgrim Fathers, left England because they disagreed with affairs in church and state, yet remembered that they were English men and women. New England is, in truth, the most English of all England's old colonies. Even now, after so many generations of severance, it is possible to recognise in the American of New England stock a nearer relation of the Englishman than in many cases of Canadians who often pride themselves on Scots descent.

The immigrant ancestor having been clearly identified, most Americans wish to know the source of their family history in England. Here a great difficulty is often encountered. It is true that many notable English families sent some members to the New World, as well as to Ireland. I have shown that there are more known descendants of the Normans in the USA than in England. A notable instance of a well-to-do family which settled in New England was that of the Lords Baltimore (family surname Calvert) who founded and settled Maryland. There was a regular system of appointing grand proprietors who owned huge areas in the Thirteen Colonies on condition of rendering feudal dues to the Crown, which had made the grant.

For the most part, however, the emigrants from England belonged to the humbler sections of society. Many of these humble folk wished to better themselves in new conditions. Strange as it may seem, there was a widespread contemporary view that the England of the Stuarts was over-populated. Thus many persons were induced to emigrate.

Passenger lists

Lists of the emigrants have been preserved. They show shiploads of carpenters, husbandmen, spinners and the like. An awkward fact about these lists is that they rarely contain anything about places of origin. As mentioned above, the port of embarkation is no guide. Take as an example Hotten's List of Travellers which covers the period 1600–1700, and is available in book form in many libraries. This gives the names of settlers who sailed from London. The value of this list is that it may enable someone who does not know the name of his first American ancestor to name and date him, but it does not help to trace the locality in which that ancestor originated.

If the American inquirer does not know the place in England from which his ancestor hailed, the search resembles that of the needle in the haystack. I can only suggest that in the first instance he should examine his surname carefully – including the variations through which it has passed – and try to find out if it were at all uncommon in the England whence his ancestor came, or at least to discover its provenance. He can then try to trace the name in records here and look for any indication that about the time his ancestor set sail there is in the pedigree anyone who bore the same Christian name as the settler and of whom nothing more was recorded. This is not proof, of course, but at least it is a pointer to what might be a possibility of affiliation. There is no doubt that many a younger son was driven to seek his fortune overseas, and in such a case nothing except his name remains in the pedigree of the older line. I have indicated how often this must have occurred in the ancestry claimed by Anglo-Irish families, where the impossibility of proof frequently caused bitter arguments during the editing of the *Landed Gentry of Ireland* (1958).

All those men who have merely a name in the Visitation pedigrees (see page 157) had, in all probability, descendants of some kind, many of whom, by the law of averages, emigrated to America.

Most American inquirers in the above circumstances will have to content themselves with at most a probability. Above all, the searcher should guard against the legendary ancestor. Having been able to see many American pedigrees, my experience has convinced me that when the American searcher is in earnest, determined to have the truth and nothing else, the quality of his family history will be unsurpassed.

The genealogy of the Crispin family had been traced to France. It was the subject of work by twenty genealogists at once, in England, France and America. Work on this scale costs a great deal, but the result justifies the expenditure: twenty workers could not all be wrong or deceitful. The genealogies of the Hydes, the Hills, the Washingtons, the Roosevelts and many others have been worked out with the exact thoroughness to which many modern peerage pedigrees cannot attain. In the instance of Hyde, however, the link with the Hydes, the Earls of Clarendon, is not exact.

This may make many an inquirer pause, for he would have to go far before he could find as much work spent on a pedigree as there has been on the Hyde ancestry. The Washington ancestry has been traced, as might have been expected, with great care and immense detail, from the original line of the Washingtons of Washington in Co. Durham.

Burke's American Families

The above examples are given in full in *Burke's American Families with British Ancestry*, published as a separate volume by the Genealogical Publishing Company in 1975. It is illustrated with arms. Originally it formed the American Supplement to the 1939 edition of *Burke's Landed Gentry*. In the preparation of this Supplement, which contained 1600 pedigrees, every variety of American genealogy was to be found. There were naturally the cases in which no affiliation could be given, not even in a wild legend. At the beginning of the British portion of the book is the English family of Abney of Measham Hall. One of the American would-be entrants to the American section gave his ancestry for four generations in the USA, prefixing it with the bland statement that his family was derived from the Abneys. On being asked for proof, he replied that he could not prove it, but as his surname was the same as that of the English family, he had assumed that he was connected. Naturally, he was excluded.

Pitfalls

Other cases presented unexpected difficulties. An American judge, whose name for this record shall be 'Brown', had a proven descent from a tenth-generation immigrant, with a source in an English village in the seventeenth century. Perfectly genuine and respectable. Unfortunately, at the head of the pedigree was the statement that Captain John 'Brown' had commanded a company of lancers for King Harold at Hastings in 1066. Quite vain was any attempt to show that this statement was impossible, even ignoring the fact that there were 600 years of unrecorded history between the Captain and the first 'Brown' in America. The judge was adamant: the absurdity had to go in. At last, I adopted an equally absurd suggestion from a friend: ask for the date of the Captain's commission in the British Army. It worked: 'I always knew that Burke was accurate, but I guess I didn't know how accurate. You must leave out the Captain.' It was a near thing.

Take another example from the above book. We will use the pseudonym 'Smith'. There was a legend at the beginning of this family history that the Americans in question descended from a British peer. It was useless to inform the lady who provided this pedigree that no person bearing the name could be found in peerage annals. She simply insisted. At length, after some considerable searching, it was found that the ancestor was indeed the son of a peer, but illegitimate. Having made the discovery, it was with considerable misgiving that I communicated the news to the lady. I expected a most indignant letter, but she took it very reasonably, though she did add that henceforth she would have to be very careful in referring to her ancestry to her relations in the Middle West.

In this case, I heard no more about the noble descent. The stigma of illegitimacy proved too strong. I am inclined to suspect that behind the story was the belief in the possibility of a claim to a peerage, a belief shared by many trans-Atlantic inquirers.

Fraudulent genealogical work is often at the root of these erroneous ideas, as with the American judge and his company of lancers. The latter preposterous statement I later found in an old American genealogical work.

Differences in original American Colonies

There were differences in the settlements of the Thirteen Colonies which formed the original United States. Space does not permit here details of all these, but the general rules for following up American family history are as described above. Anyone wishing for details of the several original colonies may profitably consult the essays in 'Anglo-Saxon Settlement of America' in *World-Wide Family History* edited by Noel Currer-Briggs (Routledge and Kegan Paul, 1982).

Racial elements in the USA

Another feature of American genealogy is the composite character of the American population. Even in the original Thirteen Colonies, there were strains other than Anglo-Saxon. In New York alone there was a considerable Dutch element. After the independence of the United States, as the vast country was opened up, floods of immigrants arrived from all parts of Europe. There is a very powerful Irish element, also Jewish, German, Italian and Polish, among others. Intermarriage has occurred, so that to treat of American genealogy as purely Anglo-Saxon would be absurd. On the contrary, it is essential to set out the lines of research in the countries of the European continent. The following works are useful in this respect.

A. Meredyth Burke's *Prominent Families of America* is mainly Anglo-Saxon, but does include the Roosevelt pedigree. Only the first volume was published. *American Origins*, by L. G. Pine, gives the genealogical and heraldic sources available throughout Europe. Published in 1960, it is still in print in the USA. The same author's *Genealogist's Encyclopedia* (1969) gives the same type of European detail plus additional information on Israel, Japan, etc., and on the Scottish clan system.

World-Wide Family History, already mentioned, provides useful information on the many racial strands of the USA; in fact, as its name implies, it is a guide to the constituents of genealogy throughout most of the world, including Islamic genealogy, China and Japan. In *Debrett's Family Historian* (1981), by Noel Currer-Briggs and Royston Gambier, there is also a considerable range of useful information on America and Australia.

Coming now to what used to be called the Dominions – Canada, Australia and New Zealand – and the former colonies, the research may be easier than for Americans but the incentive perhaps not as great.

Canada

The earliest of the British Dominions, Canada, came into existence as a result of the Seven Years' War (1756–63) half a generation before the American War of Independence. The settlers in Canada were French, apart from a few trappers of the Hudson Bay Company. After the British Conquest, the French were guaranteed their rights, and they have maintained them, even to the extent of seeking complete independence. After the recognition by Britain in 1784 of American independence, there was an influx of some 60,000 United Empire Loyalists who were of British stock. As the eighteenth century went on, and into the nineteenth century, a large number of Highlanders came from Scotland, often at first unwillingly. The policy of the British government in overturning the Highland feudal system was reinforced by the selfish action of the Highland landowners, who saw the advantage of sheep runs in place of poor crofters. The clearances in the Highlands were economic not political. The poor clansmen were packed off in the nineteenth century to Canada where, however, they greatly increased. Many other Scots voluntarily joined them later. The same considerations as to ancestor tracing apply to the Canadian Highlanders as to other clan names in Britain.

Owing to the huge territory of Canada, population was needed and to a large extent the country has followed the example of the USA and has admitted immigrants of various nationalities. Even the best purely Canadian pedigree is unlikely to exceed some seven generations, though. An interesting exception is that of Cuthbert of Berthier, settled in Canada some 250 years ago, and holding the French Canadian seignory of Berthier.

Australia and New Zealand

In the other Dominions, the history of the British settlers begins much later than in the USA or, in many cases, Canada. Australia began to be seriously settled in the early and middle nineteenth century. New Zealand's development came after 1840, when the Maoris entered into a treaty relationship with Britain.

In most cases, Australians and New Zealanders are separated from their British stock by only a few generations – two or three perhaps, at most four. Consequently, for such families to trace their English background is not too hard, initially at least, for they have no great gap to bridge between their arrival in Australia and the present time.

The Australian or New Zealand inquirer has a great initial advantage in that these newer countries have much more elaborate forms of registration of important statistics than in Britain. In Australia and New Zealand, the birth certificate must show not only the father's and mother's names, residence and occupation, but also the birthplace of the parents. In a new country, it was no doubt felt desirable to know as much as possible about people's antecedents. An example of a form of registration of birth in New South Wales is shown below.

1	Number in Register	6742
2	When and where born	28 January 1889
		Trafalgar Terrace, Petersham
3	Name and whether present or not	Harold Knightly, not present.
4	Sex	Male
5	Name and surname, rank or profession of father, age and birthplace	Charles Albert Parker, Gentleman, 34 years. Enfield, England.
6	When and where married, previous issue living and deceased	24 August 1887, Brisbane, Queensland.
7	Mother, name and maiden surname and birthplace	Julia Sheehan, 36 years. Brisbane, Queensland.
8	Informant, signature, description and residence of informant	Chas. A. Parker, Father. Trafalgar Terrace, Petersham
9	Witnesses, accoucheur, nurse or names of witnesses	Dr Coutie Mrs Burton
10	The Registrar's name and signature follow, with date.	

There is even a section headed:

11   Name if added after registration of birth.

It is obvious how helpful this type of registration must be to searchers.

With Australian genealogy there is often a suggestion (by outsiders) of a convict having been the original founder in Australia. The history of the Australian penal settlements is not a pleasant part of British history.

The American colonies were called the Plantations, and many criminals and political deportees were sent there. Jamaica also received some very dubious characters after the English conquest under Cromwell – prostitutes accompanied (I suspect) by some of Cromwell's most unruly and least desirable soldiers.

The Americans, having asserted their independence, were no longer willing to receive England's outcasts. It appeared to the British government as almost providential that, soon afterwards, Captain Cook had discovered and annexed Australia. Here was another penal settlement.

If an Australian family does descend from a convict, it is no use being ashamed of it. No one can choose his birth bed, and if a prominent and respected family was indeed founded by a convict, it merely shows how men can make good. Moreover, it is always possible to say that the crimes for which an Englishman could be transported in 1800 have long since been abolished. My own opinion is that many of the convicts did not leave issue. Certainly the cases treated in fiction, such as Henry Kingsley's *Recollections of Geoffrey Hamlyn* or Samuel Butler's *Erewhon*, do not lead one to suppose a vigorous family life in Australia for the unwilling arrivals.

Still, if convict ancestor there be, the records show much information. The Australian sources include details of the court where conviction took place and the dates. This can then be checked with the records of the English Court. In *Debrett's Family Historian* an interesting case is cited where a man who was tried in Scotland was born in Staffordshire.

The Australian inquirer may well be able to discover details about his first generation Australian forbear. As in England (see Chapter 8) newspapers can be useful in this respect. They began in Sydney from 1803. After this, various newspapers appeared in the different Australian states, and some newspapers have been indexed as regards the announcements of births, marriages and deaths. Probably – again as in England – prolonged study of the newspapers will be found of value to the inquirer. In a new society like Australia, all sorts of entries will give rewards. The early Australian communities were comparatively small and all sorts of happenings which would not appear in English newspapers would be chronicled in the Australian journals.

Directories also began quite early in Australia, in Sydney about 1830. Obviously, these are very useful in tracing individuals and families. Post Office directories begin from about 1845. A work which can be helpful for details of families is *Burke's Colonial Gentry*, in two volumes. The Australian Society of Genealogists in Sydney is a useful body. It has existed for many years but has grown considerably in strength and importance, along with the increasing interest of Australians in both heraldry and genealogy. A high class, annual publication is *FitzHardinge's Nobiliary*, produced by Charles Bailey of Baileville, listing biographies and arms.

South Africa

British immigration to South Africa is mainly from the later nineteenth century. A Dutch settlement at the Cape of Good Hope is over 300 years old. The Cape was taken by Britain during the Napoleonic wars. The Great Trek northwards was undertaken by the Boers in order to get away from British rule. The republics of Orange Free State and Transvaal were established as independent countries and this was confirmed by the Boers' victory in the first Boer War (Majuba 1881). The Second Boer War or South African War of 1899–1902 was won by Britain. In 1910 the Union of South Africa was formed by the union of the four provinces of the Cape of Good Hope, Transvaal, Natal and Orange Free State. However, despite the official adherence of South Africa to the allied cause in two World Wars, the Boer resentment of Britain never died. In 1961, South Africa left the British Commonwealth to become a Republic.

Registration in South Africa

Registration of births, marriages and deaths for the whole of South Africa dates only from the Births, Marriages and Deaths Registration Act of 1923. Application must be made to the Registrar of Births, Marriages and Deaths, Department of the Interior, Private Bag XII4, Pretoria 0001. The starting dates for compulsory registration of the three 'vital statistics' in the four provinces were as follows:

Cape Province 1895 (Office of Registrar, c/o Population Register Building, Schoolman and Van der Walt Streets, Pretoria)
Natal 1846 (Archives Depot of the Territory, Private Bag 13250, Windhoek 9100)
Orange Free State 1902
Transvaal 1900

Other records
Previous to these comparatively late dates for universal registration, there is a great amount of information, some of it in the form of church registers, as elsewhere. Considerable detail regarding South African records from the seventeenth century is given in *World-Wide Family History*, section 33.

Former British colonies

For those of British descent who come from the various colonies such as the West Indies, there was formerly a British government publication *An Abstract of Births, Marriages and Deaths in UK and the Colonies*. A copy of the work can be seen at St Catherine's House, but I was informed by the Office of Population, Censuses and Surveys (letter, 10 March 1983) that the publication went out of print in 1971 and that there are no plans to reprint it. It was added that HMSO (PITA), PO Box 569, London SE1 9NH has a photocopy service. Many details from the above work were given in the book *Your Family Tree* by L. G. Pine (1962), now out of print but available from libraries.

In colonies such as Gibraltar and Malta, most British residents have been there on official duties, civil or military, and did not intend to settle there: few families of British extraction are found among the permanent inhabitants.

In the West Indies there are many old families, such as Robertson of Struan, whose annals are sometimes to be found in books such as *Burke's Landed Gentry*. In India there was a large Anglo-Indian community which originated from British soldiers, administrators and merchants. The records of this community are preserved in the registers of English churches and chaplaincies overseas.

A good example can be seen in the *Peerage* under the title of Lord Gardner. In the Cathedral at Bombay, to take but one instance, there are numerous memorials to English persons, deceased and buried in India. The records of the Honourable East India Company, in the British Museum, and the many books owned by the Society of Genealogists which deal with British residents in India, are invaluable for tracing such connections. The records of the former India Office are maintained at India Office Library and Records (Foreign and Commonwealth Office), 197 Blackfriars Road, London SE1. The Colonial Office papers in the PRO contain much useful information on family history.

Peerage claims

The idea of a claim to a peerage title is compounded of genuine cases combined with a misunderstanding about the rules of succession. Undoubtedly there are claimants to peerages who are genuine and who turn up in different parts of the world, as we have seen in Chapter 10.

I have known many instances in which there has been a claim to a peerage, based on genealogical grounds. Where it did not succeed, it may have been due to the claimant being unable to prove that a line senior to his own had died out. When Brigadier Annesley proved his claim to the Viscounty of Valentia, it was necessary for him to show that several lines of his family, going back over a century, were extinct. In other words, he had to prove a universal negative. Fortunately, he was able to do this and his claim was accepted by the Committee of Privileges of the House of Lords.

Apart from real claims like the above, there is a mistaken idea often found in American family histories. It is of an ancestor having been a peer or an heir to a peerage, but having set it aside in favour of a younger brother and gone off to America. This is completely false and is due to ignorance of the English or Scottish peerage law. A peerage can be taken back by the Sovereign. This is now possible under the Peerage Act of 1963, and in earlier times by the simple action of the Crown. Under the 1963 Act, however, there is a great difference from the cases in our earlier history. Now, if a peer disclaims his peerage, that is for his lifetime alone. His son or grandson or other descendant can claim it and resume it. But it cannot be passed on to another person by the holder's own wish.

15

Genealogy and Heraldry

Introduction

In *The Forsyte Saga*, John Galsworthy refers to the instinct which sends every prominent or rising family to the Heralds' College. His account of Swithin Forsyte's contact with the College is most amusing. Swithin adopted the crest and motto, but did not proceed to the suggested affiliation with the great family of Forsite spelt with an 'i'.

Sooner or later, most researchers come against the existence of a coat of arms of a family of the same name. Does the coat belong to the inquirer's family?

It is an unfortunate truism in the study of genealogy that the person who begins with an interest in heraldry often goes on to develop an interest in family history, whereas the youthful devotee of pedigrees seldom becomes a keen student of heraldry. One hears even learned genealogists saying that they know nothing of heraldry or that they wish that they knew more.

Contrary to popular opinion, it is very easy to learn the basic elements of heraldry. It is, after all, a system which was originally designed for quick understanding, in the great majority of cases by those who were illiterate. The use of symbols is coeval with civilisation and heraldry is simply the hereditary use of symbols. Some people may be put off by the technical language, but this is soon learnt in practice. There are some 800 heraldic terms. No one sets out to learn them: they simply come, once the basic elements have been learnt.

The essence of heraldry is in the shield – the frequent references, in newspapers and novels, to the crest is rubbish. A crest is part of a coat of arms, the essential ingredient of which is the shield. The groundwork of the shield is (*a*) a colour or (*b*) a metal or (*c*) a fur. The last is often a variant of ermine, which was the luxury fur of the Middle Ages.

On these groundworks are put symbols, which are known as *charges*. Some of these occur frequently, so they are known as *ordinaries*. The rest – the *extraordinaries* – may be almost anything. Herschel has a telescope in the arms to represent the giant instrument with which he discovered the planet Uranus. Again, by the use of heraldic symbols and language, it has been possible to describe most adequately the Atomic Energy Authority.

This is not the place to go into the intricacies of heraldry. There are reliable and easily understood guides to the subject. One of the simplest to follow is *Heraldry Explained*, by A. C. Fox-Davies. My own book on the subject *Teach Yourself Heraldry and Genealogy* is now out of print, but went through four editions and many reprints. It included a glossary of heraldic terms and was well illustrated.

The development of heraldry

Heraldry developed in Western Europe in the twelfth century. By that time it had become a necessity, owing to the development of body armour which made it impossible to distinguish friend from foe. A parallel development took place at the same time in Japan, though with notable differences (see *International Heraldry* by L. G. Pine). European heraldry was connected with body armour for several centuries, hence much of the language – shield, helmet, coat of arms, crest – which it retains.

Coats of arms

Arms were at first chosen by individuals and then perpetuated in their families. This is shown by many instances in medieval times when two men who were unrelated were found to be using the same arms. Gradually the European sovereigns created their own heraldic advisers, the official heralds who would make grants of arms. These heralds, in some countries, were formed into corporations.

The Heralds' College in England, the Lyon Office in Scotland and the Heraldic Office in Dublin are instances which exist now. In Spain, too, there is an heraldic organisation, and there are heraldic advisers in Denmark and Sweden, and a State Herald in South Africa.

Burke's General Armory gives an index of coats of arms in the British Isles, and contains between 80,000 and 100,000 descriptions. Not all of these are of individuals or of families, for many corporate bodies (such as universities) possess arms.

Dealing first with England and Wales, how many of these 100,000 coats are genuine? Here we must be careful not to get involved in scholarly disputes. Some heraldic writers, notably A. C. Fox-Davies, hold that only a coat registered at Heralds' College is genuine. Others, of the school of Oswald Barron, point to the fact that coats of arms were originally assumed at the owner's pleasure, as were surnames. My own contribution and opinion is given in full in my *Story of Heraldry*.

Leaving such disputes to one side, what cannot be justified is the assumption of a coat of arms simply because one's family has the same surname as that of a person whose arms are mentioned in *Burke's General Armory*. In any event, many of the entries in this work are inaccurate. For instance, one of the greatest churchmen of the nineteenth century – the Reverend John Keble, a man of real sanctity of life – is commemorated in Keble College, Oxford. The arms of Keble which formed the basis of those of the College were derived from those of a Lord Mayor of London in the sixteenth century, but whether the saintly clergyman was connected with the Lord Mayor is another matter.

Therefore, if an inquirer into family history finds a family of the same name which is armigerous, he must make further investigation to discover if there is a family connection before using the arms. One pertinent factor is the area of the country in which the armigerous family lived or lives. If it is the same as one's own, then at least the search is narrowed to a particular county. There is no descendant now of William Shakespeare, but the Shakespeare Baronets come from Warwickshire and their arms are reminiscent of those granted to the poet. One can hardly blame them for wanting to be linked to so illustrious a man.

Identity of arms and surname

There is no way to deal with an identity of arms and surname except by genealogical research. But can arms point to a connection? Yes, very definitely. The possession of the same arms in modern times – that is, in the last 200 years – may well point to a relationship.

One glaring connection arises from illegitimacy. Heraldry knows several ways of delineating illegitimacy. One of the methods used by English heralds is the bordure, which is a line running round the inside of the shield. To anyone who knows the signs of heraldry, this is a sure indication that in the ancestry there is illegitimacy. On the walls of Petworth House in Sussex one can see the bordure on the Wyndham arms. The Lords Leconfield and Egremont descend from an Earl of Egremont who forgot to get married until late in his domestic connection. Another case concerns Lord Hankey and his kinsfolk, the untitled Hankeys of Fetcham Park. The first Lord Hankey descended from a Miss Alers, his great-grandmother, and the Hankey squire of her time. The bordure on the shield gives the clue.

There are, of course, many cases where a difference mark in a coat denotes not bastardy but a junior line of the family. The heraldic charge shows the distinction from the main line of the family.

These remarks apply to all heraldic systems, but none equals in exactitude and precision that of Scotland (see Chapter 10).

The Heralds' College

The Heralds' College deals with the arms of England and Wales, the Channel Islands and the Isle of Man. There is also a jurisdiction dealing with people of English or Welsh descent in the British colonies and dominions beyond the seas. Grants are also made by Heralds' College to Americans of English and Welsh descent.

Visitations

One very important development in the work of the English heralds was the holding of the Visitations. These were examinations, county by county, under royal warrant, of the arms that were in use. These Visitations began in the reign of Henry VIII and continued to that of James II, some 160 years. They were an attempt, typical of the

Tudor period, to exercise royal control of the subject. The Visitations contain a most important body of genealogy and a mass of useful information. The originals are in the Heralds' College, but copies of the Visitations exist mainly in the publications of the Harleian Society, which are available at the Society of Genealogists and in the libraries mentioned in Chapter 7. A Visitation pedigree sketch is given at the end of this chapter.

The Heralds' College in London is not open to public inspection. Its extensive archives can be searched only by the officers of Arms, the thirteen heralds who work under the rule of the hereditary Earl Marshal, the Duke of Norfolk. The officers are members of the Court of the Sovereign and are not civil servants. Fees are charged for searches as well as for coats of arms.

Scottish heraldry

In Scotland, as explained in Chapter 10, the heraldic position is completely independent of England, and quite different. It comes under the rule of the Lord Lyon who is appointed by the Crown and has jurisdiction over Lyon Court. Scots heraldry is governed by Act of the Scots Parliament of 1672. By this Act, confirmed in 1867 by the Imperial Parliament, all Scots who bear arms or seek to do so must matriculate their arms in Lyon Court. If they do not so register, they have no right to bear the arms and are liable to severe penalties imposed by Lyon Court.

This excellent system has prevented abuses in heraldic practice. A matriculation or grant in Lyon Office applies to a man and his eldest son, but a younger son must in his turn matriculate, which then necessarily involves difference marks. Thus Scots heraldry is a great visual aid to genealogy and a Scot, asked if he has arms, can reply with his matriculation or with a plain negative. If not registered with Lyon Office, then the arms are plainly bogus.

The Scots heralds have jurisdiction of persons of Scottish descent throughout the world. I have been able to put through grants of arms for a man living in Queensland, and another in Sussex. Both could prove a Scottish domicile for a forbear.

In 1977, the Heraldry Society of Scotland was founded. All inquiries should be addressed to Dr C. D. Green, 24 Strawberrybank, Dundee DD2 1BH.

Irish heraldry

To complete the account of the British Isles, there is the Irish heraldic system. As explained in Chapter 12, this was independent of England and was managed by the Ulster King of Arms who had his office in Dublin Castle. He was an appointee of the British Crown. He continued in office after Irish independence, but after the death of Sir Neville Wilkinson in 1940, the Irish leader de Valera asked to have the office removed, as mentioned in Chapter 12. This was done and it was united with the office of Norroy King of Arms. The latter then has jurisdiction as Norroy and Ulster over the six northern counties which are part of the United Kingdom.

De Valera then instituted his own officer, a civil servant, as Chief Herald of Ireland. His office is in Dublin Castle, as was Ulster's, and he carries out the same duties. I have known and worked with the first Chief Herald, the distinguished Dr Edward MacLysaght, and with his successor, Mr Gerrard Slevin. On the principles enunciated above, I would expect Dublin Castle to exercise arms grants and control for persons of Irish birth in other parts of the world, such as the USA or Australia.

A Visitation Pedigree Sketch

In selecting the family of Hooke of Crookes for illustration of a good Visitation pedigree, I have been guided by three considerations. The family (*a*) was recorded in every one of the Heralds' Visitations of Gloucestershire, in 1583, 1623 and 1683; (*b*) is still existing, and still possesses the ancient property of Crookes; and (*c*) like other truly old landed gentry families, the Hookes are lineally traced long before the Visitations. The connected descent begins with Thomas Hooke, of *circa* 1415, whose sword is in possession of the family, and who fought at Agincourt. An ancient tradition assigns to him the grant of Crookes from Henry V. The family's muniment chest contains a marriage settlement dated 7 July 1435, in which Thomas Hooke's son, another Thomas Hooke, was contracted to Margaret, only daughter of Sir Guy Whityngton, who with his son, Robert, witnessed the marriage settlement. Sir Guy, who was Lord of the Manor of Pauntley in Gloucestershire and High Sheriff of that county in 1428, commanded a company at Agincourt. He was nephew of Sir Richard Whittington, Lord Mayor of London.

The issue of this marriage was Guy Hooke of Crookes, who was living *circa* 1470 (Visitations of Gloucestershire, 1583, and 1623; Harleian mss. 1041 and 1543, British Museum) and had issue.

Richard Hooke, of Crookes, living *circa* 1510, who married Alice, dau. of William Wirrall, and d. (will dated 18 April, proved 7 July 1547) having had issue etc, etc.

The documentation of this family as preserved in their muniment chest is very extensive and of a nature which cannot be found apart from continuous possession of land. Owing to their ownership of estates in the same area extending over a period of 550 years, the Hookes possess a very large number of documents including wills, marriage settlements, leases, purchases and sales of property, which are invaluable in tracing their family history. Clearly the sources used in tracing a more modern style genealogy – birth, marriage, and death certificates, census returns and the like – assume at most a very subordinate importance in this case.

It is of interest to note that before the connected pedigree begins in the early fifteenth century, there are for upwards of two centuries mentions of Hookes in Gloucestershire. These show how deep are the roots of the family in the county. It is in the highest degree likely that the persons mentioned below were of the same stock; in fact, in more than one case there is documentary proof that they were.

1   Walter Hoke (spelling is always varied at this date) was a juror in Gloucestershire, 1247–8.
2   Richard de la Hoke was party to an oath in an Inquisition taken at Tetbury, 1327.
3   By a charter dated 5 Nov. 1433, a certain Thomas Philpot granted to Thomas Hoke and others, all lands in the vill of Morton Folet.
4   By another charter bearing same date Thomas Philpot granted other lands to the same parties.
5   There was a presentation in 1411 of William Hoke, parson of the church of Brommester in the diocese of Hereford, to the church of Redmarley Abitot in the diocese of Worcester being in the King's gift (Calendar of Patent Rolls, G. 112).
6   In 1412, in the same record as above, Philip Hoke and Agnes his wife, are commissioners appointed to receive the oath of the

following: Guy Whityngton and Thomas Hoke, mentioned in the marriage settlement of Thomas and Margaret Hooke, 1435 (see above).

7 The chantry of St James and St Anne was founded by one John Hooke and another by licence of King Henry VI.
8 Parish of Little Dean, Trinity Chantry founded by Philip Hooke.
9 In the guide to the church of St Mary the Virgin, Newent (written by Mr Irvine E. Gray, County Records Officer for Gloucestershire) in the list of incumbents are the names of Robert Hoke, 1393, and John Hoke, 1434. The former is mentioned in the marriage settlement of 1435, as also the William Hoke, (5) above.

The pedigree of Hooke of Crookes Park is given in full in *Burke's Landed Gentry* (17th and 18th editions), although the details from (1) to (9) above do not appear in the *Landed Gentry* account, which gives the pedigree generation by generation from 1415. I am much obliged to Sqdn Ldr Douglas Hooke for supplying them and for permission to print this account.

It is perfectly clear that there were Hookes in Gloucestershire from the early thirteenth century, but the pedigree of this family is honourably distinguished from first to last by a refusal to include anything in the nature of undocumented material. Perhaps the unbroken possession of land, pedigree and coat armour for five and a half centuries – far antedating the records of more than half our peerage – precludes any desire to strain after earlier items, whose connection can, however, be assumed with a high degree of probability.

Appendix 1

Useful Addresses

General Register Offices

England and Wales
  St Catherine's House, 10 Kingsway, London WC2B 6JP

Scotland
  New Register House, Edinburgh EH1 3YT

Northern Ireland
  Oxford House, 49–55 Chichester Street, Belfast BT1 4HL

Eire
  Custom House, Dublin 1

Public Record Offices

England and Wales
  Portugal Street, London WC2A 3PH
  Chancery Lane, London WC2A 1LR
  Ruskin Avenue, Kew, Richmond, Surrey TW9 4DO

Scotland
  New Register House, Edinburgh EH1 3YT

Northern Ireland
  Oxford House, 49–55 Chichester Street, Belfast BT1 4HL

Eire
  Four Courts, Dublin 7

Local Record Offices

This section lists County Record Offices and other local repositories in England. The addresses of record offices and centres in other parts of the British Isles are given in the relevant chapters.

Avon
  Bath City Record Office, Guildhall, Bath BA1 5AW
  Bath Reference Library, 18 Queen Street, Bath BA1 2HP
  Bristol Record Office, Council House, College Green, Bristol BS1 5TR

Bedfordshire
  Bedfordshire Record Office, County Hall, Bedford MK42 9AP

Berkshire
  Berkshire Record Office, Shire Hall, Shinfield Park, Reading RG2 9XD
  Windsor Muniment Room, Guildhall, High Street, Windsor SL4 1LR

Buckinghamshire
  Buckinghamshire Record Office, County Hall, Aylesbury HP20 1UA
  Buckinghamshire Archaeological Society, The Museum, Church Street,
    Aylesbury

Cambridgeshire
  Cambridge County Record Office, Shire Hall, Castle Hill, Cambridge
    CB3 0AP
  Cambridge County Record Office, Grammar School Walk, Huntingdon
    PE18 6LF
  Cambridge University Archives, University Library, Cambridge CB3
    9DR

Cheshire
  Cheshire Record Office, The Castle, Chester CH1 2DN
  Chester Archaeological Society, Chester Public Library, St John Street,
    Chester
  Chester City Record Office, Town Hall, Chester

Cornwall
  Cornwall County Record Office, County Hall, Truro TR1 3AY
  Royal Institution of Cornwall, County Museum, Truro TR1 2SJ

Cumbria
  Cumbria County Record Office, The Castle, Carlisle CQ3 8UR
  Cumbria County Record Office, Duke Street, Barrow in Furness LA14
    1XW

Derbyshire
  Derbyshire Record Office, County Offices, Matlock DE4 3AG

Devon
  Devon Record Office, Castle Street, Exeter EX4 3PQ
  Devon and Cornwall Record Society, Westcountry Studies Library,
    Exeter EX4 3PQ
  Exeter Cathedral Library, Bishop's Palace, Exeter EX1 1HX
  West Devon Record Office, 14 Tavistock Place, Plymouth PL4 8AN

Dorset
  Dorset Record Office, County Hall, Dorchester DT1 1XJ

Durham
  Durham County Record Office, County Hall, Durham DH1 5UL
  Durham University Library, Palace Green, Durham DH1 3RN

Essex
  Essex Record Office, County Hall, Chelmsford CM1 1LX

Gloucestershire
  Gloucestershire Record Office, Gloucester GL1 3DW

Hampshire
  Hampshire Record Office, 20 Southgate Street, Winchester SO23 9EF
  Portsmouth City Record Office, 3 Museum Street, Portsmouth PO1 2LE
  Southampton City Record Office, Civic Centre, Southampton SO9 4XL

Hereford and Worcester
  Hereford and Worcester Record Office, Shire Hall, Worcester WR1
    1TR
  Hereford Record Office, Old Barracks, Harold Street, Hereford HR1
    2QX
  St Helen's Record Office, Fish Street, Worcester WR1 211N

Hertfordshire
  Hertfordshire Record Office, County Hall, Hertford SG13 8DE

Humberside
  Humberside County Record Office, County Hall, Beverley HU17 9BA

Huntingdonshire see Cambridgeshire

Kent
  Kent County Archives Office, County Hall, Maidstone ME14 1XH
  Canterbury Cathedral Archives and City Record Office, The Precincts,
    Canterbury CT1 2EG

Lancashire
  Lancashire Record Office, Bow Lane, Preston PR1 8ND

Leicestershire (includes Rutland)
  Leicester Record Office, 57 New Walk, Leicester LE1 7JB

Lincolnshire
  Lincolnshire Archives Office, The Castle, Lincoln LN1 3BA

London
  Greater London Record Office, County Hall, SE1 7PB

Manchester (Lancashire and Cheshire)
  John Rylands Library, Oxford Road, Manchester M13 9PP
  Manchester Central Library, St Peter's Square, Manchester M2 5PD
  Wigan Record Office, Town Hall, Leigh WN7 2DY

Merseyside (Lancashire and Cheshire)
  Liverpool Record Office, William Brown Street, Liverpool L3 8EW

Midlands, West
> Birmingham Reference Library, Birmingham B3 3HQ
> Dudley Archives Department, Central Library, St James' Road, Dudley
> DY1 1HR

Norfolk
> Norfolk Record Office, Central Library, Norwich NR2 1NJ

Northampton
> Northampton Record Office, Delapre Abbey, Northampton NN4 9AW

Northumberland
> Northumberland Record Office, North Gosforth, Newcastle upon Tyne
> NE3 5QX

Nottinghamshire
> Nottingham Record Office, County House, Nottingham NG1 1HR

Oxfordshire
> Oxfordshire County Record Office, County Hall, Oxford OX1 1ND

Shropshire
> Shropshire Record Office, Shirehall, Shrewsbury SY2 6ND

Somerset
> Somerset Record Office, Obridge Road, Taunton TA2 7PU

Staffordshire
> Lichfield Record Office, Public Library, Bird Street, Lichfield WS13
> 6PN
> Staffordshire Record Office, Eastgate Street, Stafford ST16 2LZ

Suffolk
> Suffolk Record Office, County Hall, Ipswich IP4 2JS
> West Suffolk Record Office, School Hall Street, Bury St Edmunds
> IP33 1RX

Surrey
> Surrey Record Office, County Hall, Kingston upon Thames KT1 2DN
> Surrey Record Office, Castle Arch, Guildford GU1 3SX

Sussex, East
> East Sussex Record Office, St Andrew's Lane, Lewes BN7 1UN

Sussex, West
> West Sussex Record Office, West Street, Chichester PO19 1RN

Tyne and Wear
> Tyne and Wear Archives Department, West Blandford Street, New-
> castle NE1 4JA

Warwickshire
> Warwick County Record Office, Priory Park, Warwick CV34 4JS

Isle of Wight
Isle of Wight County Record Office, 26 Hillside, Newport PO30 2EB

Wiltshire
Wiltshire County Record Office, County Hall, Trowbridge BA14 8JG

Yorkshire, North
North Yorkshire County Record Office, County Hall, Northallerton DL7 8SG
Borthwick Institute, St Anthony's Hall, York YO1 2PW

Yorkshire, South
South Yorkshire County Record Office, Ellin Street, Sheffield S1 4PL

Yorkshire, West
West Yorkshire Record Office, Newstead Road, Wakefield WF1 2DE
Calderdale Borough Archives Department, Central Library, Halifax HX1 5LA
Leeds Archives Department, Chaleltown Road, Leeds LS7 3AP

Other useful addresses

Federation of Family History Societies, 96 Beaumont Street, Milehouse, Plymouth, Devon PL2 3AQ
Genealogical Society of Utah, Church of Jesus Christ of Latter-Day Saints, London Library, 64 Exhibition Road, London SW7 2PA
Heralds' College, The College of Arms, Queen Victoria Street, London EC4V 4BT
Society of Genealogists, 14 Charterhouse Buildings, London EC1M 7BA

Appendix 2

Records at the PRO

Records at Kew

Records are, in general, open to inspection when they are thirty years old. The appearance of classes of records on this list does not necessarily indicate that they are open.

Admiralty (ADM)
Advisory Conciliation & Arbitration Service (CW)
Agriculture, Fisheries & Food, Ministry of (MAF)
Air Ministry (AIR)
Aviation, Ministry of (AVIA)
British Council (BW)
British Railways Board (AN)
British Transport Docks Board (BR)
British Transport Historical Records (RAIL)
Cabinet Office (CAB)
Captured Enemy Documents (GFM)
Certification Office for Trades Unions and Employers Associations (CL)
Channel Tunnel Advisory Groups (BS1)
Civil Service Commission (CSC)
Civil Service Department (BA)
Civil Service Pay Research Unit (CSPR)

Coal Industry Social Welfare Organisation (BX)
Colonial Office (CO)
Commonwealth Relations Office (DO)
Copyright Office (COPY)
Countryside Commission (COU)
Crown Agents for Overseas Governments and Administration (CAOG)
Customs & Excise, Board of (CUST)
Defence, Ministry of (DEFE)
Development Commission (D)
Distribution of Income & Wealth, Royal Commission on (BS7)
Education & Science, Department of (ED)
Elizabeth Garrett Anderson Hospital (CF)
Environment, Department of the (AT)
Environmental Pollution, Royal Commission on (CY)

Exchequer and Audit Department (AO)

Export Credits Guarantee Department (ECG)

Financial Institutions, Committee to review the functioning of (BS9)

Foreign Office (FO)

Forestry Commission (F)

Forfeited Estates, Commissioners of (FEC)

Friendly Societies, Registry of (FS)

Gambling, Royal Commission on (BS3)

General Register Office (RG) except Census Returns (RG 9–RG 10), Non-Parochial Registers and records (RG 4–RG 8) and certain other registers and associated papers (RG 18, 19, 27, 30–37, 43)

Government Actuary's Department (ACT)

Health & Social Security, Department of (BN)

Health, Ministry of (MH)

Historical Manuscripts Commission (HMC)

Home Office (HO) (except Census Returns (HO 107))

Housing & Local Government, Ministry of (HLG)

Hudson's Bay Company (BH) Microfilm. Access by permission of the Company only

Information, Central Office of (INF)

Inland Revenue, Board of (IR) except Estate Duty Registers (IR 26 and IR 27)

Irish Sailors' & Soldiers' Land Trust (AP)

Iron and Steel Board (BE)

Labour, Ministry of (LAB)

Land Registry (LAR)

Lands Tribunal (LT)

Law Commission (BC)

Local Government Boundary Commission for England (AX)

Location of Offices Bureau (AH)

Lord Chancellor's Office (LCO)

Meteorological Office (BJ)

Metropolitan Police Force (MEPO)

Monuments, Ancient & Historic in Wales and Monmouthshire, Royal Commission on (MONW)

Monuments, Historic (England), Royal Commission on (AE)

Munitions, Ministry of (MUN)

National Assistance Board (AST)

National Coal Board (COAL)

National Debt Office (NDO)

National Dock Labour Board (BK)

National Health Service, Royal Commission on (BS6)

National Incomes Commission (NICO)

National Insurance Audit Department (NIA)

National Insurance Commissioners (CT)

National Savings Department for (NSC)

National Service, Ministry of (NATS)

Operators' Licensing, Committee of enquiry into (BS4)

Ordnance Survey Department (OS)

Overseas Development, Ministry of (OD)

Parliamentary Boundary Commission (AF)

Parole Board (BV)

Paymaster General's Office (PMG)

Pensions & National Insurance, Ministry of (PIN)

Pensions Appeal Tribunal (BF)

Power, Ministry of (POWE)

Press, Royal Commission on the (BS2)

Price Commission (CX)

Prime Minister's Office (PREM)

Prison Commission (PCOM)
Public Building & Works, Ministry
of (WORK)
Public Record Office (PRO) all
classes (except transcripts (PRO
31) and certain classes of gifts
and deposits (PRO 30))*
Public Trustee Office (PT)
Public Works Loan Board (PWLB)
Reconstruction, Ministry of
(RECO)
Remploy Ltd (BM)
Research Institutes (AY)
Royal Fine Art Commission (BP)
Royal Mint (MINT)
Scientific & Industrial Research,
Department of (DSIR)

Stationery Office (STAT)
Supply, Ministry of (SUPP)
Tithe Redemption Commission
(TITH)
Trade, Board of (BT)
Transport, Ministry of (MT)
Treasury (T)
Tribunals, Council on (BL)
United Kingdom Atomic Energy
Authority (AB)
University Grants Committee
(UGC)
Value Added Tax Tribunals
(CV)
Wallace Collection (AR)
War Office (WO)
Welsh Office (BD)

Records at Chancery Lane†

Admiralty, High Court of (HCA)
Alienation Office (A)
Assize, Clerks of (ASSI)
Bankruptcy, Court of (B)
Central Criminal Court (CRIM)
Chancery (C)
Chester, Palatinate of (CHES)
Common Pleas, Court of (CP)
County Courts (AK)
Crown Estate Commissioners
(CRES)
Delegates, Court of (DEL)
Durham, Palatinate of (DURH)
Exchequer (E; LR)
General Register Office (RG) Only
Census Returns (RG 9–RG 10),
Non-Parochial Registers and
records (RG 4–RG 8) and
certain other registers and

associated papers (RG 18, 19,
27, 30–37, 43)
Home Office. Only Census
Returns 1841 and 1851 (HO
107)
Inland Revenue, Board of. Only
Estate Duty Registers (IR 26 and
IR 27)
Judicature, Supreme Court of (J)
Justices Itinerant (JUST)
King's Bench, Court of (KB)
King's Bench Prison (PRIS)
Lancaster, Duchy of (DL)
Lancaster, Palatinate of (PL)
Land Revenue Record Office
(LRRO)
Law Officers' Department (LO)
Lord Chamberlain's Department
(LC)

*PRO 30/1–3, 6–12, 16–17, 20, 22, 27, 29–33, 35–37, 39–40, 42–43, 45–46, 48,
51–52, 54–79, 81–84 are at Kew
PRO 31/20 is at Kew
PRO 30/4, 13–15, 62 are no longer held in the Public Record Office
†Some classes to be seen at Chancery Lane are housed at Hayes, Middlesex, and
notice of several working days is required.

Lord Steward's Office (LS)
Palace Court (PALA)
Peveril, Court of the Honour of (PEV)
Prerogative Court of Canterbury (PROB)
Privy Council, Judicial Committee of the (PCAP)
Privy Council Office (PC)
Privy Purse Office (PP)
Privy Seal Office (PSO)
Public Prosecutions, Director of (DPP)

Public Record Office (Transcripts) (PRO 31) and certain classes of gifts and deposits (PRO 30)*
Queen Anne's Bounty (QAB)
Requests, Court of (REQ)
Signet Office (SO)
Special Collections (SC)
Star Chamber, Court of (STAC)
State Paper Office (SP)
Treasury Solicitor (TS)
Wales, Principality of (WALE)
Wards & Liveries, Court of (WARD)

---

*PRO 30/5, 18–19, 21, 23–26, 28, 34, 38, 41, 44, 47, 49, 50, 53 and 80
PRO 31/20 is at Kew
PRO 30/4, 13–15, 62 are no longer held in the Public Record Office

Index